MW01259613

SHELLEY™ TEA WARE PATTERNS

Sheryl Burdess

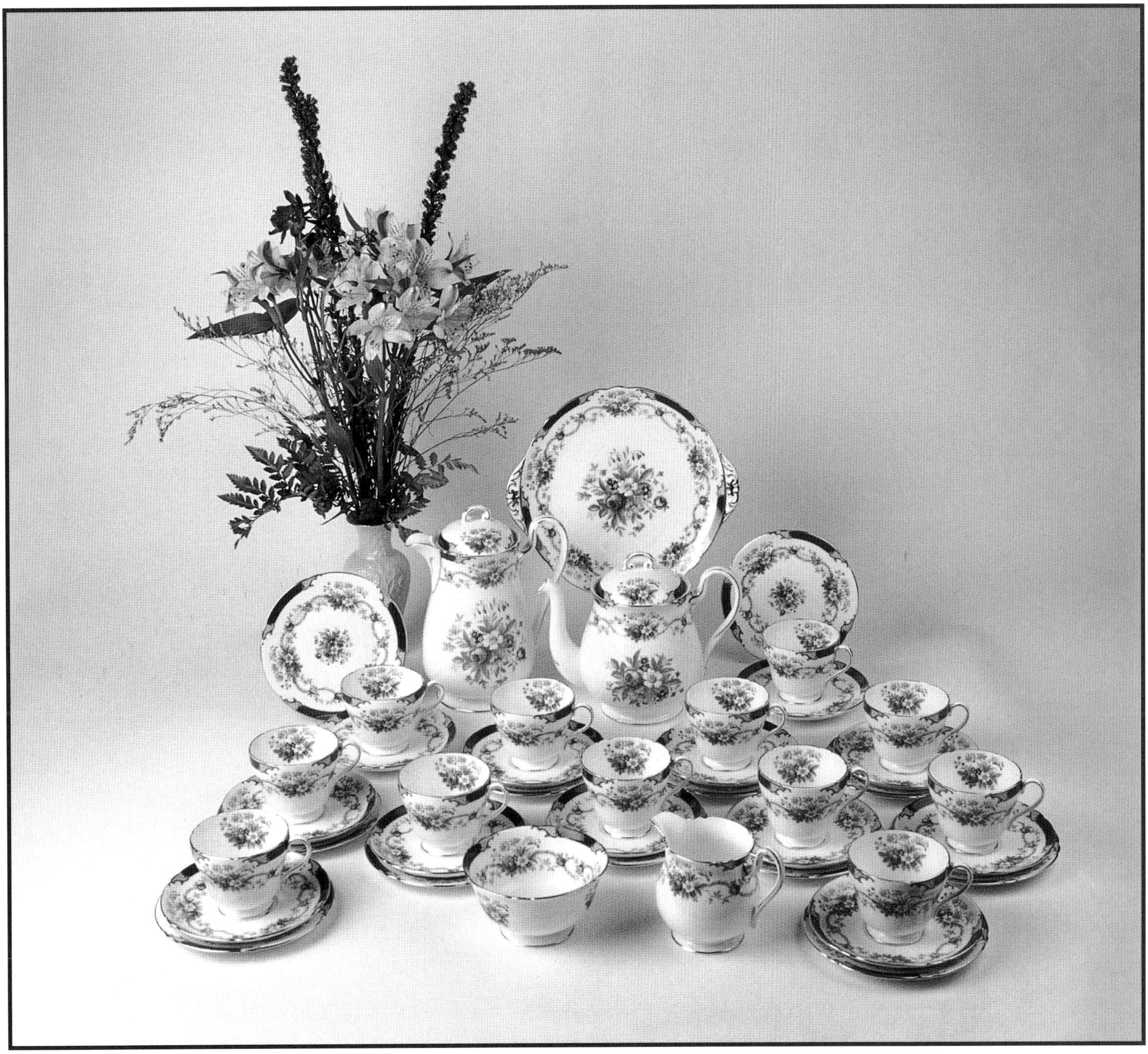

4880 Lower Valley Road, Atglen, PA 19310 USA

Dedication

To my husband, Christopher, without whom I probably would have finished writing this book much sooner.

Disclaimer

This book has been produced independently and neither the author or the publisher has any connection with either Royal Doulton Plc or the Royal Doulton International Collectors Club. Shelley is a trade mark and is registered in the UK by Royal Doulton Plc and is used in this book with the permission of Royal Doulton Plc. Any opinions expressed are those of the author and not necessarily endorsed by Royal Doulton Plc.

Library of Congress Cataloging-in-Publication Data

Burdess, Sheryl.
Shelley™ Tea Ware Patterns / By Sheryl Burdess.
p. cm.
ISBN 0-7643-1710-5 (Hardcover)
1. Shelley Potteries. 2. Wileman & Co. 3. Shelley China Ltd.
4. Drinking cups--England--Stafffordshire. I. Title.
NK4210.S53 A4 2003
738'.09424'6--dc21
2002012027

Designed by "Sue"
Type set in University Roman BT/Korinna BT

ISBN: 0-7643-1710-5
Printed in China
1 2 3 4

Published by Schiffer Publishing Ltd.
4880 Lower Valley Road
Atglen, PA 19310
Phone: (610) 593-1777; Fax: (610) 593-2002
E-mail: Schifferbk@aol.com
Please visit our web site catalog at
www.schifferbooks.com
We are always looking for people to write books on new and related subjects. If you have an idea for a book please contact us at the above address.

This book may be purchased from the publisher.
Include $3.95 for shipping.
Please try your bookstore first.
You may write for a free catalog.

In Europe, Schiffer books are distributed by
Bushwood Books
6 Marksbury Ave.
Kew Gardens
Surrey TW9 4JF England
Phone: 44 (0)20-8392-8585
Fax: 44 (0)20-8392-9876
E-mail: Bushwd@aol.com
Free postage in the UK. Europe: air mail at cost

Contents

Acknowledgments

Judy Silverman and Jerry Silverman for allowing me to photograph their truly amazing collection—also for their hospitality, encouragement, and mostly for their unconditional love and friendship. Without them this book would not have been possible.

John and Carole James for their enthusiastic help, advice, knowledge, and for allowing me to photograph their gorgeous collection.

Christie Jordano-Fasciano for her support and for allowing me to photograph her Regency coffee set.

Ris Coyne for her help with the photographs.

Christopher Burdess for his artwork, patience, and inspiration.

Bruce Waters for superbly photographing thousands of items in the U.S.A. and in the United Kingdom.

Sue Waters for her great organisational ability in helping to photograph collections in the United Kingdom.

Staff at Royal Doulton.

Pat Pedlar, Pam Burness, and Giovanni Thomson for their support, encouragement, and for putting up with me while I researched and wrote this book.

I would also like to thank all of the very many people, too numerous to mention here, who helped me with my research.

Introduction

This book documents the Shelley™ and Wileman Tea Wares™ that was produced and is still around, rather than only what is detailed in the Pattern Books.

What this Book Contains

This book gives you a brief history of the Wileman and Shelley families, the factories, and the artists who made Shelley/Wileman the highly successful company that it was. I have not covered these subjects in any depth, as other books written about Shelley have thoroughly covered the historical details. I have included a chapter on the back stamps used right through from the early Wileman days to the final years before Shelley ceased production in 1966. There is a chapter dedicated to cup shapes and another to pattern numbers, names, and descriptions.

As I have used web resources, various personal collections (and recollections!) as well as merchandise for my research, the details for each pattern number/name are not always in the same level of detail.

Terminology

Please note that British spelling is used.

Where different terms are used, I have tried to include as many of these as possible. For example, the large 9-9 1/2 inch plate included with a tea set is usually referred to in the United Kingdom as a 'bread and butter plate' and in the U.S.A as a 'cake plate'. I have thus used both terms wherever possible when referring to these plates.

Collectors' Clubs

Joining a collectors' club can be great fun and a great way of meeting people that enjoy the same things as you do. It also gives you the opportunity to learn more about Shelley and Wileman from people who are experts in this field. Most clubs hold regular meetings and shows, some of which give you the opportunity to buy and/or sell Shelley/Wileman items.

The clubs I have come across are listed alphabetically below, with the postal address and website, if applicable.

Australia
The Secretary
Australasian Shelley China Club
PO Box 819
Ballina, 2478
New South Wales
Australia

New Zealand
The Secretary
New Zealand Shelley Collectors Group
9 Fowey Avenue
Te Atatu South
Auckland 1008
New Zealand

United Kingdom
Website: www.shelley.co.uk
The Membership Secretary
The Shelley Group
15 Frolesworth Lane
Claybrooke Magna
Lutterworth
Leicestershire LE17 5AS
United Kingdom

United Sates of America
Website: www.nationalshelleychinaclub.com
The Treasurer
National Shelley China Club
591 W. 67th Ave.
Anchorage, AK 99518-1555

Families and Factories

Wileman and Shelley Families

The original potteries built in 1860 by Henry Wileman were named Foley China Works. The first Shelley to join the company was J.B. Shelley, who started work as a travelling salesperson in 1862. In 1872, J.F. Wileman and J.B. Shelley went into partnership to form Wileman & Co. In 1881 Percy Shelley also joined the company. His three sons, Norman, Jack, and Bob, joined Shelley in 1918. Bob's two sons, Alan and Donald, also joined the company in 1946.

The Company

The trade name used by Wileman & Co was Foley China. From 1890 to 1910 the name Foley, or Foley China, was used in conjunction with the name Wileman & Co. In 1910 the trade name was changed to Shelley, but between 1910 and 1916 the words 'Late Foley' were still being included in the back stamp. This caused confusion because a number of other companies were also using the name Foley, as this was the name of an area that had a lot of potteries. From 1912 the name Foley was dropped from the back stamps and only 'Shelley' was used. The company name was changed to Shelley in 1925. It became a limited company in 1929. In 1965 the name was changed yet again, this time to Shelley China Ltd.

In 1966 Shelley China Ltd came to an end when it was taken over by Allied English Potteries.

Designers and Artists

Amongst the fine artists and designers who worked for Wileman/Shelley are Frederick Rhead, who joined Wileman & Co in 1896, Walter Slater, who was appointed art director in 1905, and his son, Eric, who joined the company in 1919.

Cup Shapes

Shelley and Wileman produced a wonderful variety of cup shapes. Some of them were delicate and dainty, others were avant-gardes or elegant, while others were primarily sensible and practical. The common denominators are quality and beauty.

Documented and Undocumented

Not all the cup shapes produced are well documented in the Pattern Books. As a result, certain eagle-eyed, or lucky, collectors have discovered previously unknown cup shapes. To the knowing sleuth there are the certain little characteristics that draw your attention – perhaps a handle that looks familiar, or the gracefulness of the foot that is reminiscent of another, known, shape, or even a pattern that you know to be Shelley or Wileman on an unfamiliar shape. This all adds to the thrill of the chase and the joy of discovery.

Registration Numbers

Some of the cup shapes were registered in the Official Journal of Patents, which is available at the Public Records Office at Kew, London, United Kingdom. Various Acts of Parliament prevented a registered item from being copied. The date on which a shape was registered and the date from which it was produced are not necessarily the same. In some cases a shape was only registered when it became popular. Wherever possible I have included the registration number, which is normally preceded by 'Rd' on the base of items. Marking items with the registration number was sometimes rather inconsistent. Some earlier pieces may have an impressed registration mark, while others may also have a printed mark. Later pieces only have the printed registration number. There are pieces that are not marked with the relevant registration number at all.

Quality Ranges

Shelley/Wileman categorized many of their wares according to the quality of the items. The Bestware range consisted of the highest quality items. Any items with production faults or blemishes, such as tiny pieces of grit or firing cracks, were classified as Seconds Ware. Many of the Seconds Ware items are marked with a 2 in a circle. Any pattern numbers beginning with '2' belong to the Seconds Ware range. Some patterns were specifically designated for either Bestware or Seconds Ware, while others were produced on both.

Bestware and Seconds Ware are equally collectible. Production faults do not detract from the beauty, desirability, and collectible nature of Seconds Ware items, and some of them may indeed fetch higher prices than their Bestware counterparts, especially if they have been decorated with a rare pattern.

List of Shapes

This Chapter explores some of the Tea Wares cup shapes produced between 1870 and 1966. The shapes are listed alphabetically, with photographs and silhouettes to show you what the shapes look like. Please note that the silhouette shapes are not drawn to scale, and are the artist's impression of the shapes. I have included notes but not illustrations of shapes that were used mainly for commemorative/badged ware.

Albert

Registration number 60868 recorded in 1886. Originally named the Jubilee Flute. Tea and coffee/demitasse cups were made in this shape. Used for Bestware. Produced from c.1886-1890.

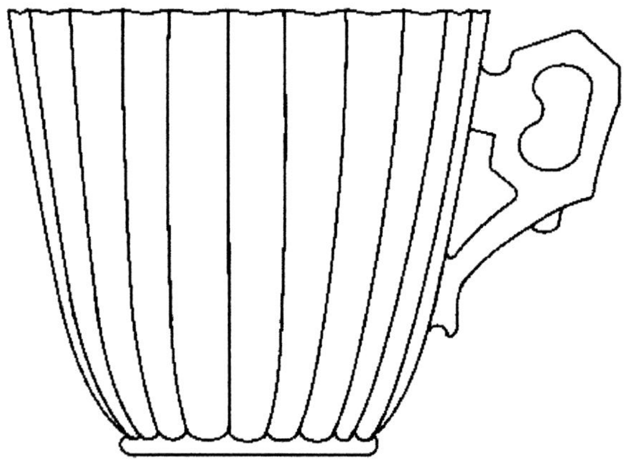

Albert silhouette

Alexandra

Registration number 60650 recorded in 1886. Originally known as Square Fluted. Also referred to as 'Alex'. Tea and coffee/demitasse cups were made in this shape. Used for Bestware and Seconds Ware. Produced from c.1887-1902.

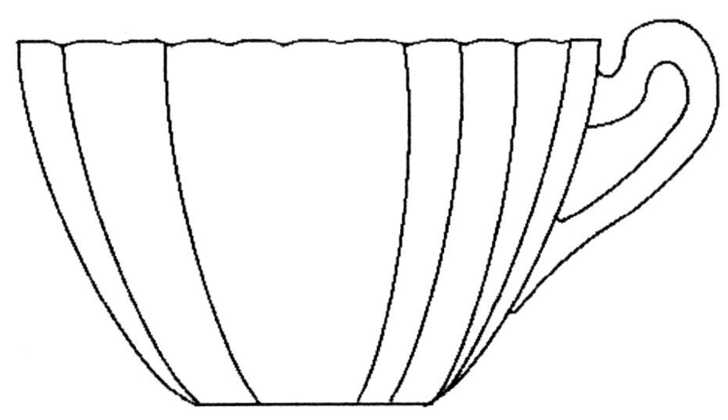

Alexandra silhouette

Alexandra

Antique

Registration number 447136 recorded in 1905. The design was based on the Square shape, or early Queen Anne, and was sometimes referred to as such. Used for Bestware. Produced from c.1905-1926.

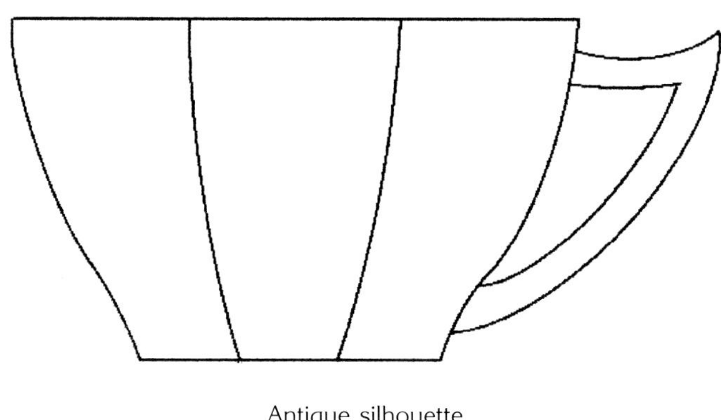

Antique silhouette

Antique

Argyle

Originally referred to as New Lily. Used for Bestware and Seconds Ware. Produced from c.1910-1914.

Argyle silhouette

Argyle

Ascot

Used for Bestware, Ideal China/Canadian Tea Wares, and Seconds Ware. Produced from c.1938-1940.

Ascot silhouette

Ascot

Atholl

Primarily designed for export to the U.S.A and Canada. Used for Bestware and Ideal China/Canadian Tea Wares. A variation of the handle was also used. Produced from c.1958-1960s.

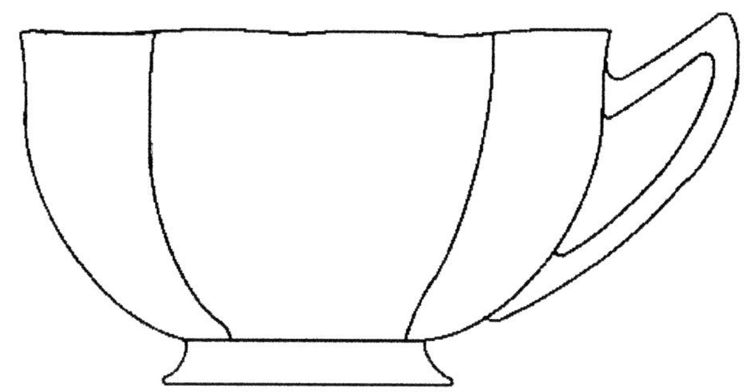

Atholl silhouette

Atholl standard handle

Atholl fancy handle

Atlantic

Identical to the Devon shape. Produced c.1941.

Atlantic silhouette

Avon

Used for Bestware, Ideal China/Canadian Tea Wares, and Seconds Ware. Produced from c.1964-1966.

Avon silhouette

Avon Coffee

Sometimes referred to as the Avon shape, making no differentiation between tea and coffee shapes. Used for Bestware, Ideal China/Canadian Tea Wares, and Seconds Ware. Produced from c.1964-1966.

Avon Coffee silhouette

Avon

Avon Coffee

Bamboo

Coffee cup. Produced c.1891.

Boston

Used for Bestware and Ideal China/Canadian Tea Wares. This shape evolved into the Lincoln shape. The only difference between the two is that the Boston has a notched foot and rim, and the Lincoln has no notches on the foot and shallower notches on the rim. Designed primarily for export. Produced from c.1963-1966.

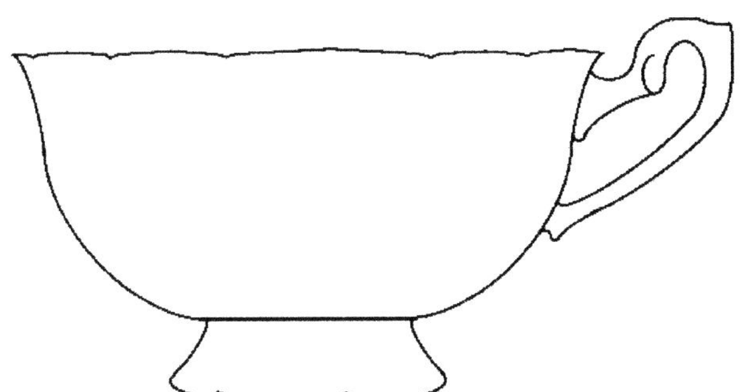

Boston silhouette

Boston

Bristol

Used for Bestware, Ideal China/Canadian Tea Wares, and Seconds Ware. Two slightly different shapes were produced. The earlier shape has a more pronounced lip than the later shape. This shape is also found in coffee/demitasse cups. Produced from c.1960-1963.

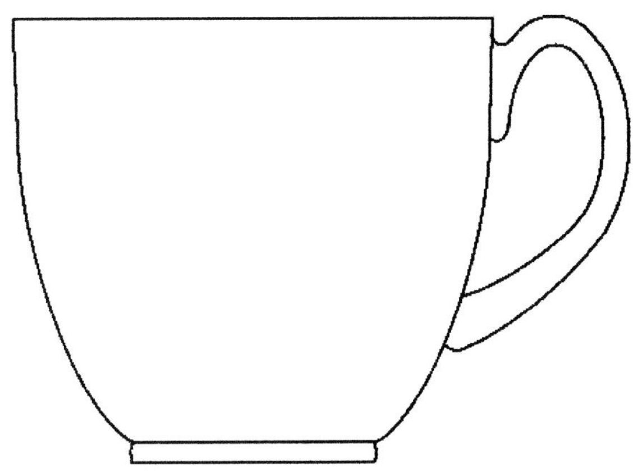

Bristol silhouette

Bute

Registration number 625614. Used for Bestware, Ideal China/Canadian Tea Wares, and Seconds Ware. Produced from c.1890-1962.

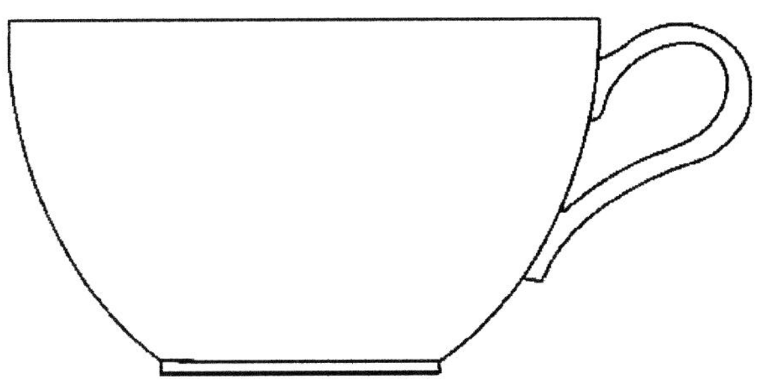

Bute silhouette

Bute

Cambridge

Used for Bestware, Ideal China/Canadian Tea Wares, and Seconds Ware. Replaced by New Cambridge. Tea and coffee/demitasse cups were made in this shape. Produced from c.1937-1954.

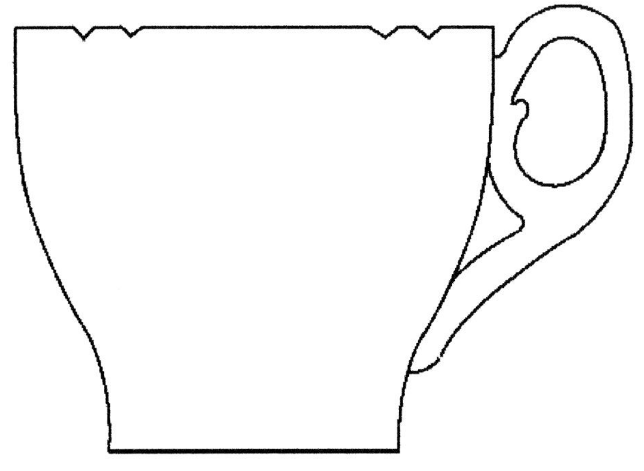

Cambridge silhouette

Cambridge

Canterbury

Miniature. Used for Bestware, Giftware, and Ideal China/ Canadian Tea Wares. An optional giftware box was available. Produced from c.1955-1966.

Canterbury silhouette

Carlisle

Used for Bestware, Ideal China/Canadian Tea Wares, and Seconds Ware. Produced from c.1950-1966.

Carlisle silhouette

Carlisle

Carlton

Used for Bestware and Seconds Ware. Produced from c.1925-1936.

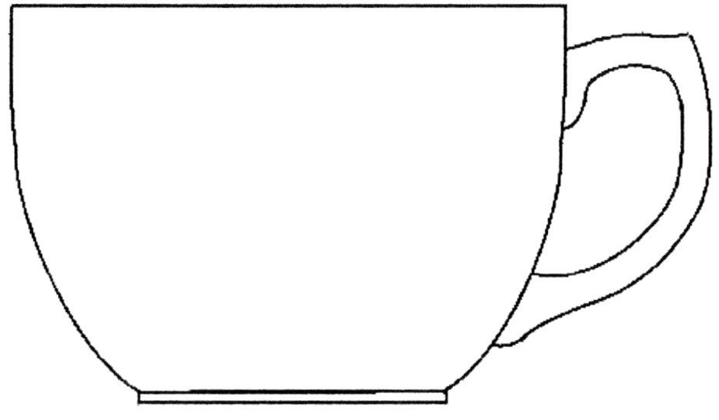

Carlton silhouette

Century

Used for Bestware and Seconds Ware. Produced from c.1895-1902.

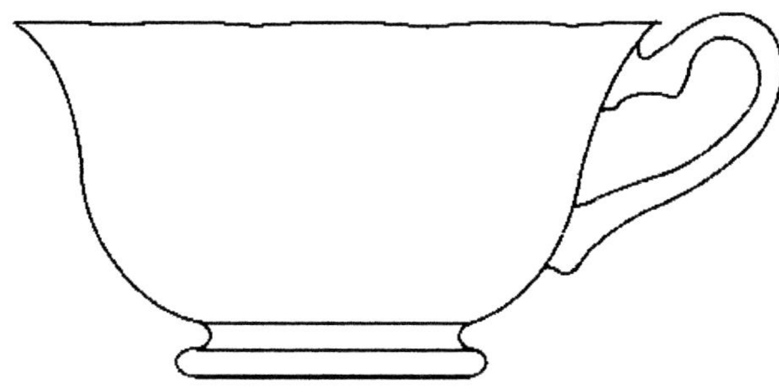

Century silhouette

Century

Chester

Used for Bestware, Ideal China/Canadian Tea Wares, and Seconds Ware. Produced from c.1931-1962.

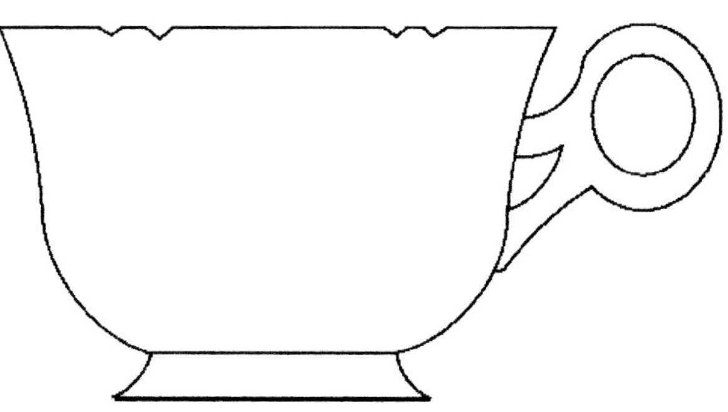

Chester silhouette

Chocolate

Large, lidded cup.

Chocolate silhouette

Court (Early)

Registration number 447137 recorded in 1905. Used for Bestware and Seconds Ware. Produced from c.1906-1913.

Court (Early) silhouette

Court (Early)

Court (Late)

Registration number 771299. Used for Bestware. Produced from c.1935-1938.

Court (Late) silhouette

Court (Late)

Dainty

Registration number 272101 recorded in 1896. Registration number 735121 is for a Dainty plate shape variation. Also referred to as Low Dainty. Designed by Rowland Morris. Extremely popular and successful shape. Used for Bestware, Ideal China/Canadian Tea Wares, and Seconds Ware. There were four variations of the Dainty shape. Sometimes the Pattern Book referred to the shape as being Dainty, but it may well have been one of these variations. Tea and coffee/demitasse cups were made in this shape. Produced from c.1896-1966. It was also produced for more than a year after Shelley was taken over in order to honour outstanding orders. *Also see Floral Dainty, Footed Dainty, Tall Dainty, and Tall Floral Dainty.*

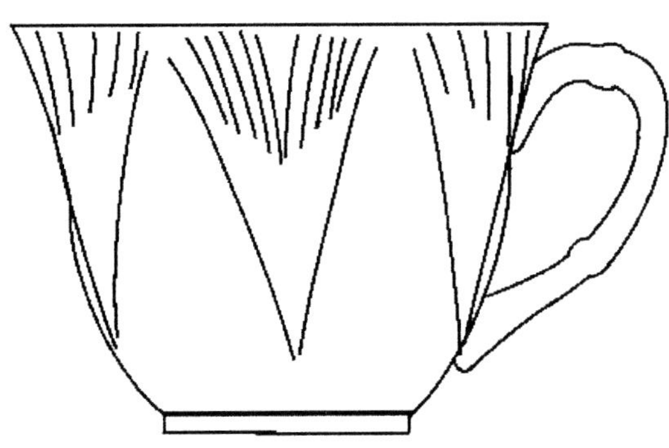

Dainty silhouette

Dainty

Daisy

Registration numbers 115510 recorded in 1888. Used for Bestware and Seconds Ware. Tea and coffee/demitasse cups were made in this shape. Produced from c.1889-1913.

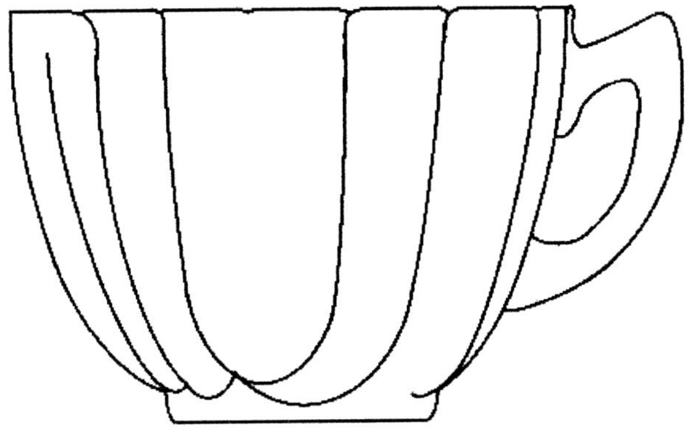

Daisy silhouette

Daisy

Devon

Used for Bestware and Ideal China/Canadian Tea Wares. Produced from c.1937-1939.

Devon silhouette

Devonshire

Used for Bestware. Produced from c.1905-1906.

Devonshire silhouette

Doric

Used for Bestware and Seconds Ware. Produced from c.1924-1932.

Doric silhouette

Doric

Dorothy (Early)

Used for Bestware and Seconds Ware. Produced from c.1906-1918.

Dorothy (Late)

Used for Bestware and Seconds Ware. Similar to the Perth shape, but the Dorothy shape has a very small foot while the Perth has no foot at all. Produced from c.1945-1953.

Dorothy (Early) silhouette

Dorothy (Early)

Dorothy (Late) silhouette

Dorothy (Late)

Edward

Used for Bestware. Produced c.1905.

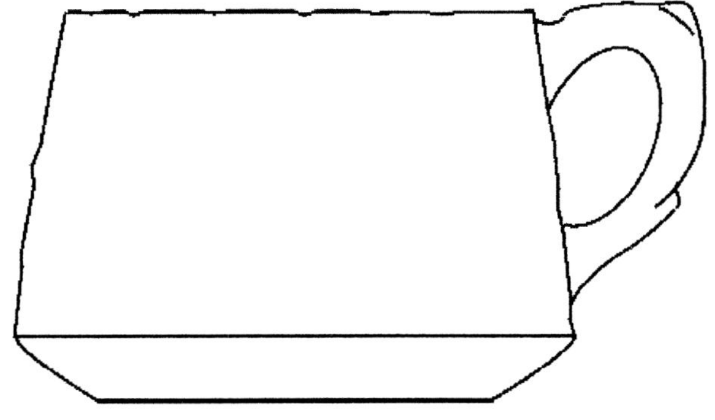

Edward silhouette

Egg

Cup is the same shape as an egg cup. The handle is similar to the old York's handle. Produced from c.1889-1890s.

Egg silhouette

Ely

Used for Bestware, Ideal China/Canadian Tea Wares, and Seconds Ware. Produced from c.1939-1960.

Ely silhouette

Ely

Empire (Early)

Registration number 108329 recorded in 1893. Used for Bestware and Seconds Ware. Produced from c.1893-1930.

Empire (Early) silhouette

Empire (Early)

Empire (Late)

Used for Bestware, Ideal China/Canadian Tea Wares, and Seconds Ware. Produced from c.1930-1939.

Empire (Late)

Empire (Late)

Eve

Registration number 756533 recorded in 1930. Used for Bestware, Ideal China/Canadian Tea Wares, and Seconds Ware. Tea and coffee/demitasse cups were made in this shape. Produced from c.1935-1942.

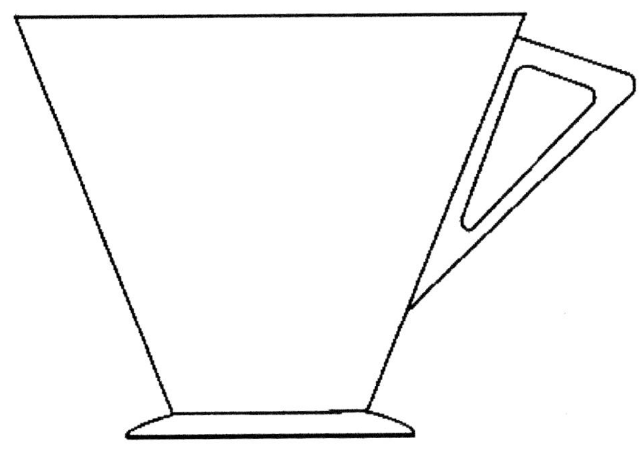

Eve silhouette

Essex

Used for Bestware and Ideal China/Canadian Tea Wares. Produced from c.1938-1940.

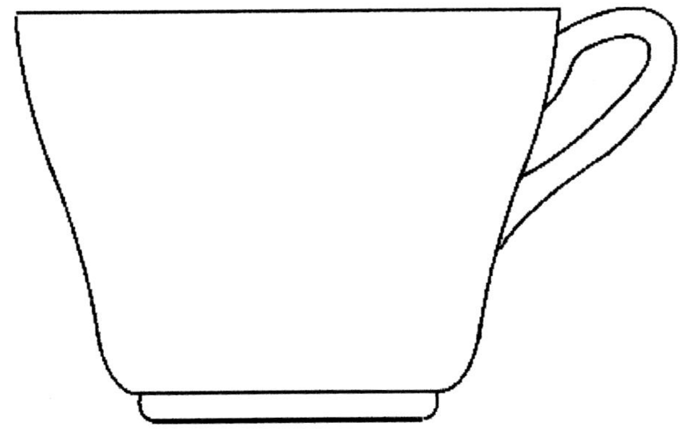

Essex silhouette

Eve

Essex

Fairy

Registration number 153594 recorded in 1890. Also referred to as New Fairy. Similar to the Violet shape, but the flute indentations are not as deep as those on the Violet shape. Used for Bestware and Seconds Ware. Produced from c.1890-1899.

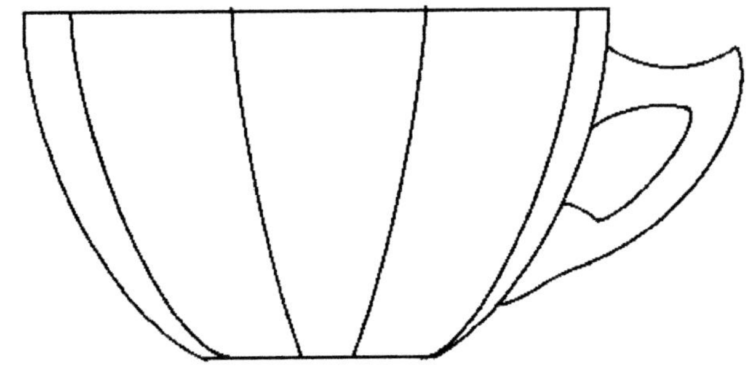

Fairy silhouette

Fairy

Floral Dainty

Figural, flower-shaped handle. Produced c.1932. *Also see Dainty, Footed Dainty, Tall Dainty, and Tall Floral Dainty.*

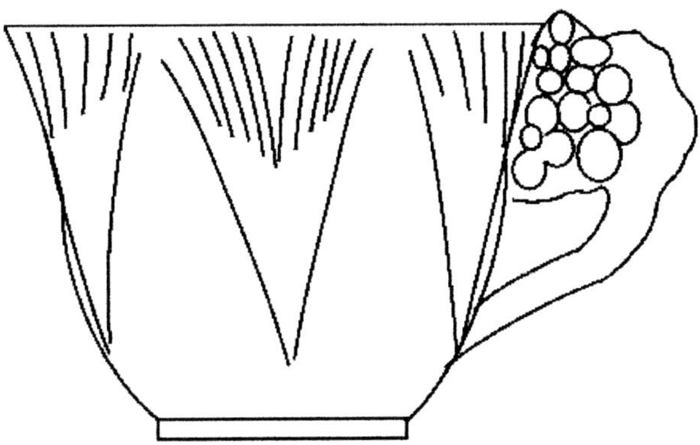

Floral Dainty silhouette

Floral Queen Anne

Figural, tulip-shaped handle. Used for Bestware. Produced c.1932.

Foley

Used for Bestware and Seconds Ware. Produced from c.1894-1910.

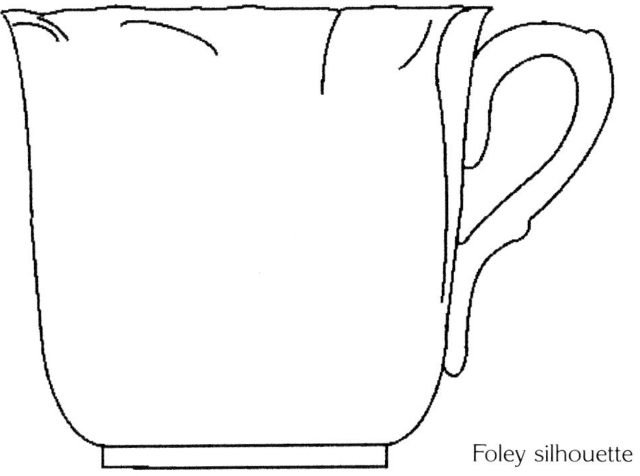

Foley silhouette

Foley Flute

Registration number 448983 recorded in 1905. Used for Bestware and Seconds Ware. Produced from c.1904-1916.

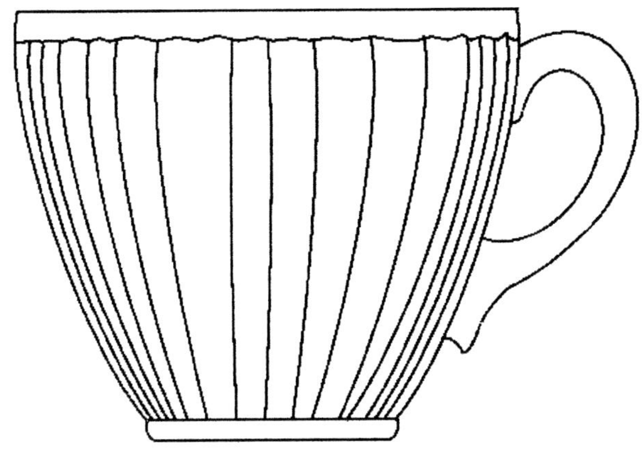

Foley Flute silhouette

Foley Flute

Footed Dainty

Used for Bestware, Ideal China/Canadian Tea Wares, and Seconds Ware. *Also see Dainty, Floral Dainty, Tall Dainty, and Tall Floral Dainty.*

Footed Dainty silhouette

Footed Dainty

Gainsborough

Similar to the Milton shape. The foot is higher than on the Milton shape. Used for Bestware and Seconds Ware. Tea and coffee/demitasse cups were made in this shape. Produced from c.1900-1965.

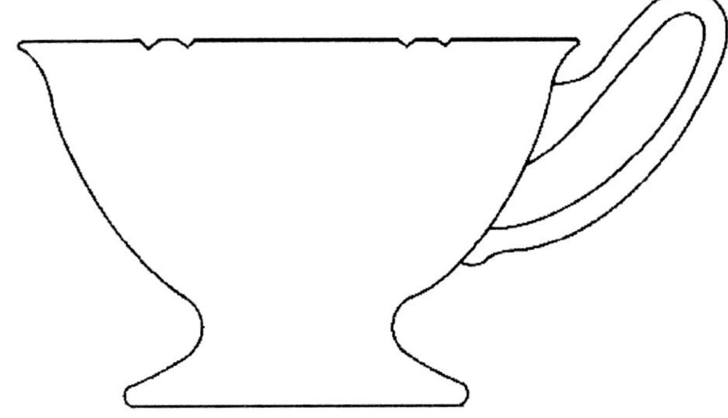

Gainsborough silhouette

Gainsborough

Gainsborough double handled soup/bouillon

Footed Oleander

Used for Bestware, Ideal China/Canadian Tea Wares, and Seconds Ware. Produced from c.1935-1962. *Also see Oleander and Tall Oleander.*

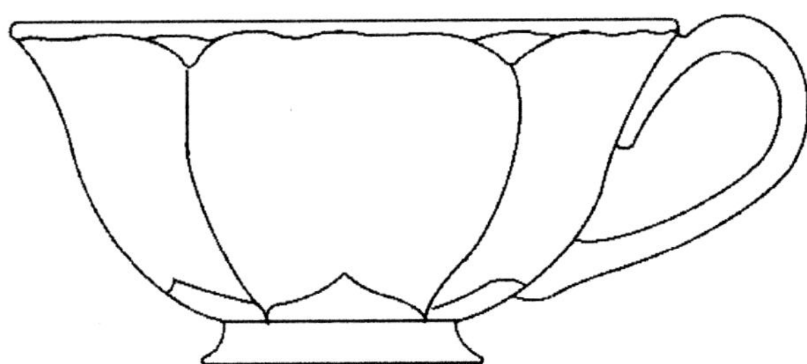

Footed Oleander silhouette

Footed Oleander

Georgian

Used for Bestware, Ideal China/Canadian Tea Wares, and Seconds Ware. Produced from c.1929-1931.

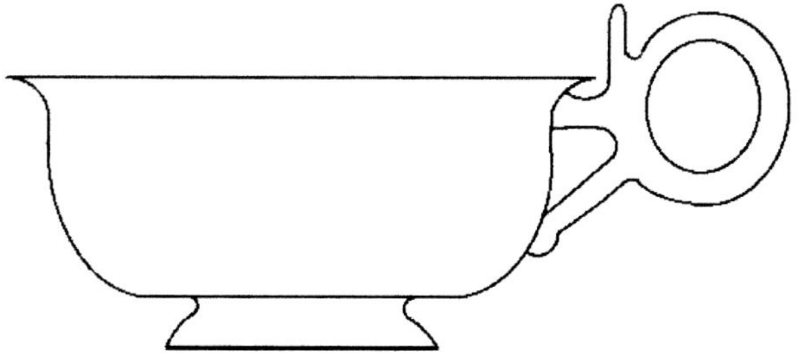

Georgian silhouette

Georgian

Henley

Hyderabad

Reputed to have been designed for a Nazam of Hyderabad.

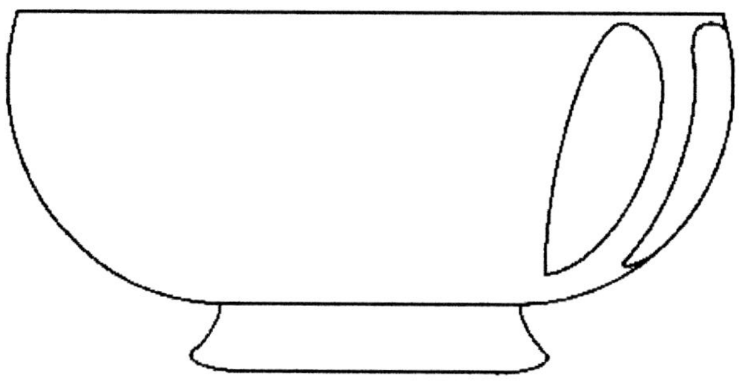

Hyderabad silhouette

Gladstone

Used for special orders of commemorative ware. Produced from c.1886-1913.

Henley

Used for Bestware, Ideal China/Canadian Tea Wares, and Seconds Ware. Tea and coffee/demitasse cups were made in this shape. Produced from c.1938-1964.

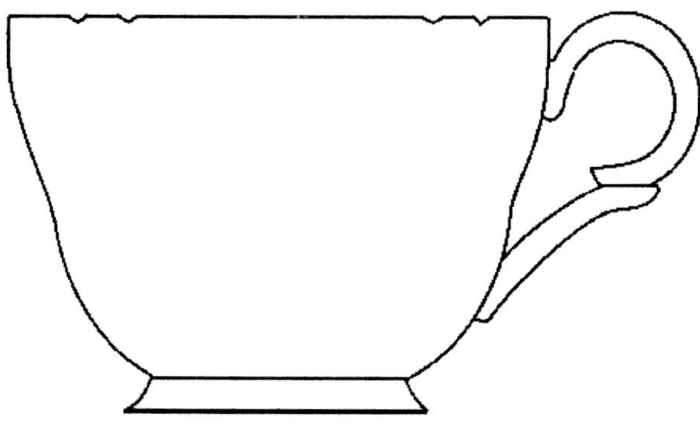

Henley silhouette

Ideal

Registration number 351373 recorded in 1900. Also known as the Scallop shape. The Pattern Books make no reference to the production of any Tea Wares, although there are examples of it in this shape.

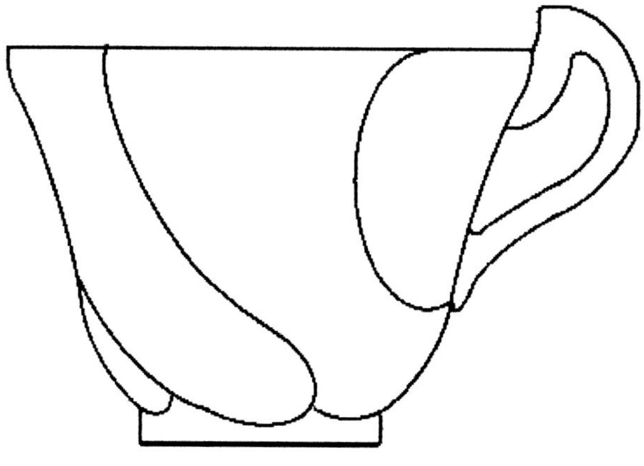

Ideal silhouette

Jubilee Flute

See Albert.

Kenneth

Named after one of Percy Shelley's twin sons, Kenneth Jack. Used for Bestware and Seconds Ware. Produced from c.1921-1926.

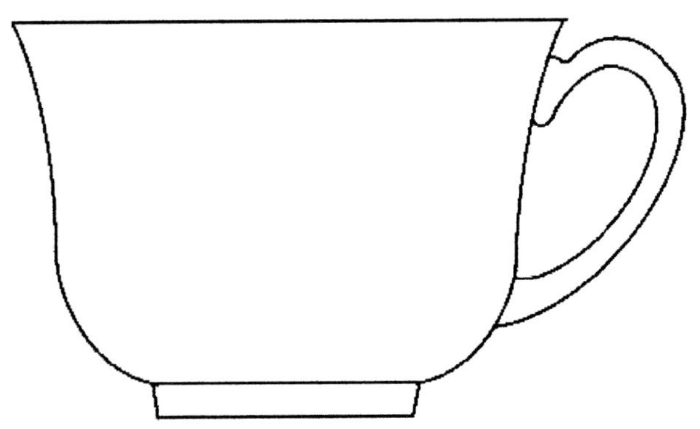

Kenneth silhouette

Kenneth

Kent

Registration number 823342. Used for Bestware. Produced from c.1937-1940.

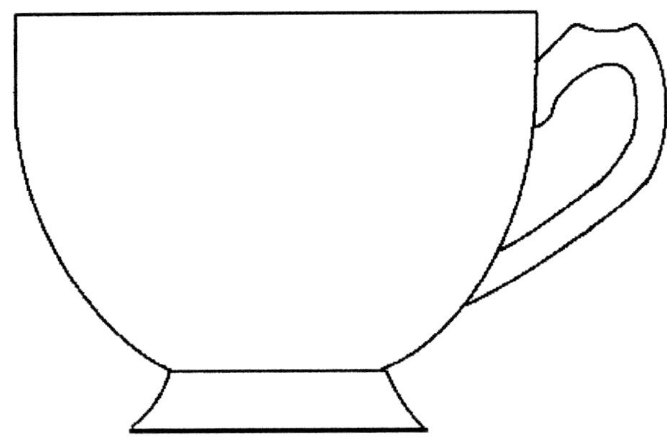

Kent silhouette

Lily (Early)

Used for Bestware and Seconds Ware. Produced from c.1888-1918.

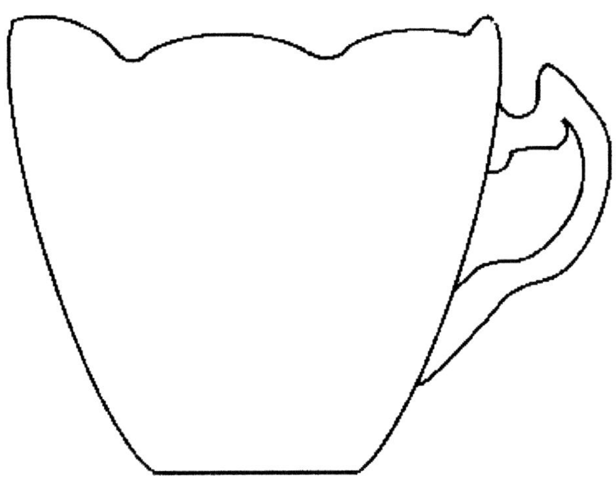

Lily (Early) silhouette

Lily (Late)

Used for Bestware and Seconds Ware. Tea and breakfast cups were made in this shape. Produced from c.1888-1918.

Lily (Late) silhouette

Lily (Late)

Lincoln

Used for Bestware and Ideal China/Canadian Tea Wares. This shape evolved from the Boston shape. The only difference between the two is that the Boston has a notched foot and rim, and the Lincoln has no notches on the foot and shallower notches on the rim. Designed primarily for export. Produced from c.1963-1966.

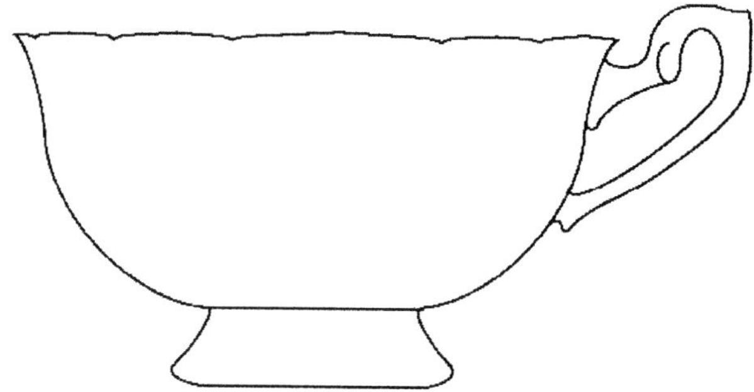

Lincoln silhouette

Lomond

Lincoln

Low Lily

Also referred to as New Lily. Used for Bestware and Seconds Ware. Produced from c.1906-1914.

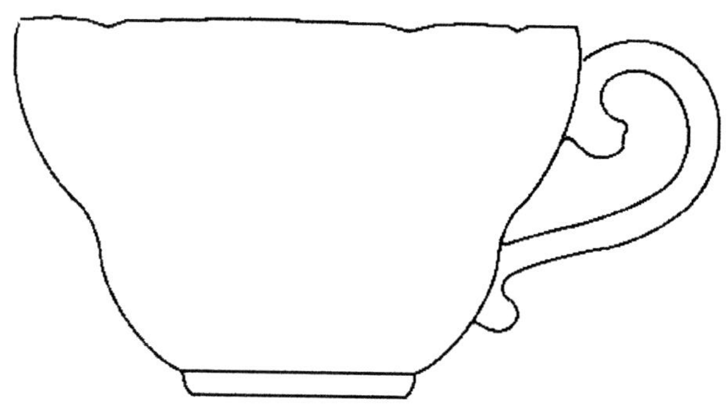

Low Lily silhouette

Lomond

Used for Bestware and Seconds Ware. Produced from c.1926-1929.

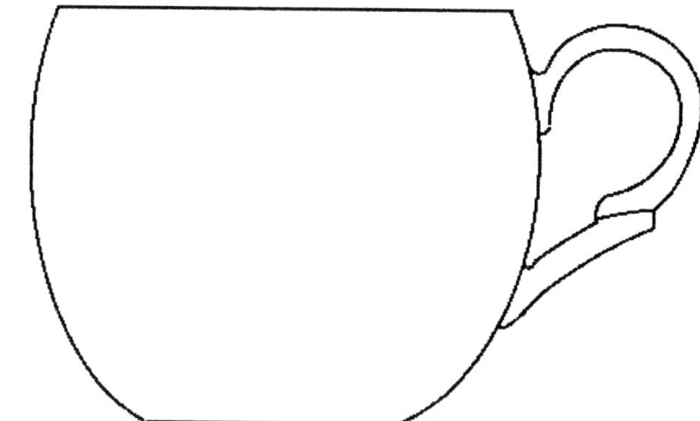

Lomond silhouette

Low Lily

Low Oleander

See Oleander.

Ludlow

Used for Bestware, Ideal China/Canadian Tea Wares, and Seconds Ware. Produced from c.1938-1966.

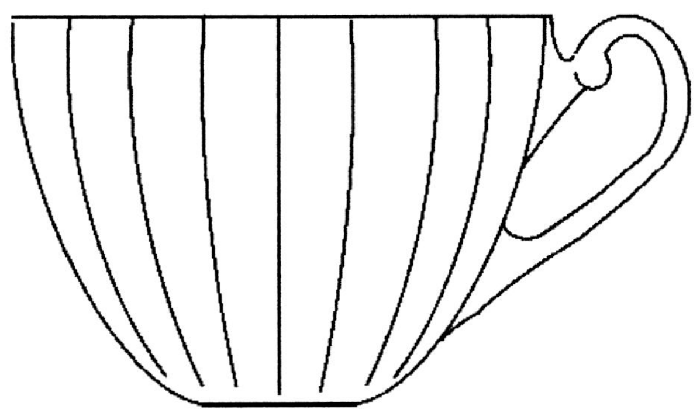

Ludlow silhouette

Ludlow

Mayfair

Registration number 771299. Used for Bestware, Ideal China/Canadian Tea Wares, and Seconds Ware. Produced from c.1932-1937.

Mayfair silhouette

Mayfair

May

Used for Bestware. Produced from c.1893-1894.

May silhouette

Milton

Similar to the Gainsborough shape. The foot is lower than on the Gainsborough shape. The earlier Milton shape has a higher foot then the later ones. Used for Bestware and Seconds Ware. Produced from c.1900-1927.

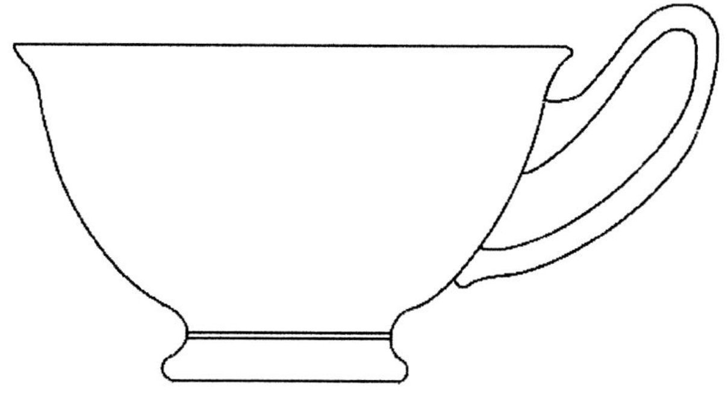

Milton silhouette

Milton

Minton

Used mainly for early patterns and special orders of commemorative ware. Produced from c.1883-1907.

Mocha

Coffee can. Used for Bestware, Ideal China/Canadian Tea Wares, and Seconds Ware. Produced from c.1913-1966. From c.1962 a larger size was produced, sometimes referred to as New Mocha.

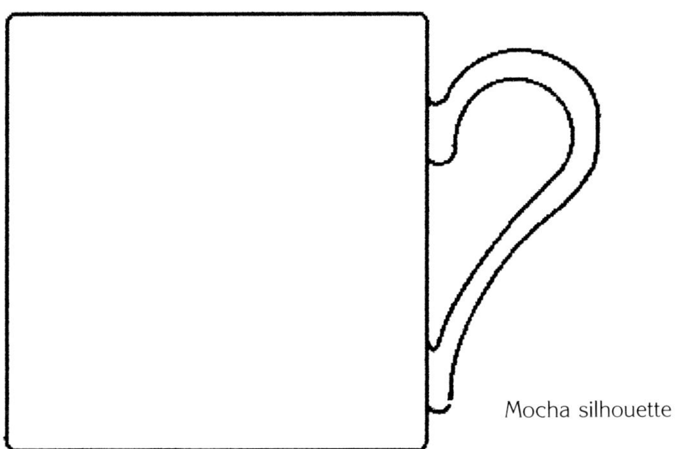

Mocha silhouette

Mocha

Mode

Registration number 756533 recorded in 1930. Used for Bestware and Seconds Ware. Produced from c.1928-1931.

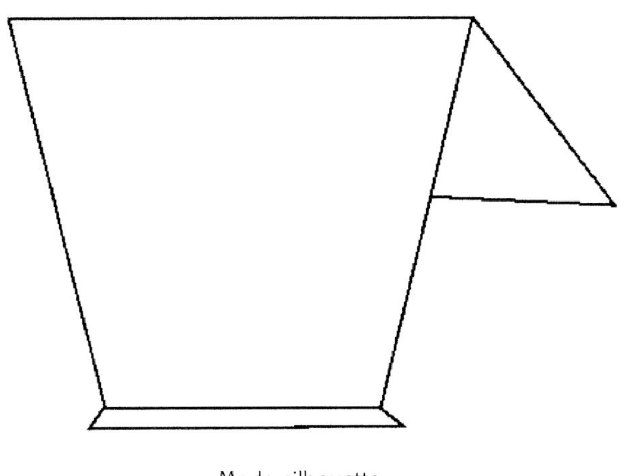

Mode silhouette

New Cambridge

Used for Bestware, Ideal China/Canadian Tea Wares, and Seconds Ware. Produced from c.1951-1962.

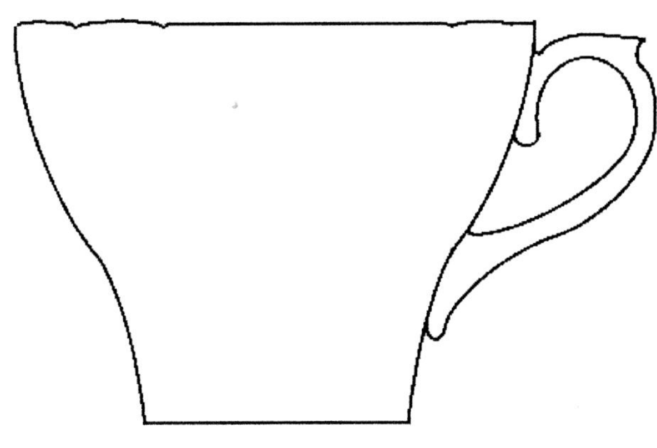

New Cambridge silhouette

New Cambridge

New Victoria

Also referred to as Victor. Used for Bestware and Ideal China/Canadian Tea Wares. Produced from c.1940s-1966.

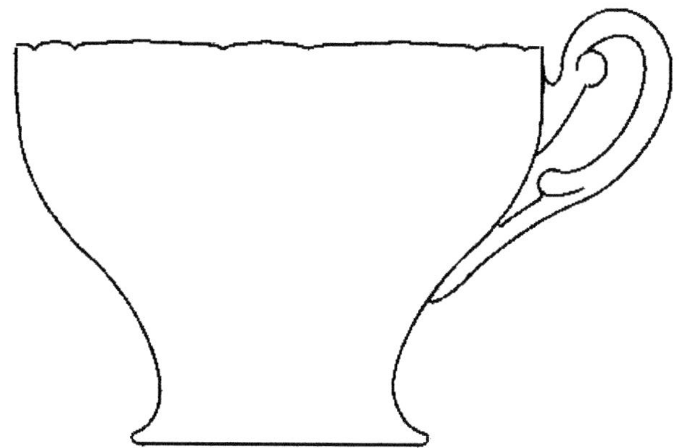

New Victoria silhouette

New Victoria

New York

Used for Bestware and Seconds Ware. Produced from c.1890-1925.

New York silhouette

New York

Norman

Named after one of Percy Shelley's sons, Percy Norman. Used for Bestware and Seconds Ware. Produced from c.1915-1924.

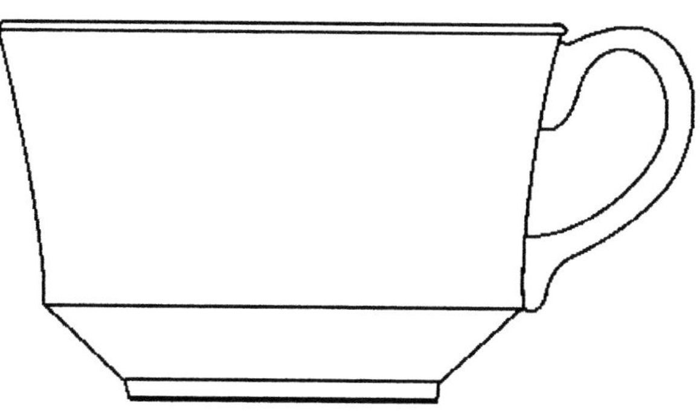

Norman silhouette

Norman

Oleander

Registration number 594382 recorded in 1912. Also referred to as Low Oleander. Used for Bestware, Ideal China/ Canadian Tea Wares, and Seconds Ware. Early production was plain white. There were three variations of the Oleander shape. Sometimes the Pattern Book referred to the shape as being Oleander, but it may well have been one of these variations. Tea and coffee/demitasse cups were made in this shape. Produced from c.1914-1962. *Also see Footed Oleander and Tall Oleander.*

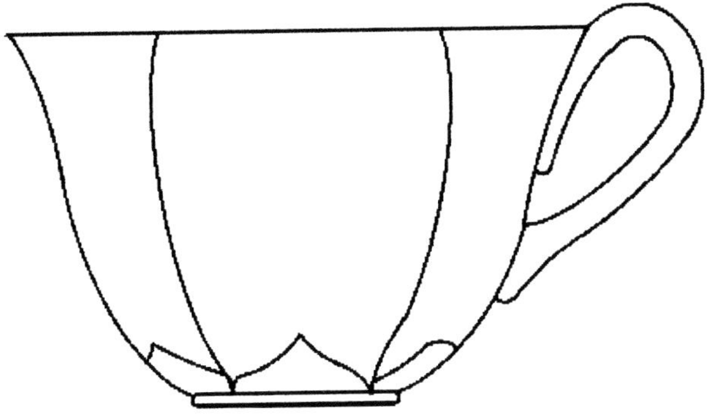

Oleander silhouette

Oleander

Ovide

Used for Bestware and Seconds Ware. Mainly used for special patterns. Large, breakfast cup. Produced from c.1956-1958.

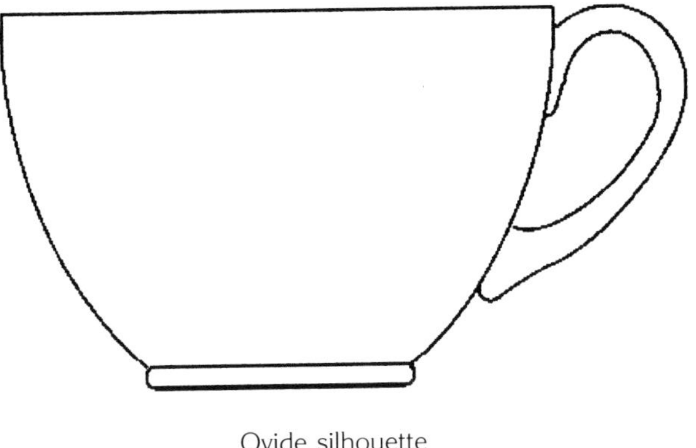

Ovide silhouette

Oxford

Registration number 795072 recorded in 1934. Used for Bestware, Ideal China/Canadian Tea Wares, and Seconds Ware. Tea and coffee/demitasse cups were made in this shape. Produced from c.1934-1940.

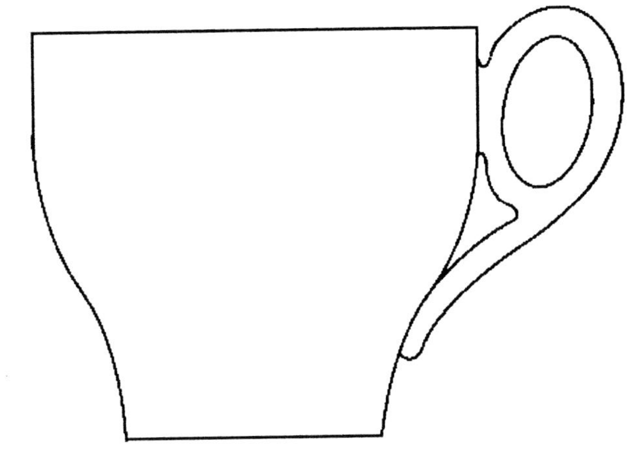

Oxford silhouette

Oxford

Paris

Used for special orders of commemorative ware. Produced from c.1887-1895.

Perth

Registration number 781613. Early cups have notched lip, later ones have a straight lip. Originally known as New Regent. Used for Bestware, Ideal China/Canadian Tea Wares, and Seconds Ware. Produced from c.1939-1962.

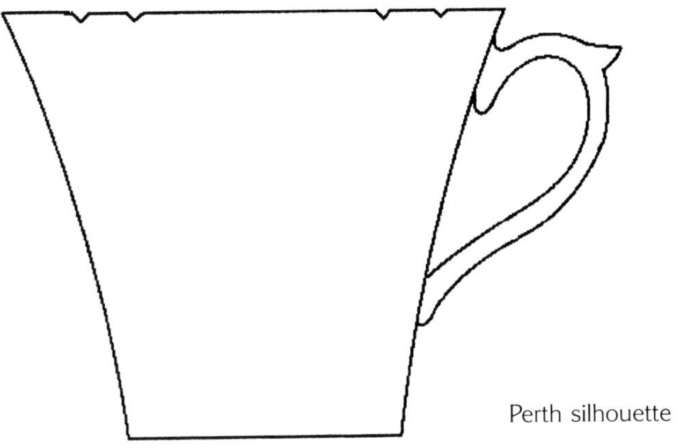

Perth silhouette

Perth

Poppy

Rare as it was only recorded against four pattern numbers. Produced c.1895.

Princess

Variation of the Queen Anne shape. Used for Bestware, Ideal China/Canadian Tea Wares, and Seconds Ware. Tea and coffee/demitasse cups were made in this shape. Produced from c.1933-1940s.

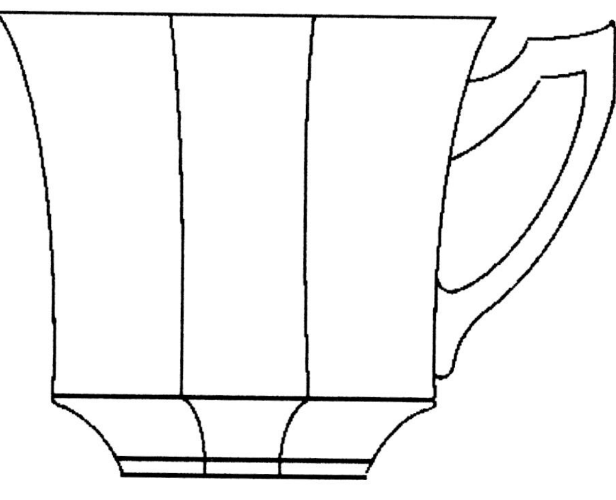

Princess silhouette

Princess

Queen Anne

Registration number 723404 recorded in 1926. Octagonal shape with four large and four smaller panels. Used for Bestware, Ideal China/Canadian Tea Wares, and Seconds Ware. Tea and coffee/demitasse cups were made in this shape. Produced from c.1926-1960s.

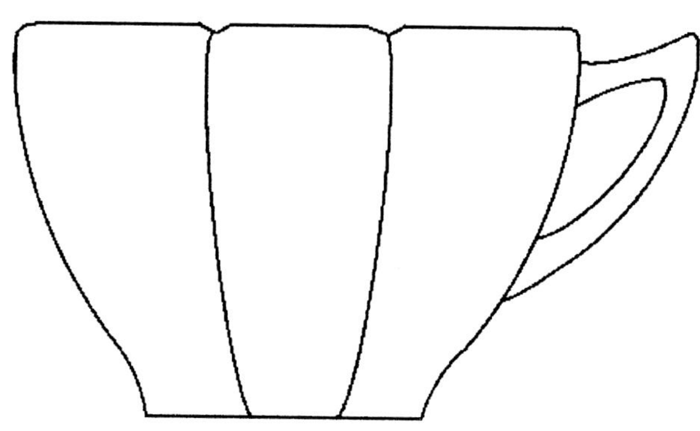

Queen Anne silhouette

Queen Anne

Regent

Registration number 781613 recorded in 1933. Used for Bestware, Ideal China/Canadian Tea Wares, and Seconds Ware. Tea and coffee/demitasse cups were made in this shape. Produced from c.1930-1962.

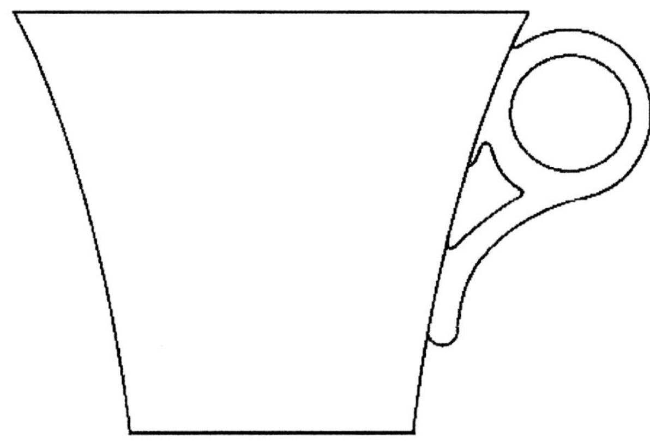

Regent silhouette

Richmond

Regent

Ripon

Used for Bestware, Ideal China/Canadian Tea Wares, and Seconds Ware. Produced from c.1937-1966.

Ripon silhouette

Richmond

Used for Bestware and Seconds Ware. Tea and coffee/ demitasse cups were made in this shape. In 1961 a variation is shown in the Pattern Books, where on a few occasions a Gainsborough handle was used on the Richmond shape. Produced from c.1938-1966.

Richmond silhouette

Ripon

Roman

Used mainly for special orders of commemorative ware. Used for Bestware and Seconds Ware. Produced from c.1886-1913.

Royal

Used for Bestware and Seconds Ware. Produced from c.1902-1916.

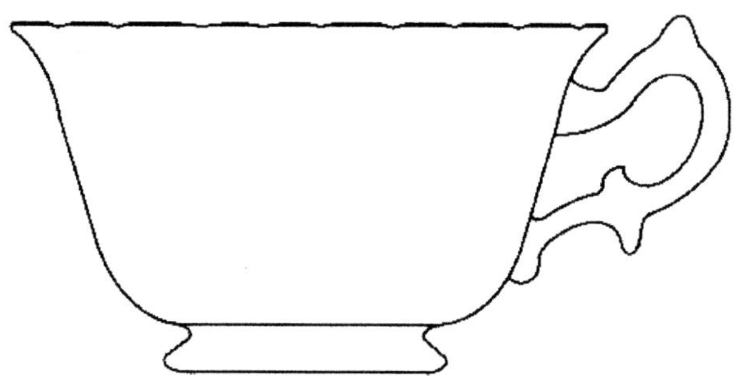

Royal silhouette

Royal

Savoy

Used for Bestware and Seconds Ware. Produced from c.1928-1933.

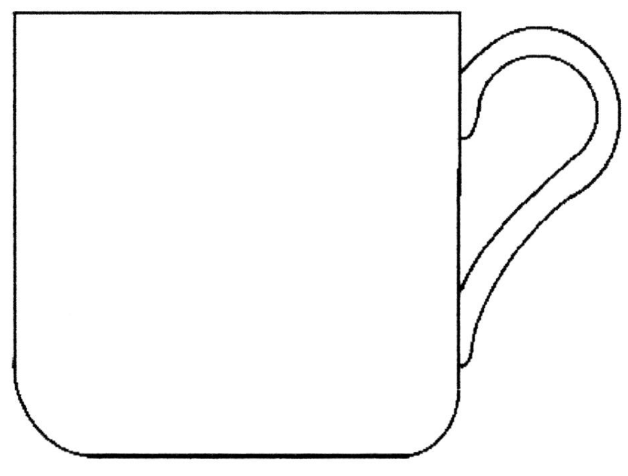

Savoy silhouette

Scallop

See Ideal.

Scandinavian Coffee

Used for Bestware and Seconds Ware. Designed for export to the Scandinavian countries. Larger than coffee cans, but smaller than a teacup.

Shell

Registration number 150035 recorded in 1890. Similar to Belleek's first period Echinus pattern, which is based on the spiny tea urchin. Tea and coffee/demitasse cups were made in this shape. Produced from c.1891-1894.

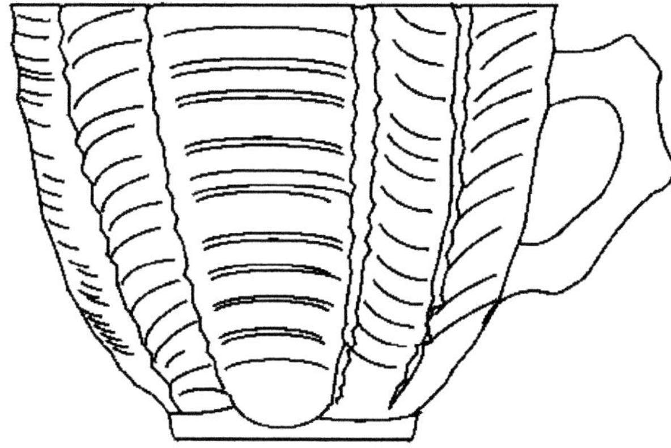

Shell silhouette

Shell

Silver

Used for special orders of commemorative ware. Used for Bestware and Seconds Ware. Produced from c.1889-1917.

Snowdrop

Registration numbers 272764 and 283973 recorded in 1896. Produced from c.1896-1914.

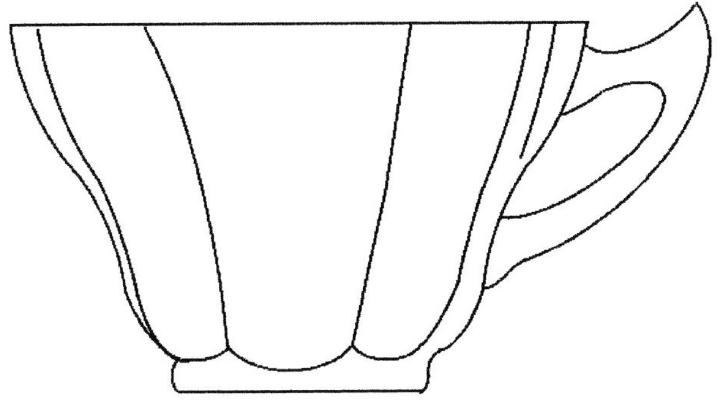

Snowdrop silhouette

Snowdrop

Special

Used for special orders.

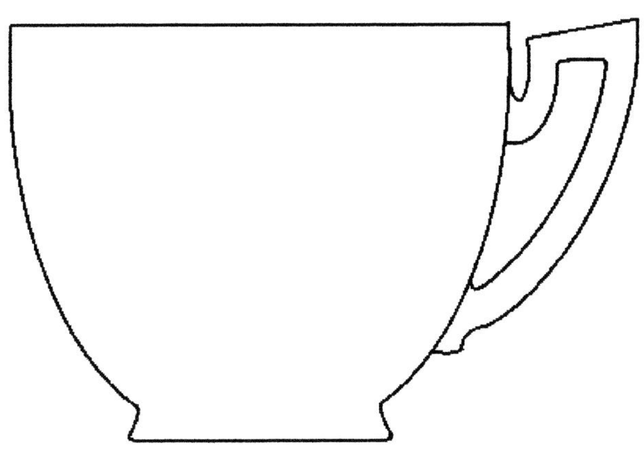

Special silhouette

Spiral

Used for Bestware and Seconds Ware.

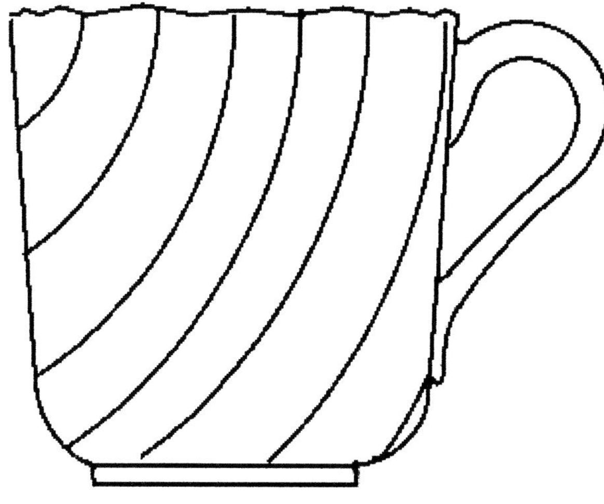

Spiral silhouette

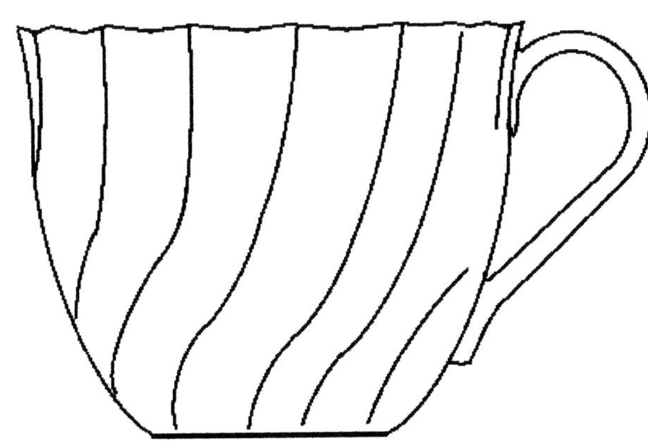

Spiral Fluted silhouette

Square

Registration number 6559 recorded in 1884. Also referred to as Square Queen Anne or Square Antique. Handle is similar to Albert. Produced from c.1884-1888.

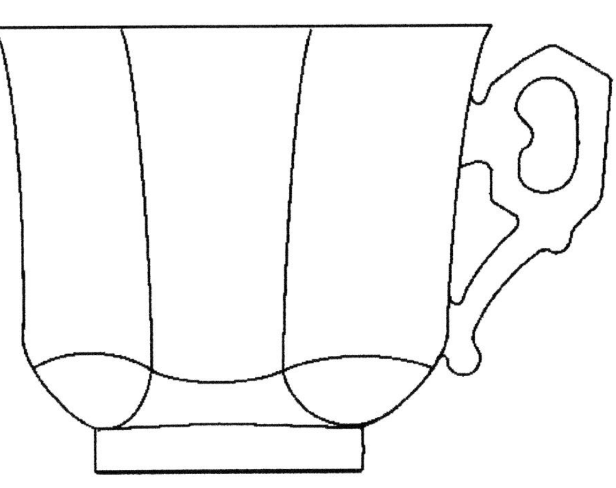

Square silhouette

Stanley

Coffee cup. Produced from c.1891-1918.

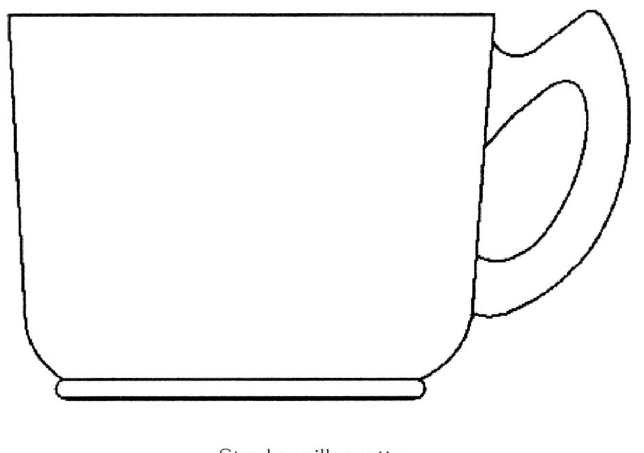

Stanley silhouette

Strand

Used for Bestware and Seconds Ware. Produced from c.1933-1940s.

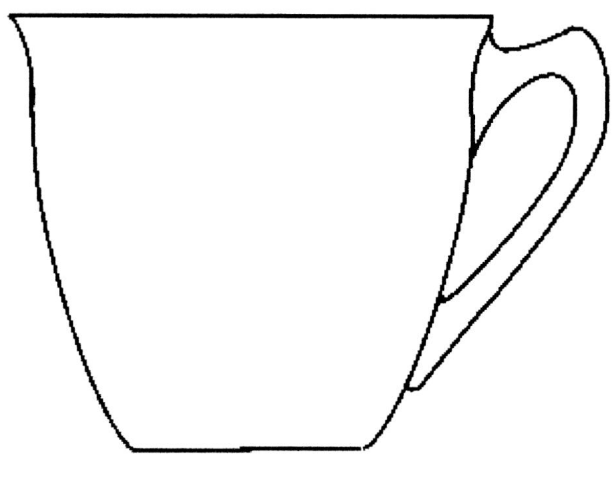

Strand silhouette

Strand

Stirling

Designed by Eric Slater. Used for Bestware and Seconds Ware. Produced from c.1956-1964.

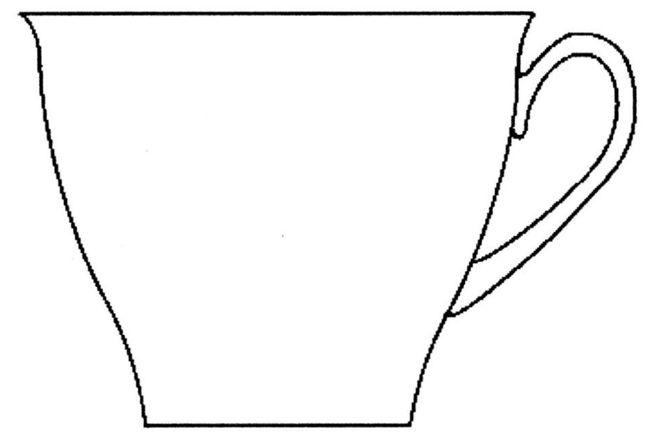

Stirling silhouette

Stirling

Stratford

Used for Bestware, Ideal China/Canadian Tea Wares, and Seconds Ware. Shown in some advertising material with a Warwick handle. Produced c.1950-1965.

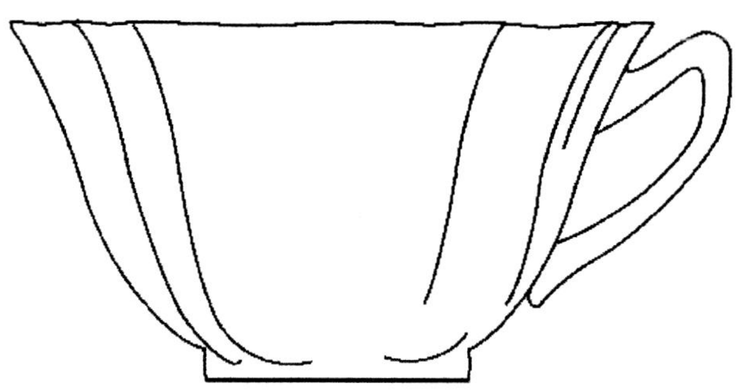

Stratford silhouette

Stratford

Tall Dainty

Registration number 272101 recorded in 1896. Designed by Rowland Morris. Extremely popular and successful shape. Used for Bestware, Ideal China/Canadian Tea Wares, and Seconds Ware. Tea and coffee/demitasse cups were made in this shape. Produced from c.1927-1966. *Also see Dainty, Floral Dainty, Footed Dainty, and Tall Floral Dainty.*

Tall Dainty silhouette

Tall Dainty

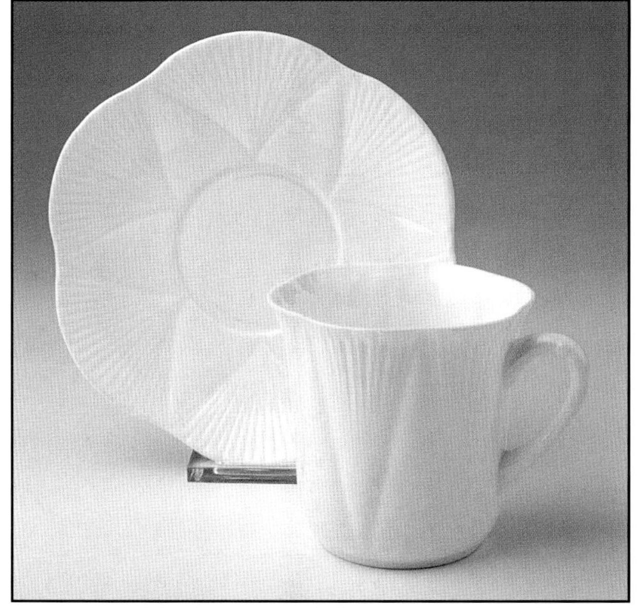

Tall Floral Dainty

Registration number 272101 recorded in 1896. Used for Ideal China/Canadian Tea Wares. Figural, flower-shaped handle. Coffee/demitasse cups were made in this shape. *Also see Dainty, Floral Dainty, Footed Dainty, and Tall Dainty.*

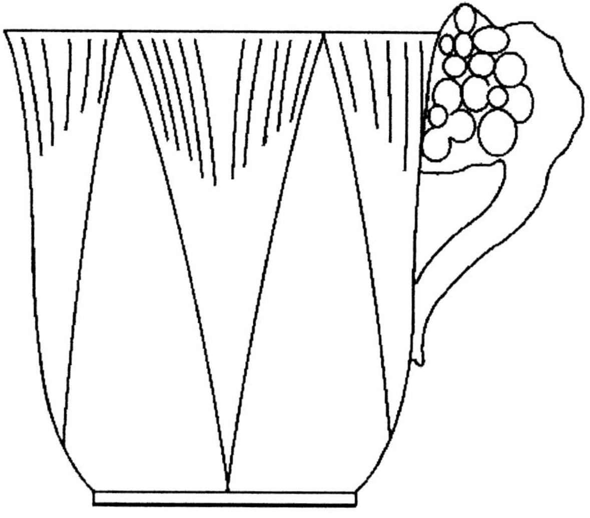

Tall Floral Dainty silhouette

Tall Oleander

Produced from c.1914-1962. *Also see Footed Oleander and Oleander.*

Tall Oleander silhouette

Turkish Can

Coffee cup. Produced from c.1887-1904.

Unhandled Coffee

Coffee cup without a handle, placed in an EPNS (Electro Plated Nickel Silver) holder.

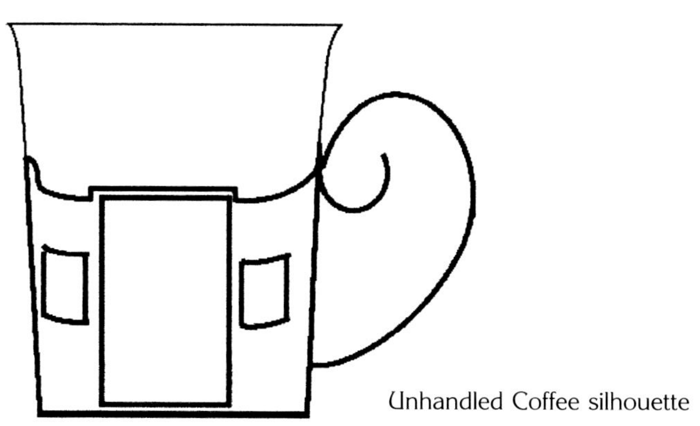

Unhandled Coffee silhouette

Unknown

A few examples of this shape have been discovered. It is one of seven currently identified shapes that have not been matched to a name. This shape has been found with Wileman 1872-1890 and Shelley 1916-1925 back stamps.

Unknown silhouette

Unnamed

A number of examples of this cup shape exist, all with the Shelley 1940-1966 back stamp and decorated with familiar Shelley patterns. The Pattern Books make no reference to this shape. It is now generally accepted as being a Royal Albert shape, produced after the takeover.

Unnamed silhouette

Unnamed

Victor

See New Victoria.

Victoria

Used for Bestware and Seconds Ware. Produced from c.1882-1922. *Also see New Victoria.*

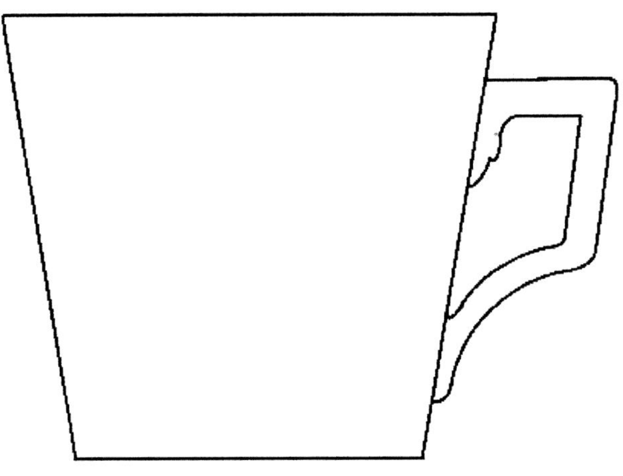

Victoria silhouette

Victoria

Vincent

Named after one of Percy Shelley's twin sons, Vincent Bob. Used for Bestware, Ideal China/Canadian Tea Wares, and Seconds Ware. The size decreased slightly in later years. There are also some variations to saucers over the years, and the plates are either round or square. Produced from c.1916-1940s.

Vincent silhouette

Vincent

Vogue

Registration number 756533 recorded in 1930. Used for Bestware and Seconds Ware. An example of Vogue with a figural handle has been noted; this handle has a moulded bunch of grapes. Produced from c.1930-1933.

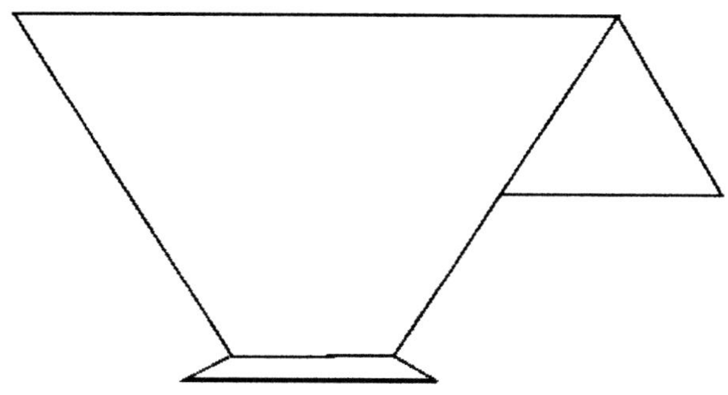

Vogue silhouette

Violet

Registration numbers 153594 and 181135 recorded in 1890 and 1896 respectively. Used for Bestware and Seconds Ware. Produced from c.1899-1913. *Also see Fairy.*

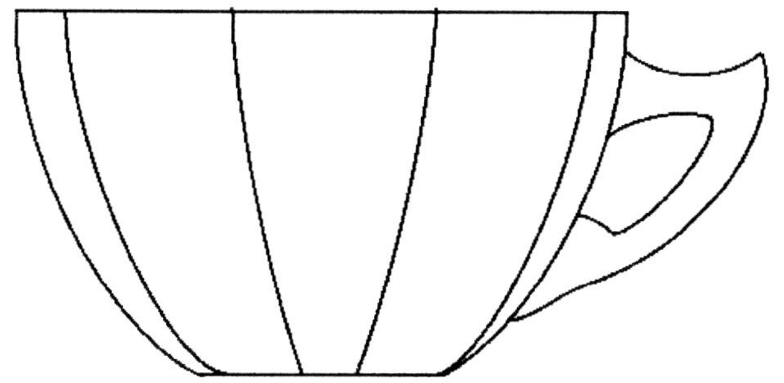

Violet silhouette

Vogue

Violet

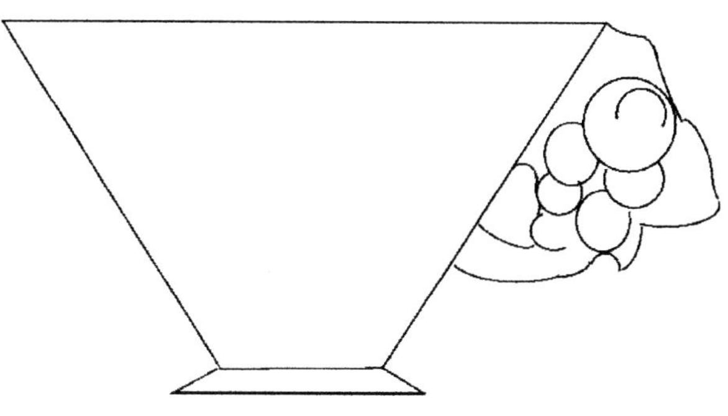

Vogue Figural Handle silhouette

Warwick

Used for Bestware, Ideal China/Canadian Tea Wares, and Seconds Ware. Produced from c.1939-1966.

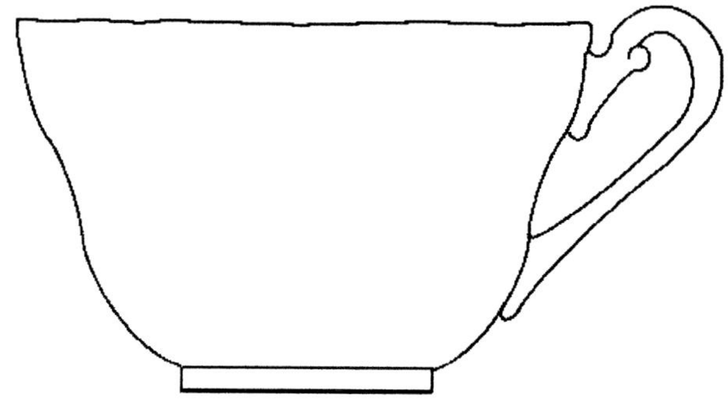

Warwick silhouette

Warwick

Westminster

Miniature. Used for Bestware, Giftware, and Ideal China/ Canadian Tea Wares. An optional giftware box was available. Produced from c.1957-1966.

Westminster silhouette

Windsor

Used for Bestware and Seconds Ware. Produced from c.1934-1964.

Windsor silhouette

Windsor

Worcester

Produced from c.1883-1925.

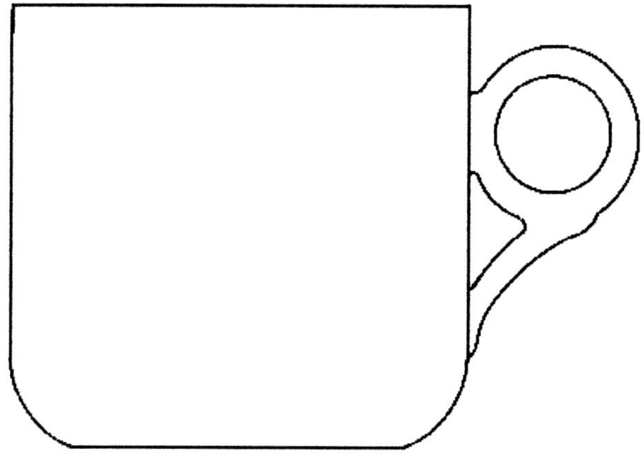

Worcester silhouette

York (Early)

Also referred to as Old York. Used for Bestware, Ideal China/Canadian Tea Wares, and Seconds Ware. Produced from c.1895-1910s.

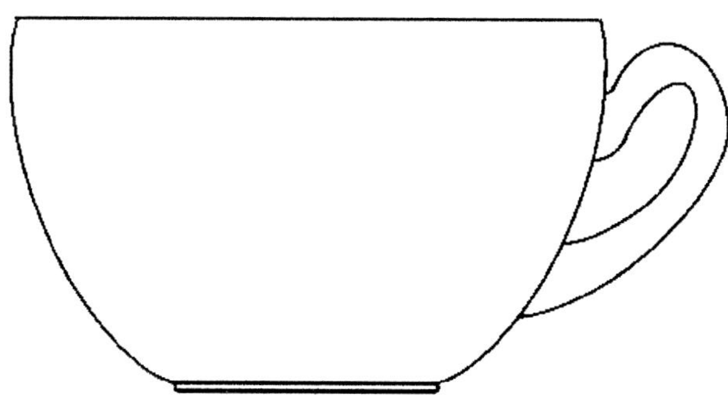

York (Early)silhouette

York (Late)

Used for Bestware, Ideal China/Canadian Tea Wares, and Seconds Ware. Produced from c.1932-1938.

York (Late) silhouette

York (Late)

Marks and Back Stamps

The marks on the base of Shelley and Wileman Tea Wares can be used to date an item. The marks included on items vary, but can include all, some, or none of the following:

Maker's Back Stamp

The maker's printed back stamp is either Wileman or Shelley. There are a number of variations, some of which are covered in this Chapter. Each variation covers a time period, e.g. the Shelley Late Foley back stamp was used from 1910 to 1916. Refer to the section below entitled *Back Stamps*.

Registration Number

Registration numbers are normally preceded by 'Rd' on the base of items. A registration number can represent a registered shape or pattern. Some earlier pieces may have an impressed registration mark only, while others may also have a printed mark. Later pieces only have the printed registration number. There are pieces that are not marked with the relevant registration number at all.

Pattern Number

Pattern numbers are either hand painted or printed. These numbers can be used to date an item, if it was accurately recorded in the Pattern Books. Some items have a printed pattern name, which may be in addition to a pattern number. Refer to the Chapter entitled *Patterns*.

Vendor's Mark

Vendor's details, where items were produced for a specific company, e.g. a mark can be found for items produced for Rowland Ward of Nairobi, Kenya, and the Lichfield mark can be found on items produced for the Canadian Cookware Company.

Canadian/Ideal China

Most of it has a printed 'Ideal China' mark. Some of the later items do not have this mark.

Seconds Ware

Most of the pattern numbers beginning with '2' are on Seconds Ware. Most Seconds ware pieces are marked with a number two in a circle. These items were considered by Shelley's stringent quality control to be sub-standard and were decorated with Seconds Ware patterns.

Painters Marks

Various dots and squiggles were used to identify the person who painted each piece. These marks were used to calculate the wages of the individuals who were paid on a piecemeal basis.

Cup Shape Letters

If pattern numbers were used on more than one cup shape, a single letter was added to the pattern number to indicate which shape it was used on. In some instances the same letter was used on more than one cup shape, so it is likely that letters were reused once a shape had gone out of production.

A	Gainsborough	N	Devon, Kenneth
B	Windsor, Milton	O	Savoy
C	Bute, Oxford	P	Vogue
D	Vincent	Q	Ely
E	Court (Late), Norman	R	Mode
F	Queen Anne	S	Empire (Late), Perth
G	Queen Anne (Tall)	T	Chester
H	Kent, Low Lily, New York	U	Eve
I	Cambridge, Oleander	V	Unknown
J	Carlton	W	Regent
K	Essex, Victoria	X	York (Late)
L	Doric, Ripon	Y	Princess
M	Mocha	Z	Henley, Strand

Back Stamps

The back stamps shown in this chapter are examples of those used on Tea Wares.

Wileman Pre-1872

Many of these items were unmarked, and therefore are not always easily identifiable. Some of them carried the initials of one of the Wileman family, such as Henry Wileman. Pieces may also have a printed pattern name, e.g. Formosa, Nankin, Seasons, Swallow, etc. The back stamp may also include the word 'Foley'.

Wileman 1870s Albert pattern produced by J.F. Wileman

Wileman 1872-1890

May include the words 'England' or 'Made in England'.

Wileman 1872-1890

Wileman Foley China 1890-1910

Includes the words 'Foley China'. This back stamp overlaps with the early Shelley back stamps, and you could find items made at the same time with either a Wileman or a Shelley 1910 back stamp.

Wileman Foley China 1890-1910

Shelley Late Foley 1910-1916

Includes the words 'Late Foley'. This back stamp overlaps with the last Wileman back stamp, and you could find items made at the same time with either a Wileman Foley China or a Shelley Late Foley back stamp.

Shelley Late Foley 1910-1916

Shelley 1912-1925

May include the words 'England' and/or 'China'. One of the variations does not have the Shelley name at all, only the words 'Made in England'.

Shelley 1912-1925

Shelley 1912-1925 variation with no Shelley shield

Shelley 1913-1926

Shelley 1912-1925 variation of Shelley shield

Shelley 1925-1940

Used on all wares.

Shelley 1925-1940

Shelley Sevres pattern 1920s-1930s

Shelley 1930-1932

Used on miniature cups and saucers between 1940 and 1966 as well as on some Tea Wares between 1930 and 1932.

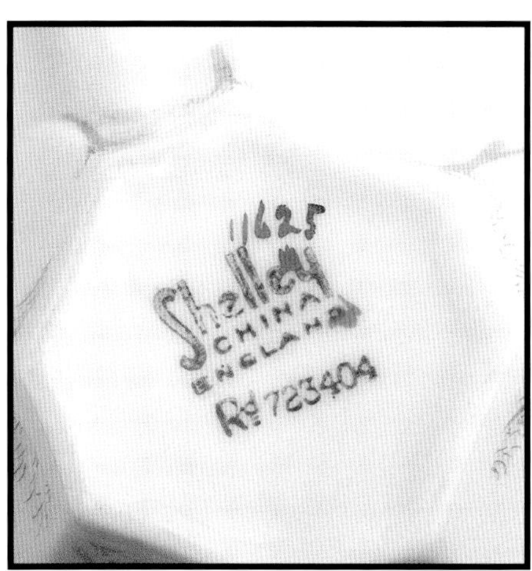

Shelley miniatures and some tea wares 1930-1932

Shelley 1940-1966

Used an all wares.

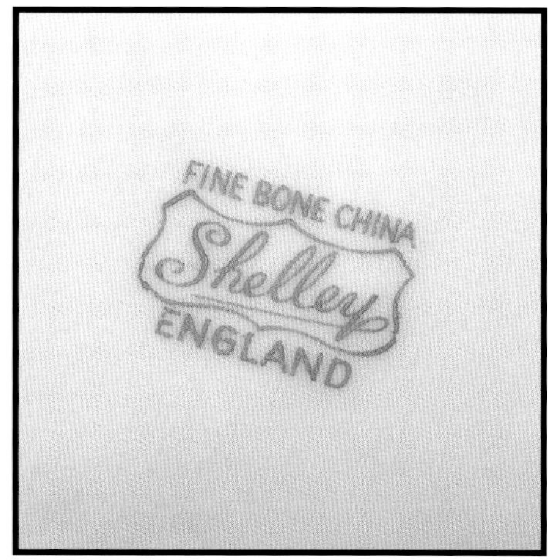

Shelley 1940-1966

Shelley Surrey Scenery pattern 1940-1966

Shelley Nairobi pattern 1940-1966

Patterns

The Shelley factory produced such a diversity of shapes and patterns, not all of which were documented thoroughly, and some not at all. This chapter explores the tea and coffee wares they produced from 1872 to 1966. Wherever possible I have described an actual example of an item. Where I have been unable to get hold of an example, I have used the pattern book details and other sources of reference to give a complete picture. As a result, the information for each pattern number is not always in the same level of detail.

This chapter lists the patterns in numerical order. Not all patterns have names, and some have unofficial names, which a number of collectors use to refer to these patterns. The descriptions in this chapter show either or both. Official names are shown in bold type.

The actual back stamp as seen on an item, or the one you may expect to find on it, is included for each pattern number.

In certain instances patterns were produced on more, or different, shapes to those listed in the pattern books. This chapter lists as many as possible, including those in the pattern books.

Unless otherwise stated, when a pattern is described, it is on the outside of the cup and on the saucer and plate.

Pattern	Description & Shapes
051	**Daisy** flowers and colour edges. Ideal China/Canadian Teaware. /B **Dainty Brown** with brown edges /M **Dainty Mauve** with mauve edges /P **Dainty Pink** with pink edges /Y **Dainty Yellow** with yellow edges /6 **Dainty Black** with gold edges /28 **Dainty Blue** with blue edges. **Backstamp(s)**: Shelley 1940-1966 **Shapes:** Cambridge, Dainty, Footed Dainty, Henley, Ludlow, Oxford, Tall Dainty

Dainty Blue Daisy 051/28 Dainty shape cup and saucer. £60-80; $80-100

Dainty Brown Daisy 051/B Dainty shape cup and saucer. £60-80; $80-100

Dainty Pink Daisy 051/P Dainty shape cup and saucer. £60-80; $130-160

Dainty Mauve Daisy 051/M Dainty shape cup and saucer. £60-80; $130-160

Dainty Yellow Daisy 051/Y Dainty shape cup and saucer. £60-150; $130-300

Ivy 052/29 Cambridge shape cup and saucer. £40-50; $80-90

Black and yellow tree 057 Oxford shape cup and saucer. £40-50; $80-100

Pattern	Description & Shapes
052	**Ivy**. Trailing orange/terracotta ivy leaves. Orange ring handle. Ideal China/ Canadian Teaware. **Backstamp(s)**: Shelley 1940-1966 **Shapes:** Cambridge, Oxford
053	**Daisy** flowers and colour edges. Ideal China/Canadian Teaware. /8 Red Daisy with orange edges and ring handle (Regent) /A **Dainty Green**. **Backstamp(s)**: Shelley 1940-1966 **Shapes:** Dainty, Regent

Dainty Green Daisy 053/A Dainty shape cup and saucer. £60-80; $130-160

054	Leaves and berries. Grey print. Two large leaf shapes with berries and leaves within them. Small leaves between the two large leaf shapes. Grey lines outside cup and on saucer. Small leaves inside cup. White ground. Coral edges and ring handle. Similar to 0176 and 0226. Ideal China/ Canadian Teaware. **Backstamp(s)**: Shelley 1940-1966 **Shapes:** Oxford, Regent
055	Plum print. Ideal China/Canadian Teaware. **Backstamp(s)**: Shelley 1940-1966 **Shapes:** Oxford
056	Floral print. Ideal China/Canadian Teaware. **Backstamp(s)**: Shelley 1940-1966 **Shapes:** Oxford
057	Yellow and black with tree in landscape. Yellow trim and handle. Ideal China/ Canadian Teaware. **Backstamp(s)**: Shelley 1940-1966 Ideal China **Shapes:** Bristol, Chester, Oxford
058	**Gorse**. Grey print. Enamelled. Green leaves, black and grey tree and leaves. Green edges. Ideal China/Canadian Teaware. /A Amber flowers and edges /R Red flowers and edges /Y Yellow flowers and edges. **Backstamp(s)**: Shelley 1940-1966 Ideal China **Shapes:** Regent, Vincent

Gorse 058 Regent shape cup, saucer, and plate; creamer and sugar. £40-50; $80-90

059	Black print. Black and grey stylised tree, grey leaves and bushes. Coral, blue, and pink flowers. Coral flower and green foliage also inside cup. White ground. Gold edges. Green ring handle. Ideal China/Canadian Teaware. **Backstamp(s)**: Shelley 1940-1966 Ideal China **Shapes:** Regent

Stylised tree 059 Regent shape cup, saucer, and plate; creamer and sugar. £40-50; $80-90

060	Floral and fern pattern. Ideal China/ Canadian Teaware. **Backstamp(s)**: Shelley 1940-1966 **Shapes:** Chester, Regent
061	Poppies and Daisies. Brown print. Coral and orange poppies, blue daisies with green and brown foliage. Flower spray inside cup. White ground. Amber edges and ring handle. Ideal China/Canadian Teaware. /BH Blue edges and handle /GH Green edges and handle. **Backstamp(s)**: Shelley 1940-1966 Ideal China **Shapes:** Chester, Oxford, Regent
062	Black print. Yellow and grey bell border inside cup and on saucer. Yellow line outside line approximately halfway between rim and base. White ground. Yellow edges and ring handle. **Backstamp(s)**: Shelley 1940-1966 Ideal China **Shapes:** Chester
063	Rose and pansy pattern. Ideal China/ Canadian Teaware. **Backstamp(s)**: Shelley 1940-1966 **Shapes:** York
064	Blossom branches. Green and black blossoms and leaves on black, thorny branches. Green edges. **Backstamp(s)**: Shelley 1940-1966 **Shapes:** Chester, Devon
065	Brown print. Floral pattern. Ideal China/ Canadian Teaware. **Backstamp(s)**: Shelley 1940-1966 **Shapes:** Devon
066	**Crocus**. Similar to 0166. Ideal China/ Canadian Teaware. /GH Green flowers /Y Yellow flowers. **Backstamp(s)**: Shelley 1940-1966 Ideal China **Shapes:** Regent
067	Tree and Hill. Similar to 0167. Ideal China/Canadian Teaware. **Backstamp(s)**: Shelley 1940-1966 **Shapes:** Regent
068	**Autumn Leaves**. Similar to 0168. Ideal China/Canadian Teaware. **Backstamp(s)**: Shelley 1940-1966 **Shapes:** Regent
069	**Harebell**. Brown print. Blue harebell in foreground against a pond and green and brown foliage. Small gate and road on plate. Small foliage sprig inside cup. White ground. Gold edges. Blue ring handle. Similar to 0169. Ideal China/ Canadian Teaware. **Backstamp(s)**: Shelley 1940-1966 Ideal China **Shapes:** Regent
070	**Phlox**. Black print. Pink and blue phlox with grey leaves. Also patterned inside cup. Blue edges and ring handle. Similar to 0170 and 0171. Ideal China/Canadian Teaware. /G Green and pink flowers; gold edges /GR Green flowers; green edges. **Backstamp(s)**: Shelley 1940-1966 Ideal China **Shapes:** Regent
071	**Phlox**. Yellow and green phlox with grey leaves. Also patterned inside cup. Yellow edges and ring handle. Ideal China/ Canadian Teaware. /G Green and pink flowers; gold edges. **Backstamp(s)**: Shelley 1940-1966 Ideal China **Shapes:** Regent
072	Stylised flowers. Ideal China/Canadian Teaware. **Backstamp(s)**: Shelley 1940-1966 **Shapes:** Oxford
073	Leaf and Flower pattern. Ideal China/ Canadian Teaware. **Backstamp(s)**: Shelley 1940-1966 **Shapes:** Devon

Pattern Description & Shapes

074 Stile and Rose pattern. Orange and blue flowers with trees and a wooden stile. Orange edges and handle. Ideal China/ Canadian Teaware.
/B Blue edges
/T Amber edges on handle.
Backstamp(s): Shelley 1940-1966
Shapes: Regent

Stile and Rose 074 Regent shape cup, saucer, and plate. £40-50; $80-90

075 Lake and Balcony. Brown print. Yellow balcony with urn of orange, yellow, and green flowers in the foreground. Lake, trees, and butterflies in the background. White ground. Yellow edges and ring handle. Ideal China/Canadian Teaware.
Backstamp(s): Shelley 1940-1966
Shapes: Oxford

Lake and Balcony 075 Oxford shape cup and saucer. £40-50; $80-100

076 Brown stylised tree and bush. Pink and blue flowers and green leaves. Green and yellow at foot of tree. Pink edges and ring handle. Ideal China/Canadian Teaware.
/GH green edges and ring handle.
Backstamp(s): Shelley 1940-1966
Shapes: Regent

077 Cornfield pattern. Ideal China/Canadian Teaware.
Backstamp(s): Shelley 1940-1966
Shapes: York

078 Balloon Tree pattern. Ideal China/ Canadian Teaware.
Backstamp(s): Shelley 1940-1966
Shapes: Oxford

079 Gate and Path print. Ideal China/ Canadian Teaware.
Backstamp(s): Shelley 1940-1966
Shapes: Devon

080 Columns and flowers pattern. Ideal China/Canadian Teaware.
Backstamp(s): Shelley 1940-1966
Shapes: Devon

081 **Bands and Shades**. Green. Ideal China/ Canadian Teaware.
/DB Dark blue
/G Grey
/M Mauve
/P Pink
/Y Orangey-yellow.
Backstamp(s): Shelley 1940-1966
Shapes: Regent

082 **Bands and Shades**. Blue. Ideal China/ Canadian Teaware.
/P Pink
/T Blue.
Backstamp(s): Shelley 1940-1966
Shapes: Regent

083 **Bands and Shades**. Brown. Ideal China/ Canadian Teaware.
Backstamp(s): Shelley 1940-1966
Shapes: Regent

084 **Bands and Shades**. Orange. Ideal China/Canadian Teaware.
Backstamp(s): Shelley 1940-1966
Shapes: Regent

085 **Rose** pattern. Green. Ideal China/ Canadian Teaware.
Backstamp(s): Shelley 1940-1966
Shapes: Devon

086 **Ivy** pattern. Green. Ideal China/Canadian Teaware.
Backstamp(s): Shelley 1940-1966
Shapes: Cambridge

087 **Daisy** pattern. Green. Ideal China/ Canadian Teaware.
Backstamp(s): Shelley 1940-1966
Shapes: Cambridge

088 **Idalium**. Enamelled pink, blue, and yellow flowers with blue branches and green and grey foliage. Ideal China/ Canadian Teaware. Same as 0190 and 11652.
Backstamp(s): Shelley 1940-1966
Shapes: Cambridge

Idalium 088 Cambridge shape cup and saucer. £40-50; $80-90

089 **Bluebird**. Ideal China/Canadian Teaware.
Backstamp(s): Shelley 1940-1966
Shapes: Dainty

090 **Lowestoft**. Ideal China/Canadian Teaware.
Backstamp(s): Shelley 1940-1966
Shapes: Dainty

091 **Chelsea**. Ideal China/Canadian Teaware.
Backstamp(s): Shelley 1940-1966
Shapes: Dainty

092 **Crabtree**. Ideal China/Canadian Teaware.
Backstamp(s): Shelley 1940-1966
Shapes: Tall Dainty

093 **Blue and Pink Daisy**. Ideal China/ Canadian Teaware.
Backstamp(s): Shelley 1940-1966
Shapes: Tall Dainty

094 **Archway of Roses**. Black print. Garden with flowers that include hollyhocks and roses. Blue butterflies. Tinted in blue, pink, brown, and green. White ground. Gold edges. Same as 0162. Ideal China/ Canadian Teaware.
Backstamp(s): Shelley 1940-1966
Shapes: Cambridge

095 **Garden Urn**. Similar to 0163. Ideal China/Canadian Teaware.
Backstamp(s): Shelley 1940-1966
Shapes: Cambridge

096 **Tulip**. Similar to 0164 and 0205. Ideal China/Canadian Teaware.
Backstamp(s): Shelley 1940-1966
Shapes: Eve

097 Dog Rose pattern. Pink and blue Dog Roses with grey leaves. Ideal China/ Canadian Teaware.
Backstamp(s): Shelley 1940-1966 Ideal China
Shapes: Cambridge

098 Autumn pattern. Ideal China/Canadian Teaware.
Backstamp(s): Shelley 1940-1966
Shapes: Vincent

099 Hydrangea pattern. Ideal China/Canadian Teaware.
Backstamp(s): Shelley 1940-1966
Shapes: Oxford

0100 Hill, tree, and lane pattern. Ideal China/ Canadian Teaware.
Backstamp(s): Shelley 1940-1966
Shapes: Vincent

0101 Syringa pattern. Ideal China/Canadian Teaware.
Backstamp(s): Shelley 1940-1966
Shapes: Vincent

0102 Poppy pattern. Ideal China/Canadian Teaware.
Backstamp(s): Shelley 1940-1966
Shapes: Devon

0103 **Wisteria**. Brown, orange, and green print. Gold edges. Amber ring handle. Ideal China/Canadian Teaware.
Backstamp(s): Shelley 1940-1966
Shapes: Cambridge

0104 Poppy pattern. Ideal China/Canadian Teaware.
Backstamp(s): Shelley 1940-1966
Shapes: Vincent

0105 **Maytime**. Small pink flowers in varying shades of pink with brown branches and green foliage. Tall Dainty Floral has pink flowers and green leaves on the figural handle. Gold edges. Ideal China/ Canadian Teaware.
Backstamp(s): Shelley 1940-1966
Shapes: Empire, Tall Dainty Floral.

0106 **Maytime**. Small pink flowers in varying shades of pink with brown branches and green foliage. Ideal China/Canadian Teaware.
Backstamp(s): Shelley 1940-1966
Shapes: Oxford

0107 **Maytime**. Small pink flowers in varying shades of pink with brown branches and green foliage. Green band. Ideal China/ Canadian Teaware.
Backstamp(s): Shelley 1940-1966
Shapes: Cambridge

0108 **Maytime**. Small pink flowers in varying shades of pink with brown branches and green foliage. Ideal China/Canadian Teaware.
/B **Peach Blossom**.
Backstamp(s): Shelley 1940-1966
Shapes: Cambridge, Chester

0109 **Maytime**. Small pink flowers in varying shades of pink with brown branches and green foliage. Ideal China/Canadian Teaware.
Backstamp(s): Shelley 1940-1966
Shapes: Cambridge, Chester

0110 **Maytime**. Chintz. Small pink flowers in varying shades of pink with brown

Pattern Description & Shapes

branches and green foliage. Inside cup has a broad band of chintz below rim on a white ground. Pale green line encircles outside cup approximately half way between the rim and the base. Saucer has a broad band of chintz along the outer edge. A band of pale green between the chintz and the white centre of the saucer. Pale green edges. Pale green ring handle and foot. Similar to 0212. Ideal China/Canadian Teaware.
Backstamp(s): Shelley 1940-1966
Shapes: Chester

Maytime 0110 Chester shape cup and saucer. £80-100; $150-200

0111 Davies **Pink, Blue, and Green Leaves Chintz**. Ideal China/Canadian Teaware.
Backstamp(s): Shelley 1940-1966
Shapes: Tall Dainty

0112 **Lowestoft**. Ideal China/Canadian Teaware.
Backstamp(s): Shelley 1940-1966
Shapes: Dainty

0113 **Yellow and Green Chintz**. Ideal China/Canadian Teaware.
Backstamp(s): Shelley 1940-1966
Shapes: Princess

0114 **Maytime**. Small pink flowers in varying shades of pink with brown branches and green foliage. Ideal China/Canadian Teaware.
Backstamp(s): Shelley 1940-1966
Shapes: Dainty

0115 **Bramble**. Ideal China/Canadian Teaware.
Backstamp(s): Shelley 1940-1966
Shapes: Tall Dainty

0116 **Bramble**. Ideal China/Canadian Teaware.
Backstamp(s): Shelley 1940-1966
Shapes: Chester, Dainty

0117 Orange floral pattern. Ideal China/Canadian Teaware.
Backstamp(s): Shelley 1940-1966
Shapes: Devon

0118 **Yellow and Green Chintz**. Ideal China/Canadian Teaware.
Backstamp(s): Shelley 1940-1966
Shapes: Cambridge

0119 **Pink, Green, and Blue Chintz**. Ideal China/Canadian Teaware.
Backstamp(s): Shelley 1940-1966
Shapes: Cambridge

0120 **Pink, Blue, and Grey Chintz**. Ideal China/Canadian Teaware.
Backstamp(s): Shelley 1940-1966
Shapes: Cambridge

0121 Colour band and gold lines. Ideal China/Canadian Teaware.
Backstamp(s): Shelley 1940-1966
Shapes: Chester

0122 **Dresden**. Ideal China/Canadian Teaware.
Backstamp(s): Shelley 1940-1966
Shapes: Chester

0123 **Chelsea**. Ideal China/Canadian Teaware.
Backstamp(s): Shelley 1940-1966
Shapes: Chester

0124 **Lowestoft**. Ideal China/Canadian Teaware.
Backstamp(s): Shelley 1940-1966
Shapes: Chester

0125 Colour band. Ideal China/Canadian Teaware.
Backstamp(s): Shelley 1940-1966
Shapes: Chester

0126 **Dresden**. Ideal China/Canadian Teaware.
Backstamp(s): Shelley 1940-1966
Shapes: Chester

0127 **Yellow Pansy**. Ideal China/Canadian Teaware.
Backstamp(s): Shelley 1940-1966
Shapes: Chester

0128 **Dresden**. Ideal China/Canadian Teaware.
Backstamp(s): Shelley 1940-1966
Shapes: Chester

0129 Blue and water green colour bands. Ideal China/Canadian Teaware.
Backstamp(s): Shelley 1940-1966
Shapes: Chester

0130 **Rose Border**. Ideal China/Canadian Teaware.
Backstamp(s): Shelley 1940-1966
Shapes: Chester

0131 Green band. Ideal China/Canadian Teaware.
Backstamp(s): Shelley 1940-1966
Shapes: Chester

0132 **Dresden**. Ideal China/Canadian Teaware.
Backstamp(s): Shelley 1940-1966
Shapes: Chester

0133 **Lowestoft**. Green bands. Ideal China/Canadian Teaware.
Backstamp(s): Shelley 1940-1966
Shapes: Regent

0134 **Lowestoft**. Yellow bands. Ideal China/Canadian Teaware.
Backstamp(s): Shelley 1940-1966
Shapes: Regent

0135 **Lowestoft**. Blue bands. Ideal China/Canadian Teaware.
Backstamp(s): Shelley 1940-1966
Shapes: Regent

0136 Print with some enamelling. Pink and blue flowers, yellow and grey grasses, and green foliage. Gold edges. Ideal China/Canadian Teaware.
Backstamp(s): Shelley 1940-1966
Shapes: Cambridge

Pattern number 0136 Cambridge shape cup, saucer, and plate. £40-50; $80-100

0137 Daisies and Sunset pattern. Blue, orange, and pink daisies. Ideal China/Canadian Teaware.
Backstamp(s): Shelley 1940-1966
Shapes: Cambridge

0138 Trees and flowers. Ideal China/Canadian Teaware.
Backstamp(s): Shelley 1940-1966
Shapes: Oxford

0139 Blossoms. Ideal China/Canadian Teaware.
Backstamp(s): Shelley 1940-1966
Shapes: Cambridge

0140 **Blossom**. Similar to 0165. Ideal China/Canadian Teaware.
Backstamp(s): Shelley 1940-1966
Shapes: Cambridge

0141 Trees and flowers. Ideal China/Canadian Teaware.
Backstamp(s): Shelley 1940-1966
Shapes: Oxford

0142 Trees and flowers. Ideal China/Canadian Teaware.
Backstamp(s): Shelley 1940-1966
Shapes: Cambridge

0143 Blue band. Ideal China/Canadian Teaware.
Backstamp(s): Shelley 1940-1966
Shapes: Ascot, Ely

0144 Green band. Ideal China/Canadian Teaware.
Backstamp(s): Shelley 1940-1966
Shapes: Ascot, Ely

0145 Stylised flowers. Ideal China/Canadian Teaware.
Backstamp(s): Shelley 1940-1966
Shapes: Henley

0146 **Pink Rose**. Ideal China/Canadian Teaware.
Backstamp(s): Shelley 1940-1966
Shapes: Henley

0147 **Blue Daisy**. Ideal China/Canadian Teaware.
Backstamp(s): Shelley 1940-1966
Shapes: Oxford

0148 Black and grey tree. Coral and blue flowers with green leaves and grass against a patch of yellow. White ground. Gold edges. Blue ring handle.
/GF green ring handle
Backstamp(s): Shelley 1940-1966 Lawleys
Shapes: Cambridge, Regent

0149 Poppies. Black print. Pink and yellow poppies with green leaves and grass. Yellow road in the left of the scene. Grey woodland in the distance. White ground. Pink edges and ring handle.
/B Includes blue flowers.
Backstamp(s): Shelley 1940-1966
Shapes: Oxford

0150 **Daisy**. Also known as **Dainty Green**. Same as 053. Ideal China/Canadian Teaware.
Backstamp(s): Shelley 1940-1966
Shapes: Oxford

0151 **Wisteria**. Brown, orange, and green print. Gold edges. Ideal China/Canadian Teaware. Same as 0103 except for ring part of handle.
Backstamp(s): Shelley 1940-1966
Shapes: Cambridge

Wisteria 0151 Cambridge shape cup, saucer, and plate. £50-60; $90-110

Pattern	Description & Shapes
0152	**Harebell**. Same as 069. Ideal China/ Canadian Teaware. **Backstamp(s)**: Shelley 1940-1966 Ideal China **Shapes:** Regent
0153	Yellow and black with tree in landscape. Same as 057. Ideal China/Canadian Teaware. **Backstamp(s)**: Shelley 1940-1966 Ideal China **Shapes:** Oxford
0154	Blue and yellow blossoms. Ideal China/ Canadian Teaware. **Backstamp(s)**: Shelley 1940-1966 Ideal China **Shapes:** Ascot
0155	Pink and green blossoms. Ideal China/ Canadian Teaware. **Backstamp(s)**: Shelley 1940-1966 Ideal China **Shapes:** Ascot
0156	Yellow and green blossoms. Ideal China/ Canadian Teaware. **Backstamp(s)**: Shelley 1940-1966 Ideal China **Shapes:** Ascot
0157	Motif and square pattern. Ideal China/ Canadian Teaware. /G Green /Y Yellow. **Backstamp(s)**: Shelley 1940-1966 Ideal China **Shapes:** Oxford
0158	Motif and triangle pattern. Ideal China/ Canadian Teaware. /B Blue /G Green /P Pink /R Red /Y Yellow. **Backstamp(s)**: Shelley 1940-1966 Ideal China **Shapes:** Oxford
0159	Graduated thin vertical blocks with black band. Similar to 0267 and 12816. Ideal China/Canadian Teaware. /B Blue /G Green /P Pink /R Red /Y Yellow. **Backstamp(s)**: Shelley 1940-1966 **Shapes:** Regent
0160	Triangles and lines. Similar to 0268 and 12817. Ideal China/Canadian Teaware. /B Blue /G Green /P Pink /R Red /Y Yellow. **Backstamp(s)**: Shelley 1940-1966 **Shapes:** Regent
0161	Colour chevrons and blocks. Same as 12818. Ideal China/Canadian Teaware. /B Blue /G Green /P Pink /R Red /Y Yellow. **Backstamp(s)**: Shelley 1940-1966 **Shapes:** Regent
0162	**Archway of Roses**. Black print. Garden with flowers that include hollyhocks and roses. Blue butterflies. Tinted in blue, pink, brown, and green. White ground. Gold edges. Similar to 094. Ideal China/ Canadian Teaware. /B Blue edges and ring handle. **Backstamp(s)**: Shelley 1940-1966 **Shapes:** Cambridge
0163	**Garden Urn**. Similar to 095. Ideal China/ Canadian Teaware. **Backstamp(s)**: Shelley 1940-1966 **Shapes:** Cambridge
0164	**Tulip**. Similar to 096 and 0205. Ideal China/Canadian Teaware. **Backstamp(s)**: Shelley 1940-1966 **Shapes:** Eve, Oxford
0165	**Blossom**. Similar to 0140. Ideal China/ Canadian Teaware. **Backstamp(s)**: Shelley 1940-1966 **Shapes:** Cambridge
0166	**Crocus**. Similar to 066. Ideal China/ Canadian Teaware. **Backstamp(s)**: Shelley 1940-1966 Ideal China **Shapes:** Regent
0167	Tree and Hill. Similar to 067. Ideal China/ Canadian Teaware. **Backstamp(s)**: Shelley 1940-1966 **Shapes:** Henley
0168	**Autumn Leaves**. Similar to 068. Ideal China/Canadian Teaware. /A Amber edges. **Backstamp(s)**: Shelley 1940-1966 **Shapes:** Henley
0169	**Harebell**. Brown print. Blue harebell in foreground against a pond and green and brown foliage. Small gate and road on plate. Small foliage sprig also inside cup. White ground. Gold edges. Similar to 069. Ideal China/Canadian Teaware. **Backstamp(s)**: Shelley 1940-1966 **Shapes:** Ascot
0170	**Phlox**. Black print. Pink and blue phlox with grey leaves. Also patterned inside cup. Gold edges. Similar to 070 and 0171. Ideal China/Canadian Teaware. **Backstamp(s)**: Shelley 1940-1966 Ideal China **Shapes:** Ascot, Henley

Blue **Phlox** 0170 Henley shape cup and saucer. £40-50; $80-100

Pattern	Description & Shapes
0171	**Phlox**. Pink and green flowers against leaves in shades of grey. Flower spray also inside cup. White ground. Gold edges. Similar to 070 and 0170. Ideal China/Canadian Teaware. **Backstamp(s)**: Shelley 1940-1966 **Shapes:** Ascot, Cambridge, Henley
0172	**Yellow Phlox**. Brown print. Yellow, orange, and green phlox with brown leaves. Phlox spray inside cup. Gold edges. Ideal China/Canadian Teaware. **Backstamp(s)**: Shelley 1940-1966 Ideal China **Shapes:** Cambridge, York
0173	**Pink Phlox**. Ideal China/Canadian Teaware. **Backstamp(s)**: Shelley 1940-1966 Ideal China **Shapes:** Cambridge, Perth
0174	**Rose**. Similar to 0191. Ideal China/ Canadian Teaware. **Backstamp(s)**: Shelley 1940-1966 Ideal China **Shapes:** Ascot, Regent
0175	Three green bands and three gold bands. Green bands inside cup. Gold edges. Green ring handle. Similar to 0227. Ideal China/Canadian Teaware. /B Blue /F Ginger /R Red. **Backstamp(s)**: Shelley 1940-1966 **Shapes:** Oxford
0176	Leaves and berries. Similar to 054 and 0226. Ideal China/Canadian Teaware. **Backstamp(s)**: Shelley 1940-1966 **Shapes:** Oxford
0177	Bands and block in shades of grey and colour variations as listed below. White ground. Coloured edges and ring handle. Similar to 0198. Same as 12316. Ideal China/Canadian Teaware. /B Blue /G Green and pale green /R Red and fawn /Y Yellow. **Backstamp(s)**: Shelley 1940-1966 **Shapes:** Oxford
0178	**Gorse**. Ideal China/Canadian Teaware. **Backstamp(s)**: Shelley 1940-1966 Ideal China **Shapes:** Cambridge
0179	**Blossom**. Ideal China/Canadian Teaware. **Backstamp(s)**: Shelley 1940-1966 Ideal China **Shapes:** Cambridge
0180	**Hydrangea**. Ideal China/Canadian Teaware. **Backstamp(s)**: Shelley 1940-1966 Ideal China **Shapes:** Henley, Mayfair
0181	**Dog Rose**. Gold print. Yellow flowers with brown and green foliage. Spray inside cup. White ground. Gold edges. Ideal China/Canadian Teaware. **Backstamp(s)**: Shelley 1940-1966 **Shapes:** Ascot

Yellow **Phlox** 0172 York shape cup and saucer. £40-50; $80-100

Yellow **Phlox** 0172 Cambridge shape demitasse cup and saucer. £40-50; $80-90

Pattern	Description & Shapes
0182	**Jasmine**. Brown print. Coral, blue, and dark pink flowers, green foliage, brown bushes on a white ground. Flowers also inside cup. Gold edges. Ideal China/ Canadian Teaware. **Backstamp(s)**: Shelley 1940-1966 **Shapes:** Ascot

Jasmine 0182 Ascot shape cup, saucer, and plate. £50-60; $90-110

0188 **Englands Charm**. Country scene. Pink flowers in the foreground, probably heather, with woods in the background. Swathe of pink flowers on inside cup below rim. Gold edges. Ideal China/ Canadian Teaware.
Backstamp(s): Shelley 1940-1966
Shapes: Cambridge

Englands Charm 0188 Cambridge shape cup, saucer, and plate. £50-60; $90-110. Teapot: £75-85, $200-300; sugar and creamer: £45-55, $80-90; bread and butter plate: £25-30, $50-60.

0183 Stylised bush. Ideal China/Canadian Teaware.
Backstamp(s): Shelley 1940-1966
Shapes: Oxford

0184 Poppies. Ideal China/Canadian Teaware.
Backstamp(s): Shelley 1940-1966
Shapes: Ascot

0185 **Melody Chintz**. Red, pink, yellow, and blue flowers on a mint green chintz background. Ideal China/Canadian Teaware.
Backstamp(s): Shelley 1940-1966
Shapes: Cambridge, Chester

0186 **Royalty**. Broad border of pink roses, green, and brown leaves on a pale green ground. Pale green handle. Gold edges. Similar to 0228. Ideal China/Canadian Teaware.
Backstamp(s): Shelley 1940-1966 Royalty
Shapes: Henley

0187 **Heather**. Countryside scene with pink heather, trees, bridge, and river. Gold edges. Similar to 0296. Ideal China/ Canadian Teaware.
Backstamp(s): Shelley 1940-1966
Shapes: Cambridge, New Cambridge, Perth

Heather 0187 Cambridge shape cup and saucer. £40-50; $50-100

0189 **Hedgerow**. Ideal China/Canadian Teaware.
Backstamp(s): Shelley 1940-1966
Shapes: Henley

0190 **Idalium**. Same as 088 and 11652. Ideal China/Canadian Teaware.
Backstamp(s): Shelley 1940-1966
Shapes: Cambridge

0191 **Rose**. Similar to 0174. Ideal China/ Canadian Teaware.
Backstamp(s): Shelley 1940-1966 Ideal China
Shapes: Regent

0192 **Posie Spray**. Orange, yellow, and blue flowers with green leaves. Pale green border, trim, and handle. White ground. Similar to 0229 and 12576. Ideal China/ Canadian Teaware.
Backstamp(s): Shelley 1940-1966 Ideal China
Shapes: Oxford

0193 **Motif**. Large pink, blue, and yellow flowers with green and grey leaves. White ground. Pink edges and handle, or ring handle. Ideal China/Canadian Teaware.
Backstamp(s): Shelley 1940-1966
Shapes: Cambridge, New Cambridge, Oxford

0194 **Blue Willow Pattern**. Oriental print on a white ground. Pattern also inside cup. Ideal China/Canadian Teaware.
/4 Red.
Backstamp(s): Shelley 1940-1966
Shapes: Henley

Right:
Heather 0187 Perth shape cup and saucer. £40-50; $50-100

Blue Willow Pattern 0194/4 Henley shape cup and saucer. £50-60; $90-110

0195 **Pink Rose Festoon**. Swathes of tiny pink roses and green leaves. White ground. Pink edges. Ideal China/Canadian Teaware.
Backstamp(s): Shelley 1940-1966
Shapes: Henley

Pink Rose Festoon 0195 Henley shape cup and saucer. £50-60; $90-110

Pattern	Description & Shapes

0196 **Melody Chintz**. Red, pink, yellow, and blue flowers on a mint green chintz background. Similar to 0210. Ideal China/Canadian Teaware.
Backstamp(s): Shelley 1940-1966
Shapes: Henley

0197 **Melody Chintz**. Red, pink, yellow, and blue flowers on a mint green chintz background. Ideal China/Canadian Teaware.
Backstamp(s): Shelley 1940-1966
Shapes: Carlisle, Ripon

Melody 0197 Carlisle shape cup, saucer, and plate. £70-80; $120-150

0198 Bands and block in shades of grey and colour variations as listed below. White ground. Coloured edges and ring handle. Similar to 0177. Same as 12316. Ideal China/Canadian Teaware.
/B Blue
/G Green and pale green
/R Red and fawn
/Y Yellow.
Backstamp(s): Shelley 1940-1966
Shapes: York

0199 **Crackle**. Pink, blue, mauve, and amber flowers and green foliage on a black and white crackle background. Gold edges. Green ring below rim on inside cup. Ideal China/Canadian Teaware.
Backstamp(s): Shelley 1940-1966
Shapes: Cambridge, Chester, Mocha

Crackle 0199 Cambridge shape cup and saucer. £60-80; $90-120c

0200 **Iris**. Blue irises. Ideal China/Canadian Teaware.
Backstamp(s): Shelley 1940-1966
Shapes: Regent

0201 **Hollyhock**. Ideal China/Canadian Teaware.
Backstamp(s): Shelley 1940-1966
Shapes: Eve

0202 **Daisy**. Ideal China/Canadian Teaware.
/B Blue
/D Green
/E Red
/41 Maroon.
Backstamp(s): Shelley 1940-1966
Shapes: Henley

0203 Brown border print and colour band. Ideal China/Canadian Teaware.
/B Blue
/D Green
/E Red
/41 Maroon.
Backstamp(s): Shelley 1940-1966
Shapes: Chester

0204 Gold border print and colour bands. Ideal China/Canadian Teaware.
/B Blue
/D Green
/E Red
/41 Maroon.
Backstamp(s): Shelley 1940-1966
Shapes: Chester

0205 **Tulip**. Similar to 096 and 0164. Ideal China/Canadian Teaware.
Backstamp(s): Shelley 1940-1966
Shapes: Cambridge

0206 **Syringa**. Ideal China/Canadian Teaware.
Backstamp(s): Shelley 1940-1966
Shapes: Cambridge

0207 **Star and Spot**. Ideal China/Canadian Teaware.
Backstamp(s): Shelley 1940-1966
Shapes: Essex

0208 **Curtain Border**. Ideal China/Canadian Teaware.
Backstamp(s): Shelley 1940-1966
Shapes: Essex

0209 **Melody**. Chintz. Red, pink, yellow, and blue flowers on a mint green chintz background. Ideal China/Canadian Teaware.
Backstamp(s): Shelley 1940-1966
Shapes: Ripon

0210 **Melody Chintz**. Red, pink, yellow, and blue flowers on a mint green chintz background. Similar to 0196. Ideal China/Canadian Teaware.
Backstamp(s): Shelley 1940-1966
Shapes: Henley

0211 **Hedgerow**. Green flowers and brown foliage on a white ground. Gold edges. Ideal China/Canadian Teaware.
Backstamp(s): Shelley 1940-1966 Hedgerow
Shapes: Cambridge, Henley

0212 **Maytime**. Chintz. Small pink flowers in varying shades of pink with brown branches and green foliage. Inside cup has a broad band of chintz below rim on a white ground. Pale green line encircles outside cup approximately half way between the rim and the base. Saucer has a broad band of chintz along the outer edge. A band of pale green between the chintz and the white centre of the saucer. Green edges. Green ring handle and foot. Similar to 0110. Ideal China/Canadian Teaware.
Backstamp(s): Shelley 1940-1966
Shapes: Chester

0213 **Blossom**. Ideal China/Canadian Teaware.
Backstamp(s): Shelley 1940-1966
Shapes: Cambridge

0214 Stylised bush, berries, and flowers. Ideal China/Canadian Teaware.
Backstamp(s): Shelley 1940-1966
Shapes: Cambridge

0215 Ratauds Floral pattern. Ideal China/Canadian Teaware.
Backstamp(s): Shelley 1940-1966
Shapes: Chester

0216 Ratauds Autumn Leaf pattern. Ideal China/Canadian Teaware.
Backstamp(s): Shelley 1940-1966
Shapes: Chester

0217 Ratauds Berries and Fruit pattern. Ideal China/Canadian Teaware.
Backstamp(s): Shelley 1940-1966
Shapes: Cambridge

0218 Ratauds Flower and Leaf pattern. Brown, yellow, and orange flowers on a white ground. Flower spray also inside cup. Gold edges. Ideal China/Canadian Teaware.
Backstamp(s): Shelley 1940-1966
Shapes: Cambridge

0219 Ratauds **Hydrangea**. Ideal China/Canadian Teaware.
Backstamp(s): Shelley 1940-1966
Shapes: Cambridge

0220 Hulmes **Wisteria**. Yellow and purple wisteria flowers with green and brown foliage on a white ground. Gold edges. Ideal China/Canadian Teaware.
Backstamp(s): Shelley 1940-1966
Shapes: Cambridge, Henley

Wisteria 0220 Henley shape cup and saucer. £40-60; $90-100

0221 Ratauds Stylised Flowers. Ideal China/Canadian Teaware.
Backstamp(s): Shelley 1940-1966
Shapes: Cambridge

0222 Hulmes Blue Floral pattern. Ideal China/Canadian Teaware.
Backstamp(s): Shelley 1940-1966
Shapes: Cambridge

0223 Ratauds Border pattern. Ideal China/Canadian Teaware.
Backstamp(s): Shelley 1940-1966
Shapes: Henley

0224 Ratauds Floral pattern. Ideal China/Canadian Teaware.
Backstamp(s): Shelley 1940-1966
Shapes: Henley

0225 Ratauds **Rose and Border**. Ideal China/Canadian Teaware.
Backstamp(s): Shelley 1940-1966
Shapes: Chester

Pattern	Description & Shapes

0226 Grey print. Two large leaf shapes with red and brown berries and fawn leaves within them. Small green leaves between the two large leaf shapes. Grey and green lines outside cup and on saucer. Small green leaves inside cup. White ground. Green edges and ring handle. Similar to 054 and 0176. Ideal China/Canadian Teaware.
Backstamp(s): Shelley 1940-1966
Shapes: Oxford

Leaves 0226 Oxford shape cup and saucer. £40-60; $90-100

0227 Three green bands and three gold bands. Green bands inside cup. Gold edges. Green ring handle. Similar to 0175. Ideal China/Canadian Teaware.
Backstamp(s): Shelley 1940-1966
Shapes: Oxford

0228 **Royalty**. Broad border of pink roses, green and brown leaves on a pale green ground. Similar to 0186. Ideal China/ Canadian Teaware.
Backstamp(s): Shelley 1940-1966
Shapes: Henley

0229 **Posies Spray**. Orange, yellow, and blue flowers with green leaves. White ground. Similar to 0192 and 12576. Ideal China/ Canadian Teaware.
Backstamp(s): Shelley 1940-1966
Shapes: Cambridge

0230 **Wild Flowers**. Similar to 12631. Ideal China/Canadian Teaware.
Backstamp(s): Shelley 1940-1966
Shapes: Cambridge

0231 **Iris**. Blue irises. Similar to 12384. Ideal China/Canadian Teaware.
Backstamp(s): Shelley 1940-1966
Shapes: Cambridge, Perth

0232 **Gentian**. Ideal China/Canadian Teaware.
Backstamp(s): Shelley 1940-1966
Shapes: Cambridge

0233 Poppies. Similar to 0273 and 12607. Ideal China/Canadian Teaware.
Backstamp(s): Shelley 1940-1966
Shapes: Perth

0234 Blossom. Similar to 12575. Ideal China/ Canadian Teaware.
Backstamp(s): Shelley 1940-1966
Shapes: Perth

0235 Purple flower print. Spray also inside cup. Ideal China/Canadian Teaware.
Backstamp(s): Shelley 1940-1966
Shapes: Dainty

0236 Poppies. Similar to 12376. Ideal China/ Canadian Teaware.
Backstamp(s): Shelley 1940-1966
Shapes: Perth

0237 Anemones. Ideal China/Canadian Teaware.
Backstamp(s): Shelley 1940-1966
Shapes: Perth

0238 **Mimosa**. Similar to 12629. Ideal China/ Canadian Teaware.
Backstamp(s): Shelley 1940-1966
Shapes: Henley, Perth

0239 **Wisteria**. Ideal China/Canadian Teaware.
Backstamp(s): Shelley 1940-1966
Shapes: Cambridge, Perth

0240 **Hollyhocks**. Similar to 12019. Ideal China/Canadian Teaware.
Backstamp(s): Shelley 1940-1966
Shapes: Cambridge

0241 Crocuses. Ideal China/Canadian Teaware.
Backstamp(s): Shelley 1940-1966
Shapes: Perth

0242 Blue flowers. Ideal China/Canadian Teaware.
Backstamp(s): Shelley 1940-1966
Shapes: Perth

0243 Yellow flowers. Ideal China/Canadian Teaware.
Backstamp(s): Shelley 1940-1966
Shapes: Cambridge

0244 Berries and leaves. Ideal China/Canadian Teaware.
Backstamp(s): Shelley 1940-1966
Shapes: Cambridge

0245 Daisies. Ideal China/Canadian Teaware.
Backstamp(s): Shelley 1940-1966
Shapes: Perth

0246 Green flowers. Ideal China/Canadian Teaware.
Backstamp(s): Shelley 1940-1966
Shapes: Perth

0247 Green and brown flowers. Ideal China/ Canadian Teaware.
Backstamp(s): Shelley 1940-1966
Shapes: Cambridge

0248 Pink and blue flowers. Ideal China/ Canadian Teaware.
Backstamp(s): Shelley 1940-1966
Shapes: Cambridge

0249 Pink and yellow flowers. Ideal China/ Canadian Teaware.
Backstamp(s): Shelley 1940-1966
Shapes: Cambridge

0250 Pink and yellow flowers. Ideal China/ Canadian Teaware.
Backstamp(s): Shelley 1940-1966
Shapes: Perth

0251 Pink and blue flowers. Ideal China/ Canadian Teaware.
Backstamp(s): Shelley 1940-1966
Shapes: Perth

0252 Pink, green, and blue flowers. Ideal China/Canadian Teaware.
Backstamp(s): Shelley 1940-1966
Shapes: Perth

0253 **Wild Flower Sprays**. Ideal China/ Canadian Teaware.
Backstamp(s): Shelley 1940-1966
Shapes: Henley

0254 **Wild Flower** border. Ideal China/ Canadian Teaware.
Backstamp(s): Shelley 1940-1966
Shapes: Bristol, Henley

0255 **Anemone**. Grey print. Pink and yellow anemones with grey and green foliage that includes ferns. Ideal China/Canadian Teaware.
Backstamp(s): Shelley 1940-1966
Shapes: Henley

Anemone 0255 Henley shape cup and saucer. £40-60; $90-100

0256 **Gorse**. Black print. Yellow leaves, black and grey trees. Gold edges. Ideal China/ Canadian Teaware.
Backstamp(s): Shelley 1940-1966 Ideal China
Shapes: Perth

0257 **Gorse**. Black print. Blue leaves, black and grey trees. Gold edges. Ideal China/ Canadian Teaware.
Backstamp(s): Shelley 1940-1966 Ideal China
Shapes: Perth

0258 **Japanese Chrysanthemum**. Ideal China/Canadian Teaware.
Backstamp(s): Shelley 1940-1966 Ideal China
Shapes: Cambridge

0259 **Wild Flower**. Flowers and green C scrolls. Ideal China/Canadian Teaware.
Backstamp(s): Shelley 1940-1966 Ideal China
Shapes: Cambridge

0260 **Poppy**. Ideal China/Canadian Teaware.
Backstamp(s): Shelley 1940-1966 Ideal China
Shapes: Perth

0261 Fir Tree. Ideal China/Canadian Teaware.
Backstamp(s): Shelley 1940-1966 Ideal China
Shapes: Perth

0262 **Poppy**. Black print. Ideal China/Canadian Teaware.
Backstamp(s): Shelley 1940-1966 Ideal China
Shapes: Henley

0263 **Poppy**. Brown print. Ideal China/ Canadian Teaware.
Backstamp(s): Shelley 1940-1966 Ideal China
Shapes: Henley

0264 **Rock Plants**. Ideal China/Canadian Teaware.
Backstamp(s): Shelley 1940-1966 Ideal China
Shapes: Perth

0265 **Wild Flower**. Ideal China/Canadian Teaware.
Backstamp(s): Shelley 1940-1966 Ideal China
Shapes: Cambridge

0266 **Wild Duck**. Ideal China/Canadian Teaware.
Backstamp(s): Shelley 1940-1966 Ideal China
Shapes: Cambridge

0267 Graduated thin vertical blocks with black band. Similar to 0159 and 12816. Ideal China/Canadian Teaware.
/B Blue
/G Green.
Backstamp(s): Shelley 1940-1966
Shapes: Regent

0268 Triangles and lines. Similar to 0160 and 12817. Ideal China/Canadian Teaware.
/B Blue
/G Green.
Backstamp(s): Shelley 1940-1966
Shapes: Regent

0269 **Fern Border**. Ideal China/Canadian Teaware.
Backstamp(s): Shelley 1940-1966
Shapes: Unknown

0270 **Blue and Pink Flowers**. Ideal China/ Canadian Teaware.
Backstamp(s): Shelley 1940-1966
Shapes: Bristol, Perth

0271 **Yellow and Pink Flowers** with grey and green leaves. Yellow bud spray inside cup. White ground. Gold edges. Ideal China/Canadian Teaware.
Backstamp(s): Shelley 1940-1966
Shapes: Bristol

0272 **Phlox**. Ideal China/Canadian Teaware.
Backstamp(s): Shelley 1940-1966
Shapes: Bristol

0273 Poppies. Similar to 0233 and 12607. Ideal China/Canadian Teaware.

Pattern	Description & Shapes

Backstamp(s): Shelley 1940-1966
Shapes: Bristol, Henley

0274 **Old Gains Festoon**. Ideal China/Canadian Teaware.
Backstamp(s): Shelley 1940-1966
Shapes: Henley

0275 **Rose and Daisy**. Green border print. White ground. Green edges and handle. Ideal China/Canadian Teaware.
/43 Pink on Cambridge shape; pink edges, white handle.
Backstamp(s): Shelley 1940-1966
Shapes: Cambridge, Dainty, Henley

Rose and Daisy 0275/43 Cambridge shape cup and saucer. £40-50; $80-100

Rose and Daisy 0275 Henley shape cup and saucer. £40-50; $80-100

0276 **Rose and Flower**. Ideal China/Canadian Teaware.
Backstamp(s): Shelley 1940-1966
Shapes: Oleander

0277 Crocus and Tree pattern. Black print. Ideal China/Canadian Teaware.
Backstamp(s): Shelley 1940-1966
Shapes: Perth

0278 Crocus and Tree pattern. Brown print. Ideal China/Canadian Teaware.
Backstamp(s): Shelley 1940-1966
Shapes: Perth

0279 Woodland. Brown print. Ideal China/Canadian Teaware.
Backstamp(s): Shelley 1940-1966
Shapes: Perth

0280 **Hawthorn Pattern**. Brown print. Ideal China/Canadian Teaware.
Backstamp(s): Shelley 1940-1966
Shapes: Cambridge

0281 **Tree Pattern**. Ideal China/Canadian Teaware.
Backstamp(s): Shelley 1940-1966
Shapes: Unknown

0282 **Rose Border**. Ideal China/Canadian Teaware.
Backstamp(s): Shelley 1940-1966
Shapes: Henley

0283 **Jasmine**. Ideal China/Canadian Teaware.
Backstamp(s): Shelley 1940-1966
Shapes: Perth

0284 **Basket Festoon**. Ideal China/Canadian Teaware.
Backstamp(s): Shelley 1940-1966
Shapes: Oleander

0285 **Pink Hedgerow**. Ideal China/Canadian Teaware.
Backstamp(s): Shelley 1940-1966
Shapes: Henley

0286 **Geranium**. Ideal China/Canadian Teaware.
Backstamp(s): Shelley 1940-1966
Shapes: Perth

0287 Landscape with trees and blossoms. Ideal China/Canadian Teaware.
Backstamp(s): Shelley 1940-1966
Shapes: Unknown

0288 **Garden Scene**. Ideal China/Canadian Teaware.
Backstamp(s): Shelley 1940-1966
Shapes: Henley

0289 **Swallow**. Ideal China/Canadian Teaware.
Backstamp(s): Shelley 1940-1966
Shapes: Bristol

0290 **Springtime**. Ideal China/Canadian Teaware.
Backstamp(s): Shelley 1940-1966
Shapes: Chester, Perth

0291 **Waterfall**. Ideal China/Canadian Teaware.
Backstamp(s): Shelley 1940-1966
Shapes: Chester, Perth

0292 Colour band. Ideal China/Canadian Teaware.
/A Amber
/B Dark blue
/G Green
/P Pink
/T Blue.
Backstamp(s): Shelley 1940-1966
Shapes: Regent

0293 **Motif** and **Vine**. Ideal China/Canadian Teaware.
Backstamp(s): Shelley 1940-1966
Shapes: Perth

0294 **Motif** and **Laurel** border. Ideal China/Canadian Teaware.
Backstamp(s): Shelley 1940-1966
Shapes: Perth

0295 **Daffodil**. Similar to 13370. Ideal China/Canadian Teaware.
Backstamp(s): Shelley 1940-1966
Shapes: Victor

0296 **Heather**. Similar to 0187. Ideal China/Canadian Teaware.
Backstamp(s): Shelley 1940-1966
Shapes: Victor

0300 **Pansy**. Ideal China/Canadian Teaware. Entered in pattern book during or after 1962.
Backstamp(s): Shelley 1940-1966
Shapes: Warwick

0301 **Daffodil Spray**. Ideal China/Canadian Teaware. Entered in pattern book during or after 1962.
Backstamp(s): Shelley 1940-1966
Shapes: Warwick

0302 **Celandine**. Ideal China/Canadian Teaware. Entered in pattern book during or after 1962.
Backstamp(s): Shelley 1940-1966
Shapes: Warwick

0303 **American Brooklime**. Ideal China/Canadian Teaware. Entered in pattern book during or after 1962.
Backstamp(s): Shelley 1940-1966
Shapes: Warwick

0304 **Hibiscus**. Ideal China/Canadian Teaware. Entered in pattern book during or after 1962.
Backstamp(s): Shelley 1940-1966
Shapes: Warwick

0305 **Lily of the Valley**. Ideal China/Canadian Teaware. Entered in pattern book during or after 1962.
Backstamp(s): Shelley 1940-1966
Shapes: Warwick

0306 **Bridesmaid**. Ideal China/Canadian Teaware. Entered in pattern book during or after 1962.
Backstamp(s): Shelley 1940-1966
Shapes: Warwick

0307 **Blue Poppy**. Ideal China/Canadian Teaware. Entered in pattern book during or after 1962.
Backstamp(s): Shelley 1940-1966
Shapes: Warwick

0308 **Thistle**. Ideal China/Canadian Teaware. Entered in pattern book during or after 1962.
Backstamp(s): Shelley 1940-1966
Shapes: Warwick

0309 **Begonia**. Ideal China/Canadian Teaware. Entered in pattern book during or after 1962.
Backstamp(s): Shelley 1940-1966
Shapes: Warwick

0310 **Stocks**. Ideal China/Canadian Teaware. Entered in pattern book during or after 1962.
Backstamp(s): Shelley 1940-1966
Shapes: Warwick

0311 **Oleander**. Ideal China/Canadian Teaware. Entered in pattern book during or after 1962.
Backstamp(s): Shelley 1940-1966
Shapes: Warwick

0312 **Primrose**. Ideal China/Canadian Teaware. Entered in pattern book during or after 1962.
Backstamp(s): Shelley 1940-1966
Shapes: Warwick

0313 **Violets**. Ideal China/Canadian Teaware. Entered in pattern book during or after 1962.
Backstamp(s): Shelley 1940-1966
Shapes: Warwick

0314 **Golden Broom**. Ideal China/Canadian Teaware. Entered in pattern book during or after 1962.
Backstamp(s): Shelley 1940-1966
Shapes: Warwick

0315 **Rambler Rose**. Ideal China/Canadian Teaware. Entered in pattern book during or after 1962.
Backstamp(s): Shelley 1940-1966
Shapes: Warwick

0316 **Heavenly Blue** outside cup and on saucer. **Bramble** inside cup. Ideal China/Canadian Teaware. Entered in pattern book during or after 1962.
Backstamp(s): Shelley 1940-1966
Shapes: Atholl

0317 **Heavenly Mauve** outside cup and on saucer. **Chantilly** inside cup and in centre of saucers. Ideal China/Canadian Teaware. Entered in pattern book during or after 1962.
Backstamp(s): Shelley 1940-1966
Shapes: Atholl

0318 **Heavenly Pink** outside cup and on saucer. **Wild Flower** inside cup. Ideal China/Canadian Teaware. Entered in pattern book during or after 1962.
Backstamp(s): Shelley 1940-1966
Shapes: Atholl

0319 **Rose, Pansy, and Forget-me-nots** on peach ground. Ideal China/Canadian Teaware. Entered in pattern book during or after 1962.
Backstamp(s): Shelley 1940-1966
Shapes: Ludlow

0320 **Rose Spray** on old gold ground. Ideal China/Canadian Teaware. Entered in pattern book during or after 1962.
Backstamp(s): Shelley 1940-1966
Shapes: Ludlow

0321 Hulmes **Roses** on pink ground. Ideal China/Canadian Teaware. Entered in pattern book during or after 1962.
Backstamp(s): Shelley 1940-1966
Shapes: Ludlow

0322 **Blue Charm** on water green ground. Ideal China/Canadian Teaware. Entered in pattern book during or after 1962.
Backstamp(s): Shelley 1940-1966
Shapes: Ludlow

0323 Hulmes **Roses** on green ground. Ideal China/Canadian Teaware. Entered in pattern book during or after 1962.
Backstamp(s): Shelley 1940-1966
Shapes: Ludlow

0324 **Yutoi** on lemon yellow ground. Ideal China/Canadian Teaware. Entered in pattern book during or after 1962.
Backstamp(s): Shelley 1940-1966
Shapes: Ludlow

0325 **Blue Poppy** on water green ground. Ideal China/Canadian Teaware. Entered in pattern book during or after 1962.
Backstamp(s): Shelley 1940-1966
Shapes: Ripon

0326 **Begonia** on pink ground. Ideal China/ Canadian Teaware. Entered in pattern book during or after 1962.
Backstamp(s): Shelley 1940-1966
Shapes: Ripon

0327 **Bridesmaid** on green ground. Ideal China/Canadian Teaware. Entered in pattern book during or after 1962.
Backstamp(s): Shelley 1940-1966
Shapes: Ripon

0328 **Harebell** on peach ground. Ideal China/ Canadian Teaware. Entered in pattern book during or after 1962.
Backstamp(s): Shelley 1940-1966
Shapes: Ripon

0329 **Ferndown** on peach ground. Ideal China/ Canadian Teaware. Entered in pattern book during or after 1962.
Backstamp(s): Shelley 1940-1966
Shapes: Ripon

0330 **Violets** on lilac ground. Ideal China/ Canadian Teaware. Entered in pattern book during or after 1962.
Backstamp(s): Shelley 1940-1966
Shapes: Ripon

0331 **Golden Broom** on old gold ground. Ideal China/Canadian Teaware. Entered in pattern book during or after 1962.
Backstamp(s): Shelley 1940-1966
Shapes: Ripon

0332 **Celandine** on ivory ground. Ideal China/ Canadian Teaware. Entered in pattern book during or after 1962.
Backstamp(s): Shelley 1940-1966
Shapes: Ripon

0333 **American Brooklime** on green ground. Ideal China/Canadian Teaware. Entered in pattern book during or after 1962.
Backstamp(s): Shelley 1940-1966
Shapes: Ripon

0334 **Thistle** on pink ground. Ideal China/ Canadian Teaware. Entered in pattern book during or after 1962.
Backstamp(s): Shelley 1940-1966
Shapes: Ripon

0335 **Rosalie** on pink ground. Ideal China/ Canadian Teaware. Entered in pattern book during or after 1962.
Backstamp(s): Shelley 1940-1966
Shapes: Ripon

0336 **Wild Anemone** on green ground. Ideal China/Canadian Teaware. Entered in pattern book during or after 1962.
Backstamp(s): Shelley 1940-1966
Shapes: Ripon

0337 **Wild Flowers** on blue ground. Ideal China/Canadian Teaware. Entered in pattern book during or after 1962.
Backstamp(s): Shelley 1940-1966
Shapes: Ripon

0338 **Wild Anemone** on green ground. Ideal China/Canadian Teaware. Entered in pattern book during or after 1962.
Backstamp(s): Shelley 1940-1966
Shapes: Ludlow

0339 **Bramble** on lemon yellow ground. Ideal China/Canadian Teaware. Entered in pattern book during or after 1962.
Backstamp(s): Shelley 1940-1966
Shapes: Ludlow

0340 **Freesia** on peach ground. Ideal China/ Canadian Teaware. Entered in pattern book during or after 1962.
Backstamp(s): Shelley 1940-1966
Shapes: Ludlow

0341 **Honeysuckle** on lilac ground. Ideal China/Canadian Teaware. Entered in pattern book during or after 1962.
Backstamp(s): Shelley 1940-1966
Shapes: Ludlow

0342 **Blue Poppy** on blue ground. Ideal China/ Canadian Teaware. Entered in pattern book during or after 1962.
Backstamp(s): Shelley 1940-1966
Shapes: Ludlow

0343 **Celandine** on water green ground. Ideal China/Canadian Teaware. Entered in pattern book during or after 1962.
Backstamp(s): Shelley 1940-1966
Shapes: Ludlow

0344 **Freesia** on lilac ground. Ideal China/ Canadian Teaware. Entered in pattern book during or after 1962.
Backstamp(s): Shelley 1940-1966
Shapes: Ludlow

0345 **Bramble** on pink ground. Ideal China/ Canadian Teaware. Entered in pattern book during or after 1962.
Backstamp(s): Shelley 1940-1966
Shapes: Ludlow

0346 Brown **Daisy** (also known as **Dainty Brown**) outside cup and on saucer. **Stocks** inside cup and centre of saucer. Ideal China/Canadian Teaware. Entered in pattern book during or after 1962.
Backstamp(s): Shelley 1940-1966
Shapes: Atholl

0347 Green **Daisy** (also known as **Dainty Green**) outside cup and on saucer. **Wild Anemone** inside cup and centre of saucer. Ideal China/Canadian Teaware. Entered in pattern book during or after 1962.
Backstamp(s): Shelley 1940-1966
Shapes: Atholl

0348 Yellow **Daisy** (also known as **Dainty Yellow**) outside cup and on saucer. **Freesia** inside cup and centre of saucer. Ideal China/Canadian Teaware. Entered in pattern book during or after 1962.
Backstamp(s): Shelley 1940-1966
Shapes: Atholl

0349 **Crochet**. Ideal China/Canadian Teaware. Entered in pattern book during or after 1962.
/S10 Blue
/S30 Green
/S39 Yellow
/S41 Lilac.
Backstamp(s): Shelley 1940-1966
Shapes: Henley

0350 **Rose Spray** and pale blue panels. Ideal China/Canadian Teaware. Entered in pattern book during or after 1963.
Backstamp(s): Shelley 1940-1966
Shapes: Footed Dainty

0351 **Heavenly Blue** and peach panels. Ideal China/Canadian Teaware. Entered in pattern book during or after 1963.
Backstamp(s): Shelley 1940-1966
Shapes: Footed Dainty

0352 **Yutoi** and lemon yellow panels. Ideal China/Canadian Teaware. Entered in pattern book during or after 1963.
Backstamp(s): Shelley 1940-1966
Shapes: Footed Dainty

0353 **Bluebell** and lemon yellow panels. **Primrose** inside cup. Ideal China/ Canadian Teaware. Entered in pattern book during or after 1963.
Backstamp(s): Shelley 1940-1966
Shapes: Footed Dainty

0354 Hulmes **Roses** and green panels. Ideal China/Canadian Teaware. Entered in pattern book during or after 1963.
Backstamp(s): Shelley 1940-1966
Shapes: Footed Dainty

0355 **Field Flowers** and green panels. Ideal China/Canadian Teaware. Entered in pattern book during or after 1963.
Backstamp(s): Shelley 1940-1966
Shapes: Footed Dainty

0356 **Blue Rock** and lilac panels. Ideal China/ Canadian Teaware. Entered in pattern book during or after 1963.
Backstamp(s): Shelley 1940-1966
Shapes: Footed Dainty

0357 **Heavenly Mauve** and green panels. Ideal China/Canadian Teaware. Entered in pattern book during or after 1963.
Backstamp(s): Shelley 1940-1966
Shapes: Footed Dainty

0358 **Stocks** and lilac panels. Ideal China/ Canadian Teaware. Entered in pattern book during or after 1963.
Backstamp(s): Shelley 1940-1966
Shapes: Dainty

0359 **Rose Spray** and green panels. Ideal China/Canadian Teaware. Entered in pattern book during or after 1963.
Backstamp(s): Shelley 1940-1966
Shapes: Dainty

0360 **Rosebud** and fawn panels. Ideal China/ Canadian Teaware. Entered in pattern book during or after 1963.
Backstamp(s): Shelley 1940-1966
Shapes: Dainty

0361 **Rose, Pansy, and Forget-me-nots** and pink panels. Ideal China/Canadian Teaware. Entered in pattern book during or after 1963.
Backstamp(s): Shelley 1940-1966
Shapes: Dainty

0362 German **Floral** and pink panels. Ideal China/Canadian Teaware. Entered in pattern book during or after 1963.
Backstamp(s): Shelley 1940-1966
Shapes: Dainty

0363 **Maroon Charm** and blue panels. Ideal China/Canadian Teaware. Entered in pattern book during or after 1963.
Backstamp(s): Shelley 1940-1966
Shapes: Dainty

0364 **Blue Rock** and water green panels. Ideal China/Canadian Teaware. Entered in pattern book during or after 1963.
Backstamp(s): Shelley 1940-1966
Shapes: Dainty

0365 **Rose and Red Daisy** and lemon yellow panels. Ideal China/Canadian Teaware. Entered in pattern book during or after 1963.
Backstamp(s): Shelley 1940-1966
Shapes: Dainty

0366 **Wild Anemone** inside cup and centre of saucer. Pink outside cup and on main part of saucer. Ideal China/Canadian Teaware. Entered in pattern book during or after 1963.
Backstamp(s): Shelley 1940-1966
Shapes: Boston

0367 **Gold Thistle** printed on coloured ground inside cup and on saucer. White ground outside cup. Gold trim, foot and handle. Similar to 0599. Ideal China/Canadian Teaware. Entered in pattern book during or after 1963.
/S3 Green
/S15 Salmon
/S39 Green
/S41 Lilac.
Backstamp(s): Shelley 1940-1966
Shapes: Lincoln

Gold Thistle 0367/S15 Lincoln shape cup and saucer. £40-60; $100-120

0368 **Fruit Centre**. Pale peach outside cup and on saucer. Gold print outside cup. Gold stippled border on inside cup and apples and various fruits in the centre of the cup. Gold edges, handle, and foot. Ideal China/Canadian Teaware. Entered in pattern book during or after 1963.
/S3 Pale green outside cup and on saucer.
Backstamp(s): Shelley 1940-1966
Shapes: Lincoln

Fruit Centre 0368/S46 Lincoln shape cup and saucer. £90-95; $150-170

Fruit Centre 0368/S46 pattern inside Lincoln shape cup.

0369 Gold roses and foliage on coloured ground inside cup and on saucer. White ground outside cup. Gold trim, foot and handle. Similar to 0600 and 0648. Ideal China/Canadian Teaware. Entered in pattern book during or after 1963.
/S3 Green
/S15 Peach
/S39 Green
/S41 Lilac.
Backstamp(s): Shelley 1940-1966
Shapes: Lincoln

0370 Gold pattern on colour ground. Ideal China/Canadian Teaware. Entered in pattern book during or after 1963.
/S3 Green
/S15 Salmon
/S39 Green
/S41 Lilac.
Backstamp(s): Shelley 1940-1966
Shapes: Lincoln

0371 Gold pattern on white ground. Ideal China/Canadian Teaware. Entered in pattern book during or after 1963.
Backstamp(s): Shelley 1940-1966
Shapes: Atholl

0372 Gold pattern on colour ground. Ideal China/Canadian Teaware. Entered in pattern book during or after 1963.
/S3 Green
/S16 Orange
/S31 Pink
/S34 Brown
/S39 Green
/S40 Green
/S41 Lilac
/S43 Water green.
Backstamp(s): Shelley 1940-1966
Shapes: Ripon

0373 Gold pattern on colour ground. Ideal China/Canadian Teaware. Entered in pattern book during or after 1963.
/S16 Orange
/S34 Brown
/S40 Green
/S41 Lilac.
Backstamp(s): Shelley 1940-1966
Shapes: Ripon

0374 Gold pattern on white ground. Ideal China/Canadian Teaware. Entered in pattern book during or after 1963.
Backstamp(s): Shelley 1940-1966
Shapes: Ripon

0375 Gold pattern on white ground. Ideal China/Canadian Teaware. Entered in pattern book during or after 1963.
Backstamp(s): Shelley 1940-1966
Shapes: Ripon

0376 Gold pattern on white ground. Ideal China/Canadian Teaware. Entered in pattern book during or after 1963.
Backstamp(s): Shelley 1940-1966
Shapes: Ripon

0377 Gold pattern on white ground. Ideal China/Canadian Teaware. Entered in pattern book during or after 1963.
Backstamp(s): Shelley 1940-1966
Shapes: Ripon

0378 Gold pattern on white ground. Ideal China/Canadian Teaware. Entered in pattern book during or after 1963.
Backstamp(s): Shelley 1940-1966
Shapes: Atholl

0379 Gold pattern on white ground. Ideal China/Canadian Teaware. Entered in pattern book during or after 1963.
Backstamp(s): Shelley 1940-1966
Shapes: Atholl

0380 Gold pattern on white ground. Ideal China/Canadian Teaware. Entered in pattern book during or after 1963.
Backstamp(s): Shelley 1940-1966
Shapes: Atholl

0381 Gold leaves and flowers on large panels outside cup and on saucer. Gold leaf border inside cup. Gold edges and foot. Ideal China/Canadian Teaware. Entered in pattern book during or after 1963.
/S15 Peach
/S39 Lemon yellow
/S40 Green
/S41 Lilac.
Backstamp(s): Shelley 1940-1966
Shapes: Atholl

Pink and gold 0381/S41 Atholl shape cup and saucer. £40-60; $100-110

0382 Gold pattern on colour ground. Ideal China/Canadian Teaware. Entered in pattern book during or after 1963.
/S15 Peach
/S39 Lemon yellow
/S40 Green
/S41 Lilac.
Backstamp(s): Shelley 1940-1966
Shapes: Atholl

0383 **Gold Peony**. Gold peonies and leaves on very coloured ground. Gold trim and handle. Similar to 0584. Ideal China/Canadian Teaware. Entered in pattern book during or after 1963.
/S9 Pink
/S10 Blue
/S15 Peach
/S39 Lemon yellow
/S40 Pale greenish blue
/S41 Lilac
Backstamp(s): Shelley 1940-1966
Shapes: Atholl

Gold peony 0383/S10 Atholl shape cup and saucer. £40-60; $100-120

0384 **Gold Thistle**. Gold peonies and leaves on very coloured ground. Gold trim and handle. Ideal China/Canadian Teaware. Entered in pattern book during or after 1963.
/S9 Pink
/S10 Blue
/S15 Peach
/S39 Lemon yellow
/S40 Pale greenish blue
/S41 Lilac.
Backstamp(s): Shelley 1940-1966
Shapes: Footed Dainty

0385 **Pyrethrum** inside cup. Green outside cup and on saucer. Ideal China/Canadian

Pattern Description & Shapes

Teaware. Entered in pattern book during or after 1963.
Backstamp(s): Shelley 1940-1966
Shapes: Boston

0386 **Blue Poppy** inside cup and centre of saucer. Water green outside cup and main part of saucer. Ideal China/Canadian Teaware. Entered in pattern book during or after 1963.
/P Special order for Niagara Parks Commission substituted **Primrose Spray**.
Backstamp(s): Shelley 1940-1966
Shapes: Boston

0387 **Bramble** inside cup and centre of saucer. Yellow outside cup and main part of saucer. Ideal China/Canadian Teaware. Entered in pattern book during or after 1963.
Backstamp(s): Shelley 1940-1966
Shapes: Boston

0388 **Honeysuckle** inside cup and centre of saucer. Green outside cup and main part of saucer. Ideal China/Canadian Teaware. Entered in pattern book during or after 1963.
Backstamp(s): Shelley 1940-1966
Shapes: Boston

0389 **Freesia** inside cup and centre of saucer. Lilac outside cup and main part of saucer. Ideal China/Canadian Teaware. Entered in pattern book during or after 1963.
Backstamp(s): Shelley 1940-1966
Shapes: Boston

0390 Gold pattern on colour ground. Similar to 0585 and 0586. Ideal China/Canadian Teaware. Entered in pattern book during or after 1963.
/S41 Lilac
/42 Blue.
Backstamp(s): Shelley 1940-1966
Shapes: Boston, Ripon

0391 Plain colour and gold print outside cup and main part of saucer. White with gold border print inside cup. Centre of saucer is white with gold print. Gold edges and handle. Ideal China/Canadian Teaware. Entered in pattern book during or after 1963.
/8 Turkish Blue
/40 Pink
/47 Royal Blue
/48 Maroon
/83 Green
/91 Drakes Neck Green.
Backstamp(s): Shelley 1940-1966
Shapes: Ripon

Royal blue and gold 0391/47 Ripon shape cup and saucer. £40-60; $100-120

0392 Gold **Fleur De Lys**. Ideal China/Canadian Teaware. Entered in pattern book during or after 1963.
Backstamp(s): Shelley 1940-1966
Shapes: Boston

0393 **Blue Daisy**. Ideal China/Canadian Teaware. Entered in pattern book during or after 1963.
Backstamp(s): Shelley 1940-1966
Shapes: Henley

0394 **Marguerite**. Ideal China/Canadian Teaware. Changed to **Melody** in June 1964. Entered in pattern book during or after 1963.
Backstamp(s): Shelley 1940-1966
Shapes: Henley

0395 **Maytime**. Ideal China/Canadian Teaware. Entered in pattern book during or after 1963.
Backstamp(s): Shelley 1940-1966
Shapes: Henley

0396 **Rock Garden**. Ideal China/Canadian Teaware. Entered in pattern book during or after 1963.
Backstamp(s): Shelley 1940-1966
Shapes: Henley

0397 **Blue Paisley Chintz**. Paisley pattern. Pale pink foot and handle. Pink edges. Also see 14042. Ideal China/Canadian Teaware. Entered in pattern book during or after 1963.
Backstamp(s): Shelley 1940-1966
Shapes: Henley

Blue Paisley Chintz 0397 Henley shape cup and saucer. £80-90; $150-180. **Blue Paisley Chintz** 14042 Henley shape cup and saucer. £80-90; $160-190

0398 **Blue Pansy**. Ideal China/Canadian Teaware. Entered in pattern book during or after 1963.
/P **Pink Glory** used instead.
Backstamp(s): Shelley 1940-1966
Shapes: Henley

0399 Lilac outside cup and on saucer. Pale green inside cup. Green handle. Ideal China/Canadian Teaware. Entered in pattern book during or after 1963.
Backstamp(s): Shelley 1940-1966
Shapes: Stratford

Lilac and green 0399 Stratford shape cup and saucer. £40-50; $80-90

0400 Pale yellow outside cup and on saucer. Pale blue inside cup and on saucer. Blue handle. Ideal China/Canadian Teaware. Entered in pattern book during or after 1963.
Backstamp(s): Shelley 1940-1966
Shapes: Stratford

Blue and yellow 0400 Stratford shape cup and saucer. £40-50; $80-90

0401 Pale blue outside cup and on saucer. Pale lilac inside cup and on saucer. Lilac handle. Ideal China/Canadian Teaware. Entered in pattern book during or after 1963.
Backstamp(s): Shelley 1940-1966
Shapes: Stratford

0402 Pale green outside cup and on saucer. Pale yellow inside cup and on saucer. Yellow handle. Ideal China/Canadian Teaware. Entered in pattern book during or after 1963.
Backstamp(s): Shelley 1940-1966
Shapes: Stratford

0403 Pale peach outside cup and on saucer. Pale green inside cup and on saucer. Green handle. Ideal China/Canadian Teaware. Entered in pattern book during or after 1963.
Backstamp(s): Shelley 1940-1966
Shapes: Stratford

0404 Pale green outside cup and on saucer. Pale pink inside cup and on saucer. Pink handle. Ideal China/Canadian Teaware. Entered in pattern book during or after 1963.
Backstamp(s): Shelley 1940-1966
Shapes: Stratford

0405 **Blue Poppy** inside cup. Lilac outside cup and on saucer. Ideal China/Canadian Teaware. Entered in pattern book during or after 1963.
Backstamp(s): Shelley 1940-1966
Shapes: Atholl

0406 **Honeysuckle** inside cup. Green outside cup and on saucer. Ideal China/Canadian Teaware. Entered in pattern book during or after 1963.
Backstamp(s): Shelley 1940-1966
Shapes: Atholl

0407 **Bramble**. Pink bramble flowers, green leaves, brown stems, against smaller grey leaves on a white ground inside cup. Lemon yellow outside cup and on saucer. Gold edges. White foot. Ideal China/ Canadian Teaware. Entered in pattern book during or after 1963.
Backstamp(s): Shelley 1940-1966.
Shapes: Atholl, Ludlow

Bramble 0407 Ludlow shape cup and saucer. £70-80; $140-160

0408 **Freesia** inside cup. Lemon yellow outside cup and on saucer. Ideal China/Canadian Teaware. Entered in pattern book during or after 1963.
Backstamp(s): Shelley 1940-1966
Shapes: Atholl

0409 Pink **Daisy** (also known as **Dainty Pink)** outside cup and on saucer. **Bramble** inside cup and centre of saucer. Ideal China/Canadian Teaware. Entered in pattern book during or after 1963.
Backstamp(s): Shelley 1940-1966
Shapes: Warwick

0410 Yellow **Daisy** (also known as **Dainty Yellow)** outside cup and on saucer. **Blue Poppy** inside cup and centre of saucer. Ideal China/Canadian Teaware. Entered in pattern book during or after 1963.
Backstamp(s): Shelley 1940-1966
Shapes: Warwick

0411 Blue **Daisy** (also known as **Dainty Blue)** outside cup and on saucer. **Syringa** inside cup and centre of saucer. Ideal China/Canadian Teaware. Entered in pattern book during or after 1963.
Backstamp(s): Shelley 1940-1966
Shapes: Warwick

0412 Mauve **Daisy** (also known as **Dainty Mauve)** outside cup and on saucer. **Freesia** inside cup and centre of saucer. Ideal China/Canadian Teaware. Entered in pattern book during or after 1963.
Backstamp(s): Shelley 1940-1966
Shapes: Warwick

0413 Green **Daisy** (also known as **Dainty Green)** outside cup and on saucer. **Honeysuckle** inside cup and centre of saucer. Ideal China/Canadian Teaware. Entered in pattern book during or after 1963.
Backstamp(s): Shelley 1940-1966
Shapes: Warwick

0414 Brown **Daisy** (also known as **Dainty Brown)** outside cup and on saucer. **Celandine** inside cup and centre of saucer. Ideal China/Canadian Teaware. Entered in pattern book during or after 1963.
Backstamp(s): Shelley 1940-1966
Shapes: Warwick

0415 **Pyrethrum** on large panels. Yellow on small panels. Ideal China/Canadian Teaware. Entered in pattern book during or after 1963.
Backstamp(s): Shelley 1940-1966
Shapes: Queen Anne

0416 **Pyrethrum** on large panels. Green on small panels. Ideal China/Canadian Teaware. Entered in pattern book during or after 1963.
Backstamp(s): Shelley 1940-1966
Shapes: Queen Anne

0417 **Rose Spray** on large panels. Lilac on small panels. Ideal China/Canadian Teaware. Entered in pattern book during or after 1963.
Backstamp(s): Shelley 1940-1966
Shapes: Queen Anne

0418 **Yutoi** on large panels. Peach on small panels. Ideal China/Canadian Teaware. Entered in pattern book during or after 1963.
Backstamp(s): Shelley 1940-1966
Shapes: Queen Anne

0419 **Rose, Pansy, and Forget-me-nots** on large panels. Blue on small panels. Ideal China/Canadian Teaware. Entered in pattern book during or after 1963.
Backstamp(s): Shelley 1940-1966
Shapes: Queen Anne

0420 **Rosebud** on large panels. Pink on small panels. Ideal China/Canadian Teaware. Entered in pattern book during or after 1963.
Backstamp(s): Shelley 1940-1966
Shapes: Queen Anne

0421 Gold pattern on colour ground. Ideal China/Canadian Teaware. Entered in pattern book during or after 1963.
/S3 Green
/S10 Blue
/S15 Peach
/S39 Lemon yellow
/S40 Pale greenish blue
/S41 Lilac.
Backstamp(s): Shelley 1940-1966
Shapes: Canterbury

0422 Gold pattern on colour ground. Ideal China/Canadian Teaware. Entered in pattern book during or after 1963.
/S3 Green
/S10 Blue
/S15 Peach
/S39 Lemon yellow
/S40 Pale greenish blue
/S41 Lilac.
Backstamp(s): Shelley 1940-1966
Shapes: Westminster

0423 **Golden Harvest**. Colour outside cup and on saucer. Ideal China/Canadian Teaware. Entered in pattern book during or after 1963.
/S2 Ivory
/S10 Blue
/S34 Brown
/S41 Lilac.
Backstamp(s): Shelley 1940-1966
Shapes: Footed Dainty

0424 **Pyrethrum** inside cup. Pink outside cup and on saucer. Ideal China/Canadian Teaware. Entered in pattern book during or after 1963.
Backstamp(s): Shelley 1940-1966
Shapes: Atholl

0425 **Wild Anemone** inside cup. Green outside cup and on saucer. Ideal China/ Canadian Teaware. Entered in pattern book during or after 1963.
Backstamp(s): Shelley 1940-1966
Shapes: Atholl

0426 **Campanula** inside cup. Lilac outside cup and on saucer. Ideal China/Canadian Teaware. Entered in pattern book during or after 1963.
Backstamp(s): Shelley 1940-1966
Shapes: Atholl

0427 **Fruit Centre** inside cup. Colour outside cup and on saucer. Ideal China/Canadian Teaware. Entered in pattern book during or after 1963.
/S3 Green
/S9 Pink
/S10 Blue
/S16 Yellow.
Backstamp(s): Shelley 1940-1966
Shapes: Footed Oleander

Fruit Centre 0427/S16 Footed Oleander cup and saucer. £90-95; $150-170

Fruit Centre 0427/S16 pattern inside Footed Oleander cup.

0428 **Bramble**. Pink bramble flowers, green leaves, brown stems, against smaller grey leaves on a white ground inside cup. Lemon yellow outside cup and on saucer. Gold edges. Ideal China/Canadian Teaware. Entered in pattern book during or after 1963.
Backstamp(s): Shelley 1940-1966.
Shapes: Stratford

Bramble 0428 Stratford shape cup and saucer. £70-80; $140-160

Pattern	Description & Shapes
0429	**Freesia**. Pink, purple, and yellow freesias and green leaves inside cup on white ground. Yellow colour outside cup and on saucer. Gold edges. Ideal China/ Canadian Teaware. Entered in pattern book during or after 1963. /S40 green **Backstamp(s)**: Shelley 1940-1966 **Shapes:** Stratford

Freesia 0429 Stratford shape cup and saucer. £60-80; $100-120

0430	**Honeysuckle** inside cup. Green outside cup and on saucer. Ideal China/Canadian Teaware. Entered in pattern book during or after 1963. **Backstamp(s)**: Shelley 1940-1966 **Shapes:** Stratford
0431	**Celandine** inside cup. Peach outside cup and on saucer. Ideal China/Canadian Teaware. Entered in pattern book during or after 1963. **Backstamp(s)**: Shelley 1940-1966 **Shapes:** Stratford
0432	**Wild Anemone** inside cup. Lilac outside cup and on saucer. Ideal China/Canadian Teaware. Entered in pattern book during or after 1963. **Backstamp(s)**: Shelley 1940-1966 **Shapes:** Stratford
0433	**Blue Poppy** inside cup. Greenish blue outside cup and on saucer. Ideal China/ Canadian Teaware. Entered in pattern book during or after 1963. **Backstamp(s)**: Shelley 1940-1966 **Shapes:** Stratford
0434	**Rose Spray** between colour bands. Ideal China/Canadian Teaware. Entered in pattern book during or after 1963. **Backstamp(s)**: Shelley 1940-1966 **Shapes:** Henley

Rose Spray 0434/S15 and 0434/S10 Henley shape cup and saucer. £40-50; $100-120

Rose Spray 0434/S39 Henley shape cup and saucer. £40-50; $80-120

Rose Spray 0434/S40 Henley shape cup and saucer. £40-50; $80-120

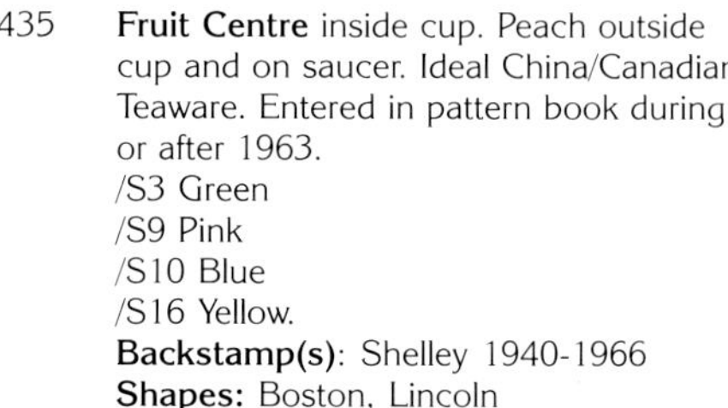

0435	**Fruit Centre** inside cup. Peach outside cup and on saucer. Ideal China/Canadian Teaware. Entered in pattern book during or after 1963. /S3 Green /S9 Pink /S10 Blue /S16 Yellow. **Backstamp(s)**: Shelley 1940-1966 **Shapes:** Boston, Lincoln

Fruit Centre 0435/S3 Lincoln cup and saucer. £90-95; $150-170

Fruit Centre 0435/S3 pattern inside Lincoln cup.

Fruit Centre 0435/S10 Lincoln shape cup and saucer. £90-95; $150-170

Fruit Centre 0435/S10 pattern inside Lincoln shape cup.

Fruit Centre 0435/S16 Lincoln cup and saucer. £90-95; $150-170

Fruit Centre 0435/S16 pattern inside Lincoln shape cup.

Pattern	Description & Shapes
0436	**Morning Glory**. Blue morning glories and green leaves. White ground. Blue edges and handle. Ideal China/Canadian Teaware. Entered in pattern book during or after 1963. **Backstamp(s)**: Shelley 1940-1966 **Shapes:** Low Oleander, Warwick
0437	**Scilla**. Blue flowers and green leaves. Spray also inside cup. Similar to 14061. Ideal China/Canadian Teaware. Entered in pattern book during or after 1963. **Backstamp(s)**: Shelley 1940-1966 **Shapes:** Low Oleander, Warwick
0438	**Blue Rose**. Ideal China/Canadian Teaware. Entered in pattern book during or after 1963. **Backstamp(s)**: Shelley 1940-1966 **Shapes:** Low Oleander, Warwick
0439	**Golden Broom**. Yellow and orange flowers with green leaves. White ground. Pale green edges and handle. Similar to 14033. Ideal China/Canadian Teaware. Entered in pattern book during or after 1963. **Backstamp(s)**: Shelley 1940-1966 **Shapes:** Low Oleander, Warwick

Golden Broom 0439 Warwick shape cup and saucer. £40-50; $80-120

0440	Hulmes **Rose Sprays**. Ideal China/ Canadian Teaware. Entered in pattern book during or after 1963. **Backstamp(s)**: Shelley 1940-1966 **Shapes:** Low Oleander, Warwick
0441	**Bridesmaid**. Similar to 14116. Ideal China/Canadian Teaware. Entered in pattern book during or after 1963. **Backstamp(s)**: Shelley 1940-1966 **Shapes:** Low Oleander, Warwick
0442	**Forget-me-nots**. Similar to 2394. Ideal China/Canadian Teaware. Entered in pattern book during or after 1963. **Backstamp(s)**: Shelley 1940-1966 **Shapes:** Low Oleander, Warwick
0443	**Chrysanthemum**. Large pink and peach chrysanthemum head surrounded by small pink and blue flowers with green foliage on a white ground. Flowers also inside cup. Pale blue edges and handle. Ideal China/Canadian Teaware. Entered in pattern book during or after 1963. **Backstamp(s)**: Shelley 1940-1966 **Shapes:** Low Oleander, Warwick
0444	**Hibiscus**. Large yellow hibiscus flowers and green foliage. Hibiscus spray inside cup. Pale green edges and handle. Ideal China/Canadian Teaware. Entered in pattern book during or after 1963. **Backstamp(s)**: Shelley 1940-1966 **Shapes:** Oleander, Warwick

Hibiscus 0444 Oleander shape cup and saucer. $50-60; $90-110

0445	**Georgian** and **Bluebell**. Ideal China/ Canadian Teaware. Entered in pattern book during or after 1963. **Backstamp(s)**: Shelley 1940-1966 **Shapes:** Low Oleander, Warwick
0446	Cappers **Pink and Yellow Rose**. Ideal China/Canadian Teaware. Entered in pattern book during or after 1963. **Backstamp(s)**: Shelley 1940-1966 **Shapes:** Low Oleander, Warwick
0447	Davies **Tulip**. Bunches of flowers, including yellow tulips, pink roses, blue, white, orange, and yellow flowers with green foliage. Pink rose also inside cup. White ground. Pale green edges and handle. Similar to 2267. Ideal China/ Canadian Teaware. Entered in pattern book during or after 1963. **Backstamp(s)**: Shelley 1940-1966 **Shapes:** Oleander, Warwick
0448	Gold pattern on colour ground. Similar to 12839. Ideal China/Canadian Teaware. Entered in pattern book during or after 1963. /41 Maroon /42 Blue. **Backstamp(s)**: Shelley 1940-1966 **Shapes:** Henley
0449	Gold pattern on colour ground. Similar to 0448 and 12839. Ideal China/Canadian Teaware. Entered in pattern book during or after 1963. /2 Fawn /8 Blue /40 Pink /73 Green. **Backstamp(s)**: Shelley 1940-1966 **Shapes:** Henley
0450	Gold Stars. Plain coloured outside cup and on saucer. White inside cup. Gold border print inside cup. Gold edges and handle. Same as 12860. Ideal China/ Canadian Teaware. Entered in pattern book during or after 1963. /S2 Peach /S5 Pink. **Backstamp(s)**: Shelley 1940-1966 **Shapes:** Ripon
0451	Gold Stars. Plain coloured outside cup and on saucer. White inside cup. Gold border print inside cup. Gold edges and handle. Same as 12860. Ideal China/ Canadian Teaware. Entered in pattern book during or after 1963. /S2 Peach /S5 Pink. **Backstamp(s)**: Shelley 1940-1966 **Shapes:** Ripon
0452	**Stocks** inside cup. Green outside cup and on saucer. Ideal China/Canadian Teaware. Entered in pattern book during or after 1964. **Backstamp(s)**: Shelley 1940-1966. **Shapes:** Boston
0453	**Honeysuckle** inside cup. Pink outside cup and on saucer. Ideal China/Canadian Teaware. Entered in pattern book during or after 1964. **Backstamp(s)**: Shelley 1940-1966. **Shapes:** Boston

Honeysuckle 0453 Lincoln shape cup and saucer. £50-60; $80-110

Pattern	Description & Shapes
0454	**Blue Poppy** inside cup. Blue outside cup and on saucer. Ideal China/Canadian Teaware. Entered in pattern book during or after 1964. **Backstamp(s)**: Shelley 1940-1966. **Shapes:** Boston
0455	**Bramble**. Pink bramble flowers, green leaves, brown stems, against smaller grey leaves on a white ground inside cup. Peach outside cup and on saucer. Plate has bramble pattern on a white centre with peach band. Gold edges. Ideal China/Canadian Teaware. Entered in pattern book during or after 1964. **Backstamp(s)**: Shelley 1940-1966. **Shapes:** Boston
0456	**Freesia** inside cup. Yellow outside cup and on saucer. Ideal China/Canadian Teaware. Entered in pattern book during or after 1964. **Backstamp(s)**: Shelley 1940-1966. **Shapes:** Boston
0457	**Celandine** inside cup. Lilac outside cup and on saucer. Ideal China/Canadian Teaware. Entered in pattern book during or after 1964. **Backstamp(s)**: Shelley 1940-1966. **Shapes:** Boston, Lincoln

Celandine 0457 Lincoln shape cup and saucer. £50-60; $80-110

0458	**Stocks** inside cup. Green outside cup and on saucer. Ideal China/Canadian Teaware. Entered in pattern book during or after 1964. **Backstamp(s)**: Shelley 1940-1966. **Shapes:** Atholl
0459	**Honeysuckle** inside cup. Pink outside cup and on saucer. Ideal China/Canadian Teaware. Entered in pattern book during or after 1964. **Backstamp(s)**: Shelley 1940-1966. **Shapes:** Atholl
0460	**Blue Poppy** inside cup. Blue outside cup and on saucer. Ideal China/Canadian Teaware. Entered in pattern book during or after 1964. **Backstamp(s)**: Shelley 1940-1966. **Shapes:** Atholl
0461	**Bramble** inside cup. Peach outside cup and on saucer. Ideal China/Canadian Teaware. Entered in pattern book during or after 1964. **Backstamp(s)**: Shelley 1940-1966. **Shapes:** Atholl
0462	**Freesia** inside cup. Yellow outside cup and on saucer. Ideal China/Canadian Teaware. Entered in pattern book during or after 1964. **Backstamp(s)**: Shelley 1940-1966. **Shapes:** Atholl
0463	**Celandine** inside cup. Lilac outside cup and on saucer. Ideal China/Canadian Teaware. Entered in pattern book during or after 1964. **Backstamp(s)**: Shelley 1940-1966. **Shapes:** Atholl

Celandine 0463 Atholl shape cup and saucer. £50-60; $120-140

0464	**Stocks** inside cup. Green outside cup and on saucer. Ideal China/Canadian Teaware. Entered in pattern book during or after 1964. **Backstamp(s)**: Shelley 1940-1966. **Shapes:** Stratford
0465	**Honeysuckle** inside cup. Pink outside cup and on saucer. Ideal China/Canadian Teaware. Entered in pattern book during or after 1964. **Backstamp(s)**: Shelley 1940-1966. **Shapes:** Stratford
0466	**Blue Poppy** inside cup. Blue outside cup and on saucer. Ideal China/Canadian Teaware. Entered in pattern book during or after 1964. **Backstamp(s)**: Shelley 1940-1966. **Shapes:** Stratford
0467	**Bramble**. Pink bramble flowers, green leaves, brown stems, against smaller grey leaves on a white ground inside cup. Peach outside cup and on saucer. Gold edges. Ideal China/Canadian Teaware. Entered in pattern book during or after 1964. **Backstamp(s)**: Shelley 1940-1966. **Shapes:** Stratford
0468	**Freesia** inside cup. Yellow outside cup and on saucer. Ideal China/Canadian Teaware. Entered in pattern book during or after 1964. **Backstamp(s)**: Shelley 1940-1966. **Shapes:** Stratford
0469	**Celandine** inside cup. Lilac outside cup and on saucer. Ideal China/Canadian Teaware. Entered in pattern book during or after 1964. **Backstamp(s)**: Shelley 1940-1966. **Shapes:** Stratford
0470	**Stocks**. Mauve, pink, and white stocks with green leaves on a white ground inside cup. Green outside cup and on saucer. Gold edges. Ideal China/Canadian Teaware. **Backstamp(s)**: Shelley 1940-1966 **Shapes:** Dainty, Ludlow
0471	**Honeysuckle**. Pink outside cup and on saucer. Pink honeysuckle and green leaves inside cup. White ground. Gold trim. Ideal China/Canadian Teaware. **Backstamp(s)**: Shelley 1940-1966 **Shapes:** Dainty, Ludlow

Honeysuckle 0471 Dainty shape cup and saucer. £70-80; $140-160

0472	**Blue Poppy**. Blue poppies and green leaves on white ground inside cup. Blue outside cup and on saucer. Gold edges. Ideal China/Canadian Teaware. Entered in pattern book during or after 1964. **Backstamp(s)**: Shelley 1940-1966 **Shapes:** Dainty, Ludlow
0473	**Bramble**. Pink bramble flowers, green leaves, brown stems, against smaller grey leaves on a white ground inside cup. Peach outside cup and on saucer. Gold edges. Ideal China/Canadian Teaware. Entered in pattern book during or after 1964. **Backstamp(s)**: Shelley 1940-1966. **Shapes:** Dainty, Ludlow
0474	**Freesia** inside cup. Yellow outside cup and on saucer. Ideal China/Canadian Teaware. Entered in pattern book during or after 1964. **Backstamp(s)**: Shelley 1940-1966. **Shapes:** Dainty, Ludlow
0475	**Celandine**. Yellow flowers and green leaves inside cup. Lilac outside cup and on saucer. Gold edges. Ideal China/Canadian Teaware. Entered in pattern book during or after 1964. **Backstamp(s)**: Shelley 1940-1966. **Shapes:** Dainty, Ludlow
0476	Gold pattern inside cup. Blue outside cup and on saucer. Ideal China/Canadian Teaware. Entered in pattern book during or after 1964. /S5IL **Debonair** inside cup. **Backstamp(s)**: Shelley 1940-1966. **Shapes:** Ludlow
0477	Gold pattern inside cup. Green outside cup and on saucer. Ideal China/Canadian Teaware. Entered in pattern book during or after 1964. **Backstamp(s)**: Shelley 1940-1966. **Shapes:** Ludlow
0478	Gold pattern inside cup. Yellow outside cup and on saucer. Ideal China/Canadian Teaware. Entered in pattern book during or after 1964. **Backstamp(s)**: Shelley 1940-1966. **Shapes:** Ludlow

Stocks 0470 Ludlow shape cup and saucer. £50-60; $110-130

Pattern **Description & Shapes**

0479 Gold pattern inside cup. Colour outside cup and on saucer. Ideal China/Canadian Teaware. Entered in pattern book during or after 1964.
Backstamp(s): Shelley 1940-1966.
Shapes: Stratford

0480 Gold leaf pattern inside cup. Turquoise outside cup and on saucer. Ideal China/Canadian Teaware. Entered in pattern book during or after 1964.
Backstamp(s): Shelley 1940-1966.
Shapes: Stratford

0481 Gold pattern inside cup. Blue outside cup and on saucer. Ideal China/Canadian Teaware. Entered in pattern book during or after 1964.
Backstamp(s): Shelley 1940-1966.
Shapes: Stratford

0482 Gold pattern inside cup. Green outside cup and on saucer. Ideal China/Canadian Teaware. Entered in pattern book during or after 1964.
Backstamp(s): Shelley 1940-1966.
Shapes: Stratford

0483 Gold border and pattern inside cup on white ground. Fawn outside cup and on saucer. Gold edges. Ideal China/Canadian Teaware. Entered in pattern book during or after 1964.
/S51 Salmon
Backstamp(s): Shelley 1940-1966.
Shapes: Stratford

0484 Gold pattern inside cup. Drakes Neck Green outside cup and on saucer. Ideal China/Canadian Teaware. Entered in pattern book during or after 1964.
Backstamp(s): Shelley 1940-1966.
Shapes: Stratford

0485 Gold pattern inside cup. Colour outside cup and on saucer. Ideal China/Canadian Teaware. Entered in pattern book during or after 1964.
Backstamp(s): Shelley 1940-1966.
Shapes: Stratford

0486 Gold pattern inside cup. Royal blue outside cup and on saucer. Ideal China/Canadian Teaware. Entered in pattern book during or after 1964.
Backstamp(s): Shelley 1940-1966.
Shapes: Stratford

0487 Gold pattern inside cup. Blue outside cup and on saucer. Ideal China/Canadian Teaware. Entered in pattern book during or after 1964.
Backstamp(s): Shelley 1940-1966.
Shapes: Stratford

0488 Gold pattern inside cup. Sand grey outside cup and on saucer. Ideal China/Canadian Teaware. Entered in pattern book during or after 1964.
Backstamp(s): Shelley 1940-1966.
Shapes: Stratford

0489 Gold pattern inside cup. Sage green outside cup and on saucer. Ideal China/Canadian Teaware. Entered in pattern book during or after 1964.
Backstamp(s): Shelley 1940-1966.
Shapes: Stratford

0490 Gold pattern inside cup. Yellow outside cup and on saucer. Ideal China/Canadian Teaware. Entered in pattern book during or after 1964.
Backstamp(s): Shelley 1940-1966.
Shapes: Stratford

0491 Gold pattern inside cup. Pink outside cup and on saucer. Ideal China/Canadian Teaware. Entered in pattern book during or after 1964.
Backstamp(s): Shelley 1940-1966.
Shapes: Stratford

0492 Gold pattern inside cup. Chinese Jade green outside cup and on saucer. Ideal China/Canadian Teaware. Entered in pattern book during or after 1964.
Backstamp(s): Shelley 1940-1966.
Shapes: Stratford

0493 Gold pattern inside cup. Yellow outside cup and on saucer. Ideal China/Canadian Teaware. Entered in pattern book during or after 1964.
Backstamp(s): Shelley 1940-1966.
Shapes: Stratford

0494 Gold pattern inside cup. Yellow outside cup and on saucer. Ideal China/Canadian Teaware. Entered in pattern book during or after 1964.
Backstamp(s): Shelley 1940-1966.
Shapes: Atholl

0495 Gold pattern inside cup. Turquoise outside cup and on saucer. Ideal China/Canadian Teaware. Entered in pattern book during or after 1964.
Backstamp(s): Shelley 1940-1966.
Shapes: Atholl

0496 Gold pattern inside cup. Red outside cup and on saucer. Ideal China/Canadian Teaware. Entered in pattern book during or after 1964.
Backstamp(s): Shelley 1940-1966.
Shapes: Atholl

0497 Gold pattern inside cup. Green outside cup and on saucer. Ideal China/Canadian Teaware. Entered in pattern book during or after 1964.
Backstamp(s): Shelley 1940-1966.
Shapes: Atholl

0498 Gold print border on white ground inside cup. Dark pink outside cup and on saucer. Gold edges. Ideal China/Canadian Teaware. Entered in pattern book during or after 1964.
Backstamp(s): Shelley 1940-1966
Shapes: Atholl

0499 Gold pattern inside cup. Green outside cup and on saucer. Ideal China/Canadian Teaware. Entered in pattern book during or after 1964.
Backstamp(s): Shelley 1940-1966.
Shapes: Atholl

0500 Gold pattern inside cup. Pink outside cup and on saucer. Ideal China/Canadian Teaware. Entered in pattern book during or after 1964.
Backstamp(s): Shelley 1940-1966.
Shapes: Atholl

0501 Gold pattern and green band inside cup and on saucer. Similar to 0604. Ideal China/Canadian Teaware. Entered in pattern book during or after 1964.
Backstamp(s): Shelley 1940-1966.
Shapes: Lincoln

0502 Gold pattern and pink band inside cup and on saucer. Ideal China/Canadian Teaware. Entered in pattern book during or after 1964.
Backstamp(s): Shelley 1940-1966.
Shapes: Lincoln

0503 Gold pattern and green band inside cup and on saucer. Ideal China/Canadian Teaware. Entered in pattern book during or after 1964.
Backstamp(s): Shelley 1940-1966.
Shapes: Lincoln

0504 Gold pattern and dark green band inside cup and on saucer. Ideal China/Canadian Teaware. Entered in pattern book during or after 1964.
Backstamp(s): Shelley 1940-1966.
Shapes: Lincoln

0505 Gold pattern and brown band inside cup and on saucer. Ideal China/Canadian Teaware. Entered in pattern book during or after 1964.
Backstamp(s): Shelley 1940-1966.
Shapes: Lincoln

0506 Gold pattern and Chinese Jade green band inside cup and on saucer. Similar to 0602. Ideal China/Canadian Teaware. Entered in pattern book during or after 1964.
Backstamp(s): Shelley 1940-1966.
Shapes: Lincoln

0507 Gold pattern and turquoise band inside cup and on saucer. Ideal China/Canadian Teaware. Entered in pattern book during or after 1964.
Backstamp(s): Shelley 1940-1966.
Shapes: Lincoln

Pattern number 0507 Lincoln shape cup and saucer. £85-95; $130-160

0508 Gold pattern and yellow band inside cup and on saucer. Ideal China/Canadian Teaware. Entered in pattern book during or after 1964.
Backstamp(s): Shelley 1940-1966.
Shapes: Lincoln

0509 Gold pattern and blue band inside cup and on saucer. Ideal China/Canadian Teaware. Entered in pattern book during or after 1964.
Backstamp(s): Shelley 1940-1966.
Shapes: Lincoln

0510 Gold pattern and lemon yellow band inside cup and on saucer. Ideal China/Canadian Teaware. Entered in pattern book during or after 1964.
Backstamp(s): Shelley 1940-1966.
Shapes: Lincoln

0511 Gold pattern and peach band inside cup and on saucer. Ideal China/Canadian Teaware. Entered in pattern book during or after 1964.
Backstamp(s): Shelley 1940-1966.
Shapes: Lincoln

0512 Gold pattern and colour band inside cup and on saucer. Ideal China/Canadian Teaware. Entered in pattern book during or after 1964.
Backstamp(s): Shelley 1940-1966.
Shapes: Lincoln

0513 Gold pattern on green ground inside cup and on saucer. White border. Ideal China/Canadian Teaware. Entered in pattern book during or after 1964.
Backstamp(s): Shelley 1940-1966.
Shapes: Lincoln

0514 Gold pattern on colour ground inside cup and on saucer. White border. Ideal China/Canadian Teaware. Entered in pattern book during or after 1964.
Backstamp(s): Shelley 1940-1966.
Shapes: Lincoln

0515 Gold pattern on Drakes Neck Green inside cup and on saucer. White border. Ideal China/Canadian Teaware. Entered in pattern book during or after 1964.
Backstamp(s): Shelley 1940-1966.
Shapes: Lincoln

0516 Gold leaf border on white with Drakes Neck Green inside cup and on saucer. White border. Ideal China/Canadian Teaware. Entered in pattern book during or after 1964.
Backstamp(s): Shelley 1940-1966.
Shapes: Lincoln

0517 Gold leaf border on white with Royal Blue inside cup and on saucer. White border. Ideal China/Canadian Teaware. Entered in pattern book during or after 1964.

Pattern	Description & Shapes
	Backstamp(s): Shelley 1940-1966. **Shapes:** Lincoln
0518	Gold leaf border on white with yellow inside cup and on saucer. White border. Ideal China/Canadian Teaware. Entered in pattern book during or after 1964. **Backstamp(s)**: Shelley 1940-1966. **Shapes:** Lincoln
0519	Turquoise inside cup and on saucer with a gold leafy border. Gold edging, foot, and outer part of handle. Colour variations. Ideal China/Canadian Teaware. Entered in pattern book during or after 1963 to c. 1966. **Backstamp(s)**: Shelley 1940-1966 **Shapes:** Boston

Pattern number 0519/S58 Boston shape cup and saucer. £85-95; $130-160

0520	Gold pattern on Chinese Jade green inside cup and on saucer. White border. Ideal China/Canadian Teaware. Entered in pattern book during or after 1964. **Backstamp(s)**: Shelley 1940-1966. **Shapes:** Lincoln
0521	Gold pattern and blue inside cup and on saucer. White border. Ideal China/ Canadian Teaware. Entered in pattern book during or after 1964. **Backstamp(s)**: Shelley 1940-1966. **Shapes:** Lincoln
0522	Gold pattern and yellow inside cup and on saucer. White border. Ideal China/ Canadian Teaware. Entered in pattern book during or after 1964. **Backstamp(s)**: Shelley 1940-1966. **Shapes:** Lincoln
0523	Gold pattern and Georgian Green inside cup and on saucer. White border. Ideal China/Canadian Teaware. Entered in pattern book during or after 1964. **Backstamp(s)**: Shelley 1940-1966. **Shapes:** Lincoln
0524	Gold pattern and Drakes Neck Green inside cup and on saucer. White border. Ideal China/Canadian Teaware. Entered in pattern book during or after 1964. **Backstamp(s)**: Shelley 1940-1966. **Shapes:** Lincoln
0525	Gold pattern and maroon inside cup and on saucer. White border. Ideal China/ Canadian Teaware. Entered in pattern book during or after 1964. **Backstamp(s)**: Shelley 1940-1966. **Shapes:** Lincoln
0526	Gold pattern and Leather Green inside cup and on saucer. White border. Ideal China/Canadian Teaware. Entered in pattern book during or after 1964. **Backstamp(s)**: Shelley 1940-1966. **Shapes:** Lincoln
0527	Gold pattern and blue inside cup and on saucer. Ideal China/Canadian Teaware. Entered in pattern book during or after 1964. **Backstamp(s)**: Shelley 1940-1966. **Shapes:** Lincoln
0528	Gold pattern on blue band inside cup and on saucer. Ideal China/Canadian Teaware. Entered in pattern book during or after 1964. **Backstamp(s)**: Shelley 1940-1966. **Shapes:** Lincoln
0529	Gold pattern on turquoise band inside cup and on saucer. Ideal China/Canadian Teaware. Entered in pattern book during or after 1964. **Backstamp(s)**: Shelley 1940-1966. **Shapes:** Lincoln
0530	Gold pattern with turquoise band inside cup and on saucer. Ideal China/Canadian Teaware. Entered in pattern book during or after 1964. **Backstamp(s)**: Shelley 1940-1966. **Shapes:** Lincoln
0531	Gold pattern with turquoise band inside cup and on saucer. Ideal China/Canadian Teaware. Entered in pattern book during or after 1964. **Backstamp(s)**: Shelley 1940-1966. **Shapes:** Lincoln
0532	Gold pattern with Corn Green band inside cup and on saucer. Ideal China/ Canadian Teaware. Entered in pattern book during or after 1964. **Backstamp(s)**: Shelley 1940-1966. **Shapes:** Lincoln
0533	Gold pattern with fawn band inside cup and on saucer. Ideal China/Canadian Teaware. Entered in pattern book during or after 1964. **Backstamp(s)**: Shelley 1940-1966. **Shapes:** Lincoln
0534	Gold leaf border with yellow band inside cup and on saucer. Ideal China/Canadian Teaware. Entered in pattern book during or after 1964. **Backstamp(s)**: Shelley 1940-1966. **Shapes:** Lincoln
0535	Gold pattern with pink band inside cup and on saucer. Ideal China/Canadian Teaware. Entered in pattern book during or after 1964. **Backstamp(s)**: Shelley 1940-1966. **Shapes:** Lincoln
0536	Gold pattern with green band inside cup and on saucer. Ideal China/Canadian Teaware. Entered in pattern book during or after 1964. **Backstamp(s)**: Shelley 1940-1966. **Shapes:** Lincoln
0537	Gold pattern with yellow band inside cup and on saucer. Ideal China/Canadian Teaware. Entered in pattern book during or after 1964. **Backstamp(s)**: Shelley 1940-1966. **Shapes:** Lincoln
0538	**Fruit Centre** inside cup. Royal blue outside cup and on saucer. Ideal China/ Canadian Teaware. Entered in pattern book during or after 1964. **Backstamp(s)**: Shelley 1940-1966. **Shapes:** Atholl
0539	Gold floral and leafy borders. The cup has an arrangement of roses in pink and green inside the cup at the base. Turquoise outside cup and on saucer. Ideal China/Canadian Teaware. Entered in pattern book during or after 1964. **Backstamp(s)**: Shelley 1940-1966 **Shapes:** Atholl
0540	Gold pattern on pink ground outside cup and on saucer. Gold border inside cup. Ideal China/Canadian Teaware. Entered in pattern book during or after 1964. **Backstamp(s)**: Shelley 1940-1966. **Shapes:** Ludlow
0541	**Fruit Centre** inside cup. Mauve outside cup and on saucer. Similar to 0606. Ideal China/Canadian Teaware. Entered in pattern book during or after 1964. **Backstamp(s)**: Shelley 1940-1966. **Shapes:** Ludlow
0542	**Fruit Centre**. Ideal China/Canadian Teaware. Similar to 0605. Entered in pattern book during or after 1964. **Backstamp(s)**: Shelley 1940-1966. **Shapes:** Lincoln
0543	**Fruit Centre**. Ideal China/Canadian Teaware. Entered in pattern book during or after 1964. **Backstamp(s)**: Shelley 1940-1966. **Shapes:** Lincoln
0544	**Fruit Centre** outside cup. Drakes Neck Green inside cup and on saucer. Ideal China/Canadian Teaware. Entered in pattern book during or after 1964. Backstamp(s): Shelley 1940-1966. **Shapes:** Lincoln
0545	Gold pattern with pink band inside cup and on saucer. Ideal China/Canadian Teaware. Entered in pattern book during or after 1964. **Backstamp(s)**: Shelley 1940-1966. **Shapes:** Lincoln
0546	Gold pattern with Drakes Neck Green band inside cup and on saucer. Ideal China/Canadian Teaware. Entered in pattern book during or after 1964. **Backstamp(s)**: Shelley 1940-1966. **Shapes:** Lincoln
0547	Gold pattern with red band inside cup and on saucer. Similar to 0547. Ideal China/Canadian Teaware. Entered in pattern book during or after 1964. **Backstamp(s)**: Shelley 1940-1966. **Shapes:** Lincoln
0548	Gold pattern with Drakes Neck Green band inside cup and on saucer. Ideal China/Canadian Teaware. Entered in pattern book during or after 1964. **Backstamp(s)**: Shelley 1940-1966. **Shapes:** Lincoln
0549	Gold pattern with pink band inside cup and on saucer. Ideal China/Canadian Teaware. Entered in pattern book during or after 1964. **Backstamp(s)**: Shelley 1940-1966. **Shapes:** Lincoln
0550	**Fruit** inside cup. Colour outside cup and on saucer. Ideal China/Canadian Teaware. Entered in pattern book during or after 1964. /S47 Blue with Plums /S48 Maroon with peaches /S49 Green with pears /S50 Blue with apples /S51 Fawn with cherries /S52 Pink with grapes. **Backstamp(s)**: Shelley 1940-1966. **Shapes:** Stratford
0551	**Dubarry** inside cup. Green outside cup and on saucer. Ideal China/Canadian Teaware. Entered in pattern book during or after 1964. **Backstamp(s)**: Shelley 1940-1966. **Shapes:** Atholl
0552	**Bridesmaid** inside cup. Blue outside cup and on saucer. Ideal China/Canadian Teaware. Entered in pattern book during or after 1964. **Backstamp(s)**: Shelley 1940-1966. **Shapes:** Stratford
0553	**Bridesmaid** inside cup. Green outside cup and on saucer. Ideal China/Canadian Teaware. Entered in pattern book during or after 1964. **Backstamp(s)**: Shelley 1940-1966. **Shapes:** Stratford
0554	**Georgian** inside cup. Blue outside cup and on saucer. Ideal China/Canadian Teaware. Entered in pattern book during or after 1964. **Backstamp(s)**: Shelley 1940-1966. **Shapes:** Atholl
0555	**Georgian** inside cup. Royal blue outside cup and on saucer. Ideal China/Canadian Teaware. Entered in pattern book during

Pattern	Description & Shapes
	or after 1964., Boston: Produced for Eatons, Toronto, Canada. /S48 Maroon /S52 Pink /S54 Drakes Neck Green /S54 Leather Green. **Backstamp(s)**: Shelley 1940-1966. **Shapes:** Atholl, Boston
0556	**Bridesmaid** inside cup. Green outside cup and on saucer. Ideal China/Canadian Teaware. Entered in pattern book during or after 1964. **Backstamp(s)**: Shelley 1940-1966. **Shapes:** Atholl, Boston
0557	**Dubarry** inside cup. Yellow outside cup and on saucer. Ideal China/Canadian Teaware. Entered in pattern book during or after 1964. **Backstamp(s)**: Shelley 1940-1966. **Shapes:** Atholl
0558	Pink pattern on large panels. White small panels. Gold pattern inside cup and on panels joins. Ideal China/Canadian Teaware. Entered in pattern book during or after 1964. **Backstamp(s)**: Shelley 1940-1966. **Shapes:** Stratford
0559	White and colour alternating panels outside cup and on saucer. Gold pattern on panel joins. Gold leaf at the top of each white panel. Gold leaf border inside cup on a white ground. Gold edges and handle. Ideal China/Canadian Teaware. Entered in pattern book during or after 1964 for Shelley Walker, New York. /39 Green /40 Pink /41 Maroon /72 Black. **Backstamp(s)**: Shelley 1940-1966 **Shapes:** Stratford

Gold leaf 0559/39 Stratford shape large cup and saucer. £85-95; $130-160

Gold leaf 0559/40 Stratford shape large cup and saucer. £85-95; $130-160

Gold leaf 0559/72 Stratford shape large cup and saucer. £85-95; $130-160

0560	Green pattern on large panels. White small panels. Gold pattern inside cup and on panels joins. Ideal China/Canadian Teaware. Entered in pattern book during or after 1964. **Backstamp(s)**: Shelley 1940-1966. **Shapes:** Stratford
0561	Drakes Neck Green pattern on large panels. White small panels. Gold pattern inside cup and on panels joins. Ideal China/Canadian Teaware. Entered in pattern book during or after 1964. **Backstamp(s)**: Shelley 1940-1966. **Shapes:** Stratford
0562	**Georgian** inside cup. Ideal China/Canadian Teaware. Entered in pattern book during or after 1964 for Shelley Walker, New York. **Backstamp(s)**: Shelley 1940-1966. **Shapes:** Atholl, Boston
0563	**Summer Bouquet**. Large bouquet inside cup and centre of saucer. Roses, blue, yellow and mauve flowers with green foliage. Pink sprays outside cup. Gold border inside cup and on saucer. White ground. Gold edges. China/Canadian Teaware. Entered in pattern book during or after 1964 for Shelley Walker, New York. **Backstamp(s)**: Shelley 1940-1966 **Shapes:** Atholl, Boston

Summer Bouquet 0563 Atholl shape cup and saucer. £70-80; $140-160

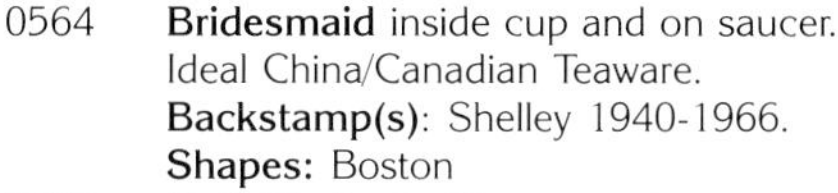

0564	**Bridesmaid** inside cup and on saucer. Ideal China/Canadian Teaware. **Backstamp(s)**: Shelley 1940-1966. **Shapes:** Boston
0565	**Fruit Centre** inside cup and on saucer. Ideal China/Canadian Teaware. Entered in pattern book during or after 1964. **Backstamp(s)**: Shelley 1940-1966. **Shapes:** Boston
0566	**Violets**. Mauve saucer. Ideal China/Canadian Teaware. Entered in pattern book during or after 1964. **Backstamp(s)**: Shelley 1940-1966. **Shapes:** Ludlow
0567	**Wild Flower**. Green saucer. Ideal China/Canadian Teaware. Entered in pattern book during or after 1964. **Backstamp(s)**: Shelley 1940-1966. **Shapes:** Ludlow
0568	**Celandine**. Yellow saucer. Ideal China/Canadian Teaware. Entered in pattern book during or after 1964. **Backstamp(s)**: Shelley 1940-1966. **Shapes:** Ludlow
0569	**Blue Rose**. Turquoise saucer. Ideal China/Canadian Teaware. Entered in pattern book during or after 1964. **Backstamp(s)**: Shelley 1940-1966. **Shapes:** Ludlow
0570	**Stocks**. Pink saucer. Ideal China/Canadian Teaware. Entered in pattern book during or after 1964. **Backstamp(s)**: Shelley 1940-1966. **Shapes:** Ludlow
0571	**Morning Glory**. Blue saucer. Ideal China/Canadian Teaware. Entered in pattern book during or after 1964. **Backstamp(s)**: Shelley 1940-1966. **Shapes:** Ludlow
0572	**Wild Anemone**. Pink saucer. Ideal China/Canadian Teaware. Entered in pattern book during or after 1964. **Backstamp(s)**: Shelley 1940-1966. **Shapes:** Ludlow
0573	**Hibiscus**. Yellow saucer. Ideal China/Canadian Teaware. Entered in pattern book during or after 1964. **Backstamp(s)**: Shelley 1940-1966. **Shapes:** Ludlow
0574	**Syringa**. Green saucer. Ideal China/Canadian Teaware. Entered in pattern book during or after 1964. **Backstamp(s)**: Shelley 1940-1966. **Shapes:** Ludlow
0575	**Blue Poppy**. Blue saucer. Ideal China/Canadian Teaware. Entered in pattern book during or after 1964. **Backstamp(s)**: Shelley 1940-1966. **Shapes:** Ludlow
0576	**Oleander**. Pink saucer. Ideal China/Canadian Teaware. Entered in pattern book during or after 1964. **Backstamp(s)**: Shelley 1940-1966. **Shapes:** Ludlow

Right:
Summer Bouquet 0563 pattern inside Atholl shape cup.

Pattern	Description & Shapes
0577	**Wild Rose**. Yellow saucer. Ideal China/ Canadian Teaware. Entered in pattern book during or after 1964. **Backstamp(s)**: Shelley 1940-1966. **Shapes:** Ludlow
0578	**Stocks** inside cup. Green outside cup and on saucer. Ideal China/Canadian Teaware. Entered in pattern book during or after 1964. **Backstamp(s)**: Shelley 1940-1966. **Shapes:** Atholl
0579	**Honeysuckle** inside cup. Pink outside cup and on saucer. Ideal China/Canadian Teaware. Entered in pattern book during or after 1964. **Backstamp(s)**: Shelley 1940-1966. **Shapes:** Atholl
0580	**Blue Poppy** inside cup. Blue outside cup and on saucer. Ideal China/Canadian Teaware. Entered in pattern book during or after 1964. **Backstamp(s)**: Shelley 1940-1966. **Shapes:** Atholl
0581	**Bramble** inside cup. Peach outside cup and on outside cup and on saucer. Gold edges. Ideal China/Canadian Teaware. Entered in pattern book during or after 1964. **Backstamp(s)**: Shelley 1940-1966. **Shapes:** Atholl
0582	**Freesia** inside cup. Yellow outside cup and on saucer. Ideal China/Canadian Teaware. Entered in pattern book during or after 1964. **Backstamp(s)**: Shelley 1940-1966. **Shapes:** Atholl
0583	**Celandine** inside cup. Lilac outside cup and on saucer. Ideal China/Canadian Teaware. Entered in pattern book during or after 1964. **Backstamp(s)**: Shelley 1940-1966. **Shapes:** Atholl
0584	**Gold Peony**. Gold peonies and leaves on colour ground. Gold trim and handle. Similar to 0383. Ideal China/Canadian Teaware. Entered in pattern book during or after 1964. /S15 Peach /S39 Lemon yellow /S40 Pale greenish blue /S41 Lilac. **Backstamp(s)**: Shelley 1940-1966 **Shapes:** Atholl
0585	Gold pattern on colour ground. Similar to 0390 and 0586. Ideal China/Canadian Teaware. Entered in pattern book during or after 1964. /S41 Lilac /42 Blue. **Backstamp(s)**: Shelley 1940-1966 **Shapes:** Ripon
0586	Gold pattern on colour ground. Similar to 0390 and 0585. Ideal China/Canadian Teaware. Entered in pattern book during or after 1964. /S47 Royal blue /S48 Maroon /S52 Pink /S53 Drakes Neck Green /S60 Sage green. **Backstamp(s)**: Shelley 1940-1966 **Shapes:** Ripon
0587	**Campanula** inside cup. Green outside cup and on saucer. Ideal China/Canadian Teaware. Entered in pattern book during or after 1964. **Backstamp(s)**: Shelley 1940-1966. **Shapes:** Stratford
0588	**Bridesmaid** inside cup. Pink outside cup and on saucer. Ideal China/Canadian Teaware. Entered in pattern book during or after 1964. **Backstamp(s)**: Shelley 1940-1966. **Shapes:** Stratford
0589	**Wild Flowers** inside cup. Blue outside cup and on saucer. Ideal China/Canadian Teaware. Entered in pattern book during or after 1964. **Backstamp(s)**: Shelley 1940-1966. **Shapes:** Stratford
0590	**Primrose** inside cup. Peach outside cup and on saucer. Ideal China/Canadian Teaware. Entered in pattern book during or after 1964. **Backstamp(s)**: Shelley 1940-1966. **Shapes:** Stratford
0591	**Wild Anemone** inside cup. Yellow outside cup and on saucer. Ideal China/ Canadian Teaware. Entered in pattern book during or after 1964. **Backstamp(s)**: Shelley 1940-1966. **Shapes:** Stratford
0592	**Violets** inside cup. Lilac outside cup and on saucer. Ideal China/Canadian Teaware. Entered in pattern book during or after 1964. **Backstamp(s)**: Shelley 1940-1966. **Shapes:** Stratford
0593	**Stocks** inside cup. Green outside cup and on saucer. Ideal China/Canadian Teaware. Entered in pattern book during or after 1964. **Backstamp(s)**: Shelley 1940-1966. **Shapes:** Stratford
0594	**Honeysuckle** inside cup. Pink outside cup and on saucer. Ideal China/Canadian Teaware. Entered in pattern book during or after 1964. **Backstamp(s)**: Shelley 1940-1966. **Shapes:** Stratford
0595	**Blue Poppy** inside cup. Royal blue outside cup and on saucer. Ideal China/ Canadian Teaware. Entered in pattern book during or after 1964. **Backstamp(s)**: Shelley 1940-1966. **Shapes:** Stratford
0596	**Bramble** inside cup. Green outside cup and on saucer. Gold edges. Ideal China/ Canadian Teaware. Entered in pattern book during or after 1964. **Backstamp(s)**: Shelley 1940-1966. **Shapes:** Stratford
0597	**Freesia** inside cup. Maroon outside cup and on saucer. Ideal China/Canadian Teaware. Entered in pattern book during or after 1964. **Backstamp(s)**: Shelley 1940-1966. **Shapes:** Stratford
0598	**Celandine** inside cup. Blue outside cup and on saucer. Ideal China/Canadian Teaware. Entered in pattern book during or after 1964. **Backstamp(s)**: Shelley 1940-1966. **Shapes:** Stratford
0599	**Gold Thistle** printed on coloured ground inside cup and on saucer. White ground outside cup. Gold trim, foot and handle. Similar to 0367. Ideal China/Canadian Teaware. Entered in pattern book during or after 1964. /S3 Green /S15 Peach S39 Lemon yellow. **Backstamp(s)**: Shelley 1940-1966 **Shapes:** Lincoln
0600	**Gold Rose**. Gold roses and foliage on coloured ground inside cup and on saucer. White ground outside cup. Gold trim, foot and handle. Similar to 0369 and 0648. Ideal China/Canadian Teaware. Entered in pattern book during or after 1964. /S9 Pink /S10 Blue /S41 Lilac. **Backstamp(s)**: Shelley 1940-1966 **Shapes:** Lincoln
0601	Alternating colour and white panels outside cup and on saucer. Gold print on white ground inside cup. Gold edges. Ideal China/Canadian Teaware. Entered in pattern book during or after 1964. /36 Malachite Green /40 Pink /41 Maroon /59 Peach /91 Drakes Neck Green /93 Light blue. **Backstamp(s)**: Shelley 1940-1966 **Shapes:** Stratford

Panels and gold print 0601/41 Stratford shape cup and saucer. £70-80; $140-160

Pattern	Description & Shapes
0602	Gold pattern and colour band inside cup and on saucer. Similar to 0506. Ideal China/Canadian Teaware. Entered in pattern book during or after 1964. /S47 Royal blue /S48 Maroon /S54 Leather Green /S58 Turquoise. **Backstamp(s)**: Shelley 1940-1966. **Shapes:** Lincoln
0602	Gold leaf pattern and colour band. Gold star inside cup. Ideal China/Canadian Teaware. Entered in pattern book during or after 1964. /S47 Royal blue /S48 Maroon /S49 Green /S53 Drakes Neck Green. **Backstamp(s)**: Shelley 1940-1966. **Shapes:** Lincoln
0604	Gold pattern and colour band inside cup and on saucer. Similar to 0501. Ideal China/Canadian Teaware. Entered in pattern book during or after 1964. /S47 Royal blue /S48 Maroon /S54 Leather Green /S58 Turquoise. **Backstamp(s)**: Shelley 1940-1966. **Shapes:** Lincoln
0605	**Fruit Centre**. Colour bands inside cup and on saucer. Ideal China/Canadian Teaware. Similar to 0542. Entered in pattern book during or after 1964., Henley: Produced for Shelley Walker, New York, U.S.A. /S48 Maroon /S53 Drakes Neck Green /S54 Leather Green /72 Black. **Backstamp(s)**: Shelley 1940-1966. **Shapes:** Henley, Lincoln
0606	**Fruit Centre** inside cup. Colour outside cup and on saucer. Similar to 0541. Ideal China/Canadian Teaware. Entered in pattern book during or after 1964. **Backstamp(s)**: Shelley 1940-1966. **Shapes:** Lincoln
0607	Gold pattern and colour bands. Gold star in centre of saucer. Ideal China/Canadian Teaware. Entered in pattern book during or after 1964. **Backstamp(s)**: Shelley 1940-1966. **Shapes:** New Victoria
0608	Gold pattern on colour ground. Ideal China/Canadian Teaware. Entered in

Pattern Description & Shapes

pattern book during or after 1964.
Backstamp(s): Shelley 1940-1966.
Shapes: New Victoria

0609 Gold pattern and colour bands. Ideal China/Canadian Teaware. Entered in pattern book during or after 1964.
Backstamp(s): Shelley 1940-1966.
Shapes: New Victoria

0610 Gold leaves. Colour outside cup and on saucer with gold leaves. Gold border pattern. White inside cup with gold border. Ideal China/Canadian Teaware. Entered in pattern book during or after 1964.
/S47 Blue
/S48 Maroon
/S49 Georgian Green
/S54 Leather Green.
Backstamp(s): Shelley 1940-1966
Shapes: New Victoria

Gold leaves 0610/S48 New Victoria shape cup and saucer. £90-100; $180-200

0611 Gold pattern and colour bands. Gold star in centre of saucer. Ideal China/Canadian Teaware. Entered in pattern book during or after 1964.
Backstamp(s): Shelley 1940-1966.
Shapes: New Victoria

0612 Gold pattern and colour bands. Ideal China/Canadian Teaware. Entered in pattern book during or after 1964.
Backstamp(s): Shelley 1940-1966.
Shapes: New Victoria

0613 Baileys **Blue Floral**. Large blue and small pink flowers with grey and green leaves on a white ground. Flower spray also inside cup. Pale blue edges and handle. Ideal China/Canadian Teaware. Entered in pattern book during or after 1965.
Backstamp(s): Shelley 1940-1966
Shapes: Low Oleander, Warwick

Blue Floral 0613 Warwick shape cup and saucer. £70-80; $140-160

0614 **Yutoi**. Ideal China/Canadian Teaware. Entered in pattern book during or after 1965.
Backstamp(s): Shelley 1940-1966.
Shapes: Low Oleander, Warwick

Yutoi Oleander shape cup and saucer. £40-60; $70-100

0615 **Wild Apple**. Ideal China/Canadian Teaware. Entered in pattern book during or after 1965.
Backstamp(s): Shelley 1940-1966.
Shapes: Low Oleander, Warwick

0616 German **Rose**. Ideal China/Canadian Teaware. Entered in pattern book during or after 1965.
Backstamp(s): Shelley 1940-1966.
Shapes: Low Oleander, Warwick

0617 **Debonair**. Ideal China/Canadian Teaware. Entered in pattern book during or after 1965.
Backstamp(s): Shelley 1940-1966.
Shapes: Low Oleander, Warwick

0618 **Blackberry**. Red and black berries with grey and green leaves on a white ground. Pale green edges and handle. Ideal China/Canadian Teaware. Entered in pattern book during or after 1965.
Backstamp(s): Shelley 1940-1966
Shapes: Low Oleander, Warwick

Blackberry 0618 Warwick shape cup and saucer. £70-80; $140-160

0619 **Chantilly** inside cup on a peach ground. Colour outside cup and on saucer. Ideal China/Canadian Teaware. Entered in pattern book during or after 1965.
/S47 Royal blue
/S48 Maroon
/S57 Blue
/S58 Turquoise.
Backstamp(s): Shelley 1940-1966.
Shapes: Lincoln

0620 **Fruit Centre** inside cup and centre of saucer. Colour band inside cup and on saucer. Ideal China/Canadian Teaware. Entered in pattern book during or after 1965.
Backstamp(s): Shelley 1940-1966.
Shapes: Lincoln

0621 **Fruit Centre** inside cup on a peach ground. Colour outside cup and on saucer. Ideal China/Canadian Teaware. Entered in pattern book during or after 1965.
/S47 Royal blue
/S48 Maroon
/S54 Leather green
/S58 Turquoise.
Backstamp(s): Shelley 1940-1966.
Shapes: Lincoln

0622 Colour inside cup and on saucer. Ivory Outside cup. Ideal China/Canadian Teaware. Entered in pattern book during or after 1965.
/S47 Royal blue
/S48 Maroon
/S54 Leather green
/ /S58 Turquoise.
Backstamp(s): Shelley 1940-1966.
Shapes: Boston

0623 **Aubusson**. Colour panels and **Chantilly** sprays. Ideal China/Canadian Teaware. Entered in pattern book during or after 1965.
Backstamp(s): Shelley 1940-1966.
Shapes: Lincoln

0624 **Georgian**. Ideal China/Canadian Teaware. Entered in pattern book during or after 1965.
Backstamp(s): Shelley 1940-1966.
Shapes: Lincoln

0625 Gold pattern and colour panels. Ideal China/Canadian Teaware. Entered in pattern book during or after 1965.
Backstamp(s): Shelley 1940-1966.
Shapes: Stratford

0626 Gold pattern and colour panels. Ideal China/Canadian Teaware. Entered in pattern book during or after 1965.
Backstamp(s): Shelley 1940-1966.
Shapes: Atholl

0627 **Violets** inside cup. Yellow outside cup and on saucer. Ideal China/Canadian Teaware. Entered in pattern book during or after 1965.
Backstamp(s): Shelley 1940-1966.
Shapes: Lincoln

0628 **Yellow Rose Spray** inside cup. Green outside cup and on saucer. Ideal China/ Canadian Teaware. Entered in pattern book during or after 1965.
Backstamp(s): Shelley 1940-1966.
Shapes: Lincoln

0629 **Dark Red Rose** inside cup. Pink outside cup and on saucer. Ideal China/Canadian Teaware. Entered in pattern book during or after 1965.
Backstamp(s): Shelley 1940-1966.
Shapes: Lincoln

0630 **Yellow Rose Spray** inside cup. Ideal China/Canadian Teaware. Entered in pattern book during or after 1965.
Backstamp(s): Shelley 1940-1966.
Shapes: Boston

0631 **Dark Red Rose** inside cup. Similar to 0676. Ideal China/Canadian Teaware. Entered in pattern book during or after 1965.
Backstamp(s): Shelley 1940-1966.
Shapes: Boston

0632 Baileys **Floral** inside cup and centre of saucer. Gold pattern outside cup. Similar to 0677. Ideal China/Canadian Teaware. Entered in pattern book during or after 1965.
Backstamp(s): Shelley 1940-1966.
Shapes: Boston

0633 **Floral Centre** inside cup and centre of saucer. Gold pattern outside cup. Ideal China/Canadian Teaware. Entered in pattern book during or after 1965.

Pattern	Description & Shapes
	Backstamp(s): Shelley 1940-1966. **Shapes:** Boston
0634	**Ambleside**. Ideal China/Canadian Teaware. Entered in pattern book during or after 1965. **Backstamp(s)**: Shelley 1940-1966. **Shapes:** Stratford
0635	**Dark Red Rose**. Ideal China/Canadian Teaware. Entered in pattern book during or after 1965. **Backstamp(s)**: Shelley 1940-1966. **Shapes:** Stratford
0636	**Orchid**. Ideal China/Canadian Teaware. Entered in pattern book during or after 1965. **Backstamp(s)**: Shelley 1940-1966. **Shapes:** Stratford
0637	**Floral Spray**. Ideal China/Canadian Teaware. Entered in pattern book during or after 1965. **Backstamp(s)**: Shelley 1940-1966. **Shapes:** Stratford
0638	Gold pattern inside cup. Green outside cup and on saucer. Ideal China/Canadian Teaware. Entered in pattern book during or after 1965. **Backstamp(s)**: Shelley 1940-1966. **Shapes:** Stratford
0639	Gold pattern inside cup. Pink outside cup and on saucer. Ideal China/Canadian Teaware. Entered in pattern book during or after 1965. **Backstamp(s)**: Shelley 1940-1966. **Shapes:** Stratford
0640	Gold pattern inside cup. Blue outside cup and on saucer. Ideal China/Canadian Teaware. Entered in pattern book during or after 1965. **Backstamp(s)**: Shelley 1940-1966. **Shapes:** Stratford
0641	Gold pattern inside cup. Peach outside cup and on saucer. Ideal China/Canadian Teaware. Entered in pattern book during or after 1965. **Backstamp(s)**: Shelley 1940-1966. **Shapes:** Stratford
0642	Gold pattern inside cup. Yellow outside cup and on saucer. Ideal China/Canadian Teaware. Entered in pattern book during or after 1965. **Backstamp(s)**: Shelley 1940-1966. **Shapes:** Stratford
0643	Gold pattern inside cup. Lilac outside cup and on saucer. Ideal China/Canadian Teaware. Entered in pattern book during or after 1965. **Backstamp(s)**: Shelley 1940-1966. **Shapes:** Stratford
0644	**Red Tapestry Rose**. Chintz. Ideal China/Canadian Teaware. Entered in pattern book during or after 1965. **Backstamp(s)**: Shelley 1940-1966. **Shapes:** Henley
0645	**Green Daisy**. Chintz. Ideal China/Canadian Teaware. Entered in pattern book during or after 1965. **Backstamp(s)**: Shelley 1940-1966. **Shapes:** Henley
0646	**Petite Floral Chintz**. Ideal China/Canadian Teaware. Entered in pattern book during or after 1965. **Backstamp(s)**: Shelley 1940-1966. **Shapes:** Henley
0647	**Georgian Chintz**. Ideal China/Canadian Teaware. Entered in pattern book during or after 1965. **Backstamp(s)**: Shelley 1940-1966. **Shapes:** Henley
0648	**Gold Rose**. Gold roses and foliage on colour ground inside cup and on saucer. White ground outside cup. Gold trim, foot and handle. Similar to 0369 and 0600. Ideal China/Canadian Teaware. Entered in pattern book during or after 1965. **Backstamp(s)**: Shelley 1940-1966 **Shapes:** Lincoln
0649	**Fleur De Lys**. Ideal China/Canadian Teaware. Entered in pattern book during or after 1965. **Backstamp(s)**: Shelley 1940-1966 **Shapes:** Lincoln
0650	Gold pattern and colour panels. Ideal China/Canadian Teaware. Entered in pattern book during or after 1965. **Backstamp(s)**: Shelley 1940-1966. **Shapes:** Atholl
0651	**Georgian** and colour bands. Ideal China/Canadian Teaware. Entered in pattern book during or after 1965. **Backstamp(s)**: Shelley 1940-1966 **Shapes:** Lincoln
0652	Gold pattern inside cup. Colour outside cup and on saucer. Similar to 0638. Ideal China/Canadian Teaware. Entered in pattern book during or after 1965. **Backstamp(s)**: Shelley 1940-1966. **Shapes:** Dainty, Ludlow
0653-0656	Gold pattern. Ideal China/Canadian Teaware. Entered in pattern book during or after 1965. **Backstamp(s)**: Shelley 1940-1966. **Shapes:** Avon
0657	Platinum pattern. Ideal China/Canadian Teaware. Entered in pattern book during or after 1965. **Backstamp(s)**: Shelley 1940-1966. **Shapes:** Avon
0658	Platinum pattern. Ideal China/Canadian Teaware. Entered in pattern book during or after 1965. **Backstamp(s)**: Shelley 1940-1966. **Shapes:** Avon
0658	Platinum pattern. Ideal China/Canadian Teaware. Entered in pattern book during or after 1965. **Backstamp(s)**: Shelley 1940-1966. **Shapes:** Avon
0659	Pattern inside cup. Ideal China/Canadian Teaware. Entered in pattern book during or after 1965. /**A** Yellow Rose Spray /B **Dark Red Rose** /C Baileys **Floral** /D **Floral** /E **Blue Floral** /F **Orchid**. **Backstamp(s)**: Shelley 1940-1966. **Shapes:** Boston
0660	Pattern on a white ground. Gold print border. Pattern also inside cup. Gold edges. Ideal China/Canadian Teaware. Entered in pattern book during or after 1965. /A **Ambleside** /B **Dark Red Rose** /C **Orchid** /D **Floral Spray** /E **Blue Floral** /F **Yellow Rose**. **Backstamp(s)**: Shelley 1940-1966 **Shapes:** Stratford
0661	Royal blue inside cup and on saucer. Gold pattern. White border. Ideal China/Canadian Teaware. Entered in pattern book during or after 1966. **Backstamp(s)**: Shelley 1940-1966. **Shapes:** Boston
0662	Pink inside cup and on saucer. Gold pattern. White border. Ideal China/Canadian Teaware. Entered in pattern book during or after 1966. **Backstamp(s)**: Shelley 1940-1966. **Shapes:** Boston
0663	Green inside cup and on saucer. Gold leaf border. Ideal China/Canadian Teaware. Entered in pattern book during or after 1966. **Backstamp(s)**: Shelley 1940-1966. **Shapes:** Boston
0664	Dark green ground with gold print inside cup and on saucer. White border on edges. White outside cup with gold ring approximately half way between rim and foot. Ideal China/Canadian Teaware. Entered in pattern book during or after 1966. **Backstamp(s)**: Shelley 1940-1966 **Shapes:** Boston, Lincoln

Green and gold 0664 Lincoln shape cup and saucer. £85-95; $130-160

Pattern	Description & Shapes
0665	Yellow band inside cup and on saucer. Gold pattern. Ideal China/Canadian Teaware. Entered in pattern book during or after 1966. **Backstamp(s)**: Shelley 1940-1966. **Shapes:** Boston
0666	Turquoise band inside cup and on saucer. Gold pattern. Ideal China/Canadian Teaware. Entered in pattern book during or after 1966. **Backstamp(s)**: Shelley 1940-1966. **Shapes:** Boston
0667	Yellow band inside cup and on saucer. Gold pattern. Ideal China/Canadian Teaware. Entered in pattern book during or after 1966. **Backstamp(s)**: Shelley 1940-1966. **Shapes:** Boston
0668	Brown band inside cup and on saucer. Gold pattern. Ideal China/Canadian Teaware. Entered in pattern book during or after 1966. **Backstamp(s)**: Shelley 1940-1966. **Shapes:** Boston
0669	Pink band inside cup and on saucer. Gold pattern. Ideal China/Canadian Teaware. Entered in pattern book during or after 1966. **Backstamp(s)**: Shelley 1940-1966. **Shapes:** Boston
0670	**Fruit Centre** inside cup on a peach ground. Red outside cup and on saucer. Ideal China/Canadian Teaware. Entered in pattern book during or after 1966. **Backstamp(s)**: Shelley 1940-1966. **Shapes:** Boston
0671	**Chantilly** inside cup on a peach ground. Royal blue outside cup and on saucer. Ideal China/Canadian Teaware. Entered in pattern book during or after 1966. **Backstamp(s)**: Shelley 1940-1966. **Shapes:** Boston
0672	**Fruit Centre** inside cup and in centre of saucer. Deep aqua band inside cup and on saucer, overlaid with a gold pattern. Ideal China/Canadian Teaware. Entered in pattern book during or after 1966. **Backstamp(s)**: Shelley 1940-1966 **Shapes:** Boston
0673	Colour on lower half of cup. Ideal China/Canadian Teaware. Entered in pattern book during or after 1966. **Backstamp(s)**: Shelley 1940-1966 **Shapes:** Henley
0674	Colour outside cup and on saucer. Gold border inside cup. Ideal China/Canadian Teaware. Entered in pattern book during

Pattern	Description & Shapes

or after 1966.
Backstamp(s): Shelley 1940-1966
Shapes: Henley

0675 Gold pattern with colour band outside cup and on saucer. Similar to 0547. Ideal China/Canadian Teaware. Entered in pattern book during or after 1966.
Backstamp(s): Shelley 1940-1966.
Shapes: Henley

0676 **Dark Red Rose** inside cup. Similar to 0631. Ideal China/Canadian Teaware. Entered in pattern book during or after 1966.
Backstamp(s): Shelley 1940-1966.
Shapes: Henley

0677 Baileys **Floral** inside cup and centre of saucer. Gold pattern outside cup. Similar to 0632. Ideal China/Canadian Teaware. Entered in pattern book during or after 1966.
Backstamp(s): Shelley 1940-1966.
Shapes: Henley

0678 **Cherry Fruit Centre** inside and outside cup as well as in the centre of the saucer. Gold border pattern. Ideal China/Canadian Teaware. Entered in pattern book during or after 1966.
Backstamp(s): Shelley 1940-1966.
Shapes: Boston, Henley

0679 **Pear Fruit Centre** inside and outside cup as well as in the centre of the saucer. Gold border pattern. Ideal China/Canadian Teaware. Entered in pattern book during or after 1966.
Backstamp(s): Shelley 1940-1966.
Shapes: Boston, Henley

0680 **Plum Fruit Centre** inside and outside cup as well as in the centre of the saucer. Gold border pattern. Ideal China/Canadian Teaware. Entered in pattern book during or after 1966.
Backstamp(s): Shelley 1940-1966.
Shapes: Boston, Henley

0681 **Apple Fruit Centre** inside and outside cup as well as in the centre of the saucer. Gold border pattern. Ideal China/Canadian Teaware. Entered in pattern book during or after 1966.
Backstamp(s): Shelley 1940-1966.
Shapes: Boston, Henley

0682 **Grapes Fruit Centre** inside and outside cup as well as in the centre of the saucer. Gold border pattern. Ideal China/Canadian Teaware. Entered in pattern book during or after 1966.
Backstamp(s): Shelley 1940-1966.
Shapes: Boston, Henley

0683 **Peach Fruit Centre** inside and outside cup as well as in the centre of the saucer. Gold border pattern. Ideal China/Canadian Teaware. Entered in pattern book during or after 1966.
Backstamp(s): Shelley 1940-1966.
Shapes: Boston, Henley

0684 **Bridesmaid** inside cup. Colour outside cup and on saucer. Gold border pattern inside cup. Ideal China/Canadian Teaware. Entered in pattern book during or after 1966.
Backstamp(s): Shelley 1940-1966.
Shapes: Atholl

0685 **Fruit Centre** inside cup. Colour outside cup and on saucer. Gold border pattern inside cup. Ideal China/Canadian Teaware. Entered in pattern book during or after 1966.
Backstamp(s): Shelley 1940-1966.
Shapes: Lincoln

0686 Gold border pattern inside cup. Colour outside cup and on saucer. Ideal China/Canadian Teaware. Entered in pattern book during or after 1966.
Backstamp(s): Shelley 1940-1966.
Shapes: Lincoln

0687 **Fruit Centre** outside cup. Colour inside cup and on saucer. Ideal China/Canadian Teaware. Entered in pattern book during or after 1966.
Backstamp(s): Shelley 1940-1966.
Shapes: Lincoln

0688 Gold border pattern inside cup. Colour outside cup and on saucer. Ideal China/Canadian Teaware. Entered in pattern book during or after 1966.
Backstamp(s): Shelley 1940-1966.
Shapes: Lincoln

0689 **Flowers of Gold** on colour ground inside cup and on saucer. White ground outside cup. Gold trim, foot and handle. Ideal China/Canadian Teaware. Entered in pattern book during or after 1965.
Backstamp(s): Shelley 1940-1966
Shapes: Boston

0690 **Chantilly** inside cup on a peach ground. Colour outside cup and on saucer. Ideal China/Canadian Teaware. Entered in pattern book during or after 1966.
Backstamp(s): Shelley 1940-1966.
Shapes: Lincoln

0691 **Fruit Centre** inside cup and front. Colour band inside cup and on saucer. Ideal China/Canadian Teaware. Entered in pattern book during or after 1966.
Backstamp(s): Shelley 1940-1966.
Shapes: Lincoln

0692 **Random Harvest** inside cup. Green outside cup and on saucer. Ideal China/Canadian Teaware. Entered in pattern book during or after 1966.
Backstamp(s): Shelley 1940-1966.
Shapes: New Victoria

0693 **High Summer** inside cup. Pink outside cup and on saucer. Ideal China/Canadian Teaware. Entered in pattern book during or after 1966.
Backstamp(s): Shelley 1940-1966.
Shapes: New Victoria

0694 **English Garden** inside cup. Blue outside cup and on saucer. Ideal China/Canadian Teaware. Entered in pattern book during or after 1966.
Backstamp(s): Shelley 1940-1966.
Shapes: New Victoria

0695 **Orchid** inside cup. Peach outside cup and on saucer. Ideal China/Canadian Teaware. Entered in pattern book during or after 1966.
Backstamp(s): Shelley 1940-1966.
Shapes: New Victoria

0696 **Coniston** inside cup. Yellow outside cup and on saucer. Ideal China/Canadian Teaware. Entered in pattern book during or after 1966.
Backstamp(s): Shelley 1940-1966.
Shapes: New Victoria

0697 **Violets** inside cup. Lilac outside cup and on saucer. Ideal China/Canadian Teaware. Entered in pattern book during or after 1966.
Backstamp(s): Shelley 1940-1966.
Shapes: New Victoria

0698 Colour on lower half of cup. Ideal China/Canadian Teaware. Entered in pattern book during or after 1966.
Backstamp(s): Shelley 1940-1966
Shapes: Lincoln

0699 **Gold Rose**. Colour outside cup and on saucer. Ideal China/Canadian Teaware. Entered in pattern book during or after 1966.
Backstamp(s): Shelley 1940-1966.
Shapes: New Victoria

0700 Colour panels with gold pattern. Ideal China/Canadian Teaware. Entered in pattern book during or after 1966.
Backstamp(s): Shelley 1940-1966
Shapes: Lincoln

0701 Pattern inside cup. Gold pattern outside cup and on saucer. Ideal China/Canadian Teaware. Entered in pattern book during or after 1966.
/A **Random Harvest**
/B **High Summer**
/C **English Garden**
/D **Orchid**
/E **Coniston**
/F **Violets**
/G **Rambler Rose**
/H **Wild Flowers**
/I **Stocks**
/J **Violets**
/K **Lilac**
/L **Blue Rock**.
Backstamp(s): Shelley 1940-1966
Shapes: Dainty

0702 Plain colours. Ideal China/Canadian Teaware. Entered in pattern book during or after 1966.
Backstamp(s): Shelley 1940-1966
Shapes: Atholl

0703 **Gold Fleur De Lys** on colour band. Ideal China/Canadian Teaware. Entered in pattern book during or after 1966.
Backstamp(s): Shelley 1940-1966.
Shapes: New Victoria

0704 **Blue Primrose**. Ideal China/Canadian Teaware. Entered in pattern book during or after 1966.
Backstamp(s): Shelley 1940-1966.
Shapes: Henley

0705 **Pink Primrose**. Ideal China/Canadian Teaware. Entered in pattern book during or after 1966.
Backstamp(s): Shelley 1940-1966.
Shapes: Henley

0706 **Yellow Marguerite**. Ideal China/Canadian Teaware. Entered in pattern book during or after 1966.
Backstamp(s): Shelley 1940-1966.
Shapes: Henley

0707 **Green Marguerite**. Ideal China/Canadian Teaware. Entered in pattern book during or after 1966.
Backstamp(s): Shelley 1940-1966.
Shapes: Henley

0708 **Black Maytime**. Ideal China/Canadian Teaware. Entered in pattern book during or after 1966.
Backstamp(s): Shelley 1940-1966.
Shapes: Henley

0709 **Primrose** inside cup. Yellow outside cup and on saucer. Ideal China/Canadian Teaware. Entered in pattern book during or after 1966.
Backstamp(s): Shelley 1940-1966.
Shapes: Boston

0710 **Wild Anemone** inside cup. Pink outside cup and on saucer. Ideal China/Canadian Teaware. Entered in pattern book during or after 1966.
Backstamp(s): Shelley 1940-1966.
Shapes: Boston

0711 **Blue Rock** inside cup. Blue outside cup and on saucer. Ideal China/Canadian Teaware. Entered in pattern book during or after 1966.
Backstamp(s): Shelley 1940-1966.
Shapes: Boston

0712 **Rosebud** inside cup. Lilac outside cup and on saucer. Ideal China/Canadian Teaware. Entered in pattern book during or after 1966.
Backstamp(s): Shelley 1940-1966.
Shapes: Boston

0713 **Rose Spray** inside cup. Green outside cup and on saucer. Ideal China/Canadian Teaware. Entered in pattern book during or after 1966.
Backstamp(s): Shelley 1940-1966.
Shapes: Boston

0714 **Rose, Pansy, and Forget-me-nots** inside cup. Peach outside cup and on saucer. Ideal China/Canadian Teaware. Entered in pattern book during or after 1966.
Backstamp(s): Shelley 1940-1966.
Shapes: Boston

0715 **Stocks**. Green saucer. Ideal China/Canadian Teaware. Entered in pattern book during or after 1966.

Pattern	Description & Shapes
	Backstamp(s): Shelley 1940-1966. **Shapes:** Avon Coffee
0716	**Honeysuckle**. Pink saucer. Ideal China/ Canadian Teaware. Entered in pattern book during or after 1966. **Backstamp(s)**: Shelley 1940-1966. **Shapes:** Avon Coffee
0717	**Blue Poppy**. Blue saucer. Ideal China/ Canadian Teaware. Entered in pattern book during or after 1966. **Backstamp(s)**: Shelley 1940-1966. **Shapes:** Avon Coffee
0718	**Bramble**. Peach saucer. Ideal China/ Canadian Teaware. Entered in pattern book during or after 1966. **Backstamp(s)**: Shelley 1940-1966. **Shapes:** Avon Coffee
0719	**Freesia**. Yellow saucer. Ideal China/ Canadian Teaware. Entered in pattern book during or after 1966. **Backstamp(s)**: Shelley 1940-1966. **Shapes:** Avon Coffee
0720	**Celandine**. Lilac saucer. Ideal China/ Canadian Teaware. Entered in pattern book during or after 1966. **Backstamp(s)**: Shelley 1940-1966. **Shapes:** Avon Coffee
0721	**Gold Thistle** on colour. Ideal China/ Canadian Teaware. Entered in pattern book during or after 1966. **Backstamp(s)**: Shelley 1940-1966. **Shapes:** Lincoln
904	Special pattern. Horse and hounds hunting scene on a white ground. Gold edges. **Backstamp(s)**: Shelley 1940-1966 **Shapes:** Bute
970	Special pattern. Fish and water plants on a white ground. Gold edges. **Backstamp(s)**: Shelley 1940-1966 **Shapes:** Bute
978	Special pattern. Ducks in flight on a white ground. Gold edges. **Backstamp(s)**: Shelley 1940-1966 **Shapes:** Bute

Special pattern number 978 Bute shape cup and saucer. £60-70; $100-120

Pattern	Description & Shapes
2001	**Rose Border**. Seconds ware. Entered in pattern book during or after 1919. **Backstamp(s)**: Shelley 1912-1925 **Shapes:** Bute, Victoria
2002	Plain colour inside cup and on saucer. White outside cup and centre of saucer. Seconds ware. Entered in pattern book during or after 1919. /A Pink. **Backstamp(s)**: Shelley 1912-1925 **Shapes:** Gainsborough
2003	Pale pink outside cup and on saucer. Dark pink inside cup. Gold edges and handle. Seconds ware. Entered in pattern book during or after 1919. **Backstamp(s)**: Shelley 1912-1925 **Shapes:** Gainsborough
2004	**Chatsworth**. Same as 11065. Seconds ware. Entered in pattern book during or after 1919. **Backstamp(s)**: Shelley 1912-1925 **Shapes:** Bute, New York
2005	**Wilson**. Same as 11117. Entered in pattern book during or after 1919. Seconds ware. **Backstamp(s)**: Shelley 1912-1925 **Shapes:** Bute, New York
2006	**Rose Border**. Pink roses on a black ground. Entered in pattern book during or after 1919. Seconds ware. **Backstamp(s)**: Shelley 1912-1925 **Shapes:** Bute, New York
2007	Hulmes **Lowestoft**. Same as 8630. Entered in pattern book during or after 1919. Seconds ware. **Backstamp(s)**: Shelley 1912-1925 **Shapes:** Bute, New York
2008	**Black Dice Border**. White ground. Gold edges. Same as 10816. Entered in pattern book during or after 1919. Seconds ware. **Backstamp(s)**: Shelley 1912-1925 **Shapes:** New York
2009	**Rose Spray**. Entered in pattern book during or after 1919. Seconds ware. **Backstamp(s)**: Shelley 1912-1925 **Shapes:** New York
2010	**Shamrock**. Same as 8064. Entered in pattern book during or after 1919. Seconds ware. **Backstamp(s)**: Shelley 1912-1925 **Shapes:** Bute
2011	**Chatsworth**. Entered in pattern book during or after 1919. Seconds ware. **Backstamp(s)**: Shelley 1912-1925 **Shapes:** Unknown
2012	**Rose**. Pink roses and blue border. Same as 11150. Entered in pattern book during or after 1921. Seconds ware. **Backstamp(s)**: Shelley 1912-1925 **Shapes:** Unknown
2013	**Rose Border**. Pink roses on a green panel. Gold edges. Same as 11133. Entered in pattern book during or after 1921. Seconds ware. **Backstamp(s)**: Shelley 1912-1925 **Shapes:** Unknown
2014	**Rose Border**. Pink roses on a violet panel. Gold edges. Entered in pattern book during or after 1921. Seconds ware. **Backstamp(s)**: Shelley 1912-1925 **Shapes:** Unknown
2015	**Rose Border**. Pink roses on a broad violet border. Also within the border are single purple flower sprigs within a white oval. Border is inside cup, on saucer, and plate. Outside cup has a gold ring approximately halfway between rim and foot. White ground. Gold edges. Same as 11135. Entered in pattern book during or after 1921. Seconds ware. **Backstamp(s)**: Shelley 1912-1925 **Shapes:** Gainsborough
2016	**Rose Border**. Border is inside cup, on saucer, and plate. Outside cup has a gold ring approximately halfway between rim and foot. Fawn ground. Gold edges and handle. Same as 11136. Entered in pattern book during or after 1921. Seconds ware. **Backstamp(s)**: Shelley 1912-1925 **Shapes:** Unknown
2017	**Grecian Border**. Same as 10796. Entered in pattern book during or after 1921. Seconds ware. **Backstamp(s)**: Shelley 1912-1925 **Shapes:** Unknown
2018	**Fuchsia**. Same as 10675. Entered in pattern book during or after 1921. Seconds ware. **Backstamp(s)**: Shelley 1912-1925 **Shapes:** Unknown
2019	**Double Diamond**. Same as 11164. Entered in pattern book during or after 1921. Seconds ware. **Backstamp(s)**: Shelley 1912-1925 **Shapes:** Unknown
2020	**Rose Border**. Blue print. Same as 11086. Entered in pattern book during or after 1921. Seconds ware. **Backstamp(s)**: Shelley 1912-1925 **Shapes:** Unknown
2021	Plain colours. White centre of saucer. Entered in pattern book during or after 1921. Seconds ware. **Backstamp(s)**: Shelley 1912-1925 **Shapes:** Unknown
2022	**Swallow**. Blue print. Same as 10413. Entered in pattern book during or after 1921. Seconds ware. **Backstamp(s)**: Shelley 1912-1925 **Shapes:** Bute
2023	**Jewel**. Black jewel and chain border print on white ground. Gold edges. Same as 10893. Entered in pattern book during or after 1921. Seconds ware. **Backstamp(s)**: Shelley 1912-1925 **Shapes:** Bute
2024	**Rose, Thistle, and Shamrock**. Same as 11120/23. Entered in pattern book during or after 1921. Seconds ware. **Backstamp(s)**: Shelley 1912-1925 **Shapes:** Norman, Vincent
2025	Blue **Roses**. Blue print. Roses and leaves on a white ground. Blue edges. Same as 8311. Entered in pattern book during or after 1921. Seconds ware. **Backstamp(s)**: Shelley 1912-1925 **Shapes:** Unknown
2026	**Oak Leaf Border**. Border with trailing, light purple oak leaves. White ground. Gold edges. Same as 9592. Entered in pattern book during or after 1921. Seconds ware. **Backstamp(s)**: Shelley 1912-1925 **Shapes:** Unknown
2027	**Oak Leaf Border**. Border with trailing, light purple oak leaves. White ground. Gold edges. Same as 9592. Entered in pattern book during or after 1921. Seconds ware. **Backstamp(s)**: Shelley 1912-1925 **Shapes:** Unknown
2028	**Cairo**. Cerise, blue, green, and purple. Cerise, daisy-like flowers with blue centres. White ground. Same as 11211. Entered in pattern book during or after 1921. Seconds ware. **Backstamp(s)**: Shelley 1912-1925 **Shapes:** Unknown
2029	**Red Narrow Border**. Same as 10399. Entered in pattern book during or after 1921. Seconds ware. **Backstamp(s)**: Shelley 1912-1925 **Shapes:** Unknown
2030	**Festoon**. Black bows and chain border on a white ground. Same as 11246. Entered in pattern book during or after 1921. Seconds ware. **Backstamp(s)**: Shelley 1912-1925 **Shapes:** Kenneth
2031	**Black Border**. Same as 11225. Entered in pattern book during or after 1923. Seconds ware. **Backstamp(s)**: Shelley 1912-1925 **Shapes:** Unknown
2032	**Red Border**. Same print as 11206. Entered in pattern book during or after 1923. Seconds ware. **Backstamp(s)**: Shelley 1912-1925 **Shapes:** Unknown
2033	**Jewel**. Black jewel and chain border print on white ground. Black edges. Same as 11256. Entered in pattern book during or after 1923. Seconds ware **Backstamp(s)**: Shelley 1912-1925 **Shapes:** Bute
2034	**Laurel Border**. Same as 11257. Entered in pattern book during or after 1923. Seconds ware **Backstamp(s)**: Shelley 1912-1925 **Shapes:** Unknown

Pattern	Description & Shapes

2035 **Laurel and Rose Border**. Same as 11236. Entered in pattern book during or after 1923. Seconds ware
Backstamp(s): Shelley 1912-1925
Shapes: Unknown

2036 **Greek Border**. Same as 11247. Entered in pattern book during or after 1923. Seconds ware
Backstamp(s): Shelley 1912-1925
Shapes: Unknown

2038 **Cairo**. Purple. Same as 11212. Entered in pattern book during or after 1923. Seconds ware.
Backstamp(s): Shelley 1912-1925
Shapes: Unknown

2039 **Celtic**. Same as 11266. Entered in pattern book during or after 1923. Seconds ware.
Backstamp(s): Shelley 1912-1925
Shapes: Kenneth

2040 **Blue and Red Berries**. Same as 11259. Entered in pattern book during or after 1924. Seconds ware.
Backstamp(s): Shelley 1912-1925
Shapes: Kenneth, Norman, Vincent

2041 **Powder Blue and Chinese Flowers**. Also known as **Mandarin**. Mottled blue border with narrow gold bands on either side of it. Pink roses and grey leaves against the blue border. Same as 11258. Entered in pattern book during or after 1924. Seconds ware.
Backstamp(s): Shelley 1912-1925
Shapes: Kenneth, Milton, Norman, Vincent

2042 **Persian**. Same as 11260. Entered in pattern book during or after 1924. Seconds ware.
Backstamp(s): Shelley 1912-1925
Shapes: Kenneth, Norman, Vincent

2043 **Chelsea**. Same as 11280. Entered in pattern book during or after 1924. Seconds ware.
Backstamp(s): Shelley 1912-1925
Shapes: Bute, New York

2044 **Fruit Basket**. Same as 11364/6. Entered in pattern book during or after 1924. Seconds ware.
Backstamp(s): Shelley 1912-1925
Shapes: Unknown

2045 **Vase of Flowers**. Same as 11370/6. Entered in pattern book during or after 1924. Seconds ware.
Backstamp(s): Shelley 1912-1925
Shapes: Unknown

2046 **Cameo**. Dancers within a black cameo. Yellow ground. Black edges and handle. Same as 11350. Entered in pattern book during or after 1924. Seconds ware.
Backstamp(s): Shelley 1912-1925
Shapes: Vincent

2047 **Cameo**. Dancers within a black cameo. Colour ground. Black edges and handle. Same as 11350. Entered in pattern book during or after 1924. Seconds ware.
Backstamp(s): Shelley 1912-1925
Shapes: Doric

2048 **Rose Sprays**. Entered in pattern book during or after 1924. Seconds ware.
Backstamp(s): Shelley 1912-1925
Shapes: Doric

2049 **Bell**. Same as 11233. Entered in pattern book during or after 1924. Seconds ware.
Backstamp(s): Shelley 1912-1925
Shapes: Doric, Milton

2050 Black and yellow. Same as 11323. Entered in pattern book during or after 1924. Seconds ware.
Backstamp(s): Shelley 1912-1925
Shapes: Doric

2051 **Thistle**. Same as 11368. Entered in pattern book during or after 1924. Seconds ware.
Backstamp(s): Shelley 1912-1925
Shapes: Doric

2052 **Vine**. Same as 11369. Entered in pattern book during or after 1924. Seconds ware.
Backstamp(s): Shelley 1912-1925
Shapes: Milton

2053 **Chelsea**. Sprays of blue, burgundy, and black flowers and leaves on a white ground. Pattern also inside cup. Deep blue border inside cup, on saucer, and plate. Entered in pattern book during or after 1924. Seconds ware.
Backstamp(s): Shelley 1912-1925
Shapes: Gainsborough

Chelsea 2053 Gainsborough shape cup, saucer, and plate. £40-50; $80-100

2054 **Wreath of Roses**. Entered in pattern book during or after 1924. Seconds ware.
Backstamp(s): Shelley 1912-1925
Shapes: Gainsborough

2055 **Black Dice**. Entered in pattern book during or after 1924. Seconds ware.
Backstamp(s): Shelley 1912-1925
Shapes: Carlton

2056 **Laurel Border**. Entered in pattern book during or after 1926. Seconds ware.
Backstamp(s): Shelley 1925-1940
Shapes: Savoy

2057 **Vine**. Same as 11429. Entered in pattern book during or after 1926. Seconds ware.
Backstamp(s): Shelley 1925-1940
Shapes: Unknown

2058 **Versailles**. Same as 11426. Entered in pattern book during or after 1926. Seconds ware.
Backstamp(s): Shelley 1925-1940
Shapes: Gainsborough

2059 **Hampton Court**. Same as 11427. Entered in pattern book during or after 1926. Seconds ware.
Backstamp(s): Shelley 1925-1940
Shapes: Gainsborough

2060 **Rose Spray**. Same as 11494. Entered in pattern book during or after 1927. Seconds ware.
Backstamp(s): Shelley 1925-1940
Shapes: Unknown

2061 **Cairo**. Yellow. Entered in pattern book during or after 1927. Seconds ware.
Backstamp(s): Shelley 1925-1940
Shapes: New York

2062 Gold band. Entered in pattern book during or after 1927.
Backstamp(s): Shelley 1925-1940
Shapes: Bute

2063 **Comport of Fruit**. Entered in pattern book during or after 1927. Seconds ware.
Backstamp(s): Shelley 1925-1940
Shapes: Milton

2064 Worcester. Black border pattern on yellow ground inside cup and on saucer. White outside cup encircled with a black line at base of handle level. Black edges. Same as 11459. Seconds ware. Entered in pattern book during or after 1927.
Backstamp(s): Shelley 1925-1940
Shapes: Milton

Worcester border 2064/Y Milton shape cup and saucer. £40-50; $80-100

2065 **Rose and Bead**. Same as 10775. Entered in pattern book during or after 1927. Seconds ware.
Backstamp(s): Shelley 1925-1940
Shapes: Gainsborough

2066 **Rose and Pansy**. Same as 11235. Entered in pattern book during or after 1927. Seconds ware.
Backstamp(s): Shelley 1925-1940
Shapes: Gainsborough

2067 **Basket of Flowers**. Same as 11371. Entered in pattern book during or after 1927. Seconds ware.
Backstamp(s): Shelley 1925-1940
Shapes: Gainsborough

2068 **Versailles**. Same as 11426. Entered in pattern book during or after 1927. Seconds ware.
Backstamp(s): Shelley 1925-1940
Shapes: Gainsborough

2069 **Hampton Court**. Same as 11427. Entered in pattern book during or after 1927. Seconds ware.
Backstamp(s): Shelley 1925-1940
Shapes: Gainsborough

2070 **Chatsworth**. Same as 11065. Entered in pattern book during or after 1927. Seconds ware.
Backstamp(s): Shelley 1925-1940
Shapes: Gainsborough

2071 **Chelsea**. Yellow ground. Same as 11280. Entered in pattern book during or after 1927. Seconds ware.
Backstamp(s): Shelley 1925-1940
Shapes: Unknown

2072 **Chatsworth**. Same as 11065. Entered in pattern book during or after 1927. Seconds ware.
Backstamp(s): Shelley 1925-1940
Shapes: Unknown

2073 **Poppy**. Same as 11326. Entered in pattern book during or after 1927. Seconds ware.
Backstamp(s): Shelley 1925-1940
Shapes: Gainsborough

2074 **Rose and Dice**. Entered in pattern book during or after 1927. Seconds ware.
Backstamp(s): Shelley 1925-1940
Shapes: Gainsborough, Vincent

2075 **Plum and Apple**. Entered in pattern book during or after 1927. Seconds ware.
Backstamp(s): Shelley 1925-1940
Shapes: Lomond, Milton

2076 **Grey and Buff Border**. Entered in pattern book during or after 1927. Seconds ware.
Backstamp(s): Shelley 1925-1940
Shapes: Lomond, Milton

2077 Stylised fruit in blue, black, green, yellow, and orange on a black white ground. Gold trim. Entered in pattern book during or after 1927. Seconds ware.
Backstamp(s): Shelley 1925-1940
Shapes: Doric, Queen Anne

Stylised fruit 2077 Queen Anne shape cup, saucer, and plate. £70-80; $150-180

Pattern	Description & Shapes
2078	Davies Border. Entered in pattern book during or after 1927. Seconds ware. **Backstamp(s)**: Shelley 1925-1940 **Shapes:** Lomond
2079	Details unknown. Entered in pattern book during or after 1927. Seconds ware. **Backstamp(s)**: Shelley 1925-1940 **Shapes:** Gainsborough
2080	**Rose**. Same as 11199. Entered in pattern book during or after 1927. Seconds ware. **Backstamp(s)**: Shelley 1925-1940 **Shapes:** Gainsborough
2081	**Vine**. Same as 11429. Entered in pattern book during or after 1927. Seconds ware. **Backstamp(s)**: Shelley 1925-1940 **Shapes:** Gainsborough
2082	**Rose**. Same as 11190. Entered in pattern book during or after 1927. Seconds ware. **Backstamp(s)**: Shelley 1925-1940 **Shapes:** Gainsborough
2083	**House**. Entered in pattern book during or after 1927. Seconds ware. **Backstamp(s)**: Shelley 1925-1940 **Shapes:** Gainsborough
2084	Floral. Entered in pattern book during or after 1927. Seconds ware. **Backstamp(s)**: Shelley 1925-1940 **Shapes:** Unknown
2085	**Willow**. Entered in pattern book during or after 1927. Seconds ware. **Backstamp(s)**: Shelley 1925-1940 **Shapes:** Unknown
2086	**Bluebird**. Birds, bunches of pink roses and green foliage. Gold edges. Entered in pattern book during or after 1927. Seconds ware. **Backstamp(s)**: 1925-1940 **Shapes:** Queen Anne

Bluebird 2086 Queen Anne shape cup, saucer, and plate. £70-80; $150-180

Pattern	Description & Shapes
2087	**Black Crackle**. Pink, blue, mauve, and amber flowers and green foliage on a black and white crackle background. Gold edges and black handle. Entered in pattern book during or after 1927. Seconds ware. **Backstamp(s)**: 1925-1940 **Shapes:** Queen Anne

Left:
Black Crackle 2087 Queen Anne shape cup, saucer, and plate. £70-80; $150-180

Black Crackle 2087 Queen Anne shape cup, saucer, and plate. £70-80; $150-180. Sugar and creamer. £60-70; $130-170

Pattern	Description & Shapes
2088	**Garland of Flowers**. Black garland pattern and trim. White ground. Same as 11504. Entered in pattern book during or after 1927. Seconds ware. **Backstamp(s)**: Shelley 1925-1940 **Shapes:** Queen Anne
2089	**Lowestoft**. Same as 11595. Entered in pattern book during or after 1927. Seconds ware. **Backstamp(s)**: Shelley 1925-1940 **Shapes:** Gainsborough, Queen Anne
2090	**Cherries**. Same as 11153. Entered in pattern book during or after 1927. Seconds ware. **Backstamp(s)**: Shelley 1925-1940 **Shapes:** Vincent
2091	**Basket of Fruit**. Brown print. Blue, yellow, orange, and green fruit in black baskets. Baskets linked by garlands of fruit and geometric pattern. Same as 11366. Entered in pattern book during or after 1927. Seconds ware. **Backstamp(s)**: Shelley 1925-1940 **Shapes:** Vincent
2092	**Bunch of Fruit**. Same as 11444. Entered in pattern book during or after 1927. Seconds ware. **Backstamp(s)**: Shelley 1925-1940 **Shapes:** Lomond
2093	**Leaves and Berries**. Same as 11431. Entered in pattern book during or after 1927. Seconds ware. **Backstamp(s)**: Shelley 1925-1940 **Shapes:** Lomond
2094	**Rose Spray**. Same as 11494. Entered in pattern book during or after 1927. Seconds ware. **Backstamp(s)**: Shelley 1925-1940 **Shapes:** Dainty, Lomond
2095	**Berries and Blocks**. Same as 11450. Entered in pattern book during or after 1927. Seconds ware. **Backstamp(s)**: Shelley 1925-1940 **Shapes:** Gainsborough, Kenneth
2096	**Blossom**. Entered in pattern book during or after 1927. Seconds ware. **Backstamp(s)**: Shelley 1925-1940 **Shapes:** Unknown
2097	**Dainty Rose**. Same as 11450. Entered in pattern book during or after 1927. Seconds ware. **Backstamp(s)**: Shelley 1925-1940 **Shapes:** Queen Anne
2098	Butchers large **Rose**. Large pink and mauve roses, tiny pink flowers and green leaves. White ground. Mauve edges. Seconds ware. **Backstamp(s)**: Shelley 1925-1940 **Shapes:** Queen Anne

Rose 2098 Queen Anne shape cup and saucer. £70-80; $150-180

Pattern	Description & Shapes
2103	**Bird and Tree**. Also known as **Swallow Print**. Same as 11349. Entered in pattern book during or after 1927. Seconds ware. **Backstamp(s)**: Shelley 1925-1940 **Shapes:** Vincent
2104	Butchers **Blue Dresden**. Entered in pattern book during or after 1927. Seconds ware. **Backstamp(s)**: Shelley 1925-1940 **Shapes:** Unknown
2105	**Poppy**. Similar to 11326. Entered in pattern book during or after 1927. Seconds ware. **Backstamp(s)**: Shelley 1925-1940 **Shapes:** Unknown
2106	**Rose and Pansy**. Same as 11235. Entered in pattern book during or after 1927. Seconds ware. **Backstamp(s)**: Shelley 1925-1940 **Shapes:** Vincent
2107	**Daisy**. Same as 11608. Entered in pattern book during or after 1927.

Pattern	Description & Shapes
	Seconds ware. **Backstamp(s)**: Shelley 1925-1940 **Shapes:** Lomond
2108	**Idalium**. Same as 11652. Entered in pattern book during or after 1927. Seconds ware. **Backstamp(s)**: Shelley 1925-1940 **Shapes:** Gainsborough, Georgian
2109	**Black Vine Leaf**. Brown print. Black leaf with green edges. Stylised red, orange, and blue fruit. Brown stem and tendrils. Brown printed border of grape vines. White ground. Green edges. Same as 11699. Seconds ware. **Backstamp(s)**: Shelley 1925-1940 **Shapes:** Vincent
2110	Cornfield. Black print. Golden yellow cornfield flanked by grey trees and green grass. Orange flowers in the foreground. Grey woodland in the distance. Yellow sun between treetops. Two birds to the right of the scene. White ground. Green edges. Entered in pattern book during or after 1927. Seconds ware. **Backstamp(s)**: Shelley 1925-1940 **Shapes:** Queen Anne

Cornfield 2110 Queen Anne shape cup, saucer, and plate. £70-80; $150-180

2111	Iris in a stream. Blue iris with grey and green foliage. Grey and pink bushes and trees in the ground. Blue edges. Entered in pattern book during or after 1927. Seconds ware. **Backstamp(s)**: Shelley 1925-1940 **Shapes:** Queen Anne

Iris in a stream 2111 Queen Anne shape cup, saucer, and plate. £70-80; $150-180

2112	Lake scene. Trees, flowers, fields, and bridge. Blue and yellow butterflies. White ground. Entered in pattern book during or after 1927. Seconds ware. **Backstamp(s)**: Shelley 1925-1940 **Shapes:** Queen Anne, Tall Dainty

Lake scene 2112 Tall Dainty shape twenty-one-piece tea set. £300-350; $700-900

2113	Archway of Roses. Black print. Garden with flowers that include hollyhocks and roses. Blue butterflies. Tinted in blue, pink, brown, and green. White ground. Mauve edges. Entered in pattern book during or after 1928. Seconds ware. **Backstamp(s)**: Shelley 1925-1940 **Shapes:** Queen Anne
2114	Stylised black tree, red, and yellow fruit with green leaves on a white ground. Green grass at base of tree. Yellow cornfield, green shrubs, and grey woodland in the background. Turquoise edges. Entered in pattern book during or after 1928. Seconds ware. **Backstamp(s)**: Shelley 1925-1940 **Shapes:** Queen Anne

Tree 2114 Queen Anne shape cup, saucer, and plate. £70-80; $150-180

2115	Country Cottage with red roof. Yellow edges. Entered in pattern book during or after 1928. Seconds ware. **Backstamp(s)**: Shelley 1925-1940 **Shapes:** Mode, Queen Anne
2116	Stile and Roses. Entered in pattern book during or after 1928. Seconds ware. **Backstamp(s)**: Shelley 1925-1940 **Shapes:** Queen Anne
2117	Lake and Balcony. Entered in pattern book during or after 1928. Seconds ware. **Backstamp(s)**: Shelley 1925-1940 **Shapes:** Queen Anne
2118	Stylised Bush. Entered in pattern book during or after 1928. Seconds ware. **Backstamp(s)**: Shelley 1925-1940 **Shapes:** Queen Anne
2119	Stream and Delphiniums. Black print. Blue delphiniums, green, and grey shrubs on left of stream. Grey bridge over blue stream. Yellow flowers on right bank of stream with and grey bushes. Coral butterfly. White ground. Turquoise edges. Entered in pattern book during or after 1930. Seconds ware. **Backstamp(s)**: Shelley 1925-1940 **Shapes:** Queen Anne
2120	Japonica. Entered in pattern book during or after 1930. Seconds ware. **Backstamp(s)**: Shelley 1925-1940 **Shapes:** Queen Anne
2121	Gate and Path. Black print. Coral and white flowers in the foreground. Yellow path leading up to a gate. Grey bushes and trees. Blue butterflies. White ground. Green edges. Entered in pattern book during or after 1930. Seconds ware. Gainsborough: Pattern inside cup and on saucer. White outside cup with line approximately halfway between rim and base. **Backstamp(s)**: Shelley 1925-1940 **Shapes:** Gainsborough, Queen Anne

Gate and Path 2121 Gainsborough shape cup and saucer. £40-50; $80-100

2122	**Jazz Fruit**. Same as 11585. Entered in pattern book during or after 1930. Seconds ware. **Backstamp(s)**: Shelley 1925-1940 **Shapes:** Doric
2123	Floral. Entered in pattern book during or after 1930. Seconds ware. **Backstamp(s)**: Shelley 1925-1940 **Shapes:** Doric
2124	**Jewel**. Blue jewel and chain print with green and coral enamelling. Same as 8910. Entered in pattern book during or after 1930. Seconds ware. **Backstamp(s)**: Shelley 1925-1940

Pattern Description & Shapes

Shapes: Bute

2125 **Urn of Flowers**. Same as 11600. Entered in pattern book during or after 1930. Seconds ware.
Backstamp(s): Shelley 1925-1940
Shapes: New York

2126 Ornament and border print. Same as 11506. Entered in pattern book during or after 1930. Seconds ware.
Backstamp(s): Shelley 1925-1940
Shapes: Norman

2127 **Jazz Fruit**. Same as 2122 and 11585. Entered in pattern book during or after 1930. Seconds ware.
Backstamp(s): Shelley 1925-1940
Shapes: Unknown

2128 **Chelsea**. Same as 11280. Entered in pattern book during or after 1930. Seconds ware.
Backstamp(s): Shelley 1925-1940
Shapes: Low Queen Anne, Tall Queen Anne

2129 **Lowestoft**. Small sprays of pink, blue, and yellow flowers with green leaves on a white ground. Black leafy border. Jade green edges. Same as 11690. Entered in pattern book during or after 1930. Seconds ware.
Backstamp(s): Shelley 1925-1940
Shapes: Low Queen Anne, Tall Queen Anne

Lowestoft 2129 Queen Anne shape cup, saucer, and plate. £70-80; $150-180

Lowestoft 2129 Queen Anne shape demi-tasse cup and saucer. £60-70; $120-140

2131 Ratauds **Azalea**. Entered in pattern book during or after 1930. Seconds ware.
Backstamp(s): Shelley 1925-1940
Shapes: Tall Queen Anne

2132 **Kenwood**. Large bunches of flowers that include roses in shades of pink, white lilies, white daisies, and green leaves. Small sprays near rim. Dark pink edges. Entered in pattern book during or after 1930. Seconds ware.
Backstamp(s): Shelley 1925-1940
Shapes: Queen Anne

2133 **Daisy**. Same as 11582. Entered in pattern book during or after 1930. Seconds ware.
Backstamp(s): Shelley 1925-1940
Shapes: Vincent

2134 **Crabtree**. Same as 11651. Entered in pattern book during or after 1930. Seconds ware.
Backstamp(s): Shelley 1925-1940
Shapes: Milton

2135 The Traveller. Entered in pattern book during or after 1930. Seconds ware.
Backstamp(s): Shelley 1925-1940
Shapes: Empire, Mode, Queen Anne, Vogue

2136 Canoe. Entered in pattern book during or after 1930. Seconds ware.
Backstamp(s): Shelley 1925-1940
Shapes: Empire, Mode, Queen Anne, Vogue

2137 Woman with Parasol. Entered in pattern book during or after 1930. Seconds ware.
Backstamp(s): Shelley 1925-1940
Shapes: Empire, Mode, Queen Anne, Vogue

2138 Guitar print. Man and woman with fan and guitar. Entered in pattern book during or after 1930. Seconds ware.
Backstamp(s): Shelley 1925-1940
Shapes: Empire, Mode, Queen Anne, Vogue

2139 Window print. Lady and gentleman walking. Entered in pattern book during or after 1930. Seconds ware.
Backstamp(s): Shelley 1925-1940
Shapes: Empire, Mode, Queen Anne, Vogue

2140 Watering Flowers. Woman in thirties-style orange dress and black and white apron watering flowers with a green watering can. Blue, orange, and yellow flowers with green foliage. Orange edges. White ground. Entered in pattern book during or after 1930. Seconds ware.
Backstamp(s): Shelley 1925-1940 Copyright
Shapes: Empire, Mode, Queen Anne, Vogue

2141 Flower Seller. Grey print. Patterned inside cup and on saucer. Two women dressed in brown, thirties-style clothing. One is standing with an armful of flowers. The other is a flower seller and is seated amongst baskets of flowers. Flowers are orange and yellow with some green foliage. Orange line on saucer, outside cup and handle. Orange edges. White ground. Entered in pattern book during or after 1930. Seconds ware.
Backstamp(s): Shelley 1925-1940
Shapes: Empire, Mode, Queen Anne, Vogue

Kenwood 2132 Queen Anne shape cup, saucer, and plate. £70-80; $100-140

2142 Woman writing. Entered in pattern book during or after 1930. Seconds ware.
Backstamp(s): Shelley 1925-1940
Shapes: Empire, Mode, Queen Anne, Vogue

2143 Woman and fan. Man and woman walking through glass door. Entered in pattern book during or after 1930. Seconds ware.
Backstamp(s): Shelley 1925-1940
Shapes: Empire, Mode, Queen Anne, Vogue

2144 Balustrade print. Grey print. Man and woman sitting on balustrade. Both dressed in Thirties clothes. Woman in yellow dress, man in black suit. Green trees. White ground. Blue edges and ring on saucer. Entered in pattern book during or after 1930. Seconds ware.
Backstamp(s): Shelley 1925-1940
Shapes: Empire, Mode, Queen Anne, Vogue

2145 Woman and posy. Entered in pattern book during or after 1930. Seconds ware.
Backstamp(s): Shelley 1925-1940
Shapes: Empire, Mode, Queen Anne, Vogue

2146 Woman and whippets. Entered in pattern book during or after 1930. Seconds ware.
Backstamp(s): Shelley 1925-1940
Shapes: Empire, Mode, Queen Anne, Vogue

2147 **Scattered Rose**. Same as 11599. Entered in pattern book during or after 1930. Seconds ware.
Backstamp(s): Shelley 1925-1940
Shapes: Dainty

Flower Seller 2141 Vogue shape cup and saucer. £150-200; $300-400

2148 **Scattered Rose**. Blue print. Same as 11599. Entered in pattern book during or after 1930. Seconds ware.
Backstamp(s): Shelley 1925-1940
Shapes: Dainty

2149 **Scattered Rose**. Green print. Same as 11599. Entered in pattern book during or after 1930. Seconds ware.
Backstamp(s): Shelley 1925-1940
Shapes: Dainty

2150 Butchers **Fruit**. Entered in pattern book during or after 1930. Seconds ware.
Backstamp(s): Shelley 1925-1940
Shapes: Vogue

2151 Butchers **Crocus**. Entered in pattern book during or after 1930. Seconds ware.
Backstamp(s): Shelley 1925-1940
Shapes: Mode

Pattern	Description & Shapes

2152 Butchers **Hollyhock**. Blue hollyhocks, yellow flowers, pink roses, and green leaves on a white ground. Jade green edges. Entered in pattern book during or after 1930. Seconds ware.
/6 Yellow edges.
Backstamp(s): Shelley 1925-1940
Shapes: Queen Anne

Hollyhock 2152/6 Queen Anne shape cup, saucer, and plate. £70-90; $120-230

2153 **Crabtree**. Entered in pattern book during or after 1931. Seconds ware.
Backstamp(s): Shelley 1925-1940
Shapes: Spoutless Teapot

2154 Hulmes **Rose**. Entered in pattern book during or after 1931. Seconds ware.
Backstamp(s): Shelley 1925-1940
Shapes: Spoutless Teapot

2155 Pale blue band. Entered in pattern book during or after 1931. Seconds ware.
Backstamp(s): Shelley 1925-1940
Shapes: Gainsborough

2156 Butchers **Plum and Yellow Leaves**. Same as 11886. Entered in pattern book during or after 1931. Seconds ware.
Backstamp(s): Shelley 1925-1940
Shapes: Unknown

2157 Butchers **Fruit, Leaves and Butterfly**. Same as 11887. Entered in pattern book during or after 1931. Seconds ware.
Backstamp(s): Shelley 1925-1940
Shapes: Unknown

2158 Primula. Entered in pattern book during or after 1931. Seconds ware.
Backstamp(s): Shelley 1925-1940
Shapes: Unknown

2159 Tulips. Entered in pattern book during or after 1931. Seconds ware.
Backstamp(s): Shelley 1925-1940
Shapes: Unknown

2160 Iris and Stream. Black print. Country scene. Stream flanked by grey trees and purple irises with green leaves. Gate and rising sun. White ground. Blue edges. Seconds ware.
/13 Blue edges
Backstamp(s): Brown Shelley
Shapes: Doric, Regent

2161 Gladioli and Cottage. Entered in pattern book during or after 1931. Seconds ware.
Backstamp(s): Shelley 1925-1940
Shapes: Unknown

2162 Poppy and Stile. Entered in pattern book during or after 1931. Seconds ware.
Backstamp(s): Shelley 1925-1940
Shapes: Unknown

2163 Daffodil and Tree. Daffodils and green grass in the foreground set against grey trees, clouds, and yellow tinted sky. White ground. Blue edges. Entered in pattern book during or after 1931. Seconds ware.
Backstamp(s): Shelley 1925-1940
Shapes: Queen Anne

2164 Crocus. Yellow, blue, and purple crocuses with green leaves. Grey tree. White ground. Entered in pattern book during or after 1931. Seconds ware.
Backstamp(s): Shelley 1925-1940
Shapes: Regent

2165 Dog Rose and Field. Yellow, blue, and purple crocuses with green leaves. Grey tree. White ground. Entered in pattern book during or after 1931. Seconds ware.
Backstamp(s): Shelley 1925-1940
Shapes: Regent

2166 Pink Harebell. Black print. Pink harebell, green leaves, and buds in the foreground against grey trees and bushes. Green grass at base of flowers. Skyline tinted yellow. White ground. Orange edges. Entered in pattern book during or after 1931. Seconds ware.
Backstamp(s): Shelley 1925-1940
Shapes: Regent

2167 Yellow buttercups. Green and grey foliage and trees. Black print. White ground. Green edges. Entered in pattern book during or after 1931. Seconds ware.
Backstamp(s): Shelley 1925-1940
Shapes: Regent

Buttercups 2167 Regent shape cup, saucer, and plate. £50-70; $90-110

2168 Red Flowers. Entered in pattern book during or after 1931. Seconds ware.
Backstamp(s): Shelley 1925-1940
Shapes: Unknown

2169 Delphiniums. Blue delphiniums, pink hollyhocks, green leaves, grey foliage, yellow sky. White ground. Blue edges. Entered in pattern book during or after 1931. Seconds ware.
Backstamp(s): Shelley 1925-1940
Shapes: Unknown

2170 **Lowestoft**. Same as 11595. Entered in pattern book during or after 1931. Seconds ware.
Backstamp(s): Shelley 1925-1940
Shapes: Unknown

Daffodil 2163 Queen Anne shape cup, saucer, and plate. £70-90; $150-200

2171 **Japan**. Entered in pattern book during or after 1931. Seconds ware.
Backstamp(s): Shelley 1925-1940
Shapes: Unknown, Vincent

2172 Floral Motif. Entered in pattern book during or after 1931. Seconds ware.
Backstamp(s): Shelley 1925-1940
Shapes: Vincent

2173 Plain blue. Entered in pattern book during or after 1931. Seconds ware.
Backstamp(s): Shelley 1925-1940
Shapes: Queen Anne

2174 Syringa. Entered in pattern book during or after 1931. Seconds ware.
Backstamp(s): Shelley 1925-1940
Shapes: Unknown

2175 Morning Glory. Entered in pattern book during or after 1931. Seconds ware.
Backstamp(s): Shelley 1925-1940
Shapes: Unknown

2176 Phlox. Entered in pattern book during or after 1931. Seconds ware.
Backstamp(s): Shelley 1925-1940
Shapes: Unknown

2177 Narcissus. Entered in pattern book during or after 1931. Seconds ware.
Backstamp(s): Shelley 1925-1940
Shapes: Unknown

2178 Poppy. Entered in pattern book during or after 1931. Seconds ware.
Backstamp(s): Shelley 1925-1940
Shapes: Unknown

2179 Acacia. Entered in pattern book during or after 1931. Seconds ware.
Backstamp(s): Shelley 1925-1940
Shapes: Unknown

2180 Butchers **Blue Bird**. Same as 11888. Entered in pattern book during or after 1931. Seconds ware.
Backstamp(s): Shelley 1925-1940
Shapes: Unknown

2181 Primula. Same as 12345. Entered in pattern book during or after 1931. Seconds ware.
Backstamp(s): Shelley 1925-1940
Shapes: Regent

2182 Primula. Same as 12344. Entered in pattern book during or after 1931. Seconds ware.
Backstamp(s): Shelley 1925-1940
Shapes: Regent

2183 Dog Rose. Same as 12339. Entered in pattern book during or after 1931. Seconds ware.
Backstamp(s): Shelley 1925-1940
Shapes: Regent

2184 Dog Rose. Same as 12338. Entered in pattern book during or after 1931. Seconds ware.
Backstamp(s): Shelley 1925-1940
Shapes: Regent

2185 Anemone. Same as 12343. Entered in pattern book during or after 1931. Seconds ware.
Backstamp(s): Shelley 1925-1940
Shapes: Regent

2186 Anemone. Same as 12342. Entered in pattern book during or after 1935. Seconds ware.
Backstamp(s): Shelley 1925-1940
Shapes: Regent

2187 Davies **Green and Yellow Leaves. Entered** in pattern book during or after 1935. Seconds ware.
Backstamp(s): Shelley 1925-1940
Shapes: Oxford, Regent

2188 Davies **Pink, Blue, and Grey Leaves**. Entered in pattern book during or after 1935. Seconds ware.
Backstamp(s): Shelley 1925-1940
Shapes: Oxford, Regent

2189 Davies **Pink, Blue, and Green Leaves**. Entered in pattern book during or after 1935. Seconds ware.

Pattern	Description & Shapes
	Backstamp(s): Shelley 1925-1940 **Shapes:** Oxford, Regent
2190	Davies Leaves. Entered in pattern book during or after 1935. Seconds ware. **Backstamp(s)**: Shelley 1925-1940 **Shapes:** Princess Coffee
2191	**Daisy**. Same as 12216. Entered in pattern book during or after 1935. Seconds ware. **Backstamp(s)**: Shelley 1925-1940 **Shapes:** Oxford, Regent
2194	Syringa. Entered in pattern book during or after 1935. Seconds ware. **Backstamp(s)**: Shelley 1925-1940 **Shapes:** Unknown
2195	Morning Glory. Entered in pattern book during or after 1935. Seconds ware. **Backstamp(s)**: Shelley 1925-1940 **Shapes:** Unknown
2196	Phlox. Entered in pattern book during or after 1935. Seconds ware. **Backstamp(s)**: Shelley 1925-1940 **Shapes:** Unknown
2197	Narcissus. Entered in pattern book during or after 1935. Seconds ware. **Backstamp(s)**: Shelley 1925-1940 **Shapes:** Unknown
2198	Poppy. Entered in pattern book during or after 1935. Seconds ware. **Backstamp(s)**: Shelley 1925-1940 **Shapes:** Unknown
2199	Acacia. Entered in pattern book during or after 1935. Seconds ware. **Backstamp(s)**: Shelley 1925-1940 **Shapes:** Unknown
2200	Syringa. Yellow Syringa flowers with green and fawn foliage. Blue or green edges and ring handle on Regent. Entered in pattern book during or after 1935. Seconds ware. **Backstamp(s)**: Shelley 1925-1940 **Shapes:** Eve, Regent, Queen Anne

Syringa 2200 Queen Anne shape cup, saucer, and plate. £70-90; $150-200

Syringa 2200 Regent shape coffee pot. £90-110; $220-280

2202	Phlox. Brown print. Pink and blue phlox flowers with brown leaves. Green edges and ring handle. Seconds ware. /B Blue edges and ring handle. **Backstamp(s)**: Shelley 1925-1940 **Shapes:** Regent

Phlox 2202 Regent shape cup and saucer. £60-70; $100-120

2203	Narcissus. Yellow, amber, and green narcissi against a white ground. Orange edges and handle, ring handle on Regent. Seconds ware. **Backstamp(s)**: Black Shelley 1912-1925; Shelley 1925-1940 **Shapes:** Dainty, Princess, Queen Anne, Regent

Syringa 2200 Eve shape coffee pot. £100-120; $250-300

Syringa 2200 Regent shape cup and saucer. £60-70; $100-120

Narcissus 2203 Dainty shape cup and saucer. £70-80; $140-160

Syringa 2200 Eve shape demitasse cup and saucer. £50-70; $80-110

2201	Morning Glory. Pink and blue convolvulus flowers with green and brown foliage against a white ground. Mauve edges. Entered in pattern book during or after 1935. Seconds ware. **Backstamp(s)**: Shelley 1925-1940 **Shapes:** Queen Anne

Morning Glory 2201 Queen Anne shape cup, saucer, and plate. £80-100; $180-200

Narcissus 2203 Princess shape cup, saucer, and plate. £80-100; $150-180

Narcissus 2203 Queen Anne shape cup, saucer, and plate. £80-100; $150-180

Pattern	Description & Shapes
2204	Poppy. Entered in pattern book during or after 1935. Seconds ware. **Backstamp(s)**: Shelley 1925-1940 **Shapes:** Unknown
2205	Acacia. Brown print. Pink and blue acacia flowers with green and brown shaded foliage. Pink edges and ring handle. Seconds ware. **Backstamp(s)**: Shelley 1925-1940 **Shapes:** Regent
2206	**Daisy**. Same as 12087/28. Entered in pattern book during or after 1935. Seconds ware. **Backstamp(s)**: Shelley 1925-1940 **Shapes:** Dainty
2207	**Motif**. Same as 12293. Entered in pattern book during or after 1935. Seconds ware. **Backstamp(s)**: Shelley 1925-1940 **Shapes:** Eve, Regent
2208	**Motif**. Same as 12294. Entered in pattern book during or after 1935. Seconds ware. **Backstamp(s)**: Shelley 1925-1940 **Shapes:** Eve, Regent
2209	Blue bands and lines. Entered in pattern book during or after 1935. Seconds ware. **Backstamp(s)**: Shelley 1925-1940 **Shapes:** Regent
2210	Green bands and lines. Entered in pattern book during or after 1935. Seconds ware. **Backstamp(s)**: Shelley 1925-1940 **Shapes:** Oxford, Regent
2211	Brown bands and lines. Entered in pattern book during or after 1935. Seconds ware. **Backstamp(s)**: Shelley 1925-1940 **Shapes:** Regent
2212	**Motif**. Entered in pattern book during or after 1935. Seconds ware. **Backstamp(s)**: Shelley 1925-1940 **Shapes:** Regent
2213	**Phlox**. Yellow. Entered in pattern book during or after 1935. Seconds ware. **Backstamp(s)**: Shelley 1925-1940 **Shapes:** Regent
2214	**Phlox**. Blue. Entered in pattern book during or after 1935. Seconds ware. **Backstamp(s)**: Shelley 1925-1940 **Shapes:** Oxford, Regent
2215	Brown and grey bands and lines. Entered in pattern book during or after 1935. Seconds ware. **Backstamp(s)**: Shelley 1925-1940 **Shapes:** Regent
2216	Black and grey bands and lines. Entered in pattern book during or after 1935. Seconds ware. **Backstamp(s)**: Shelley 1925-1940 **Shapes:** Eve, Oxford, Regent
2217	Colour bands. Entered in pattern book during or after 1935. Seconds ware. **Backstamp(s)**: Shelley 1925-1940 **Shapes:** Oxford, Regent
2218	Grey and Colour bands. Entered in pattern book during or after 1935. Seconds ware. **Backstamp(s)**: Shelley 1925-1940 **Shapes:** Regent
2219	Stylised fruit. Entered in pattern book during or after 1935. Seconds ware. **Backstamp(s)**: Shelley 1925-1940 **Shapes:** Regent
2220	Blocks and lines. Entered in pattern book during or after 1935. Seconds ware. **Backstamp(s)**: Shelley 1925-1940 **Shapes:** Oxford, Regent
2221	Scene with butterflies. Entered in pattern book during or after 1935. Seconds ware. **Backstamp(s)**: Shelley 1925-1940 **Shapes:** Unknown
2222	Jasmine. Orange and yellow flowers with green leaves on a white ground. Orange edges. Entered in pattern book during or after 1935. Seconds ware. **Backstamp(s)**: Shelley 1940-1966 **Shapes:** Strand
2223	Violets and butterflies. Entered in pattern book during or after 1935. Seconds ware. **Backstamp(s)**: Shelley 1940-1966 **Shapes:** Unknown
2224	Hydrangeas and butterflies. Entered in pattern book during or after 1935. Seconds ware. **Backstamp(s)**: Shelley 1940-1966 **Shapes:** Unknown
2225	Daisies and butterflies. Brown print. Blue and orange daisies with green and brown foliage. Blue edges and ring handle. Entered in pattern book during or after 1935. Seconds ware. **Backstamp(s)**: Shelley 1940-1966 **Shapes:** Mayfair

Daisies 2225 Mayfair shape cup, saucer, and plate. £70-80; $120-150

Cape Gooseberry 2226 Regent shape coffee pot. £120-150; $250-300. Sugar and creamer. £60-70; $100-120

Pattern	Description & Shapes
2226	Cape Gooseberry and butterflies. Orange gooseberries and brown leaves on a white ground. Green edges and ring handle on Regent. Entered in pattern book during or after 1935. Seconds ware. **Backstamp(s)**: Shelley 1940-1966 **Shapes:** Regent, York
2227	Australian Scenes. Entered in pattern book during or after 1935. Seconds ware. **Backstamp(s)**: Shelley 1940-1966 **Shapes:** Eve
2228	Australian Scenes. Entered in pattern book during or after 1935. Seconds ware. **Backstamp(s)**: Shelley 1940-1966 **Shapes:** Queen Anne
2229	Details unknown. Entered in pattern book during or after 1935. Seconds ware. **Backstamp(s)**: Shelley 1940-1966 **Shapes:** Eve
2230	Colour band with grey and black shading. Entered in pattern book during or after 1935. Seconds ware. **Backstamp(s)**: Shelley 1940-1966 **Shapes:** Oxford
2231	Stile and Rose with butterflies. Entered in pattern book during or after 1935. Seconds ware. **Backstamp(s)**: Shelley 1940-1966 **Shapes:** Unknown
2232	Lake and Balcony with butterflies. Entered in pattern book during or after 1935. Seconds ware. **Backstamp(s)**: Shelley 1940-1966 **Shapes:** Unknown
2233	Stylised with butterflies. Entered in pattern book during or after 1935. Seconds ware. **Backstamp(s)**: Shelley 1940-1966 **Shapes:** Unknown
2234	Cornfield with butterflies. Orange sun between brown trees. Entered in pattern book during or after 1935. Seconds ware. **Backstamp(s)**: Shelley 1940-1966 **Shapes:** Henley
2235	Balloon Tree with butterflies. Entered in pattern book during or after 1935. Seconds ware. **Backstamp(s)**: Shelley 1940-1966 **Shapes:** Unknown
2236	Gate and Path with butterflies. Entered in pattern book during or after 1935. Seconds ware. **Backstamp(s)**: Shelley 1940-1966 **Shapes:** Unknown
2237	Swirls. Grey and amber. Entered in pattern book during or after 1935. Same as 12405. Seconds ware. **Backstamp(s)**: Shelley 1940-1966 **Shapes:** Unknown

Pattern	Description & Shapes
2238	Silver Sage. Entered in pattern book during or after 1935. Same as 12548. Seconds ware. **Backstamp(s)**: Shelley 1940-1966 **Shapes:** Unknown
2239	Poppy. Entered in pattern book during or after 1935. Same as 12549. Seconds ware. **Backstamp(s)**: Shelley 1940-1966 **Shapes:** Unknown
2240	Floral. Entered in pattern book during or after 1935. Same as 12531. Seconds ware. **Backstamp(s)**: Shelley 1940-1966 **Shapes:** Unknown
2241	**Autumn**. Entered in pattern book during or after 1935. Same as 12565. Seconds ware. **Backstamp(s)**: Shelley 1940-1966 **Shapes:** Unknown
2242	Sunset and Flowers. Entered in pattern book during or after 1935. Same as 11691. Seconds ware. **Backstamp(s)**: Shelley 1940-1966 **Shapes:** Unknown
2243	Blossom. Entered in pattern book during or after 1935. Same as 12584. Seconds ware. **Backstamp(s)**: Shelley 1940-1966 **Shapes:** Unknown
2244	Sunset and Flowers. Brown print. Same as 11691. Entered in pattern book during or after 1935. Seconds ware. **Backstamp(s)**: Shelley 1940-1966 **Shapes:** Vincent
2245	**Native Rose**. Australian flowers. Entered in pattern book during or after 1935. Seconds ware. **Backstamp(s)**: Shelley 1940-1966 **Shapes:** Vincent
2246	**Flannel Flower**. Australian flowers. Entered in pattern book during or after 1935. Seconds ware. **Backstamp(s)**: Shelley 1940-1966 **Shapes:** Vincent
2247	**Carnation**. Entered in pattern book during or after 1935. Seconds ware. **Backstamp(s)**: Shelley 1940-1966 **Shapes:** Vincent
2248	**Wattle Flower**. Australian flowers. Entered in pattern book during or after 1935. Seconds ware. **Backstamp(s)**: Shelley 1940-1966 **Shapes:** Vincent
2249	**Yellow Pansy** and **Laurel Border**. Entered in pattern book during or after 1935. Seconds ware. **Backstamp(s)**: Shelley 1940-1966 **Shapes:** Gainsborough
2250	Warwick **Rose**. Pink roses, blue, and yellow flowers with green foliage on a white ground. One spray also inside cup. Dark green edges. Entered in pattern book during or after 1935. Seconds ware. **Backstamp(s)**: Shelley 1940-1966 **Shapes:** Dainty, Ely, Perth, Queen Anne
2251	**Motif**. Pink, blue, and yellow flowers with green leaves. Flower spray inside cup. White ground. Pink edges. Same as 0193. Entered in pattern book during or after 1935. Seconds ware. **Backstamp(s)**: Wileman 1872-1890 **Shapes:** Ely, Eve, Mode, Oxford
2252	**Idalium**. Same as 088. Entered in pattern book during or after 1935. Seconds ware. **Backstamp(s)**: Shelley 1940-1966 **Shapes:** Unknown
2253	**Wisteria**. Entered in pattern book during or after 1935. Seconds ware. **Backstamp(s)**: Shelley 1940-1966 **Shapes:** Oxford
2254	**Laburnum**. Same as 12420. Entered in pattern book during or after 1935. Seconds ware. **Backstamp(s)**: Shelley 1940-1966 **Shapes:** Eve, Oxford
2255	**Carnation**. Entered in pattern book during or after 1935. Seconds ware. **Backstamp(s)**: Shelley 1940-1966 **Shapes:** Unknown
2256	**Posy Spray** and **Border**. Entered in pattern book during or after 1935. Seconds ware. **Backstamp(s)**: Shelley 1940-1966 **Shapes:** Ascot, Eve, Gainsborough, Ripon
2257	Warwick **Rose Sprays** and border same as 11427 **Hampton Court**. Entered in pattern book during or after 1935. Seconds ware. **Backstamp(s)**: Shelley 1940-1966 **Shapes:** Ascot, Eve, Gainsborough, Ripon
2258	**Carnation** and border same as 11425 **Versailles**. Entered in pattern book during or after 1935. Seconds ware. **Backstamp(s)**: Shelley 1940-1966 **Shapes:** Gainsborough
2259	Ratauds **Pink Rose**. Same as 0146. Entered in pattern book during or after 1935. Seconds ware. **Backstamp(s)**: Shelley 1940-1966 **Shapes:** Henley
2260	**Royalty**. Same as 0186. Entered in pattern book during or after 1935. Seconds ware. **Backstamp(s)**: Shelley 1940-1966 **Shapes:** Unknown
2261	**Royalty**. Entered in pattern book during or after 1935. Seconds ware. **Backstamp(s)**: Shelley 1940-1966 **Shapes:** Oleander
2263	Hulmes **Rose and Yellow Flowers** and border same as 11427 **Hampton Court**. Entered in pattern book during or after 1935. Seconds ware. **Backstamp(s)**: Shelley 1940-1966 **Shapes:** Gainsborough
2264	Hulmes **Rose and White Flowers** and border same as 11426 **Versailles**. Entered in pattern book during or after 1935. Seconds ware. **Backstamp(s)**: Shelley 1940-1966 **Shapes:** Gainsborough
2265	**Blossom**. Same as 13429. Entered in pattern book during or after 1935. Seconds ware. **Backstamp(s)**: Shelley 1940-1966 **Shapes:** Gainsborough
2266	**Pompadour**. Entered in pattern book during or after 1935. Seconds ware. **Backstamp(s)**: Shelley 1940-1966 **Shapes:** Oleander
2267	Davies **Tulip**. Bunches of flowers, including yellow tulips, pink roses, blue, white, orange, and yellow flowers with green foliage. Yellow tulip or pink rose also inside cup. White ground. Coloured edges and handle. Entered in pattern book during or after 1935. Seconds ware. **Backstamp(s)**: Shelley 1940-1966 **Shapes:** Dainty, Ely, Gainsborough, Footed Oleander, Oleander Low, Regent

Rose 2250 Perth shape cup and saucer. £50-60; $90-110

Davies **Tulip** 2267 Low Oleander shape demitasse cup and saucer. £50-60; $90-110

Davies **Tulip** 2267 Oleander shape large coffee pot. £120-150; $250-300

Davies **Tulip** unverified pattern number Ely shape cup and saucer. £50-60; $90-110

Davies **Tulip** unverified pattern number Gainsborough shape cup and saucer. £40-50; $80-100

Davies **Tulip** unverified pattern number Tall Dainty shape cup and saucer. £70-80; $140-160

Pattern **Description & Shapes**

2268 Hulmes **Yellow Rose**. Entered in pattern book during or after 1935. Seconds ware.
Backstamp(s): Shelley 1940-1966
Shapes: Gainsborough

2269 Hulmes **White Rose**. Entered in pattern book during or after 1935. Seconds ware.
Backstamp(s): Shelley 1940-1966
Shapes: Unknown

2270 Pink **Sheraton**. Entered in pattern book during or after 1935. Seconds ware.
Backstamp(s): Shelley 1940-1966
Shapes: Gainsborough

2271 Green **Sheraton**. Entered in pattern book during or after 1935. Seconds ware.
Backstamp(s): Shelley 1940-1966
Shapes: Gainsborough

2272 Blue **Sheraton**. Entered in pattern book during or after 1935. Seconds ware.
Backstamp(s): Shelley 1940-1966
Shapes: Gainsborough

2273 Maroon **Duchess**. Entered in pattern book during or after 1935. Seconds ware.
Backstamp(s): Shelley 1940-1966
Shapes: Gainsborough

2274 Blue **Duchess**. Entered in pattern book during or after 1935. Seconds ware.
Backstamp(s): Shelley 1940-1966
Shapes: Gainsborough

2275 Green Duchess. Entered in pattern book during or after 1935. Seconds ware.
Backstamp(s): Shelley 1940-1966
Shapes: Gainsborough

2276 Maroon **Dubarry**. Entered in pattern book during or after 1935. Seconds ware.
Backstamp(s): Shelley 1940-1966
Shapes: Gainsborough

2277 Green **Dubarry**. Entered in pattern book during or after 1935. Seconds ware.
Backstamp(s): Shelley 1940-1966
Shapes: Gainsborough

2278 Blue **Dubarry**. Entered in pattern book during or after 1935. Seconds ware.
Backstamp(s): Shelley 1940-1966
Shapes: Gainsborough

2279 Blue **Regal**. Entered in pattern book during or after 1935. Seconds ware.
Backstamp(s): Shelley 1940-1966
Shapes: Gainsborough

2280 Green **Regal**. Entered in pattern book during or after 1935. Seconds ware.
Backstamp(s): Shelley 1940-1966
Shapes: Gainsborough

2281 **Georgian** flowers and **Bluebell** sprays on a white ground. Entered in pattern book during or after 1935. Seconds ware.
Backstamp(s): Shelley 1940-1966
Shapes: Ludlow, Stratford

2282 **Hedgerow** inside cup. Pale blue outside cup and on saucer. Entered in pattern book during or after 1935. Seconds ware.
Backstamp(s): Shelley 1940-1966
Shapes: Footed Oleander

2283 **Spring Bouquet** inside cup. Salmon outside cup and on saucer. Entered in pattern book during or after 1935. Seconds ware.
Backstamp(s): Shelley 1940-1966
Shapes: Footed Oleander

2284 **Georgian** and small Hulmes **Rose** inside cup. Pink outside cup and on saucer. Entered in pattern book during or after 1935. Seconds ware.
Backstamp(s): Shelley 1940-1966
Shapes: Footed Oleander

2285 **Dubarry** inside cup. Pale green outside cup and on saucer. Entered in pattern book during or after 1935. Seconds ware.
Backstamp(s): Shelley 1940-1966
Shapes: Footed Oleander

2286 **Dresden**. Entered in pattern book during or after 1935. Seconds ware.
Backstamp(s): Shelley 1940-1966
Shapes: Gainsborough

2287 Maroon **Georgian**. Entered in pattern book during or after 1935. Seconds ware.
Backstamp(s): Shelley 1940-1966
Shapes: Chester

2288 Green **Georgian**. Entered in pattern book during or after 1935. Seconds ware.
Backstamp(s): Shelley 1940-1966
Shapes: Chester

2289 **Glorious Devon**. Same as 12734. Entered in pattern book during or after 1935. Seconds ware.
Backstamp(s): Shelley 1940-1966
Shapes: Dainty

2290 **Primrose Chintz**. Same as 13586. Entered in pattern book during or after 1935. Seconds ware.
Backstamp(s): Shelley 1940-1966
Shapes: Dainty

2291 **Blue Rock**. Same as 13586. Entered in pattern book during or after 1935. Seconds ware.
Backstamp(s): Shelley 1940-1966
Shapes: Oleander

2292 **Bridal Rose**. Same as 13586. Entered in pattern book during or after 1935. Seconds ware.
Backstamp(s): Shelley 1940-1966
Shapes: Dainty

2293 **Rock Garden Chintz**. Same as 13586. Entered in pattern book during or after 1935. Seconds ware.
Backstamp(s): Shelley 1940-1966
Shapes: Oleander

2294 **Primrose Chintz**. Similar to 13586. Entered in pattern book during or after 1935. Seconds ware.
Backstamp(s): Shelley 1940-1966
Shapes: Dainty

2295 **Wild Flowers**. Green inside cup. Entered in pattern book during or after 1935. Seconds ware.
Backstamp(s): Shelley 1940-1966
Shapes: Dainty Coffee

2296 Hulmes **Rose** and **Bluebell**. Blue inside cup. Entered in pattern book during or after 1935. Seconds ware.
Backstamp(s): Shelley 1940-1966
Shapes: Gainsborough Coffee

2297 Warwick Savage **Rose**. Pale blue inside cup. Entered in pattern book during or after 1935. Seconds ware.
Backstamp(s): Shelley 1940-1966
Shapes: Gainsborough Coffee

2298 Butchers **Crocus and Rose** and **Bluebell**. Entered in pattern book during or after 1935. Seconds ware.
Backstamp(s): Shelley 1940-1966
Shapes: Cambridge, Chester, Dainty, Gainsborough, Low Oleander, Regent, Stratford

2299 Butchers **Dresden**. Pink handle. Entered in pattern book during or after 1935. Seconds ware.
Backstamp(s): Shelley 1940-1966
Shapes: Gainsborough

2300 Butchers **Dresden**. Blue handle. Entered in pattern book during or after 1935. Seconds ware.
Backstamp(s): Shelley 1940-1966
Shapes: Gainsborough

2301 Hulmes **Dresden**. Green handle. Entered in pattern book during or after 1935. Seconds ware.
Backstamp(s): Shelley 1940-1966
Shapes: Gainsborough, Oleander, Stratford

2302 Hulmes **Dresden** and **Roses**. Entered in pattern book during or after 1935. Seconds ware.
Backstamp(s): Shelley 1940-1966
Shapes: Gainsborough, Oleander, Stratford

2303 Hulmes **Rose** and **Bluebell**. Entered in pattern book during or after 1935. Seconds ware.
Backstamp(s): Shelley 1940-1966
Shapes: Cambridge, Dainty, Oleander, Regent

2304 **Georgian** and **Bluebell**. Entered in pattern book during or after 1935. Seconds ware.
Backstamp(s): Shelley 1940-1966
Shapes: Cambridge, Dainty, Regent

2305 **Georgian** and pink band. Entered in pattern book during or after 1935. Seconds ware.
Backstamp(s): Shelley 1940-1966
Shapes: Gainsborough, Stratford

2306 Butchers **Dresden**. Large pink and yellow roses with green foliage on a white ground. Green edges, foot and handle. Seconds ware.

Dresden Richmond shape cup, saucer, and plate. £40-50; $70-90

Pattern	Description & Shapes
	Backstamp(s): Shelley 1940-1966 **Shapes:** Dainty, Gainsborough, Regent, Stratford
2307	Butchers **Dresden**. Entered in pattern book during or after 1935. Seconds ware. **Backstamp(s)**: Shelley 1940-1966 **Shapes:** Gainsborough
2308	Warwick Savage **Rose and Daisy**. Same as 13725. Entered in pattern book during or after 1935. Seconds ware. **Backstamp(s)**: Shelley 1940-1966 **Shapes:** Dainty, Henley, Oleander, Richmond, Warwick
2309	Warwick Savage **Tulip and Rose**. Same as 13726. Entered in pattern book during or after 1935. Seconds ware. **Backstamp(s)**: Shelley 1940-1966 **Shapes:** Dainty, Henley, Oleander, Richmond, Warwick
2310	Warwick Savage **Floral**. Same as 13727. Entered in pattern book during or after 1935. Seconds ware. **Backstamp(s)**: Shelley 1940-1966 **Shapes:** Dainty, Henley, Oleander, Richmond, Warwick
2311	Warwick Savage **Tulip and Rose**. Same as 13728. Entered in pattern book during or after 1935. Seconds ware. **Backstamp(s)**: Shelley 1940-1966 **Shapes:** Dainty, Henley, Oleander, Richmond, Warwick
2312	Nursery way by **J Hassall**. Entered in pattern book during or after 1935. Seconds ware. **Backstamp(s)**: Shelley 1940-1966 **Shapes:** Unknown
2313	Goors **Rose Spray**. Pale pink roses and green foliage. Gold edges. Pale blue foot and handle. Seconds ware. No foot on Ludlow or Oleander. **Backstamp(s)**: Shelley 1940-1966 **Shapes:** Gainsborough, Ludlow, Oleander, Ripon, Stratford
2314	Goors **Rose Spray**. Pale pink roses and green foliage inside cup on a white ground. Pink outside cup on saucer. Gold edges and handle. Entered in pattern book during or after 1935. Seconds ware. Pattern is outside cup on Ludlow and Ripon. **Backstamp(s)**: Shelley 1940-1966 **Shapes:** Ludlow, Oleander, Ripon

Rose Spray 2313 Ripon shape cup and saucer. £50-60; $90-110

Rose Spray 2313 Ludlow shape cup and saucer. £50-60; $110-130

Rose Spray 2314 Gainsborough shape cup and saucer. £40-50; $80-100

Pattern	Description & Shapes
2315	Butchers **Crocus and Rose** inside cup. Orange outside cup and on saucer. Entered in pattern book during or after 1935. Seconds ware. **Backstamp(s)**: Shelley 1940-1966 **Shapes:** Gainsborough, Henley, Ludlow, Stratford
2316	Enterprise **Tulip**. Pattern inside cup on white ground. Pale green outside cup and on saucer. Gold edges and handle. Entered in pattern book during or after 1935. Seconds ware., Ludlow: Pattern outside cup and pale green inside cup., Ripon: Pattern outside cup and pale green inside cup. **Backstamp(s)**: Shelley 1940-1966 **Shapes:** Gainsborough, Henley, Ludlow, Oleander, Ripon, Stratford
2317	Hulmes **Dresden** inside cup. Pale blue outside cup and on saucer. Entered in pattern book during or after 1935. Seconds ware. **Backstamp(s)**: Shelley 1940-1966 **Shapes:** Gainsborough, Henley, Ludlow, Oleander, Stratford
2318	**Georgian** and Hulmes **Rose** inside cup. Fawn outside cup and on saucer. Entered in pattern book during or after 1935. Seconds ware. **Backstamp(s)**: Shelley 1940-1966 **Shapes:** Gainsborough, Henley, Ludlow, Oleander, Ripon, Stratford
2319	Hulmes **Rose** inside cup. Mauve outside cup and on saucer. Entered in pattern book during or after 1935. Seconds ware. **Backstamp(s)**: Shelley 1940-1966 **Shapes:** Gainsborough, Henley, Ludlow, Oleander, Stratford
2320	**Lowestoft** inside cup. Entered in pattern book during or after 1935. Seconds ware. **Backstamp(s)**: Shelley 1940-1966 **Shapes:** Henley, Regent
2321	**Chinese Garden**. Border of pink roses, blue, yellow, and orange flowers with green and grey foliage. White ground. Gold edges., Gainsborough: pattern inside cup, main part of saucer and plate. White outside cup, middle of saucer and plate. Line outside cup, approximately halfway between rim and foot. Entered in pattern book during or after 1935. Seconds ware. **Backstamp(s)**: Shelley 1940-1966 **Shapes:** Gainsborough, Henley
2322	**Lowestoft**. Entered in pattern book during or after 1935. Seconds ware. **Backstamp(s)**: Shelley 1940-1966 **Shapes:** Dorothy, Regent
2323	**Sheraton** and small **Grey Crystals**. Entered in pattern book during or after 1935. Seconds ware. **Backstamp(s)**: Shelley 1940-1966 **Shapes:** Dainty, Dorothy, Gainsborough, Henley, Ludlow, Oleander, Regent, Richmond, Ripon, Stratford, Warwick
2324	**Floral** and small **Grey Crystals**. Entered in pattern book during or after 1935. Seconds ware. **Backstamp(s)**: Shelley 1940-1966 **Shapes:** Henley, Regent
2325	Rateauds **Yutoi**. Same as 13797. Entered in pattern book during or after 1935. Seconds ware. **Backstamp(s)**: Shelley 1940-1966 **Shapes:** Henley, Regent, Richmond
2326	Universal **Rose Floral** with pieces of the **Bluebell** pattern. Small bouquets of red roses, orange, and blue flowers with green foliage. Bluebell spray inside cup. Blue edges and handle. Entered in pattern book during or after 1935. Seconds ware. /P Pink.

Tulip 2316 Gainsborough shape cup and saucer. £40-50; $80-100

Right:
Tulip 2316 pattern inside Gainsborough shape cup.

Pattern	Description & Shapes
	Backstamp(s): Shelley 1940-1966 **Shapes:** Dainty, Henley, Richmond
2327	**Rose Trellis**. Pink, yellow, and blue roses with green leaves on a trellis. Pattern also inside cup. Yellow trim and handle. Yellow foot on Gainsborough and Henley. Entered in pattern book during or after 1935. Seconds ware. **Backstamp(s)**: Shelley 1940-1966 **Shapes:** Gainsborough, New Cambridge, Oxford, Windsor

Rose Trellis 2327 Windsor shape cup and saucer. £40-50; $80-100

2328 **Wild Flower** and **Blue Rock** patterns. Blue, mauve, yellow, and pink flowers with green foliage on a white ground. Small spray inside cup. Blue edges, foot and handle. Entered in pattern book during or after 1935. Seconds ware.
Backstamp(s): Shelley 1940-1966
Shapes: Cambridge, Henley, Gainsborough, Regent

Wild Flower and **Blue Rock** 2328 Henley shape cup and saucer. £40-50; $80-100

2329 **Rambler Rose**. Entered in pattern book during or after 1935. Seconds ware.
Backstamp(s): Shelley 1940-1966
Shapes: Dorothy, Regent

2330 **Stocks**, **Bridal Rose** and **Blue Rock** patterns. Blue, mauve, yellow, and pink flowers with green foliage on a white ground. Small spray inside cup. Blue edges, foot and handle. Entered in pattern book during or after 1935. Seconds ware.
Backstamp(s): Shelley 1940-1966
Shapes: Henley, Footed Oleander, Gainsborough, Regent, Richmond

2331 Small **Primrose** and **Bluebell** sprays. Gold edges and pale green handle. Entered in pattern book during or after 1935. Seconds ware.
Backstamp(s): Shelley 1940-1966
Shapes: Cambridge, Ludlow, Queen Anne, Regent, Warwick

Primrose 2331 Queen Anne shape cup and saucer. £70-80; $130-150

2332 **Georgian**. Sprigs of multi-coloured flowers around a pink rose. Gold trim and pale green handle. Entered in pattern book during or after 1935. Seconds ware.
Backstamp(s): Shelley 1940-1966
Shapes: Dainty, Low Oleander, Ludlow, Stratford, Warwick

Floral pattern 2332 Dainty shape cup and saucer. £70-80; $140-160

2333 **English Rose**. Sprigs of multi-coloured flowers around a pink rose. Gold trim and pale green handle. Entered in pattern book during or after 1935. Seconds ware.
Backstamp(s): Shelley 1940-1966
Shapes: Dainty, Gainsborough, Henley, Low Oleander, Ludlow, Stratford, Warwick

2334 Small Hulmes **Rose**. One sprig of roses inside cup. Gold edges and pale pink handle. Entered in pattern book during or after 1935. Seconds ware.
Backstamp(s): Shelley 1940-1966
Shapes: Dainty, Gainsborough, Henley, Low Oleander, Ludlow, Stratford, Warwick

Right:
Rose 2334 Dainty shape cup and saucer. £70-80; $140-160

2335 Hulmes **Rose and White Flowers**. Entered in pattern book during or after 1935. Seconds ware.
Backstamp(s): Shelley 1940-1966
Shapes: Gainsborough, Henley, Low Oleander, Ludlow, Stratford, Warwick

2336 **Sheraton** and small **Grey Crystals**. Entered in pattern book during or after 1935. Seconds ware.
Backstamp(s): Shelley 1940-1966
Shapes: Unknown

2337 Butchers **Crocus and Rose** and **Bluebell**. Entered in pattern book during or after 1935. Seconds ware.
Backstamp(s): Shelley 1940-1966
Shapes: Unknown

2338 Butchers **Rose Spray**. Pink roses with blue flowers and green foliage. White ground. Pink edges. Pink foot and handle on Footed Dainty, Gainsborough, Henley, Richmond, and Ripon. Pink ring handle on Regent. Entered in pattern book during or after 1935. Seconds ware.
Backstamp(s): Shelley 1940-1966
Shapes: Dainty, Footed Dainty, Henley, Gainsborough, Ludlow, Regent, Richmond, Ripon, Warwick

2339 Butchers **Rose Spray**. Pink roses with blue flowers and green foliage. White ground. Gold edges. Pink handle. Pink foot on Henley. Entered in pattern book during or after 1935. Seconds ware.
Backstamp(s): Shelley 1940-1966
Shapes: Dainty, Henley

2340 **Rose Trellis**. Entered in pattern book during or after 1935. Seconds ware.
Backstamp(s): Shelley 1940-1966
Shapes: Dainty

2341 Small **Primrose** and **Bluebell** sprays. Entered in pattern book during or after 1935. Seconds ware.
Backstamp(s): Shelley 1940-1966
Shapes: Stratford

2342 Warwick Savage **Rose and Daisy**. Entered in pattern book during or after 1935. Seconds ware.
Backstamp(s): Shelley 1940-1966
Shapes: Unknown

2343 Warwick Savage **Tulip and Rose**. Similar to 13728. Entered in pattern book during or after 1935. Seconds ware.
Backstamp(s): Shelley 1940-1966
Shapes: Dainty

2344 Warwick Savage **Tulip and Rose**. Similar to 13726. Entered in pattern book during or after 1935. Seconds ware.
Backstamp(s): Shelley 1940-1966
Shapes: Unknown

2345 Cappers **Pink and Yellow Rose**. Entered in pattern book during or after 1935. Seconds ware.
Backstamp(s): Shelley 1940-1966
Shapes: Bute, Dainty, Gainsborough, Regent

2346 Cappers **Pink and Yellow Rose**. Entered in pattern book during or after 1935. Seconds ware.
Backstamp(s): Shelley 1940-1966

Pattern	Description & Shapes
	Shapes: Bute, Dainty, Gainsborough, Regent
2347	German **Rose Sprays**. Large pink rose, smaller yellow rose, purple forget-me-nots, small yellow flowers, small white flowers, blue convolvulus in some of the bunches. Small spray inside cup. White ground. Blue edges and ring handle (Regent). Entered in pattern book during or after 1957. Seconds ware. /G green edges and handle (Regent) **Backstamp(s)**: Shelley 1940-1966 **Shapes:** Dainty, Oleander, Regent
2348	German **Floral Sprays**. Blue, pink, yellow, mauve flowers with green leaves. Small flower spray inside cup. White ground. Yellow handle. Entered in pattern book during or after 1957., Regent: Green ring handle., Ripon: Green foot and handle. Seconds ware. /F Fawn trim /Y Orange trim /P Pink trim. **Backstamp(s)**: Shelley 1940-1966 **Shapes:** Ludlow, Stratford, Regent, Ripon

German **Floral Sprays** Ripon shape cup and saucer. £50-70; $100-120

2349	**Wine Grape**. Green leaves and purple bunches of grapes on green vine. Scattered **Grey Crystals**. White ground. Pale green edges and handle. Pale green foot on Richmond. Entered in pattern book during or after 1957. Seconds ware. **Backstamp(s)**: Shelley 1940-1966 **Shapes:** Dainty, Regent, Richmond, Ripon, Stirling

Wine Grape 2349 Ripon shape cup and saucer. £50-70; $100-120

2350	Ratauds **Bramble**. Pink edges and handle. Entered in pattern book during or after 1957. Seconds ware. **Backstamp(s)**: Shelley 1940-1966 **Shapes:** Dainty, Regent
2351	Ratauds **Summer Bouquet**. Flowers in various shades, including pink, orange, blue, and white. Flower spray also inside cup. Blue edges and handle. Blue foot on Richmond. Entered in pattern book during or after 1957. Seconds ware. /A small flower spray on Henley **Backstamp(s)**: Shelley 1940-1966 **Shapes:** Dainty, Henley, Low Oleander, Richmond

Summer Bouquet 2351 Dainty shape cup and saucer. £70-80; $140-160

2352	**Rose Spray**. Similar to 13425. Entered in pattern book during or after 1957. Seconds ware. **Backstamp(s)**: Shelley 1940-1966 **Shapes:** Dainty, Regent
2353	Ratauds **Bramble**. Gold edges. Pink handle. Entered in pattern book during or after 1957. Seconds ware. **Backstamp(s)**: Shelley 1940-1966 **Shapes:** Dainty, Ludlow, Regent
2354	Ratauds **Summer Bouquet**. Entered in pattern book during or after 1957. Seconds ware. /A small flower spray on Henley **Backstamp(s)**: Shelley 1940-1966 **Shapes:** Dainty, Low Oleander, Richmond
2355	German **Floral Sprays**. Entered in pattern book during or after 1957. Seconds ware. **Backstamp(s)**: Shelley 1940-1966 **Shapes:** Dainty, Ludlow, Stratford
2356	**Georgian** and **Bluebell**. Entered in pattern book during or after 1957. Seconds ware. **Backstamp(s)**: Shelley 1940-1966 **Shapes:** Gainsborough
2357	Butchers **Rose Spray**. Entered in pattern book during or after 1957. Seconds ware. **Backstamp(s)**: Shelley 1940-1966 **Shapes:** Gainsborough
2358	Cappers **Pink and Yellow Rose**. Entered in pattern book during or after 1935. Seconds ware. **Backstamp(s)**: Shelley 1940-1966 **Shapes:** Footed Dainty, Gainsborough
2359	Ratauds **Bramble**. Entered in pattern book during or after 1957. Seconds ware. **Backstamp(s)**: Shelley 1940-1966 **Shapes:** Footed Dainty, Gainsborough
2360	Ratauds **Summer Bouquet**. Entered in pattern book during or after 1957. Seconds ware. **Backstamp(s)**: Shelley 1940-1966 **Shapes:** Footed Dainty, Gainsborough
2361	German **Floral Sprays**. Entered in pattern book during or after 1957. Seconds ware. **Backstamp(s)**: Shelley 1940-1966 **Shapes:** Footed Dainty, Gainsborough
2362	**Georgian** and **Bluebell**. Entered in pattern book during or after 1957. Seconds ware. **Backstamp(s)**: Shelley 1940-1966 **Shapes:** Gainsborough
2363	Blue **Sheraton**. Entered in pattern book during or after 1957. Seconds ware. **Backstamp(s)**: Shelley 1940-1966 **Shapes:** Gainsborough
2364	Green **Sheraton**. Entered in pattern book during or after 1957. Seconds ware. **Backstamp(s)**: Shelley 1940-1966 **Shapes:** Gainsborough
2365	Hulmes **Rose**. Entered in pattern book during or after 1957. Seconds ware. **Backstamp(s)**: Shelley 1940-1966 **Shapes:** Gainsborough
2366	**Serenity** and **Grey Crystals**. Pink flower with turquoise and grey leaves and stem on a white ground. Scattered grey crystals. Green edges and ring handle (Regent). Entered in pattern book during or after 1958. Seconds ware. **Backstamp(s)**: Shelley 1940-1966 **Shapes:** Regent, Richmond
2367	**Rose** and **Bluebell**. Roses in shades of pink with yellow and blue flowers, green foliage. Small bluebell sprigs. White ground. Pink or green edges and handle. Green foot on Henley. Entered in pattern book during or after 1958. Same as 13799. Seconds ware. **Backstamp(s)**: Shelley 1940-1966 **Shapes:** New Cambridge, Regent, Richmond
2368	German **Rose Sprays**. Large pink rose, smaller yellow rose, purple forget-me-nots, small yellow flowers, small white flowers, blue convolvulus in some of the bunches. Small bluebell spray inside cup on Ludlow. White ground. Gold edges. Blue handle. Entered in pattern book during or after 1958. Seconds ware. **Backstamp(s)**: Shelley 1940-1966 **Shapes:** Dainty, Ludlow

Rose Sprays 2368 Ludlow shape cup and saucer. £60-70; $90-120

2369	Pink **Sheraton**. Entered in pattern book during or after 1958. Seconds ware. **Backstamp(s)**: Shelley 1940-1966 **Shapes:** Gainsborough
2370	Cappers **Rose**. Entered in pattern book during or after 1958. Seconds ware. **Backstamp(s)**: Shelley 1940-1966 **Shapes:** Gainsborough, Warwick
2371	Cappers **Camellia**. Entered in pattern book during or after 1958. Seconds ware. **Backstamp(s)**: Shelley 1940-1966 **Shapes:** Gainsborough, Warwick
2372	German **Floral**. Entered in pattern book

Pattern Description & Shapes

during or after 1958. Seconds ware.
/A Produced for Roberts of Alsager in 1960.
Backstamp(s): Shelley 1940-1966
Shapes: Richmond

2373 German **Floral**. Entered in pattern book during or after 1958. Seconds ware.
Backstamp(s): Shelley 1940-1966
Shapes: Dainty

2374 German **Floral**. Entered in pattern book during or after 1958. Seconds ware.
Backstamp(s): Shelley 1940-1966
Shapes: Regent, Richmond

2375 German **Roses and Lily of the Valley**. Entered in pattern book during or after 1958. Seconds ware.
Backstamp(s): Shelley 1940-1966
Shapes: Gainsborough

2376 German **Green Iris**. Green and grey irises and foliage on a white ground. Iris spray also inside cup. Green edges. Green handle or ring handle (Regent). Entered in pattern book during or after 1958. Seconds ware.
Backstamp(s): Shelley 1940-1966
Shapes: Dainty, Ludlow, Regent, Richmond, Warwick

2378 **Debonair**. Flowers inside and outside cup as well as saucer include red and pink roses with blue convolvulus and foliage. Blue edges, foot and handle. Entered in pattern book during or after 1958. Seconds ware.
Backstamp(s): Shelley 1940-1966
Shapes: New Cambridge, Richmond, Ovide, Stratford, Regent

Debonair 2378 Richmond shape tennis set. £50-60; $80-100

2379 **Green Iris** on large panels. Pale green on small panels. Entered in pattern book during or after 1958. Seconds ware.
Backstamp(s): Shelley 1940-1966
Shapes: Queen Anne

2380 German **Floral** and **Pole Star** on large panels. Pale blue on small panels. Entered in pattern book during or after 1958. Seconds ware.
Backstamp(s): Shelley 1940-1966
Shapes: Queen Anne

2381 **Rose and Lily of the Valley** on large panels. Pink on small panels. Entered in pattern book during or after 1958. Seconds ware.
Backstamp(s): Shelley 1940-1966
Shapes: Queen Anne

2382 **Summer Bouquet** and **Grey Crystals** on large panels. Orange on small panels. Entered in pattern book during or after 1958. Seconds ware.
Backstamp(s): Shelley 1940-1966
Shapes: Queen Anne

2383 Universal **Eglantine**. Pink flowers and green leaves. Green edges, foot (Richmond) and handle. Entered in pattern book during or after 1959. Seconds ware.
Backstamp(s): Shelley 1940-1966
Shapes: Oleander, Queen Anne, Richmond, Stirling

Green Iris 2376 Ludlow shape cup and saucer. £60-70; $90-120

Chrysanthemum 2377 Windsor shape cup, saucer, and plate. £40-50; $90-110

Eglantine 2383 coffee pot. £80-100; $200-220

Green Iris 2376 Richmond shape cup, saucer, and plate. £40-50; $90-110

Chrysanthemum 2377/A New Cambridge shape cup and saucer. £40-50; $90-110

Eglantine 2383 Low Oleander shape cup and saucer. £40-50; $70-90

2377 German **Chrysanthemum**. Large pink and peach chrysanthemum head surrounded by small pink and blue flowers with green foliage on a white ground. Flowers also inside cup. Blue edges, foot (Richmond and Windsor) and handle. Entered in pattern book during or after 1958. Seconds ware.
/A Reversed pattern.
Backstamp(s): Shelley 1940-1966
Shapes: Dainty, Dainty Tennis Set, New Cambridge, Richmond, Windsor

Chrysanthemum 2377 Windsor shape creamer and sugar. £40-50; $90-110

Eglantine 2383 Queen Anne shape cup and saucer. £60-70; $90-120

Pattern	Description & Shapes
2384	**Orchid**. Entered in pattern book during or after 1959. Seconds ware. **Backstamp(s)**: Shelley 1940-1966 **Shapes:** Richmond
2385	**Camellia**. Entered in pattern book during or after 1959. Seconds ware. **Backstamp(s)**: Shelley 1940-1966 **Shapes:** Richmond
2386	**Rose** and **Bluebell**. Entered in pattern book during or after 1959. Similar to 13799. Seconds ware. **Backstamp(s)**: Shelley 1940-1966 **Shapes:** Dainty, Ludlow, Stratford
2387	German **Green Iris**. Green and grey irises and foliage on a white ground. Gold edges. Green handle. Entered in pattern book during or after 1959. Seconds ware. **Backstamp(s)**: Shelley 1940-1966 **Shapes:** Dainty, Stratford

Green Iris 2387 Dainty shape cup and saucer. £70-80; $140-160

Green Iris 2387 Stratford shape cup and saucer. £60-70; $90-120

Pattern	Description & Shapes
2388	German **Chrysanthemum**. Entered in pattern book during or after 1959. Seconds ware. **Backstamp(s)**: Shelley 1940-1966 **Shapes:** Dainty
2389	Universal **Eglantine**. Entered in pattern book during or after 1959. Seconds ware. **Backstamp(s)**: Shelley 1940-1966 **Shapes:** Dainty, Ludlow, Stratford
2390	**Yutoi**. Entered in pattern book during or after 1959. Seconds ware. **Backstamp(s)**: Shelley 1940-1966 **Shapes:** Dainty, Ludlow
2391	Universal **Rose Floral** and **Bluebell**. Entered in pattern book during or after 1959. Seconds ware. **Backstamp(s)**: Shelley 1940-1966 **Shapes:** Dainty
2392	Cappers **Rose**. Entered in pattern book during or after 1959. Seconds ware. **Backstamp(s)**: Shelley 1940-1966 **Shapes:** Unknown
2393	Universal **Debonair**. Entered in pattern book during or after 1959. Seconds ware. **Backstamp(s)**: Shelley 1940-1966 **Shapes:** Gainsborough
2394	**Forget-me-nots**. Similar to 0442. Entered in pattern book during or after 1959. Seconds ware. **Backstamp(s)**: Shelley 1940-1966 **Shapes:** Bute, Dainty, Oleander, Regent
2395	Cappers **Fuchsia**. Cerise centre to fuchsia flowers with white outer petals and green leaves. White ground. Dark green edges. Entered in pattern book during or after 1959. Seconds ware. **Backstamp(s)**: Shelley 1940-1966 **Shapes:** Dainty, Ludlow, Richmond, Warwick

Fuchsia 2395 Queen Anne shape cup, saucer, and plate. £60-70; $90-120

Fuchsia 2395 Richmond shape cup, saucer, and plate. £40-50; $70-90

Pattern	Description & Shapes
2396	Cappers **Strawberry**. Red fruit, white flowers and green leaves. Pale green trim and handle. Entered in pattern book during or after 1959. Seconds ware. **Backstamp(s)**: Shelley 1940-1966 **Shapes:** Dainty, Henley, Ludlow, Regent

Strawberry 2396 Ludlow shape cup and saucer. £60-70; $80-120

Pattern	Description & Shapes
2397	Cappers **Strawberry**. Entered in pattern book during or after 1959. Seconds ware. **Backstamp(s)**: Shelley 1940-1966 **Shapes:** Dainty, Warwick
2398	Cappers **Fuchsia**. Entered in pattern book during or after 1959. Seconds ware. **Backstamp(s)**: Shelley 1940-1966 **Shapes:** Dainty, Ludlow, Warwick
2399	Commercial **Forget-me-nots**. Small blue flowers and green leaves. White ground. Gold edges. Blue handle. Entered in pattern book during or after 1959. Seconds ware. **Backstamp(s)**: Shelley 1940-1966 **Shapes:** Dainty, Ludlow, Warwick
2400	Cappers **Strawberry**. Entered in pattern book during or after 1959. Seconds ware. **Backstamp(s)**: Shelley 1940-1966 **Shapes:** Ludlow, Warwick
2401	Cappers **Fuchsia**. Entered in pattern book during or after 1959. Seconds ware. **Backstamp(s)**: Shelley 1940-1966 **Shapes:** Unknown
2402	**Forget-me-nots**. Entered in pattern book during or after 1959. Seconds ware. **Backstamp(s)**: Shelley 1940-1966 **Shapes:** Unknown
2403	Warwick Savage **Floral Spray**. Entered in pattern book during or after 1959. Seconds ware. **Backstamp(s)**: Shelley 1940-1966 **Shapes:** Dainty
2404	**Harmony**. Pink and green leaves inside and outside cup. Pale green trim and handle. Entered in pattern book during or after 1959. Seconds ware. **Backstamp(s)**: Shelley 1940-1945 **Shapes:** Regent
2405	**Lyric**. Entered in pattern book during or after 1959. Seconds ware. **Backstamp(s)**: Shelley 1940-1945 **Shapes:** Regent
2406	**Rhythm**. Entered in pattern book during or after 1960. Seconds ware. **Backstamp(s)**: Shelley 1940-1945 **Shapes:** Regent
2407	**Debonair**. Flowers include red and pink roses with blue convolvulus and foliage. Gold edges. Pale blue foot and handle. Entered in pattern book during or after 1960. Seconds ware. **Backstamp(s)**: Shelley 1940-1966 **Shapes:** Henley, Ludlow

Debonair 2407 Ludlow shape cup and saucer. £50-60; $80-100

Pattern Description & Shapes

2408 Ratauds **Orchid**. Entered in pattern book during or after 1960. Seconds ware.
Backstamp(s): Shelley 1940-1966
Shapes: Unknown

2409 Ratauds **Camellia**. Entered in pattern book during or after 1960. Seconds ware.
Backstamp(s): Shelley 1940-1966
Shapes: Unknown

2410 **Green Iris**. Entered in pattern book during or after 1960. Seconds ware.
Backstamp(s): Shelley 1940-1966
Shapes: Unknown

2411 Commercial **Cornflower**. Entered in pattern book during or after 1960. Seconds ware.
Backstamp(s): Shelley 1940-1945
Shapes: Dainty, Regent, Richmond, Stratford

2412 Cappers **Christmas Rose**. Entered in pattern book during or after 1960. Seconds ware.
Backstamp(s): Shelley 1940-1945
Shapes: Dainty, Stratford

2413 Commercial **Cornflower**. Entered in pattern book during or after 1960. Seconds ware.
Backstamp(s): Shelley 1940-1945
Shapes: Dainty, Stratford

2414 Commercial **Yellow Wild Rose**. Entered in pattern book during or after 1960. Seconds ware.
Backstamp(s): Shelley 1940-1945
Shapes: Dainty, Stratford

2415 Commercial **Pink Wild Rose**. Entered in pattern book during or after 1960. Seconds ware.
Backstamp(s): Shelley 1940-1945
Shapes: Dainty, Stratford

2416 Commercial **Yellow Wild Rose**. Entered in pattern book during or after 1960. Seconds ware.
Backstamp(s): Shelley 1940-1945
Shapes: Gainsborough

2417 Commercial **Pink Wild Rose**. Entered in pattern book during or after 1960. Seconds ware.
Backstamp(s): Shelley 1940-1945
Shapes: Gainsborough

2418 Cappers **Christmas Rose**. Entered in pattern book during or after 1960. Seconds ware.
Backstamp(s): Shelley 1940-1945
Shapes: Gainsborough

2419 Mulder and Zoon **Begonia**. Entered in pattern book during or after 1960. Seconds ware.
Backstamp(s): Shelley 1940-1945
Shapes: Ely, Henley, Ludlow, Stratford

2420 Mulder and Zoon **Clematis**. Entered in pattern book during or after 1960. Seconds ware.
Backstamp(s): Shelley 1940-1945
Shapes: Ely, Henley, Stratford

2421 Mulder and Zoon **Yellow Wild Rose**. White and yellow roses with green foliage on a white ground. Rosebud also inside cup. Green handle. Gold edges. Gold foot on Ely and Henley. Seconds ware.
Backstamp(s): Shelley 1940-1945
Shapes: Ely, Henley, Ludlow, Stratford

2422 Mulder and Zoon **Orchid**. Mauve and purple orchids with green foliage on a white ground. Pale pink handle. Gold edges. Entered in pattern book during or after 1960. Seconds ware.
Backstamp(s): Shelley 1940-1945
Shapes: Dainty, Ely, Henley, Ludlow, Stratford

Orchid 2422 Ludlow shape cup and saucer. £60-70; $80-120

2423 Mulder and Zoon **Chrysanthemum**. Entered in pattern book during or after 1960. Seconds ware.
Backstamp(s): Shelley 1940-1945
Shapes: Ely, Henley, Stratford

2424 Mulder and Zoon **Pink Moss Rose**. Entered in pattern book during or after 1960. Seconds ware.
Backstamp(s): Shelley 1940-1945
Shapes: Ely, Henley, Stratford

2425 Mulder and Zoon **Yellow Moss Rose**. Entered in pattern book during or after 1960. Seconds ware.
Backstamp(s): Shelley 1940-1945
Shapes: Ely, Henley, Stratford

2426 Mulder and Zoon **Yellow Moss Rose**. Entered in pattern book during or after 1960. Seconds ware.
Backstamp(s): Shelley 1940-1945
Shapes: Ely, Henley, Stratford

2427 Ratauds **Moss Rose**. Entered in pattern book during or after 1960. Seconds ware.
Backstamp(s): Shelley 1940-1945
Shapes: Ely, Henley, Stratford

2428 Ratauds **Wild Rose**. Entered in pattern book during or after 1960. Seconds ware.
Backstamp(s): Shelley 1940-1945
Shapes: Ely, Henley, Stratford

2429 Commercial **Moss Rose**. Pink roses with green and grey leaves on a white ground. Rose spray also inside cup. Gold edges. Pink handle. Entered in pattern book during or after 1960. Seconds ware.
Backstamp(s): Shelley 1940-1945
Shapes: Dainty, Ely, Henley, Stratford

2430 Commercial **Blue Rose**. Entered in pattern book during or after 1960. Seconds ware.
Backstamp(s): Shelley 1940-1945
Shapes: Ely, Henley, Stratford

2431 Mulder and Zoon **Begonia**. Entered in pattern book during or after 1960. Seconds ware.
Backstamp(s): Shelley 1940-1945
Shapes: Warwick

2432 Mulder and Zoon **Clematis**. Entered in pattern book during or after 1960. Seconds ware.
Backstamp(s): Shelley 1940-1945
Shapes: Warwick

2433 Mulder and Zoon **Yellow Wild Rose**. Entered in pattern book during or after 1960. Seconds ware.
Backstamp(s): Shelley 1940-1945
Shapes: Warwick

2434 Mulder and Zoon **Orchid**. Entered in pattern book during or after 1960. Seconds ware.
Backstamp(s): Shelley 1940-1945
Shapes: Warwick

2435 Mulder and Zoon **Chrysanthemum**. Entered in pattern book during or after 1960. Seconds ware.
Backstamp(s): Shelley 1940-1945
Shapes: Warwick

2436 Mulder and Zoon **Pink Moss Rose**. Entered in pattern book during or after 1960. Seconds ware.
Backstamp(s): Shelley 1940-1945
Shapes: Warwick

2437 Mulder and Zoon **Yellow Moss Rose**. Entered in pattern book during or after 1960. Seconds ware.
Backstamp(s): Shelley 1940-1945
Shapes: Warwick

2438 Mulder and Zoon **Dawn Rose**. Pink and yellow roses, black stems, and grey-green leaves on a white ground. Gold edges and handle. Entered in pattern book during or after 1960. Seconds ware.
Backstamp(s): Shelley 1940-1945
Shapes: Warwick

2439 Ratauds **Moss Rose**. Entered in pattern book during or after 1960. Seconds ware.
Backstamp(s): Shelley 1940-1945
Shapes: Warwick

2440 Ratauds **Wild Pink Rose**. Entered in pattern book during or after 1960. Seconds ware.
Backstamp(s): Shelley 1940-1945
Shapes: Warwick

2441 Commercial **Moss Rose**. Entered in pattern book during or after 1960. Seconds ware.
Backstamp(s): Shelley 1940-1945
Shapes: Warwick

2442 Commercial **Blue Rose**. Entered in pattern book during or after 1960. Seconds ware.
Backstamp(s): Shelley 1940-1945
Shapes: Warwick

2443 **Caprice**. Entered in pattern book during or after 1960. Seconds ware.
Backstamp(s): Shelley 1940-1945
Shapes: Unknown

2444 **Summer Bouquet**. Entered in pattern book during or after 1961. Seconds ware.
Backstamp(s): Shelley 1940-1945
Shapes: Unknown

2445 Baileys **Sweet Pea**. Entered in pattern book during or after 1961. Seconds ware.
Backstamp(s): Shelley 1940-1945
Shapes: Unknown

2446 Baileys **Peace Rose**. Entered in pattern book during or after 1961. Seconds ware.
Backstamp(s): Shelley 1940-1945
Shapes: Unknown

2447 Baileys **Gaytime**. Entered in pattern book during or after 1961. Seconds ware.
Backstamp(s): Shelley 1940-1945
Shapes: Unknown

2448 Baileys **Pink and Yellow Rose**. Entered in pattern book during or after 1961. Seconds ware.
Backstamp(s): Shelley 1940-1945
Shapes: Unknown

2449 Baileys **Azalea**. Entered in pattern book during or after 1961. Seconds ware.

Pattern Description & Shapes

Backstamp(s): Shelley 1940-1945
Shapes: Unknown

2450 Baileys **Orchid**. Orchids in shades of pink, dashes of yellow with green foliage on a white ground. Orchid and foliage also inside cup. Pink handle. Gold edges. Entered in pattern book during or after 1961. Seconds ware.
Backstamp(s): Shelley 1940-1945
Shapes: Dainty

Orchid 2450 Dainty shape cup and saucer. £70-80; $140-160

2451 Baileys **White Wild Rose**. Entered in pattern book during or after 1961. Seconds ware.
Backstamp(s): Shelley 1940-1945
Shapes: Dainty

2452 Baileys **Yellow Rose**. Entered in pattern book during or after 1961. Seconds ware.
Backstamp(s): Shelley 1940-1945
Shapes: Dainty

2453 Baileys **Pink Rhododendron**. Entered in pattern book during or after 1961. Seconds ware.
Backstamp(s): Shelley 1940-1945
Shapes: Dainty

2454 Baileys **White Rose**. Entered in pattern book during or after 1961. Seconds ware.
Backstamp(s): Shelley 1940-1945
Shapes: Dainty

2455 Hitching **September**. Entered in pattern book during or after 1961. Seconds ware.
Backstamp(s): Shelley 1940-1945
Shapes: Warwick

2456 Johnson Matthey **Evening Star**. Entered in pattern book during or after 1962. Seconds ware.
Backstamp(s): Shelley 1940-1945
Shapes: Dainty, Windsor

2457 Baileys **Pink and Grey Flower**. Entered in pattern book during or after 1962. Seconds ware.
Backstamp(s): Shelley 1940-1945
Shapes: Windsor

2458 Baileys **Wild Apple**. Pink and green apples and leaves on a white ground. Sprig also inside cup. Pink edges, foot and handle. Entered in pattern book during or after 1962. Seconds ware.
Backstamp(s): Shelley 1940-1945
Shapes: Richmond

Right:
Wild Apple 2458 Richmond shape cup, saucer, and plate. £40-50; $70-90. Creamer and sugar plate. £40-50; $70-90

2459 Baileys **Dogwood**. Entered in pattern book during or after 1962. Seconds ware.
Backstamp(s): Shelley 1940-1945
Shapes: Mocha, Ovide, Windsor

2460 Baileys **Bramble**. Entered in pattern book during or after 1962. Seconds ware.
Backstamp(s): Shelley 1940-1945
Shapes: Ludlow

2461 Baileys **Fuchsia**. Entered in pattern book during or after 1962. Seconds ware.
Backstamp(s): Shelley 1940-1945
Shapes: Ludlow

2462 Baileys **Pink and Grey Flower**. Entered in pattern book during or after 1962. Seconds ware.
Backstamp(s): Shelley 1940-1945
Shapes: Dainty

2463 Johnson Matthey **Evening Star**. Entered in pattern book during or after 1962. Seconds ware.
Backstamp(s): Shelley 1940-1945
Shapes: Dainty

2464 Baileys **Yellow Rose**. Entered in pattern book during or after 1962. Seconds ware.
Backstamp(s): Shelley 1940-1945
Shapes: Stratford

2465 Baileys **Contemporary Rose**. Entered in pattern book during or after 1962. Seconds ware.
Backstamp(s): Shelley 1940-1945
Shapes: Warwick

2466 Johnson Matthey **Geisha Girl**. Entered in pattern book during or after 1962. Seconds ware.
Backstamp(s): Shelley 1940-1945
Shapes: Stratford

2467 **Forget-me-nots**. Entered in pattern book during or after 1962. Seconds ware.
Backstamp(s): Shelley 1940-1945
Shapes: Stratford

2468 Johnson Matthey **Nosegay**. Entered in pattern book during or after 1962. Seconds ware.
Backstamp(s): Shelley 1940-1945
Shapes: Dainty

Evening Star 2456 Windsor shape cup and saucer. £40-50; $70-90

2469 Baileys **Wild Apple**. Pink and green apples and leaves on a white ground. Sprig also inside cup. Gold edges. Entered in pattern book during or after 1962. Seconds ware.
Backstamp(s): Shelley 1940-1945
Shapes: Ludlow

Wild Apple 2469 Ludlow shape cup and saucer. £50-60; $80-100

2470 Baileys **Bramble**. Green edges and handle. Entered in pattern book during or after 1962. Seconds ware.
Backstamp(s): Shelley 1940-1945
Shapes: Dainty

2471 Baileys **Fuchsia**. Entered in pattern book during or after 1962. Seconds ware.
Backstamp(s): Shelley 1940-1945
Shapes: Dainty

2472 Baileys **Yellow Rose**. Entered in pattern book during or after 1962. Seconds ware.
Backstamp(s): Shelley 1940-1945
Shapes: Dainty

2473 Johnson Matthey **Geisha Girl**. Entered in pattern book during or after 1962. Seconds ware.
Backstamp(s): Shelley 1940-1945
Shapes: Dainty

2474 Baileys **Wild Apple**. Entered in pattern book during or after 1962. Seconds ware.
Backstamp(s): Shelley 1940-1945
Shapes: Dainty

2475 Baileys **Love in a Mist** and **Grasses**. Entered in pattern book during or after 1963. Seconds ware.

Pattern	Description & Shapes
	Backstamp(s): Shelley 1940-1945 **Shapes:** Windsor
2476	**Enchantment**. Entered in pattern book during or after 1963. Seconds ware. **Backstamp(s)**: Shelley 1940-1945 **Shapes:** Windsor
2477	**Morning Glory**. Entered in pattern book during or after 1963. Seconds ware. **Backstamp(s)**: Shelley 1940-1945 **Shapes:** Dainty
2478	**Primrose**. Entered in pattern book during or after 1963. Seconds ware. **Backstamp(s)**: Shelley 1940-1945 **Shapes:** Dainty
2479	**Georgian** and **Bluebell**. Entered in pattern book during or after 1963. Seconds ware. **Backstamp(s)**: Shelley 1940-1945 **Shapes:** Dainty
2480	Butchers **Chrysanthemum**. Entered in pattern book during or after 1963. Seconds ware. **Backstamp(s)**: Shelley 1940-1945 **Shapes:** Dainty
2481	Small **Rose Spray**. Entered in pattern book during or after 1963. Seconds ware. **Backstamp(s)**: Shelley 1940-1945 **Shapes:** Dainty
2482	**Anemone**. Entered in pattern book during or after 1963. Seconds ware. **Backstamp(s)**: Shelley 1940-1945 **Shapes:** Dainty

Anemone 2482 Dainty shape cup and saucer. £50-60; $80-100

Anemone 2482 Ludlow shape cup and saucer. £50-60; $80-100

Pattern	Description & Shapes
2483	Johnson Matthey **Lime Grove**. Entered in pattern book during or after 1963. Seconds ware. **Backstamp(s)**: Shelley 1940-1945 **Shapes:** Windsor
2484	Johnson Matthey **Mayfair**. Entered in pattern book during or after 1963. Seconds ware. **Backstamp(s)**: Shelley 1940-1945 **Shapes:** Windsor
2485	Johnson Matthey **Kensington**. Entered in pattern book during or after 1963. Seconds ware. **Backstamp(s)**: Shelley 1940-1945 **Shapes:** Windsor
2486	**Georgian Chintz**. Entered in pattern book during or after 1963. Seconds ware. **Backstamp(s)**: Shelley 1940-1945 **Shapes:** Ripon
2487	Baileys **Rose Chintz**. Entered in pattern book during or after 1963. Seconds ware. **Backstamp(s)**: Shelley 1940-1945 **Shapes:** Ripon
2488	Baileys **Paisley Chintz**. Entered in pattern book during or after 1963. Seconds ware. **Backstamp(s)**: Shelley 1940-1945 **Shapes:** Ripon
2489	Rarauds **Pansy Chintz**. Entered in pattern book during or after 1963. Seconds ware. **Backstamp(s)**: Shelley 1940-1945 **Shapes:** Ripon
2490	Floral pattern inside cup. Plain colour outside cup and on saucer. Gold edges. White handle. Entered in pattern book during or after 1963. Seconds ware. /A **Golden Broom** and green /B **Dawn Rose** and lilac /C **Yellow Rose** and blue /D German **Floral** and pink. **Backstamp(s)**: Shelley 1940-1945 **Shapes:** Footed Dainty
2491	German **Chrysanthemum**. Large pink and peach chrysanthemum head surrounded by small pink and blue flowers with green foliage on a white ground. Flowers also inside cup. Entered in pattern book during or after 1963. Seconds ware. **Backstamp(s)**: Shelley 1940-1966 **Shapes:** Windsor
2492	**Rose Spray Chintz**. Entered in pattern book during or after 1963. Seconds ware. **Backstamp(s)**: Shelley 1940-1966 **Shapes:** Ripon
2493	Baileys **Yellow Rose**. Entered in pattern book during or after 1963. Seconds ware. **Backstamp(s)**: Shelley 1940-1945 **Shapes:** Scandinavian Coffee, Tall Dainty
2494	Rarauds **Moss Rose**. Entered in pattern book during or after 1963. Seconds ware. **Backstamp(s)**: Shelley 1940-1945 **Shapes:** Scandinavian Coffee, Tall Dainty
2495	Cappers **Strawberry**. Entered in pattern book during or after 1963. Seconds ware. **Backstamp(s)**: Shelley 1940-1966 **Shapes:** Scandinavian Coffee, Tall Dainty
2496	Johnson Matthey **Kensington**. Entered in pattern book during or after 1963. Seconds ware. **Backstamp(s)**: Shelley 1940-1945 **Shapes:** Dainty
2497	**Tulip and Rose Floral**. Entered in pattern book during or after 1963. Seconds ware. **Backstamp(s)**: Shelley 1940-1966 **Shapes:** Stratford
2498	Hitching **Halcyon**. Entered in pattern book during or after 1963. Seconds ware. **Backstamp(s)**: Shelley 1940-1966 **Shapes:** Stratford
2499	Johnson Matthey blue **Carolina**. Entered in pattern book during or after 1963. Seconds ware. **Backstamp(s)**: Shelley 1940-1945 **Shapes:** Ludlow
2500	**Country Garden**. Entered in pattern book during or after 1963. Seconds ware. **Backstamp(s)**: Shelley 1940-1945 **Shapes:** Ludlow
2501	Johnson Matthey **Mayfair**. Entered in pattern book during or after 1963. Seconds ware. **Backstamp(s)**: Shelley 1940-1945 **Shapes:** Warwick
2502	**Dubarry** and **Rosebud**. Floral Pink, white, yellow, and blue flowers with green foliage on a white ground. Gold edges and blue handle. Entered in pattern book during or after 1964. Seconds ware. **Backstamp(s)**: Shelley 1940-1966 **Shapes:** Dainty, Ludlow

Dubarry and **Rosebud** 2502 Dainty shape cup and saucer. £60-70; $80-100

Dubarry and **Rosebud** 2502 Ludlow shape cup and saucer. £60-70; $80-100

Pattern	Description & Shapes

2503 **Daffodil Spray**. Entered in pattern book during or after 1964. Seconds ware.
Backstamp(s): Shelley 1940-1966
Shapes: Warwick

2504 **Harebell** and **Grasses**. Mauve harebells and green foliage on a white ground. Gold edges. Green handle. Entered in pattern book during or after 1964. Seconds ware.
Backstamp(s): Shelley 1940-1966
Shapes: Warwick

Harebell and **Grasses** 2504 Warwick shape cup and saucer. £60-70; $80-100

2505 Maroon **Charm**. Small maroon flowers on a white ground. Flower spray inside cup. Gold edges. Pink handle. Entered in pattern book during or after 1964. Seconds ware.
Backstamp(s): Shelley 1940-1966
Shapes: Dainty, Ludlow

Maroon **Charm** 2505 Ludlow shape cup and saucer. £60-70; $80-100

2506 Blue **Charm**. Small blue flowers on a white ground. Flower spray inside cup. Gold edges. Pale blue handle. Entered in pattern book during or after 1964. Seconds ware.
Backstamp(s): Shelley 1940-1966
Shapes: Dainty, Ludlow

Blue **Charm** 2506 Ludlow shape cup and saucer. £60-70; $80-100

2507 **Golden Broom**. Entered in pattern book during or after 1964. Seconds ware.
Backstamp(s): Shelley 1940-1966
Shapes: Dainty

2508 **Rosalie**. Entered in pattern book during or after 1964. Seconds ware.
Backstamp(s): Shelley 1940-1966
Shapes: Dainty

2509 **Georgian** and **Rosebud**. Gold edges and blue handle. Entered in pattern book during or after 1964. Seconds ware.
Backstamp(s): Shelley 1940-1966
Shapes: Dainty

Georgian and **Rosebud** 2509 Dainty shape cup and saucer. £60-70; $80-100

2510 **Anemone**. Entered in pattern book during or after 1963. Entered in pattern book during or after 1964. Seconds ware.
Backstamp(s): Shelley 1940-1945
Shapes: Dainty

2511 **Scilla**. Blue flowers and green leaves. White ground. Gold edges. Blue handle. Entered in pattern book during or after 1964. Seconds ware.
Backstamp(s): Shelley 1940-1966
Shapes: Dainty

2512 **Roses, Pansies, and Forget-me-nots**. Same as 13424. Entered in pattern book during or after 1964. Seconds ware.
Backstamp(s): Shelley 1940-1966
Shapes: Windsor

2512 **Roses Spray**. Same as 13545. Entered in pattern book during or after 1964. Seconds ware.
Backstamp(s): Shelley 1940-1966
Shapes: Windsor

2513 **Blue Poppy**. Same as 14168. Entered in pattern book during or after 1964. Seconds ware.
Backstamp(s): Shelley 1940-1966
Shapes: Windsor

2515 **Blue Empress**. Bunches of flowers that include pink roses, blue, and yellow flowers, green and grey foliage. White ground. Gold trim. Similar to 14029. Entered in pattern book during or after 1964. Seconds ware.
Backstamp(s): Shelley 1940-1966
Shapes: Carlisle, Gainsborough

2516 Maroon **Empress**. Similar to 14024. Entered in pattern book during or after 1964. Seconds ware.
Backstamp(s): Shelley 1940-1966
Shapes: Unknown

2517 **Blue Rock**. Similar to 13591. Entered in pattern book during or after 1964. Seconds ware.
Backstamp(s): Shelley 1940-1966
Shapes: Carlisle

2518 **Maroon Viscount**. Entered in pattern book during or after 1964. Seconds ware.
Backstamp(s): Shelley 1940-1966
Shapes: Gainsborough

2519 **Rosalie**. Entered in pattern book during or after 1964. Seconds ware.
Backstamp(s): Shelley 1940-1966
Shapes: Bristol Coffee, Dainty, Ripon

2520 Ratauds **Yutoi**. Entered in pattern book during or after 1964. Seconds ware.
Backstamp(s): Shelley 1940-1966
Shapes: Unknown

2521 **Georgian**. Entered in pattern book during or after 1964. Seconds ware.
Backstamp(s): Shelley 1940-1966
Shapes: Windsor

2522 **Columbine**. Entered in pattern book during or after 1964. Seconds ware.
Backstamp(s): Shelley 1940-1966
Shapes: Richmond

2523 **Daphne** and **Debonair**. Entered in pattern book during or after 1964. Seconds ware.
Backstamp(s): Shelley 1940-1966
Shapes: Windsor

2524 **Daphne**. Entered in pattern book during or after 1964. Seconds ware.
Backstamp(s): Shelley 1940-1966
Shapes: Windsor

2525 **Georgian** and **Bluebell**. Entered in pattern book during or after 1964. Seconds ware.
Backstamp(s): Shelley 1940-1945
Shapes: Dainty

2526 Ratauds **Dark Red Rose**. Entered in pattern book during or after 1964. Seconds ware.
Backstamp(s): Shelley 1940-1966
Shapes: Dainty

2527 **Charm**. Entered in pattern book during or after 1964. Seconds ware.
/B Blue **Charm**
/M Maroon **Charm**.
Backstamp(s): Shelley 1940-1966
Shapes: Richmond

2528 **Primrose**. Same as 13430. Entered in pattern book during or after 1964. Seconds ware.
Backstamp(s): Shelley 1940-1966
Shapes: Carlisle

2529 **Campanula**. Similar to 13886. Entered in pattern book during or after 1964. Seconds ware.
Backstamp(s): Shelley 1940-1966
Shapes: Carlisle

2530 **Stocks**. Same as 13428. Entered in pattern book during or after 1964. Seconds ware.
Backstamp(s): Shelley 1940-1966
Shapes: Carlisle

2531 **Sycamore**. Entered in pattern book during or after 1965. Seconds ware.
Backstamp(s): Shelley 1940-1966
Shapes: Windsor

2532 **Spring Bouquet**. Entered in pattern book during or after 1965. Seconds ware.
Backstamp(s): Shelley 1940-1966
Shapes: Windsor

2533 Green **Empress**. Similar to 14028. Entered in pattern book during or after 1965. Seconds ware.
Backstamp(s): Shelley 1940-1966
Shapes: Gainsborough, Richmond

Pattern **Description & Shapes**

2534 Green **Dubarry** and **Georgian**. Entered in pattern book during or after 1965. Seconds ware.
Backstamp(s): Shelley 1940-1966
Shapes: Gainsborough

2535 Blue **Dubarry** and **Georgian**. Entered in pattern book during or after 1965. Seconds ware.
Backstamp(s): Shelley 1940-1966
Shapes: Gainsborough

2536 Maroon **Dubarry** and **Georgian**. Entered in pattern book during or after 1965. Seconds ware.
Backstamp(s): Shelley 1940-1966
Shapes: Gainsborough

2537 Blue **Dubarry**, and **Georgian** and forget-me-nots from **Rosebud**. Entered in pattern book during or after 1965. Seconds ware.
Backstamp(s): Shelley 1940-1966
Shapes: Gainsborough

2538 Green **Dubarry**, and **Georgian** and forget-me-nots from **Rosebud**. Entered in pattern book during or after 1965. Seconds ware.
Backstamp(s): Shelley 1940-1966
Shapes: Carlisle

2539 Baileys **Bramble**. Green edges and handle. Entered in pattern book during or after 1965. Seconds ware.
Backstamp(s): Shelley 1940-1966
Shapes: Carlisle

2540 Baileys **Fuchsia**. Entered in pattern book during or after 1965. Seconds ware.
Backstamp(s): Shelley 1940-1966
Shapes: Carlisle

2541 Johnson Matthey **English Garden**. Entered in pattern book during or after 1966. Seconds ware.
Backstamp(s): Shelley 1940-1966
Shapes: Carlisle

2542 Johnson Matthey **Purple Noon**. Entered in pattern book during or after 1966. Seconds ware.
Backstamp(s): Shelley 1940-1966
Shapes: Carlisle, Warwick

2543 Baileys **Acorn**. Entered in pattern book during or after 1965. Seconds ware.
Backstamp(s): Shelley 1940-1966
Shapes: Carlisle

2544 Baileys **Wild Apple**. Entered in pattern book during or after 1965. Seconds ware.
Backstamp(s): Shelley 1940-1966
Shapes: Carlisle

2545 Baileys **Bramble**. Gold edges. Entered in pattern book during or after 1965. Seconds ware.
Backstamp(s): Shelley 1940-1966
Shapes: Carlisle

2546 Blue **Charm**. Entered in pattern book during or after 1965. Seconds ware.
Backstamp(s): Shelley 1940-1966
Shapes: Avon

2547 German **Green Iris**. Green and grey irises and foliage on a white ground. Gold edges. Green handle. Entered in pattern book during or after 1965. Seconds ware.
Backstamp(s): Shelley 1940-1966
Shapes: Avon

2548 **June Morning**. Entered in pattern book during or after 1965. Seconds ware.
Backstamp(s): Shelley 1940-1966
Shapes: Avon

2549 **Golden Broom**. Entered in pattern book during or after 1965. Seconds ware.
Backstamp(s): Shelley 1940-1966
Shapes: Mocha

2550 **Blue Iris**. Entered in pattern book during or after 1965. Seconds ware.
Backstamp(s): Shelley 1940-1966
Shapes: Mocha

2551 **Wild Apple**. Entered in pattern book during or after 1965. Seconds ware.
Backstamp(s): Shelley 1940-1966
Shapes: Mocha

2552 **Hibiscus**. Entered in pattern book during or after 1965. Seconds ware.
Backstamp(s): Shelley 1940-1966
Shapes: Mocha

2553 Baileys **Blue Floral Spray**. Entered in pattern book during or after 1965. Seconds ware.
Backstamp(s): Shelley 1940-1966
Shapes: Ludlow, Warwick

2554 John Matthey **Barley Mow**. Entered in pattern book during or after 1965. Seconds ware.
Backstamp(s): Shelley 1940-1966
Shapes: Dainty

2555 **Thistle**. Similar to 13820. Entered in pattern book during or after 1965. Seconds ware.
Backstamp(s): Shelley 1940-1966
Shapes: Ludlow, Warwick

2556 **Violets**. Similar to 13821. Entered in pattern book during or after 1965. Seconds ware.
Backstamp(s): Shelley 1940-1966
Shapes: Ludlow, Warwick

2557 **Wild Flowers**. Similar to 13668. Entered in pattern book during or after 1965. Seconds ware.
Backstamp(s): Shelley 1940-1966
Shapes: Dainty, Warwick

2558 **Pansy**. Similar to 13823. Entered in pattern book during or after 1965. Seconds ware.
Backstamp(s): Shelley 1940-1966
Shapes: Dainty, Warwick

2559 Baileys **Rose**. Entered in pattern book during or after 1966. Seconds ware.
Backstamp(s): Shelley 1940-1966
Shapes: Dainty

2560 Baileys **Pink and White Wild Rose**. Entered in pattern book during or after 1966. Seconds ware.
Backstamp(s): Shelley 1940-1966
Shapes: Dainty

2561 Baileys **Yellow Floral Sprays**. Entered in pattern book during or after 1966. Seconds ware.
Backstamp(s): Shelley 1940-1966
Shapes: Dainty

2562 Johnson Matthey **Ambleside**. Entered in pattern book during or after 1966. Seconds ware.
Backstamp(s): Shelley 1940-1966
Shapes: Ripon

2563 Baileys **Black and Grey Floral Sprays**. Entered in pattern book during or after 1966. Seconds ware.
Backstamp(s): Shelley 1940-1966
Shapes: Unknown

2564 Baileys **Rose Sprays**. Entered in pattern book during or after 1966. Seconds ware.
Backstamp(s): Shelley 1940-1966
Shapes: Unknown

2565 Baileys **Dark Rose Sprays**. Entered in pattern book during or after 1966. Seconds ware.
Backstamp(s): Shelley 1940-1966
Shapes: Unknown

2566 **Blue Iris**. Entered in pattern book during or after 1966. Seconds ware.
Backstamp(s): Shelley 1940-1966
Shapes: Warwick

2567 **Hibiscus**. Entered in pattern book during or after 1966. Seconds ware.
Backstamp(s): Shelley 1940-1966
Shapes: Avon

2568 **Anemone**. Entered in pattern book during or after 1966. Seconds ware.
Backstamp(s): Shelley 1940-1966
Shapes: Avon

2569 **Wild Apple**. Entered in pattern book during or after 1966. Seconds ware.
Backstamp(s): Shelley 1940-1966
Shapes: Avon

2570 Pattern on cup. Plain colour on saucer. Entered in pattern book during or after 1966. Seconds ware.
Syringa with pale green
Rambler Rose with pink
Blue Iris with pale blue
Wild Anemone with salmon
Thistle with yellow
Debonair with lilac.
Backstamp(s): Shelley 1940-1966
Shapes: Dainty

2571 Pattern on cup. Plain colour on saucer. Entered in pattern book during or after 1966. Seconds ware.
Eglantine with pale green
Honeysuckle with pink
Rose and Red Daisy with pale blue
Wild Rose with salmon
Celandine with yellow
Country Garden with lilac.
Backstamp(s): Shelley 1940-1966
Shapes: Ludlow

3348 **Ivy Pattern**. Rustic handle. Entered in pattern book during or after 1882.
Backstamp(s): Wileman 1872-1890
Shapes: Unverified

3349-3365 **Japonica and Bird**. Entered in pattern book during or after 1882.
Backstamp(s): Wileman 1872-1890
Shapes: Unverified

3366-3369 **Blackberry**. Entered in pattern book during or after 1882.
Backstamp(s): Wileman 1872-1890
Shapes: Unverified

3370 **Japonica**. Entered in pattern book during or after 1882.
Backstamp(s): Wileman 1872-1890
Shapes: Unverified

3371 **Blackberry**. Entered in pattern book during or after 1882.
Backstamp(s): Wileman 1872-1890
Shapes: Unverified

3372 **Japonica**. Entered in pattern book during or after 1882.
Backstamp(s): Wileman 1872-1890
Shapes: Unverified

3373 **Japonica**. Rustic handle. Entered in pattern book during or after 1882.
Backstamp(s): Wileman 1872-1890
Shapes: Unverified

3374 **Blackberry**. Entered in pattern book during or after 1882.
Backstamp(s): Wileman 1872-1890
Shapes: Unverified

3375 **Dog Rose**. Entered in pattern book during or after 1882.
Backstamp(s): Wileman 1872-1890
Shapes: Unverified

3376 **Blackberry**. Entered in pattern book during or after 1882.
Backstamp(s): Wileman 1872-1890
Shapes: Unverified

3380 **Printed Wreaths**. Entered in pattern book during or after 1882.
Backstamp(s): Wileman 1872-1890
Shapes: Unverified

3381 **Floral Border**. Entered in pattern book during or after 1882.
Backstamp(s): Wileman 1872-1890
Shapes: Unverified

3382-3383 **Japonica and Bird**. Entered in pattern book during or after 1882.
Backstamp(s): Wileman 1872-1890
Shapes: Unverified

3384 **Bird**. Entered in pattern book during or after 1882.
Backstamp(s): Wileman 1872-1890
Shapes: Unverified

3384 **Rose**. Entered in pattern book during or after 1882.
Backstamp(s): Wileman 1872-1890
Shapes: Unverified

3391 **Blackberry**. Entered in pattern book during or after 1882.
Backstamp(s): Wileman 1872-1890

Pattern	Description & Shapes
	Shapes: Unverified
3392	**Verbena**. Entered in pattern book during or after 1882. **Backstamp(s)**: Wileman 1872-1890 **Shapes:** Unverified
3393	**Hawthorn and Passion Flower**. Entered in pattern book during or after 1882. **Backstamp(s)**: Wileman 1872-1890 **Shapes:** Unverified
3395	**Apple Blossom**. Entered in pattern book during or after 1882. **Backstamp(s)**: Wileman 1872-1890 **Shapes:** Unverified
3396	**Hawthorn Blossom**. Entered in pattern book during or after 1882. **Backstamp(s)**: Wileman 1872-1890 **Shapes:** Unverified
3397	**Sprigs and Berries**. Entered in pattern book during or after 1882. **Backstamp(s)**: Wileman 1872-1890 **Shapes:** Unverified
3398	**Sunflower**. Entered in pattern book during or after 1882. **Backstamp(s)**: Wileman 1872-1890 **Shapes:** Unverified
3399-3407	**Small Floral Borders**. Entered in pattern book during or after 1882. **Backstamp(s)**: Wileman 1872-1890 **Shapes:** Unverified
3409	**Moss Rose**. Entered in pattern book during or after 1882. **Backstamp(s)**: Wileman 1872-1890 **Shapes:** Unverified
3410	**Japonica and Bird**. Entered in pattern book during or after 1882. **Backstamp(s)**: Wileman 1872-1890 **Shapes:** Unverified
3411	**Sunflower**. Entered in pattern book during or after 1882. **Backstamp(s)**: Wileman 1872-1890 **Shapes:** Unverified
3412	**Floral Border**. Entered in pattern book during or after 1882. **Backstamp(s)**: Wileman 1872-1890 **Shapes:** Victoria
3413	**Wild Rose**. Entered in pattern book during or after 1882. **Backstamp(s)**: Wileman 1872-1890 **Shapes:** Unverified
3414	Fine black line. Entered in pattern book during or after 1882. **Backstamp(s)**: Wileman 1872-1890 **Shapes:** Unverified
3415	Fine red line. Entered in pattern book during or after 1882. **Backstamp(s)**: Wileman 1872-1890 **Shapes:** Unverified
3416	Red edge. Entered in pattern book during or after 1882. **Backstamp(s)**: Wileman 1872-1890 **Shapes:** Unverified
3417-3419	**Printed Palm**. Entered in pattern book during or after 1882. **Backstamp(s)**: Wileman 1872-1890 **Shapes:** Minton, Worcester
3420-3421	**Rose Wreaths and Forget-me-nots**. Entered in pattern book during or after 1882. **Backstamp(s)**: Wileman 1872-1890 **Shapes:** Unverified
3422	**Thistle**. Entered in pattern book during or after 1882. **Backstamp(s)**: Wileman 1872-1890 **Shapes:** Unverified
3423	**Sprig and Leaf**. Entered in pattern book during or after 1882. **Backstamp(s)**: Wileman 1872-1890 **Shapes:** Unverified
3424-3425	**Japan Blue and Red**. Entered in pattern book during or after 1882. **Backstamp(s)**: Wileman 1872-1890 **Shapes:** Unverified
3426	**Wild Rose**. Entered in pattern book during or after 1882. **Backstamp(s)**: Wileman 1872-1890 **Shapes:** Unverified
3428-3429	**Apple Blossom**. Entered in pattern book during or after 1882. **Backstamp(s)**: Wileman 1872-1890 **Shapes:** Unverified
3430-3431	**Blackthorn**. Entered in pattern book during or after 1882. **Backstamp(s)**: Wileman 1872-1890 **Shapes:** Unverified
3432	**Blackberry**. Entered in pattern book during or after 1882. **Backstamp(s)**: Wileman 1872-1890 **Shapes:** Unverified
3433	Children against country scene. Entered in pattern book during or after 1882. **Backstamp(s)**: Wileman 1872-1890 **Shapes:** Unverified
3434	**Japonica**. Enamelled. Entered in pattern book during or after 1882. **Backstamp(s)**: Wileman 1872-1890 **Shapes:** Unverified
3435	**Birds**. Enamelled. Entered in pattern book during or after 1882. **Backstamp(s)**: Wileman 1872-1890 **Shapes:** Unverified
3446-3447	**Birds**. Entered in pattern book during or after 1882. **Backstamp(s)**: Wileman 1872-1890 **Shapes:** Minton, Worcester
3448	**Wild Roses and Butterfly**. Entered in pattern book during or after 1882. **Backstamp(s)**: Wileman 1872-1890 **Shapes:** Victoria
3449-3453	**Border Pattern**. Entered in pattern book during or after 1882. **Backstamp(s)**: Wileman 1872-1890 **Shapes:** Unverified
3462-3463	**Ivy**. Entered in pattern book during or after 1882. **Backstamp(s)**: Wileman 1872-1890 **Shapes:** Unverified
3464	**Japan Blue and Red**. Black and red heart shaped pattern on white ground. Gold edges. Same as 3692, 7004, 7019, and 10169. Entered in pattern book during or after 1882. **Backstamp(s)**: Wileman 1872-1890 **Shapes:** Victoria, Victoria Breakfast
3466	Entered in pattern book during or after 1882. **Backstamp(s)**: Wileman 1872-1890 **Shapes:** Victoria
3467-3468	**Border Pattern**. Entered in pattern book during or after 1882. **Backstamp(s)**: Wileman 1872-1890 **Shapes:** Unverified
3469	**Japan**. Black and red heart shaped pattern on white ground. Gold edges. Entered in pattern book during or after 1882. **Backstamp(s)**: Wileman 1872-1890 **Shapes:** Victoria
3470	**Border Pattern**. Entered in pattern book during or after 1882. **Backstamp(s)**: Wileman 1872-1890 **Shapes:** Unverified
3475	**Blackthorn**. Entered in pattern book during or after 1882. **Backstamp(s)**: Wileman 1872-1890 **Shapes:** Unverified
3476	**Japan**. Entered in pattern book during or after 1882. **Backstamp(s)**: Wileman 1872-1890 **Shapes:** Square Queen Anne
3477-3478	**Ivy**. Same as 3462. Entered in pattern book during or after 1882. **Backstamp(s)**: Wileman 1872-1890 **Shapes:** Victoria
3479	**Ivy**. Entered in pattern book during or after 1882. **Backstamp(s)**: Wileman 1872-1890 **Shapes:** Victoria
3480	Entered in pattern book during or after 1882. **Backstamp(s)**: Wileman 1872-1890 **Shapes:** Victoria
3481	**Ivy**. Entered in pattern book during or after 1882. **Backstamp(s)**: Wileman 1872-1890 **Shapes:** Victoria
3482	**Wild Roses and Butterfly**. Entered in pattern book during or after 1882. **Backstamp(s)**: Wileman 1872-1890 **Shapes:** Victoria
3483-3487	**Gothic Border**. Entered in pattern book during or after 1882. **Backstamp(s)**: Wileman 1872-1890 **Shapes:** Victoria
3488	**Ivy**. Entered in pattern book during or after 1882. **Backstamp(s)**: Wileman 1872-1890 **Shapes:** Daisy, Square Queen Anne
3489	**Wild Roses and Butterfly**. Entered in pattern book during or after 1882. **Backstamp(s)**: Wileman 1872-1890 **Shapes:** Square Queen Anne
3490	**Blackberry**. Entered in pattern book during or after 1882. **Backstamp(s)**: Wileman 1872-1890 **Shapes:** Square Queen Anne
3491-3493	**Wild Roses and Butterfly**. Entered in pattern book during or after 1882. **Backstamp(s)**: Wileman 1872-1890 **Shapes:** Square Queen Anne
3494-3495	**Ivy**. Entered in pattern book during or after 1882. **Backstamp(s)**: Wileman 1872-1890 **Shapes:** Square Queen Anne
3496-3197	**Blackberry**. Entered in pattern book during or after 1882. **Backstamp(s)**: Wileman 1872-1890 **Shapes:** Square Queen Anne
3498	**Thistle Border**. Entered in pattern book during or after 1882. **Backstamp(s)**: Wileman 1872-1890 **Shapes:** Square Queen Anne
3499	**Ivy**. Entered in pattern book during or after 1882. **Backstamp(s)**: Wileman 1872-1890 **Shapes:** Square Queen Anne, Victoria
3500-3503	**Clematis**. Entered in pattern book during or after 1882. **Backstamp(s)**: Wileman 1872-1890 **Shapes:** Victoria
3504-3507	**Clematis**. Entered in pattern book during or after 1882. **Backstamp(s)**: Wileman 1872-1890 **Shapes:** Square Queen Anne
3508	**Border Print**. Entered in pattern book during or after 1882. **Backstamp(s)**: Wileman 1872-1890 **Shapes:** Victoria
3509	Maroon, gold, and fawn pattern. Gold lines on panel join. Panels of fawn crosshatched lines on ivory ground. Gold triangular panels of crosshatched lines and bells on small panels. Maroon ground. Gold edges and handle. Entered in pattern book during or after 1882-1886. **Backstamp(s)**: Wileman 1872-1890 **Shapes:** Square Queen Anne
3510	**Gothic Border**. Same as 3483. Entered in pattern book during or after 1882. **Backstamp(s)**: Wileman 1872-1890 **Shapes:** Victoria
3511-	

Pattern	Description & Shapes
3514	**Printed Season Views**. Entered in pattern book during or after 1882. **Backstamp(s)**: Wileman 1872-1890 **Shapes:** Square Queen Anne
3515-3522	**Border Print**. Entered in pattern book during or after 1882. **Backstamp(s)**: Wileman 1872-1890 **Shapes:** Victoria
3527	**Japonica Flowers**. Entered in pattern book during or after 1882. **Backstamp(s)**: Wileman 1872-1890 **Shapes:** Victoria
3528	**Border Design**. Entered in pattern book during or after 1882. **Backstamp(s)**: Wileman 1872-1890 **Shapes:** Victoria
3529-3531	**Orchids**. Entered in pattern book during or after 1882. **Backstamp(s)**: Wileman 1872-1890 **Shapes:** Square Queen Anne
3532	**Japan Oriental Flowers**. Orange flowers with black stems and leaves on a white ground. Entered in pattern book during or after 1882-1886. **Backstamp(s)**: Wileman 1872-1890 **Shapes:** Square Queen Anne, Victoria, Worcester
3533	Blue line border. Entered in pattern book during or after 1882. **Backstamp(s)**: Wileman 1872-1890 **Shapes:** Victoria
3534	**Blackberries**. Entered in pattern book during or after 1882. **Backstamp(s)**: Wileman 1872-1890 **Shapes:** Minton, Victoria
3535	**Wild Roses and Butterfly**. Entered in pattern book during or after 1882. **Backstamp(s)**: Wileman 1872-1890 **Shapes:** Minton, Victoria
3536-3537	**Apple Blossom**. Entered in pattern book during or after 1882. **Backstamp(s)**: Wileman 1872-1890 **Shapes:** Minton, Victoria
3538	**Blackberry**. Entered in pattern book during or after 1882. **Backstamp(s)**: Wileman 1872-1890 **Shapes:** Minton, Victoria
3539	**Wild Roses and Butterfly**. Entered in pattern book during or after 1882. **Backstamp(s)**: Wileman 1872-1890 **Shapes:** Minton, Victoria
3540	**Japonica Flowers**. Entered in pattern book during or after 1882. **Backstamp(s)**: Wileman 1872-1890 **Shapes:** Minton, Victoria
3541	**Printed Season Views**. Entered in pattern book during or after 1882. **Backstamp(s)**: Wileman 1872-1890 **Shapes:** Minton, Victoria
3542	**Ivy**. Entered in pattern book during or after 1882. **Backstamp(s)**: Wileman 1872-1890 **Shapes:** Square Queen Anne
3543	**Japan Oriental Rose**. Orange and black roses and leaves. White ground. Gold edges. **Backstamp(s)**: Wileman 1872-1890 **Shapes:** Square Queen Anne, Victoria, Worcester
3544	**Thistle**. Entered in pattern book during or after 1882-1886. **Backstamp(s)**: Wileman 1872-1890 **Shapes:** Square Queen Anne, Victoria, Worcester
3545	**Thistle**. Dark pink thistles on a pale pink ground. Gold edges. Entered in pattern book during or after 1882-1886. **Backstamp(s)**: Wileman 1872-1890 **Shapes:** Square Queen Anne, Victoria, Worcester
3546	**Thistle**. Entered in pattern book during or after 1882-1886. **Backstamp(s)**: Wileman 1872-1890 **Shapes:** Square Queen Anne, Victoria, Worcester
3547	**Thistle**. Entered in pattern book during or after 1882-1886. **Backstamp(s)**: Wileman 1872-1890 **Shapes:** Square Queen Anne, Victoria, Worcester
3548	**Gothic Border**. Same as 3483. Entered in pattern book during or after 1882-1886. **Backstamp(s)**: Wileman 1872-1890 **Shapes:** Victoria
3549-3553	**Roses**. Entered in pattern book during or after 1882-1886. **Backstamp(s)**: Wileman 1872-1890 **Shapes:** Square Queen Anne, Victoria
3554	**Japan Oriental Flowers**. Red flowers with black stems and leaves on a white ground. Entered in pattern book during or after 1882-1886. **Backstamp(s)**: Wileman 1872-1890 **Shapes:** Victoria
3555	**Japan Oriental Flowers**. Red flowers with blue stems and leaves on a white ground. Entered in pattern book during or after 1882-1886. **Backstamp(s)**: Wileman 1872-1890 **Shapes:** Victoria
3556	**Wild Rose**. Entered in pattern book during or after 1882. **Backstamp(s)**: Wileman 1872-1890 **Shapes:** Square Queen Anne
3558	**Thistle**. Entered in pattern book during or after 1882-1886. **Backstamp(s)**: Wileman 1872-1890 **Shapes:** Victoria
3559	**Apple Blossom**. Entered in pattern book during or after 1882-1886. **Backstamp(s)**: Wileman 1872-1890 **Shapes:** Square Queen Anne
3560	**Japan Flowers and Tree**. Entered in pattern book during or after 1882-1886. **Backstamp(s)**: Wileman 1872-1890 **Shapes:** Victoria
3561	**Japan Flowers and Tree**. Entered in pattern book during or after 1882-1886. **Backstamp(s)**: Wileman 1872-1890 **Shapes:** Square Queen Anne
3562	**Japan Flowers and Tree**. Entered in pattern book during or after 1882-1886. **Backstamp(s)**: Wileman 1872-1890 **Shapes:** Victoria
3563	**Japan Flowers and Tree**. Entered in pattern book during or after 1882-1886. **Backstamp(s)**: Wileman 1872-1890 **Shapes:** Square Queen Anne
3567	Turquoise and gold. Entered in pattern book during or after 1886. **Backstamp(s)**: Wileman 1872-1890 **Shapes:** Square Queen Anne
3568-3575	Entered in pattern book during or after 1886. **Backstamp(s)**: Wileman 1872-1890 **Shapes:** Square Queen Anne
3576-3578	**Blackberries**. Entered in pattern book during or after 1886. **Backstamp(s)**: Wileman 1872-1890 **Shapes:** Square Queen Anne, Victoria
3581	**Thistle Border**. Same as 6816. Entered in pattern book during or after 1886. **Backstamp(s)**: Wileman 1872-1890 **Shapes:** Victoria
3582	**Floral Border**. Same as 6815. Entered in pattern book during or after 1886. **Backstamp(s)**: Wileman 1872-1890 **Shapes:** Minton, Victoria
3588	**Sprigs**. Entered in pattern book during or after 1886. **Backstamp(s)**: Wileman 1872-1890 **Shapes:** Victoria
3589	**Thistle**. Entered in pattern book during or after 1886. **Backstamp(s)**: Wileman 1872-1890 **Shapes:** Victoria
3590-3592	**Bands**. Entered in pattern book during or after 1886. **Backstamp(s)**: Wileman 1872-1890 **Shapes:** Victoria
3593	Entered in pattern book during or after 1886. **Backstamp(s)**: Wileman 1872-1890 **Shapes:** Square Queen Anne, Victoria
3594-3596	**Bands**. Entered in pattern book during or after 1886. **Backstamp(s)**: Wileman 1872-1890 **Shapes:** Victoria
3598-3599	**Roses**. Entered in pattern book during or after 1886. **Backstamp(s)**: Wileman 1872-1890 **Shapes:** Victoria
3604-3605	**Bramble**. Entered in pattern book during or after 1886. **Backstamp(s)**: Wileman 1872-1890 **Shapes:** Victoria, Worcester
3607	**Bramble**. Entered in pattern book during or after 1886. **Backstamp(s)**: Wileman 1872-1890 **Shapes:** Victoria, Worcester
3608	**Thistle Border**. Entered in pattern book during or after 1886. **Backstamp(s)**: Wileman 1872-1890 **Shapes:** Square Queen Anne
3609	Same as 3480. Entered in pattern book during or after 1886. **Backstamp(s)**: Wileman 1872-1890 **Shapes:** Square Queen Anne, Victoria
3610-3613	**Clover**. Coloured print. Clover flowers, cloverleaves, daisy-like flowers, grass, and leaves. White ground. Gold edges. Entered in pattern book during or after 1886. **Backstamp(s)**: Wileman 1872-1890 **Shapes:** Square Queen Anne
3614-3616	**Scenery**. Entered in pattern book during or after 1886. **Backstamp(s)**: Wileman 1872-1890 **Shapes:** Square Queen Anne
3617	**Scenery**. Enamelled. Entered in pattern book during or after 1886. **Backstamp(s)**: Wileman 1872-1890 **Shapes:** Square Queen Anne
3619	**Wild Roses and Butterfly**. Entered in pattern book during or after 1886. **Backstamp(s)**: Wileman 1872-1890 **Shapes:** Square Queen Anne
3620	Same as 3229. Entered in pattern book during or after 1886. **Backstamp(s)**: Wileman 1872-1890 **Shapes:** Square Queen Anne, Victoria
3621	**Clover**. Terracotta print. Clover flowers, cloverleaves, daisy-like flowers, grass, and leaves. White ground. Gold edges. Entered in pattern book during or after 1886. **Backstamp(s)**: Wileman 1872-1890 **Shapes:** Square Queen Anne
3622	Same as 3313. Entered in pattern book during or after 1886. **Backstamp(s)**: Wileman 1872-1890 **Shapes:** Square Queen Anne, Victoria
3623-3624	**Roses**. Entered in pattern book during or after 1886. **Backstamp(s)**: Wileman 1872-1890 **Shapes:** Square Queen Anne, Victoria
3625-3628	**Clover**. Coloured print. Clover flowers, cloverleaves, daisy-like flowers, grass, and leaves. White ground. Gold edges. Entered in pattern book during or after 1886. **Backstamp(s)**: Wileman 1872-1890 **Shapes:** Victoria
3632	**Japan Black Border**. Same as 6471.

Pattern **Description & Shapes**

Entered in pattern book during or after 1886.
Backstamp(s): Wileman 1872-1890
Shapes: Jubilee Flute

3633 **Japan Oriental Flowers**. Orange flowers with black stems and leaves on a white ground. Entered in pattern book during or after 1882-1886.
Backstamp(s): Wileman 1872-1890
Shapes: Jubilee Flute

3634-3636 **Thistle**. Entered in pattern book during or after 1886.
Backstamp(s): Wileman 1872-1890
Shapes: Jubilee Flute

3637-3639 **Clover**. Coloured print. Clover flowers, cloverleaves, daisy-like flowers, grass, and leaves. White ground. Gold edges. Entered in pattern book during or after 1886.
Backstamp(s): Wileman 1872-1890
Shapes: Jubilee Flute

3640 **Wild Roses and Butterfly**. Entered in pattern book during or after 1886.
Backstamp(s): Wileman 1872-1890
Shapes: Jubilee Flute

3641 **Clover**. Enamelled. Clover flowers, cloverleaves, daisy-like flowers, grass, and leaves. White ground. Gold edges. Entered in pattern book during or after 1886.
Backstamp(s): Wileman 1872-1890
Shapes: Jubilee Flute

3642 **Japan Blue and Red**. Special Order. Entered in pattern book during or after 1887.
Backstamp(s): Wileman 1872-1890
Shapes: Turkish Cans

3644 **Japan Black Border**. Same as 3632. Entered in pattern book during or after 1887.
Backstamp(s): Wileman 1872-1890
Shapes: Square Queen Anne

3645-3647 **Bramble**. Entered in pattern book during or after 1887.
Backstamp(s): Wileman 1872-1890
Shapes: Jubilee Flute

3648-3650 **Shamrock**. Entered in pattern book during or after 1887.
Backstamp(s): Wileman 1872-1890
Shapes: Jubilee Flute

3651 **Clover**. Coloured print. Clover flowers, cloverleaves, daisy-like flowers, grass, and leaves. White ground. Gold edges. Entered in pattern book during or after 1887.
Backstamp(s): Wileman 1872-1890
Shapes: Jubilee Flute

3656-3658 **Thistle**. Entered in pattern book during or after 1887.
Backstamp(s): Wileman 1872-1890
Shapes: Victoria

3659-3660 **Shamrock**. Entered in pattern book during or after 1887.
Backstamp(s): Wileman 1872-1890
Shapes: Albert

3661 **Bramble**. Entered in pattern book during or after 1887.
Backstamp(s): Wileman 1872-1890
Shapes: Albert

3663 **Bramble**. Entered in pattern book during or after 1887.
Backstamp(s): Wileman 1872-1890
Shapes: Victoria

3664 **Shamrock**. Entered in pattern book during or after 1887.
Backstamp(s): Wileman 1872-1890
Shapes: Victoria

3665-3667 **Shamrock**. Entered in pattern book during or after 1887.
Backstamp(s): Wileman 1872-1890
Shapes: Square Queen Anne

3669-3671 **Shamrock**. Entered in pattern book during or after 1887.
Backstamp(s): Wileman 1872-1890
Shapes: Victoria

3672 **Shamrock**. Entered in pattern book during or after 1887.
Backstamp(s): Wileman 1872-1890
Shapes: Albert

3673 Same as 3176. Entered in pattern book during or after 1887.
Backstamp(s): Wileman 1872-1890
Shapes: Victoria

3674 Same as 3302. Entered in pattern book during or after 1887.
Backstamp(s): Wileman 1872-1890
Shapes: Minton

3675 **Japan Black**. Entered in pattern book during or after 1887.
Backstamp(s): Wileman 1872-1890
Shapes: Albert

3676-3678 **Bramble**. Entered in pattern book during or after 1887.
Backstamp(s): Wileman 1872-1890
Shapes: Square Queen Anne

3679-3681 **Clover**. Coloured print. Clover flowers, cloverleaves, daisy-like flowers, grass, and leaves. White ground. Gold edges. Entered in pattern book during or after 1887.
Backstamp(s): Wileman 1872-1890
Shapes: Square Queen Anne

3682-3684 **Shamrock**. Entered in pattern book during or after 1887.
Backstamp(s): Wileman 1872-1890
Shapes: Square Queen Anne

3685 **Shamrock**. Entered in pattern book during or after 1887.
Backstamp(s): Wileman 1872-1890
Shapes: Albert

3690 **Japan Blue**. Entered in pattern book during or after 1887.
Backstamp(s): Wileman 1872-1890
Shapes: Albert

3691 **Wild Roses and Butterfly**. Entered in pattern book during or after 1887.
Backstamp(s): Wileman 1872-1890
Shapes: Albert

3692 **Japan Blue and Red**. Black and red heart shaped pattern on white ground. Gold edges. Same as 3464, 7004, 7019, and 10169. Entered in pattern book during or after 1882.
Backstamp(s): Wileman 1872-1890
Shapes: Victoria

3694 **Clover**. Coloured print. Clover flowers, cloverleaves, daisy-like flowers, grass, and leaves. White ground. Gold edges. Entered in pattern book during or after 1887.
Backstamp(s): Wileman 1872-1890
Shapes: Albert

3695-3697 **Shamrock**. Entered in pattern book during or after 1887.
Backstamp(s): Wileman 1872-1890
Shapes: Square Fluted

3698-3700 **Thistle**. Entered in pattern book during or after 1887.
Backstamp(s): Wileman 1872-1890
Shapes: Square Fluted

3701-3703 **Bramble**. Entered in pattern book during or after 1887.
Backstamp(s): Wileman 1872-1890
Shapes: Square Fluted

3704-3706 **Clover**. Coloured print. Clover flowers, cloverleaves, daisy-like flowers, grass, and leaves. White ground. Gold edges. Entered in pattern book during or after 1887.
Backstamp(s): Wileman 1872-1890
Shapes: Square Fluted

3707 **Clover**. Enamelled. Clover flowers, cloverleaves, daisy-like flowers, grass, and leaves. White ground. Gold edges. Entered in pattern book during or after 1887.
Backstamp(s): Wileman 1872-1890
Shapes: Alexandra, Square Queen Anne

3708 **Wild Roses and Butterfly**. Entered in pattern book during or after 1887.
Backstamp(s): Wileman 1872-1890
Shapes: Alexandra, Square Queen Anne

3709-3710 **Roses**. Entered in pattern book during or after 1887.
Backstamp(s): Wileman 1872-1890
Shapes: Alexandra, Square Queen Anne

3711-3721 **Floral Sprigs**. Entered in pattern book during or after 1887.
Backstamp(s): Wileman 1872-1890
Shapes: Victoria

3722 **Cornflowers**. Coloured flowers on a white ground. Gilded edges and stroke on handle. Chequered diamond border inside rim of cup and centre of saucer. Entered in pattern book during or after 1887.
Backstamp(s): Wileman 1872-1890
Shapes: Alexandra

3723 **Cornflower**. Carmine Cornflowers on a white ground. Gilded edges and stroke on handle. Red and black diamond check border inside rim of cup and centre of saucer. Entered in pattern book during or after 1887.
Backstamp(s): Wileman 1872-1890
Shapes: Alexandra, Square Queen Anne

Cornflowers 3723 Alexandra shape cup, saucer, and plate. £60-70; $80-100

3724 **Cornflower**. Coloured flowers on a white ground. Gilded edges and stroke on handle. Chequered diamond border inside rim of cup and centre of saucer. Entered in pattern book during or after 1887.
Backstamp(s): Wileman 1872-1890
Shapes: Alexandra

3725 **Japan**. Red, black, and gold on a white ground
Backstamp(s): Wileman 1872-1890
Shapes: Alexandra

3727 **Shamrock**. Entered in pattern book during or after 1887.
Backstamp(s): Wileman 1872-1890
Shapes: Albert

3728-3729 **Floral**. Entered in pattern book during or after 1887.
Backstamp(s): Wileman 1872-1890
Shapes: Alexandra

3730 **Japan Black**. Red and yellow with brown stems and leaves. White ground. Gold

Pattern Description & Shapes

edges. Entered in pattern book during or after 1887.
Backstamp(s): Wileman 1872-1890
Shapes: Alexandra, Daisy, Lily, Square Queen Anne

3737 **Japan Blue and Red**. Entered in pattern book during or after 1887.
Backstamp(s): Wileman 1872-1890
Shapes: Alexandra

3738 **Clover**. Coloured print. Clover flowers, cloverleaves, daisy-like flowers, grass, and leaves. White ground. Gold edges. Entered in pattern book during or after 1887.
Backstamp(s): Wileman 1872-1890
Shapes: Alexandra

3739 **Clover**. Pink print. Clover flowers, cloverleaves, daisy-like flowers, grass, and leaves. White ground. Gold edges. Entered in pattern book during or after 1887.
Backstamp(s): Wileman 1872-1890
Shapes: Alexandra

3740 **Clover**. Coloured print. Clover flowers, cloverleaves, daisy-like flowers, grass, and leaves. White ground. Gold edges. Entered in pattern book during or after 1887.
Backstamp(s): Wileman 1872-1890
Shapes: Alexandra

3741 Entered in pattern book during or after 1887.
Backstamp(s): Wileman 1872-1890
Shapes: Victoria

3743 Entered in pattern book during or after 1887.
Backstamp(s): Wileman 1872-1890
Shapes: Paris

3744 **Dolly Varden**. Blue and white. Geometric sections of small flowers. Flower spray also inside cup. Gold edges. White handle. Entered in pattern book during or after 1887.
Backstamp(s): Wileman 1872-1890
Shapes: Alexandra

Dolly Varden 3744 Alexandra shape demitasse cup, saucer, and plate. £80-90; $150-180

3745 **Dolly Varden**. Pink and white. Geometric sections of small flowers. Flower spray also inside cup. Gold edges. White handle. Entered in pattern book during or after 1887.
Backstamp(s): Wileman 1872-1890
Shapes: Alexandra

3746 **Dolly Varden**. Brown and white. Geometric sections of small flowers. Flower spray also inside cup. Gold edges. White handle. Entered in pattern book during or after 1887.
Backstamp(s): Wileman 1872-1890
Shapes: Alexandra

3747-3749 **Dolly Varden**. Coloured and white. Geometric sections of small flowers. Flower spray also inside cup. Gold edges. White handle. Entered in pattern book during or after 1887.
Backstamp(s): Wileman 1872-1890
Shapes: Alexandra

3750 **Dolly Varden**. Pale turquoise and white. Geometric sections of small flowers. Flower spray also inside cup. Gold edges. White handle. Entered in pattern book during or after 1887.
Backstamp(s): Wileman 1872-1890
Shapes: Alexandra, Worcester

3753-3757 **Honeysuckle**. Entered in pattern book during or after 1887.
Backstamp(s): Wileman 1872-1890
Shapes: Alexandra

3758 **Honeysuckle**. Enamelled. Entered in pattern book during or after 1887.
Backstamp(s): Wileman 1872-1890
Shapes: Alexandra

3759 **Honeysuckle**. Enamelled. Entered in pattern book during or after 1887.
Backstamp(s): Wileman 1872-1890
Shapes: Square Queen Anne

3760-3761 **Honeysuckle**. Entered in pattern book during or after 1887.
Backstamp(s): Wileman 1872-1890
Shapes: Square Queen Anne

3764 **Honeysuckle**. Enamelled. Entered in pattern book during or after 1887.
Backstamp(s): Wileman 1872-1890
Shapes: Square Queen Anne

3765 **Clover**. Coloured print. Clover flowers, cloverleaves, daisy-like flowers, grass, and leaves. White ground. Gold edges. Entered in pattern book during or after 1887.
Backstamp(s): Wileman 1872-1890
Shapes: Alexandra

3766 **Japan Honeysuckle**. Red and black. Entered in pattern book during or after 1887.
Backstamp(s): Wileman 1872-1890
Shapes: Square Alexandra, Queen Anne

3767-3770 **Honeysuckle**. Entered in pattern book during or after 1887.
Backstamp(s): Wileman 1872-1890
Shapes: Albert

3771 **Honeysuckle**. Enamelled. Entered in pattern book during or after 1887.
Backstamp(s): Wileman 1872-1890
Shapes: Albert

3774 Gold. Entered in pattern book during or after 1886.
Backstamp(s): Wileman 1872-1890
Shapes: Square Queen Anne, Victoria

3775 **Japan**. Red, black, and gold on a white ground. Entered in pattern book during or after 1887.
Backstamp(s): Wileman 1872-1890
Shapes: Worcester

3778-3781 **Cornflower**. Coloured flowers on a white ground. Gilded edges and stroke on handle. Chequered diamond border inside rim of cup and centre of saucer. Entered in pattern book during or after 1887.
Backstamp(s): Wileman 1872-1890
Shapes: Albert

3782-3786 **Honeysuckle**. Entered in pattern book during or after 1887.
Backstamp(s): Wileman 1872-1890
Shapes: Victoria

3788 **Floral Sprig**. Entered in pattern book during or after 1887.
Backstamp(s): Wileman 1872-1890
Shapes: Minton

3789 **Cornflower**. Coloured flowers on a white ground. Gilded edges and stroke on handle. Chequered diamond border inside rim of cup and centre of saucer. Entered in pattern book during or after 1887.
Backstamp(s): Wileman 1872-1890
Shapes: Alexandra

3791-3794 **Sprigs**. Entered in pattern book during or after 1887.
Backstamp(s): Wileman 1872-1890
Shapes: Victoria

3795 **Jasmine**. Enamelled. Entered in pattern book during or after 1887.
Backstamp(s): Wileman 1872-1890
Shapes: Victoria

3796 **Dolly Varden**. Coloured and white. Geometric sections of small flowers. Flower spray also inside cup. Gold edges. White handle. Entered in pattern book during or after 1887.
Backstamp(s): Wileman 1872-1890
Shapes: Victoria, Worcester

3797-3799 **Oak Border**. Border with trailing oak leaves. White ground. Gold edges. Entered in pattern book during or after 1887.
Backstamp(s): Wileman 1872-1890
Shapes: Victoria, Worcester

3800 **Oak Border**. Terracotta border with trailing oak leaves. White ground. Gold edges. Entered in pattern book during or after 1887.
Backstamp(s): Wileman 1872-1890; Unmarked pieces have been found
Shapes: Victoria, Worcester

3801 **Oak Border**. Border with trailing oak leaves. White ground. Gold edges. Entered in pattern book during or after 1887.
Backstamp(s): Wileman 1872-1890
Shapes: Victoria, Worcester

3802-3805 **Bramble**. Entered in pattern book during or after 1887.
Backstamp(s): Wileman 1872-1890
Shapes: Victoria

3806-3809 **Thistle**. Entered in pattern book during or after 1887.
Backstamp(s): Wileman 1872-1890
Shapes: Victoria

3810-3813 **Shamrock**. Entered in pattern book during or after 1887.
Backstamp(s): Wileman 1872-1890
Shapes: Victoria

3814-3817 **Seasons**. Entered in pattern book during or after 1887.
Backstamp(s): Wileman 1872-1890
Shapes: Victoria

3818-3821 **Daisy and Butterfly**. Entered in pattern book during or after 1887.
Backstamp(s): Wileman 1872-1890
Shapes: Lily

3833 **Oak Border**. Border with trailing oak leaves. White ground. Gold edges. Entered in pattern book during or after 1887.
Backstamp(s): Wileman 1872-1890
Shapes: Victoria, Worcester

3834 **Japanese Rose**. Entered in pattern book during or after 1887.
Backstamp(s): Wileman 1872-1890
Shapes: Alexandra

3835 **Japanese Rose**. Entered in pattern book during or after 1887.
Backstamp(s): Wileman 1872-1890
Shapes: Lily

3836 **Japanese Rose**. Entered in pattern book during or after 1887.
Backstamp(s): Wileman 1872-1890
Shapes: Alexandra

3837 **Japanese Rose**. Entered in pattern book during or after 1887.
Backstamp(s): Wileman 1872-1890

Pattern Description & Shapes

Shapes: Lily

3838 **Japanese Rose**. Entered in pattern book during or after 1887.
Backstamp(s): Wileman 1872-1890
Shapes: Alexandra

3839 **Japanese Rose**. Entered in pattern book during or after 1887.
Backstamp(s): Wileman 1872-1890
Shapes: Lily

3840 **Japanese Rose**. Entered in pattern book during or after 1887.
Backstamp(s): Wileman 1872-1890
Shapes: Alexandra

3841 **Japanese Rose**. Entered in pattern book during or after 1887.
Backstamp(s): Wileman 1872-1890
Shapes: Lily

3842 **Gold and Silver Thorns**. Gold flowers and thorny stems on a pale ground. White inside cup. Gold edges and handle. Entered in pattern book during or after 1887.
Backstamp(s): Wileman 1872-1890
Shapes: Alexandra

3843 **Gold and Silver Thorns**. Gold flowers and thorny stems on a pale ground. White inside cup. Gold edges and handle. Entered in pattern book during or after 1887.
Backstamp(s): Wileman 1872-1890
Shapes: Lily

3844 **Gold and Silver Thorns**. Gold flowers and thorny stems on a pale pink ground. White inside cup. Gold edges and handle. Entered in pattern book during or after 1887.
Backstamp(s): Wileman 1872-1890
Shapes: Alexandra

3845 **Gold and Silver Thorns**. Gold flowers and thorny stems on a pale ground. White inside cup. Gold edges and handle. Entered in pattern book during or after 1887.
Backstamp(s): Wileman 1872-1890
Shapes: Lily

3846 **Gold and Silver Thorns**. Gold flowers and thorny stems on a pale ground. White inside cup. Gold edges and handle. Entered in pattern book during or after 1887.
Backstamp(s): Wileman 1872-1890
Shapes: Alexandra

3847 **Gold and Silver Thorns**. Gold flowers and thorny stems on a pale ground. White inside cup. Gold edges and handle. Entered in pattern book during or after 1887.
Backstamp(s): Wileman 1872-1890
Shapes: Lily

3848 **Gold and Silver Thorns**. Gold flowers and thorny stems on a pale ground. White inside cup. Gold edges and handle. Entered in pattern book during or after 1887.
Backstamp(s): Wileman 1872-1890
Shapes: Alexandra

3849 **Gold and Silver Thorns**. Gold flowers and thorny stems on a pale ground. White inside cup. Gold edges and handle. Entered in pattern book during or after 1887.
Backstamp(s): Wileman 1872-1890
Shapes: Lily

3850 **Gold and Silver Thorns**. Gold flowers and thorny stems on a pale ground. White inside cup. Gold edges and handle. Entered in pattern book during or after 1887.
Backstamp(s): Wileman 1872-1890
Shapes: Alexandra

3851 **Gold and Silver Thorns**. Gold flowers and thorny stems on a pale ground. White inside cup. Gold edges and handle. Entered in pattern book during or after 1887.
Backstamp(s): Wileman 1872-1890
Shapes: Lily

3852 **Japan**. Enamelled in black and red.
Backstamp(s): Wileman 1872-1890; Unmarked
Shapes: Lily

3853-3855 **Gold Border**. Entered in pattern book during or after 1887.
Backstamp(s): Wileman 1872-1890
Shapes: Worcester

3856 Same as 3480. Entered in pattern book during or after 1887.
Backstamp(s): Wileman 1872-1890
Shapes: Victoria

3857 **Floral Sprigs**. Same as 3713. Entered in pattern book during or after 1887.
Backstamp(s): Wileman 1872-1890
Shapes: Victoria

3858 Blue and pink edges. Entered in pattern book during or after 1887.
Backstamp(s): Wileman 1872-1890
Shapes: Minton

3859 **Bands**. Entered in pattern book during or after 1887.
Backstamp(s): Wileman 1872-1890
Shapes: Minton

3860 **Shamrock**. Entered in pattern book during or after 1887.
Backstamp(s): Wileman 1872-1890
Shapes: Worcester

3861-3867 **Panelled Prints**. Entered in pattern book during or after 1887.
Backstamp(s): Wileman 1872-1890
Shapes: Lily

3868 **Gold and Silver Thorns**. Same as 3847. Gold flowers and thorny stems on a pale ground. White inside cup. Gold edges and handle. Entered in pattern book during or after 1887.
Backstamp(s): Wileman 1872-1890
Shapes: Lily

3869 **Gold Border**. Same as 3853. Entered in pattern book during or after 1887.
Backstamp(s): Wileman 1872-1890
Shapes: Worcester

3870-3872 **Margarette**. Flowers and leaves. White ground. Gold edges. Entered in pattern book during or after 1888
Backstamp(s): Wileman Foley 1890-1910; Shelley Late Foley 1910-1916; unmarked pieces have been found
Shapes: Lily

3873 **Margarette**. Orange or pale turquoise flowers and leaves. White ground. Gold edges. Entered in pattern book during or after 1888
Backstamp(s): Wileman Foley 1890-1910; Shelley Late Foley 1910-1916; unmarked pieces have been found
Shapes: Lily

Margarette 3873 New York shape cup and saucer. £40-£50; $70-90

3874-3878 **Margarette**. Flowers and leaves. White ground. Gold edges. Entered in pattern book during or after 1888
Backstamp(s): Wileman Foley 1890-1910; Shelley Late Foley 1910-1916; unmarked pieces have been found
Shapes: Lily

3879 **Oak Border**. Turquoise border with trailing oak leaves. White ground. Gold edges. Entered in pattern book during or after 1887.
Backstamp(s): Wileman 1872-1890
Shapes: Victoria

Oak Border 3879 Victoria shape cup and saucer. £40-£50; $70-90

3880-3883 **Oak Border**. Turquoise border with trailing oak leaves. White ground. Gold edges. Entered in pattern book during or after 1887.
Backstamp(s): Wileman 1872-1890
Shapes: Victoria

3885 **Panelled Prints**. Entered in pattern book during or after 1887.
Backstamp(s): Wileman 1872-1890
Shapes: Lily

3886-3887 **Gold and Silver Thorns**. Same as 3847. Gold flowers and thorny stems on a pale ground. White inside cup. Gold edges and handle. Entered in pattern book during or after 1887/1888.
Backstamp(s): Wileman 1872-1890
Shapes: Alexandra

3888 Narrow border. Two gold lines below border. White ground. Gold edges. Entered in pattern book during or after 1887/1888.
Backstamp(s): Wileman Foley 1890-1910
Shapes: Victoria

3889 Narrow blue border. Two gold lines below border. White ground. Gold edges. Entered in pattern book during or after 1887/1888.
Backstamp(s): Wileman Foley 1890-1910
Shapes: Victoria

3890 Narrow border. Two gold lines below border. White ground. Gold edges. Entered in pattern book during or after 1887/1888.
Backstamp(s): Wileman Foley 1890-1910
Shapes: Victoria

3891 **Red Narrow Border**. Similar to 10399. Two gold lines below red border. White ground. Gold edges. Entered in pattern book during or after 1909 and was still in production in 1919 when numbers were transferred from the old to the new pattern books.
Backstamp(s):
Shapes: Victoria

Pattern	Description & Shapes
3892-3896	Narrow border. Two gold lines below border. White ground. Gold edges. Entered in pattern book during or after 1887/1888. **Backstamp(s)**: Wileman Foley 1890-1910 **Shapes:** Victoria
3897	**Gold Border**. Entered in pattern book during or after 1887/1888. **Backstamp(s)**: Wileman 1872-1890 **Shapes:** Worcester
3899	Special order. Entered in pattern book during or after 1887/1888. **Backstamp(s)**: Wileman 1872-1890 **Shapes:** Egg
3907	**Daisy Wreath**. Red and black. Entered in pattern book during or after 1889. **Backstamp(s)**: Wileman 1872-1890 **Shapes:** Lily
3914	**Floral Sprigs**. Entered in pattern book during or after 1889. **Backstamp(s)**: Wileman 1872-1890 **Shapes:** Victoria
3915	**Buttercups**. Enamelled. Entered in pattern book during or after 1889. **Backstamp(s)**: Wileman 1872-1890 **Shapes:** Alexandra
3923	**Gold Sprigs**. Entered in pattern book during or after 1889. **Backstamp(s)**: Wileman 1872-1890 **Shapes:** Minton
3927	Same as 3480. Entered in pattern book during or after 1889. **Backstamp(s)**: Wileman 1872-1890 **Shapes:** Alexandra
3928	**Floral Sprigs**. Entered in pattern book during or after 1889. **Backstamp(s)**: Wileman 1872-1890 **Shapes:** Alexandra
3929	Same as 3593. Entered in pattern book during or after 1889. **Backstamp(s)**: Wileman 1872-1890 **Shapes:** Alexandra
3930	**Floral Sprigs**. Entered in pattern book during or after 1889. **Backstamp(s)**: Wileman 1872-1890 **Shapes:** Alexandra
3931	**Japan Oriental Flowers**. Red flowers with black stems and leaves on a white ground. Entered in pattern book during or after 1889. **Backstamp(s)**: Wileman 1872-1890 **Shapes:** Lily
3932-3938	**Ornament Festooned**. Entered in pattern book during or after 1889. **Backstamp(s)**: Wileman 1872-1890 **Shapes:** Lily
3942	**Japan**. Same as 3725. Red, black, and gold on a white ground. Entered in pattern book during or after 1889. **Backstamp(s)**: Wileman 1872-1890 **Shapes:** Alexandra
3944-3949	**Wild Rose**. Entered in pattern book during or after 1889. **Backstamp(s)**: Wileman 1872-1890 **Shapes:** Alexandra
3950	**Wild Rose**. Entered in pattern book during or after 1889. **Backstamp(s)**: Wileman 1872-1890 **Shapes:** Worcester
3951-3952	**Wild Rose**. Entered in pattern book during or after 1889. **Backstamp(s)**: Wileman 1872-1890 **Shapes:** Alexandra
3953	**Chrysanthemum Sprigs**. Entered in pattern book during or after 1889. **Backstamp(s)**: Wileman 1872-1890 **Shapes:** Lily
3956-3959	**Chrysanthemum Sprigs**. Entered in pattern book during or after 1889. **Backstamp(s)**: Wileman 1872-1890 **Shapes:** Lily
3966	**Japan**. Red and black. Entered in pattern book during or after 1889. **Backstamp(s)**: Wileman 1872-1890 **Shapes:** Daisy
3967	**Ornament Festooned**. Same as 3934. Entered in pattern book during or after 1889. **Backstamp(s)**: Wileman 1872-1890 **Shapes:** Lily
3968-3970	**Sprigs**. Entered in pattern book during or after 1889. **Backstamp(s)**: Wileman 1872-1890 **Shapes:** Alexandra
3971	**Japan**. Same as 3852. Enamelled in black and red. Entered in pattern book during or after 1889. **Backstamp(s)**: Wileman 1872-1890; Unmarked **Shapes:** Lily
3973	**Chrysanthemum Sprays**. Entered in pattern book during or after 1889. **Backstamp(s)**: Wileman 1872-1890 **Shapes:** Lily
3974	**Flowers and Butterflies**. Entered in pattern book during or after 1889. **Backstamp(s)**: Wileman 1872-1890 **Shapes:** Lily
3975	**Flowers and Butterflies**. Entered in pattern book during or after 1889. **Backstamp(s)**: Wileman 1872-1890 **Shapes:** Albert
3980	**Aster Sprays**. Flowers on a white ground. Gold edges. Entered in pattern book during or after 1889. **Backstamp(s)**: Wileman Foley 1890-1910 **Shapes:** Victoria
3981	**Aster Sprays**. Gold flowers on a white ground. Gold edges. Entered in pattern book during or after 1889. **Backstamp(s)**: Wileman Foley 1890-1910 **Shapes:** Alexandra

Aster Sprays 3981 Alexandra shape cup, saucer, and plate. £30-50; $80-100

Pattern	Description & Shapes
3982	**Aster Sprays**. Entered in pattern book during or after 1889. **Backstamp(s)**: Wileman Foley 1890-1910 **Shapes:** Lily
3983	**Aster Sprays**. Entered in pattern book during or after 1889. **Backstamp(s)**: Wileman Foley 1890-1910 **Shapes:** Worcester
3984	**Aster Sprays**. Entered in pattern book during or after 1889. **Backstamp(s)**: Wileman Foley 1890-1910 **Shapes:** Minton Breakfast
3985	**Aster Sprays**. Entered in pattern book during or after 1889. **Backstamp(s)**: Wileman Foley 1890-1910 **Shapes:** Daisy
3989	**Floral Border**. Entered in pattern book during or after 1889. **Backstamp(s)**: Wileman Foley 1890-1910 **Shapes:** Alexandra
3990-3992	**Jasmine**. Entered in pattern book during or after 1889. **Backstamp(s)**: Wileman Foley 1890-1910 **Shapes:** Albert Coffee
3995	**Floral Edge**. Entered in pattern book during or after 1889. **Backstamp(s)**: Wileman Foley 1890-1910 **Shapes:** Albert Coffee
3996	**Floral Edge**. Entered in pattern book during or after 1889. **Backstamp(s)**: Wileman Foley 1890-1910 **Shapes:** Alexandra
3997-4003	**Jungle Sheet**. Entered in pattern book during or after 1889. **Backstamp(s)**: Wileman Foley 1890-1910 **Shapes:** Albert Coffee
4006	**Dolly Varden**. Same as 3744. Blue and white. Geometric sections of small flowers. Flower spray also inside cup. Gold edges. White handle. Entered in pattern book during or after 1887. **Backstamp(s)**: Wileman 1872-1890 **Shapes:** Alexandra
4007	**Bramble**. Entered in pattern book during or after 1889. **Backstamp(s)**: Wileman Foley 1890-1910 **Shapes:** Alexandra

Bramble chintz turquoise Alexandra shape cup, saucer, and plate. £70-£100; $150-180

Pattern	Description & Shapes
4008	**Bramble**. Entered in pattern book during or after 1889. **Backstamp(s)**: Wileman Foley 1890-1910 **Shapes:** Albert
4009	**Thistle**. Entered in pattern book during or after 1889. **Backstamp(s)**: Wileman Foley 1890-1910 **Shapes:** Alexandra
4010	**Thistle**. Entered in pattern book during or after 1889. **Backstamp(s)**: Wileman Foley 1890-1910 **Shapes:** Albert
4011	**Margarette**. Same as 3870. Flowers and leaves. White ground. Gold edges. Entered in pattern book during or after 1889.

Pattern | Description & Shapes

Backstamp(s): Wileman Foley 1890-1910; Shelley Late Foley 1910-1916; unmarked pieces have been found
Shapes: Lily

4012 **Oak Border**. Same as 3797. Border with trailing oak leaves. White ground. Gold edges. Entered in pattern book during or after 1889.
Backstamp(s): Wileman 1872-1890; Wileman Foley 1890-1910
Shapes: Victoria, Worcester

4017 **Chrysanthemum Sprigs**. Same as 3953. Entered in pattern book during or after 1889.
Backstamp(s): Wileman 1872-1890; Wileman Foley 1890-1910
Shapes: Lily

4023 **Japan Red**. Entered in pattern book during or after 1889.
Backstamp(s): Wileman 1872-1890; Wileman Foley 1890-1910
Shapes: Lily

4024 **Japan Red**. Entered in pattern book during or after 1889.
Backstamp(s): Wileman 1872-1890; Wileman Foley 1890-1910
Shapes: Alexandra

4026-4031 **Jungle Sheet**. Special order. Entered in pattern book during or after 1889.
Backstamp(s): Wileman Foley 1890-1910
Shapes: Daisy, Lily

4033 Entered in pattern book during or after 1889.
Backstamp(s): Wileman 1872-1890
Shapes: Minton Irish

4035 **Dolly Varden**. Same as 3744. Blue and white. Geometric sections of small flowers. Flower spray also inside cup. Gold edges. White handle. Entered in pattern book during or after 1889.
Backstamp(s): Wileman 1872-1890
Shapes: Alexandra

4036 Same as 3889. Narrow blue border. Two gold lines below border. White ground. Gold edges. Entered in pattern book during or after 1887/1888.
Backstamp(s): Wileman Foley 1890-1910
Shapes: Victoria

4037 **Border Design**. Special Order. Entered in pattern book during or after 1889.
Backstamp(s): Wileman 1872-1890; Wileman Foley 1890-1910
Shapes: Victoria

4041 **Clover**. Coloured print. Clover flowers, cloverleaves, daisy-like flowers, grass, and leaves. White ground. Gold edges. Entered in pattern book during or after 1889.
Backstamp(s): Wileman 1872-1890
Shapes: Lily

4043-4049 Plain colour outside cup, on saucer and plate. White inside cup. Gold edges and handle. Entered in pattern book during or after 1889.
Backstamp(s): Wileman 1872-1890; Wileman Foley 1890-1910
Shapes: Alexandra, Dainty, Daisy, Snowdrop

4050 Turquoise outside cup, on saucer, and plate. White inside cup. Gold edges and handle. Entered in pattern book during or after 1889.
Backstamp(s): Wileman 1872-1890; Wileman Foley 1890-1910; No backstamp, impressed registration mark only
Shapes: Alexandra, Dainty, Daisy, Snowdrop

4051-4058 Plain colour outside cup, on saucer, and plate. White inside cup. Gold edges and handle. Entered in pattern book during or after 1889.
Backstamp(s): Wileman 1872-1890; Wileman Foley 1890-1910
Shapes: Alexandra, Dainty, Daisy, Snowdrop

4061-4070 **Daisy Border Print**. Entered in pattern book during or after 1889.
Backstamp(s): Wileman 1872-1890; Wileman Foley 1890-1910
Shapes: Victoria

4071-4072 **Daisy Border Print**. Entered in pattern book during or after 1889. Seconds ware.
Backstamp(s): Wileman 1872-1890; Wileman Foley 1890-1910
Shapes: Bute

4073-4074 **Daisy Border Print**. Entered in pattern book during or after 1889. Seconds ware.
Backstamp(s): Wileman 1872-1890; Wileman Foley 1890-1910
Shapes: New York

4075-4084 **Daisy Border Print**. Entered in pattern book during or after 1889.
Backstamp(s): Wileman 1872-1890; Wileman Foley 1890-1910
Shapes: Lily

4086-4087 **Daisy Border Print**. Entered in pattern book during or after 1889.
Backstamp(s): Wileman 1872-1890; Wileman Foley 1890-1910
Shapes: Lily

4090 **Wild Rose**. Same as 3944. Entered in pattern book during or after 1889.
Backstamp(s): Wileman 1872-1890
Shapes: Alexandra

4091-4092 **Gold and Silver Thorns**. Same as 3846. Gold flowers and thorny stems on a pale ground. White inside cup. Gold edges and handle. Entered in pattern book during or after 1889.
Backstamp(s): Wileman 1872-1890
Shapes: Alexandra

4093 **Thistle**. Entered in pattern book during or after 1889.
Backstamp(s): Wileman 1872-1890
Shapes: Alexandra

4094 **Brambles**. Entered in pattern book during or after 1889.
Backstamp(s): Wileman 1872-1890
Shapes: Alexandra

4096 **Panelled Design**. Entered in pattern book during or after 1890.
Backstamp(s): Wileman Foley 1890-1910
Shapes: Alexandra

4097 **Dresden Flowers**. Entered in pattern book during or after 1890.
Backstamp(s): Wileman Foley 1890-1910
Shapes: Alexandra

Pattern number 4050 Alexandra shape cup, saucer, and plate. £70-£100; $130-155

4098 **Dresden Flowers**. Entered in pattern book during or after 1890.
Backstamp(s): Wileman Foley 1890-1910
Shapes: Lily

4100 **Gold Thorns**. Entered in pattern book during or after 1890.
Backstamp(s): Wileman Foley 1890-1910
Shapes: Daisy

4101-4102 **Gold and Silver Thorns**. Gold flowers and thorny stems on a pale ground. White inside cup. Gold edges and handle. Entered in pattern book during or after 1890.
Backstamp(s): Wileman 1872-1890
Shapes: Daisy

4104-4109 **Dresden Flowers**. Entered in pattern book during or after 1890.
Backstamp(s): Wileman Foley 1890-1910
Shapes: Alexandra

4116 **Spray and Butterfly**. Entered in pattern book during or after 1890.
Backstamp(s): Wileman Foley 1890-1910
Shapes: Victoria

4117 **Spray and Butterfly**. Entered in pattern book during or after 1890.
Backstamp(s): Wileman Foley 1890-1910
Shapes: Lily

4118 **Spray and Butterfly**. Entered in pattern book during or after 1890.
Backstamp(s): Wileman Foley 1890-1910
Shapes: Alexandra

4122 **Thistle**. Entered in pattern book during or after 1890. Seconds ware.
Backstamp(s): Wileman Foley 1890-1910
Shapes: Lily

4123 **Bramble**. Entered in pattern book during or after 1890. Seconds ware.
Backstamp(s): Wileman Foley 1890-1910
Shapes: Alexandra, Daisy

4124 **Clover**. Entered in pattern book during or after 1890. Seconds ware.
Backstamp(s): Wileman Foley 1890-1910
Shapes: Alexandra, Daisy

4125 **Thistle**. Entered in pattern book during or after 1890. Seconds ware.
Backstamp(s): Wileman Foley 1890-1910
Shapes: Alexandra, Daisy

4126 **Bramble**. Entered in pattern book during or after 1890. Seconds ware.
Backstamp(s): Wileman Foley 1890-1910
Shapes: Lily

4127 **Sunflower**. Entered in pattern book during or after 1890. Seconds ware.
Backstamp(s): Wileman Foley 1890-1910
Shapes: Lily

4128-4130 **Jungle Sheet**. Entered in pattern book during or after 1890. Seconds ware.
Backstamp(s): Wileman Foley 1890-1910
Shapes: Daisy

4131 **Jungle Sheet**. Entered in pattern book during or after 1890. Seconds ware.
Backstamp(s): Wileman Foley 1890-1910
Shapes: Fairy

4132 **Clover**. Entered in pattern book during or after 1890. Seconds ware.
Backstamp(s): Wileman Foley 1890-1910

Pattern Description & Shapes

Shapes: Fairy

4133 **Thistle**. Entered in pattern book during or after 1890. Seconds ware.
Backstamp(s): Wileman Foley 1890-1910
Shapes: Fairy

4134 **Daisy Border**. Entered in pattern book during or after 1890. Seconds ware.
Backstamp(s): Wileman Foley 1890-1910
Shapes: Fairy

4135 **Jungle Sheet**. Entered in pattern book during or after 1890. Seconds ware.
Backstamp(s): Wileman Foley 1890-1910
Shapes: Fairy

4136-4137 **Star Pattern**. Entered in pattern book during or after 1890. Seconds ware.
Backstamp(s): Wileman Foley 1890-1910
Shapes: Fairy

4138-4139 **Lace Border**. Entered in pattern book during or after 1890. Seconds ware.
Backstamp(s): Wileman Foley 1890-1910
Shapes: Lily

4140 **Dresden Flowers**. Entered in pattern book during or after 1890. Seconds ware.
Backstamp(s): Wileman Foley 1890-1910
Shapes: Daisy

4141 **Jungle Sheet**. Entered in pattern book during or after 1890. Seconds ware.
Backstamp(s): Wileman Foley 1890-1910
Shapes: Daisy

4142 **Clover**. Entered in pattern book during or after 1890. Seconds ware.
Backstamp(s): Wileman Foley 1890-1910
Shapes: Daisy

4143-4144 **Jungle Sheet**. Entered in pattern book during or after 1890. Seconds ware.
Backstamp(s): Wileman Foley 1890-1910
Shapes: Lily

4145 **Lace Border**. Entered in pattern book during or after 1890. Seconds ware.
Backstamp(s): Wileman Foley 1890-1910
Shapes: Lily

4146-4148 **Jungle Sheet**. Entered in pattern book during or after 1890. Seconds ware.
Backstamp(s): Wileman Foley 1890-1910
Shapes: Alexandra

4149 **Thistle**. Entered in pattern book during or after 1890. Seconds ware.
Backstamp(s): Wileman Foley 1890-1910
Shapes: Alexandra, Daisy

4150 **Jungle Sheet**. Entered in pattern book during or after 1890. Seconds ware.
Backstamp(s): Wileman Foley 1890-1910
Shapes: Lily

4151 **Basket of Flowers**. Flowers in shades of blue on a white ground. Sprig of flowers inside cup. Gold edges. Entered in pattern book during or after 1890.
Backstamp(s): Wileman Foley 1890-1910
Shapes: Alexandra

4152-4158 **Basket of Flowers**. Flowers on a white ground. Sprig of flowers inside cup. Gold edges. Entered in pattern book during or after 1890.
Backstamp(s): Wileman Foley 1890-1910
Shapes: Alexandra

4159 **Basket of Flowers**. Flowers in shades of brown and yellow on a white ground. Sprig of flowers inside cup. Gold edges. Entered in pattern book during or after 1890.
Backstamp(s): Wileman Foley 1890-1910
Shapes: Alexandra

4160-4162 **Basket of Flowers**. Flowers on a white ground. Sprig of flowers inside cup. Gold edges. Entered in pattern book during or after 1890.
Backstamp(s): Wileman Foley 1890-1910
Shapes: Alexandra

4164 **Dresden Flowers**. Entered in pattern book during or after 1890.
Backstamp(s): Wileman Foley 1890-1910
Shapes: Alexandra

4165-4167 **Border Sprays**. Entered in pattern book during or after 1890.
Backstamp(s): Wileman Foley 1890-1910
Shapes: Victoria

4168-4170 **Daisy Border**. Entered in pattern book during or after 1890.
Backstamp(s): Wileman Foley 1890-1910
Shapes: Albert Coffee

4171-4176 **Star Pattern**. Entered in pattern book during or after 1890.
Backstamp(s): Wileman Foley 1890-1910
Shapes: Fairy

4177 **Star Pattern**. Terracotta. Entered in pattern book during or after 1890.
Backstamp(s): Wileman Foley 1890-1910
Shapes: Fairy

4178-4182 **Star Pattern**. Entered in pattern book during or after 1890.
Backstamp(s): Wileman Foley 1890-1910
Shapes: Fairy

4184 Gold with beading. Entered in pattern book during or after 1890.
Backstamp(s): Wileman 1872-1890
Shapes: Shell

4185 White with stippled gold border on edge of saucer, rim of inside, and outside cup. Gold handle.
Backstamp(s): Wileman Foley 1890-1910
Shapes: Empire, Foley, Shell

Pattern number 4185 Shell shape cup and saucer. £30-50; $75-85

4191-4202 **Basket of Flowers**. Flowers on a white ground. Sprig of flowers inside cup. Gold edges. Entered in pattern book during or after 1890.
Backstamp(s): Wileman Foley 1890-1910
Shapes: Lily

4211-4222 **Dresden Flowers**. Entered in pattern book during or after 1891.
Backstamp(s): Wileman Foley 1890-1910
Shapes: Lily

4226-4230 **Border Pattern**. Entered in pattern book during or after 1891.
Backstamp(s): Wileman Foley 1890-1910
Shapes: Fairy

4231-4242 **Dresden Flowers**. Entered in pattern book during or after 1891.
Backstamp(s): Wileman Foley 1890-1910
Shapes: Fairy

4243 **Dresden Flowers**. Enamelled. Entered in pattern book during or after 1891.
Backstamp(s): Wileman Foley 1890-1910
Shapes: Fairy

4244 **Border Pattern**. Entered in pattern book during or after 1891.
Backstamp(s): Wileman Foley 1890-1910
Shapes: Fairy

4245 **Fern Border**. Ferns and border. Pattern also inside cup. White ground. Gold trim. Entered in pattern book during or after 1891.
Backstamp(s): Wileman Foley 1890-1910
Shapes: Victoria

4247 **Japan Oriental Flowers**. Same as 7005. Red flowers on a white ground. Gold edges. Entered in pattern book during or after 1891.
Backstamp(s): Wileman 1872-1890; Wileman Foley 1890-1910
Shapes: Turkish Coffee Can

4248 **Japan Oriental Flowers**. Red and black flowers on a white ground. Gold edges. Entered in pattern book during or after 1891.
Backstamp(s): Wileman 1872-1890; Wileman Foley 1890-1910
Shapes: Turkish Coffee Can

4249 **Dolly Varden**. Same as 3744. Coloured and white. Geometric sections of small flowers. Flower spray also inside cup. Gold edges. White handle. Entered in pattern book during or after 1891.
Backstamp(s): Wileman Foley 1890-1910
Shapes: Alexandra

4253 **Japan Oriental Flowers**. Gold, peach, and orange flowers on a white ground. Gold edges. Entered in pattern book during or after 1891.
Backstamp(s): Wileman Foley 1890-1910
Shapes: Fairy

Japan Oriental Flowers 4253 Fairy shape cup, saucer, and plate. £70-80; $140-160

Pattern	Description & Shapes
4254	**Dolly Varden**. Same as 3744. Geometric sections of small flowers. Flower spray also inside cup. Gold edges. White handle. Entered in pattern book during or after 1891. **Backstamp(s)**: Wileman Foley 1890-1910 **Shapes:** Alexandra
4255	**Japan Blue and Red**. Same as 7223. Entered in pattern book during or after 1891. **Backstamp(s)**: Wileman Foley 1890-1910 **Shapes:** Fairy
4256	**Bramble**. Entered in pattern book during or after 1891. **Backstamp(s)**: Wileman Foley 1890-1910 **Shapes:** Gladstone
4258	**Panelled Prints**. Same as 3862. Entered in pattern book during or after 1891. **Backstamp(s)**: Wileman Foley 1890-1910 **Shapes:** Lily
4260	**Gold Lines and Sprigs**. Entered in pattern book during or after 1891. **Backstamp(s)**: Wileman 1872-1890; Wileman Foley 1890-1910 **Shapes:** Victoria
4261	**Dolly Varden**. Same as 3744. Geometric sections of small flowers. Flower spray also inside cup. Gold edges. White handle. Entered in pattern book during or after 1891. **Backstamp(s)**: Wileman Foley 1890-1910 **Shapes:** Alexandra
4262	**Japan**. Same as 3852. Enamelled in black and red. Entered in pattern book during or after 1891. **Backstamp(s)**: Wileman Foley 1890-1910 **Shapes:** Fairy
4263	**Margarette**. Entered in pattern book during or after 1891. **Backstamp(s)**: Wileman Foley 1890-1910 **Shapes:** Lily
4264-4265	**Daisy Border**. Special order. Entered in pattern book during or after 1891. **Backstamp(s)**: Wileman Foley 1890-1910 **Shapes:** Lily
4268-4269	**Border Pattern**. Same as 4228. Entered in pattern book during or after 1891. **Backstamp(s)**: Wileman Foley 1890-1910 **Shapes:** Daisy
4271-4282	**Daisy Border**. Entered in pattern book during or after 1891. **Backstamp(s)**: Wileman Foley 1890-1910 **Shapes:** Fairy
4287	**Daisy Border**. Entered in pattern book during or after 1891. **Backstamp(s)**: Wileman Foley 1890-1910 **Shapes:** Albert Coffee
4288-4291	**Shell Pattern**. Special order. Entered in pattern book during or after 1891. **Backstamp(s)**: Wileman Foley 1890-1910 **Shapes:** Daisy
4292-4297	**Gothic Border**. Same as 3483. Entered in pattern book during or after 1891. **Backstamp(s)**: Wileman Foley 1890-1910 **Shapes:** Victoria
4300	**Convolvulus Print**. Entered in pattern book during or after 1891. **Backstamp(s)**: Wileman Foley 1890-1910 **Shapes:** Fairy
4301-4302	**Gold Chrysanthemum**. Entered in pattern book during or after 1891. **Backstamp(s)**: Wileman Foley 1890-1910 **Shapes:** Fairy
4303-4306	**Sprig Border**. Entered in pattern book during or after 1891. **Backstamp(s)**: Wileman Foley 1890-1910 **Shapes:** Fairy
4307	Same as 3889. Narrow blue border. Two gold lines below border. White ground. Gold edges. Entered in pattern book during or after 1891. **Backstamp(s)**: Wileman **Shapes:** Victoria
4308-4310	**Border Pattern**. Same as 4244. Entered in pattern book during or after 1891. **Backstamp(s)**: Wileman Foley 1890-1910 **Shapes:** Fairy
4311-4316	**Floral Display**. Flowers radiating from the centre of the saucer in a star formation. Shell lobes decorated with small flowers between points of star. Inside cup has flowers graduating from the rim of the cup to the base. Cascades of flowers on panels outside the cup. Entered in pattern book during or after 1891. **Backstamp(s)**: Wileman Foley 1890-1910 **Shapes:** Shell
4317	**Floral Display**. Terracotta flowers radiating from the centre of the saucer in a star formation. Shell lobes decorated with small flowers between points of star. Inside cup has flowers graduating from the rim of the cup to the base. Cascades of flowers on panels outside the cup. Entered in pattern book during or after 1891. **Backstamp(s)**: Wileman Foley 1890-1910 **Shapes:** Shell

Floral Display 4317 Shell shape cup, saucer, and plate; $70-100

Pattern	Description & Shapes
4318-4319	**Floral Display**. Flowers radiating from the centre of the saucer in a star formation. Shell lobes decorated with small flowers between points of star. Inside cup has flowers graduating from the rim of the cup to the base. Cascades of flowers on panels outside the cup. Entered in pattern book during or after 1891. **Backstamp(s)**: Wileman Foley 1890-1910 **Shapes:** Shell
4320	**Floral Display**. Turquoise Flowers radiating from the centre of the saucer in a star formation. Shell lobes decorated with small flowers between points of star. Inside cup has flowers graduating from the rim of the cup to the base. Cascades of flowers on panels outside the cup. White ground. Gold edges. Entered in pattern book during or after 1891. **Backstamp(s)**: Wileman Foley 1890-1910 **Shapes:** Shell
4321-4322	**Floral Display**. Flowers radiating from the centre of the saucer in a star formation. Shell lobes decorated with small flowers between points of star. Inside cup has flowers graduating from the rim of the cup to the base. Cascades of flowers on panels outside the cup. Entered in pattern book during or after 1891. **Backstamp(s)**: Wileman Foley 1890-1910 **Shapes:** Shell
4326	**Japan**. Same as 3852. Enamelled in black and red. Entered in pattern book during or after 1891. **Backstamp(s)**: Wileman Foley 1890-1910 **Shapes:** Fairy
4328	**Ivy Border**. Trailing ivy leaves. White ground. Gold trim. Entered in pattern book during or after 1891. **Backstamp(s)**: Wileman 1872-1890; Wileman Foley 1890-1910 **Shapes:** Stanley Coffee
4329	**Ivy Border**. Trailing ivy leaves. White ground. Gold trim. Entered in pattern book during or after 1891. **Backstamp(s)**: Wileman 1872-1890; Wileman Foley 1890-1910 **Shapes:** Bamboo Coffee
4330	**Border Pattern**. Same as 4230. Entered in pattern book during or Wileman Foley 1890-19101891. **Backstamp(s)**: Wileman Foley 1890-1910 **Shapes:** Fairy
4331-4336	**Ivy Border**. Trailing ivy leaves. White ground. Gold trim. Entered in pattern book during or after 1891. Wileman Foley 1890-1910 **Backstamp(s)**: Wileman Foley 1890-1910 Fairy
4337	**Ivy Border**. Trailing terracotta ivy leaves. White ground. Gold trim. Entered in pattern book during or after 1891. **Backstamp(s)**: Wileman Foley 1890-1910 **Shapes:** Fairy, Lily, Lily Breakfast
4338-4339	**Ivy Border**. Trailing ivy leaves. White ground. Gold trim. Entered in pattern book during or after 1891. **Backstamp(s)**: Wileman Foley 1890-1910 **Shapes:** Fairy
4340	**Ivy Border**. Turquoise trailing ivy leaves. White ground. Gold trim. Entered in pattern book during or after 1891. **Backstamp(s)**: Wileman Foley 1890-1910 **Shapes:** Fairy
4341-4345	**Ivy Border**. Trailing ivy leaves. White ground. Gold trim. Entered in pattern book during or after 1891. **Backstamp(s)**: Wileman Foley 1890-1910 **Shapes:** Fairy
4346	**Sunflower and Leaf Border**. Orange

Pattern Description & Shapes

and blue pattern on a white ground. Border inside cup. Gold edges. Entered in pattern book during or after 1891.
Backstamp(s): Wileman Foley 1890-1910
Shapes: Fairy

4348 **Sunflower and Leaf Border**. Orange and blue pattern on a white ground. Border inside cup. Gold edges. Entered in pattern book during or after 1891.
Backstamp(s): Wileman Foley 1890-1910
Shapes: Fairy

4349-4350 **Jungle Sheet**. Entered in pattern book during or after 1891.
Backstamp(s): Wileman Foley 1890-1910
Shapes: Fairy

4351-4352 **Jungle Sheet**. Entered in pattern book during or after 1891.
Backstamp(s): Wileman Foley 1890-1910
Shapes: Lily

4353 **Bramble**. Entered in pattern book during or after 1891.
Backstamp(s): Wileman
Shapes: Fairy

4354-4355 **Jungle Sheet**. Entered in pattern book during or after 1891.
Backstamp(s): Wileman Foley 1890-1910
Shapes: Lily

4356-4357 **Gold Sprigs**. Entered in pattern book during or after 1891.
Backstamp(s): Wileman Foley 1890-1910
Shapes: Alexandra

4358-4361 **Chain Border**. Entered in pattern book during or after 1891.
Backstamp(s): Wileman Foley 1890-1910
Shapes: Victoria Breakfast

4362-4363 **Jungle Sheet**. Entered in pattern book during or after 1891.
Backstamp(s): Wileman Foley 1890-1910
Shapes: Lily

4364 **Ivy**. Entered in pattern book during or after 1891.
Backstamp(s): Wileman Foley 1890-1910
Shapes: Daisy

4370-4377 **Border Pattern**. Entered in pattern book during or after 1891.
Backstamp(s): Wileman Foley 1890-1910
Shapes: Daisy, Fairy

4378-4379 **Gold Chrysanthemum**. Same as 4301. Entered in pattern book during or after 1891.
Backstamp(s): Wileman Foley 1890-1910
Shapes: Daisy, Fairy

4580 **Dresden Flowers**. Enamelled. Entered in pattern book during or after 1891.
Backstamp(s): Wileman Foley 1890-1910
Shapes: Alexandra

4582 **Stippled Colours**. White with stippled and shaded blue, beige, and turquoise border on edge of saucer, rim of inside and outside cup. Coloured handle. Entered in pattern book during or after 1892.
Backstamp(s): Wileman Foley 1890-1910
Shapes: Shell

4583-4590 **Stippled Colours**. White with stippled border on edge of saucer, rim of inside and outside cup. Coloured handle. Entered in pattern book during or after 1892.
Backstamp(s): Wileman Foley 1890-1910
Shapes: Shell

4589 **Stippled Colours**. White with dark turquoise border on edge of saucer, rim of inside and outside cup. Darker turquoise handle. Entered in pattern book during or after 1892.
Backstamp(s): Wileman Foley 1890-1910
Shapes: Shell

4583-4590 **Stippled Colours**. White with stippled border on edge of saucer, rim of inside and outside cup. Coloured handle. Entered in pattern book during or after 1892.
Backstamp(s): Wileman Foley 1890-1910
Shapes: Shell

4592-4598 **Inside Colours**. Entered in pattern book during or after 1892.
Backstamp(s): Wileman Foley 1890-1910
Shapes: Shell

4605-4610 **Inside Colours**. Entered in pattern book during or after 1892.
Backstamp(s): Wileman
Shapes: Alexandra, Fairy

4619 **Dresden Flowers**. Entered in pattern book during or after 1892.
Backstamp(s): Wileman Foley 1890-1910
Shapes: Fairy

4623 **Dresden Flowers**. Enamelled. Entered in pattern book during or after 1892.
Backstamp(s): Wileman Foley 1890-1910
Shapes: Daisy, Empire, Fairy

4625-4626 **Dresden Flowers**. Enamelled. Entered in pattern book during or after 1892.
Backstamp(s): Wileman Foley 1890-1910
Shapes: Fairy

4629 **Gold Edge**. Enamelled. Entered in pattern book during or after 1892.
Backstamp(s): Wileman Foley 1890-1910
Shapes: Alexandra

4630 **Chrysanthemum**. Entered in pattern book during or after 1892.
Backstamp(s): Wileman
Shapes: Daisy

4631-4642 **Jungle Sheet**. Entered in pattern book during or after 1892.
Backstamp(s): Wileman Foley 1890-1910
Shapes: Victoria

4646-4648 **Ivy Border**. Special order. Trailing ivy leaves. White ground. Gold edges. Entered in pattern book during or after 1892. Seconds ware.
Backstamp(s): Wileman Foley 1890-1910
Shapes: Lily

4649 **Ivy Border**. Special order. Mauve and purple trailing ivy leaves. White ground. Gold edges. Entered in pattern book during or after 1892. Seconds ware.
Backstamp(s): Wileman Foley 1890-1910
Shapes: Daisy, Lily

4650 **Ivy Border**. Special order. Trailing turquoise ivy leaves. White ground. Gold edges. Entered in pattern book during or after 1892. Seconds ware.
Backstamp(s): Wileman Foley 1890-1910
Shapes: Daisy, Lily

4651 **Ivy Border**. Special order. Trailing ivy leaves. White ground. Gold edges. Entered in pattern book during or after 1892. Seconds ware.
Backstamp(s): Wileman Foley 1890-1910
Shapes: Lily

4652 **Sunflower and Leaf Border**. Same as 4346. Orange and blue pattern on a white ground. Border inside cup. Gold edges. Entered in pattern book during or after 1891.
Backstamp(s): Wileman Foley 1890-1910
Shapes: Alexandra

4653 **Jungle Sheet**. Entered in pattern book during or after 1892.
Backstamp(s): Wileman
Shapes: Daisy

4657 **Margarette**. Same as 3875. Flowers and leaves. White ground. Gold edges. Entered in pattern book during or after 1892
Backstamp(s): Wileman Foley 1890-1910
Shapes: Lily

4658 **Outside Colour**. Entered in pattern book during or after 1892.
Backstamp(s): Wileman Foley 1890-1910
Shapes: Alexandra

4660 **Jungle Sheet**. Entered in pattern book during or after 1892.
Backstamp(s): Wileman Foley 1890-1910
Shapes: Fairy

4663-4668 **Outside Colour**. Entered in pattern book during or after 1892.
Backstamp(s): Wileman Foley 1890-1910
Shapes: Shell

4671-4682 **Sunflower Border**. Entered in pattern book during or after 1892.
Backstamp(s): Wileman Foley 1890-1910
Shapes: Victoria

4689 **Japan Blue**. Same as 3690. Entered in pattern book during or after 1892.
Backstamp(s): Wileman 1872-1890; Wileman Foley 1890-1910
Shapes: May

4691-4704 **Ivy Border**. Trailing ivy leaves. White ground. Gold edges. Entered in pattern book during or after 1893.
Backstamp(s): Wileman 1872-1890; Wileman Foley 1890-1910
Shapes: Fairy

4707-4709 **Jungle Sheet**. Entered in pattern book during or after 1893.
Backstamp(s): Wileman 1872-1890; Wileman Foley 1890-1910
Shapes: Daisy

4711-4716 **Kensington Print**. Coloured print, also inside cup. White ground. Gold edges. Entered in pattern book during or after 1893.
Backstamp(s): Wileman Foley 1890-1910
Shapes: Lily

4717 **Kensington Print**. Brown, terracotta, blue/turquoise, or pink print, also inside cup. White ground. Gold edges. Entered in pattern book during or after 1893.
Backstamp(s): Wileman Foley 1890-1910
Shapes: Lily

4718 **Kensington Print**. Purple print, also inside cup. White ground. Gold edges.

Entered in pattern book during or after 1893.
Backstamp(s): Wileman Foley 1890-1910
Shapes: Lily

Kensington Print 4718 Lily shape cup, saucer, and plate. £40-£50; $70-90

4719-4724 **Kensington Print**. Coloured print, also inside cup. White ground. Gold edges. Entered in pattern book during or after 1893.
Backstamp(s): Wileman Foley 1890-1910
Shapes: Lily

4726 **Kensington Print**. Coloured print, also inside cup. White ground. Gold edges. Entered in pattern book during or after 1893.
Backstamp(s): Wileman Foley 1890-1910
Shapes: Lily

4731-4736 **Wild Flowers**. Coloured flowers. White ground. Gold trim. Entered in pattern book during or after 1893.
Backstamp(s): Wileman Foley 1890-1910
Shapes: Victoria

4737 **Wild Flowers**. Terracotta coloured flowers. White ground. Gold trim. Entered in pattern book during or after 1893.
Backstamp(s): Wileman Foley 1890-1910
Shapes: Victoria

4738-4742 **Wild Flowers**. Coloured flowers. White ground. Gold trim. Entered in pattern book during or after 1893.
Backstamp(s): Wileman Foley 1890-1910
Shapes: Victoria

4751-4763 **Basket of Flowers**. Baskets of flowers and garlands. Pattern also inside cup. Gold edges. Entered in pattern book during or after 1893.
Backstamp(s): Wileman Foley 1890-1910
Shapes: Daisy

4770-4779 **Shaded Ground**. Entered in pattern book during or after 1893.
Backstamp(s): Wileman Foley 1890-1910
Shapes: Shell

4780 **Flower Print**. Enamelled. Entered in pattern book during or after 1893.
Backstamp(s): Wileman Foley 1890-1910
Shapes: Fairy

4781 **Flower Print**. Enamelled. Entered in pattern book during or after 1893.
Backstamp(s): Wileman Foley 1890-1910
Shapes: May

4782 **Flower Print**. Enamelled. Entered in pattern book during or after 1893.
Backstamp(s): Wileman Foley 1890-1910
Shapes: Fairy

4783-4784 **Flower Print**. Enamelled. Entered in pattern book during or after 1893.
Backstamp(s): Wileman Foley 1890-1910
Shapes: May

4785 **Daisy Print**. Entered in pattern book during or after 1893, but was apparently not sold.
Backstamp(s): Wileman Foley 1890-1910
Shapes: May

4791-4802 **Basket of Flowers**. Baskets of flowers and garlands. Pattern also inside cup. Gold edges. Entered in pattern book during or after 1893. Seconds ware.
Backstamp(s): Wileman Foley 1890-1910
Shapes: Fairy

4807-4810 **Shaded Colours**. Entered in pattern book during or after 1893.
Backstamp(s): Wileman Foley 1890-1910
Shapes: Daisy

4811-4822 **Ivy Border**. Entered in pattern book during or after 1893.
Backstamp(s): Wileman Foley 1890-1910
Shapes: Victoria

4827 **Shaded Colours**. Entered in pattern book during or after 1893.
Backstamp(s): Wileman Foley 1890-1910
Shapes: Daisy

4828 **Shaded Colours**. Entered in pattern book during or after 1893.
Backstamp(s): Wileman Foley 1890-1910
Shapes: Shell

4831-4843 **Ivy Border**. Entered in pattern book during or after 1893.
Backstamp(s): Wileman Foley 1890-1910
Shapes: May

4851-4862 **Jungle Sheet**. Entered in pattern book during or after 1893.
Backstamp(s): Wileman Foley 1890-1910
Shapes: May

4871-4882 **Ivy Border**. Entered in pattern book during or after 1893. Seconds ware.
Backstamp(s): Wileman Foley 1890-1910
Shapes: Fairy

4890 White with stippled and shaded border on edge of saucer, rim of inside and outside cup. Coloured handle. Entered in pattern book during or after 1893.
Backstamp(s): Wileman Foley 1890-1910
Shapes: Shell

4891-4898 **Star Border**. Entered in pattern book during or after 1893.
Backstamp(s): Wileman Foley 1890-1910
Shapes: Fairy

4899 **Star Border**. Fawn print. Pattern also inside cup. White ground. Gold edges. Entered in pattern book during or after 1893.
Backstamp(s): Wileman Foley 1890-1910
Shapes: Fairy

4900-4902 **Star Border**. Entered in pattern book during or after 1893.
Backstamp(s): Wileman Foley 1890-1910
Shapes: Fairy

4911-4916 **Ivy Pattern**. Entered in pattern book during or after 1893.
Backstamp(s): Wileman Foley 1890-1910
Shapes: Daisy, Empire

4917 **Ivy Pattern**. Trailing terracotta ivy leaves. White ground. Gold trim. Entered in pattern book during or after 1893.
Backstamp(s): Wileman Foley 1890-1910
Shapes: Daisy, Empire, Worcester

4918 **Ivy Border**. Trailing mauve ivy leaves. White ground. Gold trim. Entered in pattern book during or after 1893.
Backstamp(s): Wileman 1872-1890; Wileman Foley 1890-1910
Shapes: Daisy, Empire

4919-4927 **Ivy Pattern**. Entered in pattern book during or after 1893.
Backstamp(s): Wileman Foley 1890-1910
Shapes: Daisy, Empire

4931-4945 **Lace Border**. Entered in pattern book during or after 1893.
Backstamp(s): Wileman Foley 1890-1910
Shapes: May

4951-4962 **Lace Border**. Gold. Entered in pattern book during or after 1893.
Backstamp(s): Wileman Foley 1890-1910
Shapes: May

4971-4976 **Fern**. Ferns and border. Pattern also inside cup. White ground. Gold trim. Entered in pattern book during or after 1893.
Backstamp(s): Wileman Foley 1890-1910
Shapes: Empire

4977 **Fern**. Orange ferns and border. Pattern also inside cup. White ground. Gold trim. Entered in pattern book during or after 1893.
Backstamp(s): Wileman 1872-1890; Wileman Foley 1890-1910
Shapes: Empire

4978 **Fern**. Ferns and border. Pattern also inside cup. White ground. Gold trim. Entered in pattern book during or after 1893.
Backstamp(s): Wileman Foley 1890-1910
Shapes: Empire

Star Border 4899 Fairy shape cup and saucer. £40-£50; $70-90

Pattern	Description & Shapes
4979	**Fern**. Brown ferns and border. Pattern also inside cup. White ground. Gold trim. Entered in pattern book during or after 1893. **Backstamp(s)**: Wileman 1872-1890; Wileman Foley 1890-1910 **Shapes:** Empire
4980	**Fern**. Turquoise ferns and border. Pattern also inside cup. White ground. Gold trim. Entered in pattern book during or after 1893. **Backstamp(s)**: Wileman 1872-1890; Wileman Foley 1890-1910 **Shapes:** Empire
4982	**Fern**. Green ferns and border. Pattern also inside cup. White ground. Gold trim. Entered in pattern book during or after 1893. **Backstamp(s)**: Wileman Foley 1890-1910 **Shapes:** Empire
4983-4985	**Fern**. Ferns and border. Pattern also inside cup. White ground. Gold trim. Entered in pattern book during or after 1893. **Backstamp(s)**: Wileman Foley 1890-1910 **Shapes:** Empire
4991-5004	**Lace Border**. Entered in pattern book during or after 1893. **Backstamp(s)**: Wileman Foley 1890-1910 **Shapes:** Roman
5011-5012	**Buttercups**. Enamelled. Entered in pattern book during or after 1893. **Backstamp(s)**: Wileman Foley 1890-1910 **Shapes:** Fairy
5017-5018	**Buttercups**. Enamelled. Entered in pattern book during or after 1893. **Backstamp(s)**: Wileman Foley 1890-1910 **Shapes:** Fairy
5022-5023	**Kensington Pattern**. Coloured flowers. White ground. Gold edges. Entered in pattern book during or after 1893. **Backstamp(s)**: Wileman Foley 1890-1910 **Shapes:** Lily
5024	**Kensington Pattern**. Purple and fawn flowers. White ground. Gold edges. Entered in pattern book during or after 1893. **Backstamp(s)**: Wileman 1872-1890; Wileman Foley 1890-1910 **Shapes:** Lily
5025	**Kensington Print**. Pale blue or pink and fawn flowers. White ground. Gold edges. Entered in pattern book during or after 1893. **Backstamp(s)**: Wileman Foley 1890-1910 **Shapes:** Lily
5026	**Kensington Pattern**. Mauve and green flowers. White ground. Gold edges. Entered in pattern book during or after 1893. **Backstamp(s)**: Wileman 1872-1890; Wileman Foley 1890-1910 **Shapes:** Lily
5027-5030	**Kensington Pattern**. Coloured flowers. White ground. Gold edges. Entered in pattern book during or after 1893. **Backstamp(s)**: Wileman 1872-1890; Wileman Foley 1890-1910 **Shapes:** Lily
5032-5035	**Basket of Flowers**. Baskets of flowers and garlands. Pattern also inside cup. Gold edges. Entered in pattern book during or after 1893. **Backstamp(s)**: Wileman Foley 1890-1910 **Shapes:** Daisy
5042	**Ivy Print**. Trailing ivy leaves in two pale shades. Pattern also inside cup. White ground. Gold edges. Entered in pattern book during or after 1893. **Backstamp(s)**: Wileman Foley 1890-1910 **Shapes:** Empire
5043	**Ivy Print**. Trailing ivy leaves in pale green and fawn. Pattern also inside cup. White ground. Gold edges. Entered in pattern book during or after 1893. **Backstamp(s)**: Wileman Foley 1890-1910 **Shapes:** Empire
5044	**Ivy**. Trailing ivy leaves in pale mauve and fawn. Pattern also inside cup. White ground. Gold edges. Entered in pattern book during or after 1893. **Backstamp(s)**: Wileman Foley 1890-1910 **Shapes:** Empire
5045	**Ivy**. Trailing ivy leaves in pale blue or pink and fawn. Pattern also inside cup. White ground. Gold edges. Entered in pattern book during or after 1893. **Backstamp(s)**: Wileman Foley 1890-1910 **Shapes:** Empire
5052	**Ivy Print**. Trailing ivy leaves in autumnal shades. Pattern also inside cup. White ground. Gold edges. Entered in pattern book during or after 1893. **Backstamp(s)**: Wileman Foley 1890-1910 **Shapes:** Fairy
5053	**Lace Border**. Autumnal shades. Entered in pattern book during or after 1893. **Backstamp(s)**: Wileman Foley 1890-1910 **Shapes:** May
5054	**Star Border**. Autumnal shades. Entered in pattern book during or after 1893. **Backstamp(s)**: Wileman Foley 1890-1910 **Shapes:** Fairy
5055	**Ground Colour**. Shaded autumnal colours. Entered in pattern book during or after 1893. **Backstamp(s)**: Wileman Foley 1890-1910 **Shapes:** Shell
5058	**Ground Colour**. Entered in pattern book during or after 1893. **Backstamp(s)**: Wileman Foley 1890-1910 **Shapes:** Empire
5061	**Shaded Ground**. Entered in pattern book during or after 1893. **Backstamp(s)**: Wileman Foley 1890-1910 **Shapes:** Empire
5065-5066	**Daisy Spray**. Entered in pattern book during or after 1893. **Backstamp(s)**: Wileman Foley 1890-1910 **Shapes:** Empire
5067	**Ground Colour**. Shaded autumnal colours. Entered in pattern book during or after 1893. **Backstamp(s)**: Wileman Foley 1890-1910 **Shapes:** Empire
5068	**Ivy Print**. Entered in pattern book during or after 1893. **Backstamp(s)**: Wileman Foley 1890-1910 **Shapes:** Daisy, Empire, Fairy
5070	**Wreath Border**. Entered in pattern book during or after 1893. **Backstamp(s)**: Wileman Foley 1890-1910 **Shapes:** Empire
5071-5073	**Rococo Ornament**. Entered in pattern book during or after 1893. **Backstamp(s)**: Wileman Foley 1890-1910 **Shapes:** Fairy
5076	**Clover**. Enamelled. Clover flowers, cloverleaves, daisy-like flowers, grass, and leaves. White ground. Gold edges. Entered in pattern book during or after 1893. **Backstamp(s)**: Wileman Foley 1890-1910 **Shapes:** May
5077	**Poppies**. Enamelled. Entered in pattern book during or after 1893. **Backstamp(s)**: Wileman 1872-1890; Wileman Foley 1890-1910 **Shapes:** Fairy
5078-5079	**Roses**. Enamelled. Entered in pattern book during or after 1893. **Backstamp(s)**: Wileman 1872-1890; Wileman Foley 1890-1910 **Shapes:** Lily
5080-5081	**Poppies**. Enamelled. Entered in pattern book during or after 1893. **Backstamp(s)**: Wileman 1872-1890; Wileman Foley 1890-1910 **Shapes:** Fairy
5084-5085	**Roses**. Enamelled. Entered in pattern book during or after 1893. **Backstamp(s)**: Wileman 1872-1890 **Shapes:** Lily
5086	**Ivy Print**. Trailing ivy leaves in autumnal shades. Pattern also inside cup. White ground. Gold edges. Entered in pattern book during or after 1893. **Backstamp(s)**: Wileman Foley 1890-1910 **Shapes:** Daisy, Empire
5087-5090	**Ivy Print**. Shaded, trailing ivy leaves. Pattern also inside cup. White ground. Gold edges. Entered in pattern book during or after 1893. **Backstamp(s)**: Wileman Foley 1890-1910 **Shapes:** Fairy
5091-5096	**Ivy Print**. Trailing ivy leaves. Pattern also inside cup. White ground. Gold edges. Entered in pattern book during or after 1893. **Backstamp(s)**: Wileman Foley 1890-1910 **Shapes:** Lily

Kensington Print 5025 Lily shape seven-piece sandwich/cake set. £50-70; $90-120. Creamer. £20-30; $40-50

Pattern	Description & Shapes
5097	**Ivy Print**. Terracotta, trailing ivy leaves. Pattern also inside cup. White ground. Gold edges. Entered in pattern book during or after 1893. **Backstamp(s)**: Wileman Foley 1890-1910 **Shapes:** Lily

Ivy Print 5097 Lily shape cup, saucer, and plate. £40-£50; $70-90

5098-5106 **Ivy Print**. Trailing ivy leaves. Pattern also inside cup. White ground. Gold edges. Entered in pattern book during or after 1893.
Backstamp(s): Wileman Foley 1890-1910
Shapes: Lily

5111 **Poppies**. Enamelled. Entered in pattern book during or after 1893.
Backstamp(s): Wileman 1872-1890; Wileman Foley 1890-1910
Shapes: Daisy

5112-5116 **Sunflower**. Special order. Entered in pattern book during or after 1893. Seconds ware.
Backstamp(s): Wileman Foley 1890-1910
Shapes: Lily

5118 **Shaded Ground**. Entered in pattern book during or after 1893.
Backstamp(s): Wileman 1872-1890; Wileman Foley 1890-1910
Shapes: Daisy, Empire

5119-5123 **Shaded Ground**. Entered in pattern book during or after 1893.
Backstamp(s): Wileman 1872-1890; Wileman Foley 1890-1910
Shapes: Daisy

5126-5130 **Shaded Ground**. Entered in pattern book during or after 1893.
Backstamp(s): Wileman 1872-1890; Wileman Foley 1890-1910
Shapes: Empire

5135 **Fern Border**. Same as 4245. Ferns and border. Pattern also inside cup. White ground. Gold trim. Entered in pattern book during or after 1891.
Backstamp(s): Wileman Foley 1890-1910
Shapes: Victoria

5136 **Fern Border**. Same as 4245. Ferns and border. Pattern also inside cup. White ground. Gold trim. Entered in pattern book during or after 1891.
Backstamp(s): Wileman Foley 1890-1910
Shapes: Lily

5137 **Ivy Print**. Pink, blue, and beige shades. Entered in pattern book during or after 1893.
Backstamp(s): Wileman Foley 1890-1910
Shapes: Shell

5138 **Blackberries**. Pink, blue, and beige shades. Entered in pattern book during or after 1893.
Backstamp(s): Wileman Foley 1890-1910
Shapes: Daisy

5139 **Shaded Ground**. Entered in pattern book during or after 1893.
Backstamp(s): Wileman 1872-1890; Wileman Foley 1890-1910
Shapes: Empire

5140 **Sunflower and Leaf Border**. Same as 4346. Orange and blue pattern on a white ground. Border inside cup. Gold edges. Entered in pattern book during or after 1893.
Backstamp(s): Wileman Foley 1890-1910
Shapes: Fairy

5141-5143 Entered in pattern book during or after 1894.
Backstamp(s): Wileman Foley 1890-1910
Shapes: Empire

5151-5164 **Rococo Ornament**. Entered in pattern book during or after 1894.
Backstamp(s): Wileman Foley 1890-1910
Shapes: Empire

5171-5185 **Blackberries**. Entered in pattern book during or after 1894.
Backstamp(s): Wileman Foley 1890-1910
Shapes: Daisy

5191-5195 **Shaded Ground**. Entered in pattern book during or after 1893.
Backstamp(s): Wileman Foley 1890-1910 1872-1890
Shapes: Century, Daisy

5202 **Blackberries**. Entered in pattern book during or after 1894.
Backstamp(s): Wileman Foley 1890-1910
Shapes: Daisy

5203 **Blackberries**. Green and peach on a white ground. Pattern also around inside edge of cup. Gold edges. Entered in pattern book during or after 1894.
Backstamp(s): Wileman Foley 1890-1910
Shapes: Daisy

5204-5205 **Blackberries**. Entered in pattern book during or after 1894.
Backstamp(s): Wileman Foley 1890-1910
Shapes: Daisy

5211-5225 **Daises Print**. Entered in pattern book during or after 1894.
Backstamp(s): Wileman Foley 1890-1910
Shapes: Foley

5232 **Fern Border**. Same as 4245 and 5136. Ferns and border. Pattern also inside cup. White ground. Gold trim. Entered in pattern book during or after 1891.
Backstamp(s): Wileman Foley 1890-1910
Shapes: Lily

5233 Entered in pattern book during or after 1894.
Backstamp(s): Wileman Foley 1890-1910
Shapes: Empire

5234 **Diamond Design**. Entered in pattern book during or after 1894.
Backstamp(s): Wileman Foley 1890-1910
Shapes: Empire

5235 Same as 3480. Entered in pattern book during or after 1894.
Backstamp(s): Wileman Foley 1890-1910
Shapes: Victoria Breakfast

5238-5242 **Shaded Ground**. Entered in pattern book during or after 1894.
Backstamp(s): Wileman 1872-1890; Wileman Foley 1890-1910
Shapes: Foley

5243-5258 **Plain Ground**. Entered in pattern book during or after 1894.
Backstamp(s): Wileman 1872-1890; Wileman Foley 1890-1910
Shapes: Dainty, Daisy, Empire, Foley, Snowdrop

5262-6265 **Ivy Pattern**. Entered in pattern book during or after 1893.
Backstamp(s): Wileman 1872-1890; Wileman Foley 1890-1910
Shapes: Empire

5291-5300 **Plain Ground**. Entered in pattern book during or after 1894.
Backstamp(s): Wileman 1872-1890; Wileman Foley 1890-1910
Shapes: Alexandra, Daisy, Empire, Fairy

5303-5304 **Jungle Print**. Entered in pattern book during or after 1893. Seconds ware.
Backstamp(s): Wileman Foley 1890-1910
Shapes: Alexandra, Daisy

5308 **Chrysanthemum**. Enamelled. Entered in pattern book during or after 1894.
Backstamp(s): Wileman Foley 1890-1910
Shapes: Fairy, Lily

5309 **Poppies**. Enamelled. Entered in pattern book during or after 1894.
Backstamp(s): Wileman Foley 1890-1910
Shapes: Fairy, Lily

5310 **Poppies**. Same as 6848. Enamelled. Entered in pattern book during or after 1894.
Backstamp(s): Wileman Foley 1890-1910
Shapes: Lily

5311 **Poppies**. Enamelled. Entered in pattern book during or after 1894.
Backstamp(s): Wileman Foley 1890-1910
Shapes: Fairy

5312-5315 **Ivy Print**. Entered in pattern book during or after 1894.
Backstamp(s): Wileman Foley 1890-1910
Shapes: Fairy

5322 **Rococo Design**. Gold print. Entered in pattern book during or after 1894.
Backstamp(s): Wileman Foley 1890-1910
Shapes: Daisy, Empire

5323-5338 **Plain Ground**. Entered in pattern book during or after 1894.
Backstamp(s): Wileman Foley 1890-1910
Shapes: Alexandra, Daisy, Empire, Foley

5351-5365 **Plain Colours**. Entered in pattern book during or after 1894.
Backstamp(s): Wileman Foley 1890-1910
Shapes: Shell

5372-5380 **Stippled Colours**. Same as 4582. White with stippled border on edge of saucer, rim of inside, and outside cup. Coloured handle. Entered in pattern book during or after 1892.
Backstamp(s): Wileman Foley 1890-

1910
Shapes: Foley

5388 **Daisy Print**. Enamelled. Entered in pattern book during or after 1894.
Backstamp(s): Wileman Foley 1890-1910
Shapes: Lily

5389 **Chrysanthemum**. Enamelled. Entered in pattern book during or after 1894.
Backstamp(s): Wileman Foley 1890-1910
Shapes: Lily

5390 **Poppies**. Enamelled. Entered in pattern book during or after 1894.
Backstamp(s): Wileman Foley 1890-1910
Shapes: Lily

5391 **Roses**. Enamelled. Entered in pattern book during or after 1894.
Backstamp(s): Wileman Foley 1890-1910
Shapes: Lily

5392 **Clover**. Enamelled. Entered in pattern book during or after 1894.
Backstamp(s): Wileman Foley 1890-1910
Shapes: Lily

5393 **Berries**. Enamelled. Entered in pattern book during or after 1894.
Backstamp(s): Wileman Foley 1890-1910
Shapes: Lily

5396 Narrow border. Two gold lines below border. White ground. Gold edges. Entered in pattern book during or after 1894.
Backstamp(s): Wileman Foley 1890-1910
Shapes: Egg

5398 **Ivy Print**. Entered in pattern book during or after 1895.
Backstamp(s): Wileman Foley 1890-1910
Shapes: Worcester

5402-5405 **Shaded Ground**. Entered in pattern book during or after 1895.
Backstamp(s): Wileman Foley 1890-1910
Shapes: Daisy

5412 **Ivy Pattern**. Entered in pattern book during or after 1895.
Backstamp(s): Wileman Foley 1890-1910
Shapes: Egg, York

5413-5415 **Ivy Pattern**. Entered in pattern book during or after 1895.
Backstamp(s): Wileman Foley 1890-1910
Shapes: Egg

5422-5424 **Garland of Roses**. Entered in pattern book during or after 1895.
Backstamp(s): Wileman Foley 1890-1910
Shapes: Foley

5429-5430 Entered in pattern book during or after 1895.
Backstamp(s): Wileman Foley 1890-1910
Shapes: Empire, Foley

5431 **Japan Derby**. Orange and gold flowers with black leaves. Black sections on large panels with gold, crosshatched, foliage print. White ground. Gold edges. Entered in pattern book during or after 1895.
Backstamp(s): Wileman Foley 1890-1910; Unmarked pieces have been found
Shapes: Daisy

5432 Special order. Green pattern on white ground. Entered in pattern book during or after 1895.
Backstamp(s): Wileman Foley 1890-1910
Shapes: Empire, Foley

5433 **Shaded Ground**. Entered in pattern book during or after 1895.
Backstamp(s): Wileman Foley 1890-1910
Shapes: Foley

5449 Entered in pattern book during or after 1895.
Backstamp(s): Wileman Foley 1890-1910
Shapes: Empire

5451-5464 **Floral Spray with Scroll**. Entered in pattern book during or after 1895.
Backstamp(s): Wileman Foley 1890-1910
Shapes: Egg, York

5472-5475 **Floral Spray with Scroll**. Entered in pattern book during or after 1895.
Backstamp(s): Wileman Foley 1890-1910
Shapes: York

5483 **Daisies**. Entered in pattern book during or after 1895.
Backstamp(s): Wileman Foley 1890-1910
Shapes: Foley

5486-5493 **Shaded Ground**. Entered in pattern book during or after 1895.
Backstamp(s): Wileman Foley 1890-1910
Shapes: Foley

5506-5514 **Shaded Ground**. Entered in pattern book during or after 1895.
Backstamp(s): Wileman Foley 1890-1910
Shapes: Foley

5604-5610 **Ivy Print**. Shaded, trailing ivy leaves. Pattern also inside cup. White ground. Gold edges. Entered in pattern book during or after 1895.
Backstamp(s): Wileman Foley 1890-1910
Shapes: Daisy, Empire

5615-5621 **Shaded Ground**. For export only to the U.S.A. Entered in pattern book during or after 1895.
Backstamp(s): Wileman Foley 1890-1910
Shapes: York

5622-5625 **Trailing Violets Print**. Coloured print. Trailing daisies and violets. Print also inside cup. White ground. Gold edges. Entered in pattern book during or after 1895.
Backstamp(s): Wileman Foley 1890-1910
Shapes: Century

5631-5645 **Trailing Violets Print**. Coloured print. Trailing daisies and violets. Print also inside cup. White ground. Gold edges. Entered in pattern book during or after 1895.
Backstamp(s): Wileman Foley 1890-1910
Shapes: Century

5651-5657 **Trailing Violets Print**. Coloured print. Trailing daisies and violets. Print also inside cup. White ground. Gold edges. Entered in pattern book during or after 1895.
Backstamp(s): Wileman Foley 1890-1910
Shapes: Century

5658 **Trailing Violets Print**. Mauve print. Trailing daisies and violets. Print also inside cup. White ground. Gold edges. Entered in pattern book during or after 1895.
Backstamp(s): Wileman Foley 1890-1910
Shapes: Century

Trailing Violets Print 5658 Century shape cup, saucer, and plate. £40-£50; $70-90

5659-5663 **Trailing Violets Print**. Coloured print. Trailing daisies and violets. Print also inside cup. White ground. Gold edges. Entered in pattern book during or after 1895.
Backstamp(s): Wileman Foley 1890-1910
Shapes: Century

5666 **Trailing Violets Print**. Coloured print. Trailing daisies and violets. Print also inside cup. White ground. Gold edges. Entered in pattern book during or after 1895.
Backstamp(s): Wileman Foley 1890-1910
Shapes: Century

5671-5685 **Daisy Border Pattern**. Entered in pattern book during or after 1895.
Backstamp(s): Wileman Foley 1890-1910
Shapes: Dainty Coffee

5692 **Trailing Violets Print**. Enamelled, coloured print. Trailing daisies and violets. Print also inside cup. White ground. Gold edges. Entered in pattern book during or after 1895.
Backstamp(s): Wileman Foley 1890-1910
Shapes: Century

5693 **Roses and Forget-me-nots Border**. Entered in pattern book during or after 1896.
Backstamp(s): Wileman Foley 1890-1910
Shapes: York

5695 **Ivy Print**. Entered in pattern book during or after 1896.
Backstamp(s): Wileman Foley 1890-1910
Shapes: York

5696 **Ivy Print**. Entered in pattern book during or after 1896.
Backstamp(s): Wileman Foley 1890-1910
Shapes: Century

5697-5699 **Panelled Gold Border Decoration**. Entered in pattern book during or after 1896.
Backstamp(s): Wileman Foley 1890-1910
Shapes: Daisy, Empire

5700 **Chrysanthemum**. Enamelled. Entered in pattern book during or after 1896.
Backstamp(s): Wileman Foley 1890-1910
Shapes: Century

Pattern	Description & Shapes
5701	**Chrysanthemum**. Enamelled. Entered in pattern book during or after 1896. **Backstamp(s)**: Wileman Foley 1890-1910 **Shapes:** Empire
5702-5705	**Ivy Pattern**. Entered in pattern book during or after 1896. **Backstamp(s)**: Wileman Foley 1890-1910 **Shapes:** Century
5710	**Holland Pattern**. Entered in pattern book during or after 1896. **Backstamp(s)**: Wileman Foley 1890-1910 **Shapes:** Egg, York
5711-5712	**Keswick Pattern**. Entered in pattern book during or after 1896. **Backstamp(s)**: Wileman Foley 1890-1910 **Shapes:** York
5713	**Panelled Gold Border Decoration**. Entered in pattern book during or after 1896. **Backstamp(s)**: Wileman Foley 1890-1910 **Shapes:** Daisy, Empire
5714	**Panelled Gold Border Decoration**. Entered in pattern book during or after 1896. **Backstamp(s)**: Wileman Foley 1890-1910 **Shapes:** Daisy
5715	**Violet Print**. Blue, purple, and yellow violets with green and brown foliage. Spray also inside cup. Gold edges. Entered in pattern book during or after 1896. **Backstamp(s)**: Wileman Foley 1890-1910 **Shapes:** Daisy
5716-5720	**Shaded Ground**. For export only to the U.S.A. Entered in pattern book during or after 1896. **Backstamp(s)**: Wileman Foley 1890-1910 **Shapes:** York
5721	**Gold Scroll and Leaf Design**. Entered in pattern book during or after 1896. **Backstamp(s)**: Wileman Foley 1890-1910 **Shapes:** Snowdrop
5722	**Daisy Clusters Print**. Entered in pattern book during or after 1896. **Backstamp(s)**: Wileman Foley 1890-1910 **Shapes:** Snowdrop
5723	**Daisy Clusters Print**. Entered in pattern book during or after 1896. **Backstamp(s)**: Wileman Foley 1890-1910 **Shapes:** Empire
5725-5728	**Rococo Design**. Gold print. Entered in pattern book during or after 1896. **Backstamp(s)**: Wileman Foley 1890-1910 **Shapes:** Empire
5729	**Dresden Print**. Same as 6874. Entered in pattern book during or after 1896. **Backstamp(s)**: Wileman Foley 1890-1910 **Shapes:** Century
5730-5735	**Plain Ground**. Entered in pattern book during or after 1896. **Backstamp(s)**: Wileman Foley 1890-1910 **Shapes:** Daisy
5743	**Shaded Ground**. Entered in pattern book during or after 1896. **Backstamp(s)**: Wileman Foley 1890-1910 **Shapes:** York
5746-5748	**Diamond Design**. Entered in pattern book during or after 1896. **Backstamp(s)**: Wileman Foley 1890-1910 **Shapes:** Empire
5749-5750	Entered in pattern book during or after 1896. **Backstamp(s)**: Wileman Foley 1890-1910 **Shapes:** Foley
5751-5752	Same as 6605. Entered in pattern book during or after 1896. **Backstamp(s)**: Wileman Foley 1890-1910 **Shapes:** Foley
5753	**Poppy**. Enamelled. Entered in pattern book during or after 1896. **Backstamp(s)**: Wileman Foley 1890-1910 **Shapes:** Empire
5754	**Rococo Design**. Same as 5322. Gold print. Entered in pattern book during or after 1896. **Backstamp(s)**: Wileman Foley 1890-1910 **Shapes:** Daisy, Empire
5755-5763	**Shaded Ground**. Entered in pattern book during or after 1896. **Backstamp(s)**: Wileman Foley 1890-1910 **Shapes:** Dainty
5766-5769	**Diamonds and Shields**. Same as 6903. Gold design. Entered in pattern book during or after 1896. **Backstamp(s)**: Wileman Foley 1890-1910 **Shapes:** Daisy
5771-5785	**Ivy Pattern**. Entered in pattern book during or after 1896. Seconds ware. **Backstamp(s)**: Wileman Foley 1890-1910 **Shapes:** Century
5791-5802	**Gold Sprigs and Leaf Design**. Same as 6904. Entered in pattern book during or after 1896. **Backstamp(s)**: Wileman Foley 1890-1910 **Shapes:** Empire
5803-5810	**Gold Sprigs and Leaf Design**. Same as 6905. Panelled. Entered in pattern book during or after 1896. **Backstamp(s)**: Wileman Foley 1890-1910 **Shapes:** Snowdrop
5812-5813	**Cameo Print**. Pattern also inside cup. Entered in pattern book during or after 1896. **Backstamp(s)**: Wileman Foley 1890-1910 **Shapes:** Snowdrop
5814	**Cameo Print**. Lavender cameos. Pattern also inside cup. Entered in pattern book during or after 1896. **Backstamp(s)**: Wileman Foley 1890-1910 **Shapes:** Snowdrop
5815	**Cameo Print**. Pattern also inside cup. Entered in pattern book during or after 1896. **Backstamp(s)**: Wileman Foley 1890-1910 **Shapes:** Snowdrop
5821	**Cameo Print**. Two shades. Entered in pattern book during or after 1896. **Backstamp(s)**: Wileman Foley 1890-1910 **Shapes:** Snowdrop
5822	**Cameo Print**. Pink and Green cameo design. Gold trim. **Backstamp(s)**: Wileman Foley 1890-1910 **Shapes:** Snowdrop
5823	**Cameo Print**. Two shades. Entered in pattern book during or after 1896. **Backstamp(s)**: Wileman Foley 1890-1910 **Shapes:** Snowdrop
5832-5836	**Daisy Clusters Print**. Entered in pattern book during or after 1896. **Backstamp(s)**: Wileman Foley 1890-1910 **Shapes:** Empire
5842-5845	**Surrey Scenery Print**. Entered in pattern book during or after 1896. **Backstamp(s)**: Wileman Foley 1890-1910 **Shapes:** Century
5851-5852	**Surrey Scenery Print**. Entered in pattern book during or after 1896. **Backstamp(s)**: Wileman Foley 1890-1910 **Shapes:** Century
5854	**Surrey Scenery Print**. Entered in pattern book during or after 1896. **Backstamp(s)**: Wileman Foley 1890-1910 **Shapes:** Century
5857-5860	**Surrey Scenery Print**. Entered in pattern book during or after 1896. **Backstamp(s)**: Wileman Foley 1890-1910 **Shapes:** Century
5871	**Ivy Print**. Entered in pattern book during or after 1896. **Backstamp(s)**: Wileman Foley 1890-1910 **Shapes:** Empire
5872	**Poppy Print**. Entered in pattern book during or after 1896. **Backstamp(s)**: Wileman Foley 1890-1910 **Shapes:** Foley
5873-5882	**Shaded Ground**. Entered in pattern book during or after 1896. **Backstamp(s)**: Wileman Foley 1890-1910 **Shapes:** Dainty
5891	**Fern Print**. Small, daisy-like flowers and ferns. Pattern also inside cup. White ground. Gold trim. Entered in pattern book during or after 1896.

Right:
Cameo Print 5814 Snowdrop shape cup, saucer, and plate. £80-100; $150-200

Pattern	Description & Shapes
	Backstamp(s): Wileman Foley 1890-1910 **Shapes:** Lily
5892	**Fern Print**. Small, pink daisy-like flowers and ferns. Pattern also inside cup. White ground. Gold trim. Entered in pattern book during or after 1896. **Backstamp(s)**: Wileman Foley 1890-1910 **Shapes:** Lily
5893	**Fern Print**. Small, daisy-like flowers and ferns. Pattern also inside cup. White ground. Gold trim. Entered in pattern book during or after 1896. **Backstamp(s)**: Wileman Foley 1890-1910 **Shapes:** Lily
5894	**Fern Print**. Small, blue and fawn, daisy-like flowers and ferns. Pattern also inside cup. White ground. Gold trim. Entered in pattern book during or after 1896. **Backstamp(s)**: Wileman Foley 1890-1910 **Shapes:** Lily
5896	**Fern Print**. Small, green daisy-like flowers and ferns. Pattern also inside cup. White ground. Gold trim. Entered in pattern book during or after 1896. **Backstamp(s)**: Wileman Foley 1890-1910 **Shapes:** Lily
5897	**Fern Print**. Small, terracotta, daisy-like flowers and ferns. Pattern also inside cup. White ground. Gold trim. Entered in pattern book during or after 1896. **Backstamp(s)**: Wileman Foley 1890-1910 **Shapes:** Lily
5898-5899	**Fern Print**. Small, daisy-like flowers and ferns. Pattern also inside cup. White ground. Gold trim. Entered in pattern book during or after 1896. **Backstamp(s)**: Wileman Foley 1890-1910 **Shapes:** Lily
5900	**Fern Print**. Small blue daisy-like flowers and ferns. Pattern also inside cup. White ground. Gold trim. Entered in pattern book during or after 1896. **Backstamp(s)**: Wileman Foley 1890-1910 **Shapes:** Lily

Fern Print 5900 Lily shape cup, saucer, and plate. £40-£50; $70-90

Pattern	Description & Shapes
5902	**Fern Print**. Small, daisy-like flowers and ferns. Pattern also inside cup. White ground. Gold trim. Entered in pattern book during or after 1896. **Backstamp(s)**: Wileman Foley 1890-1910 **Shapes:** Lily
5905-5906	**Fern Print**. Small, daisy-like flowers and ferns. Pattern also inside cup. White ground. Gold trim. Entered in pattern book during or after 1896. **Backstamp(s)**: Wileman Foley 1890-1910 **Shapes:** Lily
5911-5912	**Daisy Clusters Print**. Entered in pattern book during or after 1896. **Backstamp(s)**: Wileman Foley 1890-1910 **Shapes:** Empire
5914	**Daisy Clusters Print**. Entered in pattern book during or after 1896. **Backstamp(s)**: Wileman Foley 1890-1910 **Shapes:** Empire
5917-5920	**Daisy Clusters Print**. Entered in pattern book during or after 1896. **Backstamp(s)**: Wileman Foley 1890-1910 **Shapes:** Empire
5922	**Daisy Clusters Print**. Entered in pattern book during or after 1896. **Backstamp(s)**: Wileman Foley 1890-1910 **Shapes:** Empire
5931	**Cameo Print**. Pattern also inside cup. Entered in pattern book during or after 1896. **Backstamp(s)**: Wileman Foley 1890-1910 **Shapes:** Snowdrop
5932	**Cameo Print**. Pink cameos. Pattern also inside cup. Entered in pattern book during or after 1896. **Backstamp(s)**: Wileman Foley 1890-1910 **Shapes:** Snowdrop
5934	**Cameo Print**. Pattern also inside cup. Entered in pattern book during or after 1896. **Backstamp(s)**: Wileman Foley 1890-1910 **Shapes:** Snowdrop
5937-5940	**Cameo Print**. Pattern also inside cup. Entered in pattern book during or after 1896. **Backstamp(s)**: Wileman Foley 1890-1910 **Shapes:** Snowdrop
5942	**Cameo Print**. Pattern also inside cup. Entered in pattern book during or after 1896. **Backstamp(s)**: Wileman Foley 1890-1910 **Shapes:** Snowdrop
5945-5946	**Cameo Print**. Pattern also inside cup. Entered in pattern book during or after 1896. **Backstamp(s)**: Wileman Foley 1890-1910 **Shapes:** Snowdrop
5951	**Mixed Single Flower Pattern**. Same as 6922. Enamelled. Entered in pattern book during or after 1896. **Backstamp(s)**: Wileman Foley 1890-1910 **Shapes:** Dainty
5952-5955	**Fern Print**. Entered in pattern book during or after 1896. **Backstamp(s)**: Wileman Foley 1890-1910 **Shapes:** Lily, Royal
5975	Same as 6839. Entered in pattern book during or after 1897. **Backstamp(s)**: Wileman Foley 1890-1910 **Shapes:** Daisy, Empire
5978-5979	**Mixed Single Flower Pattern**. Enamelled. Entered in pattern book during or after 1897. **Backstamp(s)**: Wileman Foley 1890-1910 **Shapes:** Snowdrop
5981	**Trailing Violets Print**. Coloured print. Trailing daisies and violets. Print also inside cup. White ground. Gold edges. Entered in pattern book during or after 1897. **Backstamp(s)**: Wileman Foley 1890-1910 **Shapes:** Lily
5984	**Trailing Violets Print**. Coloured print. Trailing daisies and violets. Print also inside cup. White ground. Gold edges. Entered in pattern book during or after 1897. **Backstamp(s)**: Wileman Foley 1890-1910 **Shapes:** Lily
5987-5990	**Trailing Violets Print**. Coloured print. Trailing daisies and violets. Print also inside cup. White ground. Gold edges. Entered in pattern book during or after 1897. **Backstamp(s)**: Wileman Foley 1890-1910 **Shapes:** Lily
5994	**Trailing Violets Print**. Coloured print. Trailing daisies and violets. Print also inside cup. White ground. Gold edges. Entered in pattern book during or after 1897. **Backstamp(s)**: Wileman Foley 1890-1910 **Shapes:** Lily
5981	**Trailing Violets Print**. Coloured print. Trailing daisies and violets. Print also inside cup. White ground. Gold edges. Entered in pattern book during or after 1897. **Backstamp(s)**: Wileman Foley 1890-1910 **Shapes:** Lily
5996	**Flowers with Scroll Border**. Entered in pattern book during or after 1897. **Backstamp(s)**: Wileman Foley 1890-1910 **Shapes:** Century
6001	**Ivy Print**. Entered in pattern book during or after 1897. **Backstamp(s)**: Wileman Foley 1890-1910 **Shapes:** Dainty
60012-6006	**Sprig Decoration**. Panelled. Entered in pattern book during or after 1890. **Backstamp(s)**: Wileman Foley 1890-1910 **Shapes:** Lily
6007-6014	**Border Pattern**. Entered in pattern book during or after 1890. **Backstamp(s)**: Wileman Foley 1890-1910 **Shapes:** Lily
6015-6020	**Border Pattern**. Panelled. Entered in pattern book during or after 1890. **Backstamp(s)**: Wileman 1872-1890; v **Shapes:** Lily
6021	Blue **Jungle Print**. Entered in pattern book during or after 1890. **Backstamp(s)**: Wileman 1872-1890; Wileman Foley 1890-1910 **Shapes:** Daisy
6022	Pink **Jungle Print**. Entered in pattern book during or after 1890. **Backstamp(s)**: Wileman 1872-1890; Wileman Foley 1890-1910 **Shapes:** Daisy
6023	Brown **Jungle Print**. Entered in pattern book during or after 1890. **Backstamp(s)**: Wileman 1872-1890 **Shapes:** Daisy
6024-	

Pattern **Description & Shapes**

6025 **Jungle Print**. Entered in pattern book during or after 1890.
Backstamp(s): Wileman 1872-1890
Shapes: Daisy

6026 Grey **Jungle Print**. Entered in pattern book during or after 1890.
Backstamp(s): Wileman 1872-1890
Shapes: Daisy, Daisy Bouillon Cup

6027 **Jungle Print**. Profusion of small orange flowers and foliage. White ground. Gold edges. Entered in pattern book during or after 1890.
Backstamp(s): Wileman Foley 1890-1910; Unmarked pieces have been found
Shapes: Daisy

Jungle Print 6027 Daisy shape cup, saucer, and plate. £70-90; $120-160. Creamer. £20-40; $50-60. Cake/bread and butter plate. £20-40; $60-80

6028 **Chrysanthemum**. Entered in pattern book during or after 1890.
Backstamp(s): Wileman Foley 1890-1910
Shapes: Lily

6029 **Convolvulus**. Entered in pattern book during or after 1890.
Backstamp(s): Wileman Foley 1890-1910
Shapes: Lily

6030 **Japan Derby**. Orange and gold flowers with black leaves. Black sections on large panels with gold, crosshatched, foliage print. White ground. Gold edges. Entered in pattern book during or after 1909.
Backstamp(s): Wileman Foley 1890-1910; Unmarked pieces have been found
Shapes: Daisy

6031 **Daisy Wreath Print**. Entered in pattern book during or after 1890.
Backstamp(s): Wileman 1872-1890; Wileman Foley 1890-1910
Shapes: Daisy

6032-6036 **Convolvulus**. Entered in pattern book during or after 1890.
Backstamp(s): Wileman 1872-1890; Wileman Foley 1890-1910
Shapes: Lily

6038-6040 **Chrysanthemum**. Entered in pattern book during or after 1890.
Backstamp(s): Wileman 1872-1890; Wileman Foley 1890-1910
Shapes: Lily

6044-6047 **Border Print**. Entered in pattern book during or after 1890.
Backstamp(s):
Shapes: Lily

6050 **Border Print**. Entered in pattern book during or after 1890.
Backstamp(s): Wileman 1872-1890; Wileman Foley 1890-1910
Shapes: Lily

6051-6056 **Sunflower**. Entered in pattern book during or after 1890.
Backstamp(s): Wileman 1872-1890; Wileman Foley 1890-1910
Shapes: Lily

6057 **Sunflower**. Turquoise sunflowers, trailing tendrils, and daises. White ground. Gold edges. Entered in pattern book during or after 1890.
Backstamp(s): Wileman 1872-1890; Wileman Foley 1890-1910; Unmarked pieces have been found
Shapes: Lily

Sunflower 6057 Lily shape cup and saucer. £40-50; $80-100. Sugar and creamer. £40-50; $80-100. Cake/bread and butter plate. £20-40; $60-80

6058-6059 **Sunflower**. Entered in pattern book during or after 1890.
Backstamp(s): Wileman 1872-1890; Wileman Foley 1890-1910
Shapes: Lily

6060-6061 **Panelled Decoration**. 6061 is the same as 7879. Entered in pattern book during or after 1890.
Backstamp(s): Wileman 1872-1890; Wileman Foley 1890-1910
Shapes: Daisy

6062 **Panelled Decoration**. Entered in pattern book during or after 1890.
Backstamp(s): Wileman 1872-1890; Wileman Foley 1890-1910
Shapes: Lily

6063 **Border Decoration**. Entered in pattern book during or after 1890.
Backstamp(s): Wileman 1872-1890; Wileman Foley 1890-1910
Shapes: Lily

6064-6067 **Convolvulus**. Entered in pattern book during or after 1890.
Backstamp(s):
Shapes: Lily

6069-6070 **Chrysanthemum**. Entered in pattern book during or after 1890.
Backstamp(s): Wileman 1872-1890; Wileman Foley 1890-1910
Shapes: Lily

6075 **Japan Blue and Red**. Gold edges. Entered in pattern book during or after 1890.
Backstamp(s): Wileman 1872-1890
Shapes: Daisy

6076 **Birds Nest Design**. Entered in pattern book during or after 1890.
Backstamp(s): Wileman 1872-1890; Wileman Foley 1890-1910
Shapes: Daisy

6077 **Birds Nest Design**. Entered in pattern book during or after 1890.
Backstamp(s): Wileman 1872-1890; Wileman Foley 1890-1910
Shapes: Lily

6078 **Daisy Wreath**. Same as 6031. Entered in pattern book during or after 1890.
Backstamp(s): Wileman 1872-1890; Wileman Foley 1890-1910
Shapes: Worcester

6079 **Convolvulus**. Entered in pattern book during or after 1890.
Backstamp(s): Wileman 1872-1890; Wileman Foley 1890-1910
Shapes: Lily

6088 Turquoise **Jungle Print**. Profusion of small turquoise flowers and foliage. White ground. Gold edges. Entered in pattern book during or after 1890.
Backstamp(s): Wileman Foley 1890-1910
Shapes: Daisy

6088 **Jungle Print**. Entered in pattern book during or after 1890.
Backstamp(s):
Shapes: Daisy

6090-6094 **Gold Sprig Decoration**. Panelled. Entered in pattern book during or after 1890.
Backstamp(s): Wileman 1872-1890; Wileman Foley 1890-1910
Shapes: Daisy

6095-6099 **Convolvulus**. 6099 is the same as 6475. Entered in pattern book during or after 1890.
Backstamp(s): Wileman 1872-1890; Wileman Foley 1890-1910
Shapes: Daisy

6102-6104 **Sprig Border Design**. Entered in pattern book during or after 1890.
Backstamp(s):
Shapes: Lily

6105 **Convolvulus**. Entered in pattern book during or after 1890.
Backstamp(s): Wileman 1872-1890; Wileman Foley 1890-1910
Shapes: Lily

6106-6110 **Flowering Reed**. Entered in pattern book during or after 1890.
Backstamp(s): Wileman 1872-1890; Wileman Foley 1890-1910
Shapes: Daisy

6125-6127 **Diamond Design**. Same as 5746-5748 and 6302-6305. Entered in pattern book during or after 1890.
Backstamp(s): Wileman 1872-1890; Wileman Foley 1890-1910
Shapes: Daisy

6128 **Flowers**. Entered in pattern book during or after 1890.
Backstamp(s):
Shapes: Daisy

6129 **Folded Panel Design**. Entered in pattern book during or after 1890.
Backstamp(s): Wileman 1872-1890; Wileman Foley 1890-1910
Shapes: Daisy

6130 **Buttercups**. Enamelled. Entered in pattern book during or after 1890.

Pattern Description & Shapes

Backstamp(s): Wileman 1872-1890; Wileman Foley 1890-1910
Shapes: Daisy

6131 **Buttercups**. Enamelled. Entered in pattern book during or after 1890.
Backstamp(s): Wileman 1872-1890; Wileman Foley 1890-1910
Shapes: Lily

6133 **Buttercups**. Entered in pattern book during or after 1890.
Backstamp(s): Wileman 1872-1890; Wileman Foley 1890-1910
Shapes: Daisy

6134 **Buttercups**. Entered in pattern book during or after 1890.
Backstamp(s): Wileman 1872-1890; Wileman Foley 1890-1910
Shapes: Lily

6135-6136 **Buttercups**. Entered in pattern book during or after 1890.
Backstamp(s): Wileman 1872-1890; Wileman Foley 1890-1910
Shapes: Daisy

6143-6152 **Lace Border Design**. Entered in pattern book during or after 1890.
Backstamp(s): Wileman 1872-1890; Wileman Foley 1890-1910
Shapes: Lily

6154-6157 **Lace Border Design**. Entered in pattern book during or after 1890.
Backstamp(s): Wileman 1872-1890; Wileman Foley 1890-1910
Shapes: Lily

6161 **Lace Border Design**. Entered in pattern book during or after 1890.
Backstamp(s): Wileman 1872-1890; Wileman Foley 1890-1910
Shapes: Lily

6162-6165 **Gold Sprigs**. Entered in pattern book during or after 1890.
Backstamp(s): Wileman 1872-1890; Wileman Foley 1890-1910
Shapes: Daisy

6166-6168 **Gold Sprigs**. Entered in pattern book during or after 1890.
Backstamp(s): Wileman 1872-1890; Wileman Foley 1890-1910
Shapes: Lily

6169 **Japan**. Blue, red, and gold. Entered in pattern book during or after 1890.
Backstamp(s): Wileman 1872-1890; Wileman Foley 1890-1910
Shapes: Lily

6170 **Jungle Print**. Entered in pattern book during or after 1890.
Backstamp(s): Wileman 1872-1890; Wileman Foley 1890-1910
Shapes: Daisy

6171 **Jungle Print**. Fawn. Entered in pattern book during or after 1890.
Backstamp(s): Wileman 1872-1890;
Shapes: Daisy, Daisy Bouillon Cup

6172-6173 **Rococo Design**. 6172 is the same as 6290, 6292, 6820, 6821-6822, 9267-6269, 9585, and 9683. Gold print. Entered in pattern book during or after 1890.
Backstamp(s): Wileman 1872-1890; Wileman Foley 1890-1910
Shapes: Daisy

6174-6175 **Rose Branches**. Entered in pattern book during or after 1890.
Backstamp(s): Wileman 1872-1890; Wileman Foley 1890-1910
Shapes: Daisy

6176-6178 **Rococo Design**. Gold print. Entered in pattern book during or after 1890.
Backstamp(s): Wileman 1872-1890; Wileman Foley 1890-1910
Shapes: Daisy

6179 **Rococo Design**. Gold print. Entered in pattern book during or after 1890.
Backstamp(s): Wileman 1872-1890; Wileman Foley 1890-1910
Shapes: Lily

6180 **Gold Sprigs**. Same as 6162. Entered in pattern book during or after 1890.
Backstamp(s): Wileman 1872-1890; Wileman Foley 1890-1910
Shapes: Daisy

6181-6183 **Rococo Design**. Entered in pattern book during or after 1890.
Backstamp(s): Wileman 1872-1890; Wileman Foley 1890-1910
Shapes: Daisy

6184 **Flowering Reed**. Same as 6107. Entered in pattern book during or after 1890.
Backstamp(s): Wileman 1872-1890; Wileman Foley 1890-1910
Shapes: Daisy

6185 **Sunflower Print**. Entered in pattern book during or after 1890.
Backstamp(s): Wileman 1872-1890; Wileman Foley 1890-1910
Shapes: Lily

6186-6188 **Rococo Design**. Entered in pattern book during or after 1890.
Backstamp(s): Wileman 1872-1890; Wileman Foley 1890-1910
Shapes: Daisy

6189 **Sunflower Print**. Yellow print. Entered in pattern book during or after 1890.
Backstamp(s): Wileman 1872-1890; Wileman Foley 1890-1910
Shapes: Lily

6190 **Gold Sprigs**. Panelled. Entered in pattern book during or after 1890.
Backstamp(s): Wileman 1872-1890; Wileman Foley 1890-1910
Shapes: Daisy

6191 **Gold Sprig Border**. Entered in pattern book during or after 1890.
Backstamp(s): Wileman 1872-1890; Wileman Foley 1890-1910
Shapes: Daisy

6192 **Dresden Flowers**. Enamelled. Entered in pattern book during or after 1890.
Backstamp(s): Wileman 1872-1890; Wileman Foley 1890-1910
Shapes: Daisy

6193 **Dresden Flowers**. Entered in pattern book during or after 1890.
Backstamp(s): Wileman 1872-1890; Wileman Foley 1890-1910
Shapes: Daisy

6206 **Dresden Flowers**. Enamelled. Entered in pattern book during or after 1890.
Backstamp(s): Wileman 1872-1890; Wileman Foley 1890-1910
Shapes: Daisy

6209-6210 **Sprig Border**. Entered in pattern book during or after 1890.
Backstamp(s): Wileman 1872-1890; Wileman Foley 1890-1910
Shapes: Daisy

6211 **Japan Derby**. Same as 6030. Orange and gold flowers with black leaves. Black sections on large panels with gold, crosshatched, foliage print. White ground. Gold edges. Entered in pattern book during or after 1890.
Backstamp(s): Wileman 1872-1890; Wileman Foley 1890-1910
Shapes: Daisy

6212 **Japan Red and Gold**. Entered in pattern book during or after 1890.
Backstamp(s): Wileman 1872-1890; Wileman Foley 1890-1910
Shapes: Daisy

6213 **Japan Red and Gold**. Entered in pattern book during or after 1890.
Backstamp(s): Wileman 1872-1890; Wileman Foley 1890-1910
Shapes: Lily

6214 **Floral Sprigs**. Same as 3719. Entered in pattern book during or after 1890.
Backstamp(s): Wileman 1872-1890; Wileman Foley 1890-1910
Shapes: Daisy

6215-6219 **Rococo Design**. Entered in pattern book during or after 1890.
Backstamp(s): Wileman 1872-1890; Wileman Foley 1890-1910
Shapes: Daisy

6220-6221 **Sprig Border**. Same as 6210 and 6308. Entered in pattern book during or after 1890.
Backstamp(s): Wileman 1872-1890; Wileman Foley 1890-1910
Shapes: Daisy

6222-6223 **Rococo Design**. Stippled gold. Entered in pattern book during or after 1890.
Backstamp(s): Wileman 1872-1890; Wileman Foley 1890-1910
Shapes: Daisy

6224 **Gold Sprig Decoration**. Same as 6091. Panelled. Stippled Gold. Entered in pattern book during or after 1890.
Backstamp(s): Wileman 1872-1890; Wileman Foley 1890-1910
Shapes: Daisy

6225 **Gold Sprig Decoration**. Same as 6092. Panelled. Stippled Gold. Entered in pattern book during or after 1890.
Backstamp(s): Wileman 1872-1890; Wileman Foley 1890-1910
Shapes: Daisy

6226 **Gold Sprig Decoration**. Same as 6094. Panelled. Stippled Gold. Entered in pattern book during or after 1890.
Backstamp(s): Wileman 1872-1890; Wileman Foley 1890-1910
Shapes: Daisy

6227 **Rococo Design**. Same as 6216. Stippled gold. Entered in pattern book during or after 1890.
Backstamp(s):
Shapes: Daisy

6228 **Rococo Design**. Same as 6173. Gold print. Stippled gold. Entered in pattern book during or after 1890.
Backstamp(s): Wileman 1872-1890; Wileman Foley 1890-1910
Shapes: Daisy

6229 **Rococo Design**. Same as 6218. Entered in pattern book during or after 1890.
Backstamp(s): Wileman 1872-1890; Wileman Foley 1890-1910
Shapes: Daisy

Japan Derby 6211 Daisy shape cup, saucer, and plate. £70-80; $140-160

Pattern	Description & Shapes
6230	**Rococo Design**. Same as 6217. Entered in pattern book during or after 1890. **Backstamp(s)**: Wileman 1872-1890; Wileman Foley 1890-1910 **Shapes:** Daisy
6231-6236	**Paradise Print**. Floral print on white ground. Gold edges. Entered in pattern book during or after 1890. **Backstamp(s)**: Wileman 1872-1890 **Shapes:** Daisy
6237	**Paradise Print**. Terracotta floral print on white ground. Gold edges. Entered in pattern book during or after 1890. **Backstamp(s)**: Wileman 1872-1890 **Shapes:** Daisy
6238	**Paradise Print**. Floral print on white ground. Gold edges. Entered in pattern book during or after 1890. **Backstamp(s)**: Wileman 1872-1890 **Shapes:** Daisy
6239	**Paradise Print**. Brown floral print on white ground. Gold edges. Entered in pattern book during or after 1890. **Backstamp(s)**: Wileman 1872-1890 **Shapes:** Daisy
6240-6241	**Paradise Print**. Floral print on white ground. Gold edges. Entered in pattern book during or after 1890. **Backstamp(s)**: Wileman 1872-1890 **Shapes:** Daisy
6246	**Sprig Border**. Same as 6210, 6220-6221, and 6308. Stippled gold. Entered in pattern book during or after 1890. **Backstamp(s)**: Wileman 1872-1890; Wileman Foley 1890-1910 **Shapes:** Daisy
6247	**Sprig Border**. Same as 6220. Stippled gold. Entered in pattern book during or after 1890. **Backstamp(s)**: Wileman 1872-1890; Wileman Foley 1890-1910 **Shapes:** Daisy
6248	**Sprig Border**. Same as 6221. Stippled gold. Entered in pattern book during or after 1890. **Backstamp(s)**: Wileman 1872-1890; Wileman Foley 1890-1910 **Shapes:** Daisy
6249	**Sprig Border**. Same as 6219. Stippled gold. Entered in pattern book during or after 1890. **Backstamp(s)**: Wileman 1872-1890; Wileman Foley 1890-1910 **Shapes:** Daisy
6250	**Rococo Design**. Same as 6186. Stippled gold. Entered in pattern book during or after 1890. **Backstamp(s)**: Wileman 1872-1890; Wileman Foley 1890-1910 **Shapes:** Daisy
6251-6262	**New Daisy Border**. Entered in pattern book during or after 1890. **Backstamp(s)**: Wileman 1872-1890; Wileman Foley 1890-1910 **Shapes:** Lily
6266	**Rococo Design**. Same as 6188. Stippled gold. Entered in pattern book during or after 1890. **Backstamp(s)**: Wileman 1872-1890; Wileman Foley 1890-1910 **Shapes:** Daisy
6267-6270	**Sprig Border**. Same as 6210, 6220-6221, 6246, and 6308. Stippled gold. Entered in pattern book during or after 1890. **Backstamp(s)**: Wileman 1872-1890; Wileman Foley 1890-1910 **Shapes:** Daisy
6271-6282	**New Daisy Border**. Entered in pattern book during or after 1890. **Backstamp(s)**: Wileman 1872-1890; Wileman Foley 1890-1910 **Shapes:** Victoria
6286-6287	**Jungle Print**. Entered in pattern book during or after 1890. **Backstamp(s)**: Wileman 1872-1890; Wileman Foley 1890-1910 **Shapes:** Daisy
6290	**Rococo Design**. Same as 6172, 6292, 6820, 6821-6822, 9267-9269, 9585, and 9683. Gold print. Entered in pattern book during or after 1890. **Backstamp(s)**: Wileman 1872-1890; Wileman Foley 1890-1910 **Shapes:** Daisy
6291	**Sprig Border**. Same as 6209. Entered in pattern book during or after 1890. **Backstamp(s)**: Wileman 1872-1890; Wileman Foley 1890-1910 **Shapes:** Daisy
6292	**Rococo Design**. Same as 6172, 6290, 6820, 6821-6822, 9267-9269, 9585, and 9683. Gold print. Entered in pattern book during or after 1890. **Backstamp(s)**: Wileman 1872-1890; Wileman Foley 1890-1910 **Shapes:** Daisy
6293-6294	**Sprig Border**. Same as 6209, 6291, and 6309-6310. Entered in pattern book during or after 1890. **Backstamp(s)**: Wileman 1872-1890; Wileman Foley 1890-1910 **Shapes:** Daisy
6295	**Daisy Print**. Same as 6306-6307 and 6533. Entered in pattern book during or after 1890. **Backstamp(s)**: Wileman 1872-1890; Wileman Foley 1890-1910 **Shapes:** Daisy
6296-6301	Same as 6061. Entered in pattern book during or after 1890. **Backstamp(s)**: Wileman 1872-1890; Wileman Foley 1890-1910 **Shapes:** Daisy
6302-6305	**Diamond Design**. Same as 5746-5748 and 6125. Entered in pattern book during or after 1890. **Backstamp(s)**: Wileman 1872-1890; Wileman Foley 1890-1910 **Shapes:** Daisy
6306-6307	**Daisy Print**. Same as 6295 and 6533. Entered in pattern book during or after 1890. **Backstamp(s)**: Wileman 1872-1890; Wileman Foley 1890-1910 **Shapes:** Daisy
6308	**Sprig Border**. Same as 6210, 6220-6221, 6246, and 6267-6270. Stippled gold. Entered in pattern book during or after 1890. **Backstamp(s)**: Wileman 1872-1890; Wileman Foley 1890-1910 **Shapes:** Daisy
6309-6310	**Sprig Border**. Same as 6209, 6291, and 6293-6294. Entered in pattern book during or after 1890. **Backstamp(s)**: Wileman 1872-1890; Wileman Foley 1890-1910 **Shapes:** Daisy
6311	**Daisies**. Same as 6433-6435. Enamelled and shaded. Entered in pattern book during or after 1890. **Backstamp(s)**: Wileman 1872-1890; Wileman Foley 1890-1910 **Shapes:** Daisy
6312	**Hawthorn Flowers**. Enamelled. Entered in pattern book during or after 1890. **Backstamp(s)**: Wileman 1872-1890; Wileman Foley 1890-1910 **Shapes:** Daisy
6313	**Gold Decoration**. Enamelled. Entered in pattern book during or after 1890. **Backstamp(s)**: Wileman 1872-1890; Wileman Foley 1890-1910 **Shapes:** Daisy
6314	**Shell Design**. Panelled and shaded. Entered in pattern book during or after 1890. **Backstamp(s)**: Wileman 1872-1890; Wileman Foley 1890-1910 **Shapes:** Court, Daisy
6315	**Fir Cones and Foliage**. Same as 6334 and 6335. Shaded. Entered in pattern book during or after 1890. **Backstamp(s)**: Wileman 1872-1890; Wileman Foley 1890-1910 **Shapes:** Daisy
6316	**Fir Cones and Foliage**. Shaded. Entered in pattern book during or after 1890. **Backstamp(s)**: Wileman 1872-1890; Wileman Foley 1890-1910 **Shapes:** Fairy
6317	**Violet Stems**. Shaded. Entered in pattern book during or after 1890. **Backstamp(s)**: Wileman 1872-1890; Wileman Foley 1890-1910 **Shapes:** Fairy
6318	**Ivy Leaves and Berries**. Shaded. Entered in pattern book during or after 1890. **Backstamp(s)**: Wileman 1872-1890; Wileman Foley 1890-1910 **Shapes:** Fairy
6319	**Gold Border Design**. Shaded. Entered in pattern book during or after 1890. **Backstamp(s)**: Wileman 1872-1890; Wileman Foley 1890-1910 **Shapes:** Fairy
6320	**Fir Cones and Foliage**. Shaded. Entered in pattern book during or after 1890. **Backstamp(s)**: Wileman 1872-1890; Wileman Foley 1890-1910 **Shapes:** Fairy
6321	**Fern and Flower Sprays**. Shaded. Entered in pattern book during or after 1890. **Backstamp(s)**: Wileman 1872-1890; Wileman Foley 1890-1910 **Shapes:** Fairy
6322	**Jasmine Flowers**. Shaded. Entered in pattern book during or after 1890. **Backstamp(s)**: Wileman 1872-1890; Wileman Foley 1890-1910 **Shapes:** Fairy
6323	**Shaded Colours**. Entered in pattern book during or after 1890. **Backstamp(s)**: Wileman 1872-1890; Wileman Foley 1890-1910 **Shapes:** Shell
6324-6325	**Ivy Print**. 6324 is the same as 6477 and 6484. 6325 is the same as 6485. Entered in pattern book during or after 1890. **Backstamp(s)**: Wileman 1872-1890; Wileman Foley 1890-1910 **Shapes:** Shell
6326	**Hawthorn Blossoms**. Shaded. Entered in pattern book during or after 1890. **Backstamp(s)**: Wileman 1872-1890; Wileman Foley 1890-1910 **Shapes:** Daisy
6327	**Hawthorn Blossoms**. Same as 6406. Shaded. Entered in pattern book during or after 1890. **Backstamp(s)**: Wileman 1872-1890; Wileman Foley 1890-1910 **Shapes:** Court, Daisy
6328	**Strawberries**. Shaded. Entered in pattern book during or after 1890. **Backstamp(s)**: Wileman 1872-1890; Wileman Foley 1890-1910 **Shapes:** Daisy
6329	**Hawthorn Blossoms**. Shaded. Entered in pattern book during or after 1890. **Backstamp(s)**: Wileman 1872-1890; Wileman Foley 1890-1910 **Shapes:** Fairy
6330	**Peach Blossoms**. Shaded. Entered in

Pattern **Description & Shapes**

pattern book during or after 1890.
Backstamp(s): Wileman 1872-1890; Wileman Foley 1890-1910
Shapes: Fairy

6331 **Flower Design**. Border. Panelled. Entered in pattern book during or after 1890.
Backstamp(s): Wileman 1872-1890; Wileman Foley 1890-1910
Shapes: Daisy

6332-6333 **Plum Blossom**. Entered in pattern book during or after 1890.
Backstamp(s): Wileman 1872-1890; Wileman Foley 1890-1910
Shapes: Daisy

6334 **Fir Cones and Foliage**. Same as 6315. Shaded. Entered in pattern book during or after 1890.
Backstamp(s): Wileman 1872-1890; Wileman Foley 1890-1910
Shapes: Daisy

6335 **Fir Cones and Foliage**. Same as 6315 and 6334. Shaded. Entered in pattern book during or after 1890.
Backstamp(s): Wileman 1872-1890; Wileman Foley 1890-1910
Shapes: Fairy

6336-6338 **Dresden Flowers**. Entered in pattern book during or after 1890.
Backstamp(s): Wileman 1872-1890; Wileman Foley 1890-1910
Shapes: Fairy

6339 **Flower Spray and Dragonfly**. Shaded. Entered in pattern book during or after 1890.
Backstamp(s): Wileman 1872-1890; Wileman Foley 1890-1910
Shapes: Shell

6340-6341 **Decorative Border**. 6340 is the same as 6439-6441. Entered in pattern book during or after 1890.
Backstamp(s): Wileman 1872-1890; Wileman Foley 1890-1910
Shapes: Fairy

6342 **Branches with Berries**. Same as 6476. Entered in pattern book during or after 1890.
Backstamp(s): Wileman 1872-1890; Wileman Foley 1890-1910
Shapes: Fairy

6343-6344 **Decorative Border**. Entered in pattern book during or after 1890.
Backstamp(s): Wileman 1872-1890; Wileman Foley 1890-1910
Shapes: Fairy

6345 **Daisies and Ferns**. Shaded. Entered in pattern book during or after 1890.
Backstamp(s): Wileman 1872-1890; Wileman Foley 1890-1910
Shapes: Fairy

6346 **Primrose and Forget-me-nots**. Shaded. Entered in pattern book during or after 1890.
Backstamp(s): Wileman 1872-1890; Wileman Foley 1890-1910
Shapes: Shell

6347 **Daisies**. Shaded. Entered in pattern book during or after 1890.
Backstamp(s): Wileman 1872-1890; Wileman Foley 1890-1910
Shapes: Daisy

6348-6349 **Flower Spray Print**. Shaded. Entered in pattern book during or after 1890.
Backstamp(s): Wileman 1872-1890; Wileman Foley 1890-1910
Shapes: Shell

6406 **Hawthorn Blossoms**. Same as 6327. Shaded. Entered in pattern book during or after 1890.
Backstamp(s): Wileman 1872-1890; Wileman Foley 1890-1910
Shapes: Fairy

6422-6424 **Festooned Rose Print**. Entered in pattern book during or after 1890.
Backstamp(s): Wileman 1872-1890; Wileman Foley 1890-1910
Shapes: Fairy

6433-6435 **Daisies**. Same as 6311. Enamelled and shaded. Entered in pattern book during or after 1890.
Backstamp(s): Wileman 1872-1890; Wileman Foley 1890-1910
Shapes: Daisy

6436-6438 **Heath Border**. 6436 is the same as 6489 and 6490. Entered in pattern book during or after 1890.
Backstamp(s): Wileman 1872-1890; Wileman Foley 1890-1910
Shapes: Daisy

6422-6424 **Festooned Rose Print**. Entered in pattern book during or after 1890.
Backstamp(s): Wileman 1872-1890; Wileman Foley 1890-1910
Shapes: Fairy

6439-6441 **Decorative Border**. Same as 6340. Entered in pattern book during or after 1890.
Backstamp(s): Wileman 1872-1890; Wileman Foley 1890-1910
Shapes: Fairy

6471 **Japan Black Border**. Same as 3632. Entered in pattern book during or after 1890.
Backstamp(s): Wileman 1872-1890; Wileman Foley 1890-1910
Shapes: May

6472-6474 **Sprays of Flowers**. Entered in pattern book during or after 1890.
Backstamp(s): Wileman 1872-1890; Wileman Foley 1890-1910
Shapes: Shell

6475 **Convolvulus**. Same as 6099. Entered in pattern book during or after 1890.
Backstamp(s): Wileman 1872-1890; Wileman Foley 1890-1910
Shapes: Shell

6476 **Branches with Berries**. Same as 6432. Entered in pattern book during or after 1890.
Backstamp(s): Wileman 1872-1890; Wileman Foley 1890-1910
Shapes: Shell

6477 **Ivy Print**. Same as 6324 and 6484. Entered in pattern book during or after 1890.
Backstamp(s): Wileman 1872-1890; Wileman Foley 1890-1910
Shapes: Shell

6478 **Spray**. Entered in pattern book during or after 1890.
Backstamp(s): Wileman 1872-1890; Wileman Foley 1890-1910
Shapes: Victoria

6479 **Roses**. Entered in pattern book during or after 1890.
Backstamp(s): Wileman 1872-1890; Wileman Foley 1890-1910
Shapes: Fairy

6480 **Sprays**. Entered in pattern book during or after 1890.
Backstamp(s): Wileman 1872-1890; Wileman Foley 1890-1910
Shapes: Fairy

6481 **Daisies**. Entered in pattern book during or after 1890.
Backstamp(s): Wileman 1872-1890; Wileman Foley 1890-1910
Shapes: Fairy

6482 Entered in pattern book during or after 1890.
Backstamp(s): Wileman 1872-1890; Wileman Foley 1890-1910
Shapes: Fairy

6483 **Jasmine**. Entered in pattern book during or after 1890.
Backstamp(s): Wileman 1872-1890; Wileman Foley 1890-1910
Shapes: Fairy

6484 **Ivy Print**. Same as 6324 and 6477. Entered in pattern book during or after 1893.
Backstamp(s): Wileman Foley 1890-1910
Shapes: Empire

6485 **Ivy Print**. Same as 6325. Entered in pattern book during or after 1893.
Backstamp(s): Wileman Foley 1890-1910
Shapes: Empire

6486 **Ivy Print**. Same as 6325. Entered in pattern book during or after 1893.
Backstamp(s): Wileman Foley 1890-1910
Shapes: Empire

6487 **Ivy Print**. Same as 6324, 6477, and 6484. Entered in pattern book during or after 1893.
Backstamp(s): Wileman Foley 1890-1910
Shapes: Empire

6489 **Heath Border**. Same as 6436. Entered in pattern book during or after 1893.
Backstamp(s): Wileman Foley 1890-1910
Shapes: Daisy

6490 **Heath Border**. Same as 6436 and 6489. Entered in pattern book during or after 1893.
Backstamp(s): Wileman Foley 1890-1910
Shapes: Fairy

6492 **Michaelmas Daisies**. Entered in pattern book during or after 1893.
Backstamp(s): Wileman Foley 1890-1910
Shapes: Daisy

6493-6495 **Daisies**. Enamelled. Entered in pattern book during or after 1893.
Backstamp(s): Wileman Foley 1890-1910
Shapes: May

6496 **Daisies**. Enamelled. Entered in pattern book during or after 1893.
Backstamp(s): Wileman Foley 1890-1910
Shapes: Shell

6497 **Michaelmas Daisies**. Enamelled. Entered in pattern book during or after 1893.
Backstamp(s): Wileman Foley 1890-1910
Shapes: Daisy

6498 **Michaelmas Daisies**. Enamelled. Entered in pattern book during or after 1893.
Backstamp(s): Wileman Foley 1890-1910
Shapes: May

6499 **Daisies**. Entered in pattern book during or after 1893.
Backstamp(s): Wileman Foley 1890-1910
Shapes: Daisy

6501 **Daisies**. Enamelled. Entered in pattern book during or after 1893.
Backstamp(s): Wileman Foley 1890-1910
Shapes: May

6503 **Daisies**. Entered in pattern book during or after 1893.
Backstamp(s): Wileman Foley 1890-1910
Shapes: May

6504-6505 **Michaelmas Daisies**. Enamelled. Entered in pattern book during or after 1893.

Pattern Description & Shapes

Backstamp(s): Wileman Foley 1890-1910
Shapes: May

6506-6508 6506 is the same as 9006. Entered in pattern book during or after 1893.
Backstamp(s): Wileman Foley 1890-1910
Shapes: Empire, Foley, May

6509 Yellow inside cup and main part of saucer. Ivory outside cup and centre of saucer. Entered in pattern book during or after 1893.
Backstamp(s): Wileman Foley 1890-1910
Shapes: Empire, Foley, May

Yellow and ivory 6509 Empire shape cup and saucer. £40-60; $80-100

6510-6514 Entered in pattern book during or after 1893.
Backstamp(s): Wileman Foley 1890-1910
Shapes: Empire, Foley, May

6516-6517 Entered in pattern book during or after 1893.
Backstamp(s): Wileman Foley 1890-1910
Shapes: Daisy

6521-6523 Entered in pattern book during or after 1893.
Backstamp(s): Wileman Foley 1890-1910
Shapes: Empire

6531 Same as 6564-6564. Entered in pattern book during or after 1893.
Backstamp(s): Wileman Foley 1890-1910
Shapes: Empire

6532-6533 Entered in pattern book during or after 1893.
Backstamp(s): Wileman Foley 1890-1910
Shapes: Daisy

6542 Shades of peach, cream, and green. Gold edges. Entered in pattern book during or after 1893.
Backstamp(s): Wileman Foley 1890-1910
Shapes: Empire, Foley, May

6543-6547 Entered in pattern book during or after 1893.
Backstamp(s): Wileman Foley 1890-1910
Shapes: Empire

6553 **Daisy Print**. Same as 6295, 6306-6307, and 6533. Entered in pattern book during or after 1893.
Backstamp(s): Wileman Foley 1890-1910
Shapes: Daisy

6564-6565 Same as 6531. Entered in pattern book during or after 1893.
Backstamp(s): Wileman Foley 1890-1910
Shapes: Empire

6580-6587 Entered in pattern book during or after 1893.
Backstamp(s): Wileman Foley 1890-1910
Shapes: Shell

6594-6596 6594 is the same as 5233. Entered in pattern book during or after 1893.
Backstamp(s): Wileman Foley 1890-1910
Shapes: Empire

6597-6599 Entered in pattern book during or after 1893.
Backstamp(s): Wileman Foley 1890-1910
Shapes: Foley

6604 Entered in pattern book during or after 1893.
Backstamp(s): Wileman Foley 1890-1910
Shapes: Foley

6605 Same as 5751-5752. Entered in pattern book during or after 1893.
Backstamp(s): Wileman Foley 1890-1910
Shapes: Empire, Foley

6606-6611 Entered in pattern book during or after 1893.
Backstamp(s): Wileman Foley 1890-1910
Shapes: Foley

6612-6617 Entered in pattern book during or after 1893.
Backstamp(s): Wileman Foley 1890-1910
Shapes: Empire

6618-6620 Entered in pattern book during or after 1893.
Backstamp(s): Wileman Foley 1890-1910
Shapes: Foley

6621-6624 Entered in pattern book during or after 1893.
Backstamp(s): Wileman Foley 1890-1910
Shapes: Empire

6662 Entered in pattern book during or after 1894.
Backstamp(s): Wileman Foley 1890-1910
Shapes: Daisy

6663 **Japan**. Same as 6873 and 9116. Black and red pattern. White ground. Pattern also inside cup. Gold edges. Entered in pattern book during or after 1894.
Backstamp(s): Wileman Foley 1890-1910
Shapes: Fairy

6666-6667 Entered in pattern book during or after 1894.
Backstamp(s): Wileman Foley 1890-1910
Shapes: Fairy

6668 Entered in pattern book during or after 1894.
Backstamp(s): Wileman Foley 1890-1910
Shapes: Lily

6669 Entered in pattern book during or after 1894.
Backstamp(s): Wileman Foley 1890-1910
Shapes: Fairy

6671-6676 Entered in pattern book during or after 1894.
Backstamp(s): Wileman Foley 1890-1910
Shapes: Foley

6678-6688 Entered in pattern book during or after 1894.
Backstamp(s): Wileman Foley 1890-1910
Shapes: Foley

6713 Entered in pattern book during or after 1894.
Backstamp(s): Wileman Foley 1890-1910
Shapes: Fairy

6714-6715 Entered in pattern book during or after 1894.
Backstamp(s): Wileman Foley 1890-1910
Shapes: Foley

6727 Entered in pattern book during or after 1894.
Backstamp(s): Wileman Foley 1890-1910
Shapes: Dainty, Foley

6728-6731 Entered in pattern book during or after 1894.
Backstamp(s): Wileman Foley 1890-1910
Shapes: Foley

6736-6738 Entered in pattern book during or after 1894.
Backstamp(s): Wileman Foley 1890-1910
Shapes: Empire

6743-6745 Entered in pattern book during or after 1894.
Backstamp(s): Wileman Foley 1890-1910
Shapes: Foley

6750-6757 Entered in pattern book during or after 1894.
Backstamp(s): Wileman Foley 1890-1910
Shapes: Foley

6785 Entered in pattern book during or after 1894.
Backstamp(s): Wileman Foley 1890-1910
Shapes: Foley

6795-6798 Same as 5749-5750. Entered in pattern book during or after 1894.
Backstamp(s): Wileman Foley 1890-1910
Shapes: Foley

6802-6805 **Daisies**. Shaded. Entered in pattern book during or after 1893.
Backstamp(s): Wileman Foley 1890-1910
Shapes: Foley

6811 Same as 6878, 9002, and 9076. Entered in pattern book during or after 1894.
Backstamp(s): Wileman Foley 1890-1910
Shapes: Daisy, Foley

6813 **Floral Sprigs**. Same as 3719 and 6214. Entered in pattern book during or after 1895.
Backstamp(s): Wileman Foley 1890-1910
Shapes: Lily, Victoria

6814 Same as 3714. Entered in pattern book during or after 1895.
Backstamp(s): Wileman Foley 1890-1910
Shapes: Lily, Victoria

Pattern	Description & Shapes
6815	**Floral Border**. Same as 3582. Entered in pattern book during or after 1895. **Backstamp(s)**: Wileman Foley 1890-1910 **Shapes:** Lily, Victoria
6816	**Thistle Border**. Same as 3581. Entered in pattern book during or after 1895. **Backstamp(s)**: Wileman Foley 1890-1910 **Shapes:** Lily, Victoria
6817	**Rococo Ornament**. Entered in pattern book during or after 1895. **Backstamp(s)**: Wileman Foley 1890-1910 **Shapes:** Egg, York
6820	**Rococo Design**. Same as Same as 6172, 6290, 6292, 6821-6822, 9267-9269, 9585, and 9683. Gold print. Entered in pattern book during or after 1895. **Backstamp(s)**: Wileman Foley 1890-1910 **Shapes:** Empire
6821-6822	**Rococo Design**. Same as Same as 6172, 6290, 6292, 6820, 9267-9269, 9585, and 9683. Gold print. Entered in pattern book during or after 1895. **Backstamp(s)**: Wileman Foley 1890-1910 **Shapes:** Daisy, Empire
6827	Entered in pattern book during or after 1895. **Backstamp(s)**: Wileman Foley 1890-1910 **Shapes:** Fairy
6828	Same as 5751-5752 and 6605. Entered in pattern book during or after 1895. **Backstamp(s)**: Wileman Foley 1890-1910 **Shapes:** Empire
6829-6831	**Violets**. Entered in pattern book during or after 1895. **Backstamp(s)**: Wileman Foley 1890-1910 **Shapes:** Daisy
6833-6834	Entered in pattern book during or after 1895. **Backstamp(s)**: Wileman Foley 1890-1910 **Shapes:** Century
6835-6840	6839 is the same as 5975. Entered in pattern book during or after 1895. **Backstamp(s)**: Wileman Foley 1890-1910 **Shapes:** Daisy
6841-6842	**Panelled Gold Border Decoration**. Entered in pattern book during or after 1895. **Backstamp(s)**: Wileman Foley 1890-1910 **Shapes:** Daisy, Empire
6843	**Panelled Gold Border Decoration**. Entered in pattern book during or after 1895. **Backstamp(s)**: Wileman Foley 1890-1910 **Shapes:** Daisy
6844-6847	**Panelled Gold Border Decoration**. 6845 is the same as 6854. Entered in pattern book during or after 1895. **Backstamp(s)**: Wileman Foley 1890-1910 **Shapes:** Daisy
6848	**Poppies**. Same as 5310. Enamelled. Entered in pattern book during or after 1895. **Backstamp(s)**: Wileman Foley 1890-1910 **Shapes:** Century
6849	**Chrysanthemum**. Enamelled. Entered in pattern book during or after 1895. **Backstamp(s)**: Wileman Foley 1890-1910 **Shapes:** Century
6850-6851	**Dresden Flowers**. Enamelled. Entered in pattern book during or after 1895. **Backstamp(s)**: Wileman Foley 1890-1910 **Shapes:** Century
6852	**Poppy**. Enamelled. Entered in pattern book during or after 1895. **Backstamp(s)**: Wileman Foley 1890-1910 **Shapes:** Century
6853	**Garland of Flowers and Ornament**. Enamelled. Entered in pattern book during or after 1895. **Backstamp(s)**: Wileman Foley 1890-1910 **Shapes:** Daisy
6854	**Panelled Gold Border Decoration**. Same as 6845. Entered in pattern book during or after 1895. **Backstamp(s)**: Wileman Foley 1890-1910 **Shapes:** Daisy
6855-6856	**Dresden Flowers**. Entered in pattern book during or after 1895. **Backstamp(s)**: Wileman Foley 1890-1910 **Shapes:** Century
6857	**Garland of Flowers and Ornament**. Entered in pattern book during or after 1895. **Backstamp(s)**: Wileman Foley 1890-1910 **Shapes:** Daisy
6858-6859	**Shaded Ground**. Entered in pattern book during or after 1895. **Backstamp(s)**: Wileman Foley 1890-1910 **Shapes:** Dainty
6860	**Solid Ground**. Entered in pattern book during or after 1895. **Backstamp(s)**: Wileman Foley 1890-1910 **Shapes:** Dainty
6861-6862	**Shaded Ground**. Entered in pattern book during or after 1895. **Backstamp(s)**: Wileman Foley 1890-1910 **Shapes:** Poppy
6863	**Autumnal Tints**. Entered in pattern book during or after 1895. **Backstamp(s)**: Wileman Foley 1890-1910 **Shapes:** Poppy
6864-6866	**Chrysanthemum**. 6865 is the same as 6884. Entered in pattern book during or after 1895. **Backstamp(s)**: Wileman Foley 1890-1910 **Shapes:** Century
6868	**Poppy Print**. Entered in pattern book during or after 1895. **Backstamp(s)**: Wileman Foley 1890-1910 **Shapes:** Foley
6869	Entered in pattern book during or after 1895. **Backstamp(s)**: Wileman Foley 1890-1910 **Shapes:** Dainty
6870	**Gold Border Design**. Entered in pattern book during or after 1895. **Backstamp(s)**: Wileman Foley 1890-1910 **Shapes:** Poppy
6871-6872	Entered in pattern book during or after 1895. **Backstamp(s)**: Wileman Foley 1890-1910 **Shapes:** Dainty
6873	**Japan**. Same as 6663, 6873, and 9116. Black and red pattern. White ground. Pattern also inside cup. Gold edges. Entered in pattern book during or after 1895. **Backstamp(s)**: Wileman Foley 1890-1910 **Shapes:** Century
6874	**Dresden Groups**. Same as 5729. Entered in pattern book during or after 1895. **Backstamp(s)**: Wileman Foley 1890-1910 **Shapes:** Century
6875	**Dresden Groups**. Entered in pattern book during or after 1895. **Backstamp(s)**: Wileman Foley 1890-1910 **Shapes:** Century, Royal
6876	**Poppy**. Enamelled. Entered in pattern book during or after 1895. **Backstamp(s)**: Wileman Foley 1890-1910 **Shapes:** Foley
6877	**Forget-me-nots**. Entered in pattern book during or after 1895. **Backstamp(s)**: Wileman Foley 1890-1910 **Shapes:** Foley
6878	Same as 6811, 9002, and 9076. Entered in pattern book during or after 1895. **Backstamp(s)**: Wileman Foley 1890-1910 **Shapes:** Foley
6879	**Violets**. Enamelled. Entered in pattern book during or after 1895. **Backstamp(s)**: Wileman Foley 1890-1910 **Shapes:** Empire
6880	**Violets**. Enamelled. Entered in pattern book during or after 1895. **Backstamp(s)**: Wileman Foley 1890-1910 **Shapes:** Daisy
6881	**Violets**. Enamelled. Entered in pattern book during or after 1895. **Backstamp(s)**: Wileman Foley 1890-1910 **Shapes:** Century
6882	**Daisy Clusters**. Entered in pattern book during or after 1895. **Backstamp(s)**: Wileman Foley 1890-1910 **Shapes:** Century
6883	**Kensington Print**. Entered in pattern book during or after 1895. **Backstamp(s)**: Wileman Foley 1890-1910 **Shapes:** Empire
6884	**Chrysanthemum**. Same as 6865. Entered in pattern book during or after 1895. **Backstamp(s)**: Wileman Foley 1890-1910 **Shapes:** Foley
6885	**Kensington Print**. Entered in pattern book during or after 1895. **Backstamp(s)**: Wileman Foley 1890-1910 **Shapes:** Lily
6886	**Kensington Print**. Enamelled. Entered in pattern book during or after 1895. **Backstamp(s)**: Wileman Foley 1890-1910 **Shapes:** Lily
6887	**Japan**. Black and red pattern. White ground. Gold edges. Entered in pattern book during or after 1895. **Backstamp(s)**: Wileman Foley 1890-1910 **Shapes:** Daisy
6888	**Japan Blue**. Vibrant Imari orange, indigo, and gold colours. Patterned inside cup. Outside cup is patterned on a white ground. Gold trim. Entered in

Pattern Description & Shapes

pattern book during or after 1895.
Backstamp(s): Wileman; The Foley China Wileman
Shapes: Empire

6889 **Plain Ground**. Entered in pattern book during or after 1895.
Backstamp(s): Wileman Foley 1890-1910
Shapes: Empire, Foley

6891 **Chrysanthemum**. Pink and mauve chrysanthemums with green foliage on a white ground. Entered in pattern book during or after 1895.
Backstamp(s): Wileman Foley 1890-1910
Shapes: Empire

6892-6893 **Chrysanthemum** flowers and green foliage on a white ground. Pattern also inside cup. Gold edges. Entered in pattern book during or after 1895.
Backstamp(s): Wileman Foley 1890-1910
Shapes: Empire

Chrysanthemum 6892 Empire shape cup, saucer, and plate. £70-80; $150-200

6897 **Fern Print**. Entered in pattern book during or after 1895.
Backstamp(s): Wileman Foley 1890-1910
Shapes: Century

6901 **Blue Scenery**. Entered in pattern book during or after 1896.
Backstamp(s): Wileman Foley 1890-1910
Shapes: Century

6903 **Diamonds and Shields**. Same as 5766-5769. Gold design. Entered in pattern book during or after 1896.
Backstamp(s): Wileman Foley 1890-1910
Shapes: Daisy

6904 **Gold Sprigs and Leaf Design**. Same as 5791-5802. Entered in pattern book during or after 1896.
Backstamp(s): Wileman Foley 1890-1910
Shapes: Empire

6905 **Gold Sprigs and Leaf Design**. Same as 5803-5810. Panelled. Entered in pattern book during or after 1896.
Backstamp(s): Wileman Foley 1890-1910
Shapes: Snowdrop

6907-6908 **Surrey Scenery**. Enamelled. Entered in pattern book during or after 1896.
Backstamp(s): Wileman Foley 1890-1910
Shapes: Century

6909-6910 **Fern Print**. Entered in pattern book during or after 1896.
Backstamp(s): Wileman Foley 1890-1910
Shapes: Century

6911-6912 **Cameo**. Enamelled. Entered in pattern book during or after 1896.
Backstamp(s): Wileman Foley 1890-1910
Shapes: Snowdrop

6914 **Daisy Cluster**. Entered in pattern book during or after 1896.
Backstamp(s): Wileman Foley 1890-1910
Shapes: Empire

6915-6916 **Daisy Cluster**. Entered in pattern book during or after 1896.
Backstamp(s): Wileman Foley 1890-1910
Shapes: Empire

6917 **Daisy Cluster**. Pale peach, yellow, and blue daisies with green foliage on a white ground. Pattern also inside cup. Gold Edges. Entered in pattern book during or after 1896.
Backstamp(s): Wileman Foley 1890-1910
Shapes: Empire

6918-6919 **Fern Print**. Entered in pattern book during or after 1896.
Backstamp(s): Wileman Foley 1890-1910
Shapes: Century

6920-6922 **Mixed single Flower Pattern**. 6922 is the same as 5951. Entered in pattern book during or after 1896.
Backstamp(s): Wileman Foley 1890-1910
Shapes: Dainty

6923-6925 **Rose with Small Flowers in Panels**. Coloured and gold panels. Large roses and foliage on gold panels. Small flowers and foliage on coloured panels. Large rose on white ground inside cup and centre of plate. Centre of saucer is white. Gold edges and handle. Entered in pattern book during or after 1896.
Backstamp(s): Wileman Foley 1890-1910
Shapes: Snowdrop

6926 **Rose with Small Flowers in Panels**. Turquoise and gold panels. Large yellow and brown roses and foliage on gold panels. Small white flowers and blue foliage on turquoise panels. Large yellow rose on white ground inside cup and centre of plate. Centre of saucer is white. Gold edges and handle. Entered in pattern book during or after 1896.
Backstamp(s): Wileman Foley 1890-1910
Shapes: Snowdrop

6927-6928 **Rose with Small Flowers in Panels**. Coloured and gold panels. Large roses and foliage on gold panels. Small flowers and foliage on coloured panels. Large rose on white ground inside cup and centre of plate. Centre of saucer is white. Gold edges and handle. Entered in pattern book during or after 1896. Wileman Foley 1890-1910
Backstamp(s): Wileman Foley 1890-1910
Shapes: Snowdrop

6929 **Chrysanthemum**. Entered in pattern book during or after 1896.
Backstamp(s): Wileman Foley 1890-1910
Shapes: Snowdrop

6936-6937 **Poppy**. Entered in pattern book during or after 1896.
Backstamp(s): Wileman Foley 1890-1910
Shapes: Snowdrop

6939-6940 **Poppy**. Enamelled. Entered in pattern book during or after 1896.
Backstamp(s): Wileman Foley 1890-1910
Shapes: Snowdrop

6941-6943 **Lilac**. Enamelled. Entered in pattern book during or after 1896.
Backstamp(s): Wileman Foley 1890-1910
Shapes: Snowdrop

6944 **Poppy**. Orange poppies. Dark blue leaves. Green stems. White ground. Gold edges. Entered in pattern book during or after 1896.
Backstamp(s): Wileman Foley 1890-1910
Shapes: Snowdrop

6945-6947 **Poppy**. Entered in pattern book during or after 1896.
Backstamp(s): Wileman Foley 1890-1910
Shapes: Snowdrop

6948-6949 **Trailing Violets**. Entered in pattern book during or after 1896.
Backstamp(s): Wileman Foley 1890-1910
Shapes: Empire

6950 **Japan**. Black and red. Entered in pattern book during or after 1896.
Backstamp(s): Wileman Foley 1890-1910
Shapes: Snowdrop

6954 **Shamrock**. Enamelled. Entered in pattern book during or after 1898.
Backstamp(s): Wileman Foley 1890-1910
Shapes: Snowdrop

6956 **Thistle**. Entered in pattern book during or after 1898.
Backstamp(s): Wileman Foley 1890-1910
Shapes: Snowdrop

6961 **Orchids**. Entered in pattern book during or after 1898.
Backstamp(s): Wileman Foley 1890-1910
Shapes: Empire

6962 **Roses and Snowdrops**. Entered in pattern book during or after 1898.
Backstamp(s): Wileman Foley 1890-1910
Shapes: Dainty

6963 **Roses**. Entered in pattern book during or after 1898.
Backstamp(s): Wileman Foley 1890-1910
Shapes: Lily

6974 **Chrysanthemum**. Enamelled. Entered in pattern book during or after 1898.
Backstamp(s): Wileman Foley 1890-1910
Shapes: Dainty

6979-6980 **Japan**. Enamelled. Entered in pattern book during or after 1898.
Backstamp(s): Wileman Foley 1890-1910
Shapes: Dainty

6981 **Japan**. Blue and red. Entered in pattern book during or after 1898.
Backstamp(s): Wileman Foley 1890-1910
Shapes: Snowdrop

6982 **Japan**. Blue and red. Entered in pattern book during or after 1898.
Backstamp(s): Wileman Foley 1890-1910
Shapes: Daisy

6983-6988 **Japanese Rose**. Crimson and vermilion

Pattern **Description & Shapes**

roses with green, orange, and turquoise foliage on a white ground. Gold edges. Entered in pattern book during or after 1898.
Backstamp(s): Wileman Foley 1890-1910
Shapes: Snowdrop

6989 **Chrysanthemum**. Entered in pattern book during or after 1898.
Backstamp(s): Wileman Foley 1890-1910
Shapes: Daisy

6994 **Star Design**. Same as 9097-9100. Each piece has one large, six-pointed star. The points of these stars are curled. There is an eight-pointed star between each of the large star points on a white ground. Coloured band on outside rim of cup, edge of saucer and plate. Inside cup is white with bands of colour and an eight-pointed star. Entered in pattern book during or after 1898.
Backstamp(s): Wileman Foley 1890-1910
Shapes: Snowdrop

6998 **Japan**. Blue and red. Entered in pattern book during or after 1898.
Backstamp(s): Wileman Foley 1890-1910
Shapes: Snowdrop

7004 **Japan**. Black and orange heart shaped pattern on white ground. Gold edges. Same as 3464, 3692, 7019, and 10169. Entered in pattern book during or after 1899.
Backstamp(s): Wileman Foley 1890-1910
Shapes: Turkish Cans

7005 **Japan Blue**. Same as 4247. Entered in pattern book during or after 1899.
Backstamp(s): Wileman Foley 1890-1910
Shapes: Turkish Cans

7006 Entered in pattern book during or after 1899.
Backstamp(s): Wileman Foley 1890-1910
Shapes: Turkish Cans

7018 **Thistle**. Entered in pattern book during or after 1899.
Backstamp(s): Wileman Foley 1890-1910
Shapes: Snowdrop

7019 **Japan**. Black and orange heart shaped pattern on white ground. Gold edges. Same as 3464, 3692, 7004, and 10169. Entered in pattern book during or after 1899.
Backstamp(s): Wileman Foley 1890-1910
Shapes: Turkish Cans

7033-7038 Entered in pattern book during or after 1899.
Backstamp(s): Wileman Foley 1890-1910
Shapes: Snowdrop

7042-7043 Entered in pattern book during or after 1899.
Backstamp(s): Wileman Foley 1890-1910
Shapes: Snowdrop

7044 Entered in pattern book during or after 1899.
Backstamp(s): Wileman Foley 1890-1910
Shapes: Century

7045 Entered in pattern book during or after 1899.
Backstamp(s): Wileman Foley 1890-1910
Shapes: Snowdrop

7046 Entered in pattern book during or after 1899.
Backstamp(s): Wileman Foley 1890-1910
Shapes: Century

7063 Entered in pattern book during or after 1899.
Backstamp(s): Wileman Foley 1890-1910
Shapes: Lily Breakfast

7064 Entered in pattern book during or after 1899.
Backstamp(s): Wileman Foley 1890-1910
Shapes: Snowdrop

7065 Entered in pattern book during or after 1899.
Backstamp(s): Wileman Foley 1890-1910
Shapes: Daisy

7066 Entered in pattern book during or after 1899.
Backstamp(s): Wileman Foley 1890-1910
Shapes: Foley

7068 Entered in pattern book during or after 1900.
Backstamp(s): Wileman Foley 1890-1910
Shapes: Violet

7069 **Petunia Design**. Entered in pattern book during or after 1900.
Backstamp(s): Wileman Foley 1890-1910
Shapes: Snowdrop

7070 Tiny deep blue flowers and green leaves. Entered in pattern book during or after 1900.
Backstamp(s): Wileman Foley 1890-1910
Shapes: Century, New York, Warwick

7072-7073 7072 is the same as 7284-7285 and 10093. Entered in pattern book during or after 1900.
Backstamp(s): Wileman Foley 1890-1910
Shapes: Gainsborough

7074 **Japan**. Blue, orange, yellow, and pink oriental flowers. Same as 9518. Entered in pattern book during or after 1900.
Backstamp(s): Wileman Foley 1890-1910
Shapes: Gainsborough

7075 Entered in pattern book during or after 1900.
Backstamp(s): Wileman 1890-1910
Shapes: Gainsborough

7076 Entered in pattern book during or after 1900.
Backstamp(s): Wileman Foley 1890-1910
Shapes: Foley

7081-7082 Entered in pattern book during or after 1900.
Backstamp(s): Wileman Foley 1890-1910
Shapes: Century

7083 Patterned inside and outside cup. Gold trim. Entered in pattern book during or after 1900.
Backstamp(s): Wileman 1890-1910
Shapes: Gainsborough

7084 Same as 7258. Navy blue and gold pattern. Patterned inside and outside cup. Gold trim. Entered in pattern book during or after 1900.
Backstamp(s): Wileman 1890-1910
Shapes: Gainsborough

Right:
Blue and gold 7084 Gainsborough shape cup and saucer. £40-50; $80-100

7085 Patterned inside and outside cup. Gold trim. Entered in pattern book during or after 1900.
Backstamp(s): Wileman 1890-1910
Shapes: Gainsborough

7086-7094 7088 is the same as 7255 and 7294. 7093 is the same as 7344 and 7377. 7094 is the same as 7378. Entered in pattern book during or after 1900.
Backstamp(s): Wileman Foley 1890-1910
Shapes: Century

7095 Same as 7277. Entered in pattern book during or after 1900.
Backstamp(s): Wileman 1890-1910
Shapes: Gainsborough

7096-7100 7097 is the same as 7286-7287 and 7334. 7099 is the same as 7320. Entered in pattern book during or after 1900.
Backstamp(s): Wileman Foley 1890-1910
Shapes: Century

7101-7121 **Thistle**. 7108 is the same as 7272, 7452, and 9341. 7114 is the same as 7441. 7115 is the same as 7280. 7116 is the same as 7290. 7117 is the same as 7291. 7118 is the same as 7281. 7119 is the same as 7310, 7314, and 7899-7902. Entered in pattern book during or after 1900.
Backstamp(s): Wileman 1890-1910
Shapes: Gainsborough

7122 Same as 7293. Entered in pattern book during or after 1900.
Backstamp(s): Wileman Foley 1890-1910
Shapes: Century

7123 Same as 7288-7289. Entered in pattern book during or after 1900.
Backstamp(s): Wileman 1890-1910
Shapes: Gainsborough

7125-7131 7125 is the same as 7267 and 7270-7271. 7126 is the same as 7268. 7127 is the same as 7269. Entered in pattern book during or after 1900.
Backstamp(s): Wileman 1890-1910
Shapes: Gainsborough

7132-7136 Entered in pattern book during or after 1900.
Backstamp(s): Wileman Foley 1890-1910
Shapes: Century

7137-7146 Same as 7283 and 7312-7313. Entered in pattern book during or after 1900.
Backstamp(s): Wileman 1890-1910
Shapes: Gainsborough

7147 Entered in pattern book during or after 1900.
Backstamp(s): Wileman Foley 1890-1910
Shapes: Century

Pattern	Description & Shapes
7148-7150	7148 is the same as 7276. Entered in pattern book during or after 1900. **Backstamp(s)**: Wileman 1890-1910 **Shapes:** Gainsborough
7152	Entered in pattern book during or after 1900. **Backstamp(s)**: Wileman 1890-1910 **Shapes:** Gainsborough
7223	**Japan Blue and Red.** Same as 4255. Entered in pattern book during or after 1900. **Backstamp(s)**: Wileman 1890-1910 **Shapes:** Gainsborough
7225-7229	Entered in pattern book during or after 1900. **Backstamp(s)**: Wileman 1890-1910 **Shapes:** Gainsborough
7235-7240	Entered in pattern book during or after 1900. **Backstamp(s)**: Wileman 1890-1910 **Shapes:** Gainsborough
7244-7247	**Carnations and Floral Band**. Entered in pattern book during or after 1900. **Backstamp(s)**: Wileman Foley 1890-1910 **Shapes:** Violet
7248-7249	**Basket of Flowers**. Enamelled. Entered in pattern book during or after 1900. **Backstamp(s)**: Wileman 1890-1910 **Shapes:** Gainsborough
7250	**Snowdrops**. Enamelled. Entered in pattern book during or after 1900. **Backstamp(s)**: Wileman Foley 1890-1910 **Shapes:** Daisy
7254	**Blue Delph**. Entered in pattern book during or after 1900. **Backstamp(s)**: Wileman Foley 1890-1910 **Shapes:** Foley Coffee
7255	Same as 7088 and 7394. Entered in pattern book during or after 1900. **Backstamp(s)**: Wileman 1890-1910 **Shapes:** Gainsborough
7256	**Carnations**. Entered in pattern book during or after 1900. **Backstamp(s)**: Wileman 1890-1910 **Shapes:** Gainsborough
7257	Entered in pattern book during or after 1900. **Backstamp(s)**: Wileman Foley 1890-1910 **Shapes:** Violet
7258	Same as 7084. Navy blue and gold pattern. Patterned inside and outside cup. Gold trim. Entered in pattern book during or after 1900. **Backstamp(s)**: Wileman 1890-1910 **Shapes:** Gainsborough
7267	Same as 7125 and 7270-7271. Entered in pattern book during or after 1900. **Backstamp(s)**: Wileman 1890-1910 **Shapes:** Gainsborough
7268	Same as 7126. Entered in pattern book during or after 1900. **Backstamp(s)**: Wileman 1890-1910 **Shapes:** Gainsborough
7269	Same as 7127. Entered in pattern book during or after 1900. **Backstamp(s)**: Wileman 1890-1910 **Shapes:** Gainsborough
7270-7271	Same as 7125 and 7267. Entered in pattern book during or after 1900. **Backstamp(s)**: Wileman 1890-1910 **Shapes:** Gainsborough
7270-7275	**Thistle**. Same as 7108 and 9341. Entered in pattern book during or after 1900. **Backstamp(s)**: **Shapes:** Gainsborough
7276	Same as 7148. Entered in pattern book during or after 1900. **Backstamp(s)**: Wileman 1890-1910 **Shapes:** Gainsborough
7277	Same as 7095. Entered in pattern book during or after 1900. **Backstamp(s)**: Wileman 1890-1910 **Shapes:** Gainsborough
7279	Entered in pattern book during or after 1900. **Backstamp(s)**: Wileman 1890-1910 **Shapes:** Gainsborough
7280	**Thistle**. Same as 7115. Entered in pattern book during or after 1900. **Backstamp(s)**: Wileman 1890-1910 **Shapes:** Gainsborough
7281	**Thistle**. Same as 7118. Entered in pattern book during or after 1900. **Backstamp(s)**: Wileman 1890-1910 **Shapes:** Gainsborough
7282	Entered in pattern book during or after 1900. **Backstamp(s)**: Wileman 1890-1910 **Shapes:** Gainsborough
7283	Same as 7146 and 7312-7313. Entered in pattern book during or after 1900. **Backstamp(s)**: Wileman 1890-1910 **Shapes:** Gainsborough
7284-7285	Same as 7072 and 10093. Entered in pattern book during or after 1900. **Backstamp(s)**: Wileman 1890-1910 **Shapes:** Gainsborough
7286-7287	Same as 7097 and 7334. Entered in pattern book during or after 1900. **Backstamp(s)**: Wileman 1890-1910 **Shapes:** Gainsborough
7288-7289	Same as 7123. Entered in pattern book during or after 1900. **Backstamp(s)**: Wileman 1890-1910 **Shapes:** Gainsborough
7290	**Thistle**. Same as 7116. Entered in pattern book during or after 1900. **Backstamp(s)**: Wileman 1890-1910 **Shapes:** Gainsborough
7291	**Thistle**. Same as 7117. Entered in pattern book during or after 1900. **Backstamp(s)**: Wileman 1890-1910 **Shapes:** Gainsborough
7293	Same as 7122. Entered in pattern book during or after 1902. **Backstamp(s)**: Wileman Foley 1890-1910 **Shapes:** Gainsborough
7294	Same as 7088 and 7255. Entered in pattern book during or after 1902. **Backstamp(s)**: Wileman Foley 1890-1910 **Shapes:** Gainsborough
7310	**Thistle**. Same as 7119, 7314, and 7899-7902. Entered in pattern book during or after 1902. **Backstamp(s)**: Wileman Foley 1890-1910 **Shapes:** Gainsborough
7312-7313	Same as 7146 and 7283. Entered in pattern book during or after 1902. **Backstamp(s)**: Wileman Foley 1890-1910 **Shapes:** Gainsborough
7314	**Thistle**. Same as 7119, 7310, and 7899-7902. Entered in pattern book during or after 1902. **Backstamp(s)**: Wileman Foley 1890-1910 **Shapes:** Gainsborough
7320	Same as 7099. Entered in pattern book during or after 1902. **Backstamp(s)**: Wileman Foley 1890-1910; Wileman Foley 1890-1910 **Shapes:** Century
7321-7324	**Rose Sprays**. Same as 7238, 7461, 9514-9516, and 9885. Entered in pattern book during or after 1902. **Backstamp(s)**: Wileman Foley 1890-1910 **Shapes:** Gainsborough
7326-7327	**Small Cornflowers**. Entered in pattern book during or after 1902. **Backstamp(s)**: Wileman Foley 1890-1910 **Shapes:** Gainsborough
7328	**Cornflowers**. Entered in pattern book during or after 1902. **Backstamp(s)**: Wileman Foley 1890-1910 **Shapes:** Gainsborough
7333	**Small Cornflowers**. Entered in pattern book during or after 1902. **Backstamp(s)**: Wileman Foley 1890-1910 **Shapes:** Gainsborough
7334	Same as 7097 and 7286-7287. Entered in pattern book during or after 1902. **Backstamp(s)**: Wileman Foley 1890-1910 **Shapes:** Gainsborough
7335	**Roses, Pansies and Forget-me-nots**. Entered in pattern book during or after 1902. **Backstamp(s)**: Wileman Foley 1890-1910 **Shapes:** Gainsborough
7344	Same as 7093 and 7377. Entered in pattern book during or after 1902. **Backstamp(s)**: Wileman Foley 1890-1910 **Shapes:** Gainsborough
7357-7358	**Small Cornflowers**. Entered in pattern book during or after 1902. **Backstamp(s)**: Wileman Foley 1890-1910 **Shapes:** Gainsborough
7359	**Cornflower Border**. Entered in pattern book during or after 1902. **Backstamp(s)**: Wileman Foley 1890-1910 **Shapes:** Gainsborough
7363-7368	**Anemones**. Entered in pattern book during or after 1902. **Backstamp(s)**: Wileman Foley 1890-1910 **Shapes:** Gainsborough
7372-7376	Entered in pattern book during or after 1902. **Backstamp(s)**: Wileman Foley 1890-1910 **Shapes:** Gainsborough
7377	Same as 7093 and 7344. Entered in pattern book during or after 1902. **Backstamp(s)**: Wileman Foley 1890-1910 **Shapes:** Gainsborough
7378	Same as 7094. Entered in pattern book during or after 1902. **Backstamp(s)**: Wileman Foley 1890-1910 **Shapes:** Gainsborough
7288	**Carnation**. Entered in pattern book during or after 1902. **Backstamp(s)**: Wileman Foley 1890-1910 **Shapes:** Gainsborough
7411	**Carnation**. Entered in pattern book during or after 1902. **Backstamp(s)**: Wileman Foley 1890-1910 **Shapes:** Gainsborough
7412-7413	**Cyclamen**. Entered in pattern book during or after 1902. **Backstamp(s)**: Wileman Foley 1890-1910 **Shapes:** Gainsborough

Pattern **Description & Shapes**

7415 **Cyclamen**. Entered in pattern book during or after 1902.
Backstamp(s): Wileman Foley 1890-1910
Shapes: Gainsborough

7416 **Carnation**. Entered in pattern book during or after 1902.
Backstamp(s): Wileman Foley 1890-1910
Shapes: Gainsborough

7417-7421 **Cyclamen**. Entered in pattern book during or after 1902.
Backstamp(s): Wileman Foley 1890-1910
Shapes: Gainsborough

7424-7425 Entered in pattern book during or after 1902.
Backstamp(s): Wileman Foley 1890-1910
Shapes: Gainsborough

7426-7427 Entered in pattern book during or after 1902.
Backstamp(s): Wileman Foley 1890-1910
Shapes: Dainty

7428-7430 Entered in pattern book during or after 1902.
Backstamp(s): Wileman Foley 1890-1910
Shapes: Foley

7441 **Thistle**. Same as 7114. Entered in pattern book during or after 1902.
Backstamp(s): Wileman Foley 1890-1910
Shapes: Gainsborough

7442 **Dresden Flower**. Entered in pattern book during or after 1902.
Backstamp(s): Wileman Foley 1890-1910
Shapes: Gainsborough

7443-7446 Entered in pattern book during or after 1902.
Backstamp(s): Wileman Foley 1890-1910
Shapes: Dainty

7447 **Sprig of Roses**. Same as 9581, 9590-9591, 9892, 10106, and 10114. Small sprigs of pink roses and green leaves. Gold trim. Entered in pattern book during or after 1902 and was still in production in 1919 when numbers were transferred from the old to the new pattern books.
Backstamp(s): Wileman 1873-1890; Wileman The Foley 1890-1910; Shelley 1912-1925
Shapes: Dainty, Dainty Moustache cup, Gainsborough, Milton, Royal

Sprig of Roses 7447 Large plate. £30-40; $40-60. Dainty shape, small creamer and sugar. £70-80; $140-160. Baby plate. £60-70; $100-120

7448 Entered in pattern book during or after 1902.
Backstamp(s): Wileman Foley 1890-1910
Shapes: Gainsborough

7452 **Thistle**. Same as 7108, 7272, and 9341. Entered in pattern book during or after 1902.
Backstamp(s): Wileman Foley 1890-1910
Shapes: Gainsborough

7461 **Rose Sprays**. Same as 7238, 7321-7324, 9514-9516, and 9885. Entered in pattern book during or after 1902.
Backstamp(s): Wileman Foley 1890-1910
Shapes: Gainsborough

7462-7463 Entered in pattern book during or after 1902.
Backstamp(s): Wileman Foley 1890-1910
Shapes: Royal

7465 Entered in pattern book during or after 1902.
Backstamp(s): Wileman Foley 1890-1910
Shapes: Royal Coffee

7466 Entered in pattern book during or after 1902.
Backstamp(s): Wileman Foley 1890-1910
Shapes: Royal

7469-7472 Entered in pattern book during or after 1902.
Backstamp(s): Wileman Foley 1890-1910
Shapes: Royal Bouillon

7474-7483 Entered in pattern book during or after 1902.
Backstamp(s): Wileman Foley 1890-1910
Shapes: Royal

7487-7495 For export only to the U.S.A. Entered in pattern book during or after 1902.
Backstamp(s): Wileman Foley 1890-1910
Shapes: Gainsborough

7497 Entered in pattern book during or after 1902.
Backstamp(s): Wileman Foley 1890-1910
Shapes: Royal

7501 Entered in pattern book during or after 1902.
Backstamp(s): Wileman Foley 1890-1910
Shapes: Royal

7506-7509 Entered in pattern book during or after 1902.
Backstamp(s): Wileman Foley 1890-1910
Shapes: Royal

7511 Entered in pattern book during or after 1902.
Backstamp(s): Wileman Foley 1890-1910
Shapes: Royal

7520-7521 Entered in pattern book during or after 1902.
Backstamp(s): Wileman Foley 1890-1910
Shapes: Royal

7536 **Woodcocks**. Entered in pattern book during or after 1902.
Backstamp(s): Wileman Foley 1890-1910
Shapes: Gainsborough

7537-7539 Entered in pattern book during or after 1902.
Backstamp(s): Wileman Foley 1890-1910
Shapes: Royal

7542 Entered in pattern book during or after 1902.
Backstamp(s): Wileman Foley 1890-1910
Shapes: Royal

7550 Entered in pattern book during or after 1902.
Backstamp(s): Wileman Foley 1890-1910
Shapes: Royal

7553-7558 Entered in pattern book during or after 1902.
Backstamp(s): Wileman Foley 1890-1910
Shapes: Royal

7559 Entered in pattern book during or after 1902.
Backstamp(s): Wileman Foley 1890-1910
Shapes: Gainsborough

7563 Entered in pattern book during or after 1902.
Backstamp(s): Wileman Foley 1890-1910
Shapes: Foley

7570 Entered in pattern book during or after 1902 and was still in production in 1919 when numbers were transferred from the old to the new pattern books.
Backstamp(s): Wileman Foley 1890-1910
Shapes: Bute

7575 Entered in pattern book during or after 1902.
Backstamp(s): Wileman Foley 1890-1910
Shapes: Royal

7580-7581 Entered in pattern book during or after 1902.
Backstamp(s): Wileman Foley 1890-1910
Shapes: Royal

7583 Entered in pattern book during or after 1902.
Backstamp(s): Wileman Foley 1890-1910
Shapes: Dainty

7584 Entered in pattern book during or after 1902.
Backstamp(s): Wileman Foley 1890-1910
Shapes: Gainsborough

7598 Entered in pattern book during or after 1902.
Backstamp(s): Wileman Foley 1890-1910
Shapes: Royal

7605 Entered in pattern book during or after 1902.
Backstamp(s): Wileman Foley 1890-1910
Shapes: Gainsborough

7612 Entered in pattern book during or after 1902.
Backstamp(s): Wileman Foley 1890-1910
Shapes: Snowdrop

7613 Entered in pattern book during or after 1902.
Backstamp(s): Wileman Foley 1890-1910
Shapes: Royal

7615 Entered in pattern book during or after 1902.

Pattern	Description & Shapes
	Backstamp(s): Wileman Foley 1890-1910 **Shapes:** Dainty
7618-7619	Entered in pattern book during or after 1902. **Backstamp(s)**: Wileman Foley 1890-1910 **Shapes:** Royal
7622-7624	Entered in pattern book during or after 1902. **Backstamp(s)**: Wileman Foley 1890-1910 **Shapes:** Royal
7628-7647	Entered in pattern book during or after 1902. **Backstamp(s)**: Wileman Foley 1890-1910 **Shapes:** Royal
7649-7654	Entered in pattern book during or after 1902. **Backstamp(s)**: Wileman Foley 1890-1910 **Shapes:** Royal
7656-7663	Entered in pattern book during or after 1902. **Backstamp(s)**: Wileman Foley 1890-1910 **Shapes:** Royal
7665-7683	Entered in pattern book during or after 1902. **Backstamp(s)**: Wileman Foley 1890-1910 **Shapes:** Royal
7684	Orange Poppies. Brown print. Orange poppies, brown and green leaves, and stems on a white ground. Flowers also inside cup. Patches of mottled brown along rim. Gold edges. Entered in pattern book during or after 1902. **Backstamp(s)**: Wileman Foley 1890-1910 **Shapes:** Gainsborough
7685-7715	Entered in pattern book during or after 1902. **Backstamp(s)**: Wileman Foley 1890-1910 **Shapes:** Royal
7716	For export to the U.S.A. Entered in pattern book during or after 1902. **Backstamp(s)**: Wileman Foley 1890-1910 **Shapes:** Roman
7717-7718	For export to the U.S.A. Entered in pattern book during or after 1902. **Backstamp(s)**: Wileman Foley 1890-1910 **Shapes:** New York
7719-7722	Entered in pattern book during or after 1902. **Backstamp(s)**: Wileman Foley 1890-1910 **Shapes:** Royal
7724-7727	Entered in pattern book during or after 1902. **Backstamp(s)**: Wileman Foley 1890-1910 **Shapes:** Royal
7730-7733	Entered in pattern book during or after 1902. **Backstamp(s)**: Wileman Foley 1890-1910 **Shapes:** Royal
7743-7745	Entered in pattern book during or after 1902. **Backstamp(s)**: Wileman Foley 1890-1910 **Shapes:** Royal
7749-7755	Entered in pattern book during or after 1902. **Backstamp(s)**: Wileman Foley 1890-1910 **Shapes:** Royal
7762	**Goblins**. Entered in pattern book during or after 1902. **Backstamp(s)**: Wileman Foley 1890-1910 **Shapes:** Gainsborough
7763-7766	Entered in pattern book during or after 1902. **Backstamp(s)**: Wileman Foley 1890-1910 **Shapes:** Royal
7769-7770	Entered in pattern book during or after 1902. **Backstamp(s)**: Wileman Foley 1890-1910 **Shapes:** Royal
7772-7773	Entered in pattern book during or after 1902. **Backstamp(s)**: Wileman Foley 1890-1910 **Shapes:** Royal
7774	**Primroses**. Entered in pattern book during or after 1902. **Backstamp(s)**: Wileman Foley 1890-1910 **Shapes:** Dainty
7776-7777	Entered in pattern book during or after 1902. **Backstamp(s)**: Wileman Foley 1890-1910 **Shapes:** Royal
7778-7782	Entered in pattern book during or after 1904. **Backstamp(s)**: Wileman Foley 1890-1910 **Shapes:** Royal
7783-7785	Entered in pattern book during or after 1904. **Backstamp(s)**: Wileman Foley 1890-1910 **Shapes:** Gainsborough
7786	Entered in pattern book during or after 1904. **Backstamp(s)**: Wileman Foley 1890-1910 **Shapes:** Royal
7788	Entered in pattern book during or after 1904. **Backstamp(s)**: Wileman Foley 1890-1910 **Shapes:** Royal
7789	George Logan Tulips. George Logan was a contemporary of Rennie Mackintosh, and was part of the 'Glasgow School'. Burgundy, turquoise, and purple tulips with green leaves. Beige shapes at the base of the tulip stems. White ground. Gold edges. Entered in pattern book during or after 1904. **Backstamp(s)**: Wileman Foley 1890-1910 **Shapes:** Gainsborough
7790	Entered in pattern book during or after 1904. **Backstamp(s)**: Wileman Foley 1890-1910 **Shapes:** Gainsborough
7791	Entered in pattern book during or after 1904. **Backstamp(s)**: Wileman Foley 1890-1910 **Shapes:** Royal
7792	Entered in pattern book during or after 1904. **Backstamp(s)**: Wileman Foley 1890-1910 **Shapes:** Gainsborough
7793	Entered in pattern book during or after 1904. **Backstamp(s)**: Wileman Foley 1890-1910 **Shapes:** Royal Coffee
7794	**Japan**. Entered in pattern book during or after 1904. **Backstamp(s)**: Wileman Foley 1890-1910 **Shapes:** Royal
7796	Entered in pattern book during or after 1904. **Backstamp(s)**: Wileman Foley 1890-1910 **Shapes:** Royal
7797	Entered in pattern book during or after 1904. **Backstamp(s)**: Wileman Foley 1890-1910 **Shapes:** Royal Breakfast
7798-7805	7804 is the same as 7891. Entered in pattern book during or after 1904. **Backstamp(s)**: Wileman Foley 1890-1910 **Shapes:** Royal
7806	Entered in pattern book during or after 1904. **Backstamp(s)**: Wileman Foley 1890-1910 **Shapes:** Foley Flute
7807-7824	Entered in pattern book during or after 1904. **Backstamp(s)**: Wileman Foley 1890-1910 **Shapes:** Royal
7825	Entered in pattern book during or after 1904. **Backstamp(s)**: Wileman Foley 1890-1910 **Shapes:** Gainsborough
7832	**Japan**. Entered in pattern book during or after 1904. **Backstamp(s)**: Wileman Foley 1890-1910 **Shapes:** Royal
7833	Entered in pattern book during or after 1904. **Backstamp(s)**: Wileman Foley 1890-1910 **Shapes:** Royal
7835-7837	Entered in pattern book during or after 1904. **Backstamp(s)**: Wileman Foley 1890-1910 **Shapes:** Royal
7838	Entered in pattern book during or after 1904. **Backstamp(s)**: Wileman Foley 1890-1910 **Shapes:** Royal Coffee
7839-7840	7839 is the same as 7896. 7840 is the same as 7894 and 9897. Entered in pattern book during or after 1904. **Backstamp(s)**: Wileman Foley 1890-1910 **Shapes:** Foley Flute, Royal
7841	Entered in pattern book during or after 1904. **Backstamp(s)**: Wileman Foley 1890-1910 **Shapes:** Royal
7842	Entered in pattern book during or after 1904. **Backstamp(s)**: Wileman Foley 1890-1910 **Shapes:** Gainsborough
7843	Gold and turquoise border on large panels. Gold and turquoise motif on

Pattern Description & Shapes

small panels. Gold lines on panel joins Gold ring round centre of saucer and plate. White ground. Gold edges. Entered in pattern book during or after 1904.
Backstamp(s): Wileman Foley 1890-1910; Shelley 1912-1925
Shapes: Antique, Square

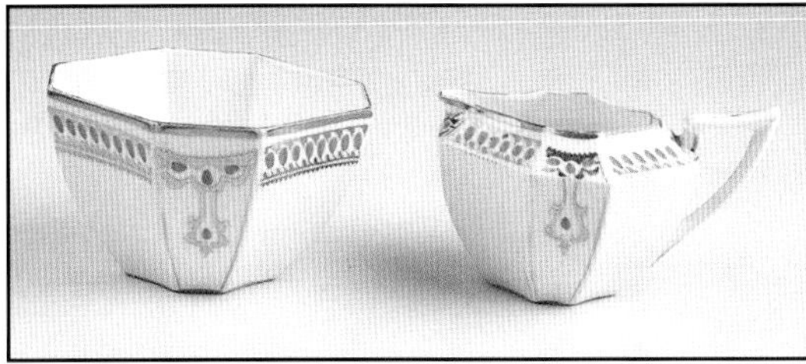

Gold and turquoise 7843 Antique shape creamer and sugar. £60-80; $90-120

Gold and turquoise 7843 Antique shape cup, saucer, and plate. £70-90; $100-140

7844 **Japan**. Blue and Red. Entered in pattern book during or after 1904.
Backstamp(s): Wileman Foley 1890-1910
Shapes: Antique

7845 **Japan**. Blue and Red. Entered in pattern book during or after 1904.
Backstamp(s): Wileman Foley 1890-1910
Shapes: Royal

7846 **Japan**. Entered in pattern book during or after 1904.
Backstamp(s): Wileman Foley 1890-1910
Shapes: Royal

7847 Entered in pattern book during or after 1904.
Backstamp(s): Wileman Foley 1890-1910
Shapes: Royal

7851 Entered in pattern book during or after 1904.
Backstamp(s): Wileman Foley 1890-1910
Shapes: Devonshire

7861 Entered in pattern book during or after 1904.
Backstamp(s): Wileman Foley 1890-1910
Shapes: Devonshire

7862 **Irises**. Entered in pattern book during or after 1904.
Backstamp(s): Wileman Foley 1890-1910
Shapes: Devonshire

7863-7864 Entered in pattern book during or after 1904.
Backstamp(s): Wileman Foley 1890-1910
Shapes: Devonshire

7865-7866 Entered in pattern book during or after 1904.
Backstamp(s): Wileman Foley 1890-1910
Shapes: Gainsborough

7867 Entered in pattern book during or after 1904.
Backstamp(s): Wileman Foley 1890-1910
Shapes: Devonshire

7868 **Japan**. Blue and Red. Entered in pattern book during or after 1904.
Backstamp(s): Wileman Foley 1890-1910
Shapes: Antique

7871-7873 **Apple Blossom**. Enamelled. Entered in pattern book during or after 1904.
Backstamp(s): Wileman Foley 1890-1910
Shapes: Edward

7874 **Apple Blossom**. Branches of pink blossoms. Gold edges. Green, pink, and yellow handle. Entered in pattern book during or after 1904.
Backstamp(s): Wileman Foley 1890-1910
Shapes: Edward

7875-7877 **Apple Blossom**. Tinted. Entered in pattern book during or after 1904.
Backstamp(s): Wileman Foley 1890-1910
Shapes: Edward

7878 **Apple Blossom**. Gold. Entered in pattern book during or after 1904.
Backstamp(s): Wileman Foley 1890-1910
Shapes: Edward

7879 **Panelled Decoration**. Same as 6061. Entered in pattern book during or after 1904.
Backstamp(s): Wileman Foley 1890-1910
Shapes: Court, Empire

7880-7881 7880 is the same as 7895. Entered in pattern book during or after 1890.
Backstamp(s): Wileman Foley 1890-1910
Shapes: Gainsborough

7882-7883 Entered in pattern book during or after 1890.
Backstamp(s): Wileman Foley 1890-1910
Shapes: Antique

7884 Same as 7898. Entered in pattern book during or after 1890.
Backstamp(s): Wileman Foley 1890-1910
Shapes: Dainty

7889-7890 Entered in pattern book during or after 1890.
Backstamp(s): Wileman Foley 1890-1910
Shapes: Antique

7891 Same as 7804. Entered in pattern book during or after 1904.
Backstamp(s): Wileman Foley 1890-1910
Shapes: Royal

7893 Entered in pattern book during or after 1904.
Backstamp(s): Wileman Foley 1890-1910
Shapes: Royal

7894 Same as 7840 and 7897. Entered in pattern book during or after 1904.
Backstamp(s): Wileman Foley 1890-1910
Shapes: Foley Flute, Royal

7895 Same as 7880. Entered in pattern book during or after 1904.
Backstamp(s): Wileman Foley 1890-1910
Shapes: Devonshire

7896 Same as 7839. Entered in pattern book during or after 1904.
Backstamp(s): Wileman Foley 1890-1910
Shapes: New York

7897 Same as 7840 and 7894. Entered in pattern book during or after 1904.
Backstamp(s): Wileman Foley 1890-1910
Shapes: New York

7898 Same as 7884. Entered in pattern book during or after 1904.
Backstamp(s): Wileman Foley 1890-1910
Shapes: Dainty

7899-7902 Same as 7119, 7310, and 7314. Entered in pattern book during or after 1904.
Backstamp(s): Wileman Foley 1890-1910
Shapes: Royal

7903 Entered in pattern book during or after 1904.
Backstamp(s): Wileman Foley 1890-1910
Shapes: Gainsborough

7906 Entered in pattern book during or after 1904.
Backstamp(s): Wileman Foley 1890-1910
Shapes: Royal

7910-7912 Entered in pattern book during or after 1904.
Backstamp(s): Wileman Foley 1890-1910
Shapes: Antique

7913 Entered in pattern book during or after 1904.
Backstamp(s): Wileman Foley 1890-1910
Shapes: Royal

7914 Entered in pattern book during or after 1904.
Backstamp(s): Wileman Foley 1890-1910
Shapes: Gainsborough

7915-7917 Entered in pattern book during or after 1904.
Backstamp(s): Wileman Foley 1890-1910
Shapes: Royal

7920 Entered in pattern book during or after 1904.
Backstamp(s): Wileman Foley 1890-1910
Shapes: Royal

7923 Entered in pattern book during or after 1904.
Backstamp(s): Wileman Foley 1890-1910
Shapes: Dorothy

7924 Olympic Torch. Green torch and pink flames. Scattered solid green stars. White ground. Green edges. Entered in pattern book during or after 1907.

Olympic Torch 7924 Dorothy shape cup, saucer, and plate. £60-90; $180-230

Pattern	Description & Shapes
	Backstamp(s): Wileman Foley 1890-1910; Shelley 1912-1925; Copyright **Shapes:** Dorothy
7925	Pink thistle on green stem with green leaves. Green edges. **Backstamp(s)**: Wileman Foley 1890-1910; Shelley 1910-1925 **Shapes:** Dorothy
7926-7928	7926 is the same as 8100. Entered in pattern book during or after 1904. **Backstamp(s)**: Wileman Foley 1890-1910 **Shapes:** Dorothy
7930	Entered in pattern book during or after 1904. **Backstamp(s)**: Wileman Foley 1890-1910 **Shapes:** Gainsborough
7933	Entered in pattern book during or after 1907. **Backstamp(s)**: Wileman Foley 1890-1910 **Shapes:** Gainsborough
7934	Entered in pattern book during or after 1907. **Backstamp(s)**: Wileman Foley 1890-1910 **Shapes:** Dorothy
7935	Entered in pattern book during or after 1907. **Backstamp(s)**: Wileman Foley 1890-1910 **Shapes:** New York
7936	Entered in pattern book during or after 1907. **Backstamp(s)**: Wileman Foley 1890-1910 **Shapes:** Royal
7941	Entered in pattern book during or after 1907. **Backstamp(s)**: Wileman Foley 1890-1910 **Shapes:** Royal
7944	Entered in pattern book during or after 1907. **Backstamp(s)**: Wileman Foley 1890-1910 **Shapes:** Royal
7945-7946	Entered in pattern book during or after 1907 and was still in production in 1919 when numbers were transferred from the old to the new pattern books. **Backstamp(s)**: Wileman Foley 1890-1910 **Shapes:** Gainsborough, Milton, Royal
7956	Entered in pattern book during or after 1907. **Backstamp(s)**: Wileman Foley 1890-1910 **Shapes:** Royal
7957	Entered in pattern book during or after 1907. **Backstamp(s)**: Wileman Foley 1890-1910 **Shapes:** Gainsborough
7966	Entered in pattern book during or after 1907. **Backstamp(s)**: Wileman Foley 1890-1910 **Shapes:** Royal
7975	Entered in pattern book during or after 1907. **Backstamp(s)**: Wileman Foley 1890-1910 **Shapes:** Royal
7976	Entered in pattern book during or after 1907 and was still in production in 1919 when numbers were transferred from the old to the new pattern books. **Backstamp(s)**: **Shapes:** Gainsborough, Milton, Royal
7977	**Peter Pan**. Entered in pattern book during or after 1907. **Backstamp(s)**: Wileman Foley 1890-1910 **Shapes:** Dorothy
7981	Entered in pattern book during or after 1907. **Backstamp(s)**: Wileman Foley 1890-1910 **Shapes:** Royal
7982-7984	Entered in pattern book during or after 1907. **Backstamp(s)**: Wileman Foley 1890-1910 **Shapes:** Dorothy
7991	Entered in pattern book during or after 1907. **Backstamp(s)**: Wileman Foley 1890-1910 **Shapes:** Royal
8014	Entered in pattern book during or after 1907. **Backstamp(s)**: Wileman Foley 1890-1910 **Shapes:** Royal
8015	Entered in pattern book during or after 1907 and was still in production in 1919 when numbers were transferred from the old to the new pattern books. **Backstamp(s)**: Wileman Foley 1890-1910 **Shapes:** Bute, Gainsborough, Milton, Royal
8017	Entered in pattern book during or after 1907 and was still in production in 1919 when numbers were transferred from the old to the new pattern books. **Backstamp(s)**: Wileman Foley 1890-1910 **Shapes:** Bute, Gainsborough, Milton, Royal
8018	Entered in pattern book during or after 1907. **Backstamp(s)**: Wileman Foley 1890-1910 **Shapes:** Royal
8020	Entered in pattern book during or after 1907. **Backstamp(s)**: Wileman Foley 1890-1910 **Shapes:** Royal
8021	Entered in pattern book during or after 1907. **Backstamp(s)**: Wileman Foley 1890-1910 **Shapes:** Gainsborough
8022	Entered in pattern book during or after 1907. **Backstamp(s)**: Wileman Foley 1890-1910 **Shapes:** Royal
8024	Entered in pattern book during or after 1907 and was still in production in 1919 when numbers were transferred from the old to the new pattern books. **Backstamp(s)**: Wileman Foley 1890-1910 **Shapes:** Bute
8035	Entered in pattern book during or after 1907. **Backstamp(s)**: Wileman Foley 1890-1910 **Shapes:** Bute
8038	Entered in pattern book during or after 1907 and was still in production in 1919 when numbers were transferred from the old to the new pattern books. **Backstamp(s)**: Wileman Foley 1890-1910 **Shapes:** Bute
8039	Entered in pattern book during or after 1907. **Backstamp(s)**: Wileman Foley 1890-1910 **Shapes:** Bute
8040	**Roses**. Entered in pattern book during or after 1907. **Backstamp(s)**: Wileman Foley 1890-1910 **Shapes:** Dainty
8044	**Japan**. Entered in pattern book during or after 1907. **Backstamp(s)**: Wileman Foley 1890-1910 **Shapes:** Dorothy
8045	Entered in pattern book during or after 1907. **Backstamp(s)**: Wileman Foley 1890-1910 **Shapes:** Low Lily
8051	**Japan**. Entered in pattern book during or after 1907. **Backstamp(s)**: Wileman Foley 1890-1910 **Shapes:** Dorothy
8053-8054	**Japan**. Entered in pattern book during or after 1907. **Backstamp(s)**: Wileman Foley 1890-1910 **Shapes:** Gainsborough
8058	Entered in pattern book during or after 1907. **Backstamp(s)**: Wileman Foley 1890-1910 **Shapes:** Foley Flute, Royal
8061	Entered in pattern book during or after 1907. **Backstamp(s)**: Wileman Foley 1890-1910 **Shapes:** Royal
8062	Entered in pattern book during or after 1907. **Backstamp(s)**: Wileman Foley 1890-1910 **Shapes:** Gainsborough
8063	**Rose Sprays**. Posies of purple flowers linked by green garlands. Scattered small flowers in groups of three. Border inside cup. White ground. Gold edges. Entered in pattern book during or after 1907. **Backstamp(s)**: Shelley Late Foley 1910-1916 **Shapes:** Dorothy
8064	**Shamrocks**. Two-shamrock sprigs on white ground. Green edges and handle. Entered in pattern book during or after 1908 and was still in production in 1919 when numbers were transferred from the old to the new pattern books. **Backstamp(s)**: Wileman Foley 1890-1910; Shelley Late Foley 1910-1916 **Shapes:** Bute, Mocha, New York, Norman, Vincent

Shamrocks 8064 Bute shape cup and saucer. £40-£50; $75-85

Pattern	Description & Shapes
8066	Entered in pattern book during or after 1907. **Backstamp(s)**: Wileman Foley 1890-1910 **Shapes:** Bute
8070	**Vine Border**. Green vines and black grapes. Dark green edges. Entered in

Pattern **Description & Shapes**

pattern book during or after 1907. A chocolate set is pictured in the UK Shelley Group magazine Issue 55 page 12.
Backstamp(s): Wileman Foley 1890-1910; Shelley Late Foley 1910-1916
Shapes: Bute, Chocolate Cup

8075-8076 Entered in pattern book during or after 1907.
Backstamp(s): Wileman Foley 1890-1910
Shapes: Royal

8085 Entered in pattern book during or after 1907.
Backstamp(s): Wileman Foley 1890-1910
Shapes: Bute

8086 Entered in pattern book during or after 1907.
Backstamp(s): Wileman Foley 1890-1910
Shapes: Royal

8087 Entered in pattern book during or after 1907.
Backstamp(s): Wileman Foley 1890-1910
Shapes: Bute

8091 Entered in pattern book during or after 1907.
Backstamp(s): Wileman Foley 1890-1910
Shapes: Worcester Breakfast

8092 Entered in pattern book during or after 1908.
Backstamp(s): Wileman Foley 1890-1910
Shapes: Dorothy

8093 Entered in pattern book during or after 1908.
Backstamp(s): Wileman Foley 1890-1910
Shapes: Royal

8094 **Rose**. Entered in pattern book during or after 1908.
Backstamp(s): Wileman Foley 1890-1910
Shapes: Bute

8095 **Rose**. Entered in pattern book during or after 1908.
Backstamp(s): Wileman Foley 1890-1910
Shapes: Gainsborough

8096 Entered in pattern book during or after 1908.
Backstamp(s): Wileman Foley 1890-1910
Shapes: Royal

8097 Entered in pattern book during or after 1908.
Backstamp(s): Wileman Foley 1890-1910
Shapes: Dorothy

8100 Same as 7926. Entered in pattern book during or after 1908.
Backstamp(s): Wileman Foley 1890-1910
Shapes: Dorothy

8101 Entered in pattern book during or after 1908.
Backstamp(s): Wileman Foley 1890-1910
Shapes: Bute

8103-8104 Entered in pattern book during or after 1908.
Backstamp(s): Wileman Foley 1890-1910
Shapes: Bute

8106 Entered in pattern book during or after 1908.
Backstamp(s): Wileman Foley 1890-1910
Shapes: Bute

8108 Entered in pattern book during or after 1908 and was still in production in 1919 when numbers were transferred from the old to the new pattern books.
Backstamp(s): Wileman Foley 1890-1910: Shelley Late Foley 1910-1916
Shapes: Bute, Royal

8110 **Sheraton**. Gold bands and green garlands. Gold edges. Entered in pattern book during or after 1908.
Backstamp(s): Wileman Foley 1890-1910
Shapes: Royal

8111 Entered in pattern book during or after 1908.
Backstamp(s): Wileman Foley 1890-1910
Shapes: Antique

8112-8113 Entered in pattern book during or after 1908.
Backstamp(s): Wileman Foley 1890-1910
Shapes: Snowdrop

8114 Entered in pattern book during or after 1908.
Backstamp(s): Wileman Foley 1890-1910
Shapes: Dainty

8115 Entered in pattern book during or after 1908 and was still in production in 1919 when numbers were transferred from the old to the new pattern books.
Backstamp(s): Wileman Foley 1890-1910: Shelley Late Foley 1910-1916
Shapes: Bute

8116 Entered in pattern book during or after 1908.
Backstamp(s): Wileman Foley 1890-1910
Shapes: Gainsborough

8117 Entered in pattern book during or after 1908 and was still in production in 1919 when numbers were transferred from the old to the new pattern books.
Backstamp(s): Wileman Foley 1890-1910: Shelley Late Foley 1910-1916
Shapes: Gainsborough, Milton

8119 Entered in pattern book during or after 1908.
Backstamp(s): Wileman Foley 1890-1910
Shapes: Dainty

8120 Entered in pattern book during or after 1908.
Backstamp(s): Wileman Foley 1890-1910
Shapes: Snowdrop

8121 Entered in pattern book during or after 1908.
Backstamp(s): Wileman Foley 1890-1910
Shapes: Dainty

8122 Entered in pattern book during or after 1908.
Backstamp(s): Wileman Foley 1890-1910
Shapes: Antique

8123-8124 Entered in pattern book during or after 1908.
Backstamp(s): Wileman Foley 1890-1910
Shapes: Gainsborough

8125 Entered in pattern book during or after 1908.
Backstamp(s): Wileman Foley 1890-1910
Shapes: Snowdrop

8126-8127 Entered in pattern book during or after 1908.
Backstamp(s): Wileman Foley 1890-1910
Shapes: Gainsborough

8128-8129 Entered in pattern book during or after 1909.
Backstamp(s): Wileman Foley 1890-1910
Shapes: Bute

8130 **Water Lilies**. Entered in pattern book during or after 1909.
Backstamp(s): Wileman Foley 1890-1910
Shapes: Dorothy

8132 Entered in pattern book during or after 1909.
Backstamp(s): Wileman Foley 1890-1910
Shapes: Dorothy

8140-8141 Entered in pattern book during or after 1909.
Backstamp(s):
Shapes: Gainsborough

8148 Entered in pattern book during or after 1909 and was still in production in 1919 when numbers were transferred from the old to the new pattern books.
Backstamp(s): Wileman Foley 1890-1910; Shelley Late Foley 1910-1916
Shapes: Gainsborough, Milton

8153 Pink roses surrounded by green wreath. Green garlands link wreathes. Blue bows and ribbons at top of wreath. White ground. Gold edges. Entered in pattern book during or after 1909.
Backstamp(s): Shelley Late Foley 1910-1916
Shapes: Gainsborough

8163 Entered in pattern book during or after 1909.
Backstamp(s): Wileman Foley 1890-1910; Shelley Late Foley 1910-1916
Shapes: Gainsborough

8164 **Japan**. Blue and red. Entered in pattern book during or after 1909.
Backstamp(s): Wileman Foley 1890-1910; Shelley Late Foley 1910-1916
Shapes: Gainsborough

8168 Entered in pattern book during or after 1909.
Backstamp(s): Wileman Foley 1890-1910; Shelley Late Foley 1910-1916
Shapes: Bute

8176 Entered in pattern book during or after 1909.
Backstamp(s): Wileman Foley 1890-1910; Shelley Late Foley 1910-1916
Shapes: Dorothy

8189 **Blue Swallows**. Entered in pattern book during or after 1909 and was still in production in 1919 when numbers were transferred from the old to the new pattern books.
Backstamp(s): Wileman Foley 1890-1910; Shelley Late Foley 1910-1916
Shapes: Bute

8190 **Blue Swallows**. Gold Border with blue swallows. White ground. Ripon has gold edges, foot and handle. Entered in

Blue Swallows 8190 Ripon shape cup and saucer. £60-90; $180-200

Pattern	Description & Shapes
	pattern book during or after 1909 and was still in production in 1919 when numbers were transferred from the old to the new pattern books. **Backstamp(s)**: Wileman Foley 1890-1910; Shelley Late Foley 1910-1916 **Shapes:** Bute, Mocha, New York, Ripon
8192	Entered in pattern book during or after 1909. **Backstamp(s)**: Wileman Foley 1890-1910; Shelley Late Foley 1910-1916 **Shapes:** New York
8194-8195	**Blue Storks**. Entered in pattern book during or after 1909. **Backstamp(s)**: Wileman Foley 1890-1910; Shelley Late Foley 1910-1916 **Shapes:** Bute
8202	Entered in pattern book during or after 1909 and was still in production in 1919 when numbers were transferred from the old to the new pattern books. **Backstamp(s)**: Wileman Foley 1890-1910; Shelley Late Foley 1910-1916 **Shapes:** Gainsborough, Milton
8205	Entered in pattern book during or after 1909. **Backstamp(s)**: Wileman Foley 1890-1910; Shelley Late Foley 1910-1916 **Shapes:** Gainsborough
8209	**Hankow**. Orange dragon print. Entered in pattern book during or after 1909. **Backstamp(s)**: Wileman Foley 1890-1910; Shelley Late Foley 1910-1916 **Shapes:** Royal
8218	Entered in pattern book during or after 1909. **Backstamp(s)**: Wileman Foley 1890-1910; Shelley Late Foley 1910-1916 **Shapes:** Antique
8219	Entered in pattern book during or after 1909. **Backstamp(s)**: Wileman Foley 1890-1910; Shelley Late Foley 1910-1916 **Shapes:** Royal
8225	Entered in pattern book during or after 1909. **Backstamp(s)**: Shelley Late Foley 1910-1916 **Shapes:** Royal, Worcester Coffee
8233	Entered in pattern book during or after 1910. **Backstamp(s)**: Shelley 1912-1925 **Shapes:** Bute
8236	Entered in pattern book during or after 1909. **Backstamp(s)**: Shelley Late Foley 1910-1916 **Shapes:** Royal
8241	Entered in pattern book during or after 1909. **Backstamp(s)**: Shelley Late Foley 1910-1916 **Shapes:** Gainsborough, Milton
8242	Entered in pattern book during or after 1909. **Backstamp(s)**: Shelley Late Foley 1910-1916 **Shapes:** Gainsborough
8244	**Peacock Feathers**. Entered in pattern book during or after 1909. **Backstamp(s)**: Shelley Late Foley 1910-1916 **Shapes:** Dorothy
8245	Entered in pattern book during or after 1909. **Backstamp(s)**: Shelley Late Foley 1910-1916 **Shapes:** Bute
8246	Entered in pattern book during or after 1909. **Backstamp(s)**: Shelley Late Foley 1910-1916 **Shapes:** Dorothy
8247-8248	Entered in pattern book during or after 1909. **Backstamp(s)**: Shelley Late Foley 1910-1916 **Shapes:** Bute
8249	Entered in pattern book during or after 1909. **Backstamp(s)**: Shelley Late Foley 1910-1916 **Shapes:** Gainsborough
8250	Entered in pattern book during or after 1909. **Backstamp(s)**: Shelley Late Foley 1910-1916 **Shapes:** Bute
8251	Entered in pattern book during or after 1909. **Backstamp(s)**: Shelley Late Foley 1910-1916 **Shapes:** Royal
8252-8257	**Gold Borders**. Entered in pattern book during or after 1910 for export to U.S.A. **Backstamp(s)**: Shelley Late Foley 1910-1916 **Shapes:** Unknown
8258	Entered in pattern book during or after 1909. **Backstamp(s)**: Shelley Late Foley 1910-1916 **Shapes:** Bute
8259	Entered in pattern book during or after 1910. **Backstamp(s)**: Shelley Late Foley 1910-1916 **Shapes:** Bute
8275	Entered in pattern book during or after 1910. **Backstamp(s)**: Shelley Late Foley 1910-1916 **Shapes:** Gainsborough
8280-8281	Entered in pattern book during or after 1910. **Backstamp(s)**: Shelley Late Foley 1910-1916 **Shapes:** Bute
8284	Entered in pattern book during or after 1910. **Backstamp(s)**: Shelley Late Foley 1910-1916 **Shapes:** New York
8285	Entered in pattern book during or after 1910. **Backstamp(s)**: Shelley Late Foley 1910-1916 **Shapes:** Bute
8286	Seconds ware. Entered in pattern book during or after 1910. **Backstamp(s)**: Shelley Late Foley 1910-1916 **Shapes:** Bute
8287	Entered in pattern book during or after 1910. **Backstamp(s)**: Shelley Late Foley 1910-1916 **Shapes:** Bute
8289-8290	Entered in pattern book during or after 1910. **Backstamp(s)**: Shelley Late Foley 1910-1916 **Shapes:** Victoria
8291	Entered in pattern book during or after 1910. **Backstamp(s)**: **Shapes:** Foley Flute
8292	Entered in pattern book during or after 1910. **Backstamp(s)**: Shelley Late Foley 1910-1916 **Shapes:** New York
8293	**Pomegranate Royal**. Entered in pattern book during or after 1910. **Backstamp(s)**: Shelley Late Foley 1910-1916 **Shapes:** Argyle
8294	Entered in pattern book during or after 1910. **Backstamp(s)**: Shelley Late Foley 1910-1916 **Shapes:** Gainsborough
8295	**Forget-me-nots**. Entered in pattern book during or after 1910. **Backstamp(s)**: Shelley Late Foley 1910-1916 **Shapes:** Dainty
8296	**Double Roses**. Entered in pattern book during or after 1910. **Backstamp(s)**: Shelley Late Foley 1910-1916 **Shapes:** Gainsborough
8297	**Louis Panel with Roses**. Entered in pattern book during or after 1910. **Backstamp(s)**: Shelley Late Foley 1910-1916 **Shapes:** Gainsborough
8298	**Bell Wreath with Roses**. Entered in pattern book during or after 1910. **Backstamp(s)**: Shelley Late Foley 1910-1916 **Shapes:** Gainsborough
8299	**Key and Roses**. Entered in pattern book during or after 1910. **Backstamp(s)**: Shelley Late Foley 1910-1916 **Shapes:** Gainsborough
8300	**Ribbon and Roses**. Entered in pattern book during or after 1910. **Backstamp(s)**: Shelley Late Foley 1910-1916 **Shapes:** Gainsborough
8301	**Circles around Roses**. Entered in pattern book during or after 1910. **Backstamp(s)**: Shelley Late Foley 1910-1916 **Shapes:** Gainsborough
8302	**Festoons and Fruit**. Green garlands and posies of pink roses inside cup and on saucer. Posy on base of inside cup. Dontil border inside cup and edge of saucer. Fawn/gold ring outside cup approximately half way between rim and foot. White ground. Gold edges. Entered in pattern book during or after 1910. **Backstamp(s)**: Shelley Late Foley 1910-1916 **Shapes:** Gainsborough, Milton
8303-8305	**Rose Sprays**. Entered in pattern book during or after 1910. **Backstamp(s)**: Shelley Late Foley 1910-1916 **Shapes:** Gainsborough
8306	**Strawberries**. Entered in pattern book during or after 1910. **Backstamp(s)**: Shelley Late Foley 1910-1916 **Shapes:** Bute
8307	**Rose and Violets**. Entered in pattern book during or after 1910. **Backstamp(s)**: Shelley Late Foley 1910-1916 **Shapes:** Bute
8308	**Rose Border**. Entered in pattern book during or after 1910. **Backstamp(s)**: Shelley Late Foley 1910-1916 **Shapes:** Gainsborough
8309	**Cornflower**. Purple flowers and green leaves on a white ground. Gold edges. Entered in pattern book during or after 1910. **Backstamp(s)**: Shelley Late Foley 1910-1916 **Shapes:** Violet

Cornflower 8309 Violet shape cup and saucer. £60-90; $140-160

Pattern	Description & Shapes
8310	**Cornflower**. Entered in pattern book during or after 1910. **Backstamp(s)**: Shelley Late Foley 1910-1916 **Shapes:** Dainty
8311	Blue **Roses**. Blue print. Roses and leaves on a white ground. Blue edges. Entered in pattern book during or after 1910. **Backstamp(s)**: Shelley 1912-1925 **Shapes:** Bute, New York, Norman, Vincent
8312	**Ivy Design**. Entered in pattern book during or after 1911. **Backstamp(s)**: Shelley Late Foley 1910-1916 **Shapes:** New York
8313	Entered in pattern book during or after 1911. **Backstamp(s)**: Shelley Late Foley 1910-1916 **Shapes:** Gainsborough
8314	Entered in pattern book during or after 1911. **Backstamp(s)**: Shelley Late Foley 1910-1916 **Shapes:** Argyle
8315	Entered in pattern book during or after 1911. **Backstamp(s)**: Shelley Late Foley 1910-1916 **Shapes:** New York
8316	Entered in pattern book during or after 1911. **Backstamp(s)**: Shelley Late Foley 1910-1916 **Shapes:** Gainsborough
8317	Entered in pattern book during or after 1911. **Backstamp(s)**: Shelley Late Foley 1910-1916 **Shapes:** Royal
8318	Entered in pattern book during or after 1911. **Backstamp(s)**: Shelley Late Foley 1910-1916 **Shapes:** Dorothy, Gainsborough, Milton, Vincent
8319	Entered in pattern book during or after 1911. **Backstamp(s)**: Shelley Late Foley 1910-1916 **Shapes:** New York
8320	**Cloisonné**. Blue. Entered in pattern book during or after 1911. **Backstamp(s)**: Shelley 1912-1925 **Shapes:** Unknown
8322	Entered in pattern book during or after 1911. **Backstamp(s)**: Shelley Late Foley 1910-1916 **Shapes:** Bute
8331	Entered in pattern book during or after 1911. **Backstamp(s)**: Shelley Late Foley 1910-1916 **Shapes:** Gainsborough
8334	Entered in pattern book during or after 1911. **Backstamp(s)**: Shelley Late Foley 1910-1916 **Shapes:** Gainsborough
8335	Entered in pattern book during or after 1911. **Backstamp(s)**: Shelley Late Foley 1910-1916 **Shapes:** Worcester
8336	Entered in pattern book during or after 1911. **Backstamp(s)**: Shelley Late Foley 1910-1916 **Shapes:** Bute
8339	Entered in pattern book during or after 1911. **Backstamp(s)**: Shelley Late Foley 1910-1916 **Shapes:** Bute
8360	Entered in pattern book during or after 1911. **Backstamp(s)**: Shelley Late Foley 1910-1916 **Shapes:** New York
8368	Entered in pattern book during or after 1911. **Backstamp(s)**: Shelley Late Foley 1910-1916 **Shapes:** Worcester Coffee
8369	Entered in pattern book during or after 1911. **Backstamp(s)**: Shelley Late Foley 1910-1916 **Shapes:** Royal
8373	Entered in pattern book during or after 1911. **Backstamp(s)**: Shelley Late Foley 1910-1916 **Shapes:** New York
8374	Entered in pattern book during or after 1911. **Backstamp(s)**: Shelley Late Foley 1910-1916 **Shapes:** Spiral Fluted
8375-8378	Entered in pattern book during or after 1911. **Backstamp(s)**: Shelley Late Foley 1910-1916 **Shapes:** Dorothy
8381-8283	Entered in pattern book during or after 1911. **Backstamp(s)**: Shelley Late Foley 1910-1916 **Shapes:** Dorothy
8384	Entered in pattern book during or after 1911. **Backstamp(s)**: Shelley Late Foley 1910-1916 **Shapes:** New York
8393	Entered in pattern book during or after 1911. **Backstamp(s)**: Shelley Late Foley 1910-1916 **Shapes:** Bute
8394	Entered in pattern book during or after 1911. **Backstamp(s)**: Shelley Late Foley 1910-1916 **Shapes:** Dorothy
8398	Entered in pattern book during or after 1911. **Backstamp(s)**: Shelley Late Foley 1910-1916 **Shapes:** Victoria
8399	Entered in pattern book during or after 1911. **Backstamp(s)**: Shelley Late Foley 1910-1916 **Shapes:** Bute, New York, Worcester Coffee
8401	Entered in pattern book during or after 1911. **Backstamp(s)**: Shelley Late Foley 1910-1916 **Shapes:** Bute, Worcester Coffee
8402	Entered in pattern book during or after 1911. **Backstamp(s)**: Shelley Late Foley 1910-1916 **Shapes:** Bute, Worcester Coffee
8403	Entered in pattern book during or after 1911. **Backstamp(s)**: Shelley Late Foley 1910-1916 **Shapes:** New York
8404	Entered in pattern book during or after 1911. **Backstamp(s)**: Shelley Late Foley 1910-1916 **Shapes:** Bute
8406	Entered in pattern book during or after 1911. **Backstamp(s)**: Shelley Late Foley 1910-1916 **Shapes:** Gainsborough
8407	Entered in pattern book during or after 1911. **Backstamp(s)**: Shelley Late Foley 1910-1916 **Shapes:** Gainsborough
8408	Entered in pattern book during or after 1911. **Backstamp(s)**: Shelley Late Foley 1910-1916 **Shapes:** Royal
8409-8410	Entered in pattern book during or after 1911. **Backstamp(s)**: Shelley Late Foley 1910-1916 **Shapes:** Dorothy
8411-8413	Entered in pattern book during or after 1911. **Backstamp(s)**: Shelley Late Foley 1910-1916 **Shapes:** Bute
8414	Fawn print. Border of scrolls, circles, and small, pale pink roses. White ground. Gold edges. Entered in pattern book during or after 1911. **Backstamp(s)**: Shelley Late Foley 1910-1916 **Shapes:** New York
8415-8416	Coloured print. Border of scrolls, circles, and small roses. White ground. Gold edges. Entered in pattern book during or after 1911. **Backstamp(s)**: Shelley Late Foley 1910-1916 **Shapes:** New York
8417-8418	Entered in pattern book during or after 1911. **Backstamp(s)**: Shelley Late Foley 1910-1916 **Shapes:** Argyle
8419	Entered in pattern book during or after 1911. **Backstamp(s)**: Shelley Late Foley 1910-1916 **Shapes:** Bute
8422	Entered in pattern book during or after 1911. **Backstamp(s)**: Shelley Late Foley 1910-1916 **Shapes:** Bute
8424-8427	Entered in pattern book during or after 1911. **Backstamp(s)**: Shelley Late Foley 1910-1916 **Shapes:** Dorothy
8428-8432	Entered in pattern book during or after 1911. **Backstamp(s)**: Shelley Late Foley 1910-

Pattern	Description & Shapes
	1916 **Shapes:** Bute
8433-8434	Entered in pattern book during or after 1911. **Backstamp(s)**: Shelley Late Foley 1910-1916 **Shapes:** Argyle
8435-8438	Entered in pattern book during or after 1911. **Backstamp(s)**: Shelley Late Foley 1910-1916 **Shapes:** Gainsborough
8439-8442	Entered in pattern book during or after 1911. **Backstamp(s)**: Shelley Late Foley 1910-1916 **Shapes:** Royal
8443-8444	Entered in pattern book during or after 1911. **Backstamp(s)**: Shelley Late Foley 1910-1916 **Shapes:** Dorothy
8445	Entered in pattern book during or after 1911. **Backstamp(s)**: Shelley Late Foley 1910-1916 **Shapes:** Bute
8446-8447	Entered in pattern book during or after 1911. **Backstamp(s)**: Shelley Late Foley 1910-1916 **Shapes:** Gainsborough
8448	Entered in pattern book during or after 1911. **Backstamp(s)**: Shelley Late Foley 1910-1916 **Shapes:** New York
8478-8479	Entered in pattern book during or after 1911. **Backstamp(s)**: Shelley Late Foley 1910-1916 **Shapes:** Victoria
8480	Entered in pattern book during or after 1911. **Backstamp(s)**: Shelley Late Foley 1910-1916 **Shapes:** Gainsborough
8481	Entered in pattern book during or after 1911. **Backstamp(s)**: Shelley Late Foley 1910-1916 **Shapes:** Dorothy
8482	Entered in pattern book during or after 1911. **Backstamp(s)**: Shelley Late Foley 1910-1916 **Shapes:** Gainsborough
8483	Entered in pattern book during or after 1911. **Backstamp(s)**: Shelley Late Foley 1910-1916 **Shapes:** Dorothy
8484	Entered in pattern book during or after 1911. **Backstamp(s)**: Shelley Late Foley 1910-1916 **Shapes:** Gainsborough
8485	Entered in pattern book during or after 1911. **Backstamp(s)**: Shelley Late Foley 1910-1916 **Shapes:** Bute
8486	Entered in pattern book during or after 1911. **Backstamp(s)**: Shelley Late Foley 1910-1916 **Shapes:** Gainsborough
8487	Entered in pattern book during or after 1911. **Backstamp(s)**: Shelley Late Foley 1910-1916 **Shapes:** Bute
8488	Entered in pattern book during or after 1911. **Backstamp(s)**: Shelley Late Foley 1910-1916 **Shapes:** Dorothy
8489	Entered in pattern book during or after 1911. **Backstamp(s)**: Shelley Late Foley 1910-1916 **Shapes:** Gainsborough
8490-8491	Entered in pattern book during or after 1911. **Backstamp(s)**: Shelley Late Foley 1910-1916 **Shapes:** Dorothy
8492	Entered in pattern book during or after 1911. **Backstamp(s)**: Shelley Late Foley 1910-1916 **Shapes:** Gainsborough
8493	Entered in pattern book during or after 1911. **Backstamp(s)**: Shelley Late Foley 1910-1916 **Shapes:** Gainsborough, Milton
8498	Entered in pattern book during or after 1912. **Backstamp(s)**: Shelley Late Foley 1910-1916; Shelley 1912-1925 **Shapes:** Dorothy
8508	Entered in pattern book during or after 1912. **Backstamp(s)**: Shelley Late Foley 1910-1916; Shelley 1912-1925 **Shapes:** Empire
8524	**Ashbourne**. Purple, orange, black, green, and gold flowers and leaves on a white ground. White border, then a purple and gold border. Gold edges. Entered in pattern book during or after 1912. **Backstamp(s)**: Shelley Late Foley 1910-1916; Shelley 1912-1925 **Shapes:** Gainsborough, Milton, Vincent

Ashbourne 8524 large plate. £60-70; $100-120. Small plate. £30-40; $50-60. Covered sugar bowl. £70-80; $110-140. Gainsborough shape cup and saucer. £70-80; $120-160

Pattern	Description & Shapes
8528	Entered in pattern book during or after 1912. **Backstamp(s)**: Shelley Late Foley 1910-1916; Shelley 1912-1925 **Shapes:** Gainsborough
8529	Entered in pattern book during or after 1912. **Backstamp(s)**: Shelley Late Foley 1910-1916; Shelley 1912-1925 **Shapes:** Bute
8530	Entered in pattern book during or after 1912. **Backstamp(s)**: Shelley Late Foley 1910-1916; Shelley 1912-1925 **Shapes:** Victoria
8531-8532	Entered in pattern book during or after 1912. **Backstamp(s)**: Shelley Late Foley 1910-1916; Shelley 1912-1925 **Shapes:** Royal
8533-8534	Entered in pattern book during or after 1912. **Backstamp(s)**: Shelley Late Foley 1910-1916; Shelley 1912-1925 **Shapes:** New York
8536	Entered in pattern book during or after 1912. **Backstamp(s)**: Shelley Late Foley 1910-1916; Shelley 1912-1925 **Shapes:** New York
8537	Entered in pattern book during or after 1912. **Backstamp(s)**: Shelley Late Foley 1910-1916; Shelley 1912-1925 **Shapes:** Bute
8638	Brown print. Brown, crosshatched border with scrolls, small pink roses and chains inside cup, saucer and plate. Gold line outside cup approximately halfway between rim and base of cup. Gold edges. Entered in pattern book during or after 1912. **Backstamp(s)**: Shelley Late Foley 1910-1916; Shelley 1912-1925 **Shapes:** Gainsborough
8539	Entered in pattern book during or after 1912. **Backstamp(s)**: Shelley Late Foley 1910-1916; Shelley 1912-1925 **Shapes:** Victoria
8540	Entered in pattern book during or after 1912. **Backstamp(s)**: Shelley Late Foley 1910-1916; Shelley 1912-1925 **Shapes:** Bute
8541	Entered in pattern book during or after 1912. **Backstamp(s)**: Shelley Late Foley 1910-1916; Shelley 1912-1925 **Shapes:** Roman
8543	Entered in pattern book during or after 1912. **Backstamp(s)**: Shelley Late Foley 1910-1916; Shelley 1912-1925 **Shapes:** Bute
8544	Entered in pattern book during or after 1912. **Backstamp(s)**: Shelley Late Foley 1910-1916; Shelley 1912-1925 **Shapes:** Lily
8545	Green and salmon flower border. Entered in pattern book during or after 1912. **Backstamp(s)**: Shelley Late Foley 1910-1916; Shelley 1912-1925 **Shapes:** Victoria
8546	Entered in pattern book during or after 1912. **Backstamp(s)**: Shelley Late Foley 1910-1916; Shelley 1912-1925 **Shapes:** Dorothy
8547	Entered in pattern book during or after 1912. **Backstamp(s)**: Shelley Late Foley 1910-1916; Shelley 1912-1925 **Shapes:** Gainsborough
8548-8549	Entered in pattern book during or after 1912. **Backstamp(s)**: Shelley Late Foley 1910-1916; Shelley 1912-1925 **Shapes:** Victoria
8550	Entered in pattern book during or after 1912.

Pattern	Description & Shapes
	Backstamp(s): Shelley Late Foley 1910-1916; Shelley 1912-1925 **Shapes:** Worcester
8551	Entered in pattern book during or after 1912. **Backstamp(s)**: Shelley Late Foley 1910-1916; Shelley 1912-1925 **Shapes:** New York
8552	Entered in pattern book during or after 1912. **Backstamp(s)**: Shelley Late Foley 1910-1916; Shelley 1912-1925 **Shapes:** Dorothy
8553	Entered in pattern book during or after 1912. **Backstamp(s)**: Shelley Late Foley 1910-1916; Shelley 1912-1925 **Shapes:** Bute
8554-8555	Entered in pattern book during or after 1912. **Backstamp(s)**: Shelley Late Foley 1910-1916; Shelley 1912-1925 **Shapes:** Dainty
8557	Entered in pattern book during or after 1912. **Backstamp(s)**: Shelley Late Foley 1910-1916; Shelley 1912-1925 **Shapes:** New York Roman
8558	Entered in pattern book during or after 1912. **Backstamp(s)**: Shelley Late Foley 1910-1916; Shelley 1912-1925 **Shapes:** Bute
8559	Entered in pattern book during or after 1912. **Backstamp(s)**: Shelley Late Foley 1910-1916; Shelley 1912-1925 **Shapes:** New York
8560	Entered in pattern book during or after 1912. **Backstamp(s)**: Shelley Late Foley 1910-1916; Shelley 1912-1925 **Shapes:** Dorothy
8561	Entered in pattern book during or after 1912. **Backstamp(s)**: Shelley Late Foley 1910-1916; Shelley 1912-1925 **Shapes:** Royal
8563	Entered in pattern book during or after 1912. **Backstamp(s)**: Shelley Late Foley 1910-1916; Shelley 1912-1925 **Shapes:** Bute
8574	Entered in pattern book during or after 1912. **Backstamp(s)**: Shelley Late Foley 1910-1916; Shelley 1912-1925 **Shapes:** Milton
8575	Entered in pattern book during or after 1912. **Backstamp(s)**: Shelley Late Foley 1910-1916; Shelley 1912-1925 **Shapes:** New York
8580	Entered in pattern book during or after 1912. **Backstamp(s)**: Shelley Late Foley 1910-1916; Shelley 1912-1925 **Shapes:** Lily
8581	Entered in pattern book during or after 1912. Seconds ware. **Backstamp(s)**: Shelley Late Foley 1910-1916; Shelley 1912-1925 **Shapes:** New York
8582	Entered in pattern book during or after 1912. **Backstamp(s)**: Shelley Late Foley 1910-1916; Shelley 1912-1925 **Shapes:** New York
8583-8585	Entered in pattern book during or after 1912. **Backstamp(s)**: Shelley Late Foley 1910-1916; Shelley 1912-1925 **Shapes:** Gainsborough
8587	Entered in pattern book during or after 1912. **Backstamp(s)**: Shelley Late Foley 1910-1916; Shelley 1912-1925 **Shapes:** Bute
8588	Entered in pattern book during or after 1912. **Backstamp(s)**: Shelley Late Foley 1910-1916; Shelley 1912-1925 **Shapes:** New York
8589	Entered in pattern book during or after 1912. **Backstamp(s)**: Shelley Late Foley 1910-1916; Shelley 1912-1925 **Shapes:** Gainsborough
8590	Entered in pattern book during or after 1912. **Backstamp(s)**: Shelley Late Foley 1910-1916; Shelley 1912-1925 **Shapes:** Empire
8591-8592	Entered in pattern book during or after 1912. **Backstamp(s)**: Shelley Late Foley 1910-1916; Shelley 1912-1925 **Shapes:** Lily
8594	Entered in pattern book during or after 1912. **Backstamp(s)**: Shelley Late Foley 1910-1916; Shelley 1912-1925 **Shapes:** Gainsborough
8613-8614	Entered in pattern book during or after 1912. **Backstamp(s)**: Shelley Late Foley 1910-1916; Shelley 1912-1925 **Shapes:** Bute
8615	Entered in pattern book during or after 1912. **Backstamp(s)**: Shelley Late Foley 1910-1916; Shelley 1912-1925 **Shapes:** Gainsborough
8616-8617	Entered in pattern book during or after 1912. **Backstamp(s)**: Shelley Late Foley 1910-1916; Shelley 1912-1925 **Shapes:** Dorothy
8618	Entered in pattern book during or after 1912. **Backstamp(s)**: Shelley Late Foley 1910-1916; Shelley 1912-1925 **Shapes:** Dorothy, Gainsborough, Milton, Vincent
8619-8622	Entered in pattern book during or after 1912. **Backstamp(s)**: Shelley Late Foley 1910-1916; Shelley 1912-1925 **Shapes:** Gainsborough
8623-8624	Entered in pattern book during or after 1912. **Backstamp(s)**: Shelley Late Foley 1910-1916; Shelley 1912-1925 **Shapes:** Bute
8625	Entered in pattern book during or after 1912. **Backstamp(s)**: Shelley Late Foley 1910-1916; Shelley 1912-1925 **Shapes:** Gainsborough
8626	Entered in pattern book during or after 1912. **Backstamp(s)**: Shelley Late Foley 1910-1916; Shelley 1912-1925 **Shapes:** Bute, Gainsborough, Milton, New York, Vincent
8627	Pink roses on gold medallions with green chains on a white ground. Gold edges. Entered in pattern book during or after 1912. **Backstamp(s)**: Shelley Late Foley 1910-1916; Shelley 1912-1925 **Shapes:** Bute, Gainsborough, Milton, New York, Unhandled Coffee, Vincent

Pink roses on gold medallions 8627 Gainsborough shape cup and saucer. £40-50; $80-100

Pink roses on gold medallions 8627 Gainsborough shape twenty-one-piece tea set. £250-350; $550-750. Twenty-one-piece demitasse coffee set. £200-300; $500-700. Teapot. £70-90; $120-150. Lidded hot water jug. £40-50; $70-80

Pattern	Description & Shapes
8628-8629	Entered in pattern book during or after 1912. **Backstamp(s)**: Shelley Late Foley 1910-1916; Shelley 1912-1925 **Shapes:** Argyle
8630	Hulmes **Lowestoft**. Entered in pattern book during or after 1912. **Backstamp(s)**: Shelley Late Foley 1910-1916; Shelley 1912-1925 **Shapes:** Dainty
8631-8632	Entered in pattern book during or after 1912. **Backstamp(s)**: Shelley Late Foley 1910-1916; Shelley 1912-1925 **Shapes:** New York
8633	Entered in pattern book during or after 1912. **Backstamp(s)**: Shelley Late Foley 1910-1916; Shelley 1912-1925 **Shapes:** Gainsborough
8634	Entered in pattern book during or after 1912. **Backstamp(s)**: Shelley Late Foley 1910-1916; Shelley 1912-1925 **Shapes:** Dainty
8635	Entered in pattern book during or after

Pattern	Description & Shapes
	1912.
	Backstamp(s): Shelley Late Foley 1910-1916; Shelley 1912-1925 **Shapes:** Bute
8636-8637	Entered in pattern book during or after 1912. **Backstamp(s):** Shelley Late Foley 1910-1916; Shelley 1912-1925 **Shapes:** Dorothy
8638-8639	Entered in pattern book during or after 1912. **Backstamp(s):** Shelley Late Foley 1910-1916; Shelley 1912-1925 **Shapes:** Gainsborough
8640-8641	Entered in pattern book during or after 1912. **Backstamp(s):** Shelley Late Foley 1910-1916; Shelley 1912-1925 **Shapes:** Bute
8642	Vermillion print. Border of scrolls, circles, and small, bright pink roses. White ground. Gold edges. Entered in pattern book during or after 1912. **Backstamp(s):** Shelley Late Foley 1910-1916 **Shapes:** New York
8643	Coloured print. Border of scrolls, circles, and small roses. White ground. Gold edges. Entered in pattern book during or after 1912. **Backstamp(s):** Shelley Late Foley 1910-1916 **Shapes:** New York
8644	Entered in pattern book during or after 1912. **Backstamp(s):** Shelley Late Foley 1910-1916; Shelley 1912-1925 **Shapes:** Bute
8646	Entered in pattern book during or after 1912. **Backstamp(s):** Shelley Late Foley 1910-1916; Shelley 1912-1925 **Shapes:** Gainsborough
8647	Entered in pattern book during or after 1912. **Backstamp(s):** Shelley Late Foley 1910-1916; Shelley 1912-1925 **Shapes:** Dorothy, Milton, Vincent
8648	Entered in pattern book during or after 1912. **Backstamp(s):** Shelley Late Foley 1910-1916; Shelley 1912-1925 **Shapes:** Gainsborough, Milton, Vincent
8649	Entered in pattern book during or after 1912. **Backstamp(s):** Shelley Late Foley 1910-1916; Shelley 1912-1925 **Shapes:** Bute
8650	Entered in pattern book during or after 1912. **Backstamp(s):** Shelley Late Foley 1910-1916; Shelley 1912-1925 **Shapes:** Dorothy
8651	Entered in pattern book during or after 1912. **Backstamp(s):** Shelley Late Foley 1910-1916; Shelley 1912-1925 **Shapes:** Gainsborough, Milton
8652	Floral sprays. Pink roses, purple forget-me-nots, mauve flowers with green foliage on a white ground. Gold edges. Entered in pattern book during or after 1912. **Backstamp(s):** Shelley 1912-1925 **Shapes:** New York
8653	Green and blue parrot sitting on branch. Pink roses and green leaves. White ground. Entered in pattern book during or after 1912. **Backstamp(s):** Shelley 1912-1925 **Shapes:** Bute, Norman
8654	Entered in pattern book during or after 1912. **Backstamp(s):** Shelley Late Foley 1910-1916; Shelley 1912-1925 **Shapes:** Dorothy
8655	Pink roses with green and grey leaves. Entered in pattern book during or after 1912. **Backstamp(s):** Shelley Late Foley 1910-1916; Shelley 1912-1925 **Shapes:** Dorothy, Gainsborough, Vincent
8656	Entered in pattern book during or after 1912. **Backstamp(s):** Shelley Late Foley 1910-1916; Shelley 1912-1925 **Shapes:** Gainsborough
8657	Entered in pattern book during or after 1912. **Backstamp(s):** Shelley Late Foley 1910-1916; Shelley 1912-1925 **Shapes:** Dorothy
8658	Entered in pattern book during or after 1912. **Backstamp(s):** Shelley Late Foley 1910-1916; Shelley 1912-1925 **Shapes:** Bute, Dorothy, Vincent
8661	Entered in pattern book during or after 1912. Seconds ware. **Backstamp(s):** Shelley Late Foley 1910-1916; Shelley 1912-1925 **Shapes:** Royal
8662	Border of small rose bouquets, garlands of green leaves against a dark green Greek Key band. White ground. Gold edges. Entered in pattern book during or after 1912/1913. Seconds ware. **Backstamp(s):** Shelley 1912-1925 **Shapes:** Bute, Gainsborough
8663	Entered in pattern book during or after 1912. Seconds ware. **Backstamp(s):** Shelley Late Foley 1910-1916; Shelley 1912-1925 **Shapes:** New York
8664	Entered in pattern book during or after 1912. Seconds ware. **Backstamp(s):** Shelley Late Foley 1910-1916; Shelley 1912-1925 **Shapes:** Gainsborough
8665	Entered in pattern book during or after 1912. Seconds ware. **Backstamp(s):** Shelley Late Foley 1910-1916; Shelley 1912-1925 **Shapes:** Royal
8666	Entered in pattern book during or after 1912. Seconds ware. **Backstamp(s):** Shelley Late Foley 1910-1916; Shelley 1912-1925 **Shapes:** New York
8667	Entered in pattern book during or after 1912. Seconds ware. **Backstamp(s):** Shelley Late Foley 1910-1916; Shelley 1912-1925 **Shapes:** Gainsborough
8668-8669	Entered in pattern book during or after 1912. Seconds ware. **Backstamp(s):** Shelley Late Foley 1910-1916; Shelley 1912-1925 **Shapes:** Dainty
8670	Entered in pattern book during or after 1912. **Backstamp(s):** Shelley Late Foley 1910-1916; Shelley 1912-1925 **Shapes:** Gainsborough
8674-8675	Entered in pattern book during or after 1912. **Backstamp(s):** Shelley Late Foley 1910-1916; Shelley 1912-1925 **Shapes:** Bute
8676	Entered in pattern book during or after 1912. **Backstamp(s):** Shelley Late Foley 1910-1916; Shelley 1912-1925 **Shapes:** Dorothy
8677	Entered in pattern book during or after 1912. **Backstamp(s):** Shelley Late Foley 1910-1916; Shelley 1912-1925 **Shapes:** Bute
8678	Entered in pattern book during or after 1912. **Backstamp(s):** Shelley Late Foley 1910-1916; Shelley 1912-1925 **Shapes:** New York
8679	Entered in pattern book during or after 1912. **Backstamp(s):** Shelley Late Foley 1910-1916; Shelley 1912-1925 **Shapes:** Unhandled Coffee
8703	Sprays of pink roses and small blue flowers with green foliage on a white ground. Spray also inside cup. Gold edges. Seconds ware. **Backstamp(s):** Shelley Late Foley 1912-1916 **Shapes:** New York
8680	Entered in pattern book during or after 1912. **Backstamp(s):** Shelley Late Foley 1910-1916; Shelley 1912-1925 **Shapes:** Roman
8681	Entered in pattern book during or after 1912. **Backstamp(s):** Shelley Late Foley 1910-1916; Shelley 1912-1925 **Shapes:** New York
8682	Entered in pattern book during or after 1912. **Backstamp(s):** Shelley Late Foley 1910-1916; Shelley 1912-1925 **Shapes:** Bute
8684	Entered in pattern book during or after 1913. **Backstamp(s):** Shelley Late Foley 1910-1916; Shelley 1912-1925 **Shapes:** Victoria
8688	Entered in pattern book during or after 1913. **Backstamp(s):** Shelley Late Foley 1910-1916; Shelley 1912-1925 **Shapes:** Bute
8691-8692	Entered in pattern book during or after 1913. **Backstamp(s):** Shelley Late Foley 1910-1916; Shelley 1912-1925 **Shapes:** Bute
8693	Entered in pattern book during or after 1913. **Backstamp(s):** Shelley Late Foley 1910-1916; Shelley 1912-1925 **Shapes:** Dorothy
8695	Entered in pattern book during or after 1913. Seconds ware. **Backstamp(s):** Shelley Late Foley 1910-1916; Shelley 1912-1925 **Shapes:** Gainsborough
8696	Entered in pattern book during or after 1913. Seconds ware. **Backstamp(s):** Shelley Late Foley 1910-1916; Shelley 1912-1925 **Shapes:** Violet
8697-8700	Entered in pattern book during or after 1913. Seconds ware. **Backstamp(s):** Shelley Late Foley 1910-1916; Shelley 1912-1925 **Shapes:** Dorothy
8701	Entered in pattern book during or after 1913. Seconds ware. **Backstamp(s):** Shelley Late Foley 1910-1916; Shelley 1912-1925 **Shapes:** Lily
8702	Entered in pattern book during or after 1913. Seconds ware. **Backstamp(s):** Shelley Late Foley 1910-1916; Shelley 1912-1925 **Shapes:** Bute
8703	Entered in pattern book during or after 1913. Seconds ware. **Backstamp(s):** Shelley Late Foley 1910-1916; Shelley 1912-1925 **Shapes:** New York
8704	Entered in pattern book during or after

Pattern	Description & Shapes
	1913. Seconds ware. **Backstamp(s)**: Shelley Late Foley 1910-1916; Shelley 1912-1925 **Shapes:** Dainty
8705	Entered in pattern book during or after 1913. Seconds ware. **Backstamp(s)**: Shelley Late Foley 1910-1916; Shelley 1912-1925 **Shapes:** Court
8706	Entered in pattern book during or after 1913. Seconds ware. **Backstamp(s)**: Shelley Late Foley 1910-1916; Shelley 1912-1925 **Shapes:** Low Lily
8707	Entered in pattern book during or after 1913. **Backstamp(s)**: Shelley Late Foley 1910-1916; Shelley 1912-1925 **Shapes:** Roman
8708	Entered in pattern book during or after 1913. **Backstamp(s)**: Shelley Late Foley 1910-1916; Shelley 1912-1925 **Shapes:** Milton
8709	Entered in pattern book during or after 1913. **Backstamp(s)**: Shelley Late Foley 1910-1916; Shelley 1912-1925 **Shapes:** Antique
8710	Entered in pattern book during or after 1913. **Backstamp(s)**: Shelley Late Foley 1910-1916; Shelley 1912-1925 **Shapes:** Violet
8711-8712	Entered in pattern book during or after 1913. **Backstamp(s)**: Shelley Late Foley 1910-1916; Shelley 1912-1925 **Shapes:** Argyle
8714	Entered in pattern book during or after 1913. **Backstamp(s)**: Shelley Late Foley 1910-1916; Shelley 1912-1925 **Shapes:** Gainsborough
8715-8721	Entered in pattern book during or after 1913. Seconds ware. **Backstamp(s)**: Shelley Late Foley 1910-1916; Shelley 1912-1925 **Shapes:** Way Spiral
8722	Entered in pattern book during or after 1913. Seconds ware. **Backstamp(s)**: Shelley Late Foley 1910-1916; Shelley 1912-1925 **Shapes:** Empire
8723	Entered in pattern book during or after 1913. Seconds ware. **Backstamp(s)**: Shelley Late Foley 1910-1916; Shelley 1912-1925 **Shapes:** Gainsborough
8724	Entered in pattern book during or after 1913. Seconds ware. **Backstamp(s)**: Shelley Late Foley 1910-1916; Shelley 1912-1925 **Shapes:** Dorothy
8725	Entered in pattern book during or after 1913. Seconds ware. **Backstamp(s)**: Shelley Late Foley 1910-1916; Shelley 1912-1925 **Shapes:** Gainsborough
8726	Entered in pattern book during or after 1913. Seconds ware. **Backstamp(s)**: Shelley Late Foley 1910-1916; Shelley 1912-1925 **Shapes:** New York
8727	Entered in pattern book during or after 1913. Seconds ware. **Backstamp(s)**: Shelley Late Foley 1910-1916; Shelley 1912-1925 **Shapes:** Violet
8728	Entered in pattern book during or after 1913. Seconds ware. **Backstamp(s)**: Shelley Late Foley 1910-1916; Shelley 1912-1925 **Shapes:** Bute
8729	Entered in pattern book during or after 1913. Seconds ware. **Backstamp(s)**: Shelley Late Foley 1910-1916; Shelley 1912-1925 **Shapes:** Court
8730	Entered in pattern book during or after 1913. **Backstamp(s)**: Shelley Late Foley 1910-1916; Shelley 1912-1925 **Shapes:** Bute
8731	Entered in pattern book during or after 1913. **Backstamp(s)**: Shelley Late Foley 1910-1916; Shelley 1912-1925 **Shapes:** Gainsborough
8732	Entered in pattern book during or after 1913. **Backstamp(s)**: Shelley Late Foley 1910-1916; Shelley 1912-1925 **Shapes:** Dorothy
8733	Entered in pattern book during or after 1913. **Backstamp(s)**: Shelley Late Foley 1910-1916; Shelley 1912-1925 **Shapes:** Gainsborough
8734	Entered in pattern book during or after 1913. **Backstamp(s)**: Shelley Late Foley 1910-1916; Shelley 1912-1925 **Shapes:** Bute, Dorothy
8735	Entered in pattern book during or after 1913. Seconds ware. **Backstamp(s)**: Shelley Late Foley 1910-1916; Shelley 1912-1925 **Shapes:** Bute
8736	Entered in pattern book during or after 1913. Seconds ware. **Backstamp(s)**: Shelley Late Foley 1910-1916; Shelley 1912-1925 **Shapes:** Lily
8737	Entered in pattern book during or after 1913. **Backstamp(s)**: Shelley Late Foley 1910-1916; Shelley 1912-1925 **Shapes:** Roman
8738-8739	Entered in pattern book during or after 1913. **Backstamp(s)**: Shelley Late Foley 1910-1916; Shelley 1912-1925 **Shapes:** Gainsborough
8740-8745	Entered in pattern book during or after 1913. **Backstamp(s)**: Shelley Late Foley 1910-1916; Shelley 1912-1925 **Shapes:** Mocha
8752	Entered in pattern book during or after 1913. **Backstamp(s)**: Shelley Late Foley 1910-1916; Shelley 1912-1925 **Shapes:** Gainsborough
8761-8762	Entered in pattern book during or after 1913. **Backstamp(s)**: Shelley Late Foley 1910-1916; Shelley 1912-1925 **Shapes:** Bute
8763-8765	Entered in pattern book during or after 1913. Seconds ware. **Backstamp(s)**: Shelley Late Foley 1910-1916; Shelley 1912-1925 **Shapes:** Bute
8766	Entered in pattern book during or after 1913. **Backstamp(s)**: Shelley Late Foley 1910-1916; Shelley 1912-1925 **Shapes:** Dorothy
8769-8770	Entered in pattern book during or after 1913. **Backstamp(s)**: Shelley Late Foley 1910-1916; Shelley 1912-1925 **Shapes:** Gainsborough
8771	Entered in pattern book during or after 1913. Seconds ware. **Backstamp(s)**: Shelley Late Foley 1910-1916; Shelley 1912-1925 **Shapes:** Gainsborough
8772	Entered in pattern book during or after 1913. **Backstamp(s)**: Shelley Late Foley 1910-1916; Shelley 1912-1925 **Shapes:** Bute
8774	Entered in pattern book during or after 1913. **Backstamp(s)**: Shelley Late Foley 1910-1916; Shelley 1912-1925 **Shapes:** Bute
8775	Plain colours. White centre of saucer. Entered in pattern book during or after 1913. **Backstamp(s)**: Shelley Late Foley 1910-1916; Shelley 1912-1925 **Shapes:** Antique, Dainty, Mocha, New York, Norman, Stanley Coffee Pot, Vincent
8786	Entered in pattern book during or after 1913. **Backstamp(s)**: Shelley Late Foley 1910-1916; Shelley 1912-1925 **Shapes:** Antique, Dainty, Mocha, New York, Norman, Stanley Coffee Pot, Vincent
8787	**Maytime**. Half chintz and green. Small pink flowers in varying shades of pink with brown branches and green foliage. Entered in pattern book during or after 1913. Seconds ware. **Backstamp(s)**: Shelley 1925-1940 **Shapes:** Unknown
8794	Entered in pattern book during or after 1913. **Backstamp(s)**: Shelley Late Foley 1910-1916; Shelley 1912-1925 **Shapes:** Gainsborough, Royal
8795	Entered in pattern book during or after 1913. **Backstamp(s)**: Shelley Late Foley 1910-1916; Shelley 1912-1925 **Shapes:** Gladstone
8796	Entered in pattern book during or after 1913. **Backstamp(s)**: Shelley Late Foley 1910-1916; Shelley 1912-1925 **Shapes:** Bute
8797	Entered in pattern book during or after 1913. **Backstamp(s)**: Shelley Late Foley 1910-1916; Shelley 1912-1925 **Shapes:** New York
8798	Entered in pattern book during or after 1913. **Backstamp(s)**: Shelley Late Foley 1910-1916; Shelley 1912-1925 **Shapes:** Lily
8802	Entered in pattern book during or after 1913. **Backstamp(s)**: Shelley Late Foley 1910-1916; Shelley 1912-1925 **Shapes:** Mocha
8804	Entered in pattern book during or after 1913. **Backstamp(s)**: Shelley Late Foley 1910-1916; Shelley 1912-1925 **Shapes:** Gainsborough, Royal
8806-8808	Entered in pattern book during or after 1913. Seconds ware. **Backstamp(s)**: Shelley Late Foley 1910-1916; Shelley 1912-1925 **Shapes:** Argyle
8809	Entered in pattern book during or after 1913. **Backstamp(s)**: Shelley Late Foley 1910-1916; Shelley 1912-1925 **Shapes:** Empress Teapot, Victoria
8810	American samples. Entered in pattern book during or after 1913. **Backstamp(s)**: Shelley Late Foley 1910-1916; Shelley 1912-1925 **Shapes:** Unknown

Pattern Description & Shapes

8811 **Indian Peony**. American sample. Entered in pattern book during or after 1913.
Backstamp(s): Shelley Late Foley 1910-1916; Shelley 1912-1925
Shapes: Gainsborough, Milton

8812 **Indian Peony**. American sample. Entered in pattern book during or after 1913.
Backstamp(s): Shelley Late Foley 1910-1916; Shelley 1912-1925
Shapes: Gainsborough

8813 **Indian Tree Border**. American sample. Entered in pattern book during or after 1913.
Backstamp(s): Shelley Late Foley 1910-1916; Shelley 1912-1925
Shapes: Bute

8814 **Jacobean**. Entered in pattern book during or after 1913.
Backstamp(s): Shelley Late Foley 1910-1916; Shelley 1912-1925
Shapes: New York

8820-8825 American samples. Entered in pattern book during or after 1913.
Backstamp(s): Shelley Late Foley 1910-1916; Shelley 1912-1925
Shapes: Mocha

8826 **Jacobean**. Entered in pattern book during or after 1913.
Backstamp(s): Shelley Late Foley 1910-1916; Shelley 1912-1925
Shapes: Royal

8827 Entered in pattern book during or after 1913.
Backstamp(s): Shelley Late Foley 1910-1916; Shelley 1912-1925
Shapes: Gainsborough

8830 Entered in pattern book during or after 1913.
Backstamp(s): Shelley Late Foley 1910-1916; Shelley 1912-1925
Shapes: Gainsborough

8831 **Festoon**. Entered in pattern book during or after 1913. Seconds ware.
Backstamp(s): Shelley Late Foley 1910-1916; Shelley 1912-1925
Shapes: Gainsborough

8832 **Lowestoft**. Small sprays of pink, blue, and yellow flowers with green leaves on a white ground. Entered in pattern book during or after 1913. Seconds ware.
Backstamp(s): Shelley Late Foley 1910-1916; Shelley 1912-1925
Shapes: Daisy

8833 **Festoon**. Entered in pattern book during or after 1913. Seconds ware.
Backstamp(s): Shelley Late Foley 1910-1916; Shelley 1912-1925
Shapes: Lily

8834 **Festoon**. Entered in pattern book during or after 1913. Seconds ware.
Backstamp(s): Shelley Late Foley 1910-1916; Shelley 1912-1925
Shapes: Gainsborough

8835 Entered in pattern book during or after 1913.
Backstamp(s): Shelley Late Foley 1910-1916; Shelley 1912-1925
Shapes: Victoria

8842-8847 **Solid Colours**. Entered in pattern book during or after 1913.
Backstamp(s): Shelley Late Foley 1910-1916; Shelley 1912-1925
Shapes: Mocha

8863-8894 **Border Patterns**. For export to U.S.A. Entered in pattern book during or after 1913.
Backstamp(s): Shelley Late Foley 1910-1916; Shelley 1912-1925
Shapes: Gainsborough

8895 **Apple Sprays**. Entered in pattern book during or after 1913.
Backstamp(s): Shelley Late Foley 1910-1916; Shelley 1912-1925
Shapes: Bute, New York Teapot

8896-8899 Entered in pattern book during or after 1913.
Backstamp(s): Shelley Late Foley 1910-1916; Shelley 1912-1925
Shapes: Bute

8900-8901 Entered in pattern book during or after 1913.
Backstamp(s): Shelley Late Foley 1910-1916; Shelley 1912-1925
Shapes: Gainsborough

8902-8904 Entered in pattern book during or after 1913.
Backstamp(s): Shelley Late Foley 1910-1916; Shelley 1912-1925
Shapes: Bute

8905 Entered in pattern book during or after 1913.
Backstamp(s): Shelley Late Foley 1910-1916; Shelley 1912-1925
Shapes: Dorothy

8906 Entered in pattern book during or after 1913.
Backstamp(s): Shelley Late Foley 1910-1916; Shelley 1912-1925
Shapes: Gainsborough

8907 Entered in pattern book during or after 1913.
Backstamp(s): Shelley Late Foley 1910-1916; Shelley 1912-1925
Shapes: Bute

8908 **Jewel and Chain**. Black pattern with blue and black enamelling. Art nouveau border **outside cup** and on saucer. Entered in pattern book during or after 1913.
Backstamp(s): Shelley 1912-1925
Shapes: Bute

8909 **Jewel and Chain**. Black pattern with pink and black enamelling. Art nouveau border **outside cup** and on saucer. Entered in pattern book during or after 1913.
Backstamp(s): Shelley 1912-1925
Shapes: Bute

8910 **Jewel and Chain**. Black pattern with green and black enamelling. Art nouveau border **outside cup** and on saucer. Entered in pattern book during or after 1913.
Backstamp(s): Shelley 1912-1925
Shapes: Bute

Jewel and Chain 8910 Bute shape cup, saucer, and plate. £40-£50; $75-85

8911 Entered in pattern book during or after 1913.
Backstamp(s): Shelley Late Foley 1910-1916; Shelley 1912-1925
Shapes: Bute

8912-8918 Entered in pattern book during or after 1913.
Backstamp(s): Shelley Late Foley 1910-1916; Shelley 1912-1925
Shapes: Gainsborough

8919 **Pink Apples**. Black ground. Entered in pattern book during or after 1913.
Backstamp(s): Shelley Late Foley 1910-1916; Shelley 1912-1925
Shapes: Bute

8920 Entered in pattern book during or after 1913.
Backstamp(s): Shelley Late Foley 1910-1916; Shelley 1912-1925
Shapes: Gainsborough

8921 Entered in pattern book during or after 1913. Seconds ware.
Backstamp(s): Shelley Late Foley 1910-1916; Shelley 1912-1925
Shapes: Gainsborough

8922 Entered in pattern book during or after 1914. Seconds ware.
Backstamp(s): Shelley Late Foley 1910-1916; Shelley 1912-1925
Shapes: Bute

8923-8924 Entered in pattern book during or after 1914.
Backstamp(s): Shelley Late Foley 1910-1916; Shelley 1912-1925
Shapes: Snowdrop

8927 Entered in pattern book during or after 1914.
Backstamp(s): Shelley Late Foley 1910-1916; Shelley 1912-1925
Shapes: Mocha

8931-8934 Entered in pattern book during or after 1914.
Backstamp(s): Shelley Late Foley 1910-1916; Shelley 1912-1925
Shapes: Mocha

8935 Entered in pattern book during or after 1914.
Backstamp(s): Shelley Late Foley 1910-1916; Shelley 1912-1925
Shapes: Bute

8936 Entered in pattern book during or after 1914.
Backstamp(s): Shelley Late Foley 1910-1916; Shelley 1912-1925
Shapes: Dorothy

8937 Entered in pattern book during or after 1914. Seconds ware.
Backstamp(s): Shelley Late Foley 1910-1916; Shelley 1912-1925
Shapes: Gainsborough

8938-8946 Entered in pattern book during or after 1914.
Backstamp(s): Shelley Late Foley 1910-1916; Shelley 1912-1925
Shapes: Bute, Mocha

8952 Entered in pattern book during or after 1914.
Backstamp(s): Shelley Late Foley 1910-1916; Shelley 1912-1925
Shapes: Milton

8953 Entered in pattern book during or after 1914.
Backstamp(s): Shelley Late Foley 1910-1916; Shelley 1912-1925
Shapes: Gainsborough

8959 Entered in pattern book during or after 1914.
Backstamp(s): Shelley Late Foley 1910-1916; Shelley 1912-1925
Shapes: New York

8960 Entered in pattern book during or after 1914.
Backstamp(s): Shelley Late Foley 1910-1916; Shelley 1912-1925
Shapes: Gainsborough

8961 Entered in pattern book during or after 1914.
Backstamp(s): Shelley Late Foley 1910-1916; Shelley 1912-1925
Shapes: Bute

8962 Entered in pattern book during or after

Pattern **Description & Shapes**

1914. Seconds ware.
Backstamp(s): Shelley Late Foley 1910-1916; Shelley 1912-1925
Shapes: York

8963 Entered in pattern book during or after 1914. Seconds ware.
Backstamp(s): Shelley Late Foley 1910-1916; Shelley 1912-1925
Shapes: Low Lily

8964-8965 Entered in pattern book during or after 1914.
Backstamp(s): Shelley Late Foley 1910-1916; Shelley 1912-1925
Shapes: Gainsborough

8966 Entered in pattern book during or after 1914.
Backstamp(s): Shelley Late Foley 1910-1916; Shelley 1912-1925
Shapes: New York

8967 Entered in pattern book during or after 1914.
Backstamp(s): Shelley Late Foley 1910-1916; Shelley 1912-1925
Shapes: Bute

8968-8979 Entered in pattern book during or after 1914.
Backstamp(s): Shelley Late Foley 1910-1916; Shelley 1912-1925
Shapes: Oleander

8980-8985 Entered in pattern book during or after 1914.
Backstamp(s): Shelley Late Foley 1910-1916; Shelley 1912-1925
Shapes: Gainsborough

8986 Entered in pattern book during or after 1914.
Backstamp(s): Shelley Late Foley 1910-1916; Shelley 1912-1925
Shapes: Bute, Mocha

8987 Entered in pattern book during or after 1914.
Backstamp(s): Shelley Late Foley 1910-1916; Shelley 1912-1925
Shapes: Gainsborough, Mocha

8988 Entered in pattern book during or after 1914.
Backstamp(s): Shelley Late Foley 1910-1916; Shelley 1912-1925
Shapes: Gainsborough

8989-8990 Entered in pattern book during or after 1914.
Backstamp(s): Shelley Late Foley 1910-1916; Shelley 1912-1925
Shapes: Mocha

8991-8993 **Silk Pattern**. Entered in pattern book during or after 1914.
Backstamp(s): Shelley Late Foley 1910-1916; Shelley 1912-1925
Shapes: Mocha

8994 **Parrot Pattern**. Entered in pattern book during or after 1914.
Backstamp(s): Shelley Late Foley 1910-1916; Shelley 1912-1925
Shapes: Gainsborough

8995-8996 Entered in pattern book during or after 1914.
Backstamp(s): Shelley Late Foley 1910-1916; Shelley 1912-1925
Shapes: Gainsborough

8997-8999 Entered in pattern book during or after 1914.
Backstamp(s): Shelley Late Foley 1910-1916; Shelley 1912-1925
Shapes: Bute

9000-9001 Entered in pattern book during or after 1914.
Backstamp(s): Shelley Late Foley 1910-1916; Shelley 1912-1925
Shapes: Gainsborough

9002 Same as 6811, 6878, and 9076. Entered in pattern book during or after 1897.
Backstamp(s): Wileman Foley 1890-1910
Shapes: Dainty

9003 **Poppy**. Same as 5753. Enamelled. Entered in pattern book during or after 1897.
Backstamp(s): Wileman Foley 1890-1910
Shapes: Dainty

9005 **Shaded Ground**. Same as 5875. Entered in pattern book during or after 1897.
Backstamp(s): Wileman Foley 1890-1910
Shapes: Dainty

9006 Same as 6506. Entered in pattern book during or after 1897.
Backstamp(s): Wileman Foley 1890-1910
Shapes: Empire, Foley

9011-9028 **Star Design, Cluster of Flowers**. Entered in pattern book during or after 1897.
Backstamp(s): Wileman Foley 1890-1910
Shapes: Dainty

9032-9035 **Star Design, Cluster of Flowers**. Entered in pattern book during or after 1897.
Backstamp(s): Wileman Foley 1890-1910
Shapes: Dainty

9044 **Cluster of Daisies**. Entered in pattern book during or after 1897.
Backstamp(s): Wileman Foley 1890-1910
Shapes: Empire

9050 **Gold Sprigs and Leaf Design**. Same as 5805. Panelled. Entered in pattern book during or after 1897.
Backstamp(s): Wileman Foley 1890-1910
Shapes: Snowdrop Bouillon

9051 **Gold Sprigs and Leaf Design**. Same as 5809. Panelled. Entered in pattern book during or after 1897.
Backstamp(s): Wileman Foley 1890-1910
Shapes: Snowdrop Bouillon

9052-9055 **Trailing Violets Print**. Same as 5622. Coloured print. Trailing daisies and violets. Print also inside cup. White ground. Gold edges. Entered in pattern book during or after 1895.
Backstamp(s): Wileman Foley 1890-1910
Shapes: Dainty, Snowdrop

9056 **Trailing Violets Print**. Pink and turquoise trailing daisies and violets. Pattern also inside cup. White ground. Gold edges. Entered in pattern book during or after 1895.
Backstamp(s): Wileman Foley 1890-1910
Shapes: Dainty, Snowdrop

9057 **Trailing Violets Print**. Same as 5622. Coloured print. Trailing daisies and violets. Print also inside cup. White ground. Gold edges. Entered in pattern book during or after 1895.
Backstamp(s): Wileman Foley 1890-1910
Shapes: Dainty, Snowdrop

9058 **Trailing Violets Print**. Brown and turquoise trailing daisies and violets. Pattern also inside cup. White ground. Gold edges. Entered in pattern book during or after 1895.
Backstamp(s): Wileman Foley 1890-1910
Shapes: Dainty, Snowdrop

9059 **Daisies Print**. Trailing orange daisies and green foliage on a white ground. Pattern also inside cup. Gold edges. Entered in pattern book during or after 1897.
Backstamp(s): Wileman Foley 1890-1910
Shapes: Snowdrop

9062-9065 **Daisies Print**. Trailing daisies and foliage on a white ground. Pattern also inside cup. Gold edges. Entered in pattern book during or after 1897. Seconds ware.
Backstamp(s): Wileman Foley 1890-1910
Shapes: Dainty

9066 **Surrey Scenery**. Entered in pattern book during or after 1897.
Backstamp(s): Wileman Foley 1890-1910
Shapes: Century

9067 Daisies Print. Trailing turquoise daisies and brown foliage on a white ground. Pattern also inside cup. Gold edges. Entered in pattern book during or after 1897.
Backstamp(s): Wileman Foley 1890-1910
Shapes: Snowdrop

9068 **Daisies**. Enamelled. Entered in pattern book during or after 1897.
Backstamp(s): Wileman Foley 1890-1910
Shapes: Roman

9076 Same as 6811, 6878, and 9002. Entered in pattern book during or after 1898.
Backstamp(s): Wileman Foley 1890-1910
Shapes: Dainty

9077 **Star Design**, Cluster of Flowers. Entered in pattern book during or after 1898.
Backstamp(s): Wileman Foley 1890-1910
Shapes: Dainty

9079 **Daisies**. Enamelled. Entered in pattern book during or after 1898.
Backstamp(s): Wileman Foley 1890-1910
Shapes: Roman

9082 **Fern Print**. Entered in pattern book during or after 1898.
Backstamp(s): Wileman Foley 1890-1910
Shapes: Lily

9083 **Chrysanthemum Print**. Enamelled. Entered in pattern book during or after 1898.
Backstamp(s): Wileman Foley 1890-1910
Shapes: Dainty, Snowdrop

9084 **Chrysanthemum Print**. Entered in pattern book during or after 1898.
Backstamp(s): Wileman Foley 1890-1910
Shapes: Dainty, Snowdrop

9097 **Star Design**. Each piece has one large, six-pointed emerald green star. The points of the green stars are curled. There is an eight-pointed, yellow star between each of the green star points on a white ground. Emerald green band on outside rim of cup, edge of saucer and plate. Inside cup is white with bands of green border and a yellow star. Entered in pattern book during or after 1898.
Backstamp(s): Wileman Foley 1890-1910
Shapes: Snowdrop

9098-9100 **Star Design**. Same as 6994. Each piece has one large, six-pointed star. The points of the large stars are curled. There is an eight-pointed star between each of the large star points on a white ground. Band on outside rim of cup, edge of saucer and plate. Inside cup is white with bands of border and a small star. Entered in pattern book during or after 1898.

Pattern Description & Shapes

Backstamp(s): Wileman Foley 1890-1910
Shapes: Snowdrop

9102-9109 **Floral Print with Scroll Border**. Entered in pattern book during or after 1899.
Backstamp(s): Wileman Foley 1890-1910
Shapes: Empire

9115 **Floral Print with Scroll Border**. Entered in pattern book during or after 1899.
Backstamp(s): Wileman Foley 1890-1910
Shapes: Empire

9116 **Japan**. Same as 6663 and 6873. Blue and red pattern. White ground. Pattern also inside cup. Gold edges. Entered in pattern book during or after 1899.
Backstamp(s): Wileman Foley 1890-1910
Shapes: New Fairy

9117 **Japan**. Same as 3852 and 4326. Enamelled in blue and red. Entered in pattern book during or after 1899.
Backstamp(s): Wileman Foley 1890-1910
Shapes: New Fairy

9118 **Daisy Wreath Print**. Entered in pattern book during or after 1899.
Backstamp(s): Wileman Foley 1890-1910
Shapes: Daisy

9119 **Japan**. Same as 6887. Blue and red pattern. White ground. Gold edges. Entered in pattern book during or after 1899.
Backstamp(s): Wileman Foley 1890-1910
Shapes: Daisy

9120 **Chrysanthemum**. Enamelled in blue. Entered in pattern book during or after 1899.
Backstamp(s): Wileman Foley 1890-1910
Shapes: Daisy

9121 **Surrey Scenery**. Entered in pattern book during or after 1899.
Backstamp(s): Wileman Foley 1890-1910
Shapes: Violet

9122 **Fern Print**. Same as 6897. Deep-blue ferns. Entered in pattern book during or after 1899.
Backstamp(s): Wileman Foley 1890-1910
Shapes: Violet

9127 **Sunflower and Leaf Border**. Orange and blue Imari type pattern on a white ground. Border also inside cup. Gold edges. Entered in pattern book during or after 1899.

Sunflower and Leaf Border 9127 Violet shape cup, saucer, and plate. £60-90; $90-110

Backstamp(s): Wileman Foley 1890-1910
Shapes: Violet, Violet Moustache Cup

9131-9145 **Sprays of Poppies**. Entered in pattern book during or after 1899.
Backstamp(s): Wileman Foley 1890-1910
Shapes: New Fairy

9151-9161 **Petunia**. Art nouveau type design. Flowers and stems. White ground. Gold edges. Entered in pattern book during or after 1899.
Backstamp(s): Wileman Foley 1890-1910
Shapes: Snowdrop

9162 **Petunia**. Green art nouveau type design. Green flowers and stems. White ground. Gold edges. Entered in pattern book during or after 1899.
Backstamp(s): Wileman Foley 1890-1910
Shapes: Snowdrop

9163-9164 **Petunia**. Art nouveau type design. Flowers and stems. White ground. Gold edges. Entered in pattern book during or after 1899.
Backstamp(s): Wileman Foley 1890-1910
Shapes: Snowdrop

9166 **Petunia**. Art nouveau type design. Flowers and stems. White ground. Gold edges. Entered in pattern book during or after 1899.
Backstamp(s): Wileman Foley 1890-1910
Shapes: Snowdrop

9171-9186 **Snowdrops**. Entered in pattern book during or after 1899.
Backstamp(s): Wileman Foley 1890-1910
Shapes: Daisy

(*Is a number missing here? Thanks.)Snowdrops. Panels with Entered in pattern book during or after 1899.
Backstamp(s): Wileman Foley 1890-1910
Shapes: Daisy

9171-9186 **Snowdrops**. Entered in pattern book during or after 1899.
Backstamp(s): Wileman Foley 1890-1910
Shapes: Daisy

9196-9197 Same as 7045. Entered in pattern book during or after 1899.
Backstamp(s): Wileman Foley 1890-1910
Shapes: Snowdrop

9199 **Fern Print**. Same as 6897 and 9122. Deep-blue ferns. Entered in pattern book during or after 1899.
Backstamp(s): Wileman Foley 1890-1910
Shapes: Lily

9202 **Blue Scenery**. Same as 6901. Deep-blue ferns. Entered in pattern book during or after 1899.
Backstamp(s): Wileman Foley 1890-1910
Shapes: Violet

9211-9228 **Roses Border Print**. Entered in pattern book during or after 1900.
Backstamp(s): Wileman Foley 1890-1910
Shapes: Foley

9321-9250 **Storks Print**. Entered in pattern book during or after 1900.
Backstamp(s): Wileman Foley 1890-1910
Shapes: New York

9254-9255 **Chrysanthemum Print**. Same as 9083. Enamelled. Entered in pattern book during or after 1900.
Backstamp(s): Wileman Foley 1890-1910
Shapes: Snowdrop

9256 **Star Design**. Same as 6994. Each piece has one large, six-pointed star. The points of these stars are curled. There is an eight-pointed star between each of the large star points on a white ground. Coloured band on outside rim of cup, edge of saucer and plate. Inside cup is white with bands of colour and an eight-pointed star. Entered in pattern book during or after 1900.
Backstamp(s): Wileman Foley 1890-1910
Shapes: Snowdrop

9258 Same as 7044. Entered in pattern book during or after 1900.
Backstamp(s): Wileman Foley 1890-1910
Shapes: Century

9259-9260 Same as 7064. Entered in pattern book during or after 1900.
Backstamp(s): Wileman Foley 1890-1910
Shapes: Snowdrop

9261 **Trailing Violets Print**. Same as 5692. Enamelled, coloured print. Trailing daisies and violets. Print also inside cup. White ground. Gold edges. Entered in pattern book during or after 1900.
Backstamp(s): Wileman Foley 1890-1910
Shapes: Violet

9267-9269 **Rococo Design**. Same as 6172, 6290, 6292, 6820, 9585, and 9683. Gold print. Entered in pattern book during or after 1900.
Backstamp(s): Wileman Foley 1890-1910
Shapes: Empire

9279-9282 **Daisy Border**. Entered in pattern book during or after 1901.
Backstamp(s): Wileman Foley 1890-1910
Shapes: Dainty

9287 **Snowdrops**. Entered in pattern book during or after 1901.
Backstamp(s): Wileman Foley 1890-1910
Shapes: Daisy

9289 **Floral Print with Scroll Border**. Same as 9106. Entered in pattern book during or after 1901.
Backstamp(s): Wileman Foley 1890-1910
Shapes: Empire

9291-9303 **Basket of Flowers**. Baskets of flowers and garlands. Pattern also inside cup. Colour variations include blue and terracotta. Gold edges. Entered in pattern book during or after 1901. Also see 13629 Basket Festoon.
Backstamp(s): Wileman Foley 1890-1910
Shapes: Gainsborough

9304 **Basket of Flowers**. Blue print. Baskets of flowers and garlands. Pattern also inside cup. Gold edges. Entered in pattern book during or after 1901. Also see 13629 Basket Festoon.
Backstamp(s): Wileman Foley 1890-1910
Shapes: Gainsborough

9305-9308 **Basket of Flowers**. Baskets of flowers and garlands. Pattern also inside cup. Colour variations include blue and

terracotta. Gold edges. Entered in pattern book during or after 1901. Also see 13629 Basket Festoon.
Backstamp(s): Wileman Foley 1890-1910
Shapes: Gainsborough

9311-9328 **Dresden Flowers**. Entered in pattern book during or after 1901.
Backstamp(s): Wileman Foley 1890-1910
Shapes: Lily

9331 **Cameo**. Vermillion cameos. Pattern also inside cup. Entered in pattern book during or after 1901.
Backstamp(s): Wileman Foley 1890-1910
Shapes: Snowdrop

9332-9334 **Cameo**. Entered in pattern book during or after 1901.
Backstamp(s): Wileman Foley 1890-1910
Shapes: Snowdrop

9335 **Cameo**. Pale turquoise cameos. Pattern also inside cup. Entered in pattern book during or after 1901.
Backstamp(s): Wileman Foley 1890-1910
Shapes: Snowdrop

9339 **Daisies**. Enamelled. Orange daisies against shades of blue-green, which graduate through to white. Pattern also inside cup. Gold edges. Entered in pattern book during or after 1901.
Backstamp(s): Wileman Foley 1890-1910
Shapes: Empire

9340 **Daisies**. Enamelled. Daisies against shades, which graduate through to white. Pattern also inside cup. Gold edges. Entered in pattern book during or after 1901.
Backstamp(s): Wileman Foley 1890-1910
Shapes: Snowdrop

9341 **Thistle**. Same as 7108, 7272, and 7452. Enamelled. Pink shaded ground fading to ivory. Green thistle. Thistle sprig also inside cup. Gold edges. Entered in pattern book during or after 1901.
Backstamp(s): Wileman Foley 1890-1910
Shapes: Snowdrop

9342 **Violet Print**. Same as 5715. Enamelled. Entered in pattern book during or after 1901.
Backstamp(s): Wileman Foley 1890-1910
Shapes: Daisy

9343 **Poppy**. Same as 5753 and 9003. Enamelled. Entered in pattern book during or after 1901.
Backstamp(s): Wileman Foley 1890-1910
Shapes: Dainty

9344 **Chrysanthemum**. Same as 6892. Enamelled. Entered in pattern book during or after 1901.
Backstamp(s): Wileman Foley 1890-1910
Shapes: Empire

9345 **Stylised Flower and Stem**. Same as 7069. Entered in pattern book during or after 1901.
Backstamp(s): Wileman Foley 1890-1910
Shapes: Snowdrop

9345 **Stylised Flower and Stem**. Same as 7069. Entered in pattern book during or after 1901.
Backstamp(s): Wileman Foley 1890-1910
Shapes: Snowdrop

9346 **Gold Scroll and Leaf Design**. Same as 6905. Panelled. Entered in pattern book during or after 1901.
Backstamp(s): Wileman Foley 1890-1910
Shapes: Snowdrop

9347 **Panelled Gold Border Decoration**. Same as 6842. Panelled. Entered in pattern book during or after 1901.
Backstamp(s): Wileman Foley 1890-1910
Shapes: Empire

9351-9365 **Carnations and Border**. Entered in pattern book during or after 1901.
Backstamp(s): Wileman Foley 1890-1910
Shapes: Violet

9366 **Carnations and Border**. Green print. Dark green border with white flowers. Lighter green carnation print on either side of border and inside rim of cup. White ground. Gold edges. Entered in pattern book during or after 1901.
Backstamp(s): Wileman Foley 1890-1910
Shapes: Violet

9367-9368 **Carnations and Border**. Entered in pattern book during or after 1901.
Backstamp(s): Wileman Foley 1890-1910
Shapes: Violet

9471 **Stork Print**. Entered in pattern book during or after 1901.
Backstamp(s): Wileman Foley 1890-1910
Shapes: New York

9474 **Roses Border Print**. Same as 9218. Entered in pattern book during or after 1901.
Backstamp(s): Wileman Foley 1890-1910
Shapes: Foley

9482 **Panelled Gold Border Decoration**. Same as 6842 and 9347. Entered in pattern book during or after 1901.
Backstamp(s): Wileman Foley 1890-1910
Shapes: Empire

9483 **Margarette**. Same as 3873. Orange or pale turquoise flowers and leaves. White ground. Gold edges. Entered in pattern book during or after 1901.
Backstamp(s): Wileman Foley 1890-1910; Shelley Late Foley 1910-1916
Shapes: New York

9484 **Panelled Gold Border Decoration**. Same as 6842, 9347, and 9482. Entered in pattern book during or after 1901.
Backstamp(s): Wileman Foley 1890-1910
Shapes: Empire

9485-9487 **Shaded Half Down**. Entered in pattern book during or after 1901.
Backstamp(s): Wileman Foley 1890-1910
Shapes: Foley

9488-9490 **Shaded Half Down**. Entered in pattern book during or after 1901.
Backstamp(s): Wileman Foley 1890-1910
Shapes: Lily

9491-9493 **Shaded Half Down**. Entered in pattern book during or after 1901.
Backstamp(s): Wileman Foley 1890-1910
Shapes: Daisy

9494-9496 **Shaded Half Down**. Entered in pattern book during or after 1901.
Backstamp(s): Wileman Foley 1890-1910
Shapes: Dainty

9497-9499 **Shaded Half Down**. Entered in pattern book during or after 1901.
Backstamp(s): Wileman Foley 1890-1910
Shapes: Snowdrop

9500-9502 **Shaded Half Down**. Entered in pattern book during or after 1901.
Backstamp(s): Wileman Foley 1890-1910
Shapes: Violet

9503-9505 **Shaded Half Down**. Entered in pattern book during or after 1901.
Backstamp(s): Wileman Foley 1890-1910
Shapes: Empire

9506 **Shaded Ground**. Entered in pattern book during or after 1901.
Backstamp(s): Wileman Foley 1890-1910
Shapes: Dainty

9511 Same as 7073. Entered in pattern book during or after 1901.
Backstamp(s): Wileman Foley 1890-1910
Shapes: Gainsborough

9512 **Dresden Flowers**. Entered in pattern book during or after 1901.
Backstamp(s): Wileman Foley 1890-1910
Shapes: Dainty

9512 **Dresden Flowers**. Entered in pattern book during or after 1901.
Backstamp(s): Wileman Foley 1890-1910
Shapes: Dainty

9514-9516 **Rose Sprays**. Same as 7238, 7321-7324, 7461, and 9885. Entered in pattern book during or after 1901.
Backstamp(s): Wileman Foley 1890-1910
Shapes: Gainsborough

9518 **Japan**. Blue, orange, yellow, and pink oriental flowers. Same as 7074. Entered in pattern book during or after 1901.
Backstamp(s): Wileman Foley 1890-1910
Shapes: Gainsborough

9519 Same as 9138. Entered in pattern book during or after 1901.
Backstamp(s): Wileman Foley 1890-1910
Shapes: Lily

9520 **Carnations and Border**. Same as 9366. Green print. Dark green border with white flowers. Lighter green carnation print on either side of border and inside rim of cup. White ground. Gold edges. Entered in pattern book during or after 1901.
Backstamp(s): Wileman Foley 1890-1910
Shapes: Lily

9521 **Trailing Violets Print**. Same as 5622 and 9058. Coloured print. Trailing daisies and violets. Print also inside cup. White ground. Gold edges. Entered in pattern book during or after 1895.
Backstamp(s): Wileman Foley 1890-1910
Shapes: Lily

9523 **Daisies**. Shaded. Same as 6805. Entered in pattern book during or after 1901.
Backstamp(s): Wileman Foley 1890-1910
Shapes: Lily

9524 **Daises Print**. Same as 5217. Entered in pattern book during or after 1901.
Backstamp(s): Wileman Foley 1890-1910
Shapes: Lily

9525 **Japanese Border Print**. Entered in pattern book during or after 1901.
Backstamp(s): Wileman Foley 1890-1910
Shapes: Lily

Pattern **Description & Shapes**

9529 **Panelled Gold Border Decoration**. Same as 6842, 9347, 9482, and 9484. Entered in pattern book during or after 1901.
Backstamp(s): Wileman Foley 1890-1910
Shapes: Empire

9533-9536 **Wild Rose Sprays**. Entered in pattern book during or after 1902. Seconds ware.
Backstamp(s): Wileman Foley 1890-1910
Shapes: Violet

9538-9541 **Daisy Border**. Entered in pattern book during or after 1902. Seconds ware.
Backstamp(s): Wileman Foley 1890-1910
Shapes: Daisy

9553 **Stork Print**. Same as 9471. Entered in pattern book during or after 1902.
Backstamp(s): Wileman Foley 1890-1910
Shapes: New York

9581 **Sprig of Roses**. Same as 7447, 9590-9591, 9892, 10106, and 10114. Small sprigs of pink roses and green leaves. Gold trim. Entered in pattern book during or after 1902.
Backstamp(s): Wileman Foley 1890-1910
Shapes: Gainsborough

9582 Same as 7294. Entered in pattern book during or after 1902.
Backstamp(s): Wileman Foley 1890-1910
Shapes: Gainsborough, Royal

9583 **Oak Leaf**. Border with trailing, light purple oak leaves. White ground. Gold edges. Entered in pattern book during or after 1902.
Backstamp(s): Wileman Foley 1890-1910
Shapes: Gainsborough, Royal

9584 Same as 7294. Entered in pattern book during or after 1902.
Backstamp(s): Wileman Foley 1890-1910
Shapes: Gainsborough, Royal

9585 **Rococo Design**. Same as 6172, 6290, 6292, 6820, 9267-9269, and 9683. Gold print. Entered in pattern book during or after 1902.
Backstamp(s): Wileman Foley 1890-1910
Shapes: Royal

9586-9587 **Shaded Ground**. Entered in pattern book during or after 1902.
Backstamp(s): Wileman Foley 1890-1910
Shapes: Dainty

9590-9591 **Sprig of Roses**. Same as 7447, 9581, 9892, 10106, and 10114. Small sprigs of pink roses and green leaves. Gold trim. Entered in pattern book during or after 1902.
Backstamp(s): Wileman Foley 1890-1910
Shapes: Gainsborough

9592 **Oak Leaf Border**. Border with trailing, green oak leaves. White ground. Gold edges. Entered in pattern book during or after 1902 and was still in production in 1919 when numbers were transferred from the old to the new pattern books.
Backstamp(s): Wileman 1872-1890; Wileman Foley 1890-1910
Shapes: Victoria

9593 **Oak Leaf Border**. Border with trailing oak leaves. White ground. Gold edges. Entered in pattern book during or after 1902 and was still in production in 1919 when numbers were transferred from the old to the new pattern books.
Backstamp(s): Wileman 1872-1890; Wileman Foley 1890-1910
Shapes: Victoria

9594 **Shaded Ground**. Same as 5873. Entered in pattern book during or after 1902.
Backstamp(s): Wileman Foley 1890-1910
Shapes: Dainty

9595 **Shaded Ground**. Same as 5861. Entered in pattern book during or after 1902.
Backstamp(s): Wileman Foley 1890-1910
Shapes: Dainty

9596-9599 **Carnations and Border**. Same as 9351. Entered in pattern book during or after 1902.
Backstamp(s): Wileman Foley 1890-1910
Shapes: Violet

9603-9606 **Wild Rose Sprays**. Entered in pattern book during or after 1902.
Backstamp(s): Wileman Foley 1890-1910
Shapes: Lily

9611-9630 **Coloured Fibre**. Entered in pattern book during or after 1902.
Backstamp(s): Wileman Foley 1890-1910
Shapes: Royal

9631-9633 **Carnation**. Entered in pattern book during or after 1902.
Backstamp(s): Wileman Foley 1890-1910
Shapes: Snowdrop

9635 Same as 7580. Entered in pattern book during or after 1902.
Backstamp(s): Wileman Foley 1890-1910
Shapes: Royal

9636-9638 **Lilac**. Entered in pattern book during or after 1902.
Backstamp(s): Wileman Foley 1890-1910
Shapes: Snowdrop

9641-9643 **Double Poppy**. Entered in pattern book during or after 1902.
Backstamp(s): Wileman Foley 1890-1910
Shapes: Dainty

9646-9648 **Old Chrysanthemum**. Entered in pattern book during or after 1902.
Backstamp(s): Wileman Foley 1890-1910
Shapes: Violet

9651-9653 **Dandelion**. Entered in pattern book during or after 1902.
Backstamp(s): Wileman Foley 1890-1910
Shapes: Violet

9654-9655 **Blue Fibre**. Entered in pattern book during or after 1902.
Backstamp(s): Wileman Foley 1890-1910
Shapes: Royal

9656 Same as 7466. Entered in pattern book during or after 1902.
Backstamp(s): Wileman Foley 1890-1910
Shapes: Royal

9657 **Dresden Flowers**. Entered in pattern book during or after 1902.
Backstamp(s): Wileman Foley 1890-1910
Shapes: Royal

9658 **Indian Tree**. Same as 7479. Enamelled. Entered in pattern book during or after 1902 and was still in production in 1919 when numbers were transferred from the old to the new pattern books.
Backstamp(s): Wileman Foley 1890-1910
Shapes: Gainsborough, Milton, Royal

Indian Tree 9658 Gainsborough shape cup, saucer, and plate. £40-50; $80-100

9659 Same as 7424. Entered in pattern book during or after 1902.
Backstamp(s): Wileman Foley 1890-1910
Shapes: Royal

9660 Same as 7425. Entered in pattern book during or after 1902.
Backstamp(s): Wileman Foley 1890-1910
Shapes: Royal

9662-9665 **Wild Roses Print**. Entered in pattern book during or after 1902. Seconds ware.
Backstamp(s): Wileman
Shapes: Violet

9666 **Plain Ground**. Entered in pattern book during or after 1902 and was still in production in 1919 when numbers were transferred from the old to the new pattern books.
Backstamp(s): Wileman
Shapes: Antique, Dainty

9667-9680 **Plain Ground**. Entered in pattern book during or after 1902.
Backstamp(s): Wileman Foley 1890-1910
Shapes: Antique, Dainty

9683 **Rococo Design**. Same as Same as 6172, 6290, 6292, 6820, 9267-9269, and 9585. Gold print. Entered in pattern book during or after 1903.
Backstamp(s): Wileman Foley 1890-1910
Shapes: Royal

9691-9697 **Lily Prints with Rings**. Entered in pattern book during or after 1903.
Backstamp(s): Wileman Foley 1890-1910
Shapes: Royal

9698 **Lily Prints with Rings**. Mauve pattern on white ground inside cup, on saucer and plate. Lily sprays outside cup. Entered in pattern book during or after 1903.
Backstamp(s): Wileman Foley 1890-1910
Shapes: Royal

Opposite page, bottom left:
Lily Prints with Rings 9698 Royal shape cup, saucer, and plate. £60-90; $90-110

Pattern Description & Shapes

9699-9709 **Lily Prints with Rings**. Entered in pattern book during or after 1903.
Backstamp(s): Wileman Foley 1890-1910
Shapes: Royal

9715-9716 **Daisy Border**. Entered in pattern book during or after 1903.
Backstamp(s): Wileman Foley 1890-1910
Shapes: Violet

9717 **Carnations and Border**. Same as 9351 and 9596. Entered in pattern book during or after 1903.
Backstamp(s): Wileman Foley 1890-1910
Shapes: New York

9718 **Carnations and Border**. Same as 9351 and 9599. Entered in pattern book during or after 1903.
Backstamp(s): Wileman Foley 1890-1910
Shapes: New York

9725 **Anemones**. Same as 7365. Entered in pattern book during or after 1903.
Backstamp(s): Wileman Foley 1890-1910
Shapes: Gainsborough

9735 **Lily Prints with Rings**. Same as 9691. Entered in pattern book during or after 1903.
Backstamp(s): Wileman Foley 1890-1910
Shapes: Royal

9736 **Roses**. Enamelled. Entered in pattern book during or after 1903.
Backstamp(s): Wileman Foley 1890-1910
Shapes: Gainsborough

9737-9738 **Daisies**. Entered in pattern book during or after 1903.
Backstamp(s): Wileman Foley 1890-1910
Shapes: Dainty

9739 **Clover**. Enamelled. Entered in pattern book during or after 1903.
Backstamp(s): Wileman Foley 1890-1910
Shapes: Dainty

9741 **Chrysanthemum**. Entered in pattern book during or after 1903.
Backstamp(s): Wileman Foley 1890-1910
Shapes: Dainty

9742 **Cornflower**. Entered in pattern book during or after 1903.
Backstamp(s): Wileman Foley 1890-1910
Shapes: Dainty

9743 **Violets**. Entered in pattern book during or after 1903.
Backstamp(s): Wileman Foley 1890-1910
Shapes: Dainty

9744 **Violets**. Pink, blue, and yellow flowers with green leaves. Flower spray also inside cup. White ground. Gold edges. Entered in pattern book during or after 1903.
Backstamp(s): Wileman Foley 1890-1910
Shapes: Daisy

Violets 9744 Daisy shape cup, saucer, and plate. £60-90; $90-110

9746-9748 **Floral Print with Scroll Border**. Same as 9106 and 9289. Entered in pattern book during or after 1903.
Backstamp(s): Wileman Foley 1890-1910
Shapes: Daisy

9749 **Trailing Violets Print**. Same as 5658. Mauve print. Trailing daisies and violets. Print also inside cup. White ground. Gold edges. Entered in pattern book during or after 1903.
Backstamp(s): Wileman Foley 1890-1910
Shapes: Snowdrop

9755 **Floral Sprays**. Entered in pattern book during or after 1903. Seconds ware.
Backstamp(s): Wileman Foley 1890-1910
Shapes: Dainty

9756 **Floral Sprays**. Entered in pattern book during or after 1903. Seconds ware.
Backstamp(s): Wileman Foley 1890-1910
Shapes: Daisy

9757 **Floral Sprays**. Entered in pattern book during or after 1903. Seconds ware.
Backstamp(s): Wileman Foley 1890-1910
Shapes: Foley

9758 **Floral Sprays**. Entered in pattern book during or after 1903. Seconds ware.
Backstamp(s): Wileman Foley 1890-1910
Shapes: Lily

9760 **Forget-me-nots and Maiden Fern**. Same as 7686. Entered in pattern book during or after 1903.
Backstamp(s): Wileman Foley 1890-1910
Shapes: Royal

9761 **Rose Pansy**. Same as 7335. Entered in pattern book during or after 1903.
Backstamp(s): Wileman Foley 1890-1910
Shapes: Dainty, Gainsborough

9762 **Clover**. Same as 7677. Entered in pattern book during or after 1903.
Backstamp(s): Wileman Foley 1890-1910
Shapes: Dainty

9764 **Japan Blue**. Same as 6888. Vibrant Imari orange, indigo, and gold colours. Patterned inside cup. Outside cup is patterned on a white ground. Gold trim. Entered in pattern book during or after 1903.
Backstamp(s): Wileman Foley 1890-1910
Shapes: Gainsborough

9765 Same as 7643. Entered in pattern book during or after 1903.
Backstamp(s): Wileman Foley 1890-1910
Shapes: Dainty

9766 **Japan Red**. Entered in pattern book during or after 1903.
Backstamp(s): Wileman Foley 1890-1910
Shapes: Royal

9771-9776 **Chain Border Design**. Entered in pattern book during or after 1903.
Backstamp(s): Wileman Foley 1890-1910
Shapes: Violet

9777 **Chain Border Design**. Terracotta print. Entered in pattern book during or after 1903.
Backstamp(s): Wileman Foley 1890-1910
Shapes: Violet

9778-9790 **Chain Border Design**. Entered in pattern book during or after 1903.
Backstamp(s): Wileman Foley 1890-1910
Shapes: Violet

9791-9796 **Grass Print**. Entered in pattern book during or after 1903.
Backstamp(s): Wileman Foley 1890-1910
Shapes: Foley

9797 **Grass Print**. Terracotta print on white ground. Border inside cup. Gold edges. Entered in pattern book during or after 1903.
Backstamp(s): Wileman Foley 1890-1910
Shapes: Foley

9798-9810 **Grass Print**. Entered in pattern book during or after 1903.
Backstamp(s): Wileman Foley 1890-1910
Shapes: Foley

9811-9830 **Floral Sprays and Scroll**. Entered in pattern book during or after 1903.
Backstamp(s): Wileman Foley 1890-1910
Shapes: Lily

9831-9850 **Anemones Print**. Entered in pattern book during or after 1903.
Backstamp(s): Wileman Foley 1890-1910
Shapes: Dainty

9851-9869 **Sprays and Border Design**. Entered in pattern book during or after 1903.
Backstamp(s): Wileman Foley 1890-1910
Shapes: Daisy

9870 **Sprays and Border Design**. Entered in pattern book during or after 1904.
Backstamp(s): Wileman Foley 1890-1910
Shapes: Daisy

9872 **Japan**. Same as 7019 using special gilt. Entered in pattern book during or after 1904.
Backstamp(s): Wileman Foley 1890-1910
Shapes: Foley

9874-9876 **Goblins**. Same as 7762. Entered in pattern book during or after 1904.
Backstamp(s): Wileman Foley 1890-1910
Shapes: Gainsborough

Pattern **Description & Shapes**

9877 **Floral Sprays and Scroll**. Same as 9811. Entered in pattern book during or after 1904.
Backstamp(s): Wileman Foley 1890-1910
Shapes: Violet

9882 **Festoon of Roses**. Same as 7733. Entered in pattern book during or after 1904.
Backstamp(s): Wileman Foley 1890-1910
Shapes: Royal

9885 **Rose Sprays**. Same as 7238, 7321-7324, 7461, and 9514-9516. Entered in pattern book during or after 1904.
Backstamp(s): Wileman Foley 1890-1910
Shapes: Royal Coffee

9888-9889 **Japan**. Entered in pattern book during or after 1904.
Backstamp(s): Wileman Foley 1890-1910
Shapes: Turkish Cans

9890 Same as 7006. Entered in pattern book during or after 1904.
Backstamp(s): Wileman Foley 1890-1910
Shapes: Turkish Cans

9892 **Sprig of Roses**. Same as 7447, 9581, 9590-9591, 10106, and 10114. Small sprigs of pink roses and green leaves. Gold trim. Entered in pattern book during or after 1904.
Backstamp(s): Wileman Foley 1890-1910
Shapes: Foley

9893-9894 **Festoon of Roses**. Same as 7733 and 9882. Entered in pattern book during or after 1904.
Backstamp(s): Wileman Foley 1890-1910
Shapes: Dainty

9895 **Shaded Ground**. Same as 5875 and 9005. Entered in pattern book during or after 1904.
Backstamp(s): Wileman Foley 1890-1910
Shapes: Dainty

9897 **Anemones**. Same as 7367. Entered in pattern book during or after 1904.
Backstamp(s): Wileman Foley 1890-1910
Shapes: Royal

9898 **Plain Ground**. Same as 9666. Entered in pattern book during or after 1902.
Backstamp(s): Wileman Foley 1890-1910
Shapes: Dainty

9899 **Plain Ground**. Entered in pattern book during or after 1904. Seconds ware.
Backstamp(s): Wileman Foley 1890-1910
Shapes: Dainty

9900 **Plain Ground**. White outside cup, saucer, and plate. Bright yellow inside cup. Gold edge and handle. Entered in pattern book during or after 1904. Seconds ware.
Backstamp(s): Wileman Foley 1890-1910
Shapes: Dainty

9901 **Plain Ground**. Entered in pattern book during or after 1904. Seconds ware.
Backstamp(s): Wileman Foley 1890-1910
Shapes: Dainty

9902-9905 **Floral Print with Scroll Border**. Same as 9102. Entered in pattern book during or after 1904.
Backstamp(s): Wileman Foley 1890-1910
Shapes: Violet

9906 **Japan**. Entered in pattern book during or after 1904.
Backstamp(s): Wileman Foley 1890-1910
Shapes: Royal

9907 **Floral Sprays**. Same as 9756. Entered in pattern book during or after 1904.
Backstamp(s): Wileman Foley 1890-1910
Shapes: Foley Flute

9908 **Floral Sprays**. Same as 9755. Entered in pattern book during or after 1904.
Backstamp(s): Wileman Foley 1890-1910
Shapes: Foley Flute

9909 **Floral Sprigs**. Same as 9757. Entered in pattern book during or after 1904.
Backstamp(s): Wileman Foley 1890-1910
Shapes: Lily

9910 **Floral Sprigs**. Same as 9757. Entered in pattern book during or after 1904.
Backstamp(s): Wileman Foley 1890-1910
Shapes: Foley Flute

9911-9919 **Border Violet Print**. Trailing violets and foliage. White ground. Gold edges. Entered in pattern book during or after 1904.
Backstamp(s): Wileman Foley 1890-1910
Shapes: Foley Flute

9920 **Violet Border Print**. Turquoise trailing violets and foliage. White ground. Gold edges. Entered in pattern book during or after 1904.
Backstamp(s): Wileman Foley 1890-1910
Shapes: Foley Flute

Violet Border Print 9920 Foley Flute cup, saucer, and plate. £60-90; $90-110

9921-9930 **Violet Border Print**. Trailing violets and foliage. White ground. Gold edges. Entered in pattern book during or after 1904.
Backstamp(s): Wileman Foley 1890-1910
Shapes: Foley Flute

9932-9935 **Basket of Flowers**. Entered in pattern book during or after 1904.
Backstamp(s): Wileman Foley 1890-1910
Shapes: Gainsborough

9937 **Primula**. Enamelled. Entered in pattern book during or after 1905.
Backstamp(s): Wileman Foley 1890-1910
Shapes: Dainty

9944 **Floral Sprays**. Same as 9758. Entered in pattern book during or after 1905.
Backstamp(s): Wileman Foley 1890-1910
Shapes: Foley Flute, Royal

9945 **Rose Sprays**. Entered in pattern book during or after 1905.
Backstamp(s): Wileman Foley 1890-1910
Shapes: Foley Flute, Royal

9947 **Wreath with Roses**. Same as 7598. Entered in pattern book during or after 1905.
Backstamp(s): Wileman Foley 1890-1910
Shapes: Royal

9948 **Oak Leaf Pattern**. Same as 9592. Entered in pattern book during or after 1905.
Backstamp(s): Wileman Foley 1890-1910
Shapes: Victoria

9951-9952 **Oak Leaf Pattern**. Same as 9592. Entered in pattern book during or after 1905.
Backstamp(s): Wileman Foley 1890-1910
Shapes: Victoria

9961-9964 **Daisies**. Same as 9056. Entered in pattern book during or after 1905.
Backstamp(s): Wileman Foley 1890-1910
Shapes: Victoria

9965-9968 **Basket of Flowers**. Same as 9102. Entered in pattern book during or after 1905.
Backstamp(s): Wileman Foley 1890-1910
Shapes: Victoria

9969-9972 **Anemones**. Same as 9831. Entered in pattern book during or after 1905.
Backstamp(s): Wileman Foley 1890-1910
Shapes: Victoria

9973-9978 **Ivy Border**. Entered in pattern book during or after 1905.
Backstamp(s): Wileman Foley 1890-1910
Shapes: Victoria

9981-9986 **Chain Border Design**. Same as 9771. Entered in pattern book during or after 1905.
Backstamp(s): Wileman Foley 1890-1910
Shapes: Victoria

9989-9994 **Grass Print**. Same as 9791. Entered in pattern book during or after 1905.
Backstamp(s): Wileman 1872-1890
Shapes: Victoria

10002-10005 **Rose Sprays**. Entered in pattern book during or after 1905.
Backstamp(s): Wileman Foley 1890-1910
Shapes: Lily

10011-10030 **Floral Garland Border**. Entered in pattern book during or after 1906.
Backstamp(s): Wileman Foley 1890-1910
Shapes: Antique Square

10031-10045 **Rose Sprays**. Entered in pattern book during or after 1906.
Backstamp(s): Wileman Foley 1890-1910
Shapes: Lily

10046 **Rose Sprays**. Green Rose Sprays on white ground. Gold edges. Entered in pattern book during or after 1906.
Backstamp(s): Wileman Foley 1890-1910
Shapes: Lily

10047 **Rose Sprays**. Blue Rose Sprays on white

Pattern Description & Shapes

ground. Gold edges. Entered in pattern book during or after 1906.
Backstamp(s): Wileman Foley 1890-1910; Shelley 1910-1925
Shapes: Lily

10048-10050 **Rose Sprays**. Entered in pattern book during or after 1906.
Backstamp(s): Wileman Foley 1890-1910
Shapes: Lily

10051-10066 **Floral Chains**. Chain border. Floral swags. White ground. Gold edges. Entered in pattern book during or after 1906.
Backstamp(s): Wileman Foley 1890-1910
Shapes: Court

10067 **Floral Chains**. Blue print. Chain border. Floral swags. White ground. Gold edges. Entered in pattern book during or after 1906.
Backstamp(s): Wileman Foley 1890-1910
Shapes: Court

Green **Floral Chains** 10067 Court shape cup and saucer. $60. Sugar and creamer. $70

10068-10070 **Floral Chains**. Chain border. Floral swags. White ground. Gold edges. Entered in pattern book during or after 1906.
Backstamp(s): Wileman Foley 1890-1910
Shapes: Court

10071-10090 **Rose Sprays with Scroll Border**. Entered in pattern book during or after 1906.
Backstamp(s): Wileman Foley 1890-1910
Shapes: Devonshire

10091-10092 Same as 7818. Entered in pattern book during or after 1906.
Backstamp(s): Wileman Foley 1890-1910
Shapes: Royal

10093 Same as 7072 and 7284-7285. Entered in pattern book during or after 1906.
Backstamp(s): Wileman Foley 1890-1910
Shapes: Royal

10094 Same as 7779. Entered in pattern book during or after 1906.
Backstamp(s): Wileman Foley 1890-1910
Shapes: Royal

10095 Same as 7279. Entered in pattern book during or after 1906.
Backstamp(s): Wileman Foley 1890-1910
Shapes: Royal

10096-10098 Same as 7690. Entered in pattern book during or after 1906.
Backstamp(s): Wileman Foley 1890-1910
Shapes: Royal

10102-10103 Same as 7424 and 9659. Entered in pattern book during or after 1906.
Backstamp(s): Wileman Foley 1890-1910
Shapes: Gainsborough

10106 **Sprig of Roses**. Same as 7447, 9581, 9590-9591, 9892, and 10114. Small sprigs of pink roses and green leaves. Gold trim. Entered in pattern book during or after 1906.
Backstamp(s): Wileman Foley 1890-1910
Shapes: Gainsborough

10107 **Wild Roses**. Same as 7866. Entered in pattern book during or after 1906.
Backstamp(s): Wileman Foley 1890-1910
Shapes: Gainsborough

10108 **Daisies**. Same as 9961. Entered in pattern book during or after 1906.
Backstamp(s): Wileman Foley 1890-1910
Shapes: Lily

10109-10111 Same as 7818. Entered in pattern book during or after 1906.
Backstamp(s): Wileman Foley 1890-1910
Shapes: Royal

10112-10113 **Banded**. Entered in pattern book during or after 1906.
Backstamp(s): Wileman Foley 1890-1910
Shapes: Foley Flute, Royal

10114 **Sprig of Roses**. Same as 7447, 9581, 9590-9591, 9892, and 1010. Small sprigs of pink roses and green leaves. Gold trim. Entered in pattern book during or after 1906.
Backstamp(s): Wileman Foley 1890-1910
Shapes: Dainty

10115 **Rose Festoon and Bows**. Same as 7733. Entered in pattern book during or after 1906.
Backstamp(s): Wileman Foley 1890-1910
Shapes: Royal

10122-10125 **Floral Print with Scroll Border**. Same as 9102. Entered in pattern book during or after 1906. Seconds ware.
Backstamp(s): Wileman Foley 1890-1910
Shapes: Foley Flute, Royal

10126 **Clover Leaf**. Entered in pattern book during or after 1906. Seconds ware.
Backstamp(s): Wileman Foley 1890-1910
Shapes: Lily

10127 **Clover Leaf**. Entered in pattern book during or after 1906. Seconds ware.
Backstamp(s): Wileman Foley 1890-1910
Shapes: Foley Flute

10128 **Clover Leaf**. Entered in pattern book during or after 1906. Seconds ware.
Backstamp(s): Wileman Foley 1890-1910
Shapes: Lily

10132-10135 **Daisies**. Same as 9506. Entered in pattern book during or after 1906. Seconds ware.
Backstamp(s): Wileman Foley 1890-1910
Shapes: Gainsborough

10136 **Wreaths with Roses**. Entered in pattern book during or after 1906.
Backstamp(s): Wileman Foley 1890-1910
Shapes: Gainsborough

10137 **Clusters of Roses**. Entered in pattern book during or after 1906.
Backstamp(s): Wileman Foley 1890-1910
Shapes: Court

10138 **Floral Wreath**. Entered in pattern book during or after 1906.
Backstamp(s): Wileman Foley 1890-1910
Shapes: Foley Flute, Royal

10140 Same as 7819. Entered in pattern book during or after 1906.
Backstamp(s): Wileman Foley 1890-1910
Shapes: Gainsborough

10142-10144 Same as 7086. Entered in pattern book during or after 1906.
Backstamp(s): Wileman Foley 1890-1910
Shapes: Royal

10145-10146 Same as 7812. Entered in pattern book during or after 1906.
Backstamp(s): Wileman Foley 1890-1910
Shapes: Royal

10147 Same as 7691. Entered in pattern book during or after 1906.
Backstamp(s): Wileman Foley 1890-1910
Shapes: Royal

10148 Same as 7474. Entered in pattern book during or after 1906.
Backstamp(s): Wileman Foley 1890-1910
Shapes: Gainsborough

10149-10150 Same as 7815. Entered in pattern book during or after 1906.
Backstamp(s): Wileman Foley 1890-1910
Shapes: Royal

10151 Same as 7693. Entered in pattern book during or after 1906.
Backstamp(s): Wileman Foley 1890-1910
Shapes: Royal

10152 Same as 7660. Entered in pattern book during or after 1906.
Backstamp(s): Wileman Foley 1890-1910
Shapes: Royal

10153 Same as 7558. Entered in pattern book during or after 1906.
Backstamp(s): Wileman Foley 1890-1910
Shapes: Gainsborough

10154 Same as 7294. Entered in pattern book during or after 1906.
Backstamp(s): Wileman Foley 1890-1910
Shapes: Royal

10155 Same as 7538. Entered in pattern book during or after 1906.
Backstamp(s): Wileman Foley 1890-1910
Shapes: Royal

10156 **Sunflower and Leaf Border**. Same as 9127. Orange and blue Imari type pattern on a white ground. Border also inside cup. Gold edges. Entered in pattern book during or after 1906.
Backstamp(s): Wileman Foley 1890-1910
Shapes: Royal

10157 Same as 7798. Entered in pattern book during or after 1906.
Backstamp(s): Wileman Foley 1890-1910
Shapes: Gainsborough

10158 Same as 7612. Entered in pattern book during or after 1906.
Backstamp(s): Wileman Foley 1890-1910
Shapes: Gainsborough

10159 Same as 7693. Entered in pattern book

Pattern	Description & Shapes
	during or after 1906. **Backstamp(s)**: Wileman Foley 1890-1910 **Shapes:** Royal
10160-10163	Jungle Print. Entered in pattern book during or after 1906. **Backstamp(s)**: Wileman Foley 1890-1910 **Shapes:** Snowdrop
10167	**Floral Sprays**. Entered in pattern book during or after 1906. **Backstamp(s)**: Wileman Foley 1890-1910 **Shapes:** New Low Lily
10168	**Violets**. Entered in pattern book during or after 1906. **Backstamp(s)**: Wileman Foley 1890-1910 **Shapes:** New York
10169	**Japan**. Orange, black, and gold heart shaped pattern. Gold edges. Same as 3464, 3692, 7019, and 7004. Entered in pattern book during or after 1906. **Backstamp(s)**: Wileman Foley 1890-1910 **Shapes:** Dorothy
10170	Same as 7508. Entered in pattern book during or after 1906. **Backstamp(s)**: Wileman Foley 1890-1910 **Shapes:** Royal
10176-10177	Same as 7937. Entered in pattern book during or after 1906. **Backstamp(s):** Wileman Foley 1890-1910 **Shapes:** Royal
10178	**Japan Red**. Same as 4023. Imari colours – orange, black, and gold. Gold edges. Entered in pattern book during or after 1906. **Backstamp(s)**: Wileman Foley 1890-1910 **Shapes:** Dorothy
10187	**Delphic Sunset**. Same as 7332. Entered in pattern book during or after 1907. **Backstamp(s)**: Wileman Foley 1890-1910 **Shapes:** Dorothy
10191-10197	**Wreath with Rose Chain**. Entered in pattern book during or after 1907. **Backstamp(s)**: Wileman Foley 1890-1910 **Shapes:** New Low Lily
10198	**Wreath with Rose Chain**. Purple and mauve roses and chains. Entered in pattern book during or after 1907. **Backstamp(s)**: Wileman Foley 1890-1910 **Shapes:** New Low Lily
10199-10210	**Wreath with Rose Chain**. Entered in pattern book during or after 1907. **Backstamp(s)**: Wileman Foley 1890-1910 **Shapes:** New Low Lily
10211-10230	**Rose Bloom and Chains with Scroll**. Entered in pattern book during or after 1907. **Backstamp(s)**: Wileman Foley 1890-1910 **Shapes:** Dorothy
10231	Same as 7984. Entered in pattern book during or after 1907. **Backstamp(s)**: Wileman Foley 1890-1910 **Shapes:** Dorothy
10233	**Jungle Print**. Entered in pattern book during or after 1907. **Backstamp(s)**: Wileman Foley 1890-1910 **Shapes:** Snowdrop
10235	Same as 7283. Entered in pattern book during or after 1907. **Backstamp(s)**: Wileman Foley 1890-1910 **Shapes:** Gainsborough
10237	Same as 7930. Entered in pattern book during or after 1907. **Backstamp(s)**: Wileman Foley 1890-1910 **Shapes:** Gainsborough
10239	Same as 7929. Entered in pattern book during or after 1907. **Backstamp(s)**: Wileman Foley 1890-1910 **Shapes:** Dorothy
10240	**Cornflower**. Same as 7685. Entered in pattern book during or after 1907. **Backstamp(s)**: Wileman Foley 1890-1910 **Shapes:** Royal
10241	Same as 7951. Entered in pattern book during or after 1907. **Backstamp(s)**: Wileman Foley 1890-1910 **Shapes:** Royal
10242	**Wreath of Roses**. Same as 7956. Entered in pattern book during or after 1907. **Backstamp(s)**: Wileman Foley 1890-1910 **Shapes:** Bute
10243	Same as 7951. Entered in pattern book during or after 1907. **Backstamp(s)**: Wileman Foley 1890-1910 **Shapes:** Royal
10244	**Margarette**. Same as 3873. Orange or pale turquoise flowers and leaves. White ground. Gold edges. Entered in pattern book during or after 1907 **Backstamp(s)**: **Shapes:** Dorothy
10245	**Floral Wreath**. Same as 10138. Entered in pattern book during or after 1907 and was still in production in 1919 when numbers were transferred from the old to the new pattern books. **Backstamp(s)**: Wileman Foley 1890-1910 **Shapes:** New York
10251	**Banded**. Same as 10113. Entered in pattern book during or after 1907. **Backstamp(s)**: Wileman Foley 1890-1910 **Shapes:** New York
10253	**Wisteria**. Border of pendulous, purple wisteria flowers and green leaves on a white ground. Gold edges. Entered in pattern book during or after 1907. **Backstamp(s)**: Wileman Foley 1890-1910 **Shapes:** Dorothy
10254-10259	**Plain Ground**. Entered in pattern book during or after 1907. **Backstamp(s)**: Wileman Foley 1890-1910 **Shapes:** Gainsborough
10260-10266	**Plain Ground**. Entered in pattern book during or after 1907. **Backstamp(s)**: Wileman Foley 1890-1910 **Shapes:** Antique
10275	**Chain Border**. Entered in pattern book during or after 1908. **Backstamp(s)**: Wileman Foley 1890-1910 **Shapes:** Bute
10277	**Banded**. Same as 10112. Entered in pattern book during or after 1908. **Backstamp(s)**: Wileman Foley 1890-1910 **Shapes:** Foley Flute, Royal
10278-10279	Same as 8061. Entered in pattern book during or after 1908. **Backstamp(s)**: Wileman Foley 1890-1910 **Shapes:** Royal
10280-10281	Same as 8062. Entered in pattern book during or after 1908. **Backstamp(s)**: Wileman Foley 1890-1910 **Shapes:** Gainsborough
10282	**Plain Edge Line**. Entered in pattern book during or after 1908. **Backstamp(s)**: Wileman Foley 1890-1910 **Shapes:** Foley Flute, Royal
10284-10285	**Shamrocks**. Same as 8064. Two-shamrock sprigs on white ground. Green edges and handle. Entered in pattern book during or after 1908. **Backstamp(s)**: Wileman Foley 1890-1910 **Shapes:** Bute
10289	**Rose Festoon**. Same as 7952. Entered in pattern book during or after 1908. **Backstamp(s)**: Wileman Foley 1890-1910 **Shapes:** Gainsborough
10290	**Banded Edge**. Same as 8039. Entered in pattern book during or after 1908. **Backstamp(s)**: Wileman Foley 1890-1910 **Shapes:** Bute
10292-10295	**Wreath with Rose Chain**. Same as 10191. Entered in pattern book during or after 1908. Seconds ware. **Backstamp(s)**: Wileman Foley 1890-1910 **Shapes:** Low Lily
10300	**Clusters of Roses**. Same as 10137. Entered in pattern book during or after 1908. **Backstamp(s)**: Wileman Foley 1890-1910 **Shapes:** New York
10301	**Wisteria**. Same as 10253. Entered in pattern book during or after 1908. **Backstamp(s)**: Wileman Foley 1890-1910 **Shapes:** Victoria
10302-10305	**Rose Bloom and Chains with Scroll**. Same as 10211. Entered in pattern book during or after 1908. Seconds ware. **Backstamp(s)**: Wileman Foley 1890-1910 **Shapes:** Dorothy
10308	**Wisteria**. Entered in pattern book during or after 1908. **Backstamp(s)**: Wileman Foley 1890-1910 **Shapes:** Dainty
10313	**Shamrocks**. Same as 8064 and 10284-10285. Two-shamrock sprigs on white ground. Green edges and handle. Entered in pattern book during or after 1908. **Backstamp(s)**: Wileman Foley 1890-1910 **Shapes:** Bute
10316	**Clusters of Roses**. Same as 10137 and 10300. Entered in pattern book during or after 1908. **Backstamp(s):** Wileman Foley 1890-1910 **Shapes:** Victoria
10317	**Floral Wreath**. Same as 10138 and 10245. Entered in pattern book during or after 1908. **Backstamp(s)**: Wileman Foley 1890-1910 **Shapes:** Victoria
10318	**Roses and Daisy Festooned**. Entered in pattern book during or after 1908. **Backstamp(s)**: Wileman Foley 1890-1910

Pattern	Description & Shapes
	Shapes: Dainty
10319	**Vine Border**. Same as 8070. Green vines and black grapes. Dark green edges. Entered in pattern book during or after 1908. **Backstamp(s)**: Wileman Foley 1890-1910 **Shapes:** Bute
10321	Same as 8038. Entered in pattern book during or after 1908. **Backstamp(s)**: Wileman Foley 1890-1910 **Shapes:** Bute
10324-10327	**Shaded Ground**. Entered in pattern book during or after 1908. **Backstamp(s)**: Wileman Foley 1890-1910 **Shapes:** Dainty
10329	**Banded**. Same as 10113 and 10251. Entered in pattern book during or after 1908. **Backstamp(s)**: Wileman Foley 1890-1910 **Shapes:** New York
10331	Same as 8062. Entered in pattern book during or after 1908. **Backstamp(s)**: Wileman Foley 1890-1910 **Shapes:** Gainsborough
10332	Same as 8021. Entered in pattern book during or after 1908. **Backstamp(s)**: Wileman Foley 1890-1910 **Shapes:** Bute, Gainsborough
10333	**Star Border**. Orange and green stars. Border also inside cup. White ground. Gold edges. Entered in pattern book during or after 1908 and was still in production in 1919 when numbers were transferred from the old to the new pattern books. **Backstamp(s)**: Shelley 1912-1925 **Shapes:** Gainsborough, New York
10336	**Wisteria**. Entered in pattern book during or after 1908. **Backstamp(s)**: Wileman Foley 1890-1910 **Shapes:** Bute
10337	**Roses and Ribbon Border**. Same as 7976. Entered in pattern book during or after 1908. **Backstamp(s)**: Wileman Foley 1890-1910 **Shapes:** Gainsborough
10338-10340	Poppies. Same as 7584. Entered in pattern book during or after 1908. **Backstamp(s)**: Wileman Foley 1890-1910 **Shapes:** Gainsborough
10341	**Sheraton**. Same as 8110. Gold bands and green garlands. Gold edges. Entered in pattern book during or after 1908. **Backstamp(s)**: Wileman Foley 1890-1910 **Shapes:** Royal
10342	**Rose Spray**. Entered in pattern book during or after 1908. **Backstamp(s)**: Wileman Foley 1890-1910 **Shapes:** Gainsborough
10343-10346	Same as 8132. Entered in pattern book during or after 1908. **Backstamp(s)**: Wileman Foley 1890-1910 **Shapes:** Dorothy
10347	**Green Key and Rose Border**. Pattern also inside cup. White ground. Gold edges. Entered in pattern book during or after 1908. **Backstamp(s)**: Wileman Foley 1890-1910 **Shapes:** Gainsborough
10348-10349	Same as 8140. Entered in pattern book during or after 1908. **Backstamp(s)**: Wileman Foley 1890-1910 **Shapes:** Bute, Gainsborough
10350	Same as 7984 and 10231. Entered in pattern book during or after 1909. **Backstamp(s)**: Wileman Foley 1890-1910 **Shapes:** Worcester
10351	**Roses and Daisy Festooned**. Pink roses with blue and green garlands on a white ground. Gold edges. Same as 10231. Entered in pattern book during or after 1909. **Backstamp(s):** Wileman Foley 1890-1910 **Shapes:** Dorothy
10354	Same as 8106. Entered in pattern book during or after 1909. **Backstamp(s)**: Wileman Foley 1890-1910 **Shapes:** Bute
10355	**Star Border**. Same as 10333. Orange and green stars. Border also inside cup. White ground. Gold edges. Entered in pattern book during or after 1909. **Backstamp(s)**: Wileman Foley 1890-1910; Shelley 1912-1925 **Shapes:** Royal
10356	**Rose**. Same as 8094. Entered in pattern book during or after 1909. **Backstamp(s)**: Wileman **Shapes:** New York
10359	**Roses and Daisy Festooned**. Same as 10318. Entered in pattern book during or after 1909. **Backstamp(s):** **Shapes:** New York
10360	**Floral Sprays**. Same as 9758. Entered in pattern book during or after 1909. **Backstamp(s)**: Wileman Foley 1890-1910 **Shapes:** New York
10361	**Floral Sprays**. Same as 10167. Entered in pattern book during or after 1909. **Backstamp(s):** Wileman Foley 1890-1910 **Shapes:** New York
10362	Entered in pattern book during or after 1909. **Backstamp(s):** Wileman Foley 1890-1910 **Shapes:** Bute
10363	**Star Border**. Same as 10333 and 10355. Orange and green stars. Border also inside cup. White ground. Gold edges. Entered in pattern book during or after 1909. **Backstamp(s)**: Shelley 1912-1925 **Shapes:** Dorothy
10364	**Star Border**. Same as 10333, 10355, and 10363. Orange and green stars. Border also inside cup. White ground. Gold edges. Entered in pattern book during or after 1909. **Backstamp(s)**: Shelley 1912-1925 **Shapes:** New York
10365	**Wisteria**. Same as 10253 and 10301. Entered in pattern book during or after 1909. **Backstamp(s)**: Wileman Foley 1890-1910 **Shapes:** Royal
10366	**Green Key and Rose Border**. Same as 10347. Entered in pattern book during or after 1909. **Backstamp(s)**: Wileman Foley 1890-1910 **Shapes:** Royal
10367	**Star Border**. Same as 10333, 10355, 10363, and 10364. Orange and green stars. Border also inside cup. White ground. Gold edges. Entered in pattern book during or after 1909. **Backstamp(s)**: Shelley 1912-1925 **Shapes:** Bute
10369	**Clusters of Roses**. Same as 10137, 10300, and 10316. Entered in pattern book during or after 1909. **Backstamp(s):** Wileman Foley 1890-1910 **Shapes:** Dorothy
10370	**Indian Tree**. Same as 7479 and 9658. Enamelled. Entered in pattern book during or after 1909. **Backstamp(s)**: Wileman Foley 1890-1910 **Shapes:** New York Coffee
10371	**Wreath with Roses**. Same as 7598 and 9947. Entered in pattern book during or after 1909. **Backstamp(s)**: Wileman **Shapes:** New York Coffee
10374	Same as 7581. Entered in pattern book during or after 1909. **Backstamp(s):** Wileman Foley 1890-1910 **Shapes:** Victoria
10375	**Clusters of Roses**. Same as 10137, 10300, 10316, and 10369. Entered in pattern book during or after 1909. **Backstamp(s):** Wileman Foley 1890-1910 **Shapes:** Bute
10388	**Clusters of Roses**. Same as 10137, 10300, 10316, 10369, and 10375. Entered in pattern book during or after 1909. **Backstamp(s):** Wileman Foley 1890-1910 **Shapes:** Snowdrop
10389	**Daisy Clusters Print**. Same as 5918. Entered in pattern book during or after 1909. **Backstamp(s):** Wileman Foley 1890-1910 **Shapes:** Dainty
10390	**Ivy**. Same as 5045. Trailing ivy leaves in pale blue or pink and fawn. Pattern also inside cup. White ground. Gold edges. Entered in pattern book during or after 1909. **Backstamp(s)**: Wileman Foley 1890-1910 **Shapes:** Dainty
10391	**Primula**. Same as 9937. Enamelled. Entered in pattern book during or after 1909. **Backstamp(s)**: Wileman Foley 1890-1910 **Shapes:** Gainsborough
10392	**Wisteria**. Same as 10253, 10301, and 10365. Entered in pattern book during or after 1909. **Backstamp(s)**: Wileman Foley 1890-1910 **Shapes:** Gainsborough
10393	**Banded**. Same as 10112 and 10277. Entered in pattern book during or after 1909. **Backstamp(s)**: Wileman Foley 1890-1910

Green Key and Rose Border 10347
Gainsborough shape cup and saucer. £40-50; $80-100

Pattern	Description & Shapes
	Shapes: New York
10396	**Roses and Daisy Festooned**. Same as 10231 and 10351. Entered in pattern book during or after 1909. **Backstamp(s):** Wileman Foley 1890-1910 **Shapes:** Gainsborough
10397	**Rose and Shamrock Border**. Entered in pattern book during or after 1909. Seconds ware. **Backstamp(s):** Wileman Foley 1890-1910 **Shapes:** Bute
10398	**Rose and Shamrock Border**. Entered in pattern book during or after 1909. Seconds ware. **Backstamp(s):** Wileman Foley 1890-1910 **Shapes:** Dorothy
10399	**Red Narrow Border**. Two gold lines below red border. White ground. Gold edges. Entered in pattern book during or after 1909. **Backstamp(s):** Wileman Foley 1890-1910 **Shapes:** Gainsborough
10400	**Wreath**. Entered in pattern book during or after 1909. **Backstamp(s):** Wileman Foley 1890-1910 **Shapes:** Unhandled Coffee
10401	**Roses**. Entered in pattern book during or after 1909. **Backstamp(s):** Wileman Foley 1890-1910 **Shapes:** Unhandled Coffee
10402	**Banded**. Same as 7982. Entered in pattern book during or after 1909. **Backstamp(s):** Wileman Foley 1890-1910 **Shapes:** Unhandled Coffee
10403	**Ribbon Band**. Entered in pattern book during or after 1909. **Backstamp(s):** Wileman Foley 1890-1910 **Shapes:** Unhandled Coffee
10404	Same as 8192. Entered in pattern book during or after 1909. **Backstamp(s):** Wileman Foley 1890-1910 **Shapes:** Dorothy
10405	**Wisteria**. Same as 10253, 10365, and 10392. Entered in pattern book during or after 1909. **Backstamp(s):** Wileman Foley 1890-1910 **Shapes:** New York
10406	**Rose Sprays**. Same as 8063. Posies of purple flowers linked by green garlands. Scattered small flowers in groups of three. Border inside cup. White ground. Gold edges. Entered in pattern book during or after 1909. **Backstamp(s):** Wileman Foley 1890-1910; Shelley Late Foley 1910-1916 **Shapes:** New York
10407	**Green Key and Rose Border**. Same as 10347 and 10366. Entered in pattern book during or after 1909. **Backstamp(s):** Wileman **Shapes:** New York
10408	Same as 8121. Entered in pattern book during or after 1909. **Backstamp(s):** Wileman Foley 1890-1910 **Shapes:** Dainty
10409	**Vine Border**. Same as 8070 and 10319. Green vines and black grapes. Dark green edges. Entered in pattern book during or after 1909. **Backstamp(s):** Wileman Foley 1890-1910 **Shapes:** New York
10410	**Wreath with Roses**. Same as 7598, 9947, and 10371. Entered in pattern book during or after 1909. **Backstamp(s):** Wileman Foley 1890-1910 **Shapes:** Dorothy
10411	**Shamrocks**. Same as 8064, 10284-10285, and 10313. Two-shamrock sprigs on white ground. Green edges and handle. Entered in pattern book during or after 1909. **Backstamp(s):** Wileman Foley 1890-1910 **Shapes:** New York
10413	**Swallow Print**. Blue. Entered in pattern book during or after 1909. **Backstamp(s):** Wileman Foley 1890-1910 **Shapes:** Bute
10414	**Shamrocks**. Two-shamrock sprigs on white ground. Green edges and handle. Entered in pattern book during or after 1909. Seconds ware. **Backstamp(s):** Wileman Foley 1890-1910 **Shapes:** Royal
10415	**Shamrocks**. Two-shamrock sprigs on white ground. Green edges and handle. Entered in pattern book during or after 1909. Seconds ware. **Backstamp(s):** Wileman Foley 1890-1910 **Shapes:** Royal
10416	**Wisteria**. Entered in pattern book during or after 1909. Seconds ware. **Backstamp(s):** Wileman Foley 1890-1910 **Shapes:** Lily Breakfast
10417	**Vine Border**. Green vines and black grapes. Dark green edges. Entered in pattern book during or after 1909. Seconds ware. **Backstamp(s):** Wileman Foley 1890-1910 **Shapes:** Bute
10418	**Vine Border**. Green vines and black grapes. Dark green edges. Entered in pattern book during or after 1909. Seconds ware. **Backstamp(s):** Wileman Foley 1890-1910 **Shapes:** Roman
10419	**Sheraton**. Gold bands and green garlands. Gold edges. Entered in pattern book during or after 1908. **Backstamp(s):** Wileman Foley 1890-1910 **Shapes:** Royal
10425	**Shamrocks**. Two-shamrock sprigs on white ground. Green edges and handle. Entered in pattern book during or after 1909. **Backstamp(s):** Wileman Foley 1890-1910 **Shapes:** Violet Breakfast
10426	**Roses and Daisy Festooned**. Entered in pattern book during or after 1909. **Backstamp(s):** Wileman Foley 1890-1910 **Shapes:** Unhandled Coffee
10427	**Green Key and Rose Border**. Entered in pattern book during or after 1909. **Backstamp(s):** Wileman Foley 1890-1910 **Shapes:** Unhandled Coffee
10428	**Floral Wreath**. Entered in pattern book during or after 1909. **Backstamp(s):** Wileman Foley 1890-1910 **Shapes:** Bute
10429	**Vine Border**. Green vines and black grapes. Dark green edges. Entered in pattern book during or after 1909. **Backstamp(s):** Wileman Foley 1890-1910 **Shapes:** Gainsborough
10430	**Vine Border**. Green vines and black grapes. Dark green edges. Entered in pattern book during or after 1909. **Backstamp(s):** Wileman Foley 1890-1910 **Shapes:** Dorothy
10431	Same as 8243. Entered in pattern book during or after 1909. **Backstamp(s):** Wileman Foley 1890-1910 **Shapes:** Royal
10432-10433	Same as 8126. Enamelled. Entered in pattern book during or after 19909. **Backstamp(s):** Wileman Foley 1890-1910 **Shapes:** Gainsborough
10434	**Green Key and Rose Border**. Seconds ware for export to Australia. Entered in pattern book during or after 1909. **Backstamp(s):** Wileman Foley 1890-1910 **Shapes:** Gainsborough
10435	**Roses and Daisy Festooned**. Seconds ware for export to Australia. Entered in pattern book during or after 1909. **Backstamp(s):** Wileman Foley 1890-1910 **Shapes:** Dainty
10436	Enamelled. Entered in pattern book during or after 1910. **Backstamp(s):** Wileman Foley 1890-1910; Shelley Late Foley 1910-1916 **Shapes:** Gainsborough
10437	**Star Border**. Orange and green stars. Border also inside cup. White ground. Gold edges. Entered in pattern book during or after 1910. Seconds ware for export to Australia. **Backstamp(s):** Shelley 1912-1925 **Shapes:** Bute
10438	**Wisteria**. Entered in pattern book during or after 1910. Seconds ware for export to Australia. **Backstamp(s):** Wileman Foley 1890-1910; Shelley Late Foley 1910-1916 **Shapes:** Roman
10439	Entered in pattern book during or after 1910. Seconds ware for export to Australia. **Backstamp(s):** Wileman Foley 1890-1910; Shelley Late Foley 1910-1916 **Shapes:** Bute
10440	Entered in pattern book during or after 1910. **Backstamp(s):** Wileman Foley 1890-1910; Shelley Late Foley 1910-1916 **Shapes:** New York
10441	Entered in pattern book during or after 1910. Seconds ware for export to Australia. **Backstamp(s):** Wileman Foley 1890-1910; Shelley Late Foley 1910-1916 **Shapes:** Foley
10442	Entered in pattern book during or after 1910. **Backstamp(s):** Wileman Foley 1890-1910; Shelley Late Foley 1910-1916 **Shapes:** Bute
10443-10445	Entered in pattern book during or after 1910. Seconds ware for export to Australia. **Backstamp(s):** Wileman Foley 1890-1910; Shelley Late Foley 1910-1916 **Shapes:** Dorothy
10446	Entered in pattern book during or after 1910. **Backstamp(s):** Wileman Foley 1890-1910; Shelley Late Foley 1910-1916 **Shapes:** Gainsborough
10448	Entered in pattern book during or after 1910. Seconds ware. **Backstamp(s):** Wileman Foley 1890-1910; Shelley Late Foley 1910-1916 **Shapes:** Silver
10449	Entered in pattern book during or after 1910. **Backstamp(s):** Wileman Foley 1890-1910; Shelley Late Foley 1910-1916

Pattern Description & Shapes

Shapes: Empire

10450 Entered in pattern book during or after 1910.
Backstamp(s): Wileman Foley 1890-1910; Shelley Late Foley 1910-1916
Shapes: Gladstone

10443-
10445 Entered in pattern book during or after 1910. Seconds ware for export to Australia.
Backstamp(s): Wileman Foley 1890-1910; Shelley Late Foley 1910-1916
Shapes: Dorothy

10450 Pink and mauve roses with green and grey foliage. Grey printed foliage border. Green and grey leaf border inside cup. White ground. Gold edges. Entered in pattern book during or after 1914.
Backstamp(s): Shelley 1912-1925
Shapes: Gladstone, New York

10451-
10470 Entered in pattern book during or after 1910.
Backstamp(s): Wileman Foley 1890-1910; Shelley Late Foley 1910-1916
Shapes: Victoria

10471-
10486 Coloured print of roses, leaves, and stems on a white ground. Gold edges. Entered in pattern book during or after 1910.
Backstamp(s): Shelley Late Foley 1910-1916; Shelley 1912-1925
Shapes: Argyle, New Lily

10487 Turquoise Roses. Turquoise print of roses, leaves, and stems on a white ground. Gold edges. Entered in pattern book during or after 1910.
Backstamp(s): Shelley Late Foley 1910-1916; Shelley 1912-1925
Shapes: Argyle, New Lily

Turquoise Roses 10487 Argyle cup, saucer, and plate. £60-70; $120-140

10488-
10490 Coloured print of roses, leaves, and stems on a white ground. Gold edges. Entered in pattern book during or after 1910.
Backstamp(s): Shelley Late Foley 1910-1916; Shelley 1912-1925
Shapes: Argyle, New Lily

10492 Entered in pattern book during or after 1910.
Backstamp(s): Wileman Foley 1890-1910; Shelley Late Foley 1910-1916
Shapes: Gainsborough

10493 Entered in pattern book during or after 1910.
Backstamp(s): Wileman Foley 1890-1910; Shelley Late Foley 1910-1916
Shapes: Unhandled Coffee

10494 Entered in pattern book during or after 1910.
Backstamp(s): Wileman Foley 1890-1910; Shelley Late Foley 1910-1916
Shapes: Gainsborough

10495 Entered in pattern book during or after 1910.
Backstamp(s): Wileman Foley 1890-1910; Shelley Late Foley 1910-1916
Shapes: Worcester

10497 Entered in pattern book during or after 1910.
Backstamp(s): Wileman Foley 1890-1910; Shelley Late Foley 1910-1916
Shapes: Victoria

10498 Entered in pattern book during or after 1910.
Backstamp(s): Wileman Foley 1890-1910; Shelley Late Foley 1910-1916
Shapes: Royal

10499 Entered in pattern book during or after 1910.
Backstamp(s): Wileman Foley 1890-1910; Shelley Late Foley 1910-1916
Shapes: Victoria

10500 Entered in pattern book during or after 1910.
Backstamp(s): Wileman Foley 1890-1910; Shelley Late Foley 1910-1916
Shapes: Silver

10502 Entered in pattern book during or after 1910.
Backstamp(s): Wileman Foley 1890-1910; Shelley Late Foley 1910-1916
Shapes: Antique

10503 Entered in pattern book during or after 1910.
Backstamp(s): Wileman Foley 1890-1910; Shelley Late Foley 1910-1916
Shapes: Bute

10504 Entered in pattern book during or after 1910.
Backstamp(s): Wileman Foley 1890-1910; Shelley Late Foley 1910-1916
Shapes: New York

10505 Entered in pattern book during or after 1910.
Backstamp(s): Wileman Foley 1890-1910; Shelley Late Foley 1910-1916
Shapes: Victoria

10507-
10508 Entered in pattern book during or after 1910.
Backstamp(s): Wileman Foley 1890-1910; Shelley Late Foley 1910-1916
Shapes: New York

10509 Entered in pattern book during or after 1910.
Backstamp(s): Wileman Foley 1890-1910; Shelley Late Foley 1910-1916
Shapes: Gainsborough

10510-
10511 Entered in pattern book during or after 1910.
Backstamp(s): Wileman Foley 1890-1910; Shelley Late Foley 1910-1916
Shapes: New York

10512-
10513 Entered in pattern book during or after 1910.
Backstamp(s): Wileman Foley 1890-1910; Shelley Late Foley 1910-1916
Shapes: Bute

10514 Entered in pattern book during or after 1910.
Backstamp(s): Wileman Foley 1890-1910; Shelley Late Foley 1910-1916
Shapes: Gladstone

10515 Entered in pattern book during or after 1910.
Backstamp(s): Wileman Foley 1890-1910; Shelley Late Foley 1910-1916
Shapes: Gainsborough

10516 Entered in pattern book during or after 1910.
Backstamp(s): Wileman Foley 1890-1910; Shelley Late Foley 1910-1916
Shapes: Bute

10517 Entered in pattern book during or after 1910.
Backstamp(s): Wileman Foley 1890-1910; Shelley Late Foley 1910-1916
Shapes: Gainsborough

10518 Entered in pattern book during or after 1910.
Backstamp(s): Wileman Foley 1890-1910; Shelley Late Foley 1910-1916
Shapes: Roman

10519 Entered in pattern book during or after 1910.
Backstamp(s): Wileman Foley 1890-1910; Shelley Late Foley 1910-1916
Shapes: Victoria

10520 Entered in pattern book during or after 1910.
Backstamp(s): Wileman Foley 1890-1910; Shelley Late Foley 1910-1916
Shapes: New York

10524-
10525 Entered in pattern book during or after 1910.
Backstamp(s): Wileman Foley 1890-1910; Shelley Late Foley 1910-1916
Shapes: Bute

10537 Entered in pattern book during or after 1910.
Backstamp(s): Wileman Foley 1890-1910; Shelley Late Foley 1910-1916
Shapes: Bute

10541 Entered in pattern book during or after 1910.
Backstamp(s): Wileman Foley 1890-1910; Shelley Late Foley 1910-1916
Shapes: Bute

10542 Entered in pattern book during or after 1910.
Backstamp(s): Wileman Foley 1890-1910; Shelley Late Foley 1910-1916
Shapes: Gainsborough

10545 Entered in pattern book during or after 1910.
Backstamp(s): Wileman Foley 1890-1910; Shelley Late Foley 1910-1916
Shapes: Victoria

10547-
10549 Entered in pattern book during or after 1910-1914.
Backstamp(s): Wileman Foley 1890-1910; Shelley Late Foley 1910-1916
Shapes: Bute

10550 Festoons of pink roses and green leaves along a border of closely linked, green leaves. Entered in pattern book during or after 1910-1914.
Backstamp(s): Wileman Foley 1890-1910; Shelley Late Foley 1910-1916
Shapes: Dorothy

10551 Entered in pattern book during or after 1910-1914.
Backstamp(s): Wileman Foley 1890-1910; Shelley Late Foley 1910-1916
Shapes: Victoria

10552 Entered in pattern book during or after 1910-1914.
Backstamp(s): Wileman Foley 1890-1910; Shelley Late Foley 1910-1916
Shapes: Bute

10553 Entered in pattern book during or after 1910-1914.
Backstamp(s): Wileman Foley 1890-1910; Shelley Late Foley 1910-1916
Shapes: Dorothy

10554 Entered in pattern book during or after 1910-1914. Seconds ware.
Backstamp(s): Wileman Foley 1890-1910; Shelley Late Foley 1910-1916
Shapes: Gainsborough

10555 Entered in pattern book during or after 1910-1914.
Backstamp(s): Wileman Foley 1890-1910; Shelley Late Foley 1910-1916
Shapes: Bute

10557 Entered in pattern book during or after 1910-1914.
Backstamp(s): Wileman Foley 1890-

Pattern Description & Shapes

1910; Shelley Late Foley 1910-1916
Shapes: Bute

10558 Flowers in shades of pink, red, mauve, and purple with green leaves. Entered in pattern book during or after 1910-1914.
Backstamp(s): Shelley 1912-1925
Shapes: New York

Pattern number 10558 New York shape teapot and stand. £100-120; $150-200. Large jug/pitcher. £50-60; $80-100. Sugar bowl. £30-40; $50-60

10561 Entered in pattern book during or after 1910-1914.
Backstamp(s): Wileman Foley 1890-1910; Shelley Late Foley 1910-1916
Shapes: Bute, Mocha

10562 Entered in pattern book during or after 1910-1914.
Backstamp(s): Wileman Foley 1890-1910; Shelley Late Foley 1910-1916
Shapes: Dainty

10563 Entered in pattern book during or after 1910-1914.
Backstamp(s): Wileman Foley 1890-1910; Shelley Late Foley 1910-1916
Shapes: Argyle

10564-10573 Entered in pattern book during or after 1910-1914.
Backstamp(s): Wileman Foley 1890-1910; Shelley Late Foley 1910-1916
Shapes: Bute

10564-10573 Entered in pattern book during or after 1910-1914.
Backstamp(s): Wileman Foley 1890-1910; Shelley Late Foley 1910-1916
Shapes: Bute

10574 **Silk Moiré**. Entered in pattern book during or after 1910-1914.
Backstamp(s): Wileman Foley 1890-1910; Shelley Late Foley 1910-1916
Shapes: Mocha

10578 Entered in pattern book during or after 1910-1914.
Backstamp(s): Wileman Foley 1890-1910; Shelley Late Foley 1910-1916
Shapes: Antique

10579-10580 Carnation Border. Entered in pattern book during or after 1910-1914.
Backstamp(s): Wileman Foley 1890-1910; Shelley Late Foley 1910-1916
Shapes: Bute

10581-10582 Rose Border. Entered in pattern book during or after 1910-1914.
Backstamp(s): Wileman Foley 1890-1910; Shelley Late Foley 1910-1916
Shapes: New York

10583 Entered in pattern book during or after 1910-1914.
Backstamp(s): Wileman Foley 1890-1910; Shelley Late Foley 1910-1916
Shapes: New York

10584-10593 Entered in pattern book during or after 1910-1914.
Backstamp(s): Wileman Foley 1890-1910; Shelley Late Foley 1910-1916
Shapes: Bute, Mocha, New York

10595-10597 Entered in pattern book during or after 1910-1914.
Backstamp(s): Wileman Foley 1890-1910; Shelley Late Foley 1910-1916
Shapes: Bute, Mocha, New York

10598 Entered in pattern book during or after 1914.
Backstamp(s): Wileman Foley 1890-1910; Shelley Late Foley 1910-1916
Shapes: Victoria

10599 Entered in pattern book during or after 1914.
Backstamp(s): Wileman Foley 1890-1910; Shelley Late Foley 1910-1916
Shapes: Gainsborough

10600-10601 Entered in pattern book during or after 1914.
Backstamp(s): Wileman Foley 1890-1910; Shelley Late Foley 1910-1916
Shapes: Bute, Mocha

10602 Entered in pattern book during or after 1914.
Backstamp(s): Wileman Foley 1890-1910; Shelley Late Foley 1910-1916
Shapes: New York

10606-10607 Entered in pattern book during or after 1914.
Backstamp(s): Wileman Foley 1890-1910; Shelley Late Foley 1910-1916
Shapes: Bute

10608-10610 Entered in pattern book during or after 1914.
Backstamp(s): Wileman Foley 1890-1910; Shelley Late Foley 1910-1916
Shapes: Bute, Mocha

10611-10617 Entered in pattern book during or after 1914.
Backstamp(s): Wileman Foley 1890-1910; Shelley Late Foley 1910-1916
Shapes: Gainsborough

10618 **Old Sevres**. Blue and gold border with pink and amber flowers and green foliage. Birds decorate the outside cup and centre of the saucer. Registration number 648812. Entered in pattern book during or after 1914.
Backstamp(s): Shelley 1912-1925
Shapes: Bute

Old Sevres 10618 Double-handled Bute shape cup and saucer. £75-£85; $110-120

10620 Entered in pattern book during or after 1914.
Backstamp(s): Shelley Late Foley 1910-1916; Shelley 1912-1925
Shapes: Bute, Dorothy, Gainsborough, New York

10267-10268 Entered in pattern book during or after 1914.
Backstamp(s): Shelley Late Foley 1910-1916; Shelley 1912-1925
Shapes: Dorothy

10629 Entered in pattern book during or after 1914.
Backstamp(s): Shelley Late Foley 1910-1916; Shelley 1912-1925
Shapes: Gainsborough

10631-10632 Entered in pattern book during or after 1914.
Backstamp(s): Shelley Late Foley 1910-1916; Shelley 1912-1925
Shapes: Gainsborough

10633 Entered in pattern book during or after 1914.
Backstamp(s): Shelley Late Foley 1910-1916; Shelley 1912-1925
Shapes: Victoria

10636 Entered in pattern book during or after 1914.
Backstamp(s): Shelley Late Foley 1910-1916; Shelley 1912-1925
Shapes: Bute, New York

10640 Entered in pattern book during or after 1914.
Backstamp(s): Shelley Late Foley 1910-1916; Shelley 1912-1925
Shapes: Gainsborough

10641 Entered in pattern book during or after 1914.
Backstamp(s): Shelley Late Foley 1910-1916; Shelley 1912-1925
Shapes: Royal

10642-10644 Entered in pattern book during or after 1914.
Backstamp(s): Shelley Late Foley 1910-1916; Shelley 1912-1925
Shapes: Bute

10654 Entered in pattern book during or after 1914.
Backstamp(s): Shelley Late Foley 1910-1916; Shelley 1912-1925
Shapes: Gainsborough

10655-10656 Entered in pattern book during or after 1914.
Backstamp(s): Shelley Late Foley 1910-1916; Shelley 1912-1925
Shapes: Bute

10657 Entered in pattern book during or after 1914.
Backstamp(s): Shelley Late Foley 1910-1916; Shelley 1912-1925
Shapes: Victoria

10658 Blue, black, yellow, and orange border. White ground. Gold trim. Entered in pattern book during or after 1914.
Backstamp(s): Shelley 1912-1925
Shapes: Bute, Victoria

10659 Entered in pattern book during or after 1914.
Backstamp(s): Shelley Late Foley 1910-1916; Shelley 1912-1925
Shapes: New York

10661 **Cloisello**. White daisies on a mottled blue ground. Blue and white border edged with gold ring. Gold edges. Registration number 695614. Entered in pattern book during or after 1914.
Backstamp(s): Shelley Late Foley 1910-1916; Shelley 1912-1925
Shapes: Bute

Cloisello 10661 Bute shape cup and saucer. £100-£120; $150-180

Cloisello teapot and stand. £150-170; $200-250

10662 Entered in pattern book during or after 1914.
Backstamp(s): Shelley Late Foley 1910-1916; Shelley 1912-1925
Shapes: Gainsborough

10663 Entered in pattern book during or after 1914/1915.
Backstamp(s): Shelley Late Foley 1910-1916; Shelley 1912-1925
Shapes: Bute

10664 Purple leaves and pendulous flowers. White ground. Entered in pattern book during or after 1914/1915.
Backstamp(s): Wileman Foley 1890-1910; Shelley Late Foley 1910-1916; Shelley 1925-1940
Shapes: Bute

10665 Entered in pattern book during or after 1914/1915.
Backstamp(s): Shelley Late Foley 1910-1916; Shelley 1912-1925
Shapes: Bute

10666 Entered in pattern book during or after 1914/1915.
Backstamp(s): Shelley Late Foley 1910-1916; Shelley 1912-1925
Shapes: Gainsborough

10668-10671 Entered in pattern book during or after 1914/1915.
Backstamp(s): Shelley Late Foley 1910-1916; Shelley 1912-1925
Shapes: Bute

10672 Entered in pattern book during or after 1914/1915.
Backstamp(s): Shelley Late Foley 1910-1916; Shelley 1912-1925
Shapes: Gainsborough, Milton

10673-10674 Entered in pattern book during or after 1914/1915.
Backstamp(s): Shelley Late Foley 1910-1916; Shelley 1912-1925
Shapes: Bute

10675 **Fuchsia**. Entered in pattern book during or after 1914/1915.
Backstamp(s): Shelley Late Foley 1910-1916; Shelley 1912-1925
Shapes: Bute

10676 Entered in pattern book during or after 1914/1915.
Backstamp(s): Shelley Late Foley 1910-1916; Shelley 1912-1925
Shapes: New York

10677 Broad blue patterned border. White ground. Gold edges. Entered in pattern book during or after 1914/1915.
Backstamp(s): Shelley Late Foley 1910-1916
Shapes: Bute, Gainsborough, Milton

10678 **Chelsea Bird Centres**. Entered in pattern book during or after 1914/1915.
Backstamp(s): Shelley Late Foley 1910-1916; Shelley 1912-1925
Shapes: Bute

10679-10681 Entered in pattern book during or after 1914/1915.
Backstamp(s): Shelley Late Foley 1910-1916; Shelley 1912-1925
Shapes: Gainsborough

10682 Entered in pattern book during or after 1915.
Backstamp(s): Shelley Late Foley 1910-1916; Shelley 1912-1925
Shapes: Bute

10683 Entered in pattern book during or after 1915.
Backstamp(s): Shelley Late Foley 1910-1916; Shelley 1912-1925
Shapes: Roman, Worcester

10684 Entered in pattern book during or after 1915.
Backstamp(s): Shelley Late Foley 1910-1916; Shelley 1912-1925
Shapes: Dorothy

10685 Entered in pattern book during or after 1915.
Backstamp(s): Shelley Late Foley 1910-1916; Shelley 1912-1925
Shapes: Royal

10699 Entered in pattern book during or after 1915.
Backstamp(s): Shelley Late Foley 1910-1916; Shelley 1912-1925
Shapes: Gainsborough

10700 Entered in pattern book during or after 1915.
Backstamp(s): Shelley Late Foley 1910-1916; Shelley 1912-1925
Shapes: Bute

10702 Entered in pattern book during or after 1915.
Backstamp(s): Shelley Late Foley 1910-1916; Shelley 1912-1925
Shapes: Bute

10703 Produced from c 1915.
Backstamp(s): Shelley Late Foley 1910-1916; Shelley 1912-1925
Shapes: New York

10704 Border of green and purple motifs between gold lines on a white ground. Gold edges. Entered in pattern book during or after 1915.
Backstamp(s): Shelley Late Foley 1910-1916; Shelley 1912-1925
Shapes: Bute

10705 **Violet Pattern**. Pink and mauve violets with green and grey leaves on a white ground. Black, grey, and white border of tiny semicircles. Gold edges. Entered in pattern book during or after 1915.
Backstamp(s): Shelley Late Foley 1910-1916; Shelley 1912-1925
Shapes: Bute

10706 **Rose Pattern**. Entered in pattern book during or after 1915.
Backstamp(s): Shelley Late Foley 1910-1916; Shelley 1912-1925
Shapes: Bute

10707 **Rose and Forget-me-nots Pattern**. Entered in pattern book during or after 1915.
Backstamp(s): Shelley 1912-1925
Shapes: New York

10708 Entered in pattern book during or after 1915.
Backstamp(s): Shelley Late Foley 1910-1916; Shelley 1912-1925
Shapes: Royal

10713-10714 Entered in pattern book during or after 1915.
Backstamp(s): Shelley Late Foley 1910-1916; Shelley 1912-1925
Shapes: Bute

10715 Entered in pattern book during or after 1915.
Backstamp(s): Shelley Late Foley 1910-1916; Shelley 1912-1925
Shapes: Dorothy, Vincent

10716-10717 Entered in pattern book during or after 1915.
Backstamp(s): Shelley Late Foley 1910-1916; Shelley 1912-1925
Shapes: Bute

10718 Entered in pattern book during or after 1915. Seconds ware.
Backstamp(s): Shelley Late Foley 1910-1916; Shelley 1912-1925
Shapes: New York, Victoria

10719 Entered in pattern book during or after 1915.
Backstamp(s): Shelley Late Foley 1910-1916; Shelley 1912-1925
Shapes: Mocha

10721 Entered in pattern book during or after 1915.
Backstamp(s): Shelley Late Foley 1910-1916; Shelley 1912-1925
Shapes: Bute, New York

10722 Entered in pattern book during or after 1915. Seconds ware.
Backstamp(s): Shelley Late Foley 1910-1916; Shelley 1912-1925
Shapes: Spiral

10724-10725 Entered in pattern book during or after 1915. Seconds ware.
Backstamp(s): Shelley Late Foley 1910-1916; Shelley 1912-1925
Shapes: Spiral

10729-10732 Entered in pattern book during or after 1915.
Backstamp(s): Shelley Late Foley 1910-1916; Shelley 1912-1925
Shapes: Bute

10733 Entered in pattern book during or after 1915. Seconds ware.
Backstamp(s): Shelley Late Foley 1910-1916; Shelley 1912-1925
Shapes: Gainsborough

10734 Two parallel border patterns. White ground. Gold edges. Entered in pattern book during or after 1915.
Backstamp(s): Shelley Late Foley 1910-1916; Shelley 1912-1925
Shapes: Bute

10735 Entered in pattern book during or after 1915.
Backstamp(s): Shelley Late Foley 1910-1916; Shelley 1912-1925
Shapes: Gainsborough, Milton, Mocha

10736-10739 Entered in pattern book during or after 1915.
Backstamp(s): Shelley Late Foley 1910-1916; Shelley 1912-1925
Shapes: Gainsborough

10740 Entered in pattern book during or after 1915.
Backstamp(s): Shelley Late Foley 1910-1916; Shelley 1912-1925
Shapes: Bute

10741-

Pattern	Description & Shapes
10743	Morning and tea sets. Entered in pattern book during or after 1915. **Backstamp(s)**: Shelley Late Foley 1910-1916; Shelley 1912-1925 **Shapes:** Bute
10744	Entered in pattern book during or after 1915. Seconds ware. **Backstamp(s)**: Shelley Late Foley 1910-1916; Shelley 1912-1925 **Shapes:** Bute
10745	Entered in pattern book during or after 1915. **Backstamp(s)**: Shelley Late Foley 1910-1916; Shelley 1912-1925 **Shapes:** New York
10747	Entered in pattern book during or after 1915. **Backstamp(s)**: Shelley Late Foley 1910-1916; Shelley 1912-1925 **Shapes:** New York
10748	Entered in pattern book during or after 1915. **Backstamp(s)**: Shelley Late Foley 1910-1916; Shelley 1912-1925 **Shapes:** Bute
10749	Entered in pattern book during or after 1915. **Backstamp(s)**: Shelley Late Foley 1910-1916; Shelley 1912-1925 **Shapes:** Norman
10750	Roses in varying shades of pink and mauve with green and grey foliage. Broad grey, printed foliage border. Green and grey foliage border inside cup. Entered in pattern book during or after 1914. **Backstamp(s)**: Shelley 1912-1925 **Shapes:** New York
10751	Roses in varying shades of pink with green and grey foliage. Foliage border inside cup. Entered in pattern book during or after 1914. **Backstamp(s)**: Shelley 1912-1925 **Shapes:** Bute

Roses 10751 Bute shape cup, saucer, and plate. £50-60; $80-100

10752	Entered in pattern book during or after 1915. **Backstamp(s)**: Shelley Late Foley 1910-1916; Shelley 1912-1925 **Shapes:** Norman
10753	Entered in pattern book during or after 1915. **Backstamp(s)**: Shelley Late Foley 1910-1916; Shelley 1912-1925 **Shapes:** New York
10754	Entered in pattern book during or after 1915. **Backstamp(s)**: Shelley Late Foley 1910-1916; Shelley 1912-1925 **Shapes:** Gainsborough
10755	Border consisting of pink and mauve roses, green, and grey foliage, black lines above and below border. Row of black dots and circles above border. Row of white dots and circle on a narrow black band below border. White ground. Gold edges. Entered in pattern book during or after 1914. **Backstamp(s)**: Shelley 1912-1925 **Shapes:** Bute, Norman

Roses Border 10755 Bute shape cup, saucer, and plate. £50-60; $80-100

10758	Entered in pattern book during or after 1915. **Backstamp(s)**: Shelley Late Foley 1910-1916; Shelley 1912-1925 **Shapes:** New York
10760	Entered in pattern book during or after 1915. Seconds ware. **Backstamp(s)**: Shelley Late Foley 1910-1916; Shelley 1912-1925 **Shapes:** Foley Flute, Royal
10761	Entered in pattern book during or after 1915. **Backstamp(s)**: Shelley Late Foley 1910-1916; Shelley 1912-1925 **Shapes:** Gainsborough
10762	Entered in pattern book during or after 1915. **Backstamp(s)**: Shelley Late Foley 1910-1916; Shelley 1912-1925 **Shapes:** New York
10763	Entered in pattern book during or after 1915. **Backstamp(s)**: Shelley Late Foley 1910-1916; Shelley 1912-1925 **Shapes:** Gainsborough
10764-10765	Entered in pattern book during or after 1915. Seconds ware. **Backstamp(s)**: Shelley Late Foley 1910-1916; Shelley 1912-1925 **Shapes:** Dorothy
10767	Entered in pattern book during or after 1915. **Backstamp(s)**: Shelley Late Foley 1910-1916; Shelley 1912-1925 **Shapes:** New York
10768-10769	Entered in pattern book during or after 1915. **Backstamp(s)**: Shelley Late Foley 1910-1916; Shelley 1912-1925 **Shapes:** Bute
10773	Entered in pattern book during or after 1915. **Backstamp(s)**: Shelley Late Foley 1910-1916; Shelley 1912-1925 **Shapes:** Dorothy
10774	Entered in pattern book during or after 1915. **Backstamp(s)**: Shelley Late Foley 1910-1916; Shelley 1912-1925 **Shapes:** Bute
10775	**Rose and Bead**. Entered in pattern book during or after 1915. **Backstamp(s)**: Shelley Late Foley 1910-1916; Shelley 1912-1925 **Shapes:** Gainsborough, Milton
10776	Pink rose sprays and blue flower sprays on a grey ribbon-type border. White ground. Gold edges. Entered in pattern book during or after 1915. **Backstamp(s)**: Shelley Late Foley 1910-1916; Shelley 1912-1925 **Shapes:** Gainsborough, Milton
10777	Entered in pattern book during or after 1915. **Backstamp(s)**: Shelley Late Foley 1910-1916; Shelley 1912-1925 **Shapes:** Gainsborough, Milton
10778	Entered in pattern book during or after 1915. **Backstamp(s)**: Shelley Late Foley 1910-1916; Shelley 1912-1925 **Shapes:** New York
10779	Entered in pattern book during or after 1915. **Backstamp(s)**: Shelley Late Foley 1910-1916; Shelley 1912-1925 **Shapes:** Norman
10780	Entered in pattern book during or after 1915. **Backstamp(s)**: Shelley Late Foley 1910-1916; Shelley 1912-1925 **Shapes:** Victoria
10781	Entered in pattern book during or after 1915. **Backstamp(s)**: Shelley Late Foley 1910-1916; Shelley 1912-1925 **Shapes:** Bute
10782-10790	Entered in pattern book during or after 1915. **Backstamp(s)**: Shelley Late Foley 1910-1916; Shelley 1912-1925 **Shapes:** New York
10794-10795	Entered in pattern book during or after 1915. **Backstamp(s)**: Shelley Late Foley 1910-1916; Shelley 1912-1925 **Shapes:** Gainsborough
10796	**Grecian Border**. Entered in pattern book during or after 1915. **Backstamp(s)**: Shelley Late Foley 1910-1916; Shelley 1912-1925 **Shapes:** Bute, Norman
10797	Black and white chequered border with gold print below it. White ground. Entered in pattern book during or after 1915. **Backstamp(s)**: Shelley 1912-1925 **Shapes:** Norman
10798	Entered in pattern book during or after 1915. **Backstamp(s)**: Shelley Late Foley 1910-1916; Shelley 1912-1925 **Shapes:** Gainsborough
10799	Entered in pattern book during or after 1915. **Backstamp(s)**: Shelley Late Foley 1910-1916; Shelley 1912-1925 **Shapes:** Norman
10800	Entered in pattern book during or after 1915. **Backstamp(s)**: Shelley Late Foley 1910-1916; Shelley 1912-1925 **Shapes:** Gainsborough
10801-10802	Entered in pattern book during or after 1915. **Backstamp(s)**: Shelley Late Foley 1910-1916; Shelley 1912-1925 **Shapes:** Gainsborough, Milton, Mocha
10804	Yellow outside cup and main part of saucer. White inside cup and centre of saucer. Entered in pattern book during or after 1915. **Backstamp(s)**: Shelley 1912-1925 **Shapes:** Norman, Vincent

Yellow 10804 Norman shape cup and saucer. £40-50; $80-90

Pattern	Description & Shapes
10805-10811	Entered in pattern book during or after 1915. **Backstamp(s)**: Shelley Late Foley 1910-1916; Shelley 1912-1925 **Shapes:** Norman
10812	Entered in pattern book during or after 1915. **Backstamp(s)**: Shelley Late Foley 1910-1916; Shelley 1912-1925 **Shapes:** Gainsborough, Milton
10813-10815	Entered in pattern book during or after 1915. **Backstamp(s)**: Shelley Late Foley 1910-1916; Shelley 1912-1925 **Shapes:** Norman
10816	**Black Dice Border**. White ground. Gold edges. Entered in pattern book during or after 1915. **Backstamp(s)**: Shelley Late Foley 1910-1916; Shelley 1912-1925 **Shapes:** New York

Black Dice Border 10816 New York shape cup, saucer, and plate. £40-50; $70-90. Creamer and sugar plate. £40-50; $70-90. Bread and butter/cake plate. £25-35; $40-60

Pattern	Description & Shapes
10817-10820	Entered in pattern book during or after 1915. **Backstamp(s)**: Shelley Late Foley 1910-1916; Shelley 1912-1925 **Shapes:** New York
10821	Entered in pattern book during or after 1915. **Backstamp(s)**: Shelley Late Foley 1910-1916; Shelley 1912-1925 **Shapes:** Gainsborough
10822-10824	Entered in pattern book during or after 1915. **Backstamp(s)**: Shelley Late Foley 1910-1916; Shelley 1912-1925 **Shapes:** Norman
10825	Entered in pattern book during or after 1915. **Backstamp(s)**: Shelley Late Foley 1910-1916; Shelley 1912-1925 **Shapes:** Gainsborough
10826	Entered in pattern book during or after 1916. **Backstamp(s)**: Shelley Late Foley 1910-1916; Shelley 1912-1925 **Shapes:** Gainsborough
10827-10831	Entered in pattern book during or after 1916. **Backstamp(s)**: Shelley Late Foley 1910-1916; Shelley 1912-1925 **Shapes:** Oleander
10832-10836	Entered in pattern book during or after 1916. **Backstamp(s)**: Shelley Late Foley 1910-1916; Shelley 1912-1925 **Shapes:** New York
10837	Black vase of flowers cameo on a dark yellow ground. White outside cup. Entered in pattern book during or after 1916. **Backstamp(s)**: Shelley Late Foley 1910-1916; Shelley 1912-1925 **Shapes:** Gainsborough, Milton

Vase of Flowers Cameo 10837 Gainsborough shape cup and saucer. £40-60; $100-130

Pattern	Description & Shapes
10841	Entered in pattern book during or after 1916. **Backstamp(s)**: Shelley Late Foley 1910-1916; Shelley 1912-1925 **Shapes:** Gainsborough
10842-10844	Entered in pattern book during or after 1916. **Backstamp(s)**: Shelley Late Foley 1910-1916; Shelley 1912-1925 **Shapes:** Norman
10845	Entered in pattern book during or after 1916. **Backstamp(s)**: Shelley Late Foley 1910-1916; Shelley 1912-1925 **Shapes:** New York
10846	Entered in pattern book during or after 1916. **Backstamp(s)**: Shelley Late Foley 1910-1916; Shelley 1912-1925 **Shapes:** Gainsborough
10847-10848	Entered in pattern book during or after 1916. **Backstamp(s)**: Shelley Late Foley 1910-1916; Shelley 1912-1925 **Shapes:** Norman
10849	Pink and yellow roses with small blue flowers and green foliage. White ground. Gold edges. Entered in pattern book during or after 1916. **Backstamp(s)**: Shelley Late Foley 1910-1916; Shelley 1912-1925 **Shapes:** Gainsborough
10850	Entered in pattern book during or after 1916. **Backstamp(s)**: Shelley Late Foley 1910-1916; Shelley 1912-1925 **Shapes:** Norman
10856	New Foley shape used. Entered in pattern book during or after 1916. **Backstamp(s)**: Shelley Late Foley 1910-1916; Shelley 1912-1925 **Shapes:** Foley
10857	Pink roses with green leaves. Patterned on inside and outside cup. Gold trim, ring inside cup and on saucer. Entered in pattern book during or after 1916. **Backstamp(s)**: Shelley Late Foley 1910-1916; Shelley 1912-1925 **Shapes:** Gainsborough, Milton
10858	Entered in pattern book during or after 1916. **Backstamp(s)**: Shelley Late Foley 1910-1916; Shelley 1912-1925 **Shapes:** Norman
10860	Entered in pattern book during or after 1916. **Backstamp(s)**: Shelley Late Foley 1910-1916; Shelley 1912-1925 **Shapes:** Dainty
10861	Entered in pattern book during or after 1916. **Backstamp(s)**: Shelley Late Foley 1910-1916; Shelley 1912-1925 **Shapes:** Gainsborough
10862-10863	Entered in pattern book during or after 1916. **Backstamp(s)**: Shelley Late Foley 1910-1916; Shelley 1912-1925 **Shapes:** New York
10864	Entered in pattern book during or after 1916. Seconds ware. **Backstamp(s)**: Shelley Late Foley 1910-1916; Shelley 1912-1925 **Shapes:** Dainty
10869	**Shamrock Pattern**. Entered in pattern book during or after 1916. **Backstamp(s)**: Shelley Late Foley 1910-1916; Shelley 1912-1925 **Shapes:** Foley Flute, Royal
10870	Entered in pattern book during or after 1916. **Backstamp(s)**: Shelley Late Foley 1910-1916; Shelley 1912-1925 **Shapes:** Norman
10871-10872	Entered in pattern book during or after 1916. **Backstamp(s)**: Shelley Late Foley 1910-1916; Shelley 1912-1925 **Shapes:** Vincent
10873	Entered in pattern book during or after 1916. **Backstamp(s)**: Shelley Late Foley 1910-1916; Shelley 1912-1925 **Shapes:** Bute
10874	Entered in pattern book during or after 1916. **Backstamp(s)**: Shelley Late Foley 1910-1916; Shelley 1912-1925 **Shapes:** Gainsborough
10875	Entered in pattern book during or after 1916. **Backstamp(s)**: Shelley Late Foley 1910-1916; Shelley 1912-1925 **Shapes:** Norman
10876-10877	**Swansea Lace**. Entered in pattern book during or after 1916. **Backstamp(s)**: Shelley Late Foley 1910-1916; Shelley 1912-1925 **Shapes:** Royal
10878	Entered in pattern book during or after 1916. **Backstamp(s)**: Shelley Late Foley 1910-

Pattern Description & Shapes

1916; Shelley 1912-1925
Shapes: Milton
10879 Entered in pattern book during or after 1916.
Backstamp(s): Shelley Late Foley 1910-1916; Shelley 1912-1925
Shapes: Gainsborough
10880 Entered in pattern book during or after 1916.
Backstamp(s): Shelley Late Foley 1910-1916; Shelley 1912-1925
Shapes: Norman
10881 Entered in pattern book during or after 1916.
Backstamp(s): Shelley Late Foley 1910-1916; Shelley 1912-1925
Shapes: Bute
10882-10883 Entered in pattern book during or after 1916.
Backstamp(s): Shelley Late Foley 1910-1916; Shelley 1912-1925
Shapes: Norman
10884 **Haddon**. Profusion of dark pink and mauve roses with green foliage on a white ground. Gold edges and handle. Entered in pattern book during or after 1916.
Backstamp(s): Shelley 1912-1925
Shapes: Norman, Vincent

Haddon 10884 Vincent shape cup and saucer. £50-60; $90-120

10885-10887 Entered in pattern book during or after 1916.
Backstamp(s): Shelley Late Foley 1910-1916; Shelley 1912-1925
Shapes: Vincent
10888 Entered in pattern book during or after 1916.
Backstamp(s): Shelley Late Foley 1910-1916; Shelley 1912-1925
Shapes: Norman
10889-10890 Entered in pattern book during or after 1916.
Backstamp(s): Shelley Late Foley 1910-1916; Shelley 1912-1925
Shapes: Vincent
10891 Entered in pattern book during or after 1916.
Backstamp(s): Shelley Late Foley 1910-1916; Shelley 1912-1925
Shapes: Norman
10892 Entered in pattern book during or after 1916.
Backstamp(s): Shelley Late Foley 1910-1916; Shelley 1912-1925
Shapes: Gainsborough
10893 **Jewel**. Black jewel and chain border print on white ground. Gold edges. Entered in pattern book during or after 1916.
Backstamp(s): Shelley Late Foley 1910-1916; Shelley 1912-1925
Shapes: Vincent
10894 Entered in pattern book during or after 1916.
Backstamp(s): Shelley Late Foley 1910-1916; Shelley 1912-1925
Shapes: Vincent
10896 **Ashbourne**. Purple, orange, black, green, and gold flowers and leaves on a white ground. White border, then a purple and gold border. Gold edges. Entered in pattern book during or after 1916.
Backstamp(s): Shelley 1912-1925
Shapes: Vincent
10894 Entered in pattern book during or after 1916.
Backstamp(s): Shelley Late Foley 1910-1916; Shelley 1912-1925
Shapes: Vincent
10897 Entered in pattern book during or after 1916.
Backstamp(s): Shelley Late Foley 1910-1916; Shelley 1912-1925
Shapes: Bute
10901 **Swallow Pattern**. Entered in pattern book during or after 1916.
Backstamp(s): Shelley Late Foley 1910-1916; Shelley 1912-1925
Shapes: Vincent
10904 Entered in pattern book during or after 1916.
Backstamp(s): Shelley Late Foley 1910-1916; Shelley 1912-1925
Shapes: Bute
10905 Entered in pattern book during or after 1916.
Backstamp(s): Shelley Late Foley 1910-1916; Shelley 1912-1925
Shapes: Gainsborough, Milton
10906 Border of vertical black lines and pink roses with green foliage on a white ground inside cup and on saucer. Dark yellow below border inside cup and on saucer. White outside cup with gold ring approximately halfway between rim and base. Gold edges. Entered in pattern book during or after 1917.
Backstamp(s): Shelley 1912-1925; Alfred B Pearce
Shapes: Gainsborough, Milton

Yellow and black 10906 Gainsborough cup, saucer, and plate. £40-50; $80-100

10908 Border of pink roses and green leaves with black crosshatching on a white ground. Remainder of outside cup, saucer, and plate are plain coloured. Gold edges. Entered in pattern book during or after 1917.
/25 sky blue.
Backstamp(s): Shelley 1912-1925
Shapes: Norman
10909 Entered in pattern book during or after 1916.
Backstamp(s): Shelley Late Foley 1910-1916; Shelley 1912-1925
Shapes: New York
10911-10914 Entered in pattern book during or after 1916.
Backstamp(s): Shelley Late Foley 1910-1916; Shelley 1912-1925
Shapes: Bute
10918-10921 Entered in pattern book during or after 1917.
Backstamp(s): Shelley 1912-1925
Shapes: Oleander
10930 Entered in pattern book during or after 1917. Seconds ware.
Backstamp(s): Shelley 1912-1925
Shapes: New York
10931-10932 Entered in pattern book during or after 1917. Seconds ware.
Backstamp(s): Shelley 1912-1925
Shapes: Norman
10934-10935 Entered in pattern book during or after 1917. Seconds ware.
Backstamp(s): Shelley 1912-1925
Shapes: Vincent
10948-10958 Entered in pattern book during or after 1917.
Backstamp(s): Shelley 1912-1925
Shapes: Norman
10959 Entered in pattern book during or after 1917.
Backstamp(s): Shelley 1912-1925
Shapes: Gainsborough, Milton
10960 Entered in pattern book during or after 1917.
Backstamp(s): Shelley 1912-1925
Shapes: Mocha
10961-10964 Entered in pattern book during or after 1917.
Backstamp(s): Shelley 1912-1925
Shapes: Norman
10965-10969 Entered in pattern book during or after 1917.
Backstamp(s): Shelley 1912-1925
Shapes: Vincent
10970-10972 Entered in pattern book during or after 1917.
Backstamp(s): Shelley 1912-1925
Shapes: Norman
10974-10976 Entered in pattern book during or after 1917.
Backstamp(s): Shelley 1912-1925
Shapes: Gainsborough
10977 Entered in pattern book during or after 1917.
Backstamp(s): Shelley 1912-1925
Shapes: Bute
10979 Entered in pattern book during or after 1917.
Backstamp(s): Shelley 1912-1925
Shapes: New York
10989 Entered in pattern book during or after 1917. Seconds ware.
Backstamp(s): Shelley 1912-1925
Shapes: Lily
10990 Entered in pattern book during or after 1917.
Backstamp(s): Shelley 1912-1925
Shapes: Vincent
10993 Entered in pattern book during or after 1917. Seconds ware.
Backstamp(s): Shelley 1912-1925
Shapes: Silver
10995-10998 Entered in pattern book during or after 1917.
Backstamp(s): Shelley 1912-1925
Shapes: Gainsborough
11001-

Pattern	Description & Shapes
11003	Entered in pattern book during or after 1917. **Backstamp(s)**: Shelley 1912-1925 **Shapes:** Gainsborough
11004	Entered in pattern book during or after 1917. **Backstamp(s)**: Shelley 1912-1925 **Shapes:** Vincent
11005	Black, linear border print with pink roses on a white ground. Gold edges. Entered in pattern book during or after 1917. **Backstamp(s)**: Shelley 1912-1925 **Shapes:** Norman

Black border and roses 11005 Norman cup, saucer, and plate. £50-60; $90-120

Pattern	Description & Shapes
11006-11008	Entered in pattern book during or after 1917. **Backstamp(s)**: Shelley 1912-1925 **Shapes:** Vincent
11009	Entered in pattern book during or after 1917. **Backstamp(s)**: Shelley 1912-1925 **Shapes:** Norman
11010-11011	Entered in pattern book during or after 1917. **Backstamp(s)**: Shelley 1912-1925 **Shapes:** New York
11012	Entered in pattern book during or after 1917. **Backstamp(s)**: Shelley 1912-1925 **Shapes:** Norman
11013	Entered in pattern book during or after 1917. Seconds ware. **Backstamp(s)**: Shelley 1912-1925 **Shapes:** New York
11014	Entered in pattern book during or after 1917. **Backstamp(s)**: Shelley 1912-1925 **Shapes:** Dorothy
11015	Entered in pattern book during or after 1917. Seconds ware. **Backstamp(s)**: Shelley 1912-1925 **Shapes:** Bute
11016	Entered in pattern book during or after 1917. Seconds ware. **Backstamp(s)**: Shelley 1912-1925 **Shapes:** Gainsborough
11017	Entered in pattern book during or after 1917. **Backstamp(s)**: Shelley 1912-1925 **Shapes:** Norman
11018	Entered in pattern book during or after 1917. Seconds ware. **Backstamp(s)**: Shelley 1912-1925 **Shapes:** Lily
11019	Entered in pattern book during or after 1917. Seconds ware. **Backstamp(s)**: Shelley 1912-1925 **Shapes:** New York
11020	Entered in pattern book during or after 1917. **Backstamp(s)**: Shelley 1912-1925 **Shapes:** Norman, Vincent
11021-11023	Entered in pattern book during or after 1917. **Backstamp(s)**: Shelley 1912-1925 **Shapes:** Vincent
11024	Entered in pattern book during or after 1917. **Backstamp(s)**: Shelley 1912-1925 **Shapes:** Bute
11025	Entered in pattern book during or after 1917. **Backstamp(s)**: Shelley 1912-1925 **Shapes:** Gainsborough
11026	Entered in pattern book during or after 1917. **Backstamp(s)**: Shelley 1912-1925 **Shapes:** Vincent
11027-11028	Entered in pattern book during or after 1917. **Backstamp(s)**: Shelley 1912-1925 **Shapes:** Bute
11029	Entered in pattern book during or after 1918. **Backstamp(s)**: Shelley 1912-1925 **Shapes:** Bute
11030-11031	Entered in pattern book during or after 1918. **Backstamp(s)**: Shelley 1912-1925 **Shapes:** New York
11032-11034	Entered in pattern book during or after 1918. **Backstamp(s)**: Shelley 1912-1925 **Shapes:** Bute
11035	Entered in pattern book during or after 1918. **Backstamp(s)**: Shelley 1912-1925 **Shapes:** Gainsborough
11036	Entered in pattern book during or after 1918. **Backstamp(s)**: Shelley 1912-1925 **Shapes:** Dorothy
11037	Entered in pattern book during or after 1918. **Backstamp(s)**: Shelley 1912-1925 **Shapes:** Gainsborough
11038	Entered in pattern book during or after 1918. Seconds ware. **Backstamp(s)**: Shelley 1912-1925 **Shapes:** Norman
11039	Entered in pattern book during or after 1918. **Backstamp(s)**: Shelley 1912-1925 **Shapes:** Norman
11041	Entered in pattern book during or after 1918. **Backstamp(s)**: Shelley 1912-1925 **Shapes:** Bute
11042	Entered in pattern book during or after 1918. **Backstamp(s)**: Shelley 1912-1925 **Shapes:** Gainsborough
11043-11046	Entered in pattern book during or after 1918. Seconds ware. **Backstamp(s)**: Shelley 1912-1925 **Shapes:** Bute
11049	Mauve outside cup and on saucer and plate. White inside cup. Black edges and handle. Entered in pattern book during or after 1918. **Backstamp(s)**: Shelley 1912-1925 **Shapes:** Dainty, Gainsborough, Mocha, Queen Anne

Right:
Mauve 11049 Queen Anne shape cup, saucer, and plate. £60-700; $100-120

Pattern	Description & Shapes
11043-11046	Entered in pattern book during or after 1918. Seconds ware. **Backstamp(s)**: Shelley 1912-1925 **Shapes:** Bute
11050	Entered in pattern book during or after 1918. **Backstamp(s)**: Shelley 1912-1925 **Shapes:** Mocha
11051-11055	Entered in pattern book during or after 1918. **Backstamp(s)**: Shelley 1912-1925 **Shapes:** Gainsborough
11059-11061	Entered in pattern book during or after 1918. **Backstamp(s)**: Shelley 1912-1925 **Shapes:** Bute
11062-11064	Entered in pattern book during or after 1918. Seconds ware. **Backstamp(s)**: Shelley 1912-1925 **Shapes:** Norman
11065	**Chatsworth**. Sprigs of small pink roses and green foliage on a white ground. Entered in pattern book during or after 1918. **Backstamp(s)**: Shelley 1912-1925 **Shapes:** New York, Norman, Vincent

Chatsworth 11065 Norman shape cup and saucer. £40-50; $80-90. Small Globe shape teapot. £50-80; $140-160. Small creamer and sugar. £30-40; $50-60. Tray, 11 1/4 inch. £60-70; $120-150

Chatsworth 11065 Norman shape twenty-one-piece tea set. £350-400; $600-700. Vincent shape twenty-one-piece tea set (shown with Gainsborough shape creamer). £350-400; $600-700. Pin tray/bonbon dish. £30-40; $50-60. Hors d'oeuvres dish. £60-70; $100-120. Invalid feeder. £40-50; $80-90

Pattern	Description & Shapes
11066	Entered in pattern book during or after 1918. **Backstamp(s)**: Shelley 1912-1925 **Shapes:** Vincent
11068	Bright pink ground inside cup and on saucer. Border inside cup and outer edge of saucer. Pink roses and blue flowers with green leaves and diamond pattern. **Backstamp(s)**: Shelley 1912-1925 **Shapes:** Gainsborough
11074	Entered in pattern book during or after 1918. **Backstamp(s)**: Shelley 1912-1925 **Shapes:** Norman
11080	Entered in pattern book during or after 1918. **Backstamp(s)**: Shelley 1912-1925 **Shapes:** Mocha, Stanley Coffee Pot
11081-11083	Entered in pattern book during or after 1918. **Backstamp(s)**: Shelley 1912-1925 **Shapes:** Bute
11084	Entered in pattern book during or after 1918. Seconds ware. **Backstamp(s)**: Shelley 1912-1925 **Shapes:** New York
11085	Entered in pattern book during or after 1918. Seconds ware. **Backstamp(s)**: Shelley 1912-1925 **Shapes:** Gainsborough
11086	**Rose Border**. Entered in pattern book during or after 1918. Seconds ware. **Backstamp(s)**: Shelley 1912-1925 **Shapes:** Gainsborough
11087	Entered in pattern book during or after 1919. **Backstamp(s)**: Shelley 1912-1925 **Shapes:** Bute
11088	**Rose Wreath**. Entered in pattern book during or after 1919. **Backstamp(s)**: Shelley 1912-1925 **Shapes:** Vincent
11089-11090	Entered in pattern book during or after 1919. **Backstamp(s)**: Shelley 1912-1925 **Shapes:** Gainsborough
11091-11092	Entered in pattern book during or after 1919. **Backstamp(s)**: Shelley 1912-1925 **Shapes:** New York
11093	Entered in pattern book during or after 1919. **Backstamp(s)**: Shelley 1912-1925 **Shapes:** Norman
11094-11095	Entered in pattern book during or after 1919. **Backstamp(s)**: Shelley 1912-1925 **Shapes:** Vincent
11099	Entered in pattern book during or after 1919. **Backstamp(s)**: Shelley 1912-1925 **Shapes:** Norman
11100	Border of dashes. Stylised, heart-shaped motif. White ground. Entered in pattern book during or after 1919. **Backstamp(s)**: Shelley 1912-1925 **Shapes:** Vincent
11101	Entered in pattern book during or after 1919. **Backstamp(s)**: Shelley 1912-1925 **Shapes:** Vincent
11102	Entered in pattern book during or after 1919. **Backstamp(s)**: Shelley 1912-1925 **Shapes:** New York, Norman, Vincent
11103	Entered in pattern book during or after 1919. **Backstamp(s)**: Shelley 1912-1925 **Shapes:** Norman
11104	Entered in pattern book during or after 1919. **Backstamp(s)**: Shelley 1912-1925 **Shapes:** Bute
11105	Entered in pattern book during or after 1919. **Backstamp(s)**: Shelley 1912-1925 **Shapes:** Norman
11106	Entered in pattern book during or after 1919. **Backstamp(s)**: Shelley 1912-1925 **Shapes:** Gainsborough, Milton
11107	Entered in pattern book during or after 1919. **Backstamp(s)**: Shelley 1912-1925 **Shapes:** Milton
11108	Entered in pattern book during or after 1919. **Backstamp(s)**: Shelley 1912-1925 **Shapes:** Bute
11109	Entered in pattern book during or after 1919. **Backstamp(s)**: Shelley 1912-1925 **Shapes:** Gainsborough, Milton
11110	Entered in pattern book during or after 1919. Seconds ware. **Backstamp(s)**: Shelley 1912-1925 **Shapes:** Bute
11111	Entered in pattern book during or after 1919. **Backstamp(s)**: Shelley 1912-1925 **Shapes:** Dainty
11112	Entered in pattern book during or after 1919. **Backstamp(s)**: Shelley 1912-1925 **Shapes:** Bute, Gainsborough, Norman
11113	Entered in pattern book during or after 1919. **Backstamp(s)**: Shelley 1912-1925 **Shapes:** Vincent
11114	Entered in pattern book during or after 1919. **Backstamp(s)**: Shelley 1912-1925 **Shapes:** Bute, New York
11115-11116	Entered in pattern book during or after 1919. **Backstamp(s)**: Shelley 1912-1925 **Shapes:** Bute
11117	**Wilson**. Entered in pattern book during or after 1919. **Backstamp(s)**: Shelley 1912-1925 **Shapes:** Gainsborough, Milton, Norman
11118	Entered in pattern book during or after 1919. **Backstamp(s)**: Shelley 1912-1925 **Shapes:** Dainty
11120	**Rose, Thistle, and Shamrock**. Entered in pattern book during or after 1919. /23 Purple. **Backstamp(s)**: Shelley 1912-1925 **Shapes:** Unknown
11125	Entered in pattern book during or after 1919. **Backstamp(s)**: Shelley 1912-1925 **Shapes:** New York
11126	Entered in pattern book during or after 1919. **Backstamp(s)**: Shelley 1912-1925 **Shapes:** Gainsborough, Milton
11127	Entered in pattern book during or after 1919. **Backstamp(s)**: Shelley 1912-1925 **Shapes:** Vincent
11128	Entered in pattern book during or after 1919. **Backstamp(s)**: Shelley 1912-1925 **Shapes:** Gainsborough, Milton
11129	Entered in pattern book during or after 1919. **Backstamp(s)**: Shelley 1912-1925 **Shapes:** Vincent
11130	Entered in pattern book during or after 1919. **Backstamp(s)**: Shelley 1912-1925 **Shapes:** Victoria
11131	**Dorothy Perkins**. Pink roses and black foliage. Green crosshatching. White ground. Dark green edges and handle. Entered in pattern book during or after 1920/1921. **Backstamp(s)**: Shelley 1912-1925 **Shapes:** Norman, Vincent

Dorothy Perkins 11131 Norman shape cup, saucer, and plate. £50-60; $90-120

Pattern	Description & Shapes
11132	Entered in pattern book during or after 1919. **Backstamp(s)**: Shelley 1912-1925 **Shapes:** Bute
11133	**Rose Border**. Pink roses on a green panel. Gold edges. Entered in pattern book during or after 1919. **Backstamp(s)**: Shelley 1912-1925 **Shapes:** Vincent
11134	**Juno**. Pink, mauve and purple roses on a violet and black panel border. Gold edges. Entered in pattern book during or after 1919. **Backstamp(s)**: Shelley 1912-1925 Juno **Shapes:** Vincent
11135	**Rose Border**. Pink roses on a broad violet border. Also within the border are single purple flower sprigs within a white oval. Border is inside cup, on saucer, and plate. Outside cup has a gold ring approximately halfway between rim and foot. White ground. Gold edges. Entered in pattern book during or after 1919. **Backstamp(s)**: Shelley 1912-1925 **Shapes:** Gainsborough, Milton
11136	**Rose Border**. Border is inside cup, on

Pattern	Description & Shapes
	saucer, and plate. Outside cup has a gold ring approximately halfway between rim and foot. Fawn ground. Gold edges and handle. Entered in pattern book during or after 1919. **Backstamp(s)**: Shelley 1912-1925 **Shapes:** Gainsborough, Milton
11137	Entered in pattern book during or after 1919. **Backstamp(s)**: Shelley 1912-1925 **Shapes:** Norman
11138-11139	Entered in pattern book during or after 1919. **Backstamp(s)**: Shelley 1912-1925 **Shapes:** Vincent
11140	Black garland border with yellow and black pendants. Narrow black and yellow border on edges. White ground. Black trim and handle. Entered in pattern book during or after 1921. **Backstamp(s)**: Shelley 1912-1925 **Shapes:** Vincent
11141-11142	Entered in pattern book during or after 1919. **Backstamp(s)**: Shelley 1912-1925 **Shapes:** Gainsborough, Milton
11143	Entered in pattern book during or after 1919. **Backstamp(s)**: Shelley 1912-1925 **Shapes:** Milton
11144	Entered in pattern book during or after 1919. **Backstamp(s)**: Shelley 1912-1925 **Shapes:** Gainsborough
11145	Entered in pattern book during or after 1919. **Backstamp(s)**: Shelley 1912-1925 **Shapes:** Vincent
11146-11148	Entered in pattern book during or after 1919. **Backstamp(s)**: Shelley 1912-1925 **Shapes:** Milton
11149	Entered in pattern book during or after 1919. **Backstamp(s)**: Shelley 1912-1925 **Shapes:** Vincent
11150	**Rose**. Pink roses and blue border. Entered in pattern book during or after 1919. **Backstamp(s)**: Shelley 1912-1925 **Shapes:** New York
11151	Pink roses against black border on a white ground. Gold edges. Entered in pattern book during or after 1920/1921. **Backstamp(s)**: Shelley 1912-1925 **Shapes:** New York, Victoria
11152	Entered in pattern book during or after 1919. **Backstamp(s)**: Shelley 1912-1925 **Shapes:** Norman
11153	**Cherries**. Entered in pattern book during or after 1919. **Backstamp(s)**: Shelley 1912-1925 **Shapes:** Vincent
11154	Entered in pattern book during or after 1919. **Backstamp(s)**: Shelley 1912-1925 **Shapes:** Bute
11155	Entered in pattern book during or after 1919. **Backstamp(s)**: Shelley 1912-1925 **Shapes:** Vincent
11156-11162	Manufactured for Sloane & Smith. Entered in pattern book during or after 1919. **Backstamp(s)**: Shelley 1912-1925 **Shapes:** Milton
11163	Entered in pattern book during or after 1919. **Backstamp(s)**: Shelley 1912-1925 **Shapes:** Bute, New York
11164	**Double Diamond**. Entered in pattern book during or after 1919. **Backstamp(s)**: Shelley 1912-1925 **Shapes:** Bute, New York, Norman, Victoria, Vincent
11165	Entered in pattern book during or after 1919. **Backstamp(s)**: Shelley 1912-1925 **Shapes:** New York
11166	Entered in pattern book during or after 1919. **Backstamp(s)**: Shelley 1912-1925 **Shapes:** Victoria
11167	Border of grey and black geometric pattern, mauve, salmon, and green triangles with salmon diamonds border. White ground. Black edges. Entered in pattern book during or after 1920/1921. **Backstamp(s)**: Shelley 1912-1925 **Shapes:** Victoria

Diamonds and triangles 11167 Victoria shape cup, saucer, and plate. £50-60; $90-120

Pattern	Description & Shapes
11168	**Dorothy Perkins**. Yellow roses and black foliage. Black crosshatching. White ground. Black edges and handle. Entered in pattern book during or after 1920/1921. **Backstamp(s)**: Shelley 1912-1925 **Shapes:** Vincent
11169	Entered in pattern book during or after 1919. **Backstamp(s)**: Shelley 1912-1925 **Shapes:** Vincent
11170	Entered in pattern book during or after 1919. **Backstamp(s)**: Shelley 1912-1925 **Shapes:** Norman
11171	Entered in pattern book during or after 1919. **Backstamp(s)**: Shelley 1912-1925 **Shapes:** New York
11172	Entered in pattern book during or after 1919. **Backstamp(s)**: Shelley 1912-1925 **Shapes:** Norman
11173	Entered in pattern book during or after 1919. **Backstamp(s)**: Shelley 1912-1925 **Shapes:** Vincent
11174	Entered in pattern book during or after 1919. **Backstamp(s)**: Shelley 1912-1925 **Shapes:** Gainsborough
11175	Entered in pattern book during or after 1920. **Backstamp(s)**: Shelley 1912-1925 **Shapes:** Gainsborough
11176	**Bubbles**. Pink, blue, and yellow bubbles on a black ground. Black edges and handle. Entered in pattern book during or after 1921. **Backstamp(s)**: Shelley 1912-1925 **Shapes:** Bute, Mocha

Bubbles 11176 Bute shape cup, saucer, and plate. £75-£95; $140-180

Pattern	Description & Shapes
11177-11179	**Bubbles**. Entered in pattern book during or after 1921. **Backstamp(s)**: Shelley 1912-1925 **Shapes:** Bute, Mocha
11180	Entered in pattern book during or after 1921. **Backstamp(s)**: Shelley 1912-1925 **Shapes:** New York
11181	Entered in pattern book during or after 1921. **Backstamp(s)**: Shelley 1912-1925 **Shapes:** Gainsborough
11182	**Bubbles**. Pink and yellow bubbles on a black ground. Black edges and handle. Entered in pattern book during or after 1921. **Backstamp(s)**: Shelley 1912-1925 **Shapes:** Bute
11183	**Bubbles**. Mauve and yellow bubbles on a black ground. Black edges and handle. Entered in pattern book during or after 1921. **Backstamp(s)**: Shelley 1912-1925 **Shapes:** Bute, Mocha
11184-11187	**Bubbles**. Entered in pattern book during or after 1921. **Backstamp(s)**: Shelley 1912-1925 **Shapes:** Bute
11188	**Bubbles**. Entered in pattern book during or after 1921. **Backstamp(s)**: Shelley 1912-1925 **Shapes:** Mocha
11189	Entered in pattern book during or after 1921. **Backstamp(s)**: Shelley 1912-1925 **Shapes:** Vincent
11190	**Rose**. Entered in pattern book during or after 1921. **Backstamp(s)**: Shelley 1912-1925 **Shapes:** Gainsborough
11191-11192	Entered in pattern book during or after 1921. **Backstamp(s)**: Shelley 1912-1925 **Shapes:** Norman
11193	Entered in pattern book during or after 1921. **Backstamp(s)**: Shelley 1912-1925 **Shapes:** Bute, Norman
11194	Entered in pattern book during or after 1921. **Backstamp(s)**: Shelley 1912-1925 **Shapes:** Gainsborough
11196-11197	Entered in pattern book during or after 1921. **Backstamp(s)**: Shelley 1912-1925 **Shapes:** Gainsborough
11198	**Laurel Border**. Entered in pattern book during or after 1921. **Backstamp(s)**: Shelley 1912-1925 **Shapes:** New York
11199	Small pink roses with green and grey leaves. Black linear border. White ground. Black edges. Entered in pattern book

Pattern Description & Shapes

during or after 1921.
Backstamp(s): Shelley 1912-1925
Shapes: Gainsborough

Pink roses and black lines 11199 Gainsborough shape cup, saucer, and plate. £40-50; $80-100

11200 Entered in pattern book during or after 1921.
Backstamp(s): Shelley 1912-1925
Shapes: Gainsborough

11201 Entered in pattern book during or after 1921.
Backstamp(s): Shelley 1912-1925
Shapes: Bute

11202 Entered in pattern book during or after 1921.
Backstamp(s): Shelley 1912-1925
Shapes: Gainsborough

11203 Entered in pattern book during or after 1921.
Backstamp(s): Shelley 1912-1925
Shapes: Norman

11104 Entered in pattern book during or after 1921.
Backstamp(s): Shelley 1912-1925
Shapes: Vincent

11205 Black and yellow border. White ground. Black trim and handle. Entered in pattern book during or after 1921.
Backstamp(s): Shelley 1912-1925
Shapes: Kenneth, Vincent

11206 Purple or black border pattern. White ground. Gold edges. Entered in pattern book during or after 1921.
Backstamp(s): Shelley 1912-1925
Shapes: Kenneth

Pattern number 11206 Kenneth shape cup, saucer, and plate. £50-60; $90-120

11207 Entered in pattern book during or after 1921.
Backstamp(s): Shelley 1912-1925
Shapes: New York

11208 **Cairo**. Cerise, blue, green, and purple. Cerise, daisy-like flowers with blue centres. White ground. Black edges and handle. Entered in pattern book during or after 1921.
Backstamp(s): Shelley 1912-1925 Cairo
Shapes: Mocha, Norman, Vincent

11209 **Cairo**. Purple. White ground. Black edges and handle. Entered in pattern book during or after 1921.
Backstamp(s): Shelley 1912-1925 Cairo
Shapes: Norman, Vincent

11210 **Cairo**. Yellow. White ground. Black edges and handle. Entered in pattern book during or after 1921.
Backstamp(s): Shelley 1912-1925 Cairo
Shapes: Norman, Vincent

11211 **Cairo**. Cerise, blue, green, and purple. Cerise, daisy-like flowers with blue centres. White ground. Black edges and handle. Entered in pattern book during or after 1921.
Backstamp(s): Shelley 1912-1925 Cairo
Shapes: Kenneth

11212 **Cairo**. Purple. White ground. Black edges and handle. Entered in pattern book during or after 1921.
Backstamp(s): Shelley 1912-1925 Cairo
Shapes: Kenneth

11213 **Cairo**. Yellow. White ground. Black edges and handle. Entered in pattern book during or after 1921.
Backstamp(s): Shelley 1912-1925 Cairo
Shapes: Kenneth

11214 Entered in pattern book during or after 1921.
Backstamp(s): Shelley 1912-1925
Shapes: Vincent

11215 Entered in pattern book during or after 1921.
Backstamp(s): Shelley 1912-1925
Shapes: Kenneth

11216-
11217 Entered in pattern book during or after 1921.
Backstamp(s): Shelley 1912-1925
Shapes: Mocha

11218 **Bubble Border**. Entered in pattern book during or after 1922.
Backstamp(s): Shelley 1912-1925
Shapes: Vincent

11219 **Cairo**. Coloured ground. Entered in pattern book during or after 1922.
Backstamp(s): Shelley 1912-1925
Shapes: Mocha, Norman, Vincent

11220 **Cairo**. Purple. Coloured ground. Entered in pattern book during or after 1922.
Backstamp(s): Shelley 1912-1925
Shapes: Mocha, Norman, Vincent

11221 **Cairo**. Yellow. Coloured ground. Entered in pattern book during or after 1922.
Backstamp(s): Shelley 1912-1925
Shapes: Mocha, Norman, Vincent

11222-
11224 Entered in pattern book during or after 1922.
Backstamp(s): Shelley 1912-1925
Shapes: Gainsborough

11225 **Black Border**. Manufactured for Pattersons Perfect Productions, Bishop Aukland. Entered in pattern book during or after 1922.
Backstamp(s): Shelley 1912-1925
Shapes: Kenneth

11226 Entered in pattern book during or after 1922.
Backstamp(s): Shelley 1912-1925
Shapes: Kenneth

11227 Entered in pattern book during or after 1922.
Backstamp(s): Shelley 1912-1925
Shapes: Gainsborough

11228 Entered in pattern book during or after 1922.
Backstamp(s): Shelley 1912-1925
Shapes: Norman

11229 Pink. Entered in pattern book during or after 1922.
Backstamp(s): Shelley 1912-1925
Shapes: Mocha

11230 Yellow. Entered in pattern book during or after 1922.
Backstamp(s): Shelley 1912-1925
Shapes: Mocha

11231 Green. Entered in pattern book during or after 1922.
Backstamp(s): Shelley 1912-1925
Shapes: Mocha

11232 Green. Entered in pattern book during or after 1922.
Backstamp(s): Shelley 1912-1925
Shapes: Mocha

11233 **Bell**. Black and yellow border on a white ground. Black edges. Entered in pattern book during or after 1922.
Backstamp(s): Shelley 1912-1925
Shapes: Norman

11234 Entered in pattern book during or after 1922.
Backstamp(s): Shelley 1912-1925
Shapes: Vincent

11235 **Rose and Pansy**. Entered in pattern book during or after 1922.
Backstamp(s): Shelley 1912-1925
Shapes: New York

11236 **Laurel and Rose Border**. Entered in pattern book during or after 1922.
Backstamp(s): Shelley 1912-1925
Shapes: Victoria

11237 Black, yellow, and mauve border on a white ground.
Backstamp(s): Shelley 1912-1925
Shapes: Milton

11238-
11239 Entered in pattern book during or after 1922.
Backstamp(s): Shelley 1912-1925
Shapes: Unhandled Coffee

11240 Entered in pattern book during or after 1922.
Backstamp(s): Shelley 1912-1925
Shapes: Gainsborough

11241 Entered in pattern book during or after 1922.
Backstamp(s): Shelley 1912-1925
Shapes: Vincent

11242 Entered in pattern book during or after 1922.
Backstamp(s): Shelley 1912-1925
Shapes: Gainsborough

11243 Border of purple butterflies on a white ground. Black edges. Entered in pattern book during or after 1922.
/7 Yellow ground.
Backstamp(s): Shelley 1912-1925
Shapes: Vincent

Butterfly border 11243/7 Vincent shape cup, saucer, and plate. £80-100; $150-200

Pattern	Description & Shapes
11244	Entered in pattern book during or after 1922. **Backstamp(s)**: Shelley 1912-1925 **Shapes:** Milton
11245	Entered in pattern book during or after 1922. **Backstamp(s)**: Shelley 1912-1925 **Shapes:** Norman
11246	**Festoon**. Black bows and chain border on a white ground. Entered in pattern book during or after 1922. **Backstamp(s)**: Shelley 1912-1925 **Shapes:** Kenneth, Vincent
11247	**Greek Border**. Entered in pattern book during or after 1922. **Backstamp(s)**: Shelley 1912-1925 **Shapes:** Kenneth
11248	Entered in pattern book during or after 1922. **Backstamp(s)**: Shelley 1912-1925 **Shapes:** Gainsborough
11251	Entered in pattern book during or after 1922. **Backstamp(s)**: Shelley 1912-1925 **Shapes:** Victoria
11255	Entered in pattern book during or after 1923. **Backstamp(s)**: Shelley 1912-1925 **Shapes:** Gainsborough
11256	**Jewel**. Black jewel and chain border print on white ground. Black edges. Entered in pattern book during or after 1923. **Backstamp(s)**: Shelley 1912-1925 **Shapes:** Kenneth
11257	**Laurel Border**. Entered in pattern book during or after 1923. **Backstamp(s)**: Shelley 1912-1925 **Shapes:** Kenneth
11258	**Mandarin**. Also known as **Powder Blue and Chinese Flowers**. Mottled blue border with narrow gold bands on either side of it. Pink roses and grey leaves against the blue border. White ground. Gold edges. Entered in pattern book during or after 1923. **Backstamp(s)**: Shelley 1912-1925; Shelley 1925-1940 **Shapes:** Kenneth, Vincent
11259	**Blue and Red Berries**. Also known as **Ning Poo**. Blue border. White insets with red fruit and green leaves. White ground. Gold edges. Entered in pattern book during or after 1923. **Backstamp(s)**: Shelley 1912-1925; Shelley 1925-1940 **Shapes:** Kenneth, Vincent
11260	**Persian**. Entered in pattern book during or after 1923. **Backstamp(s)**: Shelley 1912-1925 **Shapes:** Kenneth, Vincent
11261	Entered in pattern book during or after 1923. **Backstamp(s)**: Shelley 1912-1925 **Shapes:** Vincent
11262	Entered in pattern book during or after 1923. **Backstamp(s)**: Shelley 1912-1925 **Shapes:** Norman
11263	Entered in pattern book during or after 1923. **Backstamp(s)**: Shelley 1912-1925 **Shapes:** Bute
11264	Gold border with black laurel leaves. Brown chain and garland print. White ground. Gold edges. Entered in pattern book during or after 1923. **Backstamp(s)**: Shelley 1912-1925 **Shapes:** Gainsborough
11265	Entered in pattern book during or after 1923. **Backstamp(s)**: Shelley 1912-1925 **Shapes:** Vincent
11266	**Celtic**. Entered in pattern book during or after 1923. **Backstamp(s)**: Shelley 1912-1925 **Shapes:** Kenneth, Vincent
11267	Entered in pattern book during or after 1923. **Backstamp(s)**: Shelley 1912-1925 **Shapes:** Norman
11268	Entered in pattern book during or after 1923. **Backstamp(s)**: Shelley 1912-1925 **Shapes:** Gainsborough
11269	Entered in pattern book during or after 1923. **Backstamp(s)**: Shelley 1912-1925 **Shapes:** Norman
11270-11273	Entered In pattern book during or after 1923. **Backstamp(s)**: Shelley 1912-1925 **Shapes:** Milton
11274	**Hankow**. Dragon chintz. Entered in pattern book during or after 1923. **Backstamp(s)**: Shelley 1912-1925 **Shapes:** Milton
11275-11278	Entered in pattern book during or after 1923. **Backstamp(s)**: Shelley 1912-1925 **Shapes:** Milton
11279	Entered in pattern book during or after 1923. **Backstamp(s)**: Shelley 1912-1925 **Shapes:** Kenneth
11280	**Chelsea**. Sprays of blue, burgundy, and black flowers and leaves on a white ground. Border. Entered in pattern book during or after 1923. **Backstamp(s)**: Shelley 1912-1925; Shelley 1925-1940 Chelsea **Shapes:** Milton, Vincent
11281-11283	**Borgfeldt**. Entered in pattern book during or after 1923. **Backstamp(s)**: Shelley 1912-1925 **Shapes:** Milton
11284	Outer border in orange with a black Greek key border. Outside border in pink, blue, fawn, and green. White ground. Gold trim. **Backstamp(s)**: Shelley 1925-1940 **Shapes:** Gainsborough
11285	**Borgfeldt**. Entered in pattern book during or after 1923. **Backstamp(s)**: Shelley 1912-1925 **Shapes:** Gainsborough
11286	Broad green band inside cup and on saucer. White centre of inside cup, outside cup, and centre of saucer. Gold lines separate green and white areas. Narrow patterned gold band within green band inside cup and on saucer. Gold edges and handle. Entered in pattern book during or after 1923. **Backstamp(s)**: Shelley 1912-1925 **Shapes:** Gainsborough
11287	**Chelsea**. Sprays of blue, burgundy, and black flowers and leaves on a white ground. Border. Entered in pattern book during or after 1923. **Backstamp(s)**: Shelley 1925-1940 Chelsea **Shapes:** Vincent
11288-11292	Entered in pattern book during or after 1923. **Backstamp(s)**: Shelley 1912-1925 **Shapes:** Gainsborough
11298	Entered in pattern book during or after 1923. **Backstamp(s)**: Shelley 1912-1925 **Shapes:** Gainsborough
11299	**Borgfeldt**. Entered in pattern book during or after 1923. **Backstamp(s)**: Shelley 1912-1925 **Shapes:** Milton
11300	**Borgfeldt**. Entered in pattern book during or after 1923. **Backstamp(s)**: Shelley 1912-1925 **Shapes:** Gainsborough
11301	Chintz litho inside cup, band round edge of saucer, and centre of saucer. Plain colour outside cup and main part of saucer. Black edges and handle. /31 Bright yellow /40 Salmon pink. **Backstamp(s)**: Shelley 1912-1925 **Shapes:** Gainsborough, Milton

Chintz 11301/31 Milton shape cup and saucer. £40-50; $50-70

Pattern	Description & Shapes
11302	**Swansea Lace**. Chintz. Bands of chintz and plain colour. /25 Turquoise. **Backstamp(s)**: Shelley 1912-1925 **Shapes:** Gainsborough
11303	Handled urn on a stand with blue and orange flowers. Blue and orange leaves and flower garlands on either side of urn. Vermillion chequered border. White ground. Gold trim. Entered in pattern book during or after 1923. **Backstamp(s)**: Shelley 1912-1925 **Shapes:** Gainsborough, Milton, Mocha
11304	Entered in pattern book during or after 1923. **Backstamp(s)**: Shelley 1912-1925 **Shapes:** Gainsborough, Milton, Mocha
11305	Border of yellow and pink roses. White ground. Entered in pattern book during or after 1923. **Backstamp(s)**: Shelley 1912-1925 **Shapes:** Vincent
11306	Art nouveau pattern. Orange and green in a circle with three chains below it. Black linear border. Black edges. Entered in pattern book during or after 1923. **Backstamp(s)**: Shelley 1912-1925 **Shapes:** Kenneth
11309	Entered in pattern book during or after 1923. **Backstamp(s)**: Shelley 1912-1925 **Shapes:** Vincent
11310	Entered in pattern book during or after 1923. **Backstamp(s)**: Shelley 1912-1925 **Shapes:** Bute
11311-11313	Entered in pattern book during or after 1923. **Backstamp(s)**: Shelley 1912-1925 **Shapes:** Vincent
11314	Entered in pattern book during or after 1923. **Backstamp(s)**: Shelley 1912-1925 **Shapes:** Worcester
11315	Entered in pattern book during or after 1923. **Backstamp(s)**: Shelley 1912-1925 **Shapes:** Mocha
11316	Entered in pattern book during or after 1923. **Backstamp(s)**: Shelley 1912-1925 **Shapes:** Vincent
11317	Entered in pattern book during or after 1923.

Pattern	Description & Shapes
	Backstamp(s): Shelley 1912-1925 **Shapes:** Milton
11318-11319	Entered in pattern book during or after 1923. **Backstamp(s)**: Shelley 1912-1925 **Shapes:** Vincent
11320	Entered in pattern book during or after 1923. **Backstamp(s)**: Shelley 1912-1925 **Shapes:** Milton, Vincent
11321	Entered in pattern book during or after 1924. **Backstamp(s)**: Shelley 1912-1925 **Shapes:** Vincent
11322	Entered in pattern book during or after 1924. **Backstamp(s)**: Shelley 1912-1925 **Shapes:** Norman
11323	Black and yellow. Entered in pattern book during or after 1924. **Backstamp(s)**: Shelley 1912-1925 **Shapes:** Kenneth
11324	Enamelled in blue, yellow, and orange on black white ground. Black edges. Entered in pattern book during or after 1923. **Backstamp(s)**: Shelley 1925-1940 **Shapes:** Vincent
11325	Entered in pattern book during or after 1924. **Backstamp(s)**: Shelley 1912-1925 **Shapes:** Vincent
11326	Red **Poppy**. Coral poppy with black stem and leaves. White ground. Entered in pattern book during or after 1924. /BG Queen Anne shape /Y Yellow poppy. **Backstamp(s)**: Shelley 1912-1925; Shelley 1925-1940 **Shapes:** Queen Anne, Vincent
11327	**Joys**. Entered in pattern book during or after 1924. **Backstamp(s)**: Shelley 1912-1925 **Shapes:** New York
11328-11329	Entered in pattern book during or after 1924. **Backstamp(s)**: Shelley 1912-1925 **Shapes:** Vincent
11330	Entered in pattern book during or after 1924. **Backstamp(s)**: Shelley 1912-1925 **Shapes:** Milton
11331-11333	Entered in pattern book during or after 1924. **Backstamp(s)**: Shelley 1912-1925 **Shapes:** Vincent
11334-11338	Entered in pattern book during or after 1924. **Backstamp(s)**: Shelley 1912-1925 **Shapes:** Gainsborough
11340	Entered in pattern book during or after 1924. **Backstamp(s)**: Shelley 1912-1925 **Shapes:** Vincent
11341	Entered in pattern book during or after 1924. **Backstamp(s)**: Shelley 1912-1925 **Shapes:** Queen Anne, Vincent
11342	Entered in pattern book during or after 1924. **Backstamp(s)**: Shelley 1912-1925 **Shapes:** Queen Anne, Gainsborough
11343	Border of yellow, coral, and mauve fruit with green and black leaves. White ground. Black edges. White handle. Entered in pattern book during or after 1924. **Backstamp(s)**: Shelley 1912-1925; Shelley 1925-1940 **Shapes:** Vincent
11344-11345	Entered in pattern book during or after 1924. **Backstamp(s)**: Shelley 1912-1925 **Shapes:** Vincent
11346	Entered in pattern book during or after 1924. **Backstamp(s)**: Shelley 1912-1925 **Shapes:** Norman
11347	Entered in pattern book during or after 1924. **Backstamp(s)**: Shelley 1912-1925 **Shapes:** Gainsborough
11348	Entered in pattern book during or after 1924. **Backstamp(s)**: Shelley 1912-1925 **Shapes:** Vincent
11349	**Swallows**. Black and orange swallows. Black, leafy tree with orange and yellow fruit. Blue lake, grey mountains. White ground. Black edges and handle. Entered in pattern book during or after 1930. **Backstamp(s)**: Shelley 1925-1940 **Shapes:** Vincent

Swallows 11349 Vincent shape cup, saucer, and plate. £50-60; $90-120

Pattern	Description & Shapes
11350	**Cameo**. Dancers within a black cameo. Yellow ground. Black edges and handle. Entered in pattern book during or after 1924. **Backstamp(s)**: Shelley 1925-1940 **Shapes:** Vincent
11351	Entered in pattern book during or after 1924. **Backstamp(s)**: Shelley 1912-1925 **Shapes:** Bute
11352	Entered in pattern book during or after 1924. **Backstamp(s)**: Shelley 1912-1925 **Shapes:** Vincent
11353	Entered in pattern book during or after 1924. **Backstamp(s)**: Shelley 1912-1925 **Shapes:** Norman
11354-11355	Entered in pattern book during or after 1924. **Backstamp(s)**: Shelley 1912-1925 **Shapes:** Vincent
11356-11358	Entered in pattern book during or after 1924. **Backstamp(s)**: Shelley 1912-1925 **Shapes:** Doric
11359	**Cameo Dancing**. Figure in black on powder blue ground. Entered in pattern book during or after 1924. **Backstamp(s)**: Shelley 1912-1925 **Shapes:** Vincent
11360-11363	Entered in pattern book during or after 1924. **Backstamp(s)**: Shelley 1912-1925 **Shapes:** Doric
11364	**Fruit Basket**. Entered in pattern book during or after 1924. /6 Black. **Backstamp(s)**: Shelley 1912-1925 **Shapes:** Unknown
11365	Entered in pattern book during or after 1924. **Backstamp(s)**: Shelley 1912-1925 **Shapes:** Vincent
11366	**Basket of Fruit**. Black print. Blue, yellow, orange, and green fruit in black baskets. Baskets linked by garlands of fruit and geometric pattern. Entered in pattern book during or after 1924. **Backstamp(s)**: Shelley 1912-1925 **Shapes:** Doric
11367	Entered in pattern book during or after 1924. **Backstamp(s)**: Shelley 1912-1925 **Shapes:** Doric
11368	**Thistle**. Entered in pattern book during or after 1924. **Backstamp(s)**: Shelley 1912-1925 **Shapes:** Doric
11369	**Vine**. Entered in pattern book during or after 1924. **Backstamp(s)**: Shelley 1912-1925 **Shapes:** Doric
11370	**Vase of Flowers**. Entered in pattern book during or after 1924. /6 Black. **Backstamp(s)**: Shelley 1912-1925 **Shapes:** Doric
11371	**Basket of Flowers**. Entered in pattern book during or after 1924. **Backstamp(s)**: Shelley 1912-1925 **Shapes:** Doric
11372-11373	Entered in pattern book during or after 1924. **Backstamp(s)**: Shelley 1912-1925 **Shapes:** Doric
11374-11375	Entered in pattern book during or after 1924. **Backstamp(s)**: Shelley 1912-1925 **Shapes:** Gainsborough
11376	Entered in pattern book during or after 1924. **Backstamp(s)**: Shelley 1912-1925 **Shapes:** Milton, Mocha
11384-11385	Entered in pattern book during or after 1924. **Backstamp(s)**: Shelley 1912-1925 **Shapes:** Doric
11386	Entered in pattern book during or after 1925. **Backstamp(s)**: Shelley 1912-1925; Shelley 1925-1940 **Shapes:** Doric
11387	Entered in pattern book during or after 1925. **Backstamp(s)**: Shelley 1912-1925; Shelley 1925-1940 **Shapes:** Gainsborough
11388	Entered in pattern book during or after 1925. **Backstamp(s)**: Shelley 1912-1925; Shelley 1925-1940 **Shapes:** Vincent
11389-11391	Entered in pattern book during or after 1925. **Backstamp(s)**: Shelley 1912-1925; Shelley 1925-1940 **Shapes:** Doric
11392	Gold print. Coral fruit with green leaves. Gold edges and handle. Entered in pattern book during or after 1925. **Backstamp(s)**: Shelley 1912-1925 **Shapes:** Vincent
11393	Entered in pattern book during or after 1925. **Backstamp(s)**: Shelley 1912-1925; Shelley 1925-1940 **Shapes:** Vincent
11394-11398	Entered in pattern book during or after 1925.

Pattern	Description & Shapes
	Backstamp(s): Shelley 1912-1925; Shelley 1925-1940 **Shapes:** Dainty
11399-11401	Entered in pattern book during or after 1925. **Backstamp(s)**: Shelley 1912-1925; Shelley 1925-1940 **Shapes:** Gainsborough
11402-11403	Entered in pattern book during or after 1925. **Backstamp(s)**: Shelley 1912-1925; Shelley 1925-1940 **Shapes:** Vincent
11405	Entered in pattern book during or after 1925. **Backstamp(s)**: Shelley 1912-1925; Shelley 1925-1940 **Shapes:** Gainsborough
11406	Entered in pattern book during or after 1925. **Backstamp(s)**: Shelley 1912-1925; Shelley 1925-1940 **Shapes:** Vincent
11407	Entered in pattern book during or after 1925. **Backstamp(s)**: Shelley 1912-1925; Shelley 1925-1940 **Shapes:** Gainsborough
11408	Entered in pattern book during or after 1925. **Backstamp(s)**: Shelley 1912-1925; Shelley 1925-1940 **Shapes:** Bute
11410-11411	Entered in pattern book during or after 1925. **Backstamp(s)**: Shelley 1912-1925; Shelley 1925-1940 **Shapes:** Milton
11412	Entered in pattern book during or after 1925. **Backstamp(s)**: Shelley 1912-1925; Shelley 1925-1940 **Shapes:** Bute
11413-11414	Entered in pattern book during or after 1925. **Backstamp(s)**: Shelley 1912-1925; Shelley 1925-1940 **Shapes:** Vincent
11415	Entered in pattern book during or after 1925. **Backstamp(s)**: Shelley 1912-1925; Shelley 1925-1940 **Shapes:** Gainsborough
11416-11417	Entered in pattern book during or after 1925. **Backstamp(s)**: Shelley 1912-1925; Shelley 1925-1940 **Shapes:** Doric
11418	Entered in pattern book during or after 1925. **Backstamp(s)**: Shelley 1912-1925; Shelley 1925-1940 **Shapes:** Carlton
11419	Entered in pattern book during or after 1925. **Backstamp(s)**: Shelley 1912-1925; Shelley 1925-1940 **Shapes:** Worcester
11420-11421	Entered in pattern book during or after 1925. **Backstamp(s)**: Shelley 1912-1925; Shelley 1925-1940 **Shapes:** Doric
11422	Deep blue outer border enclosed in gold lines. Inner border has vases of turquoise and yellow flowers with brown leaves linked by fawn garlands. White ground. Gold trim. Entered in pattern book during or after 1925. **Backstamp(s)**: Shelley 1912-1925 **Shapes:** Vincent
11423-11424	Entered in pattern book during or after 1925. **Backstamp(s)**: Shelley 1912-1925; Shelley 1925-1940 **Shapes:** Vincent
11425	Orange and mauve fruit with green leaves on a white ground. Entered in pattern book during or after 1925. **Backstamp(s)**: Shelley 1912-1925; Shelley 1925-1940 **Shapes:** Vincent
11426	**Versailles**. Inside cup, saucer, and plate have long-tailed birds in blue, red, yellow, and green; red, yellow, and orange fruit with green leaves. Outside cup also has fruit. Teal and gold border inside cup and edges of saucer and plate. White ground. Gold edges. Entered in pattern book during or after 1925. **Backstamp(s)**: Shelley 1912-1925 Versailles **Shapes:** Doric, Gainsborough

Versailles 11426 Doric shape cup, saucer, and plate. £50-60; $90-120

Versailles 11426 Gainsborough shape cup, saucer, and plate. £40-50; $80-100

Pattern	Description & Shapes
11427	**Hampton Court**. Basket of fruit and flowers on a white ground. Border inside cup and edge of saucer includes leaves, fruit, and flowers. Gold edges. Entered in pattern book during or after 1925. **Backstamp(s)**: Shelley 1912-1925 Hampton Court **Shapes:** Doric, Gainsborough

Right:
Hampton Court 11427 Doric shape cup and saucer. £50-60; $90-120

Pattern	Description & Shapes
11428	Entered in pattern book during or after 1925. **Backstamp(s)**: Shelley 1912-1925; Shelley 1925-1940 **Shapes:** Kenneth
11429	**Vine**. Entered in pattern book during or after 1925. **Backstamp(s)**: Shelley 1912-1925; Shelley 1925-1940 **Shapes:** Kenneth
11430	Fruit and Jewel. Black print. Orange, yellow, and purple fruit. Purple motifs on either side of fruit groups. Chain border. White ground. Entered in pattern book during or after 1925. **Backstamp(s)**: Shelley 1925-1940 **Shapes:** Vincent
11431	**Leaves and Berries**. Entered in pattern book during or after 1925. **Backstamp(s)**: Shelley 1912-1925; Shelley 1925-1940 **Shapes:** Vincent
11432	Entered in pattern book during or after 1925. **Backstamp(s)**: Shelley 1912-1925; Shelley 1925-1940 **Shapes:** New York
11434	Entered in pattern book during or after 1925. **Backstamp(s)**: Shelley 1912-1925; Shelley 1925-1940 **Shapes:** Doric
11436-11437	Entered in pattern book during or after 1925. **Backstamp(s)**: Shelley 1912-1925; Shelley 1925-1940 **Shapes:** Doric
11438-11439	Entered in pattern book during or after 1925. **Backstamp(s)**: Shelley 1912-1925; Shelley 1925-1940 **Shapes:** Vincent
11440	Entered in pattern book during or after 1925. **Backstamp(s)**: Shelley 1912-1925; Shelley 1925-1940 **Shapes:** Doric
11441	Coral, yellow, blue, and mauve fruit, black and green leaves against a white band. Yellow below patterned band. Black edges and handle. Entered in pattern book during or after 1925. /32 Yellow outside cup and on main part of saucer; pattern inside cup and centre of saucer on a white ground; black edges and handle. **Backstamp(s)**: Shelley 1925-1940 **Shapes:** Gainsborough, Milton
11442	Entered in pattern book during or after 1925. **Backstamp(s)**: Shelley 1912-1925; Shelley 1925-1940 **Shapes:** Doric
11443	Entered in pattern book during or after 1925. **Backstamp(s)**: Shelley 1912-1925;

Pattern	Description & Shapes
	Shelley 1925-1940 **Shapes:** Vincent
11444	**Bunch of Fruit**. Entered in pattern book during or after 1925. **Backstamp(s)**: Shelley 1912-1925; Shelley 1925-1940 **Shapes:** Doric
11445	Entered in pattern book during or after 1925. **Backstamp(s)**: Shelley 1912-1925; Shelley 1925-1940 **Shapes:** Doric
11446-11447	Entered in pattern book during or after 1925. **Backstamp(s)**: Shelley 1912-1925; Shelley 1925-1940 **Shapes:** Vincent
11448	Entered in pattern book during or after 1925. **Backstamp(s)**: Shelley 1912-1925; Shelley 1925-1940 **Shapes:** Doric
11449	Entered in pattern book during or after 1925. **Backstamp(s)**: Shelley 1912-1925; Shelley 1925-1940 **Shapes:** Vincent
11450	**Berries and Blocks**. Entered in pattern book during or after 1925. **Backstamp(s)**: Shelley 1912-1925; Shelley 1925-1940 **Shapes:** Doric, Kenneth, Mocha
11451	Entered in pattern book during or after 1925. **Backstamp(s)**: Shelley 1912-1925; Shelley 1925-1940 **Shapes:** Doric
11452	Entered in pattern book during or after 1925. **Backstamp(s)**: Shelley 1912-1925; Shelley 1925-1940 **Shapes:** Vincent
11453	Entered in pattern book during or after 1925. **Backstamp(s)**: Shelley 1912-1925; Shelley 1925-1940 **Shapes:** Mocha, Vincent
11454	Entered in pattern book during or after 1925. **Backstamp(s)**: Shelley 1912-1925; Shelley 1925-1940 **Shapes:** Doric
11455	Entered in pattern book during or after 1925. **Backstamp(s)**: Shelley 1912-1925; Shelley 1925-1940 **Shapes:** Vincent
11458	Entered in pattern book during or after 1926. **Backstamp(s)**: Shelley 1925-1940 **Shapes:** Gainsborough
11459	Worcester. Black border pattern on yellow ground inside cup and on saucer. White outside cup encircled with a black line at base of handle level. Black edges. Seconds ware. Entered in pattern book during or after 1926. **Backstamp(s)**: Shelley 1925-1940 **Shapes:** Gainsborough
11468	Entered in pattern book during or after 1926. **Backstamp(s)**: Shelley 1925-1940 **Shapes:** Lomond, Vincent
11469-11470	Entered in pattern book during or after 1926. **Backstamp(s)**: Shelley 1925-1940 **Shapes:** Milton
11471-11474	Entered in pattern book during or after 1926. **Backstamp(s)**: Shelley 1925-1940 **Shapes:** Gainsborough
11475	Black print. Pink and mauve flowers with green leaves within a black semicircle on large panels. Pink flower with green leaves and stem on small panels. Leaf type design on panels joins. Dark green edges. Entered in pattern book during or after 1926 **Backstamp(s)**: Shelley 1925-1940 **Shapes:** Queen Anne

Flowers in semicircles 11475 Queen Anne shape cup, saucer, and plate. £80-100; $120-160

11476	**Black Trees**. Black print. Black trees with black and green leaves. Coral, blue, yellow, and purple stylised fruit. Grey flowers. Black edges. Similar to 11697. Entered in pattern book during or after 1926 **Backstamp(s)**: Shelley 1925-1940 **Shapes:** Queen Anne

Black Trees 11476 Queen Anne shape cup, saucer, and plate. £80-100; $120-160

11477	Unnamed. *Very rare*. Pink and blue cornflowers. Black net pattern on panel joins. White ground. Entered in pattern book during or after 1926. Not included in the 1928 catalogue. **Backstamp(s)**: Shelley 1925-1940 **Shapes:** Queen Anne
11478	Bands of pink roses with green leaves inside cup and on saucer. Rose sprigs outside cup. Gold dontil edge inside cup and on saucer. White ground. Gold edges. Entered in pattern book during or after 1926. **Backstamp(s)**: Shelley 1925-1940 **Shapes:** Gainsborough, Mocha

Right:
Pink rose 11478 Gainsborough shape cup, saucer, and plate. £40-50; $80-100

11479	**Trees and Sunset**. Silhouetted pairs of black trees on panel edges. Yellow setting sun between trees. Grey shaded landscape border on outside of cup and on saucer. White ground. Black edges. Entered in pattern book during or after 1926. **Backstamp(s)**: Shelley 1925-1940 **Shapes:** Queen Anne

Trees and Sunset 11479 Queen Anne shape cup, saucer, and plate. £80-100; $120-160

11480	Entered in pattern book during or after 1926. **Backstamp(s)**: Shelley 1925-1940 **Shapes:** Bute
11481	Entered in pattern book during or after 1926. **Backstamp(s)**: Shelley 1925-1940 **Shapes:** Milton, Mocha
11482-11483	Entered in pattern book during or after 1926. **Backstamp(s)**: Shelley 1925-1940 **Shapes:** Doric, Mocha
11484-11485	Entered in pattern book during or after 1926. **Backstamp(s)**: Shelley 1925-1940 **Shapes:** Mocha, Vincent
11489	Entered in pattern book during or after 1926. **Backstamp(s)**: Shelley 1925-1940 **Shapes:** Mocha, Vincent
11490	Entered in pattern book during or after 1926. **Backstamp(s)**: Shelley 1925-1940 **Shapes:** Gainsborough
11494	**Rose Spray**. Floral bunches that include pink roses, pink, yellow, and blue flowers with green leaves. White ground. Mottled gold edges, also inside cup. Entered in pattern book during or after 1926. **Backstamp(s)**: Shelley 1925-1940

Pattern	Description & Shapes
11495	**Vase of Flowers**. Black print. Blue and green vase. Pink and blue flowers. Pink edges. Entered in pattern book during or after 1926. **Backstamp(s)**: Shelley 1925-1940 **Shapes:** Queen Anne

Vase of Flowers 11495 Queen Anne shape cup, saucer, and plate. £80-100; $140-180

11496 Black stylised bush and leaves. Yellow, pink, and blue fruit. Yellow and mauve border. Black linear design on panel joins. White ground. Black trim. Entered in pattern book during or after 1926.
Backstamp(s): Shelley 1925-1940
Shapes: Queen Anne

11497 **Daisy**. Black print with red enamelled daises. White ground. Black edges. Entered in pattern book during or after 1926.
/G green daisies
/M mauve daisies
/T turquoise daisies
/P pink daisies.
Backstamp(s): Shelley 1925-1940
Shapes: Queen Anne

Right:
Daisy 11497 Queen Anne shape creamer and sugar. £80-100; $120-160

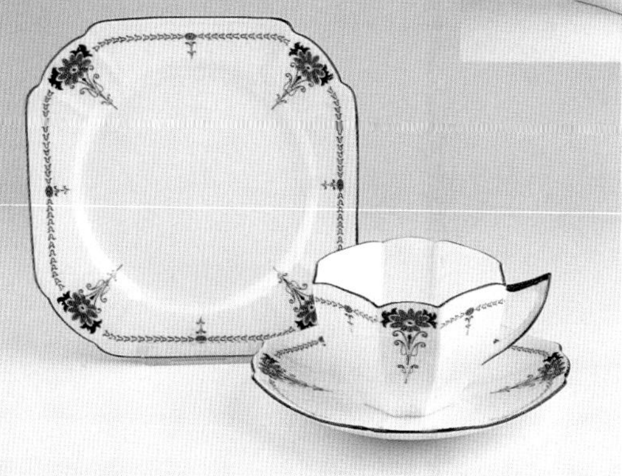

Daisy 11497 Queen Anne shape cup, saucer, and plate. £80-100; $120-160

11498 Peaches and Grapes. Black print. Pink and yellow peaches with purple and blue grapes. Grey leaves and tendrils on large panels white ground. Black edges. Entered in pattern book during or after 1926.
Backstamp(s): Shelley 1925-1940
Shapes: Queen Anne

11499 **Daisy**. Brown print with daises enamelled in gold. Gold edges. Entered in pattern book during or after 1926.
Backstamp(s): Shelley 1925-1940
Shapes: Queen Anne

Peaches and Grapes 11498 Queen Anne shape cup, saucer, and plate, £80-100; $120-160; sugar bowl and creamer, £80-100; $120-160 each.

Daisy 11499 Queen Anne shape cup, saucer, and plate. £80-100; $120-160

Pattern number 11499 Queen Anne shape cup, saucer, and plate. £80-100; $120-160

11500 Entered in pattern book during or after 1926.
Backstamp(s): Shelley 1925-1940
Shapes: Doric

11501 Garland of Fruit. Black print. Yellow, coral, orange, and blue fruit with green leaves on small panels. Fruit garlands on large panels. Chevrons on panels joins. Border consisting of yellow motifs and band of vertical lines. White ground. Black edges. Similar to 11705. Entered in pattern book during or after 1926.
Backstamp(s): Shelley 1925-1940
Shapes: Queen Anne

11502 **Pink Scroll**. Pink flowers and green enclosed by black scrolls and tendrils on a white ground. Black and pink border. Pink edges. Entered in pattern book during or after 1926.
Backstamp(s): Shelley 1925-1940
Shapes: Queen Anne

Pink Scroll 11502 Queen Anne shape cup, saucer, and plate. £80-100; $120-160

Right:
Garland of Fruit 11501 Queen Anne shape cup, saucer, and plate. £80-100; $120-160

Pattern **Description & Shapes**

11504 **Garland of Flowers**. Black garland pattern and trim. White ground. Entered in pattern book during or after 1926.
Backstamp(s): Shelley 1925-1940
Shapes: Queen Anne

Garland of Flowers 11504 Queen Anne shape cup, saucer, and plate. £80-100; $120-160

11505 Panelled fruit pattern against a black diamond with orange, blue, and black garlands. Entered in pattern book during or after 1926.
Backstamp(s): Shelley 1925-1940
Shapes: Queen Anne

Fruit and diamonds 11505 Queen Anne shape cup, saucer, and plate. £80-100; $120-160

11506 Ornament and border print. Entered in pattern book during or after 1926.
Backstamp(s): Shelley 1925-1940
Shapes: Doric, Mocha

11507 Entered in pattern book during or after 1926.
Backstamp(s): Shelley 1925-1940
Shapes: Doric

11508 Entered in pattern book during or after 1926.
Backstamp(s): Shelley 1925-1940
Shapes: Doric, Mocha

11509 Entered in pattern book during or after 1926.
Backstamp(s): Shelley 1925-1940
Shapes: Mocha, Vincent

11510 Entered in pattern book during or after 1926.
Backstamp(s): Shelley 1925-1940
Shapes: Queen Anne

11511 Panelled fruit pattern against a black diamond on yellow panels. Alternated with orange, blue, and black garlands on white panels.
Entered in pattern book during or after 1926.
Backstamp(s): Shelley 1925-1940
Shapes: Queen Anne

Fruit and black diamonds 11511/31 Queen Anne shape cup, saucer, and plate. £80-100; $120-160. Sugar bowl and creamer. £70-90; $100-140

11512 **Garland of Flowers**. Black garland pattern and trim. Coloured ground. Entered in pattern book during or after 1926.
/1 Pink
/31 Yellow.
Backstamp(s): Shelley 1925-1940
Shapes: Queen Anne

Garland of Flowers 11512/31 Queen Anne shape cup, saucer, and plate. £80-100; $120-160

Garland of Flowers 11512/1 Queen Anne shape cup, saucer, and plate. £80-100; $120-160

11513 **Trees and Sunset**. Silhouetted pairs of black trees on panel edges. Yellow setting sun between trees. Grey and green shaded landscape border on outside of cup and on saucer. Coral ground. Black edges. Entered in pattern book during or after 1926.
Backstamp(s): Shelley 1925-1940
Shapes: Queen Anne

Right:
Trees and Sunset 11513 Queen Anne shape cup, saucer, and plate. £100-120; $170-190

Trees and Sunset 11513 Queen Anne shape demitasse cup and saucer. £90-110; $160-180. Demitasse creamer. £50-60; $90-110

Pattern	Description & Shapes
11514	**Trees and Sunset**. Silhouetted pairs of black trees on panel edges. Yellow setting sun between trees. Grey and green shaded landscape border on outside of cup and on saucer. Greenish-blue/aqua ground. Black edges. Entered in pattern book during or after 1926. **Backstamp(s)**: Shelley 1925-1940 **Shapes:** Queen Anne

Trees and Sunset 11514 Queen Anne shape cup, saucer, and plate. £80-100; $120-160

Pattern	Description & Shapes
11515	Black art deco litho on white ground, hand-enamelled in fruit and leaves in blue, yellow, and green. November 1926. **Backstamp(s)**: Shelley 1925-1940 **Shapes:** Vincent
11516	Entered in pattern book during or after 1926. **Backstamp(s)**: Shelley 1925-1940 **Shapes:** Kenneth, Mocha
11517	Entered in pattern book during or after 1926. **Backstamp(s)**: Shelley 1925-1940 **Shapes:** Gainsborough
11518	Entered in pattern book during or after 1926. **Backstamp(s)**: Shelley 1925-1940 **Shapes:** Doric
11519	Entered in pattern book during or after 1926. **Backstamp(s)**: Shelley 1925-1940 **Shapes:** Tall Dainty
11520	**Garland of Flowers**. Black garland pattern and trim. White ground. Entered in pattern book during or after 1926. **Backstamp(s)**: Shelley 1925-1940 **Shapes:** Queen Anne, Tall Dainty
11521	Entered in pattern book during or after 1926. **Backstamp(s)**: Shelley 1925-1940 **Shapes:** Doric
11522	**Sprig of Roses**. Small sprigs of pink roses and green leaves. Gold trim. **Backstamp(s)**: Shelley 1925-1940 **Shapes:** Dainty
11523	Entered in pattern book during or after 1926. **Backstamp(s)**: Shelley 1925-1940 **Shapes:** Dainty
11524	Black print. Pink and mauve flowers with green leaves within a black semicircle on large panels. Plain colour on small panels. Leaf type design on panels joins. Dark green edges. Entered in pattern book during or after 1926 **Backstamp(s)**: Shelley 1925-1940 **Shapes:** Queen Anne
11525	**Vase of Flowers**. Small panels are pink. Black print on large white panels with blue and green vase, ink and blue flowers. Pink edges. **Backstamp(s)**: Shelley 1925-1940 **Shapes:** Queen Anne
11526-11528	Entered in pattern book during or after 1926. **Backstamp(s)**: Shelley 1925-1940 **Shapes:** Gainsborough
11529-11536	Entered in pattern book during or after 1926. **Backstamp(s)**: Shelley 1925-1940 **Shapes:** Lomond
11537	Entered in pattern book during or after 1926. **Backstamp(s)**: Shelley 1925-1940 **Shapes:** Vincent
11538	Entered in pattern book during or after 1926. **Backstamp(s)**: Shelley 1925-1940 **Shapes:** Gainsborough
11539	Gold border with triangular frames with rose sprays on small panels. Coloured ground. Gold edges and handle. Similar to 11827. Entered in pattern book during or after 1927. **Backstamp(s)**: Shelley 1925-1940 **Shapes:** Queen Anne
11540	Maroon, gold, and fawn pattern. Gold lines on panel joins. Panels of fawn crosshatched lines on ivory ground. Gold triangular panels of crosshatched lines and bells on small panels. Maroon ground. Gold edges and handle. Entered in pattern book during or after 1927. **Backstamp(s)**: Shelley 1925-1940 **Shapes:** Queen Anne
11541	Gold vine and trellis print on salmon ground. Entered in pattern book during or after 1927. **Backstamp(s)**: Shelley 1925-1940 **Shapes:** Queen Anne
11542	Gold vine and trellis print on green ground. Entered in pattern book during or after 1927. **Backstamp(s)**: Shelley 1925-1940 **Shapes:** Queen Anne
11543-11545	Entered in pattern book during or after 1927. **Backstamp(s)**: Shelley 1925-1940 **Shapes:** Gainsborough
11546-11547	Entered in pattern book during or after 1927. **Backstamp(s)**: Shelley 1925-1940 **Shapes:** Lomond
11548	Gold vine and trellis print on pink ground. Entered in pattern book during or after 1927. **Backstamp(s)**: Shelley 1925-1940 **Shapes:** Queen Anne
11549-11550	Entered in pattern book during or after 1927. **Backstamp(s)**: Shelley 1925-1940 **Shapes:** Gainsborough
11551	Gold vine and trellis print on white ground. Entered in pattern book during or after 1927. **Backstamp(s)**: Shelley 1925-1940 **Shapes:** Queen Anne
11552	Entered in pattern book during or after 1927. **Backstamp(s)**: Shelley 1925-1940 **Shapes:** Gainsborough
11553	Gold leafy trees. Green, yellow, orange, and blue balloons. White ground. Gold trim. Entered in pattern book during or after 1927. **Backstamp(s)**: Shelley 1925-1940 **Shapes:** Lomond

Right:
Gold leafy trees and balloons 11553 Lomond shape cup, saucer, and plate. £50-60; $90-120

Pattern	Description & Shapes
11554-11558	Entered in pattern book during or after 1927. **Backstamp(s)**: Shelley 1925-1940 **Shapes:** Lomond
11559	Entered in pattern book during or after 1927. **Backstamp(s)**: Shelley 1925-1940 **Shapes:** Gainsborough
11560	Entered in pattern book during or after 1927. **Backstamp(s)**: Shelley 1925-1940 **Shapes:** Vincent
11561	**Blue Iris**. Irises with green leaves on small panels. Yellow and red stylised fruit and grey leaves on large panels. Dots and circles on panel joins. White ground. Dark blue edges. Entered in pattern book during or after 1927. **Backstamp(s)**: Shelley 1925-1940 **Shapes:** Queen Anne

Blue Iris 11561 Queen Anne shape cup, saucer, and plate. £80-100; $120-160

Blue Iris 11561 Queen Anne shape demitasse cup and saucer. £70-90; $100-140

Pattern	Description & Shapes
11562	Bananas. Black print. Large bunch of bananas with leaves on small panels. Smaller bunches on large panels. White ground. Similar to 11693 and 11706. Entered in pattern book during or after 1927. **Backstamp(s)**: Shelley 1925-1940 **Shapes:** Queen Anne
11563	Fruit Border. Black print. Border of coral, blue, and yellow fruit. Yellow fruit and grey leaves on small panels. Grey leaves on large panels. Grey chain pattern on panels joins. White ground. Orange edges. Entered in pattern book during or after 1927. /BE Black edges. **Backstamp(s)**: Shelley 1925-1940 **Shapes:** Queen Anne

Fruit Border 11563 Queen Anne shape cup, saucer, and plate. £80-100; $120-160

11564	Pink and blue flowers with green foliage on small panels. Flowers and leaf border. Pink chevrons half the length of the panel joins. Pink edges. Entered in pattern book during or after 1927. **Backstamp(s)**: Shelley 1925-1940 **Shapes:** Queen Anne
11565	Fruit Border. Black print. Border of coral, blue, and yellow fruit. Yellow fruit and grey leaves on small panels. Grey leaves on large panels. Grey chain pattern on panels joins. White ground. Orange edges. Entered in pattern book during or after 1927. **Backstamp(s)**: Shelley 1925-1940 **Shapes:** Queen Anne

Fruit Border 11565 Queen Anne shape cup, saucer, and plate. £80-100; $120-160

11566	**Bowl of Fruit**. Black print. Black bowl with in coral, yellow, pink, and purple fruit. White ground. Orange edges. Entered in pattern book during or after 1927. **Backstamp(s)**: Shelley 1925-1940 **Shapes:** Queen Anne

Bowl of Fruit 11566 Queen Anne shape cup, saucer, and plate. £80-100; $120-160

11567	Wreathes of fruit and flowers in black, orange, red, mauve, green, and blue. Thin black border outside cup and on saucer. Entered in pattern book during or after 1927. **Backstamp(s)**: Shelley 1925-1940 **Shapes:** Vincent
11568	Black print. Red roses with green leaves on black art nouveau motif. Black line and motif inside cup. White ground. Black edges. Entered in pattern book during or after 1927. **Backstamp(s)**: Shelley 1925-1940 **Shapes:** Doric
11569	Entered in pattern book during or after 1927. **Backstamp(s)**: Shelley 1925-1940 **Shapes:** Doric
11570-11572	Entered in pattern book during or after 1927. **Backstamp(s)**: Shelley 1925-1940 **Shapes:** Vincent
11573	Entered in pattern book during or after 1927. **Backstamp(s)**: Shelley 1925-1940 **Shapes:** Doric
11574	**Bunch of Grapes**. Mauve and black grapes with green leaves on small panels. Grey leaves and tendrils on large panels. Yellow, coral, and blue fruit with green leaves on saucer and centre of plate. White ground. Yellow edges. Entered in pattern book during or after 1927. **Backstamp(s)**: Shelley 1925-1940 **Shapes:** Queen Anne

11575	**Black Leafy Tree**. Enamelled in blue, pink, orange, and coral. White ground. Black edges. Entered in pattern book during or after 1927. **Backstamp(s)**: Shelley 1925-1940 **Shapes:** Queen Anne

Black Leafy Tree 11575 Queen Anne demitasse shape creamer and sugar. £70-90; $100-120

Black Leafy Tree 11575 Queen Anne shape creamer. £50-60; $80-90

Black Leafy Tree 11575 Queen Anne shape cup, saucer, and plate. £80-100; $120-160

Bunch of Grapes 11574 Queen Anne shape cup, saucer, and plate. £80-100; $120-160

Pattern	Description & Shapes

11576 Small panels are white and have black and green jardinière with a stylised black bush and orange, blue, yellow, and coral fruit and leaves. Large panels are plain coloured – dark pink or blue. The pink panels are rarer than the blue. Black linear pattern on panels joins and around jardinière and bush in centre of plate. Black edges. Entered in pattern book during or after 1927.
/34 pink
Backstamp(s): Shelley 1925-1940
Shapes: Queen Anne

Jardinière and stylised bush 11576 Queen Anne shape large teapot. £250-300; $400-500. Cup, saucer, and plate. £80-100; $120-160

11577 Fruit Border. Brown print. Border of coral, blue, and yellow fruit. Yellow fruit and brown leaves on small panels. Brown leaves on large panels. Brown chain pattern on panels joins. Coloured ground. Gold edges. Entered in pattern book during or after 1927.
Backstamp(s): Shelley 1925-1940
Shapes: Queen Anne

11578 **Blue Iris**. Irises with green leaves on small panels. Yellow and red stylised fruit and grey leaves on large panels. Dots and circles on panel joins. Coloured ground on large panels. White ground on small panels. Gold edges. Entered in pattern book during or after 1927.
Backstamp(s): Shelley 1925-1940
Shapes: Queen Anne

11579 **Bowl of Fruit**. Black print. Black bowl with fruit in coral, yellow, pink, and purple on white panels. Alternating panels are mauve. Entered in pattern book during or after 1927.
Backstamp(s): Shelley 1925-1940
Shapes: Queen Anne

Bowl of Fruit 11579 Queen Anne shape cup, saucer, and plate. £80-100; $120-160

11580 Entered in pattern book during or after 1927.
Backstamp(s): Shelley 1925-1940
Shapes: Milton

11581 Plain colour on small panels. Black feathered, scroll print on a white ground on large panels. Blacks spots on panel joins. Black edges. Entered in pattern book during or after 1927.
/31 Yellow
/4 Green.
Backstamp(s): Shelley 1925-1940
Shapes: Queen Anne

Green and white panels 11581/4 Queen Anne shape cup, saucer, and plate. £80-100; $120-160

Turquoise and white panels 11581 Queen Anne shape cup, saucer, and plate. £80-100; $120-160

Right:
Yellow and white panels 11581/31 Queen Anne shape cup, saucer, and plate. £80-100; $120-160

11582 Entered in pattern book during or after 1927.
Backstamp(s): Shelley 1925-1940
Shapes: Vincent

11583 Entered in pattern book during or after 1927.
Backstamp(s): Shelley 1925-1940
Shapes: Milton, Mocha

11584 Entered in pattern book during or after 1927.
Backstamp(s): Shelley 1925-1940
Shapes: Lomond

11585 **Jazz Fruit**. Entered in pattern book during or after 1927.
Backstamp(s): Shelley 1925-1940
Shapes: Vincent

11586 Gold swirl with orange, mauve, and yellow flame flowers and tendrils. Black edges. Entered in pattern book during or after 1927.
Backstamp(s): Shelley 1925-1940
Shapes: Vincent

11587-11588 Entered in pattern book during or after 1927.
Backstamp(s): Shelley 1925-1940
Shapes: Vincent

11589 Tall, thin black stems and tendrils with green leaves on panel joins. Black leaves and fruit or flowers in blue and yellow below rim. Dark yellow/orange edges. Entered in pattern book during or after 1927.
Backstamp(s): Shelley 1925-1940
Shapes: Queen Anne

11590 Large Fruit. Brown print. Large yellow stylised fruit with red spot, black tendrils, green, brown, and blue leaves on a white ground on the small panels. Border with mauve and coral dots and circles, with leafy swathes below it. White ground. Gold edges. Entered in pattern book during or after 1927.
Backstamp(s): Shelley 1925-1940
Shapes: Queen Anne

Large Fruit 11590 Queen Anne shape cup, saucer, and plate. £80-100; $120-160

Pattern	Description & Shapes
11591	Large Fruit. Black print. Large yellow stylised fruit with red spot, black tendrils, green, black, and blue leaves on a white ground on the small panels. Plain colour on large panels. Border with black and coral dots and circles, with leafy swathes below it. Entered in pattern book during or after 1927. /8 Blue. **Backstamp(s)**: Shelley 1925-1940 **Shapes:** Queen Anne

Large Fruit 11591/8 Queen Anne shape cup, saucer, and plate. £80-100; $120-160

11592 **Black Leafy Tree**. Gold print. Enamelled in blue, pink, orange, and coral. White ground. Gold edges. Entered in pattern book during or after 1927.
Backstamp(s): Shelley 1925-1940
Shapes: Queen Anne

11595 **Lowestoft**. Small sprays of pink, blue, and yellow flowers with green leaves on a white ground. Black leafy border. Gold edges. Entered in pattern book during or after 1928.
Backstamp(s): Shelley 1925-1940
Shapes: Lomond, Mocha, Queen Anne, Vincent

Lowestoft 11595 Queen Anne shape cup, saucer, and plate. £80-100; $120-160

11597 Entered in pattern book during or after 1928.
Backstamp(s): Shelley 1925-1940
Shapes: Vincent

11598 Entered in pattern book during or after 1928.
Backstamp(s): Shelley 1925-1940
Shapes: Carlton, Savoy

11599 **Scattered Rose**. Entered in pattern book during or after 1928.
Backstamp(s): Shelley 1925-1940
Shapes: Carlton, Savoy

11600 **Urn of Flowers**. Entered in pattern book during or after 1928.
Backstamp(s): Shelley 1925-1940
Shapes: Lomond

11601 Entered in pattern book during or after 1928.
Backstamp(s): Shelley 1925-1940
Shapes: Lomond

11602 Leafy Branches. Black print. Black branches, black and green leaves, coral flowers. Yellow border. White ground. Blue edges. Entered in pattern book during or after 1928.
Backstamp(s): Shelley 1925-1940
Shapes: Lomond

11603 Stylised black tree with blue, red, and yellow flowers. Green at base of tree with blades of grass and small yellow flowers. Border of small dots outside cup and on saucer. Band of flowers and leaves separate dots from made part of cup and on saucer. White ground. Dark blue edges. Entered in pattern book during or after 1928.
Backstamp(s): Shelley 1925-1940
Shapes: Vincent

Stylised tree and flowers 11603 Vincent shape cup, saucer, and plate. £50-60; $90-120

11604 Cottage-1. Black print on outside cup, centre of saucer and plates. Body of saucer and outer border of plate are plain coloured. Cottage with chimneys. Grey trees partly enamelled in black. Green fields. Yellow road. Fence and gate across road. Smoke rising from chimney on cup. White ground. Black edges and handle. Entered in pattern book during or after 1928.
Cake/bread and butter plate has pattern in middle of plate surrounded by plain green.
Backstamp(s): Shelley 1925-1940
Shapes: Queen Anne

Cottage-1 11604 Queen Anne shape cup, saucer, and plate. £150-200; $250-300

11605 Combination and variation of **My Garden** on cup and saucer and **Archway of Roses** on plate. Garden with flowers that include hollyhocks and roses. Sundial on cup. Enamelled in blue, pink, yellow, and green. Pattern outside cup, centre of saucer and plate. Saucer and plate have border of pale grey trees. White ground. Orange edges. Entered in pattern book during or after 1928.
Backstamp(s): Shelley 1925-1940
Shapes: Lomond

11606 **Archway of Roses**. Black print. Garden with flowers that include hollyhocks and roses. Blue butterflies. Enamelled in blue, pink, yellow, and green. White ground. Blue edges. Entered in pattern book during or after 1928. Also seem in demitasse size.
/O orange edges
/G green edges
/M mauve edges.
Backstamp(s): Shelley 1925-1940
Shapes: Queen Anne

Archway of Roses 11606 Queen Anne shape cup, saucer, and plate. £80-100; $120-160

Archway of Roses 11606 Queen Anne shape demitasse cup and saucer. £70-90; $100-140

Archway of Roses 11606/G Queen Anne shape cup, saucer, and plate. £80-100; $140-180

Pattern	Description & Shapes
11607	**My Garden**. Black print. Garden with flowers that include hollyhocks and roses. Sundial on plate. Enamelled in blue, pink, yellow, and green. Pattern outside cup, centre of saucer and plate. Saucer and plate have border of pale grey trees. Yellow band on saucer and plate below border. White ground. Blue edges and handle. Entered in pattern book during or after 1928. **Backstamp(s)**: Shelley 1925-1940; Shelley 1940-1966 **Shapes:** Cambridge, Queen Anne

My Garden 11607 Queen Anne shape cup, saucer, and plate. £80-100; $120-160

11608	**Daisy**. Entered in pattern book during or after 1928. **Backstamp(s)**: Shelley 1925-1940 **Shapes:** Vincent
11609	Jardiniere. Pink, yellow, and green flowers on black branches in a green, mauve, and black jardiniere on a white ground. Border of green leaves on a white ground. Yellow band at base of cup, round centre of saucer and shoulder of plate. Entered in pattern book during or after 1928. **Backstamp(s)**: Shelley 1925-1940 **Shapes:** Queen Anne

Jardinière 11609 Queen Anne shape cup, saucer, and plate. £80-100; $120-160

11610	Black outside cup and on saucer. Coloured inside cup and handle. Entered in pattern book during or after 1928. /A Green /B Yellow /C Red /D Grey /E Blue /F Turquoise. **Backstamp(s)**: Shelley 1925-1940 **Shapes:** Queen Anne
11611	Standard Rose Bush. Coral roses, black stem. Grey border. White ground. Red edges. Teal handle. Entered in pattern book during or after 1928. **Backstamp(s)**: Shelley 1925-1940 **Shapes:** Doric
11612	Medallion. White flower on a black medallion with delicate garland and linear border. Entered in pattern book during or after 1928. **Backstamp(s)**: Shelley 1925-1940 **Shapes:** Queen Anne

Medallion 11612 Queen Anne shape cup, saucer, and plate. £80-100; $120-160

11613	Entered in pattern book during or after 1928. **Backstamp(s)**: Shelley 1925-1940 **Shapes:** Lomond
11614	Tall black tree. Enamelling at base in green, orange, mauve, and yellow. Blue edges, half handle, foot and border on saucer. **Backstamp(s)**: Shelley 1925-1940 **Shapes:** Lomond
11615	Entered in pattern book during or after 1928. **Backstamp(s)**: Shelley 1925-1940 **Shapes:** Lomond
11617	**Garden** Urn. Brown print. Enamelled in pink, blue, coral, yellow, and mauve. Garden scene. Urn of flowers. Pink, blue, mauve, and yellow flowers. Tall mauve and yellow flowers could be hollyhocks. Fawn trees in the background. White ground. Mauve edges. Entered in pattern book during or after 1928. /G green edges /P pink edges. **Backstamp(s)**: Shelley 1925-1940 **Shapes:** Queen Anne, Cambridge

Garden Urn 11617 Queen Anne shape cup, saucer, and plate. £80-100; $120-160

Garden Urn 11617 Cambridge shape cup and saucer. £40-50; $80-100

11618	**Garden Urn**. Brown print. Green edges and handle. Entered in pattern book during or after 1928. **Backstamp(s)**: Shelley 1925-1940 **Shapes:** Vincent
11619	Orange flowers and black leaves. Orange edges. White ground. Entered in pattern book during or after 1928. **Backstamp(s)**: Shelley 1925-1940 **Shapes:** Queen Anne

Orange Flowers 11619 Queen Anne shape cup, saucer, and plate. £80-100; $120-160

Orange Flowers 11619 Queen Anne shape demitasse cup and saucer. £70-90; $110-150

11620	Entered in pattern book during or after 1928. **Backstamp(s)**: Shelley 1925-1940 **Shapes:** Vincent
11621	Cottage-2. Thatched cottage with brick chimneys. Cottage garden type flowers enamelled in blue, coral, yellow, and orange with green leaves. Grey trees. White ground. Dark yellow edges and

Pattern	Description & Shapes
	handle. Entered in pattern book during or after 1928. Also see 11836. **Backstamp(s)**: Shelley 1925-1940 **Shapes:** Queen Anne

Cottage-2 11621 Queen Anne shape cup, saucer, and plate. £150-200; $250-300

11622-
11623 Entered in pattern book during or after 1928.
Backstamp(s): Shelley 1925-1940
Shapes: Vincent

11624 Balloon Tree. Black tree with green leaves. Green grass at foot of tree. Green and purple bushes in the distance. Orange, blue, mauve, and yellow balloons against the tree. Balloons and leaves also inside cup. Yellow banded border. Blue edges. Entered in pattern book during or after 1928. Also see 11839.
Backstamp(s): Shelley 1925-1940
Shapes: Queen Anne

Balloon Tree 11624 Queen Anne shape cup, saucer, and plate. £80-100; $120-160

11625 Damsons enamelled in green on a brown and grey pattern. Green edges. Entered in pattern book during or after 1928.
Backstamp(s): Shelley 1925-1940
Shapes: Queen Anne

Right:
Damsons 11625 Queen Anne shape cup, saucer, and plate. £80-100; $120-160

11627 Entered in pattern book during or after 1928.
Backstamp(s): Shelley 1925-1940
Shapes: Queen Anne

11628 **Garland of Flowers**. Black garland pattern and trim. White ground. Entered in pattern book during or after 1926 for export to Canada.
Backstamp(s): Shelley 1925-1940
Shapes: Queen Anne

11629 **Pansies**. Black print. Purple pansy with green leaves on small panels. Tiny dots above pansy. Small yellow flowers and green leaves on large panels. Chevrons on panel joins. White ground. Purple edges. Entered in pattern book during or after 1928
Backstamp(s): Shelley 1925-1940
Shapes: Queen Anne

Pansies 11629 Queen Anne shape cup, saucer, and plate. £80-100; $120-160

11630 Coral, purple, and yellow flowers with green leaves and grey tendrils on a white ground. Dark blue edges. Entered in pattern book during or after 1928.
Backstamp(s): Shelley 1925-1940
Shapes: Queen Anne

Flowers 11630 Queen Anne shape cup, saucer, and plate. £80-100; $120-160

11631 Diamonds. Green diamond within a yellow diamond on a black motif, which has scrolled edges, and has below it red and blue fruit with green leaves on small panels. Black and grey scrolled motif on large panels. White ground. Yellow edges. Entered in pattern book during or after 1928.
Backstamp(s): Shelley 1925-1940
Shapes: Queen Anne

Diamonds 11631 Queen Anne shape cup, saucer, and plate. £80-100; $120-160

11632 Damsons enamelled in orange on a black and grey pattern. White ground. Orange edges. Entered in pattern book during or after 1928.
Backstamp(s): Shelley 1925-1940
Shapes: Queen Anne

Damsons 11632 Queen Anne shape cup, saucer, and plate. £80-100; $120-160

11633 Cottage. Brown print. Timbered and thatched cottage set amongst trees and a cottage garden. Produced from 1928.
Backstamp(s): Shelley 1925-1940
Shapes: Doric

11634 Damsons enamelled in orange on a black and grey pattern. Yellow ground. Black edges. Entered in pattern book during or after 1928.
Backstamp(s): Shelley 1925-1940
Shapes: Queen Anne

Opposite page, bottom left:
Damsons 11634 Queen Anne shape cup, saucer, and plate. £80-100; $120-160

Pattern	Description & Shapes

11635 **Pansies**. Black print. Purple pansy with green leaves on small panels on a white ground. Tiny dots above pansy. Small yellow flowers and green leaves on large panels on a coloured ground. Chevrons on panel joins. Gold edges. Entered in pattern book during or after 1928.
Backstamp(s): Shelley 1925-1940
Shapes: Queen Anne

11636 Damsons enamelled in green on a red ground. Gold edges. Similar to 11629. Entered in pattern book during or after 1928.
Backstamp(s): Shelley 1925-1940
Shapes: Queen Anne

Damsons 11636 Queen Anne shape cup, saucer, and plate. £80-100; $120-160

11637 Orange flowers and black leaves. Orange edges. Coloured ground on large panels. White ground on small panels. Black edges. Similar to 11619. Entered in pattern book during or after 1928.
Backstamp(s): Shelley 1925-1940
Shapes: Queen Anne

11638 Medallion. White flower on a black medallion with delicate garland and linear border. Pink ground. Black edges. Similar to 11612. Entered in pattern book during or after 1928.
Backstamp(s): Shelley 1925-1940
Shapes: Queen Anne

11639 Entered in pattern book during or after 1928.
Backstamp(s): Shelley 1925-1940
Shapes: Lomond

11640 Tall tree and leaves in the foreground. Large sun on the horizon behind trees. White ground. Entered in pattern book during or after 1928.
Backstamp(s): Shelley 1925-1940
Shapes: Vincent

11641 Medallion. Gold print. White flower on a black medallion with delicate garland and linear border. Gold edges. Similar to 11612. Entered in pattern book during or after 1928.
Backstamp(s): Shelley 1925-1940
Shapes: Queen Anne

11642 Diamonds. Gold print. Green diamond within a yellow diamond on a black motif, which has scrolled edges, and has below it red and blue fruit with green leaves on small panels. Black and grey scrolled motif on large panels. White ground. Gold edges. Entered in pattern book during or after 1928.
Backstamp(s): Shelley 1925-1940
Shapes: Queen Anne

11643 Black outside cup and on saucer. Gold inside cup and handle. Entered in pattern book during or after 1928.
Backstamp(s): Shelley 1925-1940
Shapes: Queen Anne

11644 Garlands and dots. Gold print. Dark green border. Gold edges. Entered in pattern book during or after 1928.
Backstamp(s): Shelley 1925-1940
Shapes: Queen Anne

11645 Gold half suns and garlands on a broad pale mauve border. Gold edges. Entered in pattern book during or after 1928.
Backstamp(s): Shelley 1925-1940
Shapes: Queen Anne

11646 Entered in pattern book during or after 1928.
Backstamp(s): Shelley 1925-1940
Shapes: Gainsborough

11647 Entered in pattern book during or after 1928.
Backstamp(s): Shelley 1925-1940
Shapes: Vincent

11648 Gold leaves and butterflies. Turquoise small panels. Gold edges and handle. Entered in pattern book during or after 1929.
Backstamp(s): Shelley 1925-1940
Shapes: Queen Anne

11649 Entered in pattern book during or after 1929.
Backstamp(s): Shelley 1925-1940
Shapes: Gainsborough

11650 Cottage-1. Black print on outside cup, centre of saucer and plates. Cottage with chimneys. Grey trees partly enamelled in black. Green fields. Yellow road. Fence and gate across road. Smoke rising from chimney on cup. White ground. Black edges and handle. Entered in pattern book during or after 1929.
Backstamp(s): Shelley 1925-1940
Shapes: Queen Anne

11651 **Crabtree**. Tree in landscape with fruit enamelled in blue, orange, and yellow. Inside cup has branches and fruit. White ground. Green edges. Entered in pattern book during or after 1929.
Backstamp(s): Shelley 1925-1940
Shapes: Queen Anne

Crabtree 11651 Queen Anne shape cup, saucer, and plate. £80-100; $120-160

11652 **Idalium**. Enamelled orange, blue, and yellow flowers with blue branches and green and grey foliage. Same as 088. Entered in pattern book during or after 1929.
Backstamp(s): Shelley 1925-1940
Shapes: Vincent

11653 Gold vine and trellis print on blue ground. Gold edges and handle. Entered in pattern book during or after 1929.
Backstamp(s): Shelley 1925-1940
Shapes: Queen Anne

11654 Medallion. Gold print. Flower on a coral medallion with delicate garland and linear border. Blue ground. Gold edges. Similar to 11641. Entered in pattern book during or after 1929.
Backstamp(s): Shelley 1925-1940
Shapes: Queen Anne

11655 Entered in pattern book during or after 1929.
Backstamp(s): Shelley 1925-1940
Shapes: Vincent

11656 Colour ground outside cup and on saucer. Gold inside cup. Gold handle. Similar to 11781. Entered in pattern book during or after 1929.
Backstamp(s): Shelley 1925-1940
Shapes: Queen Anne

11657 Gold vine and trellis print on coloured ground. Gold edges and handle. Entered in pattern book during or after 1929.
Backstamp(s): Shelley 1925-1940
Shapes: Queen Anne

11658 Medallion. Gold print. Flower on a coral medallion with delicate garland and linear border. Coloured ground. Similar to 11654. Entered in pattern book during or after 1929.
Backstamp(s): Shelley 1925-1940
Shapes: Queen Anne

11659-
11662 Cottage-3. Brown print. Cottage with blue roof and door. White ground. Blue edges and handle.
Backstamp(s): Shelley 1925-1940
Shapes: Georgian

Cottage-3 11659 Georgian shape cup and saucer. £90-110; $140-170

Pattern	Description & Shapes
11663	Black leafy tree with yellow, orange, and mauve and green flowers on a white ground inside cup and on saucer. White outside cup with royal blue line halfway between rim and base. Royal blue edges. Entered in pattern book during or after 1929. **Backstamp(s)**: Shelley 1925-1940 **Shapes:** Doric, Georgian

Black leafy tree 11663 Georgian shape cup, saucer, and plate. £90-110; $140-170

11664 Flashes and Flowers. Black print. Orange, yellow, blue, and purple flowers with green foliage on small panels. Orange, white, and blue flashes in a pennant shape on large panels. Black dots and lines on panel joins, for approximately half the height of the cup. Green edges. Similar to 11665 and 11666. Entered in pattern book during or after 1929.
Backstamp(s): Shelley 1925-1940
Shapes: Queen Anne

11665 Flashes and Flowers. Black print. Orange, yellow, blue, and purple flowers with green foliage on small panels. Orange, white, and blue flashes in a pennant shape on large panels. Black dots and lines on panel joins, for approximately half the height of the cup. Green edges. Similar to 11664 and 11666. Entered in pattern book during or after 1929.
Backstamp(s): Shelley 1925-1940
Shapes: Queen Anne

11666 Flashes and Flowers. Black print. Blue and purple flowers with green foliage on small panels. Purple, white, and green flashes in a pennant shape on large panels. Black dots and lines on panel joins, for approximately half the height of the cup. White ground. Blue edges. Similar to 11664 and 11665. Entered in pattern book during or after 1929.
Backstamp(s): Shelley 1925-1940
Shapes: Queen Anne

11667 Flame Flowers. Black print. Black tree with yellow, black, and grey leaves. Coral and purple flowers at the foot of the tree with green and mauve leaves. Green band around base of cup, and centre of saucer. White ground. White ground. Orange edges. Entered in pattern book during or after 1929.
Backstamp(s): Shelley 1925-1940
Shapes: Queen Anne

Right:
Flame Flowers 11667 Queen Anne shape cup, saucer, and plate. £80-100; $120-160

11668 Garden scene. Black print. Enamelled in coral, blue, and green. Tall blue flowers, probably lupins or delphiniums with green grass at the base and grey trees in the background. Overhanging black and grey branches with orange flowers and green leaves. White ground. Blue edges. Entered in pattern book during or after 1929.
Backstamp(s): Shelley 1925-1940
Shapes: Queen Ann

Garden scene 11668 Queen Anne shape cup, saucer, and plate. £80-100; $120-160

Garden scene 11668 Queen Anne shape demitasse cup and saucer. £70-90; $110-150

11669 Blue Kingfisher. Bird on branch overhanging water. White ground. Royal blue edges. Entered in pattern book during or after 1929.
Backstamp(s): Shelley 1925-1940
Shapes: Vincent

11671-11672 Entered in pattern book during or after 1929.
Backstamp(s): Shelley 1925-1940
Shapes: Vincent

11673 Garden Scene border. Black print. White ground. Blue edges and handle. Similar to 11687. Entered in pattern book during or after 1929.
Backstamp(s): Shelley 1925-1940
Shapes: Queen Anne

11674 Balloon Tree. Black tree with green leaves. Green grass at foot of tree. Green and purple bushes in the distance. Blue, orange, mauve, and yellow balloons against the tree. Balloons and leaves also inside cup. Green edges. Similar to 11712. Entered in pattern book during or after 1929.
Backstamp(s): Shelley 1925-1940
Shapes: Queen Anne

11675 Country scene. Black print. Enamelled in pink, yellow, and orange. Flowers with green leaves bordering a path with grey trees in the background. Mauve edges. Entered in pattern book during or after 1929.
Backstamp(s): Shelley 1925-1940
Shapes: Queen Anne

Country Scene 11675 Queen Anne shape cup, saucer, and plate. £80-100; $120-160

11676 Country Bluebell. Bluebells in the foreground with green leaves, small orange and yellow flowers, and grey fern leaves. Road leading to a gate with grey trees on either side of the gate. White ground. Mauve edges. Entered in pattern book during or after 1929.
Backstamp(s): Shelley 1925-1940
Shapes: Queen Anne

Country Bluebell 11676 Queen Anne shape cup and saucer. £80-100; $120-160

Pattern	Description & Shapes

11677 Tall bushes and flowers. Black print. Green edges. Similar to 11830. Entered in pattern book during or after 1929.
Backstamp(s): Shelley 1925-1940
Shapes: Queen Anne

11678 **Sunrise and Tall Trees**. Yellow sun rising through black tall trees. Woodland in shades of grey and a field, or meadow, in yellow. Entered in pattern book during or after 1929.
/G Green edges and handle
/B Blue variation.
Backstamp(s): Shelley 1925-1940; Lawleys
Shapes: Queen Anne

Sunrise and Tall Trees 11678 Queen Anne shape cake plate with EPNS handle. £50-70; $100-120

Sunrise and Tall Trees 11678 Queen Anne shape cup, saucer, and plate. £80-100; $120-160

11679 Garden scene. Lily pond and grass with a pathway between them. Garden wall with an urn of flowers. Tall blue flowers, which could be delphiniums. Grey trees in the background. Entered in pattern book during or after 1929.
Backstamp(s): Shelley 1925-1940
Shapes: Georgian, Queen Anne

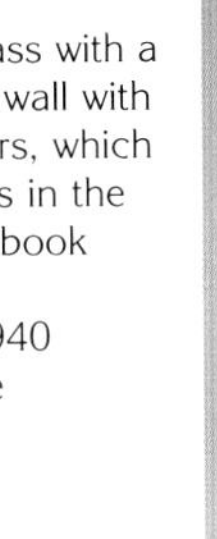

Right:
Garden scene 11679 Queen Anne shape cup, saucer, and plate. £80-100; $120-160

11680 Entered in pattern book during or after 1929.
Backstamp(s): Shelley 1925-1940
Shapes: Georgian

11681 Entered in pattern book during or after 1929.
Backstamp(s): Shelley 1925-1940
Shapes: Doric, Georgian

11682 Pink and blue flowers. Grey and black leaves and garlands. White ground. Jade green edges. Entered in pattern book during or after 1929.
Backstamp(s): Shelley 1925-1940
Shapes: Queen Anne

11683 Oriental Water Garden. Brown print. Pink and blue hollyhocks in the foreground. Green fountain in the middle distance with a yellow pagoda and grey trees in the distance. White ground. Green edges. Entered in pattern book during or after 1929.
Backstamp(s): Shelley 1925-1940
Shapes: Vincent

11684 Entered in pattern book during or after 1929.
Backstamp(s): Shelley 1925-1940
Shapes: Lomond

11685 Entered in pattern book during or after 1929.
Backstamp(s): Shelley 1925-1940
Shapes: Doric

11686 Entered in pattern book during or after 1929.
Backstamp(s): Shelley 1925-1940
Shapes: Vincent

11687 Garden Scene border. Black print. Coloured ground below border. Blue edges and handle. Similar to 11673. Entered in pattern book during or after 1929.
Backstamp(s): Shelley 1925-1940
Shapes: Queen Anne

11688-11689 Entered in pattern book during or after 1929.
Backstamp(s): Shelley 1925-1940
Shapes: Georgian

11690 **Lowestoft**. Small sprays of pink, blue, and yellow flowers with green leaves on a white ground. Black leafy border. Jade green edges. Entered in pattern book during or after 1929.
Backstamp(s): Shelley 1925-1940
Shapes: Queen Anne

11691 **Sunset and Flowers**. Black print. Enamelled in orange and white. Bright orange setting sun. Fluffy clouds. Black trees and yellow haze around sunset. Sunset reflected in water. White ground. Yellow edges. Similar to 11707 and 11860. Entered in pattern book during or after 1929.
Backstamp(s): Shelley 1925-1940
Shapes: Queen Anne

Sunset and Flowers 11691 Queen Anne shape cup, saucer, and plate. £80-100; $120-160

11692 Entered in pattern book during or after 1929.
Backstamp(s): Shelley 1925-1940
Shapes: Gainsborough

11693 Bananas. Brown print. Large bunch of coral and green bananas with leaves on small panels. Smaller bunches on large panels. White ground. Blue edges. Similar to 11562 and 11706. Entered in pattern book during or after 1929
Backstamp(s): Shelley 1925-1940
Shapes: Queen Anne

11694 Entered in pattern book during or after 1929.
Backstamp(s): Shelley 1925-1940
Shapes: Gainsborough

11695 Entered in pattern book during or after 1929.
Backstamp(s): Shelley 1925-1940
Shapes: Vincent

11696 Entered in pattern book during or after 1929.
Backstamp(s): Shelley 1925-1940
Shapes: Lomond

11697 **Black Trees**. Brown print. Black trees with black and green leaves. Orange, blue, yellow, and purple stylised fruit. Fawn flowers. Blue edges. Similar to 11476. Entered in pattern book during or after 1929.
Backstamp(s): Shelley 1925-1940
Shapes: Queen Anne

Black Trees 11697 Queen Anne shape cup and saucer. £80-100; $120-160

11698 Entered in pattern book during or after 1929.
Backstamp(s): Shelley 1925-1940
Shapes: Vincent

11699 **Black Vine Leaf**. Brown print. Black leaf with green edges. Stylised red, orange, and blue fruit. Brown stem and tendrils. Brown printed border of grape vines. White ground. Green edges. Entered in pattern book during or after 1929.

Pattern Description & Shapes

Backstamp(s): Shelley 1925-1940
Shapes: Vincent

11700 Entered in pattern book during or after 1929.
Backstamp(s): Shelley 1925-1940
Shapes: Gainsborough

11701 Entered in pattern book during or after 1929.
Backstamp(s): Shelley 1925-1940
Shapes: Vincent

11702 Blue, orange, green, and mauve fruit with yellow, orange and brown leaves. Black chains and tassels. White ground. Black edges and handle. Entered in pattern book during or after 1929.
Backstamp(s): Shelley 1925-1940
Shapes: Vincent

Fruit and leaves 11702 Vincent shape cup, saucer, and plate. £60-70; $100-120. Creamer and sugar. £60-70; $100-120

11703 Entered in pattern book during or after 1929.
Backstamp(s): Shelley 1925-1940
Shapes: Georgian

11704 Colour ground outside cup and on saucer. Mauve, orange, and green fruit with green and brown leaves inside cup. Royal blue edges. Entered in pattern book during or after 1929.
/31 Dark yellow.
Backstamp(s): Shelley 1925-1940
Shapes: Georgian

11705 Garland of Fruit. Brown print. Yellow, orange, and blue fruit with green leaves on small panels. Yellow fruit garlands on large panels. Chevrons on panels joins – approximately half the length of the cup. Border consisting or purple motifs and band of vertical lines. White ground. Blue edges. Similar to 11501. Entered in pattern book during or after 1929.
Backstamp(s): Shelley 1925-1940
Shapes: Queen Anne

Garland of Fruit 11705 Queen Anne shape cup, saucer, and plate. £80-100; $120-160

11706 Bananas. Gold print. Large bunch of yellow and orange bananas with turquoise leaves on small panels. Smaller bunches on large panels. White ground. Gold edges. Blue outside handle. Similar to 11562 and 11693. Entered in pattern book during or after 1929
Backstamp(s): Shelley 1925-1940
Shapes: Queen Anne

Bananas 11706 Queen Anne shape cup, saucer, and plate. £100-110; $150-170

11707 **Sunset and Flowers**. Gold print. Enamelled in coral and orange. Bright orange setting sun. Fluffy clouds. Black trees and yellow haze around sunset. Sunset reflected in water. White ground. Gold edges. Similar to 11691 and 11860. Entered in pattern book during or after 1929
Backstamp(s): Shelley 1925-1940
Shapes: Queen Anne

Sunset and Flowers 11707 Queen Anne shape cup, saucer, and plate. £80-100; $120-160

11708 Cottage. Brown print. Orange tiled roof with a chimney. Path leading to cottage. Green shrubbery in front of cottage. Trees behind cottage. White ground. Gold edges. Dark blue edge on handle. Entered in pattern book during or after 1929.
Backstamp(s): Shelley 1925-1940
Shapes: Vincent

11709 Entered in pattern book during or after 1929.
Backstamp(s): Shelley 1925-1940
Shapes: Gainsborough

11710-
11711 Entered in pattern book during or after 1929.
Backstamp(s): Shelley 1925-1940
Shapes: Georgian

11712 Balloon Tree. Black tree with green leaves. Green grass at foot of tree. Green and purple bushes in the distance. Pink, blue, mauve, and yellow balloons against the tree. Balloons and leaves also inside cup. White ground on cup and inside of saucer and plate. Coloured, broad, band on saucer and plate. Black edges. Similar to 11674. Entered in pattern book during or after 1930.
Backstamp(s): Shelley 1925-1940
Shapes: Queen Anne

11717 **Sweat Pea**. Brown print. Pink sweat peas with blue motifs. White ground. Blue edges. Entered in pattern book during or after 1930.
Backstamp(s): Shelley 1925-1940
Shapes: Queen Anne

11718 **Sweat Pea**. Brown print. Yellow sweat peas with brown stems, tendrils, and green leaves on small panels. Tiny, mauve, dots above sweat pea. Stylised brown leaves on panels joins. Mauve and brown motif on large panels. White ground. Mauve edges. Entered in pattern book during or after 1930.
/4 green edges
Backstamp(s): Shelley 1925-1940
Shapes: Queen Anne

Sweat Pea 11718/4 Queen Anne shape cup, saucer, and plate. £80-100; $120-160

11719 Big Leaves. Black and grey trees with large autumn coloured leaves. Blue at base of trees. Blue, coral, and yellow flowers. White ground. Dark blue edges. Produced from c. 1930.
Backstamp(s): Shelley 1925-1940
Shapes: Vincent

11720 Entered in pattern book during or after 1930.
Backstamp(s): Shelley 1925-1940
Shapes: Empire, Vincent

11721 **Sweat Pea**. Black print. Blue sweat peas with black stems, tendrils, and green leaves on small panels. Tiny, mauve, dots above sweat pea. Stylised black leaves on panels joins. Yellow and black motif on large panels. White ground. Mauve edges. Entered in pattern book during or after 1930.
Backstamp(s): Shelley 1925-1940
Shapes: Queen Anne

11722 Entered in pattern book during or after 1930.
Backstamp(s): Shelley 1925-1940
Shapes: Vincent

11723 **Sheep and Cottage**. Sheep in a field

Pattern	Description & Shapes

next to a stream with a bridge over it. Cottage and trees in the background. Black print enamelled in pink, orange, blue, green, and brown. White ground. Yellow edges. Entered in pattern book during or after 1930.
Backstamp(s): Shelley 1925-1940
Shapes: Queen Anne

Sheep and Cottage 11723 Queen Anne shape cup, saucer, and plate. £100-110; $150-170

11724 **Autumn Leaves**. Brown tree with red, yellow, brown, and green leaves. Green grass at base of tree. White ground. Green edges. Entered in pattern book during or after 1930.
Backstamp(s): Shelley 1925-1940
Shapes: Queen Anne

Autumn Leaves 11724 Queen Anne shape cup, saucer, and plate. £80-100; $120-160

11725 **Wattle**. Similar to 11728. Entered in pattern book during or after 1930.
Backstamp(s): Shelley 1925-1940
Shapes: Queen Anne

11726-11727 Entered in pattern book during or after 1930.
Backstamp(s): Shelley 1925-1940
Shapes: Vincent

11728 **Wattle**. Colour ground on large panels. Gold edges and handle. Similar to 11725. Entered in pattern book during or after 1930.
Backstamp(s): Shelley 1925-1940
Shapes: Queen Anne

11729 Diamonds. Diamond within a diamond on a black motif, which has scrolled edges, and has below it fruit with leaves on small panels. Black and grey scrolled motif on large panels. White ground. Entered in pattern book during or after 1930.
Backstamp(s): Shelley 1925-1940
Shapes: Queen Anne

11730 Peaches and Grapes. Brown print. Coral, green, and purple fruit with brown leaves on small panels. Leaves and tendrils on large panels. Brown spots on panel joins. White ground. Green edges. Entered in pattern book during or after 1930.
Backstamp(s): Shelley 1925-1940
Shapes: Queen Anne

Peaches and Grapes 11730 Queen Anne shape cup, saucer, and plate. £80-100; $120-160

11731 **Bunch of Grapes**. Brown print. Grapes with leaves on small panels. Leaves and tendrils on large panels. Fruit with green leaves on saucer and centre of plate. White ground. Green edges. Entered in pattern book during or after 1930.
Backstamp(s): Shelley 1925-1940
Shapes: Queen Anne

11732-11733 Entered in pattern book during or after 1930.
Backstamp(s): Shelley 1925-1940
Shapes: Vincent

11734 **Pansies**. Brown print. Orange pansy with green leaves on small panels. Tiny, mauve, dots above pansy. Small mauve flowers and green leaves on large panels. Chevrons on panels joins. White ground. Green edges. Entered in pattern book during or after 1930.
Backstamp(s): Shelley 1925-1940
Shapes: Queen Anne

Pansies 11734 Queen Anne shape cup, saucer, and plate. £80-100; $120-160

11735 Brown print. Panelled fruit pattern against a diamond with garlands. Similar to 11505. Entered in pattern book during or after 1930.
Backstamp(s): Shelley 1925-1940
Shapes: Queen Anne

11736 Bowl of Fruit. Brown print. Brown and black bowl with blue, yellow and orange fruit. White ground. Blue edges. Entered in pattern book during or after 1930.
/B Black print.
Backstamp(s): Shelley 1925-1940
Shapes: Queen Anne

11737 **Sweat Pea**. Black print. Blue sweat peas with black stems, tendrils, and green leaves on small panels. Tiny, mauve, dots above sweat pea. Stylised black leaves on panels joins. Yellow and black motif on large panels. White ground. Gold edges. Entered in pattern book during or after 1930.
Backstamp(s): Shelley 1925-1940
Shapes: Queen Anne

11738 Bands and triangles. Entered in pattern book during or after 1930.
Backstamp(s): Shelley 1925-1940
Shapes: Vogue

11739 J Pattern. Red J and border. Blue flowers with black stems and black and grey leaves. Border on handle and flower sprig. Red foot. Red ring round centre of saucer. White ground. Entered in pattern book during or after 1930.
Backstamp(s): Shelley 1925-1940
Shapes: Mode, Vogue

J Pattern 11739 Vogue shape cup and saucer. £100-120; $150-170

11740 J Pattern. Green J and border. Blue flowers with black stems and black and grey leaves. Border on handle and flower sprig. Green foot. Green ring round centre of saucer. White ground. Entered in pattern book during or after 1930.
Backstamp(s): Shelley 1925-1940
Shapes: Vogue

11741 Triangle with blue and orange blocks. Entered in pattern book during or after 1930.
Backstamp(s): Shelley 1925-1940
Shapes: Vogue

11742 Sunray. Entered in pattern book during or after 1930.
Backstamp(s): Shelley 1925-1940
Shapes: Vogue

11743 Sunray. Orange sun with green and yellow. Yellow edges. Green edge on handle. Entered in pattern book during or after 1930.
Backstamp(s): Shelley 1925-1940
Shapes: Vogue

11744 Blue flowers. Linear border. Entered in pattern book during or after 1930.
Backstamp(s): Shelley 1925-1940
Shapes: Vogue

11745 Mauve flowers. Linear border. Entered in pattern book during or after 1930.
Backstamp(s): Shelley 1925-1940
Shapes: Vogue

11746 Bell flower and circle. Entered in pattern book during or after 1930.
Backstamp(s): Shelley 1925-1940

Pattern	Description & Shapes
	Shapes: Vogue
11747	Sunray. Entered in pattern book during or after 1930. **Backstamp(s):** Shelley 1925-1940 **Shapes:** Vogue
11748	Chevrons. Gold print. Broad border inside cup, on saucer, and plate of blue chevrons and vertical lines. Triangle outside cup with chevron and vertical lines. Handle has border surrounding chevrons, with dots above and vertical lines below them. Gold edges. Entered in pattern book during or after 1930. **Backstamp(s):** Shelley 1925-1940 **Shapes:** Vogue
11749	Horn of Flowers. Entered in pattern book during or after 1930. **Backstamp(s):** Shelley 1925-1940 **Shapes:** Vogue
11750	Diamonds. Entered in pattern book during or after 1930. **Backstamp(s):** Shelley 1925-1940 **Shapes:** Vogue
11751	Gold print. Blue flowers. Linear border. Entered in pattern book during or after 1930. **Backstamp(s):** Shelley 1925-1940 **Shapes:** Vogue
11752	Martian. Entered in pattern book during or after 1930. **Backstamp(s):** Shelley 1925-1940 **Shapes:** Vincent
11753	Pink Hollyhocks. Green leaves and grass. Mauve wisteria and grey leaves. Small yellow flowers. Blue butterflies. Blue sky. White ground. Green edges. Entered in pattern book during or after 1930. **Backstamp(s):** Shelley 1925-1940 **Shapes:** Vincent
11754	Plain colour outside cup and on saucer. Gold inside cup. Entered in pattern book during or after 1930. **Backstamp(s):** Shelley 1925-1940 **Shapes:** Vogue
11755	Blue J and border. Coral flowers, blue stylised fruit, black stems, and black and green leaves. Blue border on solid handle surrounds a black triangle, a white line, and then a green triangle. Blue foot. Blue ring round centre of saucer. White ground. Entered in pattern book during or after 1930. **Backstamp(s):** Shelley 1925-1940 **Shapes:** Mode
11756	Stylised flower and coral band. Entered in pattern book during or after 1930. **Backstamp(s):** Shelley 1925-1940 **Shapes:** Mode
11757	Butterfly handle in black and orange. Blue, orange, and yellow enamelled flowers with green and grey leaves. Entered in pattern book during or after 1930. **Backstamp(s):** Shelley 1925-1940 **Shapes:** Mode
11758	Butterfly Wing. Entered in pattern book during or after 1930. **Backstamp(s):** Shelley 1925-1940 **Shapes:** Mode
11759	Green band and flowers. Entered in pattern book during or after 1930. **Backstamp(s):** Shelley 1925-1940 **Shapes:** Mode
11760	**Shades and Lines**. Blue, silver, and orange. Entered in pattern book during or after 1930. **Backstamp(s):** Shelley 1925-1940 **Shapes:** Mode
11761	Butterfly handle in black and orange. Blue, orange, and yellow enamelled flowers with green and grey leaves. Colour ground. Entered in pattern book during or after 1930. **Backstamp(s):** Shelley 1925-1940 **Shapes:** Mode
11762	Butterfly Wing. Entered in pattern book during or after 1930. **Backstamp(s):** Shelley 1925-1940 **Shapes:** Mode
11763	Crocus. Yellow, blue, and purple crocuses with green leaves. Blue and yellow butterflies. Green trim and handle. Entered in pattern book during or after 1930. **Backstamp(s):** Shelley 1925-1940 **Shapes:** Empire, Regent
11764-11766	Entered in pattern book during or after 1930. **Backstamp(s):** Shelley 1925-1940 **Shapes:** Empire
11767	Bluebell in the foreground with green and awn foliage. Blue edges. Entered in pattern book during or after 1930. **Backstamp(s):** Shelley 1925-1940 **Shapes:** Empire, Vincent
11768	Entered in pattern book during or after 1930. **Backstamp(s):** Shelley 1925-1940 **Shapes:** Empire
11769	Entered in pattern book during or after 1930. **Backstamp(s):** Shelley 1925-1940 **Shapes:** Doric
11770	Pink star. Segments between points of star are a pale yellow. Pink handle. Entered in pattern book during or after 1930. **Backstamp(s):** Shelley 1925-1940 **Shapes:** Dainty
11771	Horn of Flowers. Pattern inside cup. Green outside cup and on saucer. Gold edges and foot. Entered in pattern book during or after 1930. **Backstamp(s):** Shelley 1925-1940 **Shapes:** Vogue
11772	Diamonds. Orange, black, and green diamonds with grey bands and lines. Orange trim. Entered in pattern book during or after 1930. **Backstamp(s):** Shelley 1925-1940 **Shapes:** Vogue
11773	Entered in pattern book during or after 1930. **Backstamp(s):** Shelley 1925-1940 **Shapes:** Doric
11774	Horn of Flowers. Entered in pattern book during or after 1930. **Backstamp(s):** Shelley 1925-1940 **Shapes:** Vogue
11775	Chevrons. Brown print. Broad border inside cup, on saucer and plate of blue chevrons and brown vertical lines. Triangle outside cup with chevron and vertical lines. Handle has orange border surrounding blue and orange chevrons, with dots above and vertical lines below them. Orange edges and foot. Entered in pattern book during or after 1930. **Backstamp(s):** Shelley 1925-1940 **Shapes:** Vogue
11776	Green outside cup and on saucer. White inside cup and centre of saucer. Black and white chevron pattern on solid handle. Black edges and foot. Entered in pattern book during or after 1930. /3 Yellow /34 Pink /A Amber /C Special set. **Backstamp(s):** Shelley 1925-1940; Lawleys; Shelley 1930-1932 **Shapes:** Mode, Princess, Vogue
11777	Alternating gold and plain colour panels. Gold edges and handle. Entered in pattern book during or after 1930. /S10 White /24 Black /41 Red. **Backstamp(s):** Shelley 1940-1966. **Shapes:** Dainty, Queen Anne
11778	Yellow band inside cup. Yellow and blue J; red and blue fruit with green leaves outside cup and on saucer. Amber edge to handle. Centre of handle has a black triangle, a white line and a blue triangle. White ground. Yellow foot. Entered in pattern book during or after 1930. **Backstamp(s):** Shelley 1925-1940 **Shapes:** Mode
11779	**Shades and Lines**. Green, purple and orange. Entered in pattern book during or after 1930. **Backstamp(s):** Shelley 1925-1940 **Shapes:** Mode
11780	Butterfly handle. Enamelled flowers. Entered in pattern book during or after 1930. **Backstamp(s):** Shelley 1925-1940 **Shapes:** Mode
11781	Colour ground outside cup and on saucer. Gold inside cup. Gold edges and handle. Similar to 11656. Entered in pattern book during or after 1930. **Backstamp(s):** Shelley 1925-1940 **Shapes:** Queen Anne
11782	Coral flower. Entered in pattern book during or after 1930. **Backstamp(s):** Shelley 1925-1940 **Shapes:** Vogue
11783	J pattern. Bands and flowers. Entered in pattern book during or after 1930. **Backstamp(s):** Shelley 1925-1940 **Shapes:** Vogue
11784	Sunray. Entered in pattern book during or after 1930. **Backstamp(s):** Shelley 1925-1940 **Shapes:** Vogue
11785	Blocks. Entered in pattern book during or after 1930. **Backstamp(s):** Shelley 1925-1940 **Shapes:** Mode, Vogue
11786	Blocks. Entered in pattern book during or after 1930. **Backstamp(s):** Shelley 1925-1940 **Shapes:** Mode, Vogue
11787	Blocks. Entered in pattern book during or after 1930. **Backstamp(s):** Shelley 1925-1940 **Shapes:** Vogue
11788	Blocks. Entered in pattern book during or after 1930. **Backstamp(s):** Shelley 1925-1940 **Shapes:** Vogue
11789	Triangles. Triangular handle blue with black border. Blue and black triangles on a white ground. Entered in pattern book during or after 1930. **Backstamp(s):** Wileman 1872-1890 **Shapes:** Mode
11790	Large and small blocks. Entered in pattern book during or after 1930. **Backstamp(s):** Shelley 1925-1940 **Shapes:** Mode
11791	Staggered blacks. Entered in pattern book during or after 1930. **Backstamp(s):** Shelley 1925-1940 **Shapes:** Mode
11792	Squares and lines. Black print. An orange and a smaller black square with two black lines below them. Narrow black and orange border. Orange ring round centre of saucer. Entered in pattern book during or after 1930. **Backstamp(s):** Shelley 1925-1940 **Shapes:** Mode
11793-11794	Entered in pattern book during or after 1930. **Backstamp(s):** Shelley 1925-1940 **Shapes:** Empire
11796	Sunray. Manufactured for Lawleys. Entered in pattern book during or after 1930. **Backstamp(s):** Shelley 1925-1940 Lawleys **Shapes:** Vogue
11797	Sunray. Manufactured for Lawleys. Entered in pattern book during or after

Pattern	Description & Shapes
	1930. **Backstamp(s)**: Shelley 1925-1940 Lawleys **Shapes:** Vogue
11798	Entered in pattern book during or after 1930. **Backstamp(s)**: Shelley 1925-1940 **Shapes:** Empire
11799	Fruit bowl border. Lines and triangles. Green edges and handle. Entered in pattern book during or after 1930. **Backstamp(s)**: Shelley 1925-1940 **Shapes:** Vincent
11801	Border of flowers and leaves with blue triangles. Entered in pattern book during or after 1930. **Backstamp(s)**: Shelley 1925-1940 **Shapes:** Empire
11802	Blue blocks and blue-green leaves. Green edges. Entered in pattern book during or after 1930. **Backstamp(s)**: Shelley 1925-1940 **Shapes:** Doric
11803	Border of mauve, yellow, and black blocks. Green edges. Entered in pattern book during or after 1930. **Backstamp(s)**: Shelley 1925-1940 **Shapes:** Vincent
11804	Green and black circles with orange and green blocks. Orange edges. Entered in pattern book during or after 1930. **Backstamp(s)**: Shelley 1925-1940 **Shapes:** Carlton
11825	Archway of Roses. Black print. Garden with flowers that include hollyhocks and roses. Blue butterflies. Enamelled in blue, pink, yellow, and green. White ground. Gold edges and handle. Entered in pattern book during or after 1930. **Backstamp(s)**: Shelley 1925-1940 **Shapes:** Queen Anne
11826	Plain colours. Entered in pattern book during or after 1930. **Backstamp(s)**: Shelley 1925-1940 **Shapes:** Vogue
11827	Gold border with triangular frames with rose sprays on small panels. Border inside cup. Coloured ground. Gold edges and handle. Similar to 11539. Entered in pattern book during or after 1931. **Backstamp(s)**: Shelley 1925-1940 **Shapes:** Queen Anne
11828	**Trees and Sunset**. Brown print. Silhouetted pairs of black trees on panel edges. Yellow setting sun between trees. Grey and green shaded landscape border on outside of cup and on saucer. Alternating white and maize yellow panels. Black edges. Entered in pattern book during or after 1931. **Backstamp(s)**: Shelley 1925-1940 **Shapes:** Queen Anne

Trees and Sunset 11828 Queen Anne shape cup, saucer, and plate. £80-100; $120-250

Pattern	Description & Shapes
11829	Balloon Tree. Black tree with green leaves. Green grass at foot of tree. Green and purple bushes in the distance. Orange, blue, and yellow balloons against the tree. Balloons and leaves also inside cup. Yellow banded border. Blue edges. Entered in pattern book during or after 1931 for export. Also see 11624. **Backstamp(s)**: Shelley 1925-1940 **Shapes:** Queen Anne
11830	Tall bushes and flowers. Black print. Green edges. Similar to 11677 with different colours. Entered in pattern book during or after 1931 for export. **Backstamp(s)**: Shelley 1925-1940 **Shapes:** Queen Anne
11831	Flame Flowers. Black print. Black tree with yellow, black, and grey leaves. Coral and turquoise flowers at the foot of the tree with green and yellow leaves. White ground. Blue edges. Entered in pattern book during or after 1931. **Backstamp(s)**: Shelley 1925-1940 **Shapes:** Queen Anne
11832	**Black Leafy Tree**. Brown print. Enamelled in blue and green. White ground. Blue edges and handle. Entered in pattern book during or after 1931 for export. **Backstamp(s)**: Shelley 1925-1940 **Shapes:** Queen Anne
11833	Damsons enamelled in green on a brown pattern. Green edges. Entered in pattern book during or after 1931. /R Coral damsons. **Backstamp(s)**: Shelley 1925-1940 **Shapes:** Queen Anne

Damsons green 11833 Queen Anne shape cup, saucer, and plate. £80-100; $120-200

Pattern	Description & Shapes
11834	**Daisy**. Brown print with green enamelled daisies. White ground. Green edges and handle. Entered in pattern book during or after 1931. /T Turquoise daisies. **Backstamp(s)**: Shelley 1925-1940 **Shapes:** Queen Anne
11835	Cottage-1. Brown print on outside cup, centre of saucer and plates. Cottage with chimneys. Grey trees partly enamelled in black. Green fields. Yellow road. Fence and gate across road. Smoke rising from chimney on cup. White ground. Green edges and handle. Entered in pattern book during or after 1931 for export. **Backstamp(s)**: Shelley 1925-1940 **Shapes:** Queen Anne
11836	Cottage-2. Thatched cottage with brick chimneys. Cottage garden type flowers enamelled in blue, coral, yellow, and orange with green leaves. Fawn trees. Brown print. White ground. Green edges and handle. Entered in pattern book during or after 1931. Also see 11621. /GE Gold edges /O Orange edges. **Backstamp(s)**: Shelley 1925-1940 **Shapes:** Queen Anne

Cottage-2 11836 Queen Anne shape cup, saucer, and plate. £150-170; $200-300

Pattern	Description & Shapes
11837	Flower and Blocks. Black print. Mauve, stylised flower set against green and black blocks and lines on small panels. Green band and V on large panels. White ground. White edges and green edge on handle. Entered in pattern book during or after 1931. **Backstamp(s)**: Shelley 1925-1940 **Shapes:** Queen Anne

Flowers and Blocks 11837 Queen Anne shape cup, saucer, and plate. £80-100; $120-160

Pattern	Description & Shapes
11838	Flower and Blocks. Black print. Coral flower set against blocks and lines on small panels. Band and V on large panels. White ground. White edges and blue edge on handle. Entered in pattern book during or after 1931. **Backstamp(s)**: Shelley 1925-1940 **Shapes:** Queen Anne
11839	Stylised flower on small panels and tree on large panels. Grey print. Green edges and handle. Entered in pattern book during or after 1931. **Backstamp(s)**: Shelley 1925-1940 **Shapes:** Queen Anne
11840	Stylised floral pattern. Green and coral. Entered in pattern book during or after 1931. **Backstamp(s)**: Shelley 1925-1940 **Shapes:** Vogue
11841	Stylised floral pattern. Blue, orange, and green. Entered in pattern book during or after 1931. **Backstamp(s)**: Shelley 1925-1940 **Shapes:** Vogue
11842	Garden Scene. Brown print. Green edges

Pattern	Description & Shapes
	and handle. Entered in pattern book during or after 1931. /G Special order for Yeates. **Backstamp(s)**: Shelley 1925-1940 **Shapes:** Queen Anne
11843	**Bluebird**. Entered in pattern book during or after 1931. **Backstamp(s)**: Shelley 1925-1940 **Shapes:** Mode
11844	**Cornflower**. Entered in pattern book during or after 1931. **Backstamp(s)**: Shelley 1925-1940 **Shapes:** Mode
11845	**Apple**. Coral handle. Entered in pattern book during or after 1931. **Backstamp(s)**: Shelley 1925-1940 **Shapes:** Mode
11846	**Apple**. Blue handle. Entered in pattern book during or after 1931. **Backstamp(s)**: Shelley 1925-1940 **Shapes:** Mode
11847	**Apple**. Orange handle. Entered in pattern book during or after 1931. **Backstamp(s)**: Shelley 1925-1940 **Shapes:** Mode
11848	**Tulip**. Green edges. Entered in pattern book during or after 1931. **Backstamp(s)**: Shelley 1925-1940 **Shapes:** Mode
11849	**Tulip**. Orange edges. Entered in pattern book during or after 1931. **Backstamp(s)**: Shelley 1925-1940 **Shapes:** Mode
11850	**Iris**. Entered in pattern book during or after 1931. **Backstamp(s)**: Shelley 1925-1940 **Shapes:** Mode
11851	Block and stylised bell flower. Green print. Entered in pattern book during or after 1931. **Backstamp(s)**: Shelley 1925-1940 **Shapes:** Mode
11852	Block and stylised bell flower. Fawn print. Entered in pattern book during or after 1931. **Backstamp(s)**: Shelley 1925-1940 **Shapes:** Mode
11853	Block and stylised bell flower. Purple print. Entered in pattern book during or after 1931. **Backstamp(s)**: Shelley 1925-1940 **Shapes:** Mode
11854	Entered in pattern book during or after 1931. **Backstamp(s)**: Shelley 1925-1940 **Shapes:** Empire
11855	Bluebells. Entered in pattern book during or after 1931. **Backstamp(s)**: Shelley 1925-1940 **Shapes:** Mode
11856	Entered in pattern book during or after 1931. **Backstamp(s)**: Shelley 1925-1940 **Shapes:** Empire
11857-11858	Entered in pattern book during or after 1931. **Backstamp(s)**: Shelley 1925-1940 **Shapes:** Vincent
11859	Cottage-3. Brown print. Cottage with blue roof and door. White ground. Blue edges and handle. **Backstamp(s)**: Shelley 1925-1940 **Shapes:** Georgian
11860	Sunset and Flowers. Black print. Enamelled in coral and orange. Bright orange setting sun. Fluffy clouds. Black trees and yellow haze around sunset. Sunset reflected in water. Green ground. Orange edges. Similar to 11691 and 11707. Entered in pattern book during or after 1931. **Backstamp(s)**: Shelley 1925-1940 **Shapes:** Queen Anne
11861	Geometric shapes and stylised, orange flower. Blue print. Blue handle. Entered in pattern book during or after 1931. **Backstamp(s)**: Shelley 1925-1940 **Shapes:** Queen Anne
11862	Geometric shapes and stylised, coral flower. Green print. Green handle. Entered in pattern book during or after 1931. **Backstamp(s)**: Shelley 1925-1940 **Shapes:** Queen Anne
11863	Chrysanthemum. Grey print. Green edges and handle. Entered in pattern book during or after 1931. **Backstamp(s)**: Shelley 1925-1940 **Shapes:** Queen Anne
11864	Chrysanthemum. Blue print. Orange edges and handle. Entered in pattern book during or after 1931. **Backstamp(s)**: Shelley 1925-1940 **Shapes:** Queen Anne
11865	**Poppies**. Brown print. Sun at base of cup. Green edges and handle. Entered in pattern book during or after 1931. **Backstamp(s)**: Shelley 1925-1940 **Shapes:** Queen Anne
11866	**Poppies**. Black print. Sun at base of cup. Green edges and handle. Entered in pattern book during or after 1931. **Backstamp(s)**: Shelley 1925-1940 **Shapes:** Queen Anne
11867	Martian. Coral flower and bands. Entered in pattern book during or after 1931. **Backstamp(s)**: Shelley 1925-1940 **Shapes:** Mode
11868	Martian. Yellow and blue yellow flower and bands. Entered in pattern book during or after 1931. **Backstamp(s)**: Shelley 1925-1940 **Shapes:** Mode
11869	Entered in pattern book during or after 1931 for export. **Backstamp(s)**: Shelley 1925-1940 **Shapes:** Doric
11870	Entered in pattern book during or after 1931. **Backstamp(s)**: Shelley 1925-1940 **Shapes:** Empire
11871	Bluebells. Coral. Entered in pattern book during or after 1931. **Backstamp(s)**: Shelley 1925-1940 **Shapes:** Mode
11872	**Rose Arches**. Brown print. Pink roses and green leaves on tall black and brown stems. White ground. Leaf green edges. Entered in pattern book during or after 1931. **Backstamp(s)**: Shelley 1925-1940 **Shapes:** Queen Anne

Rose Arches 11872 Queen Anne shape demitasse cup and saucer. £80-100; $120-160

Pattern	Description & Shapes
11873	**Cottage and Trees**. Grey print. Blue edges and handle. Entered in pattern book during or after 1931. **Backstamp(s)**: Shelley 1925-1940 **Shapes:** Queen Anne
11874	**Corn and Poppies**. Brown print. Outside cup has cornfield and poppies in coral and shades of brown. The front panel has a landscape with brown trees, blue sky, white and yellow clouds, blue foreground, and a blue bird in flight. Saucer has corn and poppies in the lower part and the landscape scene in the upper part. White ground. Leaf green edges. Entered in pattern book during or after 1931. **Backstamp(s)**: Shelley 1925-1940 **Shapes:** Queen Anne
11875	Geometric Border. Inside cup, edge of saucer and plate have border of diagonal red, black, and grey stripes. There are two lines below the below, one black and one red. Outside cup, red line approximately half way between rim and base. Main part of saucer and plate have two widely spaced red lines. White ground. Red ring handle. Black trim. Entered in pattern book during or after 1931. **Backstamp(s)**: Shelley 1925-1940 **Shapes:** Vogue
11876	Geometric Border. Inside cup, edge of saucer, and plate have border of diagonal green, black, and grey stripes. There are two lines below the below, one black and one green. Outside cup, green line approximately half way between rim and base. Main part of saucer and plate have two widely spaced green lines. White ground. Green ring handle. Black trim. Entered in pattern book during or after 1931. **Backstamp(s)**: Shelley 1925-1940 **Shapes:** Vogue
11877	Geometric Border. Inside cup, edge of saucer and plate have border of diagonal yellow, black, and grey stripes. There are two lines below the below, one black and one yellow. Outside cup, yellow line approximately half way between rim and base. Main part of saucer and plate have two widely spaced yellow lines. White ground. Yellow ring handle. Black trim. Entered in pattern book during or after 1931. **Backstamp(s)**: Shelley 1925-1940 **Shapes:** Vogue
11878	Geometric Border. Inside cup, edge of saucer and plate have border of diagonal blue, black, and grey stripes. There are two lines below the below, one black and one blue. Outside cup, blue line approximately half way between rim and base. Main part of saucer and plate have two widely spaced blue lines. White ground. Blue ring handle. Black trim. Entered in pattern book during or after 1931. **Backstamp(s)**: Shelley 1925-1940 **Shapes:** Vogue
11879	**Fruit**. Red and black apples. Entered in pattern book during or after 1931. **Backstamp(s)**: Shelley 1925-1940 **Shapes:** Vogue
11880	**Fruit**. Green and black apples. Entered in pattern book during or after 1931. **Backstamp(s)**: Shelley 1925-1940 **Shapes:** Vogue
11881	**Moresque**. Entered in pattern book during or after 1931. **Backstamp(s)**: Shelley 1925-1940 **Shapes:** Vogue
11882-11885	Entered in pattern book during or after 1931 for Boyle, Canada. **Backstamp(s)**: Shelley 1925-1940 **Shapes:** Chester
11886	Butchers **Plum and Yellow Leaves**. Blue, orange, and yellow flowers/fruit and leaves. White ground. Blue trim. Entered in pattern book during or after 1931. **Backstamp(s)**: Shelley 1925-1940 **Shapes:** Queen Anne, Vincent

Pattern	Description & Shapes

11887 Butchers **Fruit, Leaves and Butterfly**. Entered in pattern book during or after 1931.
Backstamp(s): Shelley 1925-1940
Shapes: Doric

11888 Butchers **Blue Bird**. Birds, bunches of pink roses, and green foliage on a white ground. Blue edges. Entered in pattern book during or after 1931.
Backstamp(s): Shelley 1925-1940
Shapes: Empire, Eve, Queen Anne

Blue Bird 11888 Queen Anne shape cup, saucer, and plate. £80-100; $120-160

11889 **Fruit**. Blue and black apples. Entered in pattern book during or after 1931.
Backstamp(s): Shelley 1925-1940
Shapes: Vogue

11890 Oriental Water Garden. Brown print. Pink and blue hollyhocks in the foreground. Green fountain in the middle distance with a yellow pagoda and grey trees in the distance. White ground. Green edges. Entered in pattern book during or after 1931.
Backstamp(s): Shelley 1925-1940
Shapes: Queen Anne

Oriental Water Garden 11890 Queen Anne shape cup, saucer, and plate. £80-100; $120-160

11891 Country scene. Brown print. Enamelled in coral, orange, and green. Flowers with green leaves bordering a path with grey trees in the background. Green edges and handle. Also seen in demitasse size. Entered in pattern book during or after 1931.
Backstamp(s): Shelley 1925-1940
Shapes: Queen Anne

11892 Entered in pattern book during or after 1931.
Backstamp(s): Shelley 1925-1940
Shapes: Chester, Empire

11893 Three flowers against leaves. Grey print. Gold edges and handle. Entered in pattern book during or after 1931.
Backstamp(s): Shelley 1925-1940
Shapes: Chester, Queen Anne

11894 Border of blue, mauve, and coral flowers with green foliage on a white ground. Yellow band below border. Entered in pattern book during or after 1931.
Backstamp(s): Shelley 1925-1940
Shapes: Chester, Empire, Vincent

11895 Plums, plum blossom, and leaves. Brown print. Gold edges and handle. Entered in pattern book during or after 1931.
Backstamp(s): Shelley 1925-1940
Shapes: Queen Anne, Vincent

11896 **Apple Blossom**. Entered in pattern book during or after 1931 for export.
Backstamp(s): Shelley 1925-1940
Shapes: Mode, Vincent

11897 Diamonds. Black ground. Gold inside cup. Entered in pattern book during or after 1931.
Backstamp(s): Shelley 1925-1940
Shapes: Vogue Coffee

11898-11912 Entered in pattern book during or after 1931 for export to Canada.
Backstamp(s): Shelley 1925-1940
Shapes: Chester

11913-11916 Entered in pattern book during or after 1931.
Backstamp(s): Shelley 1925-1940
Shapes: Empire

11917 Entered in pattern book during or after 1931.
Backstamp(s): Shelley 1925-1940
Shapes: Carlton

11918 Entered in pattern book during or after 1931.
Backstamp(s): Shelley 1925-1940
Shapes: Chester, Vincent

11919-11920 Entered in pattern book during or after 1931.
Backstamp(s): Shelley 1925-1940
Shapes: Vincent

11921-11922 Entered in pattern book during or after 1931 for export to Canada.
Backstamp(s): Shelley 1925-1940
Shapes: Chester

11923 Autumn Leaves. Brown print. Autumnal coloured leaves inside cup and on saucer and plate on a yellow ground. Gold edges and ring handle. Entered in pattern book during or after 1931 for export to Canada.
Backstamp(s): Shelley 1925-1940
Shapes: Chester

Autumn Leaves 11923 Chester shape cup, saucer, and plate. £80-100; $120-160

11924-11928 Entered in pattern book during or after 1931 for export to Canada.
Backstamp(s): Shelley 1925-1940
Shapes: Chester

11929 Cottage scene. Orange and grey tiled roof with a chimney. Paved path leading to cottage. Tall blue flowers, possibly hollyhocks, in the foreground. Green shrubbery in front of cottage. Grey and green shrubs and trees behind cottage. White ground. Green edges and ring handle. Entered in pattern book during or after 1931. Made for Canadian market.
Backstamp(s): Shelley 1925-1940 Ryrie-Birks Ltd Toronto
Shapes: Chester

11930 Entered in pattern book during or after 1931 for export to Canada.
Backstamp(s): Shelley 1925-1940
Shapes: Chester

11931 Entered in pattern book during or after 1931 for export to Canada.
Backstamp(s): Shelley 1925-1940
Shapes: Dainty

11932 Entered in pattern book during or after 1931 for export to Canada.
Backstamp(s): Shelley 1925-1940
Shapes: Chester

11933-11934 Entered in pattern book during or after 1931 for export to Canada.
Backstamp(s): Shelley 1925-1940
Shapes: Dainty

11935 Gold vine and trellis print on coloured ground. Gold edges and handle. Entered in pattern book during or after 1932 for export to Canada.
Backstamp(s): Shelley 1925-1940
Shapes: Queen Anne Coffee

11939-11940 Entered in pattern book during or after 1931.
Backstamp(s): Shelley 1925-1940
Shapes: Empire

11941 Tulips. Large, blue, vertical tulips, each with one green and one grey leaf. Yellow buds. Grey print border inside cup. Blue edges and handle. Entered in pattern book during or after 1932.
Backstamp(s): Shelley 1925-1940
Shapes: Vincent

11942 Entered in pattern book during or after 1931.
Backstamp(s): Shelley 1925-1940
Shapes: Vincent

11943 Entered in pattern book during or after 1932.
Backstamp(s): Shelley 1925-1940
Shapes: Doric

11944 Brown print. Green and yellow flowers with green and brown leaves, also inside cup. White ground. Yellow edges. Entered in pattern book during or after 1932.
Backstamp(s): Shelley 1925-1940
Shapes: Empire

Green and Yellow Flowers 11944 Empire shape cup, saucer, and plate. £80-100; $120-160

Pattern	Description & Shapes

11945 Green apples with yellow and pink leaves. Entered in pattern book during or after 1932.
Backstamp(s): Shelley 1925-1940
Shapes: Empire

11946 Entered in pattern book during or after 1932.
Backstamp(s): Shelley 1925-1940
Shapes: Empire

11947 Entered in pattern book during or after 1932.
Backstamp(s): Shelley 1925-1940
Shapes: Vincent

11948 Entered in pattern book during or after 1932.
Backstamp(s): Shelley 1925-1940
Shapes: Dainty

11950 **Daisies**. Pink and orange. Entered in pattern book during or after 1932.
Backstamp(s): Shelley 1925-1940
Shapes: Eve

11951 Blue and orange flower. Entered in pattern book during or after 1932.
Backstamp(s): Shelley 1925-1940
Shapes: Eve

11952 **Crocus**. Yellow, blue, and purple crocuses with green leaves. Grey tree. Butterflies. White ground. Entered in pattern book during or after 1932.
Backstamp(s): Shelley 1925-1940
Shapes: Eve

11953-11956 Entered in pattern book during or after 1932.
Backstamp(s): Shelley 1925-1940
Shapes: Mayfair

11957 Entered in pattern book during or after 1932.
Backstamp(s): Shelley 1925-1940
Shapes: Chester

11958 Sunray. Entered in pattern book during or after 1932.
Backstamp(s): Shelley 1925-1940
Shapes: Vogue

11959 **Bands and Shades**. Green and cream. Green foot. Cream handle. White ground. Entered in pattern book during or after 1932.
/G Grey
/M Purple
/P Pink.
Backstamp(s): Shelley 1925-1940
Shapes: Chester, Eve, Vogue

Bands and Shades 11959 Eve shape cup, saucer, and plate. £60-80; $100-120

11960 **Gladiola**. Dark yellow and orange gladiola with green leaves on a white ground. Lemon yellow shades fading to white inside cup. Green edges. Entered in pattern book during or after 1932.
Backstamp(s): Shelley 1925-1940
Shapes: Eve

11961 **Gladiola**. Blue gladiola with green leaves on a white ground. Green shades fading to white inside cup. Blue edges and foot. Green handle. Entered in pattern book during or after 1932.
Backstamp(s): Shelley 1925-1940
Shapes: Eve

11962-11964 Entered in pattern book during or after 1932.
Backstamp(s): Shelley 1925-1940
Shapes: Empire

11965 **Gladiola**. Pink gladiola with green leaves on a white ground. Green shades fading to white inside cup. Blue edges and foot. Green handle. Entered in pattern book during or after 1932.
/G Green foot.
Backstamp(s): Shelley 1925-1940
Shapes: Eve

11966 Entered in pattern book during or after 1932.
Backstamp(s): Shelley 1925-1940
Shapes: Vincent

11967 Entered in pattern book during or after 1932.
Backstamp(s): Shelley 1925-1940
Shapes: Empire

11968-11970 Entered in pattern book during or after 1932.
Backstamp(s): Shelley 1925-1940
Shapes: Vincent

11971 **Crocus**. Pink, blue, and yellow crocuses with green foliage and a yellow butterfly. Border inside cup. Green edges and outer handle.
Backstamp(s): Shelley 1925-1940
Shapes: Chester, Eve

Crocus 11971 Eve shape cup and saucer. £60-80; $100-120

11972-11973 Entered in pattern book during or after 1932.
Backstamp(s): Shelley 1925-1940
Shapes: Empire

11974 Entered in pattern book during or after 1932.
Backstamp(s): Shelley 1925-1940
Shapes: Chester

11975-11976 Entered in pattern book during or after 1932.
Backstamp(s): Shelley 1925-1940
Shapes: Chester, Queen Anne

11977 Stylised floral motif. Entered in pattern book during or after 1932.
Backstamp(s): Shelley 1925-1940
Shapes: Eve

11978 Entered in pattern book during or after 1932.
Backstamp(s): Shelley 1925-1940
Shapes: Dainty

11979-11982 Entered in pattern book during or after 1932.
Backstamp(s): Shelley 1925-1940
Shapes: Chester

11983 **Crocus**. Entered in pattern book during or after 1932.
Backstamp(s): Shelley 1925-1940
Shapes: Eve

11984 Entered in pattern book during or after 1932.
Backstamp(s): Shelley 1925-1940
Shapes: Chester

11985 **Daisies**. Pink and blue. Entered in pattern book during or after 1932.
Backstamp(s): Shelley 1925-1940
Shapes: Eve

11986 Large pink and small blue flowers. Entered in pattern book during or after 1932.
Backstamp(s): Shelley 1925-1940
Shapes: Eve

11987 Entered in pattern book during or after 1932.
Backstamp(s): Shelley 1925-1940
Shapes: Chester

11988 Blue lines on a white ground.
Backstamp(s): Shelley 1925-1940
Shapes: Chester, Eve

11989 Bands and Lines. Shaded of orange to yellow bands and lines on white ground. Entered in pattern book during or after 1932.
Backstamp(s): Shelley 1925-1940
Shapes: Chester, Eve, Regent

11990 Entered in pattern book during or after 1932.
Backstamp(s): Shelley 1925-1940
Shapes: Chester

11991 Entered in pattern book during or after 1932.
Backstamp(s): Shelley 1925-1940
Shapes: Dainty Floral

11992 Coloured star. Segments between points of star are of a paler colour than the star. Figural handle with flowers. Entered in pattern book during or after 1932.
/25 blue star shaded yellow segments
Backstamp(s): Shelley 1925-1940
Shapes: Dainty Floral

11993 Apple green star. Segments between points of star are a pale yellow. Green figural handle with yellow flowers. Entered in pattern book during or after 1932.
/25 blue star shaded yellow segments
Backstamp(s): Shelley 1925-1940
Shapes: Dainty Floral

11994-11995 Entered in pattern book during or after 1932.
Backstamp(s): Shelley 1925-1940
Shapes: Dainty Floral

11996-11997 Entered in pattern book during or after 1932.
Backstamp(s): Shelley 1925-1940
Shapes: Empire

11998-11999 Entered in pattern book during or after 1932.
Backstamp(s): Shelley 1925-1940
Shapes: Carlton

12001 Yellow flowers in the foreground against grey bushes. White ground. Entered in pattern book during or after 1932.
Backstamp(s): Shelley 1925-1940
Shapes: Dainty

12003 Entered in pattern book during or after 1932.
Backstamp(s): Shelley 1925-1940
Shapes: Chester, Mayfair

12004 Blue pansies and green foliage on a white ground. Green edges. Entered in pattern book during or after 1932.
Backstamp(s): Shelley 1925-1940
Shapes: Chester, Mayfair, Vincent

12005-12006 Entered in pattern book during or after

Pattern	Description & Shapes
	1932. **Backstamp(s)**: Shelley 1925-1940 **Shapes:** Chester, Mayfair
12007	**Heather**. Countryside scene with pink heather, trees, bridge, and river. Pattern outside cup, middle of saucer, and plate. Broad, burgundy border with gold print inside cup, on saucer, and plate. Gold edges. Pale green handle. Entered in pattern book during or after 1932. **Backstamp(s)**: 1940-1966 Heather **Shapes:** Chester, Henley, Mayfair
12008	Entered in pattern book during or after 1932. **Backstamp(s)**: Shelley 1925-1940 **Shapes:** Chester, Mayfair
12009	Large, open pink wild roses with green and grey foliage on a white ground. Green edges. Entered in pattern book during or after 1932. **Backstamp(s)**: Shelley 1925-1940 **Shapes:** Chester, Mayfair

Wild roses 12009 Mayfair shape cup and saucer. £60-70; $90-120

12010-12012	Entered in pattern book during or after 1932. **Backstamp(s)**: Shelley 1925-1940 **Shapes:** Chester, Mayfair
12013-12016	Entered in pattern book during or after 1932. **Backstamp(s)**: Shelley 1925-1940 **Shapes:** Dainty Floral
12017-12018	Entered in pattern book during or after 1932. **Backstamp(s)**: Shelley 1925-1940 **Shapes:** York
12019	**Hollyhocks**. Pink hollyhocks with green foliage on a white ground. Blue shades inside cup. Blue foot and handle. Similar to 0240. Entered in pattern book during or after 1932. /4R Round plates. **Backstamp(s)**: Shelley 1925-1940 **Shapes:** Eve

Hollyhocks 12019 Eve shape cup and saucer. £60-80; $100-120

12020	**Hollyhocks**. Brown print. Yellow and orange flowers. Entered in pattern book during or after 1932. /S Produced for Nelson, Australia. **Backstamp(s)**: Shelley 1925-1940 **Shapes:** Eve
12021	**Bands and Shades**. Brown and cream. Brown foot and handle. White ground. Entered in pattern book during or after 1932. **Backstamp(s)**: Shelley 1925-1940 **Shapes:** Eve, Regent

Bands and Shades 12021 Regent shape cup and saucer. £50-60; $80-90

12022	Entered in pattern book during or after 1932. **Backstamp(s)**: Shelley 1925-1940 **Shapes:** Dainty Floral
12023	Yellow flowers with green leaves in the foreground. Grey woodland in the background with yellow tinted sky. Green figural handle with yellow flowers. White ground. Dark blue edges. Entered in pattern book during or after 1932. **Backstamp(s)**: Shelley 1925-1940 **Shapes:** Dainty Floral

Yellow flowers 12023 Dainty Floral shape cup and saucer. £70-80; $140-160

Right:
Syringa 12027 Queen Anne shape cup, saucer, and plate. £80-100; $120-160

12024	Entered in pattern book during or after 1932. **Backstamp(s)**: Shelley 1925-1940 **Shapes:** Dainty Floral
12025	**Syringa**. Blue Syringa flowers with green and fawn foliage. Blue edges and ring handle. Entered in pattern book during or after 1932. **Backstamp(s)**: Shelley 1925-1940 **Shapes:** Regent

Syringa 12025 Regent shape cup, saucer, and plate. £40-60; $60-120

12026	**Syringa**. Yellow Syringa flowers with green and fawn foliage. Green edges and ring handle. Entered in pattern book during or after 1932. **Backstamp(s)**: Shelley 1925-1940 **Shapes:** Regent
12027	**Syringa**. Pink, blue, and yellow Syringa flowers with green and grey foliage. Turquoise edges and handle. Entered in pattern book during or after 1932. **Backstamp(s)**: Shelley 1925-1940 **Shapes:** Queen Anne

Anemone 12067 Queen Anne shape cup, saucer, and plate. £80-100; $120-160

Pattern	Description & Shapes

12028-
12031 Entered in pattern book during or after 1932.
Backstamp(s): Shelley 1925-1940
Shapes: Dainty Floral

12032 **Bands and Lines**. Shades of fawn and green bands and lines on a white ground. Green ring handle. Entered in pattern book during or after 1933.
Backstamp(s): Shelley 1925-1940
Shapes: Regent

Bands and Lines 12032 Regent shape coffee pot. £150-160; $200-270. Sugar and creamer. £50-60; $80-90

12033 **Bands and Lines**. Blue bands and green lines on a white ground. Green ring handle. Entered in pattern book during or after 1932.
/G Green only
/Y Yellow and green.
Backstamp(s): Shelley 1925-1940
Shapes: Regent

12034 **Bands and Lines**. Mauve bands and green lines on a white ground. Green ring handle. Entered in pattern book during or after 1932.
Backstamp(s): Shelley 1925-1940
Shapes: Regent

12035 **Bands and Lines**. Orange bands and green lines on a white ground. Green ring handle. Entered in pattern book during or after 1932.
/A Green bands and red lines.
Backstamp(s): Shelley 1925-1940
Shapes: Regent

12036 Entered in pattern book during or after 1932.
Backstamp(s): Shelley 1925-1940
Shapes: Mocha

12037-
12038 Entered in pattern book during or after 1932.
Backstamp(s): Shelley 1925-1940
Shapes: Dainty Floral

12039 **Geometric Border**. Inside cup, edge of saucer, and plate have border of diagonal red, black, and grey stripes. There are two lines below the below, one black and one red. Outside cup, red line approximately half way between rim and base. Main part of saucer and plate have two widely spaced red lines. White ground. Red ring handle. Black trim. Entered in pattern book during or after 1932.
Backstamp(s): Shelley 1925-1940
Shapes: Regent

12040 **Geometric Border**. Inside cup, edge of saucer and plate have border of diagonal green, black, and grey stripes. There are two lines below the below, one black and one green. Outside cup, green line approximately half way between rim and base. Main part of saucer and plate have two widely spaced green lines. White ground. Green ring handle. Black trim. Entered in pattern book during or after 1932.
Backstamp(s): Shelley 1925-1940
Shapes: Regent

12041 Squares and lines. Black print. A coral block and a smaller black square with two black lines below them. Entered in pattern book during or after 1932.
Backstamp(s): Shelley 1925-1940
Shapes: Regent

12042 Tulip. Similar to 11941. Entered in pattern book during or after 1932.
Backstamp(s): Shelley 1925-1940
Shapes: Regent

12043 Blue, orange, and yellow enamelled flowers with green and grey leaves. Same as 11757. Entered in pattern book during or after 1932.
Backstamp(s): Shelley 1925-1940
Shapes: Regent

12044 Fruit bowl border. Lines and triangles. Green edges and handle. Entered in pattern book during or after 1932.
Backstamp(s): Shelley 1925-1940
Shapes: Regent

12045 Blue, linear border inside cup, with orange semicircles and green triangles. Entered in pattern book during or after 1932.
Backstamp(s): Shelley 1925-1940
Shapes: Regent

12046 Border of flowers and leaves with blue triangles. Blue ring handle. Same as 11801. Entered in pattern book during or after 1932.
Backstamp(s): Shelley 1925-1940
Shapes: Regent

12047 Blue blocks and blue-green leaves. Green edges. Same as 11802. Entered in pattern book during or after 1932.
Backstamp(s): Shelley 1925-1940
Shapes: Regent

12048 Border of mauve, yellow, and black blocks. Green edges. Same as 11803. Entered in pattern book during or after 1932.
Backstamp(s): Shelley 1925-1940
Shapes: Regent

12049 Green and black circles with orange and green blocks. Orange edges. Same as 11804. Entered in pattern book during or after 1932.
Backstamp(s): Shelley 1925-1940
Shapes: Regent

12050 Entered in pattern book during or after 1932.
Backstamp(s): Shelley 1925-1940
Shapes: York

12051 J Pattern. Pattern inside cup. Green J and border. Blue flowers with black stems and black and grey leaves. Border on handle and flower sprig. Green foot. Green ring round centre of saucer. White ground. Entered in pattern book during or after 1932.
Backstamp(s): Shelley 1925-1940
Shapes: Eve

12052 J Pattern. Pattern inside cup. Red J and border. Blue flowers with black stems and black and grey leaves. Border on handle and flower sprig. Red foot. Red ring round centre of saucer. White ground. Entered in pattern book during or after 1932.
Backstamp(s): Shelley 1925-1940
Shapes: Eve

12053 J Pattern. Pattern inside cup. Red J and border. Blue flowers with black stems and black and grey leaves. Border on handle and flower sprig. Blue foot. Blue ring round centre of saucer. White ground. Entered in pattern book during or after 1932.
Backstamp(s): Shelley 1925-1940
Shapes: Eve

12054 **Motif**. Large pink, blue, and yellow flowers with green and grey leaves. Green swirls inside cup, border of saucer, and plate. White ground, edges, and handle. Entered in pattern book during or after 1932.
Backstamp(s): Shelley 1940-1966
Shapes: Mayfair, Regent

12055-
12056 Entered in pattern book during or after 1932.
Backstamp(s): Shelley 1925-1940
Shapes: Mayfair

12057 Blue and orange flower. Same as 11951. Entered in pattern book during or after 1932.
Backstamp(s): Shelley 1925-1940
Shapes: Regent

12058 **Crocuses**. Pink, blue, and yellow crocuses with green foliage and a yellow butterfly. Border inside cup. Gold edges. Entered in pattern book during or after 1932.
Backstamp(s): Shelley 1925-1940
Shapes: Regent

12059 Blue and green flower. Entered in pattern book during or after 1932.
Backstamp(s): Shelley 1925-1940
Shapes: York

12060 Three flowers against leaves. Gold edges and handle. Entered in pattern book during or after 1932.
Backstamp(s): Shelley 1925-1940
Shapes: Queen Anne

12061 Entered in pattern book during or after 1932.
Backstamp(s): Shelley 1925-1940
Shapes: York

12062 **Spring**. Entered in pattern book during or after 1932.
Backstamp(s): Shelley 1925-1940
Shapes: Vincent, York

12063 Entered in pattern book during or after 1932.
Backstamp(s): Shelley 1925-1940
Shapes: Mayfair

12064 **Blue Iris**. Black print. Irises with leaves on small panels. Stylised fruit and leaves on large panels. Dots and circles on panel joins. White ground. Green edges and handle. Entered in pattern book during or after 1932.
Backstamp(s): Shelley 1925-1940
Shapes: Queen Anne

12065 Entered in pattern book during or after 1932.
Backstamp(s): Shelley 1925-1940
Shapes: York

12066 White with emerald green edges and handle. Figural handle has red flowers with green leaves. Entered in pattern book during or after 1932.
Backstamp(s): Shelley 1925-1940
Shapes: Dainty Floral

12067 **Anemone**. Pink, blue, and yellow anemones with green and grey leaves. White ground. Green edges and handle. Entered in pattern book during or after 1932.
/B blue edges and handle
/O orange edges and handle.
Backstamp(s): Shelley 1925-1940
Shapes: Queen Anne

12068 **Anemone**. Yellow, blue, and grey anemones with green and leaves. White ground. Green edges and handle. Entered in pattern book during or after 1932.
/Y Yellow anemones.
Backstamp(s): Shelley 1925-1940
Shapes: Queen Anne

12069 Entered in pattern book during or after 1932.
Backstamp(s): Shelley 1925-1940
Shapes: Regent

12070 **Syringa**. Brown print. Pink, blue, and orange Syringa flowers with green and fawn foliage. Green edges and ring handle. Entered in pattern book during or

Pattern **Description & Shapes**

after 1932.
Backstamp(s): Shelley 1925-1940
Shapes: Regent

12071 Entered in pattern book during or after 1932.
Backstamp(s): Shelley 1925-1940
Shapes: Mayfair

12072 **Anemone Bunch**. Pink, blue, yellow, and orange anemones with green leaves on ivory ground. Large bunches inside cup and on saucer and plate. Small bunch outside cup. Narrow peach-fawn band on outer edge of saucer and plate. Broad green band inside peach-fawn band. Green ring handle. Entered in pattern book during or after 1932.
/P pink
/N green edges
/B blue edges
/T blue.
Backstamp(s): Shelley 1925-1940
Shapes: Regent

12073 Entered in pattern book during or after 1932.
Backstamp(s): Shelley 1925-1940
Shapes: Mayfair

12074-
12075 Entered in pattern book during or after 1932.
Backstamp(s): Shelley 1925-1940
Shapes: York

12076 **Swirls**. Grey, pink, and green. Green ring handle. Entered in pattern book during or after 1932.
Backstamp(s): Shelley 1925-1940
Shapes: Regent

12077 Green shades with fawn. Green ring handle. Entered in pattern book during or after 1932.
Backstamp(s): Shelley 1925-1940
Shapes: Regent

12078 Entered in pattern book during or after 1932.
Backstamp(s): Shelley 1925-1940
Shapes: Mayfair

12079 **Anemone**. Gold edges and handle. Entered in pattern book during or after 1932.
Backstamp(s): Shelley 1925-1940
Shapes: Queen Anne

12080 **Primrose**. Green print. Gold edges and handle. Entered in pattern book during or after 1932.
Backstamp(s): Shelley 1925-1940
Shapes: Queen Anne

12081-
12082 Entered in pattern book during or after 1932.
Backstamp(s): Shelley 1925-1940
Shapes: Mayfair

12083 **Harmony Artware**. Coral and black drip design. Entered in pattern book during or after 1932.
Backstamp(s): Shelley 1925-1940
Shapes: Vogue

12084 **Harmony Artware**. Blue and mauve drip design. Entered in pattern book during or after 1932.
Backstamp(s): Shelley 1925-1940
Shapes: Vogue

12085 **Harmony Artware**. Orange, blue, and yellow drip design. Green inside cup and ring handle. Entered in pattern book during or after 1932.
Backstamp(s): Shelley 1925-1940
Shapes: Regent, Vogue

12086 Entered in pattern book during or after 1932 for export to Canada.
Backstamp(s): Shelley 1925-1940
Shapes: Dainty

12087 **Century Rose**. Entered in pattern book during or after 1932 for export to Canada.
/28 Blue
Backstamp(s): Shelley 1925-1940
Shapes: Dainty

12088 **Ivy**. Entered in pattern book during or after 1932 for export to Canada.
Backstamp(s): Shelley 1925-1940
Shapes: Dainty

12089-
12090 **Rose and Beads**. Entered in pattern book during or after 1932 for export to Canada.
Backstamp(s): Shelley 1925-1940
Shapes: Dainty

12091 **Fern Border**. Entered in pattern book during or after 1932 for export to Canada.
Backstamp(s): Shelley 1925-1940
Shapes: Dainty

12092 Brown print. Coral and green enamelling. Large flowers with entwined stems. Entered in pattern book during or after 1932.
Backstamp(s): Shelley 1925-1940
Shapes: Regent

12093 Green print. Blue enamelling. Large flowers with entwined stems. Entered in pattern book during or after 1932.
Backstamp(s): Shelley 1925-1940
Shapes: Regent

12094 Brown print. Blue, mauve, coral, and green enamelling. Large flowers with entwined stems. Entered in pattern book during or after 1932.
Backstamp(s): Shelley 1925-1940
Shapes: Regent

12095 **Crabtree**. Tree in landscape with fruit. Entered in pattern book during or after 1932.
Backstamp(s): Shelley 1925-1940
Shapes: York

12096-
12098 Entered in pattern book during or after 1932.
Backstamp(s): Shelley 1925-1940
Shapes: Dainty Floral

12099-
12102 Entered in pattern book during or after 1932.
Backstamp(s): Shelley 1925-1940
Shapes: York

12103-
12105 Entered in pattern book during or after 1932.
Backstamp(s): Shelley 1925-1940
Shapes: Chester, Empire

12106 **Sunflower**. Yellow. Entered in pattern book during or after 1932.
Backstamp(s): Shelley 1925-1940
Shapes: York

12107 **Sunflower**. Green. Entered in pattern book during or after 1932.
Backstamp(s): Shelley 1925-1940
Shapes: York

12108 **Bluebell Wood**. Woodland scene with bluebells in the foreground on a sloping bank below some trees. Road and fence to the left of the scene. Trees and foliage to the right. White ground. Blue edges. Entered in pattern book during or after 1932.
Backstamp(s): Shelley 1925-1940
Shapes: Vincent

12109 Colour ground on small panels. Ivory ground on large panels. Tulip handle. Entered in pattern book during or after 1932.
Small panels and handle:
/1 Pink ground, pink and blue tulip
/4 Green ground, yellow and green tulip
/6 Grey ground, pink and green tulip
/24 Black ground, orange and black tulip
/25 Water green ground, pink and blue tulip
/31 Orange ground, green and grey tulip.
Backstamp(s): Shelley 1925-1940
Shapes: Floral Queen Anne

12110 Three flowers against leaves. Grey print. Green edges and handle. Entered in pattern book during or after 1932 for export to Canada.
Backstamp(s): Shelley 1925-1940
Shapes: Chester, Queen Anne

12111 **Wild Rose**. Entered in pattern book during or after 1932.
Backstamp(s): Shelley 1925-1940
Shapes: Mayfair

12112-
12113 Entered in pattern book during or after 1932.
Backstamp(s): Shelley 1925-1940
Shapes: Mayfair

12114 **Violets**. Black print. Violets with a green leaf on small panels. Grey flowers on large panels. White ground. Green edges. Entered in pattern book during or after 1932.
Backstamp(s): Shelley 1925-1940
Shapes: Queen Anne

12115 Entered in pattern book during or after 1933.
Backstamp(s): Shelley 1925-1940
Shapes: York

12116 Entered in pattern book during or after 1933.
Backstamp(s): Shelley 1925-1940
Shapes: Dainty

12117 **Blue Bird**. Entered in pattern book during or after 1933.
Backstamp(s): Shelley 1925-1940
Shapes: Dainty

12118 **Roses, Pansies, and Forget-me-nots**. Entered in pattern book during or after 1933.
Backstamp(s): Shelley 1925-1940
Shapes: Dainty

12119 Entered in pattern book during or after 1933.
Backstamp(s): Shelley 1925-1940
Shapes: Dainty Floral

12120 **Violets**. Black print. Pink, mauve, and yellow violets with a green leaf on small panels. Grey flowers on large panels. White ground. Mauve edges. Entered in pattern book during or after 1933.
Backstamp(s): Shelley 1925-1940
Shapes: Queen Anne

Violets 12120 Queen Anne shape cup, saucer, and plate. £80-100; $120-160

12121 **Violets**. Black print. Pink, mauve, and yellow violets with a green leaf on a white ground on small panels. Grey flowers on large panels on a coloured ground. Gold edges. Floral Queen Anne handles are pink and blue. Entered in pattern book during or after 1933.
Backstamp(s): Shelley 1925-1940
Shapes: Floral Queen Anne, Queen Anne

12122 **Pansy**. Entered in pattern book during or after 1933.
Backstamp(s): Shelley 1925-1940
Shapes: Mayfair

12123 Sunray. Black and orange. Entered in pattern book during or after 1933.

Pattern	Description & Shapes
	Backstamp(s): Shelley 1925-1940 **Shapes:** Eve, Regent
12124	**Harmony Artware**. Green and orange drip design. Entered in pattern book during or after 1933. **Backstamp(s)**: Shelley 1925-1940 **Shapes:** Chester, Eve, Regent, Vogue
12125	**Harmony Artware**. Blue drip design. Entered in pattern book during or after 1933. **Backstamp(s)**: Shelley 1925-1940 **Shapes:** Chester, Eve, Regent, Vogue
12126	**Harmony Artware**. Blue and green drip design. Entered in pattern book during or after 1933. /M Mauve added. **Backstamp(s)**: Shelley 1925-1940 **Shapes:** Chester, Eve, Regent, Vogue
12127	**Harmony**. Orange and green drip design. Green ring handle. Entered in pattern book during or after 1933. **Backstamp(s)**: Shelley 1925-1940 **Shapes:** Chester, Eve, Regent, Vogue

Harmony 12127 Regent shape cup and saucer. £90-110; $130-170

12128	Blocks and Bands. Dark yellow and black blocks. Grey lines blow blocks. Yellow, shaded border. Grey border and yellow inside cup. White ground. Dark yellow ring handle. Entered in pattern book during or after 1933. **Backstamp(s)**: Shelley 1925-1940 **Shapes:** Eve, Regent

Blocks and Bands 12128 Regent shape cup, saucer, and plate. £50-70; $80-100

12129	Blocks and Bands. Pattern inside cup. Green enamelling. Same as 12128. Entered in pattern book during or after 1933. **Backstamp(s)**: Shelley 1925-1940 **Shapes:** Regent
12130	**Bands and Lines**. Shades of fawn and yellow bands and lines on a white ground. Orange ring handle. Entered in pattern book during or after 1933. **Backstamp(s)**: Shelley 1925-1940 **Shapes:** Regent
12131	**Bands and Lines**. Coral and black. Entered in pattern book during or after 1933. /A Amber /B Blue /G Green /O Orange. **Backstamp(s)**: Shelley 1925-1940 **Shapes:** Regent
12132	**Bands and Lines**. Shades of yellow and green bands and lines on white ground. Green ring handle. Entered in pattern book during or after 1933. /G grey /B blue Entered in pattern book during or after 1933. **Backstamp(s)**: Shelley 1925-1940 **Shapes:** Regent
12133	Green and silver bands. Inside cup, saucer, and plate, broad green and silver bands near the rim/edge. Outside cup, thin green bands near the foot. Foot has silver band. Main part of saucer has similar lines to outside cup. White ground. Entered in pattern book during or after 1933. /B Blue and silver /BL Black and silver /M Purple and silver /P Pink and silver /T Turquoise and silver. **Backstamp(s)**: Shelley 1925-1940 **Shapes:** Eve
12134	**Bands and Lines**. Entered in pattern book during or after 1933. **Backstamp(s)**: Shelley 1925-1940 **Shapes:** Vogue
12135	Blue bands and silver handle. Entered in pattern book during or after 1933. **Backstamp(s)**: Shelley 1925-1940 **Shapes:** Eve
12136	**Bands and Lines**. Red and silver. Entered in pattern book during or after 1933. **Backstamp(s)**: Shelley 1925-1940 **Shapes:** Vogue
12137	Blue band and silver lines. Entered in pattern book during or after 1933. **Backstamp(s)**: Shelley 1925-1940 **Shapes:** Eve
12138	Green band and silver lines. Entered in pattern book during or after 1933. **Backstamp(s)**: Shelley 1925-1940 **Shapes:** Eve
12139	Plain colour outside cup and on saucer. Gold inside cup. Entered in pattern book during or after 1933. /S Silver. **Backstamp(s)**: Shelley 1925-1940 **Shapes:** Eve
12140	Green and gold bands. Inside cup, saucer, and plate, broad green and gold bands near the rim/edge. Outside cup, thin green bands near the foot. Foot has gold band. Main part of saucer has similar lines to outside cup. White ground. Entered in pattern book during or after 1933. /BL black and gold /R red and gold. **Backstamp(s)**: Shelley 1925-1940 **Shapes:** Eve
12141	**Wild Rose**. Orange roses with green and yellow foliage. Rose spray inside cup. White ground. Blue edges. Entered in pattern book during or after 1933. **Backstamp(s)**: Shelley 1925-1940 **Shapes:** Mayfair, Vincent
12142	**Wild Rose**. Roses and foliage. Rose spray inside cup. Entered in pattern book during or after 1933. **Backstamp(s)**: Shelley 1925-1940 **Shapes:** Vincent
12143	**Primrose**. Entered in pattern book during or after 1933. **Backstamp(s)**: Shelley 1925-1940 **Shapes:** Vincent
12144	**Gladioli**. Green print. Yellow, blue, red, and green flowers and foliage. Blue edges and ring handle. Entered in pattern book during or after 1933. **Backstamp(s)**: Shelley 1925-1940 **Shapes:** Regent
12145	**Anemone**. Green print. Three large flowers. Entered in pattern book during or after 1933. **Backstamp(s)**: Shelley 1925-1940 **Shapes:** Regent, York
12146	**Anemone Bunch**. Pink, blue, yellow, and orange anemones with green leaves on ivory ground. Large bunches inside cup and on saucer and plate. Small bunch outside cup. Narrow blue band on outer edge of saucer and plate. Broad green band inside blue band. Blue ring handle. Entered in pattern book during or after 1933. **Backstamp(s)**: Shelley 1925-1940 **Shapes:** York
12147	**Anemone Bunch**. Yellow and orange anemones with green leaves on ivory ground. Yellow inside cup. Black line on outer edge of saucer and plate. Broad yellow band below black band. Yellow edges and dark yellow handle. Entered in pattern book during or after 1933. **Backstamp(s)**: Shelley 1925-1940 **Shapes:** York

Anemone Bunch 12147 York shape cup, saucer, and plate. £50-70; $80-100

12148	**Anemone Bunch**. Brown print. Pink, blue, yellow, and orange anemones with green leaves on ivory ground. Large bunches inside cup and on saucer and plate. Small bunch outside cup. Narrow blue band on outer edge of saucer and plate. Broad green band inside blue band. Blue ring handle. Entered in pattern book during or after 1933. **Backstamp(s)**: Shelley 1925-1940 **Shapes:** Regent
12149	**Primrose**. Entered in pattern book during or after 1933. **Backstamp(s)**: Shelley 1925-1940 **Shapes:** York
12150	Entered in pattern book during or after 1933. **Backstamp(s)**: Shelley 1925-1940 **Shapes:** York
12151	Entered in pattern book during or after 1933. **Backstamp(s)**: Shelley 1925-1940 **Shapes:** Vincent
12152	**Anemone**. Black print. Anemones with

Pattern	Description & Shapes
	leaves. White ground. Blue edges and handle. Entered in pattern book during or after 1933. **Backstamp(s)**: Shelley 1925-1940 **Shapes:** Queen Anne
12153	**Violets**. Grey print. Yellow violets with a green leaf on small panels. Grey flowers on large panels. White ground. Orange edges. Entered in pattern book during or after 1933. **Backstamp(s)**: Shelley 1925-1940 **Shapes:** Queen Anne
12154	**Violets**. Brown print. Blue violets with a green leaf on small panels. Grey flowers on large panels. White ground. Blue edges. Entered in pattern book during or after 1933. **Backstamp(s)**: Shelley 1925-1940 **Shapes:** Queen Anne
12155	**Woodland Bluebells**. Grey print. Enamelled in blue, coral, and green. Bluebells set against woodland. Pattern outside cup, saucer, and plate. Centre of saucer and blank. White ground. Green edges. Entered in pattern book during or after 1933. **Backstamp(s)**: Shelley 1925-1940 **Shapes:** Queen Anne
12156	**Woodland Bluebells**. Grey print, Enamelled in orange and green. Bluebells set against woodland. Pattern outside cup, saucer, and plate. Centre of saucer and blank. White ground. Green edges. Entered in pattern book during or after 1933. **Backstamp(s)**: Shelley 1925-1940 **Shapes:** Queen Anne
12157	**Woodland Bluebells**. Grey print, Enamelled in black, orange, and yellow. Orange bluebells set against black and grey woodland. Pattern outside cup, saucer, and plate. Centre of saucer and blank. White ground. Black edges. Entered in pattern book during or after 1933. **Backstamp(s)**: Shelley 1925-1940 **Shapes:** Queen Anne

Woodland Bluebells 12157 Queen Anne shape cup, saucer, and plate. £80-100; $120-160

12158	**Woodland Bluebells**. Black print, Bluebells set against woodland. Pattern outside cup, saucer, and plate. Centre of saucer and blank. Colour in small panels. White ground. Gold edges. Handle same colour as small panels. Entered in pattern book during or after 1933. **Backstamp(s)**: Shelley 1925-1940 **Shapes:** Queen Anne
12159-12160	Entered in pattern book during or after 1933. **Backstamp(s)**: Shelley 1925-1940 **Shapes:** York
12161	Entered in pattern book during or after 1933. **Backstamp(s)**: Shelley 1925-1940 **Shapes:** Vincent
12162-12164	Entered in pattern book during or after 1933 for export to Canada. **Backstamp(s)**: Shelley 1925-1940 **Shapes:** Dainty
12165	Green apples with yellow and pink leaves. Same as 11946. Entered in pattern book during or after 1933. **Backstamp(s)**: Shelley 1925-1940 **Shapes:** Regent
12166	**Cornflowers**. Blue cornflowers and yellow corn ears. Blue edges and ring handle. Entered in pattern book during or after 1933. **Backstamp(s)**: Shelley 1925-1940 **Shapes:** Regent
12167	**Bluebird**. Blue print. Entered in pattern book during or after 1933. **Backstamp(s)**: Shelley 1925-1940 **Shapes:** Regent
12168	**Swirls**. Shaded green, grey, and black lines and bands on white ground. Inside cup and main body of saucer are green. Green shades with grey and black outside cup and centre of saucer. Entered in pattern book during or after 1933. **Backstamp(s)**: Shelley 1925-1940 **Shapes:** Regent

Swirls 12168 Regent shape cup and saucer. £50-60; $80-90

12169	**Swirls**. Black, pink, and orange. Entered in pattern book during or after 1933. **Backstamp(s)**: Shelley 1925-1940 **Shapes:** Regent
12170	**Swirls**. Black, blue, and grey. Entered in pattern book during or after 1933. /SB Peacock green and blue. **Backstamp(s)**: Shelley 1925-1940 **Shapes:** Regent
12171	**Swirls**. Shaded yellow and green lines and bands on white ground. Inside cup and main body of saucer are yellow. Green shades and some black outside cup and centre of saucer. Entered in pattern book during or after 1933. **Backstamp(s)**: Shelley 1925-1940 **Shapes:** Regent
12172	Entered in pattern book during or after 1933. **Backstamp(s)**: Shelley 1925-1940 **Shapes:** Carlton
12173	**Century Rose**. Same as 12087. Entered in pattern book during or after 1933. **Backstamp(s)**: Shelley 1925-1940 **Shapes:** Carlton, Savoy
12174	**Ivy**. Same as 12088. Entered in pattern book during or after 1933. **Backstamp(s)**: Shelley 1925-1940 **Shapes:** Carlton, Savoy
12175	**Rose and Beads**. Same as 12090. Entered in pattern book during or after 1933. **Backstamp(s)**: Shelley 1925-1940 **Shapes:** Carlton, Savoy
12176	**Fern Border**. Same as 12091. Entered in pattern book during or after 1933. **Backstamp(s)**: Shelley 1925-1940 **Shapes:** Carlton, Savoy
12177	**Bunch of Grapes**. Brown print. Grapes with leaves on small panels. Leaves and tendrils on large panels. Fruit with green leaves on saucer and centre of plate. Various colour grounds. Gold edges. Entered in pattern book during or after 1933. **Backstamp(s)**: Shelley 1925-1940 **Shapes:** Queen Anne
12178	Peaches and Grapes. Brown print. Fruit with leaves on a white ground on small panels. Leaves and tendrils on large panels on a coloured ground. Spots on panel joins. Gold edges. Tulip handle. Entered in pattern book during or after 1933. **Backstamp(s)**: Shelley 1925-1940 **Shapes:** Floral Queen Anne
12179-12181	Entered in pattern book during or after 1933. **Backstamp(s)**: Shelley 1925-1940 **Shapes:** Dainty
12182	Three open flowers with leaves. Grey print. Gold edges. Entered in pattern book during or after 1933. **Backstamp(s)**: Shelley 1925-1940 **Shapes:** Regent
12183	**Poppies**. Black print. Red poppies. Sun at base of cup. Green edges and handle. Entered in pattern book during or after 1933. **Backstamp(s)**: Shelley 1925-1940 **Shapes:** Regent
12184	**Fruit**. Black print. Red apples. Entered in pattern book during or after 1933. **Backstamp(s)**: Shelley 1925-1940 **Shapes:** Regent
12185	**Fruit**. Black print. Green apples. Entered in pattern book during or after 1933. **Backstamp(s)**: Shelley 1925-1940 **Shapes:** Regent
12186	Apple Blossom. Black print. Pink and green blossom. Entered in pattern book during or after 1933. **Backstamp(s)**: Shelley 1925-1940 **Shapes:** Regent
12187-12188	Entered in pattern book during or after 1933. **Backstamp(s)**: Shelley 1925-1940 **Shapes:** Dainty
12189	**Phlox**. Black print. Pink and blue phlox with grey leaves. Patterned inside and outside cup. Saucer has outer blue band surrounding the patterned centre of the saucer. Blue trim and ring handle. Entered in pattern book during or after 1933. **Backstamp(s)**: Shelley 1924-1940 **Shapes:** Regent, Regent demi

Blue **Phlox** 12189 Regent shape cup, saucer, and plate. £40-50; $80-90

Pattern	Description & Shapes

12190 **Phlox**. Brown print. Yellow, orange, and green phlox with brown leaves. Patterned inside and outside cup. Saucer has outer yellow band surrounding the patterned centre of the saucer. Yellow trim and ring handle. Entered in pattern book during or after 1933.
Backstamp(s): Shelley 1924-1940
Shapes: Regent, Regent demi

Yellow **Phlox** 12190 Regent shape cup and saucer. £40-50; $80-90

12191 **Phlox**. Pink and blue flowers. Entered in pattern book during or after 1933.
Backstamp(s): Shelley 1925-1940
Shapes: York

12192 **Violets**. Gold print. Blue and mauve violets with a green leaf on small panels. Flowers on large panels. White ground. Gold edges. Gold and blue handle. Entered in pattern book during or after 1933.
Backstamp(s): Shelley 1925-1940
Shapes: Queen Anne

12193 **Violets**. Gold print. Yellow violets with a green leaf on small panels. Flowers on large panels. White ground. Gold edges. Gold and yellow handle. Entered in pattern book during or after 1933.
Backstamp(s): Shelley 1925-1940
Shapes: Queen Anne

12194 Entered in pattern book during or after 1933.
Backstamp(s): Shelley 1925-1940
Shapes: Mayfair

12195 Stylised tree. Blue and pink flowers. Gold print. Entered in pattern book during or after 1933.
Backstamp(s): Shelley 1925-1940
Shapes: Regent

12196 Pink, blue, and yellow balloons on short branches with green leaves. Gold print. Entered in pattern book during or after 1933.
Backstamp(s): Shelley 1925-1940
Shapes: Regent

12197 **Fruit**. Black print. Two red apples. Entered in pattern book during or after 1933.
Backstamp(s): Shelley 1925-1940
Shapes: Regent

12198 **Fruit**. Black print. Two green apples. Entered in pattern book during or after 1933.
Backstamp(s): Shelley 1925-1940
Shapes: Regent

12199 **Fruit**. Black print. Two orange apples. Entered in pattern book during or after 1933.
Backstamp(s): Shelley 1925-1940
Shapes: Regent

12200 **Swirls**. Mauve, green, and black. Entered in pattern book during or after 1933.
Backstamp(s): Shelley 1925-1940
Shapes: Regent

12201 **Swirls**. Brown, orange, and green. Entered in pattern book during or after 1933.
Backstamp(s): Shelley 1925-1940
Shapes: Regent

12202 **Woodland Bluebells**. Gold print, Enamelled in green and mauve. Bluebells set against woodland. Pattern outside cup, saucer, and plate. Centre of saucer and blank. White ground. Gold edges. Handle green and gold. Entered in pattern book during or after 1933.
Backstamp(s): Shelley 1925-1940
Shapes: Queen Anne

12203 **Phlox**. Gold print. Yellow and green phlox with grey leaves. Patterned inside and outside cup. Saucer has outer blue band surrounding the patterned centre of the saucer. Gold trim and ring handle. Entered in pattern book during or after 1933.
Backstamp(s): Shelley 1925-1940
Shapes: Regent

12204 **Acacia**. Black print. Yellow and orange flowers. Entered in pattern book during or after 1933.
Backstamp(s): Shelley 1925-1940
Shapes: Regent

12205 **Berries**. Entered in pattern book during or after 1933.
Backstamp(s): Shelley 1925-1940
Shapes: Regent

12206 Poppies. Woodland scene. Entered in pattern book during or after 1933.
Backstamp(s): Shelley 1925-1940
Shapes: York

12207 **Patches and Shades**. Entered in pattern book during or after 1933.
Backstamp(s): Shelley 1925-1940
Shapes: Regent

12208 Plain colour with gold band. Entered in pattern book during or after 1933.
Backstamp(s): Shelley 1925-1940
Shapes: Regent

12209 Entered in pattern book during or after 1933.
Backstamp(s): Shelley 1925-1940
Shapes: York

12210 Polka Dot. Brown print. Amber dots. Entered in pattern book during or after 1933.
Backstamp(s): Shelley 1925-1940
Shapes: Regent

12211 Polka Dot. Black print. Green dots. Entered in pattern book during or after 1933.
Backstamp(s): Shelley 1925-1940
Shapes: Regent

12212 Polka Dot. Black print. Orange dots. Entered in pattern book during or after 1933.
Backstamp(s): Shelley 1925-1940
Shapes: Regent

12213 Polka Dot. Black print. Blue dots. Blue trim and handles.
Backstamp(s):
Shapes: Regent

12214 Blue delphiniums, orange, blue, and yellow anemone-like flowers, green foliage against grey leaves. Grey tree with dashes of green and yellow. Grey and yellow shading at foot of flowers and tree. White ground. Blue edges. Entered in pattern book during or after 1933.
Backstamp(s): Shelley 1925-1940
Shapes: York

12215 Floral pattern enamelled in orange and green. Entered in pattern book during or after 1933.
Backstamp(s): Shelley 1925-1940
Shapes: Regent

12216 **Blue and Pink Daisy**. Pink and blue daisies with green leaves against shades of grey. White ground. Sky blue edges and ring handle. Entered in pattern book during or after 1933.
Backstamp(s): Shelley 1925-1940
Shapes: Oxford, Regent, Strand, Vincent

Blue and Pink Daisies 12216 Regent shape cup and saucer. £40-50; $80-90

12217 Entered in pattern book during or after 1933.
Backstamp(s): Shelley 1925-1940
Shapes: Strand

12218 Pink and blue flowers with green and grey leaves on a white ground. Flower spray also inside cup. Pale green edges and ring handle. Entered in pattern book during or after 1933.
Backstamp(s): Shelley 1925-1940
Shapes: Oxford, York

Pink and blue flowers 12218 Oxford shape cup and saucer. £40-50; $80-100

12219 **Colour Bands**. Entered in pattern book during or after 1933.
/A Brown
/B Grey
/C Green.
Backstamp(s): Shelley 1925-1940
Shapes: Regent

12220 Bands and triangles. Entered in pattern book during or after 1933.
Backstamp(s): Shelley 1925-1940
Shapes: Regent

12221 **Fruit**. Gold print. Two orange apples. Entered in pattern book during or after 1933.
Backstamp(s): Shelley 1925-1940
Shapes: Regent

12222 Blocks and Bands. Gold print. Green and yellow. Entered in pattern book during or after 1933.
Backstamp(s): Shelley 1925-1940
Shapes: Regent

12223 Polka Dot. Gold print. Green dots. Entered in pattern book during or after 1933.
Backstamp(s): Shelley 1925-1940
Shapes: Regent

12224 **Chippendale**. Enamelled in turquoise and black on black Blue edges, handle, and foot. Entered in pattern book during or after 1933.

Pattern	Description & Shapes
	Backstamp(s): Shelley 1925-1940 **Shapes:** Gainsborough, Strand
12225	Large yellow poppies with green foliage on a white ground. Green scroll border, which is also inside cup. Yellow edges. Entered in pattern book during or after 1933. **Backstamp(s)**: Shelley 1925-1940 **Shapes:** Strand
12226	Tall pink poppies and green leaves. Grey trees behind the poppies. White ground. Green edges and handle. Entered in pattern book during or after 1933. **Backstamp(s)**: Shelley 1925-1940 **Shapes:** Princess

Pink poppy 12226 Princess shape cup, saucer, and plate. £80-100; $120-160

12227 Yellow and orange poppies and green leaves. Brown trees behind the poppies. White ground. Orange edges and handle. Entered in pattern book during or after 1933.
Backstamp(s): Shelley 1925-1940
Shapes: Princess

12228 Poppies. Blue, yellow, and green. Entered in pattern book during or after 1933.
Backstamp(s): Shelley 1925-1940
Shapes: Regent

12229 Poppies. Amber, blue, and green. Entered in pattern book during or after 1933.
Backstamp(s): Shelley 1925-1940
Shapes: Regent

Poppies 12229 Regent shape cup, saucer, and plate. £60-80; $140-160

12230 Small blue and yellow phlox flowers against shades of grey. White ground. Green edges and ring handle. Entered in pattern book during or after 1933.
Backstamp(s): Shelley 1925-1940
Shapes: Regent

Floral 12230 Ludlow shape cup and saucer. £50-60; $110-130

Floral 12230 Stratford shape cup and saucer. £50-60; $110-130

12231 Small amber and yellow phlox flowers. Entered in pattern book during or after 1933.
Backstamp(s): Shelley 1925-1940
Shapes: Regent

12232 Small blue and pink phlox flowers. Entered in pattern book during or after 1933.
Backstamp(s): Shelley 1925-1940
Shapes: Regent

12233 **Silk**. Also known as Pyjama Stripe. Blue. Entered in pattern book during or after 1933.
Backstamp(s): Shelley 1925-1940
Shapes: Regent

12234 **Silk**. Also known as Pyjama Stripe. Entered in pattern book during or after 1933.
Backstamp(s): Shelley 1925-1940
Shapes: Regent

12235 **Silk**. Also known as Pyjama Stripe. Amber. Entered in pattern book during or after 1933.
Backstamp(s): Shelley 1925-1940
Shapes: Regent

12236-12239 Entered in pattern book during or after 1933.
Backstamp(s): Shelley 1925-1940
Shapes: Strand

12240 Bunches and sprays of pink roses, blue, white, and yellow flowers with green leaves. One spray also inside cup. White ground. Green edges and handle. Entered in pattern book during or after 1933.
Backstamp(s): Shelley 1925-1940
Shapes: Dainty, Strand, Stratford

12241-12242 Entered in pattern book during or after 1933.
Backstamp(s): Shelley 1925-1940
Shapes: York

12243-12247 Entered in pattern book during or after 1933.
Backstamp(s): Shelley 1925-1940
Shapes: Strand

12248 **Patches and Shades**. Graduated fawn rectangles. Colour starts from ginger, fading through to very light fawn in the last rectangle. Gold edges and ring on saucer, fawn ring handle. White ground. Patter book c. 1933.
/B blue
/BH gold handle
/G green
/Y orange.
Backstamp(s): Shelley 1925-1940
Shapes: Regent

Patches and Shades 12248/G Regent shape cup and saucer. £50-60; $80-90

12249-12254 Entered in pattern book during or after 1933.
Backstamp(s): Shelley 1925-1940
Shapes: Princess

12255 **Acacia**. Yellow and orange acacia flowers with grey shaded foliage. Orange edges and handle.
Backstamp(s): Shelley 1925-1940 "Made Expressly for Bevilles Melbourne"
Shapes: Regent

12256 **Daffodil**. Yellow. Entered in pattern book during or after 1933.
Backstamp(s): Shelley 1925-1940
Shapes: Princess

12257 **Daffodil**. Green. Entered in pattern book during or after 1933.
Backstamp(s): Shelley 1925-1940
Shapes: Princess

12258-12261 Entered in pattern book during or after 1933.
Backstamp(s): Shelley 1925-1940
Shapes: Princess

12262 **Phlox**. Green. Entered in pattern book during or after 1933.
Backstamp(s): Shelley 1925-1940
Shapes: Princess

12263 **Violets**. Pink. Entered in pattern book during or after 1933.
Backstamp(s): Shelley 1925-1940
Shapes: Princess

12264 **Coral Daisy**. Green. Entered in pattern book during or after 1933.
Backstamp(s): Shelley 1925-1940
Shapes: Princess

12265-12266 Entered in pattern book during or after 1933.
Backstamp(s): Shelley 1925-1940
Shapes: York

12267-12271 Entered in pattern book during or after

Pattern Description & Shapes

1933.
Backstamp(s): Shelley 1925-1940
Shapes: Chester

12272 Entered in pattern book during or after 1934.
Backstamp(s): Shelley 1925-1940
Shapes: York

12273 Bands in black, grey, and gold. Entered in pattern book during or after 1934.
/S Silver
Backstamp(s): Shelley 1925-1940
Shapes: Regent

12274 Dog Roses. Yellow. Entered in pattern book during or after 1934.
/B Blue.
Backstamp(s): Shelley 1925-1940
Shapes: Regent

Dog Roses 12274 Regent shape cup and saucer. £40-50; $80-90

12275 Dog Roses. Pink. Entered in pattern book during or after 1934.
/B Blue flowers included.
Backstamp(s): Shelley 1925-1940
Shapes: Regent

12276 **Dog Rose**. Yellow. Entered in pattern book during or after 1934.
Backstamp(s): Shelley 1925-1940
Shapes: Mayfair

12277 **Dog Rose**. Pink. Entered in pattern book during or after 1934.
Backstamp(s): Shelley 1925-1940
Shapes: Mayfair

12278-
12279 Entered in pattern book during or after 1934.
Backstamp(s): Shelley 1925-1940
Shapes: Mayfair

12280 Three large pink flowers with four small blue ones and green leaves. Silver edges. Silver and pink handle. Entered in pattern book during or after 1934.
Backstamp(s): Shelley 1925-1940
Shapes: Eve

12281 Three large mauve and four small flowers with green leaves. Silver edges. Silver and green handle. Entered in pattern book during or after 1934.
Backstamp(s): Shelley 1925-1940
Shapes: Eve

12282 **Sunset and Flowers**. Mauve print. Bright orange setting sun. Blue flower. Fluffy clouds. Black trees and yellow haze around sunset. Sunset reflected in water. White ground. Silver edges. Similar to 11691. Entered in pattern book during or after 1934.
Backstamp(s): Shelley 1925-1940
Shapes: Eve

12283 Poppies. Woodland scene. Same as 12206. Entered in pattern book during or after 1934.
Backstamp(s): Shelley 1925-1940
Shapes: Regent

12284 **Nemesia**. Entered in pattern book during or after 1934.
Backstamp(s): Shelley 1925-1940
Shapes: Mayfair

12285 **Nemesia**. Same as 12284. Entered in pattern book during or after 1934.
Backstamp(s): Shelley 1925-1940
Shapes: Eve

12286 **Nemesia**. Pink and blue. Entered in pattern book during or after 1934.
Backstamp(s): Shelley 1925-1940
Shapes: Regent

12287 **Apple Blossom**. Entered in pattern book during or after 1934.
Backstamp(s): Shelley 1925-1940
Shapes: Eve

12288 **Motif**. Large pink, blue, and yellow flowers Pink flower spray in centre of saucer. Blue bands and lines inside cup, border of saucer, and plate. White ground. Blue edges and ring handle. Entered in pattern book during or after 1934.
Backstamp(s): Shelley 1940-1966
Shapes: Eve, Regent

Motif 12288 Regent shape cup and saucer. £40-50; $80-90

12289 Bands. Black and green. Entered in pattern book during or after 1934.
Backstamp(s): Shelley 1925-1940
Shapes: Regent

12290 Curved line and blocks. Black, green, and silver. Entered in pattern book during or after 1934.
Backstamp(s): Shelley 1925-1940
Shapes: Regent

12291 **Bands and Lines**. Silver and grey. Entered in pattern book during or after 1934.
Backstamp(s): Shelley 1925-1940
Shapes: Eve

12292 Entered in pattern book during or after 1934.
Backstamp(s): Shelley 1925-1940
Shapes: Regent

12293 **Motif**. Entered in pattern book during or after 1934.
Backstamp(s): Shelley 1925-1940
Shapes: Eve

12294 **Motif**. Entered in pattern book during or after 1934.
Backstamp(s): Shelley 1925-1940
Shapes: Eve

12295 Border of Leaves. Gold print. Yellow, black, and brown. Entered in pattern book during or after 1934.
Backstamp(s): Shelley 1925-1940
Shapes: Regent

12296 Border of Leaves. Black print. Green, black, and brown. Entered in pattern book during or after 1934.
Backstamp(s): Shelley 1925-1940
Shapes: Regent

12297 Border of Leaves. Print in old gold. Turkish blue leaves and handle. Entered in pattern book during or after 1934.
Backstamp(s): Shelley 1925-1940
Shapes: Regent

12298 Border of Leaves. Brown print. Amber, black, and brown. Entered in pattern book during or after 1934.
Backstamp(s): Shelley 1925-1940
Shapes: Regent

12299 **Cape Gooseberry**. Orange and yellow gooseberries and brown leaves on a white ground. Orange edges and ring handle. Entered in pattern book during or after 1934.
Backstamp(s): Shelley 1925-1940
Shapes: Regent

12300 Pink and grey flowers. Pink and grey border inside cup and on saucer and plate. White ground. Pink ring handle. Entered in pattern book during or after 1934.
Backstamp(s): Shelley 1925-1940
Shapes: Oxford

Pink and grey flowers 12300 Oxford shape cup and saucer. £40-50; $80-100

12301 Yellow and grey flowers. Yellow and grey border inside cup and on saucer and plate. White ground. Yellow ring handle. Entered in pattern book during or after 1934.
Backstamp(s): Shelley 1925-1940
Shapes: Oxford

Yellow and grey flowers 12301 Oxford shape cup and saucer. £40-50; $80-100

Pattern **Description & Shapes**

12302 Bands. Coral and black. Entered in pattern book during or after 1934.
Backstamp(s): Shelley 1925-1940
Shapes: Regent

12303 **Fruit**. Black print. Two coral apples. Entered in pattern book during or after 1934.
Backstamp(s): Shelley 1925-1940
Shapes: Regent

12304 Curved line and blocks. Coral. Entered in pattern book during or after 1934.
Backstamp(s): Shelley 1925-1940
Shapes: Regent

12305 Red, grey, and silver bands. White ground. Entered in pattern book during or after 1934.
Backstamp(s): Shelley 1925-1940
Shapes: Eve

12306 **Tulip**. Brown print. Pink and yellow flowers. Entered in pattern book during or after 1934.
Backstamp(s): Shelley 1925-1940
Shapes: Eve

12307 Circle of stylised fruit. Blue and green with silver lines. Entered in pattern book during or after 1934.
Backstamp(s): Shelley 1925-1940
Shapes: Regent

12308 Circle of stylised fruit. Green tint with gold lines. Entered in pattern book during or after 1934.
/S Silver.
Backstamp(s): Shelley 1925-1940
Shapes: Regent

12309 Circle of stylised fruit. Coral tint with silver lines. Entered in pattern book during or after 1934.
Backstamp(s): Shelley 1925-1940
Shapes: Regent

12310 **Siberian Wallflower**. Entered in pattern book during or after 1934.
Backstamp(s): Shelley 1925-1940
Shapes: Oxford

12311 **Stocks**. Mauve, pink, and white stocks with green leaves. Green border on cup and on saucer. White ground. Green edges, foot and handle.
Backstamp(s): Shelley 1940-1966
Shapes: Oxford, Richmond

12312 **Polyanthus**. Pink and blue bell-like flowers with green leaves. Grey band with pink shaded border inside cup. White ground. Pink edges and ring handle. Entered in pattern book during or after 1934.
Backstamp(s): Shelley 1940-1966
Shapes: Oxford, Regent

12313 **Polyanthus**. Amber and yellow bell-like flowers with green leaves. Band with shaded border inside cup. White ground. Yellow edges and ring handle. Entered in pattern book during or after 1934.
Backstamp(s): Shelley 1925-1940
Shapes: Oxford, Regent

12314 **Violets**. Mauve print. Blue, yellow, and green flowers and leaves. Entered in pattern book during or after 1934.
Backstamp(s): Shelley 1925-1940
Shapes: Regent

12315 **Violets**. Black print. Pink and green flowers and leaves. Silver handle. Entered in pattern book during or after 1934.
Backstamp(s): Shelley 1925-1940
Shapes: Regent

12316 Bands and block in black, grey and red. Grey band inside cup. White ground. Red ring handle. Same as 0177. Similar to 0198. Entered in pattern book during or after 1934.
Backstamp(s): Shelley 1940-1966
Shapes: Oxford

Right:
Bands and blocks 12316 Oxford shape cup and saucer. £40-50; $80-100

12317 Entered in pattern book during or after 1934.
Backstamp(s): Shelley 1925-1940
Shapes: Oxford

12318 **Hydrangea**. Black print. Pink and blue flowers with green leaves. Entered in pattern book during or after 1934.
Backstamp(s): Shelley 1925-1940
Shapes: Eve

12319 **Hydrangea**. Brown print. Pale amber and yellow flowers with green leaves. Entered in pattern book during or after 1934.
Backstamp(s): Shelley 1925-1940
Shapes: Eve

12320 Entered in pattern book during or after 1934.
Backstamp(s): Shelley 1925-1940
Shapes: Oxford

12321 Acid on platinum border. Entered in pattern book during or after 1934.
/120 Gold.
Backstamp(s): Shelley 1925-1940
Shapes: Eve

12322 **Swirls**. Shaded blue and grey lines on white ground. Grey handle. Entered in pattern book during or after 1934.
Backstamp(s): Shelley 1925-1940
Shapes: Regent

12323 **Swirls**. Shaded green lines on white ground. Green handle. Entered in pattern book during or after 1934.
Backstamp(s): Shelley 1925-1940
Shapes: Regent

Swirls 12323 Regent shape cup and saucer. £50-60; $80-90

12324 **Swirls**. Shaded brown lines on white ground. Brown handle. Entered in pattern book during or after 1934.
Backstamp(s): Shelley 1925-1940
Shapes: Regent

12325 **Phlox**. Pink and green. Entered in pattern book during or after 1934.
Backstamp(s): Shelley 1925-1940
Shapes: Regent

12326 **Tulip**. Black print. Pink and yellow flowers. Entered in pattern book during or after 1934.
Backstamp(s): Shelley 1925-1940
Shapes: Eve

12327-
12328 Entered in pattern book during or after 1934.
Backstamp(s): Shelley 1925-1940
Shapes: Oxford

12329 **Poppies**. Yellow and orange poppies with green leaves. Grey shades behind the poppies. White ground. Fawn ring handle. Entered in pattern book during or after 1934.
Backstamp(s): Shelley 1925-1940
Shapes: Oxford, Regent

12330 **Poppies**. Pink and blue poppies with green leaves. Grey shades behind the poppies. White ground. Fawn ring handle. Entered in pattern book during or after 1934.
Backstamp(s): Shelley 1925-1940
Shapes: Oxford, Regent

12331-
12332 Entered in pattern book during or after 1934.
Backstamp(s): Shelley 1925-1940
Shapes: Oxford

12333 Large blue poppies with green and grey leaves on a white ground. Poppy spray also inside cup. Blue edges and ring handle. Entered in pattern book during or after 1934.
Backstamp(s): Shelley 1925-1940
Shapes: Oxford

Blue poppies 12333 Oxford shape cup and saucer. £40-50; $80-100

12334-
12335 Entered in pattern book during or after 1934.
Backstamp(s): Shelley 1925-1940
Shapes: Oxford

12336 **Lakeland**. Grey print. Bluebird in the foreground. Grey and yellow lakeland scene with trees. Yellow shaded border inside cup. White ground. Dark yellow ring handle. Entered in pattern book during or after 1934.
/P Pink instead of yellow.
Backstamp(s): Shelley 1925-1940
Shapes: Regent

Pattern	Description & Shapes
12337	**Lakeland**. Scene of lake, trees, and birds in shades of blue and grey. Blue edge and handle. Entered in pattern book during or after 1934. **Backstamp(s)**: Shelley 1925-1940 **Shapes:** Regent

Lakeland 12337 Regent shape cup, saucer, and plate. £45-65; $75-120

12338 Dog Rose. Entered in pattern book during or after 1934.
Backstamp(s): Shelley 1925-1940
Shapes: Windsor

12339 Dog Rose. Entered in pattern book during or after 1934.
Backstamp(s): Shelley 1925-1940
Shapes: Windsor

12340-12341 Entered in pattern book during or after 1934.
Backstamp(s): Shelley 1925-1940
Shapes: Windsor

12342 Anemone. Entered in pattern book during or after 1934.
Backstamp(s): Shelley 1925-1940
Shapes: Windsor

12343 Anemone. Entered in pattern book during or after 1934.
Backstamp(s): Shelley 1925-1940
Shapes: Windsor

12344 Primula. Entered in pattern book during or after 1934.
Backstamp(s): Shelley 1925-1940
Shapes: Windsor

12345 Primula. Entered in pattern book during or after 1934.
Backstamp(s): Shelley 1925-1940
Shapes: Windsor

12346-12351 Entered in pattern book during or after 1934.
Backstamp(s): Shelley 1925-1940
Shapes: Mayfair

12352 **Violets**. Blue. Entered in pattern book during or after 1934.
Backstamp(s): Shelley 1925-1940
Shapes: Mayfair

12353 **Violets**. Pink. Entered in pattern book during or after 1934.
Backstamp(s): Shelley 1925-1940
Shapes: Mayfair

12354 **Nemesia**. Gold print. Orange flowers. Entered in pattern book during or after 1934.
Backstamp(s): Shelley 1925-1940
Shapes: Regent

12355 Green **Symphony**. Entered in pattern book during or after 1934.
Backstamp(s): Shelley 1925-1940
Shapes: Regent

12356 Blue **Symphony**. Entered in pattern book during or after 1934.
Backstamp(s): Shelley 1925-1940
Shapes: Regent

12358 Fawn **Symphony**. Entered in pattern book during or after 1934.
Backstamp(s): Shelley 1925-1940
Shapes: Regent

12359 **Violets**. Blue handle. Entered in pattern book during or after 1934.
Backstamp(s): Shelley 1925-1940
Shapes: Regent

12360 **Violets**. Pink handle. Entered in pattern book during or after 1934.
Backstamp(s): Shelley 1925-1940
Shapes: Regent

12361-12363 Entered in pattern book during or after 1935.
Backstamp(s): Shelley 1925-1940
Shapes: Oxford

12364 Entered in pattern book during or after 1935.
Backstamp(s): Shelley 1925-1940
Shapes: Mayfair

12365 **Bird Stitch**. Blue and green. Entered in pattern book during or after 1935.
Backstamp(s): Shelley 1925-1940
Shapes: Unknown

12366 **Bird Stitch**. Pink and green. Entered in pattern book during or after 1935.
Backstamp(s): Shelley 1925-1940
Shapes: Unknown

12367 **Bird Stitch**. Amber. Entered in pattern book during or after 1935.
Backstamp(s): Shelley 1925-1940
Shapes: Unknown

12368 **House**. Entered in pattern book during or after 1935.
Backstamp(s): Shelley 1925-1940
Shapes: Oxford

House print (no pattern number) Oxford shape cup and saucer. £40-50; $80-100

12369 **Bell Flower**. Pink and blue. Entered in pattern book during or after 1935.
Backstamp(s): Shelley 1925-1940
Shapes: Oxford

12370 **Bell Flower**. Yellow and amber. Entered in pattern book during or after 1935.
Backstamp(s): Shelley 1925-1940
Shapes: Oxford

12371 **Gladiola**. Amber and yellow. Entered in pattern book during or after 1935.
Backstamp(s): Shelley 1925-1940
Shapes: Oxford

12372 **Gladiola**. Pink. Entered in pattern book during or after 1935.
Backstamp(s): Shelley 1925-1940
Shapes: Oxford

12373 **Bands and Lines**. Fawn. Entered in pattern book during or after 1935.
Backstamp(s): Shelley 1925-1940
Shapes: Regent

12374 **Ashbourne**. Purple, orange, black, green, and gold flowers and leaves on a white ground. White border, then a purple and gold border. Gold edges. Same as 8524. Entered in pattern book during or after 1935.
Backstamp(s): Shelley 1925-1940
Shapes: Eve, Mayfair, Regent

12375 **Apple Blossom**. Entered in pattern book during or after 1935.
Backstamp(s): Shelley 1925-1940
Shapes: Eve, Oxford, Regent

12376 Poppies. Similar to 0236. Entered in pattern book during or after 1935.
Backstamp(s): Shelley 1925-1940
Shapes: Oxford

12377-12378 Entered in pattern book during or after 1935.
Backstamp(s): Shelley 1925-1940
Shapes: Oxford

12379 **Tree**. Amber. Entered in pattern book during or after 1935.
Backstamp(s): Shelley 1925-1940
Shapes: Oxford

12380 **Tree**. Green. Entered in pattern book during or after 1935.
Backstamp(s): Shelley 1925-1940
Shapes: Oxford

12381 **Tree**. Coral. Grey and orange border. Entered in pattern book during or after 1935.
Backstamp(s): Shelley 1925-1940
Shapes: Oxford

12382 **Iris**. Amber irises with green and brown leaves on brown print. White ground. Pink edges and ring handle. Entered in pattern book during or after 1935.
Backstamp(s): Shelley 1925-1940
Shapes: Regent

12383 **Iris**. Pink irises with green and grey leaves on brown print. White ground. Amber edges and ring handle. Entered in pattern book during or after 1935.
Backstamp(s): Shelley 1925-1940
Shapes: Regent

12384 **Iris**. Blue irises with yellow centres and green and grey leaves on black print. White ground. Blue edges and ring handle (Regent). Similar to 0231. Entered in pattern book during or after 1935.
Backstamp(s): Shelley 1925-1940
Shapes: Eve, Regent

12385 **Lilac**. Pink and blue. Entered in pattern book during or after 1935.
Backstamp(s): Shelley 1925-1940
Shapes: Oxford

12386 **Lilac**. Mauve and green. Entered in pattern book during or after 1935.
Backstamp(s): Shelley 1925-1940
Shapes: Oxford

12387 **Leaf Motif**. Green. Entered in pattern book during or after 1935.
Backstamp(s): Shelley 1925-1940
Shapes: Oxford

12388 **Leaf Motif**. Coral. Entered in pattern book during or after 1935.
Backstamp(s): Shelley 1925-1940
Shapes: Oxford, Regent

12389 **Leaf Motif**. Blue. Entered in pattern book during or after 1935.
Backstamp(s): Shelley 1925-1940
Shapes: Oxford, Regent

12390 **Blossom** or **Scarlet Splurge**. Outside cup and on saucer scarlet and white flowers against grey on a white ground. Inside cup has solid scarlet border between gold lines. Saucer has border of three gold lines and then the solid scarlet border. White ground. Scarlet ring handle. Entered in pattern book during or after 1935.
Backstamp(s): Shelley 1925-1940 Scarlet Splurge
Shapes: Oxford

12391 **Blossom**. Outside cup and on saucer green and white flowers against grey on a white ground. Inside cup has solid green border between gold lines. Saucer has border of three gold lines and then the solid green border. White ground. Green ring handle. Entered in pattern book during or after 1935.
Backstamp(s): Shelley 1925-1940
Shapes: Oxford

Blossom 12391 Oxford shape cup, saucer, and plate. £40-50; $80-100

Pattern	Description & Shapes
12392	Entered in pattern book during or after 1935. **Backstamp(s)**: Shelley 1925-1940 **Shapes:** Mayfair
12393	Outside cup and middle of saucer have pink bell-like flowers with grey stems and leaves. Saucer has broad bank of deep pink. Gold dontil border inside cup and on saucer. Ivory ground. Gold edges and ring handle. Deep pink foot. Entered in pattern book during or after 1935. **Backstamp(s)**: Shelley 1925-1940 **Shapes:** Mayfair

Pink bell flowers 12393 Court shape cup, saucer, and plate. £50-60

Pattern	Description & Shapes
12394-12395	Entered in pattern book during or after 1935. **Backstamp(s)**: Shelley 1925-1940 **Shapes:** Mayfair
12396	Entered in pattern book during or after 1935. **Backstamp(s)**: Shelley 1925-1940 **Shapes:** Oxford
12397-12399	Entered in pattern book during or after 1935. **Backstamp(s)**: Shelley 1925-1940 **Shapes:** Mayfair
12400	Pale blue wash. Entered in pattern book during or after 1935. **Backstamp(s)**: Shelley 1925-1940 **Shapes:** Regent
12401	Pale green wash. Entered in pattern book during or after 1935. **Backstamp(s)**: Shelley 1925-1940 **Shapes:** Regent
12402	Entered in pattern book during or after 1935. **Backstamp(s)**: Shelley 1925-1940 **Shapes:** Mayfair
12403	Pink and blue flowers with green foliage on a shaded grey to green ground. Green inside cup. Broad, green band on saucer. Pattern in centre of saucer on white ground. Gold ring between green band and pattern. Gold dontil edge inside cup and edge of saucers and plates. Gold edges and ring handle. Entered in pattern book during or after 1935. **Backstamp(s)**: Shelley 1925-1940 **Shapes:** Court, Mayfair
12404	Spike border. Brown and black. Entered in pattern book during or after 1935. **Backstamp(s)**: Shelley 1925-1940 **Shapes:** Regent
12405	**Swirls**. Grey and amber. Entered in pattern book during or after 1935. **Backstamp(s)**: Shelley 1925-1940 **Shapes:** Regent
12406	**Archway of Roses**. Black print. Garden with flowers that include hollyhocks and roses. Blue butterflies. Enamelled in blue, pink, yellow, and green. White ground. Blue edges. Green edges and ring handle. Entered in pattern book during or after 1935. **Backstamp(s)**: Shelley 1925-1940 **Shapes:** Regent
12407-12408	Entered in pattern book during or after 1935. **Backstamp(s)**: Shelley 1925-1940 **Shapes:** Oxford
12409	**Sheep and Cottage**. Sheep in a field next to a stream with a bridge over it. Cottage and trees in the background. Black print enamelled in pink, orange, blue, green, and brown. White ground. Gold edges and ruing handle. Entered in pattern book during or after 1935. **Backstamp(s)**: Shelley 1925-1940 **Shapes:** Regent
12410	Entered in pattern book during or after 1935. **Backstamp(s)**: Shelley 1925-1940 **Shapes:** Oxford
12411	**English Chintz**. Red, blue, and yellow flowers sprays with green and grey leaves. Striped mauve border on saucer and plate. White ground. Mauve-pink edges. Green ring handle. Entered in pattern book during or after 1935. **Backstamp(s)**: Shelley 1925-1940 English Chintz **Shapes:** Oxford, Regent
12412	Three blue flowers with green leaves. Entered in pattern book during or after 1935. **Backstamp(s)**: Shelley 1925-1940 **Shapes:** Regent
12413	Three pink flowers with green leaves. Entered in pattern book during or after 1935. **Backstamp(s)**: Shelley 1925-1940 **Shapes:** Regent
12414	**Japonica**. Coral. Entered in pattern book during or after 1935. /120 Silver. **Backstamp(s)**: Shelley 1925-1940 **Shapes:** Regent
12415	**Japonica**. Pink. Entered in pattern book during or after 1935. /S Silver. **Backstamp(s)**: Shelley 1925-1940 **Shapes:** Regent
12416	Apple Blossom. Grey print. Pink and green blossoms with grey leaves and branches on an ivory ground inside and outside cup. Pink swirls at base both inside and outside cup. Saucer has grey border with pink swirls fading to ivory. Entered in pattern book during or after 1935. **Backstamp(s)**: Shelley 1925-1940 **Shapes:** Regent
12417	Entered in pattern book during or after 1935. **Backstamp(s)**: Shelley 1925-1940 **Shapes:** Mayfair
12418	**Primula**. Black print. Pink and blue flowers with green leaves. Entered in pattern book during or after 1935. **Backstamp(s)**: Shelley 1925-1940 **Shapes:** Regent
12419	**Nemesia**. Mauve print. Blue flowers with green leaves. Entered in pattern book during or after 1935. **Backstamp(s)**: Shelley 1925-1940 **Shapes:** Regent
12420	**Laburnum**. Green print. Yellow flowers. Entered in pattern book during or after 1935. /B Brown print. **Backstamp(s)**: Shelley 1925-1940 **Shapes:** Eve
12421	**Wisteria**. Mauve print. Blue flowers and green leaves. Gold edges. Entered in pattern book during or after 1935. **Backstamp(s)**: Shelley 1925-1940 **Shapes:** Eve, Oxford
12422	Entered in pattern book during or after 1935. **Backstamp(s)**: Shelley 1925-1940 **Shapes:** Court
12423	**Wildflower**. Blue. Entered in pattern book during or after 1935. **Backstamp(s)**: Shelley 1925-1940 **Shapes:** Court
12424-12425	Entered in pattern book during or after 1935. **Backstamp(s)**: Shelley 1925-1940 **Shapes:** Court
12426	**Japonica**. Coral. Entered in pattern book during or after 1935. **Backstamp(s)**: Shelley 1925-1940 **Shapes:** Regent
12427	**Japonica**. Pink. Entered in pattern book during or after 1935. **Backstamp(s)**: Shelley 1925-1940 **Shapes:** Regent
12428	**Laburnum**. Entered in pattern book during or after 1935. **Backstamp(s)**: Shelley 1925-1940 **Shapes:** Unknown
12429	**Wisteria**. Entered in pattern book during or after 1935. **Backstamp(s)**: Shelley 1925-1940 **Shapes:** Oxford
12430	Entered in pattern book during or after 1935. **Backstamp(s)**: Shelley 1925-1940 **Shapes:** Court
12431	Orange and yellow flowers against shades of fawn and brown. Yellow inside cup with gold dontil border. Gold edges, foot and ring handle. Entered in pattern book during or after 1935. **Backstamp(s)**: Shelley 1925-1940 **Shapes:** Court
12432	**Laburnum**. Bunches of pendulous dark yellow laburnum with pale green and brown foliage against muted pale brown on a buttery yellow ground. Gold edges, ring of handle and foot. Appears in Produced from for 1935. **Backstamp(s)**: Shelley 1925-1940 **Shapes:** Court
12433	Entered in pattern book during or after 1935. **Backstamp(s)**: Shelley 1925-1940 **Shapes:** Court
12434	**Loganberry**. Red berries with leaves. Entered in pattern book during or after 1935. **Backstamp(s)**: Shelley 1925-1940 **Shapes:** Eve
12435	**Loganberry**. Green berries, green and brown leaves. Ivory and green shaded ground. Entered in pattern book during or after 1935. **Backstamp(s)**: Shelley 1925-1940 **Shapes:** Eve, Regent
12436	**Loganberry**. Grey print. Yellow berries with leaves. Entered in pattern book

Pattern	Description & Shapes
	during or after 1935. **Backstamp(s)**: Shelley 1925-1940 **Shapes:** Eve
12437	Apple Blossom. Blue. Entered in pattern book during or after 1935. **Backstamp(s)**: Shelley 1925-1940 **Shapes:** Regent
12444-12449	Entered in pattern book during or after 1935. **Backstamp(s)**: Shelley 1925-1940 **Shapes:** Court
12450-12452	Entered in pattern book during or after 1936. **Backstamp(s)**: Shelley 1925-1940 **Shapes:** Court
12453	Geometric pattern. Green and grey blocks with a black strip at base of front two blocks. Grey arched line. White ground. Green edges. Entered in pattern book during or after 1935. **Backstamp(s)**: Shelley 1925-1940 **Shapes:** York
12454-12455	Entered in pattern book during or after 1935. **Backstamp(s)**: Shelley 1925-1940 **Shapes:** York
12456	Yellow and orange flowers with green and brown leaves. Amber edges. White ground. Entered in pattern book during or after 1936. **Backstamp(s)**: Shelley 1925-1940 **Shapes:** York
12457-12461	Entered in pattern book during or after 1936. **Backstamp(s)**: Shelley 1925-1940 **Shapes:** Oxford
12462	Circles, wavy lines, and bands. Green. Entered in pattern book during or after 1936. **Backstamp(s)**: Shelley 1925-1940 **Shapes:** Regent
12463	Circles, wavy lines, and bands. Blue. Entered in pattern book during or after 1936. **Backstamp(s)**: Shelley 1925-1940 **Shapes:** Regent
12464	Circles, wavy lines, and bands. Brown and amber. Entered in pattern book during or after 1936. **Backstamp(s)**: Shelley 1925-1940 **Shapes:** Regent
12465-12471	Entered in pattern book during or after 1936. **Backstamp(s)**: Shelley 1925-1940 **Shapes:** Oxford
12472	Entered in pattern book during or after 1936. **Backstamp(s)**: Shelley 1925-1940 **Shapes:** Court
12473	**Bands and Shades**. Green bands and shades inside cup and on saucer and plate. Green line approximately halfway between rim and base outside cup. Green lines at base of cup. Ivory ground. Green ring handle. Entered in pattern book during or after 1936. **Backstamp(s)**: Shelley 1925-1940 **Shapes:** Regent
12474	**Bands and Shades**. Blue bands and shades inside cup and on saucer and plate. Blue line approximately halfway between rim and base outside cup. Blue lines at base of cup. Blue ring handle. Entered in pattern book during or after 1936. **Backstamp(s)**: Shelley 1925-1940 **Shapes:** Eve, Regent
12475	**Bands and Shades**. Yellow and orange bands and shades inside cup and on saucer and plate. Line approximately halfway between rim and base outside cup. Yellow lines at base of cup. Orange ring handle. Entered in pattern book during or after 1936. **Backstamp(s)**: Shelley 1925-1940 **Shapes:** Regent
12476	Entered in pattern book during or after 1936. **Backstamp(s)**: Shelley 1925-1940 **Shapes:** Court, Mayfair
12477	Entered in pattern book during or after 1936. **Backstamp(s)**: Shelley 1925-1940 **Shapes:** Court, Mayfair
12478-12479	Entered in pattern book during or after 1936. **Backstamp(s)**: Shelley 1925-1940 **Shapes:** Oxford
12480	Bands. Entered in pattern book during or after 1936. **Backstamp(s)**: Shelley 1925-1940 **Shapes:** Eve
12481	Bands. Entered in pattern book during or after 1936. **Backstamp(s)**: Shelley 1925-1940 **Shapes:** Eve
12482	Bands. Entered in pattern book during or after 1936. **Backstamp(s)**: Shelley 1925-1940 **Shapes:** Eve
12483	**Chintz**. Entered in pattern book during or after 1936. **Backstamp(s)**: Shelley 1925-1940 **Shapes:** Oxford
12484	**Swirls**. Green. Graduated, concentric green swirls inside and outside cup and on saucer. Entered in pattern book during or after 1936. **Backstamp(s)**: Shelley 1925-1940 **Shapes:** Regent
12485	**Swirls**. Brown. Graduated, concentric brown swirls inside and outside cup and on saucer. Entered in pattern book during or after 1936. **Backstamp(s)**: Shelley 1925-1940 **Shapes:** Regent
12486	**Swirls**. Blue. Graduated, concentric blue swirls inside and outside cup and on saucer. Entered in pattern book during or after 1936. **Backstamp(s)**: Shelley 1925-1940 **Shapes:** Regent
12487	**Swirls**. Salmon. Graduated, concentric salmon swirls inside and outside cup and on saucer. Entered in pattern book during or after 1936. **Backstamp(s)**: Shelley 1925-1940 **Shapes:** Regent
12488-12489	Entered in pattern book during or after 1936. **Backstamp(s)**: Shelley 1925-1940 **Shapes:** Oxford
12490	Black print. Blue, bell-shaped flower. Entered in pattern book during or after 1936 /M green **Backstamp(s)**: Shelley 1925-1940 **Shapes:** Eve
12491	Green, bell-shaped flower with green and grey leaves. Green and grey border. Pale green band round rim. White ground. Pale green foot and handle. Entered in pattern book during or after 1936 **Backstamp(s)**: Shelley 1925-1940 **Shapes:** Eve
12495-12497	Entered in pattern book during or after 1936. **Backstamp(s)**: Shelley 1925-1940 **Shapes:** Oxford
12498	Orange band inside cup, edge of saucer, and plate. Graduated orange shading inside cup, fading from orange band to ivory towards base of cup. Outside cup, saucer, and plate have orange and yellow flowers with green leaves. White ground. Orange ring handle. Entered in pattern book during or after 1936. **Backstamp(s)**: Shelley 1925-1940 **Shapes:** Oxford
12499	Entered in pattern book during or after 1936. **Backstamp(s)**: Shelley 1925-1940 **Shapes:** Oxford
12500	Entered in pattern book during or after 1936. **Backstamp(s)**: Shelley 1925-1940 **Shapes:** Carlton
12501	Blue border band on a white ground. Entered in pattern book during or after 1936. **Backstamp(s)**: Shelley 1925-1940 **Shapes:** Carlton
12502-12503	Entered in pattern book during or after 1936. **Backstamp(s)**: Shelley 1925-1940 **Shapes:** Carlton
12504	**Silver Sage**. Entered in pattern book during or after 1936. **Backstamp(s)**: Shelley 1925-1940 **Shapes:** Regent
12505	**Bar and Leaf Motif**. Pink. Entered in pattern book during or after 1936. **Backstamp(s)**: Shelley 1925-1940 **Shapes:** Oxford
12506	**Bar and Leaf Motif**. Amber. Entered in pattern book during or after 1936. **Backstamp(s)**: Shelley 1925-1940 **Shapes:** Oxford
12507	**Bar and Leaf Motif**. Green. Entered in pattern book during or after 1936. **Backstamp(s)**: Shelley 1925-1940 **Shapes:** Oxford
12508	Entered in pattern book during or after 1936. **Backstamp(s)**: Shelley 1925-1940 **Shapes:** Oxford
12509	Entered in pattern book during or after 1936. **Backstamp(s)**: Shelley 1925-1940 **Shapes:** York
12510	**Bar and Leaf Motif**. Entered in pattern book during or after 1936. **Backstamp(s)**: Shelley 1925-1940 **Shapes:** Oxford
12511	**Spring Flowers**. Entered in pattern book during or after 1936. **Backstamp(s)**: Shelley 1925-1940 **Shapes:** Unknown
12512	**Spring Time**. Entered in pattern book during or after 1936. **Backstamp(s)**: Shelley 1925-1940 **Shapes:** Unknown
12512-12514	Entered in pattern book during or after 1936. **Backstamp(s)**: Shelley 1925-1940 **Shapes:** Court
12515	Pale pink and blue shaded flowers (possibly cranesbill) with pale olive-

Pink and blue flowers 12515 Court shape cup and saucer. £55-75; $75-95

Pattern Description & Shapes

green and grey foliage on a white ground. Gold edges, ring of handle and foot. Appears in Produced from for 1936.
Backstamp(s): Shelley 1925-1940
Shapes: Court

12516 Entered in pattern book during or after 1936.
Backstamp(s): Shelley 1925-1940
Shapes: Oxford

12517 Entered in pattern book during or after 1936.
Backstamp(s): Shelley 1925-1940
Shapes: Court

12518 Green and fawn bands. Gold pattern border. Entered in pattern book during or after 1936.
Backstamp(s): Shelley 1925-1940
Shapes: Regent

12519 Maroon and fawn bands. Gold pattern border. Entered in pattern book during or after 1936.
Backstamp(s): Shelley 1925-1940
Shapes: Regent

12520 Blue and fawn bands. Silver lines. Entered in pattern book during or after 1936.
Backstamp(s): Shelley 1925-1940
Shapes: Regent

12521 **Swirls**. Green bands of varying shades and width inside and outside cup. Outside cup is mainly white with a fawn band approximately midway between rim and base. Silver edges and ring of handle. Entered in pattern book during or after 1936.
/120 Gold.
Backstamp(s): Shelley 1925-1940
Shapes: Carlton, Oxford, Regent

12522 **Swirls**. Blue bands of varying shades and width inside and outside cup. Outside cup is mainly white with an ivory band approximately midway between rim and base. Silver edges and ring of handle. Entered in pattern book during or after 1936.
Backstamp(s): Shelley 1925-1940
Shapes: Regent

12523 **Swirls**. Green with shamrock leaves. Entered in pattern book during or after 1936.
/S Snowdrops.
Backstamp(s): Shelley 1925-1940
Shapes: Regent

12524 **Swirls**. Salmon with roses. Entered in pattern book during or after 1936.
Backstamp(s): Shelley 1925-1940
Shapes: Regent

12525 **Swirls**. Brown with leaves. Entered in pattern book during or after 1936.
Backstamp(s): Shelley 1925-1940
Shapes: Regent

12526 **Swirls**. Blue with snowdrops. Entered in pattern book during or after 1936.
Backstamp(s): Shelley 1925-1940
Shapes: Regent

12527-
12530 Entered in pattern book during or after 1936.
Backstamp(s): Shelley 1925-1940
Shapes: Oxford

12531 Floral print. Entered in pattern book during or after 1936.
Backstamp(s): Shelley 1925-1940
Shapes: Oxford

12532 Entered in pattern book during or after 1936.
Backstamp(s): Shelley 1925-1940
Shapes: Oxford

12533 **Honeysuckle**. Amber and yellow flowers with green leaves. Entered in pattern book during or after 1936.
Backstamp(s): Shelley 1925-1940
Shapes: Regent

12534 **Honeysuckle**. Pink flowers with green leaves. Entered in pattern book during or after 1936.
Backstamp(s): Shelley 1925-1940
Shapes: Regent

12535 **Swirls**. Brown and ivory. Entered in pattern book during or after 1936.
Backstamp(s): Shelley 1925-1940
Shapes: Regent

12536 Entered in pattern book during or after 1936.
Backstamp(s): Shelley 1925-1940
Shapes: Court

12537 **Blue Bird**. Entered in pattern book during or after 1936.
Backstamp(s): Shelley 1925-1940
Shapes: Oxford

12538-
12540 Entered in pattern book during or after 1936.
Backstamp(s): Shelley 1925-1940
Shapes: York

12541 Dog Roses. Yellow and green. Entered in pattern book during or after 1936.
Backstamp(s): Shelley 1925-1940
Shapes: Regent

12542 Dog Roses. Pink, blue, and green. Entered in pattern book during or after 1936.
/Y Yellow and blue flowers.
Backstamp(s): Shelley 1925-1940
Shapes: Regent

12543 Entered in pattern book during or after 1936.
Backstamp(s): Shelley 1925-1940
Shapes: Court

12544 Abstract print. Large pink flowers with, black centres, green leaves, small blue flowers with yellow centres, white sections with blue crosshatching. Peach shades fading to ivory inside cup. Peach band around centre of saucer and plate. Peach edges and handle. Entered in pattern book during or after 1937.
Backstamp(s): Shelley 1925-1940
Shapes: Oxford

12545-
12546 Entered in pattern book during or after 1936.
Backstamp(s): Shelley 1925-1940
Shapes: Oxford

12547 Entered in pattern book during or after 1936.
Backstamp(s): Shelley 1925-1940
Shapes: Mayfair

12548 Silver Sage. Entered in pattern book during or after 1936.
Backstamp(s): Shelley 1925-1940
Shapes: Mayfair

12549 Poppy. Entered in pattern book during or after 1936.
Backstamp(s): Shelley 1925-1940
Shapes: Mayfair

12550-
12551 Entered in pattern book during or after 1936.
Backstamp(s): Shelley 1925-1940
Shapes: Mayfair

12552 Entered in pattern book during or after 1936.
Backstamp(s): Shelley 1925-1940
Shapes: Oxford

12553 Entered in pattern book during or after 1936.
Backstamp(s): Shelley 1925-1940
Shapes: Court

12554-
12556 Entered in pattern book during or after 1936.
Backstamp(s): Shelley 1925-1940
Shapes: Oxford

12557 Entered in pattern book during or after 1936.
Backstamp(s): Shelley 1925-1940
Shapes: Regent

12558 **Swirls**. Blue with gold. Entered in pattern book during or after 1936.
Backstamp(s): Shelley 1925-1940
Shapes: Regent

12559 Pink, blue, green, and brown stylised flowers, leaves, and spots within a large panel. Irregularly shaped border around panel. Pink foot, handle and edges. Entered in pattern book during or after 1936.
Backstamp(s): Shelley 1925-1940
Shapes: Eve

12560 Grey scroll along edge. Graded green ground. Green flowers and grey leaves. Entered in pattern book during or after 1936.
Backstamp(s): Shelley 1925-1940
Shapes: Eve

12561-
12562 Entered in pattern book during or after 1936.
Backstamp(s): Shelley 1925-1940
Shapes: Court

12563 **Spring**. White border inside cup and edge of saucer. Green swirls inside cup and broad band on saucer. Green shamrocks outside cup and centre of saucer. White ground. Green foot line outside cup. Green handle. Entered in pattern book during or after 1936.
Backstamp(s): Shelley 1925-1940
Shapes: Regent

Spring 12563 Regent shape cup and saucer. £50-60; $80-90

12564 **Summer**. White border inside cup and edge of saucer. Salmon pink swirls inside cup and broad band on saucer. Salmon pink roses outside cup and centre of saucer. White ground. Salmon pink foot line outside cup. Salmon pink handle. Entered in pattern book during or after 1936.
Backstamp(s): Shelley 1925-1940
Shapes: Regent

Summer 12564 Regent shape cup and saucer. £50-60; $80-90

Pattern	Description & Shapes

12565 **Autumn**. White border inside cup and edge of saucer. Brown swirls inside cup and broad band on saucer. Brown leaves outside cup and centre of saucer. White ground. Brown foot line outside cup. Brown handle. Entered in pattern book during or after 1936.
Backstamp(s): Shelley 1925-1940
Shapes: Regent

Autumn 12565 Regent shape cup and saucer. £50-60; $80-90

12566 **Winter**. White border inside cup and edge of saucer. Blue swirls inside cup and broad band on saucer. Blue snowdrops outside cup and centre of saucer. White ground. Blue foot line outside cup. Blue handle. Entered in pattern book during or after 1936.
/G Green, see 12563
/P Pink, see 12564
/Y Yellow.
Backstamp(s): Shelley 1925-1940
Shapes: Regent

Winter 12566 Regent shape cup and saucer. £50-60; $80-90

12568 **Coronation Spray**. Entered in pattern book during or after 1936.
Backstamp(s): Shelley 1925-1940
Shapes: Oxford

12569-12570 Entered in pattern book during or after 1936.
Backstamp(s): Shelley 1925-1940
Shapes: Oxford

12571 **Daffodils**. Entered in pattern book during or after 1936.
Backstamp(s): Shelley 1925-1940
Shapes: Oxford

12572 Yellow, orange, green, and black stylised flowers, leaves, and spots within a large panel. Irregularly shaped yellow border around panel. Yellow foot, handle and edges. Entered in pattern book during or after 1937.
Backstamp(s): Shelley 1925-1940
Shapes: Eve

12573 **Blossom**. Blue. Entered in pattern book during or after 1936.
Backstamp(s): Shelley 1925-1940
Shapes: Oxford

12574 **Blossom**. Yellow. Entered in pattern book during or after 1936.
Backstamp(s): Shelley 1925-1940
Shapes: Oxford

12575 **Blossom**. Green. Similar to 0234. Entered in pattern book during or after 1936.
Backstamp(s): Shelley 1925-1940
Shapes: Oxford

12576 **Posie Spray**. Orange, yellow, and blue flowers with green leaves. Pale green border, trim, and handle. White ground. Similar to 0192 and 0229. Entered in pattern book during or after 1936.
Backstamp(s): Shelley 1925-1940 Posy Spray
Shapes: Cambridge, Oxford, Regent

Posie Spray 12576 Cambridge shape cup and saucer. £40-50; $80-100

Posie Spray 12576 large Regent shape teapot. £180-200; $250-300

Posie Spray 12576 Oxford shape cup, saucer, and plate. £40-50; $80-100

12577 Coral, bell-shaped flower and poppies. Entered in pattern book during or after 1936.
Backstamp(s): Shelley 1925-1940
Shapes: Regent

12578 Green, bell-shaped flower and poppies. Entered in pattern book during or after 1936.
Backstamp(s): Shelley 1925-1940
Shapes: Regent

12579 Amber, bell-shaped flower and poppies. Entered in pattern book during or after 1936.
Backstamp(s): Shelley 1925-1940
Shapes: Regent

12580 **Sunset**. Yellow. Entered in pattern book during or after 1936.
Backstamp(s): Shelley 1925-1940
Shapes: Oxford

12581 **Sunset**. Amber. Entered in pattern book during or after 1936.
Backstamp(s): Shelley 1925-1940
Shapes: Oxford

12582 Entered in pattern book during or after 1936.
Backstamp(s): Shelley 1925-1940
Shapes: Court

12583 Entered in pattern book during or after 1936.
Backstamp(s): Shelley 1925-1940
Shapes: Oxford

12584 Blossom. Entered in pattern book during or after 1936.
Backstamp(s): Shelley 1925-1940
Shapes: Oxford

12585 Orange and yellow poppies with brown foliage on a white ground. Poppy spray inside cup. Brown and yellow leaf border. Orange edges and ring handle. Entered in pattern book during or after 1937.
Backstamp(s): Shelley 1925-1940
Shapes: Oxford

12586 Entered in pattern book during or after 1936.
Backstamp(s): Shelley 1925-1940
Shapes: Oxford

12587 **Acacia**. Grey print. Blue and grey flowers with grey shaded foliage. Blue edges and handle. Entered in pattern book during or after 1936.
/G Green.
Backstamp(s): Shelley 1925-1940
Shapes: Regent

12588 **Acacia**. Yellow and orange acacia flowers with grey shaded foliage. Brown border. Orange edges and handle. Entered in pattern book during or after 1936.
Backstamp(s): Shelley 1925-1940
Shapes: Dainty, Regent

Acacia 12588 Dainty shape cup and saucer. £70-80; $140-160

Pattern	Description & Shapes
12589	Entered in pattern book during or after 1937. **Backstamp(s)**: Shelley 1925-1940 **Shapes:** Oxford
12590	Yellow poppies with grey foliage on a white ground. Poppy spray inside cup. Black, grey, and yellow border. Yellow border inside cup. Yellow edges and ring handle. Entered in pattern book during or after 1937 **Backstamp(s)**: Shelley 1925-1940 **Shapes:** Oxford

Yellow poppies 12590 Oxford shape cup, saucer, and plate. £40-50; $80-100

12591-
12592 Entered in pattern book during or after 1937.
Backstamp(s): Shelley 1925-1940
Shapes: Oxford

12593 Entered in pattern book during or after 1937.
Backstamp(s): Shelley 1925-1940
Shapes: Court

12594 Grey print. Pink blossoms with green and grey leaves. Green edges and ring handle. Entered in pattern book during or after 1937.
Backstamp(s): Shelley 1925-1940; Shelley 1940-1966
Shapes: Court

Pink blossom 12594 Court shape cup, saucer, and plate. £50-60; $80-130. Sugar and creamer. £40-50; $80-130. Bread and butter/cake plate. £20-£30; $40-60

12595-
12596 Entered in pattern book during or after 1937.
Backstamp(s): Shelley 1925-1940
Shapes: Cambridge

12597-
12599 Entered in pattern book during or after 1937.
Backstamp(s): Shelley 1925-1940
Shapes: Kent

12600 Coral, blue, and vermilion flowers with green and grey foliage. Sprig also inside cup. White ground. Mint green edges, foot and handle. Entered in pattern book during or after 1937
Backstamp(s): Shelley 1925-1940
Shapes: Kent

12601 Anemone. Entered in pattern book during or after 1937.
Backstamp(s): Shelley 1925-1940
Shapes: Kent

12602-
12606 Entered in pattern book during or after 1937.
Backstamp(s): Shelley 1925-1940
Shapes: Kent

12607 Poppies. Similar to 0233 and 0273. Entered in pattern book during or after 1937.
Backstamp(s): Shelley 1925-1940
Shapes: Kent

12608 Entered in pattern book during or after 1937.
Backstamp(s): Shelley 1925-1940
Shapes: Kent

12609-
12610 **Rose, Pansy, Forget-me-nots** chintz. Entered in pattern book during or after 1937.
Backstamp(s): Shelley 1925-1940
Shapes: Gainsborough, Kent, Ripon

12611 Entered in pattern book during or after 1937.
Backstamp(s): Shelley 1925-1940
Shapes: Kent, Ripon

12612-
12618 Entered in pattern book during or after 1937.
Backstamp(s): Shelley 1925-1940
Shapes: Kent

12619 Entered in pattern book during or after 1937.
Backstamp(s): Shelley 1925-1940
Shapes: Kent, Oxford

12620 Entered in pattern book during or after 1937.
Backstamp(s): Shelley 1925-1940
Shapes: Kent

12621 Entered in pattern book during or after 1937.
Backstamp(s): Shelley 1925-1940
Shapes: Court

12622 **Bands and Shades**. Shades of blue and fawn. Entered in pattern book during or after 1937.
Backstamp(s): Shelley 1925-1940
Shapes: Regent

12623 **Bands and Shades**. Shades of green and brown. Entered in pattern book during or after 1937.
Backstamp(s): Shelley 1925-1940
Shapes: Regent

12624 **Bands and Shades**. Shades of deep pink, salmon, and cream inside cup and on saucer. Line around outside cup and foot band. Salmon ring handle. Entered in pattern book during or after 1937.
Backstamp(s): Shelley 1925-1940
Shapes: Regent

Bands and Shades 12624 Regent shape cup and saucer. £50-60; $80-90

12625 **Bands and Shades**. Ginger. Entered in pattern book during or after 1937.
Backstamp(s): Shelley 1925-1940
Shapes: Regent

12626 **Bands and Shades**. Shades of salmon, grey, and green. Entered in pattern book during or after 1937.
Backstamp(s): Shelley 1925-1940
Shapes: Regent

12627 **Bands and Shades**. Shades of amber, brown, and grey. Entered in pattern book during or after 1937.
Backstamp(s): Shelley 1925-1940
Shapes: Regent

12628 Entered in pattern book during or after 1937.
Backstamp(s): Shelley 1925-1940
Shapes: Cambridge

12629 **Mimosa**. Similar to 0238. Entered in pattern book during or after 1937.
Backstamp(s): Shelley 1925-1940
Shapes: Cambridge

12630 Entered in pattern book during or after 1937.
Backstamp(s): Shelley 1925-1940
Shapes: Cambridge

12631 **Wild Flowers**. Blue, orange, and yellow flowers with green leaves on a white ground. Green edges. This was the original Wild Flowers pattern. See pattern number 13668 for an example of the later version. Similar to 0230. Entered in pattern book during or after 1937.
Backstamp(s): Shelley 1925-1940
Shapes: Cambridge, Regent

12632 **Winter Cherry**. Entered in pattern book during or after 1937.
Backstamp(s): Shelley 1925-1940
Shapes: Cambridge

12633 **Iris**. Entered in pattern book during or after 1937.
Backstamp(s): Shelley 1925-1940
Shapes: Cambridge

12634-
12636 Entered in pattern book during or after 1937.
Backstamp(s): Shelley 1925-1940
Shapes: Kent

12637-
12638 Entered in pattern book during or after 1937.
Backstamp(s): Shelley 1925-1940
Shapes: Chester

12639 Green outside cup and main part of saucer. White inside cup and centre of saucer. Gold edges. Entered in pattern book during or after 1937.
Backstamp(s): Shelley 1925-1940
Shapes: Cambridge

12640 Entered in pattern book during or after 1937.
Backstamp(s): Shelley 1925-1940
Shapes: Mayfair

12641-
12642 Entered in pattern book during or after 1937.
Backstamp(s): Shelley 1925-1940
Shapes: Cambridge

12643 Entered in pattern book during or after 1937.
Backstamp(s): Shelley 1925-1940
Shapes: Kent

12644 Entered in pattern book during or after 1937.
Backstamp(s): Shelley 1925-1940
Shapes: Chester

12645 Entered in pattern book during or after 1937.
Backstamp(s): Shelley 1925-1940
Shapes: Cambridge

12646 Entered in pattern book during or after 1937.
Backstamp(s): Shelley 1925-1940
Shapes: Cambridge, Chester

12647-
12648 Entered in pattern book during or after

Pattern	Description & Shapes
	1937. **Backstamp(s)**: Shelley 1925-1940 **Shapes:** Kent
12649	Pink Swirls. Broad pink border. Gold edges. **Backstamp(s)**: Pink Shelley 1925-1940 **Shapes:** Unknown
12650	**Dresden Sprays**. Entered in pattern book during or after 1937. **Backstamp(s)**: Shelley 1925-1940 **Shapes:** Devon
12651	**Wild Flowers**. Blue, orange, and yellow flowers with green leaves on a white ground. Entered in pattern book during or after 1937. **Backstamp(s)**: Shelley 1925-1940 **Shapes:** Chester
12652	**Rose Festoons**. Entered in pattern book during or after 1937. **Backstamp(s)**: Shelley 1925-1940 **Shapes:** Chester
12653-12658	Entered in pattern book during or after 1937. **Backstamp(s)**: Shelley 1925-1940 **Shapes:** Chester
12659-12664	**Dresden Sprays**. Entered in pattern book during or after 1937. **Backstamp(s)**: Shelley 1925-1940 **Shapes:** Devon
12665	Entered in pattern book during or after 1937. **Backstamp(s)**: Shelley 1925-1940 **Shapes:** Cambridge
12666	Entered in pattern book during or after 1937. **Backstamp(s)**: Shelley 1925-1940 **Shapes:** Devon
12667	**Rose** print. Entered in pattern book during or after 1937. **Backstamp(s)**: Shelley 1925-1940 **Shapes:** Devon
12668	Entered in pattern book during or after 1937. **Backstamp(s)**: Shelley 1925-1940 **Shapes:** Cambridge
12669	**Daisy** print. Green. Entered in pattern book during or after 1937. **Backstamp(s)**: Shelley 1925-1940 **Shapes:** Cambridge
12670	**Ivy**. Green print. Entered in pattern book during or after 1937. **Backstamp(s)**: Shelley 1925-1940 **Shapes:** Cambridge
12671-12676	Entered in pattern book during or after 1937. **Backstamp(s)**: Shelley 1925-1940 **Shapes:** Chester
12677	**Yellow and Green Chintz**. Entered in pattern book during or after 1937. **Backstamp(s)**: Shelley 1925-1940 **Shapes:** Cambridge
12678	**Pink, Green and Blue Chintz**. Entered in pattern book during or after 1937. **Backstamp(s)**: Shelley 1925-1940 **Shapes:** Cambridge
12679	**Pink, Blue, and Grey Chintz**. Entered in pattern book during or after 1937. **Backstamp(s)**: Shelley 1925-1940 **Shapes:** Cambridge
12680	**Surrey Scenes**. Entered in pattern book during or after 1937. **Backstamp(s)**: Shelley 1925-1940 **Shapes:** Devon
12681-12682	Entered in pattern book during or after 1937. **Backstamp(s)**: Shelley 1925-1940 **Shapes:** Devon
12683-12684	**Old Bow**. Entered in pattern book during or after 1938. **Backstamp(s)**: Shelley 1925-1940 **Shapes:** Cambridge
12685	Entered in pattern book during or after 1938. **Backstamp(s)**: Shelley 1925-1940 **Shapes:** Chester
12686-12687	**Persian**. Entered in pattern book during or after 1938. **Backstamp(s)**: Shelley 1925-1940 **Shapes:** Chester
12688-12689	Entered in pattern book during or after 1938. **Backstamp(s)**: Shelley 1925-1940 **Shapes:** Chester
12690-12692	Entered in pattern book during or after 1938. **Backstamp(s)**: Shelley 1925-1940 **Shapes:** Cambridge
12693	Floral pattern. Blue shades and brown band. Entered in pattern book during or after 1938. **Backstamp(s)**: Shelley 1925-1940 **Shapes:** Regent
12694	Entered in pattern book during or after 1938. **Backstamp(s)**: Shelley 1925-1940 **Shapes:** Oxford
12695	Entered in pattern book during or after 1938. **Backstamp(s)**: Shelley 1925-1940 **Shapes:** Cambridge, Court
12698-12699	Entered in pattern book during or after 1938. **Backstamp(s)**: Shelley 1925-1940 **Shapes:** Chester
12700	Entered in pattern book during or after 1938. **Backstamp(s)**: Shelley 1925-1940 **Shapes:** Cambridge
12701	Entered in pattern book during or after 1938. **Backstamp(s)**: Shelley 1925-1940 **Shapes:** Chester
12704-12706	Entered in pattern book during or after 1938. **Backstamp(s)**: Shelley 1925-1940 **Shapes:** Chester
12707-12708	Entered in pattern book during or after 1938. **Backstamp(s)**: Shelley 1925-1940 **Shapes:** Cambridge
12709-12711	Entered in pattern book during or after 1938. **Backstamp(s)**: Shelley 1925-1940 **Shapes:** Chester
12712	Narrow blue border inside cup below rim. Body of inside cup decorated with gold delicate floral outline on a white ground. Delicate gold scroll on the outside of the cup approximately half way between the rim and the base. Saucer has a broad band of gold delicate floral outline. A band of blue on either side of the floral band. Gold edges. Pattern number is dated c. 1938. **Backstamp(s)**: Shelley 1940-1966 **Shapes:** Chester
12713-12718	Entered in pattern book during or after 1938. **Backstamp(s)**: Shelley 1925-1940 **Shapes:** Chester
12719	**Maytime**. Entered in pattern book during or after 1938. **Backstamp(s)**: Shelley 1925-1940 **Shapes:** Cambridge
12720-12721	Entered in pattern book during or after 1938. **Backstamp(s)**: Shelley 1925-1940 **Shapes:** Chester
12722	Entered in pattern book during or after 1938. **Backstamp(s)**: Shelley 1925-1940 **Shapes:** Cambridge
12723-12724	Entered in pattern book during or after 1938. **Backstamp(s)**: Shelley 1925-1940 **Shapes:** Chester
12725	**Maytime** border. Entered in pattern book during or after 1938. **Backstamp(s)**: Shelley 1925-1940 **Shapes:** Chester
12726-12729	Entered in pattern book during or after 1938. **Backstamp(s)**: Shelley 1925-1940 **Shapes:** Chester
12730	Entered in pattern book during or after 1938. **Backstamp(s)**: Shelley 1925-1940 **Shapes:** Cambridge
12731-12732	Entered in pattern book during or after 1938. **Backstamp(s)**: Shelley 1925-1940 **Shapes:** Chester
12734	**Glorious Devon** or **Blue Devon**. Blue print on white ground. Devonshire country scene showing woman on a wooden bridge over a stream, fields, hedges, trees, and thatched cottages. Gold edges. **Backstamp(s)**: Shelley 1940-1966 Glorious Devon **Shapes:** Cambridge, Devon, New Cambridge, Oleander

Maytime cake plate on chrome stand. £50-60; $150-180

Left:
Pattern number 12712/25 Chester shape cup and saucer. £55-75; $75-95

Blue Devon 12734 Cambridge shape cup and saucer. £40-50; $80-100

Blue Devon 12734 New Cambridge shape cup and saucer. £40-50; $80-100

Blue Devon 12734 Footed Oleander shape bouillon cup and saucer. £35-50; $50-85

Blue Devon 12734 pattern inside Footed Oleander shape bouillon cup.

Pattern	Description & Shapes
12736-12739	Entered in pattern book during or after 1938. **Backstamp(s)**: Shelley 1925-1940 **Shapes:** Chester
12740	Entered in pattern book during or after 1938. **Backstamp(s)**: Shelley 1925-1940 **Shapes:** Cambridge
12741	Entered in pattern book during or after 1938. **Backstamp(s)**: Shelley 1925-1940 **Shapes:** Chester, Gainsborough
12742	**Rose**. Bouquets of flowers, including pink roses, blue, and yellow flowers with green leaves against a mottled ground inside cup and on saucer. Large rose on a white ground outside cup. Gold ring round outside cup. Gold edges. Entered in pattern book during or after 1938 **Backstamp(s)**: Shelley 1940-1966 **Shapes:** Chester, Court
12743	Entered in pattern book during or after 1938. **Backstamp(s)**: Shelley 1925-1940 **Shapes:** Chester
12744	**Carnation**. Pink carnations, small blue flowers, and green leaves. Flower spray also inside cup. Broad blue dotted border outside cup and on saucer. Blue line separates border. White ground. Gold edges. Entered in pattern book during or after 1938. **Backstamp(s)**: Shelley 1925-1940 Carnation **Shapes:** Cambridge, Gainsborough, Mocha
12745-12746	Entered in pattern book during or after 1938. **Backstamp(s)**: Shelley 1925-1940 **Shapes:** Cambridge, Gainsborough
12747	**Athens**. Narrow, gold, Greek Key pattern border. White ground. Gold edges. Entered in pattern book during or after 1938. **Backstamp(s)**: Shelley 1925-1940 Athens **Shapes:** Bute, Devon, Gainsborough, Mocha, Ripon, Windsor

Athens 12747 Gainsborough shape cup and saucer. £50-60; $90-110

Pattern	Description & Shapes
12748	Entered in pattern book during or after 1938. **Backstamp(s)**: Shelley 1925-1940 **Shapes:** Chester
12749	Narrow green border on a pale green ground. White outside cup and centre of saucer. Gold edges. Entered in pattern book during or after 1938. **Backstamp(s)**: Shelley 1925-1940 **Shapes:** Bute, Gainsborough, Mocha, Richmond, Windsor
12763-12765	Entered in pattern book during or after 1938. **Backstamp(s)**: Shelley 1925-1940 **Shapes:** Chester
12766	Entered in pattern book during or after 1938. **Backstamp(s)**: Shelley 1925-1940 **Shapes:** Oxford
12767-12768	Entered in pattern book during or after 1938. **Backstamp(s)**: Shelley 1925-1940 **Shapes:** Chester
12769	Entered in pattern book during or after 1938. **Backstamp(s)**: Shelley 1925-1940 **Shapes:** Oxford
12770-12772	Entered in pattern book during or after 1938. **Backstamp(s)**: Shelley 1925-1940 **Shapes:** Chester
12773	Entered in pattern book during or after 1938. **Backstamp(s)**: Shelley 1925-1940 **Shapes:** Devon
12774	Entered in pattern book during or after 1938. **Backstamp(s)**: Shelley 1925-1940 **Shapes:** Oxford
12775-12777	Entered in pattern book during or after 1938. **Backstamp(s)**: Shelley 1925-1940 **Shapes:** Chester
12778	**Mallards in Flight**. Brown print of mallards in flight. Brown border. Gold edges. Entered in pattern book during or after 1938. **Backstamp(s)**: Shelley 1925-1940 **Shapes:** Cambridge, Chester

Right:
Green border 12749 Gainsborough shape cup and saucer. £40-50; $80-100

Mallards in Flight 12778 Cambridge shape cup and saucer. £50-60; $80-100

Pattern	Description & Shapes
12779	Entered in pattern book during or after 1938. **Backstamp(s)**: Shelley 1925-1940 **Shapes:** Cambridge, Chester
12780	Chintz pattern. Pink and blue flowers with green foliage. Entered in pattern book during or after 1938. Backstamp(s): **Shelley 1925-1940** **Shapes:** Cambridge, Chester
12781	Chintz pattern. Pink and blue flowers with green foliage. Entered in pattern book during or after 1938. Backstamp(s): **Shelley 1925-1940** **Shapes:** Cambridge, Chester
12782	**Storks**. Entered in pattern book during or after 1938. **Backstamp(s)**: Shelley 1925-1940 **Shapes:** Cambridge, Chester

Storks (no pattern number mark) Gainsborough shape cup and saucer. £40-50; $80-100

Pattern	Description & Shapes
12783-12784	Entered in pattern book during or after 1938. **Backstamp(s)**: Shelley 1925-1940 **Shapes:** Gainsborough
12785-12787	Entered in pattern book during or after 1938. **Backstamp(s)**: Shelley 1925-1940 **Shapes:** Chester
12788	Entered in pattern book during or after 1938. **Backstamp(s)**: Shelley 1925-1940 **Shapes:** Cambridge
12789	Entered in pattern book during or after 1938. **Backstamp(s)**: Shelley 1925-1940 **Shapes:** Chester
12797	Entered in pattern book during or after 1938. **Backstamp(s)**: Shelley 1925-1940 **Shapes:** Cambridge
12798	Gold print. Entered in pattern book during or after 1938. /41 Maroon /67 Green. **Backstamp(s)**: Shelley 1925-1940; Shelley 1940-1966 **Shapes:** Cambridge, Gainsborough, Ludlow, Ripon, Stirling, Windsor
12799-12801	Entered in pattern book during or after 1938. **Backstamp(s)**: Shelley 1925-1940 **Shapes:** Chester
12802	Entered in pattern book during or after 1938. **Backstamp(s)**: Shelley 1925-1940 **Shapes:** Gainsborough
12803	Entered in pattern book during or after 1938. **Backstamp(s)**: Shelley 1925-1940 **Shapes:** Gainsborough, Henley, Richmond, Ripon, Windsor
12804-12805	Entered in pattern book during or after 1938. **Backstamp(s)**: Shelley 1925-1940 **Shapes:** Chester
12806	Entered in pattern book during or after 1938. **Backstamp(s)**: Shelley 1925-1940 **Shapes:** Gainsborough
12807	Entered in pattern book during or after 1938. **Backstamp(s)**: Shelley 1925-1940 **Shapes:** Chester
12808	Entered in pattern book during or after 1938. **Backstamp(s)**: Shelley 1925-1940 **Shapes:** Gainsborough, Henley
12809	Entered in pattern book during or after 1938. **Backstamp(s)**: Shelley 1925-1940 **Shapes:** Gainsborough
12810	Band of stylised flowers. Gold edges. Entered in pattern book during or after 1938. **Backstamp(s)**: Shelley 1925-1940 **Shapes:** Henley
12811	Entered in pattern book during or after 1938. **Backstamp(s)**: Shelley 1925-1940 **Shapes:** Henley
12812-12813	Entered in pattern book during or after 1938. **Backstamp(s)**: Shelley 1925-1940 **Shapes:** Ascot
12814-12815	Entered in pattern book during or after 1938. **Backstamp(s)**: Shelley 1925-1940 **Shapes:** Oxford
12816	Graduated thin vertical blocks with black band. Similar to 0159 and 0267. Entered in pattern book during or after 1938. /B Blue /G Green. **Backstamp(s)**: Shelley 1925-1940 **Shapes:** Regent
12817	Triangles and lines. Similar to 0160 and 0268. Entered in pattern book during or after 1938. **Backstamp(s)**: Shelley 1925-1940 **Shapes:** Regent
12818	Colour chevrons and blocks. Same as 0161. Entered in pattern book during or after 1938. **Backstamp(s)**: Shelley 1925-1940 **Shapes:** Regent
12819	Entered in pattern book during or after 1938. **Backstamp(s)**: Shelley 1925-1940 **Shapes:** Ascot
12820	Entered in pattern book during or after 1938. **Backstamp(s)**: Shelley 1925-1940 **Shapes:** Henley
12821	Entered in pattern book during or after 1938. **Backstamp(s)**: Shelley 1925-1940 **Shapes:** Ascot
12822	Entered in pattern book during or after 1938. **Backstamp(s)**: Shelley 1925-1940 **Shapes:** Henley
12823	Entered in pattern book during or after 1938. **Backstamp(s)**: Shelley 1925-1940 **Shapes:** Ascot
12824	Geometric pattern. Green and gold on black print. Thin vertical blocks and horizontal lines. Entered in pattern book during or after 1938. **Backstamp(s)**: Shelley 1925-1940 **Shapes:** Eve, Regent
12825	Geometric pattern. Blue and gold on black print. Large blue block with thin black blocks. Entered in pattern book during or after 1938. **Backstamp(s)**: Shelley 1925-1940 **Shapes:** Eve
12826	Geometric pattern. Chevrons and blocks. Pink and silver on a black print. Entered in pattern book during or after 1938. **Backstamp(s)**: Shelley 1925-1940 **Shapes:** Eve
12827-12828	Entered in pattern book during or after 1938. **Backstamp(s)**: Shelley 1925-1940 **Shapes:** Ascot
12829	Entered in pattern book during or after 1938. **Backstamp(s)**: Shelley 1925-1940 **Shapes:** Henley
12830	Entered in pattern book during or after 1938. **Backstamp(s)**: Shelley 1925-1940 **Shapes:** Cambridge
12831	Entered in pattern book during or after 1938. **Backstamp(s)**: Shelley 1925-1940 **Shapes:** Henley
12832	Entered in pattern book during or after 1938. **Backstamp(s)**: Shelley 1925-1940 **Shapes:** Ascot
12833	Entered in pattern book during or after 1938. **Backstamp(s)**: Shelley 1925-1940 **Shapes:** Henley, Ripon
12834	Entered in pattern book during or after 1938. **Backstamp(s)**: Shelley 1925-1940 **Shapes:** Ascot
12835	Entered in pattern book during or after 1938. **Backstamp(s)**: Shelley 1925-1940 **Shapes:** Cambridge
12836	Entered in pattern book during or after 1938. **Backstamp(s)**: Shelley 1925-1940 **Shapes:** Henley
12837	Entered in pattern book during or after 1938. **Backstamp(s)**: Shelley 1925-1940 **Shapes:** Ascot
12838	Entered in pattern book during or after 1938. **Backstamp(s)**: Shelley 1925-1940 **Shapes:** Henley
12839	Gold pattern on colour ground. Similar to 0448 and 0449. Entered in pattern book during or after 1938. /40 Deep salmon. **Backstamp(s)**: Shelley 1925-1940; Shelley 1940-1966 **Shapes:** Henley
12840-12841	Entered in pattern book during or after 1938. **Backstamp(s)**: Shelley 1925-1940 **Shapes:** Ascot
12842	Entered in pattern book during or after 1938. **Backstamp(s)**: Shelley 1925-1940 **Shapes:** Ascot, Ripon
12843-12845	Entered in pattern book during or after 1938. **Backstamp(s)**: Shelley 1925-1940 **Shapes:** Ascot
12846	Entered in pattern book during or after 1938. **Backstamp(s)**: Shelley 1925-1940 **Shapes:** Henley
12847	Entered in pattern book during or after 1938. **Backstamp(s)**: Shelley 1925-1940 **Shapes:** Ascot, Ripon
12848	**Orchid**. Ivory ground outside cup with a gold ring about half way down. Band of gold Orchid pattern inside cup and on saucer. Cup base and saucer centre are leaf green. Gold edges, handle and foot.

Pattern **Description & Shapes**

Entered in pattern book during or after 1938.
Backstamp(s): Shelley 1940-1966
Shapes: Gainsborough, Henley, Mocha, Richmond

12849-12850 Entered in pattern book during or after 1938.
Backstamp(s): Shelley 1925-1940
Shapes: Ascot

12851 **Sunrise and Tall Trees**. Entered in pattern book during or after 1938.
Backstamp(s): Shelley 1925-1940
Shapes: Cambridge

12852-12854 Entered in pattern book during or after 1938.
Backstamp(s): Shelley 1925-1940
Shapes: Henley

12855-12856 Entered in pattern book during or after 1938.
Backstamp(s): Shelley 1925-1940
Shapes: Ascot

12857 **Bands and Shades**. Green with floral pattern. Entered in pattern book during or after 1938.
Backstamp(s): Shelley 1925-1940
Shapes: Regent

12858 **Bands and Shades**. Blue with floral pattern. Entered in pattern book during or after 1938.
Backstamp(s): Shelley 1925-1940
Shapes: Regent

12859 Entered in pattern book during or after 1938.
Backstamp(s): Shelley 1925-1940
Shapes: Henley

12860 Gold Stars. Plain coloured outside cup and on saucer. White inside cup. Gold border print inside cup. Gold edges and handle. Same as 0450. Entered in pattern book during or after 1938.
/S2 Peach
/S5 Pink.
Backstamp(s): Shelley 1940-1966
Shapes: Gainsborough, Henley, Richmond, Ripon

Gold Stars 12860 Henley shape cup and saucer. £50-70; $80-100

Gold Stars 12860/S2 Henley shape cup and saucer. £50-70; $80-100

12861 Entered in pattern book during or after 1938.
Backstamp(s): Shelley 1925-1940
Shapes: Ascot

12862-12864 Entered in pattern book during or after 1938.
Backstamp(s): Shelley 1925-1940
Shapes: Henley

12865 Entered in pattern book during or after 1938.
Backstamp(s): Shelley 1925-1940
Shapes: Ascot

12866 Entered in pattern book during or after 1938.
Backstamp(s): Shelley 1925-1940
Shapes: Henley

12867 Entered in pattern book during or after 1938.
Backstamp(s): Shelley 1925-1940
Shapes: Cambridge

12868 Entered in pattern book during or after 1938.
Backstamp(s): Shelley 1925-1940
Shapes: Ascot, Henley

12869 **Swirls**. Green. No shades. Entered in pattern book during or after 1938.
Backstamp(s): Shelley 1925-1940
Shapes: Regent

12870 **Swirls**. Brown. No shades. Entered in pattern book during or after 1938.
Backstamp(s): Shelley 1925-1940
Shapes: Regent

12871 **Swirls**. Blue. No shades. Entered in pattern book during or after 1938.
Backstamp(s): Shelley 1925-1940
Shapes: Regent

12872 **Swirls**. Pink. No shades. Entered in pattern book during or after 1938.
Backstamp(s): Shelley 1925-1940
Shapes: Regent, Windsor

12873-12874 Entered in pattern book during or after 1938.
Backstamp(s): Shelley 1925-1940
Shapes: Henley

12875 **Swirls**. Green. Entered in pattern book during or after 1938.
/A Amber
/C Chrome green
/S Shamrock green.
Backstamp(s): Shelley 1925-1940
Shapes: Regent

12876 **Swirls**. Brown. Entered in pattern book during or after 1938.
Backstamp(s): Shelley 1925-1940
Shapes: Regent

12877 **Swirls**. Blue. Entered in pattern book during or after 1938.
Backstamp(s): Shelley 1925-1940
Shapes: Regent

12878 **Swirls**. Pink. Entered in pattern book during or after 1938.
Backstamp(s): Shelley 1925-1940
Shapes: Regent

12879 Entered in pattern book during or after 1938.
Backstamp(s): Shelley 1925-1940
Shapes: Ascot

12880 Entered in pattern book during or after 1938.
Backstamp(s): Shelley 1925-1940
Shapes: Henley

12886 Entered in pattern book during or after 1938.
Backstamp(s): Shelley 1925-1940
Shapes: Gainsborough, Richmond, Ripon, Windsor

12887 Maroon outside cup and main part of saucer. White inside cup and centre of saucer. Entered in pattern book during or after 1938.
Backstamp(s): Shelley 1925-1940
Shapes: Chester, Gainsborough, Henley

12888 Deep blue band and floral centre to cup and on saucer. Gold trim. Entered in pattern book during or after 1938.
Backstamp(s): Shelley 1940-1966
Shapes: Chester, Gainsborough

12889-12890 Entered in pattern book during or after 1938.
Backstamp(s): Shelley 1925-1940
Shapes: Henley, Kent

12891-12892 Entered in pattern book during or after 1938.
Backstamp(s): Shelley 1925-1940
Shapes: Devon, Kent

12893 Entered in pattern book during or after 1938.
Backstamp(s): Shelley 1925-1940
Shapes: Chester, Henley

12894 Gold dots on a maroon ground. Gold border. Gold edges and handle. Entered in pattern book during or after 1938.
Backstamp(s): Shelley 1925-1940
Shapes: Henley, Mocha, Ripon

12895 Entered in pattern book during or after 1938.
Backstamp(s): Shelley 1925-1940
Shapes: Henley, Kent

12896 Entered in pattern book during or after 1938.
Backstamp(s): Shelley 1925-1940
Shapes: Devon, Kent

12897 **Pandora**. Entered in pattern book during or after 1938.
Backstamp(s): Shelley 1925-1940
Shapes: Chester

12898 **Rosalie**. Entered in pattern book during or after 1938.
Backstamp(s): Shelley 1925-1940
Shapes: Chester

12899-12900 Entered in pattern book during or after 1938.
Backstamp(s): Shelley 1925-1940
Shapes: Henley

12901 Entered in pattern book during or after 1938.
Backstamp(s): Shelley 1925-1940
Shapes: Ascot

12902 Entered in pattern book during or after 1938.
Backstamp(s): Shelley 1925-1940
Shapes: Henley

12903 Entered in pattern book during or after 1938.
Backstamp(s): Shelley 1925-1940
Shapes: Henley, Kent

12913-12918 Entered in pattern book during or after 1938.
Backstamp(s): Shelley 1925-1940
Shapes: Henley

12920 Entered in pattern book during or after 1938.
Backstamp(s): Shelley 1925-1940
Shapes: Mocha

12922 Entered in pattern book during or after 1938.
Backstamp(s): Shelley 1925-1940
Shapes: Gainsborough

12923 Entered in pattern book during or after 1938.
Backstamp(s): Shelley 1925-1940
Shapes: Henley

12924 Entered in pattern book during or after 1938.
Backstamp(s): Shelley 1925-1940
Shapes: Gainsborough

12925-12927 Entered in pattern book during or after 1938.
Backstamp(s): Shelley 1925-1940
Shapes: Henley

Pattern **Description & Shapes**

12928 Entered in pattern book during or after 1938.
Backstamp(s): Shelley 1925-1940
Shapes: Mocha

12936 Entered in pattern book during or after 1938.
Backstamp(s): Shelley 1925-1940
Shapes: Chester

12938 Entered in pattern book during or after 1938.
Backstamp(s): Shelley 1925-1940
Shapes: Mocha

12939 Entered in pattern book during or after 1938.
Backstamp(s): Shelley 1925-1940
Shapes: Gainsborough, Mocha

12944 Entered in pattern book during or after 1938.
Backstamp(s): Shelley 1925-1940
Shapes: Chester, Kent

12945 Entered in pattern book during or after 1938.
Backstamp(s): Shelley 1925-1940
Shapes: Devon, Kent

12946 Entered in pattern book during or after 1938.
Backstamp(s): Shelley 1925-1940
Shapes: Chester

12947 Entered in pattern book during or after 1938.
Backstamp(s): Shelley 1925-1940
Shapes: Kent

12948 Outside cup, saucer, and plate have orange flowers and green leaves. Orange band on saucer, plate, and inside edge of cup. Inside cup has yellow below the orange band, fading into palest yellow. Ivory ground. Entered in pattern book during or after 1938.
Backstamp(s): Shelley 1925-1940 Lawleys
Shapes: Oxford

12949 Entered in pattern book during or after 1938.
Backstamp(s): Shelley 1925-1940
Shapes: Oxford

12951 Entered in pattern book during or after 1938.
Backstamp(s): Shelley 1925-1940
Shapes: Ripon

12953 Entered in pattern book during or after 1938.
Backstamp(s): Shelley 1925-1940
Shapes: Henley

12954 Entered in pattern book during or after 1938.
Backstamp(s): Shelley 1925-1940
Shapes: Ely

12955 Enamelled flowers. Brown print. Entered in pattern book during or after 1938.
Backstamp(s): Shelley 1925-1940
Shapes: Henley

12956 Entered in pattern book during or after 1938.
Backstamp(s): Shelley 1925-1940
Shapes: Ascot, Cambridge

12957 Entered in pattern book during or after 1938.
Backstamp(s): Shelley 1925-1940
Shapes: Ascot

12958 **Spaniel**. Entered in pattern book during or after 1938.
Backstamp(s): Shelley 1925-1940
Shapes: Ascot

12959 Entered in pattern book during or after 1938.
Backstamp(s): Shelley 1925-1940
Shapes: Ascot

12962 Entered in pattern book during or after 1938.
Backstamp(s): Shelley 1925-1940
Shapes: Ascot

12963 Entered in pattern book during or after 1938.
Backstamp(s): Shelley 1925-1940
Shapes: Henley

12964-12965 Entered in pattern book during or after 1938.
Backstamp(s): Shelley 1925-1940
Shapes: Ripon

12966 **Pink Hedgerow**. Entered in pattern book during or after 1938.
Backstamp(s): Shelley 1925-1940
Shapes: Henley

12967 **Green Hedgerow**. Entered in pattern book during or after 1938.
Backstamp(s): Shelley 1925-1940
Shapes: Henley

12968 **Royalty**. Entered in pattern book during or after 1938.
Backstamp(s): Shelley 1925-1940
Shapes: Henley

12969 Entered in pattern book during or after 1938.
Backstamp(s): Shelley 1925-1940
Shapes: Dainty

12970 Polka Dot. Dark green dots on a lighter green ground. Dark green trim with light green handle.
Backstamp(s):
Shapes: Dainty, Henley

12971-12972 Entered in pattern book during or after 1938.
Backstamp(s): Shelley 1925-1940
Shapes: Tall Dainty

12973 **Melody**. Chintz. Red, pink, yellow, and blue flowers on a mint green chintz background. Gold edges.
Backstamp(s): Shelley 1925-1940
Shapes: Cambridge, Chester

12974 **Melody**. Chintz. Also known as 'Half Melody'. Red, pink, yellow, and blue flowers on a mint green chintz background. Chintz band on upper outside cup, outer saucer. Gold trim. Mint green band on lower cup, centre of the saucer and lower part of handle.
Backstamp(s): Shelley 1925-1940
Shapes: Henley, Regent

12975-12976 Entered in pattern book during or after 1938.
Backstamp(s): Shelley 1925-1940
Shapes: Henley

12977 **Heather**. Entered in pattern book during or after 1938.
Backstamp(s): Shelley 1925-1940
Shapes: Cambridge, Ripon

12978 **Englands Charm**. Country scene. Pink flowers in the foreground, probably heather, with woods in the background. Swathe of pink flowers inside cup below rim. Pale blue ground. Gold edges. Entered in pattern book during or after 1938.
Backstamp(s): Shelley 1925-1940
Shapes: Cambridge, Ripon

12979 Entered in pattern book during or after 1938.
Backstamp(s): Shelley 1925-1940
Shapes: Ely

12980 Entered in pattern book during or after 1938.
Backstamp(s): Shelley 1925-1940
Shapes: Ripon

12981 Entered in pattern book during or after 1938.
Backstamp(s): Shelley 1925-1940
Shapes: Ripon

12982 **Japanese Chrysanthemums**. Entered in pattern book during or after 1938.
Backstamp(s): Shelley 1925-1940
Shapes: Cambridge

12983 Entered in pattern book during or after 1938.
Backstamp(s): Shelley 1925-1940
Shapes: Cambridge

12984 Small pink, blue, and yellow flowers with green leaves against shades of grey. Flower spray also inside cup. Pale pink ground. Gold edges. Entered in pattern book during or after 1938.
Backstamp(s): Shelley 1940-1966
Shapes: Henley

12985 Entered in pattern book during or after 1938.
Backstamp(s): Shelley 1925-1940
Shapes: Ripon

12986 **Royalty**. Entered in pattern book during or after 1938.
Backstamp(s): Shelley 1925-1940
Shapes: Henley

12987 **Maytime**. Entered in pattern book during or after 1938.
Backstamp(s): Shelley 1925-1940
Shapes: Ely

12988 Entered in pattern book during or after 1938.
Backstamp(s): Shelley 1925-1940
Shapes: Henley

12989 Entered in pattern book during or after 1938.
Backstamp(s): Shelley 1925-1940
Shapes: Ely

12990 Light green. Entered in pattern book during or after 1938.
Backstamp(s): Shelley 1925-1940
Shapes: Ascot
Bute, Cambridge, Henley, Oxford, Ripon, York

12991 Pink with green bands. Entered in pattern book during or after 1938.
Backstamp(s): Shelley 1925-1940
Shapes: Regent

12992 Bands and Lines. Shaded bands and lines on white ground. Colour variations include green, orange, blue, and salmon. Entered in pattern book during or after 1938. /S3 Green.
Backstamp(s): Shelley 1925-1940
Shapes: Eve, Regent

Englands Charm 12978 Ripon shape cup and saucer. £40-50; $50-75

Bands and Lines 12992/S3 Eve shape cup, saucer, and plate. £60-80; $100-120

Pattern	Description & Shapes

12993 Entered in pattern book during or after 1938.
Backstamp(s): Shelley 1925-1940
Shapes: Ely

12994 **Heather**. Brown bands and lines. Entered in pattern book during or after 1938.
Backstamp(s): Shelley 1925-1940
Shapes: Regent

12995 **Englands Charm** inside cup. Green bands and lines. Pink ground outside cup and on saucer. Entered in pattern book during or after 1938.
Backstamp(s): Shelley 1925-1940
Shapes: Regent

12996 **Heather**. Entered in pattern book during or after 1938.
Backstamp(s): Shelley 1925-1940
Shapes: Queen Anne

12997 **Englands Charm**. Country scene. Pink flowers in the foreground, probably heather, with woods in the background. Swathe of pink flowers inside cup below rim. Entered in pattern book during or after 1938.
Backstamp(s): Shelley 1925-1940
Shapes: Queen Anne

12998 Entered in pattern book during or after 1939.
Backstamp(s): Shelley 1925-1940
Shapes: Ripon

13000 Plain colours. Gold edges and handle on Tall Dainty. Figural, pink and blue flower handle on Dainty Floral. Entered in pattern book during or after 1939.
/S1 Dainty shapes with gold handle.
Backstamp(s): Shelley 1925-1940
Shapes: Dainty, Floral Dainty, Tall Dainty

Yellow and gold 13000/S1 Dainty shape cup and saucer. £70-80; $140-160

13001 **Gold Blossom**. Pink outside cup, green near the foot and centre of saucer. Pattern inside cup. Gold edges, foot and handle. Entered in pattern book during or after 1939.
Backstamp(s): Shelley 1925-1940; Shelley 1940-1966
Shapes: Ripon

13002 Green band outside cup. Ivory ground. Entered in pattern book during or after 1939.
Backstamp(s): Shelley 1940-1966
Shapes: Ripon

13003 Bands and gold stamps. Ivory ground. Gold edges. Entered in pattern book during or after 1939.
Backstamp(s): Shelley 1925-1940; Shelley 1940-1966
Shapes: Ely, Henley, Ripon

13004 **Gold Vine** and **Floral Spray**. Entered in pattern book during or after 1939.
Backstamp(s): Shelley 1925-1940; Shelley 1940-1966
Shapes: Cambridge, Ely, Henley, Ripon

13005 **Dark Rose**. Entered in pattern book during or after 1939.
Backstamp(s): Shelley 1925-1940; Shelley 1940-1966
Shapes: Henley

13006 **Dark Rose**. Entered in pattern book during or after 1939.
Backstamp(s): Shelley 1925-1940; Shelley 1940-1966
Shapes: Ripon

13007 **Heather**. Entered in pattern book during or after 1939.
Backstamp(s): Shelley 1925-1940; Shelley 1940-1966
Shapes: Henley

13008 **Dark Rose**. Entered in pattern book during or after 1939.
Backstamp(s): Shelley 1925-1940; Shelley 1940-1966
Shapes: Ely

13009 **Carnation**. Entered in pattern book during or after 1939.
Backstamp(s): Shelley 1940-1966
Shapes: Ely

13010 **Single Rose**. Entered in pattern book during or after 1939.
Backstamp(s): Shelley 1940-1966
Shapes: Ely, Henley

13011 **Englands Charm.** Country scene. Pink flowers in the foreground, probably heather, with woods in the background. Swathe of pink flowers inside cup below rim. Entered in pattern book during or after 1939.
Backstamp(s): Shelley 1940-1966
Shapes: Henley

13012 **Dark Rose**. Black outside cup. Entered in pattern book during or after 1939.
Backstamp(s): Shelley 1940-1966
Shapes: Ely

13013 **Open Rose**. Black outside cup. Entered in pattern book during or after 1939.
Backstamp(s): Shelley 1940-1966
Shapes: Ely

13014 **Royalty**. Black outside cup and main body of saucer. Inside cup and centre of saucer, pink roses, green and brown leaves on a white ground. Gold foot. Gold edges. Entered in pattern book during or after 1939.
Backstamp(s): Shelley 1940-1966; Royalty
Shapes: Henley

13015 **Hedgerow**. Black outside cup and main body of saucer. Pink pattern inside cup and centre of saucer. Gold foot. Gold edges. Entered in pattern book during or after 1939.
Backstamp(s): Shelley 1940-1966
Shapes: Chester

13016 **Hedgerow**. Black outside cup and main body of saucer. Green pattern inside cup and centre of saucer. Gold foot. Gold edges. Entered in pattern book during or after 1939.
Backstamp(s): Shelley 1940-1966
Shapes: Chester, Ely

13017 Savage **Rose**. Black outside cup and main body of saucer. Green pattern inside cup and centre of saucer. Gold foot. Gold edges. Entered in pattern book during or after 1939.
Backstamp(s): Shelley 1940-1966
Shapes: Warwick

13018 **Heather**. Black outside cup and main body of saucer. Pattern inside cup and centre of saucer. Gold foot. Gold edges. Entered in pattern book during or after 1939.
/W White ground inside cup.
Backstamp(s): Shelley 1940-1966
Shapes: Henley

13019 **Englands Charm**. Country scene inside cup and centre of saucer. Pink flowers in the foreground, probably heather, with woods in the background. Black outside cup and main body of saucer. Gold edges. Entered in pattern book during or after 1939.
Backstamp(s): Shelley 1940-1966
Shapes: Henley

Englands Charm 13019 Henley shape cup and saucer. £40-50; $80-100

13020 **Maytime**. Chintz. Red, pink, yellow, and blue flowers on a mint green chintz background inside cup and centre of saucer. Outside cup and body of saucer are black. Gold edges. Entered in pattern book during or after 1939.
Backstamp(s): Shelley 1925-1940
Shapes: Henley

13021 **Melody**. Chintz. Red, pink, yellow, and blue flowers on a mint green chintz background inside cup and centre of saucer. Outside cup and body of saucer are black. Gold edges. Entered in pattern book during or after 1939.
Backstamp(s): Shelley 1925-1940
Shapes: Henley

13022 **Dark Rose**. Maroon outside cup. Pink roses and flowers inside cup on an ivory ground. Gold edges. Entered in pattern book during or after 1939.
/4 Green outside cup.
Backstamp(s): Shelley 1940-1966
Shapes: Cambridge, Henley

Dark Rose 13022/4 Henley shape cup and saucer. £40-50; $80-100

13023 **Royalty**. Green outside cup and main body of saucer. Inside cup and centre of saucer, pink roses, green and brown leaves on a white ground. Gold foot. Gold edges. Entered in pattern book during or after 1939.
Backstamp(s): Shelley 1940-1966
Shapes: Cambridge

13024 **Hedgerow**. Green outside cup and main body of saucer. Pink pattern inside cup and centre of saucer. Gold foot. Gold edges. Entered in pattern book during or

Pattern	Description & Shapes
	after 1939. **Backstamp(s)**: Shelley 1940-1966 **Shapes:** Henley
13025	**Hedgerow**. Maroon outside cup and main body of saucer. Pink pattern inside cup and centre of saucer. Gold foot. Gold edges. Entered in pattern book during or after 1939. **Backstamp(s)**: Shelley 1940-1966 **Shapes:** Chester
13026	**Hedgerow**. Green outside cup and main body of saucer. Green pattern inside cup and centre of saucer. Gold foot. Gold edges. Entered in pattern book during or after 1939. **Backstamp(s)**: Shelley 1940-1966 **Shapes:** Chester
13027	Savage **Rose**. Maroon outside cup and main body of saucer. Green pattern inside cup and centre of saucer. Gold foot. Gold edges. Entered in pattern book during or after 1939. **Backstamp(s)**: Shelley 1940-1966 **Shapes:** Cambridge, Henley
13028	**Heather**. Green outside cup and main body of saucer. Pattern inside cup and centre of saucer. Gold foot. Gold edges. /W White ground inside cup. Entered in pattern book during or after 1939. **Backstamp(s)**: Shelley 1940-1966 **Shapes:** Henley
13029	**Englands Charm**. Country scene inside cup and centre of saucer. Pink flowers in the foreground, probably heather, with woods in the background. Maroon outside cup and main body of saucer. Gold foot. Gold edges. Entered in pattern book during or after 1939. **Backstamp(s)**: Shelley 1940-1966 **Shapes:** Henley
13030	**Maytime**. Chintz. Red, pink, yellow, and blue flowers on a mint green chintz background inside cup and centre of saucer. Outside cup and body of saucer are green. Gold edges. Entered in pattern book during or after 1939. **Backstamp(s)**: Shelley 1925-1940 **Shapes:** Chester
13031	**Melody**. Chintz. Red, pink, yellow, and blue flowers on a mint green chintz background inside cup and centre of saucer. Outside cup and body of saucer are maroon. Gold edges. Entered in pattern book during or after 1939. **Backstamp(s)**: Shelley 1925-1940 **Shapes:** Henley
13032	**Posy Sprays**. Green outside cup. Orange, yellow, and blue flowers with green leaves on an ivory ground inside cup. Entered in pattern book during or after 1939. **Backstamp(s)**: Shelley 1925-1940 **Shapes:** Cambridge
13033	**Carnation**. Yellow outside cup. Pattern on an ivory ground inside cup. **Backstamp(s)**: Shelley 1925-1940 **Shapes:** Cambridge
13034	**Carnation**. Maroon outside cup. Pattern on an ivory ground inside cup. Entered in pattern book during or after 1939. **Backstamp(s)**: Shelley 1925-1940 **Shapes:** Cambridge
13035	**Motif**. Pink outside cup. Large pink, blue, and yellow flowers with green and grey leaves on an n ivory ground inside cup. Gold edges and ring handle on Regent. Entered in pattern book during or after 1939. **Backstamp(s)**: Shelley 1925-1940 **Shapes:** Henley, Regent
13036	**Iceland Poppy**. Pink, mauve, and purple poppies, buds, green stems and leaves, green grass and grey bushes in the distance. Gold section above poppies. Small poppy spray and gold section inside cup. White ground. Gold edges. Entered in pattern book during or after 1939. **Backstamp(s)**: Shelley 1925-1940 **Shapes:** Cambridge
13037	**Iceland Poppy**. Brown print. Pink, mauve, and yellow poppies, buds, green stems and leaves, green grass and bushes in the distance. Yellow inside cup. White ground. Gold edges. Entered in pattern book during or after 1939. **Backstamp(s)**: Shelley 1925-1940 **Shapes:** Ely
13038	**Primrose**. Brown print. Gold edges. Entered in pattern book during or after 1939. **Backstamp(s)**: Shelley 1925-1940 **Shapes:** Ripon
13039	**Anemone**. Brown print. Gold edges. Entered in pattern book during or after 1939. **Backstamp(s)**: Shelley 1925-1940 **Shapes:** Ely
13040	**Yellow Gorse**. Brown print. Yellow edges and ring handle. Entered in pattern book during or after 1939. **Backstamp(s)**: Shelley 1925-1940 **Shapes:** Regent
13041	**Japonica**. Yellow and white flowers against shades of green on an ivory ground. Flowers also inside cup. Gold edges. Entered in pattern book during or after 1939. /GH green edges **Backstamp(s)**: Shelley 1940-1966 **Shapes:** Cambridge, Ely
13042	**Symphony**. Purple. Entered in pattern book during or after 1939. **Backstamp(s)**: Shelley 1925-1940 **Shapes:** Ely
13043	**Symphony**. Chrome. Entered in pattern book during or after 1939. **Backstamp(s)**: Shelley 1925-1940 **Shapes:** Ely
13044	**Symphony**. Beige. Entered in pattern book during or after 1939. **Backstamp(s)**: Shelley 1925-1940 **Shapes:** Ely
13045	**Symphony**. Turquoise. Entered in pattern book during or after 1939. **Backstamp(s)**: Shelley 1925-1940 **Shapes:** Ely
13046	Band of stylised flowers. Gold edges. Entered in pattern book during or after 1939. **Backstamp(s)**: Shelley 1925-1940 **Shapes:** Henley
13047	Band of stylised flowers. Gold edges. Entered in pattern book during or after 1939. **Backstamp(s)**: Shelley 1925-1940 **Shapes:** Henley
13048	**Rose**. Entered in pattern book during or after 1939. **Backstamp(s)**: Shelley 1925-1940 **Shapes:** Ely
13049	**Japanese Chrysanthemums**. Entered in pattern book during or after 1939. **Backstamp(s)**: Shelley 1925-1940 **Shapes:** Perth
13050	Enamelled flowers. Brown print. Entered in pattern book during or after 1938. **Backstamp(s)**: Shelley 1925-1940 **Shapes:** Henley
13051	Enamelled flowers. Brown print. Entered in pattern book during or after 1938. **Backstamp(s)**: Shelley 1925-1940 **Shapes:** Henley
13052	**Anemone**. Brown print. Gold edges. Entered in pattern book during or after 1939. **Backstamp(s)**: Shelley 1925-1940 **Shapes:** Perth
13053	**Blue Gorse**. Entered in pattern book during or after 1939. **Backstamp(s)**: Shelley 1925-1940 **Shapes:** Perth
13054	**Motif** outside cup. Green swirls inside cup. Entered in pattern book during or after 1939. **Backstamp(s)**: Shelley 1925-1940 **Shapes:** Regent
13055	**Motif** outside cup. Blue swirls inside cup. Entered in pattern book during or after 1939. **Backstamp(s)**: Shelley 1925-1940 **Shapes:** Regent
13056	Green outside cup and main part of saucer. White inside cup and centre of saucer. Gold edges. Entered in pattern book during or after 1939. **Backstamp(s)**: Shelley 1925-1940 **Shapes:** Cambridge
13057	Maroon outside cup and main part of saucer. White inside cup and centre of saucer. Entered in pattern book during or after 1939. **Backstamp(s)**: Shelley 1925-1940 **Shapes:** Chester, Henley
13058	Gold pattern on fawn. Gold edges. Entered in pattern book during or after 1939. **Backstamp(s)**: Shelley 1925-1940 **Shapes:** Henley
13059	Gold pattern on ivory. Gold edges. Entered in pattern book during or after 1939. **Backstamp(s)**: Shelley 1925-1940 **Shapes:** Cambridge
13060	**Basket of Flowers**. Entered in pattern book during or after 1939. **Backstamp(s)**: Shelley 1925-1940 **Shapes:** Ripon
13061	Gold pattern on green. Gold edges. Entered in pattern book during or after 1939. **Backstamp(s)**: Shelley 1925-1940 **Shapes:** Cambridge
13062	Narrow green border. Gold edges. Entered in pattern book during or after 1939. **Backstamp(s)**: Shelley 1925-1940 **Shapes:** Gainsborough
13063	Narrow blue border. Gold edges. Entered in pattern book during or after 1939. **Backstamp(s)**: Shelley 1925-1940 **Shapes:** Gainsborough
13064	**Melody**. Chintz. Red, pink, yellow, and blue flowers on a mint green chintz background. Entered in pattern book during or after 1939. **Backstamp(s)**: Shelley 1925-1940 **Shapes:** Gainsborough
13065	Floral sprays on ivory ground. Entered in pattern book during or after 1939. **Backstamp(s)**: Shelley 1925-1940 **Shapes:** Gainsborough
13066	Floral sprays on fawn ground. Entered in pattern book during or after 1939. **Backstamp(s)**: Shelley 1925-1940 **Shapes:** Gainsborough
13067	**Rose**. Entered in pattern book during or after 1939. **Backstamp(s)**: Shelley 1925-1940 **Shapes:** Gainsborough
13068	Border and floral sprays. Entered in pattern book during or after 1939. **Backstamp(s)**: Shelley 1925-1940 **Shapes:** Gainsborough
13069	Border and floral sprays. Entered in pattern book during or after 1939. **Backstamp(s)**: Shelley 1925-1940 **Shapes:** Gainsborough
13070	**Dark Rose**. Entered in pattern book during or after 1939. **Backstamp(s)**: Shelley 1925-1940 **Shapes:** Gainsborough
13071	Floral sprays. Brown border print. Entered in pattern book during or after 1939. **Backstamp(s)**: Shelley 1925-1940 **Shapes:** Gainsborough
13072	Brown print. Enamelled flowers. Entered in pattern book during or after 1939.

Pattern Description & Shapes

Backstamp(s): Shelley 1925-1940
Shapes: Gainsborough

13073 Daisy-like flowers. Entered in pattern book during or after 1939.
Backstamp(s): Shelley 1925-1940
Shapes: Gainsborough

13074 Urn and flowers. Entered in pattern book during or after 1939.
Backstamp(s): Shelley 1925-1940
Shapes: Gainsborough

13075 **Dark Rose**. Entered in pattern book during or after 1939.
Backstamp(s): Shelley 1925-1940
Shapes: Gainsborough

13076 **Open Rose**. Entered in pattern book during or after 1939.
Backstamp(s): Shelley 1925-1940
Shapes: Gainsborough

13077 Maroon band with gold print. Entered in pattern book during or after 1939.
Backstamp(s): Shelley 1925-1940
Shapes: Gainsborough

13078 Green band with gold print. Entered in pattern book during or after 1939.
Backstamp(s): Shelley 1925-1940
Shapes: Gainsborough

13079 **Open Rose**. Entered in pattern book during or after 1939.
Backstamp(s): Shelley 1925-1940
Shapes: Gainsborough

13080 Crocuses. Entered in pattern book during or after 1939.
Backstamp(s): Shelley 1925-1940
Shapes: Perth

13081 Blue flowers. Entered in pattern book during or after 1939.
Backstamp(s): Shelley 1925-1940
Shapes: Perth

13082 Hand painted yellow and pink flowers. Green swirls inside cup. Entered in pattern book during or after 1939.
Backstamp(s): Shelley 1925-1940
Shapes: Regent

13083 **Chevrons**. Grey print. Yellow and blue chevrons and spots. Entered in pattern book during or after 1939.
Backstamp(s): Shelley 1925-1940
Shapes: Regent

13084 **Chevrons**. Grey print. Turquoise and green chevrons and spots. Entered in pattern book during or after 1939.
Backstamp(s): Shelley 1925-1940
Shapes: Regent

13085 **Yellow Gorse**. Entered in pattern book during or after 1939.
Backstamp(s): Shelley 1925-1940
Shapes: Regent

13086 **Blue Gorse**. Entered in pattern book during or after 1939.
Backstamp(s): Shelley 1925-1940
Shapes: Regent

13087 **Iceland Poppy**. Entered in pattern book during or after 1939.
Backstamp(s): Shelley 1925-1940
Shapes: Perth

13088 Brown print. Enamelled flowers. Swirls inside cup and on saucer. Entered in pattern book during or after 1939.
Backstamp(s): Shelley 1925-1940
Shapes: Perth

13089 'Fishbones' - this is the term used for this pattern by the factory worker. Hand painted designs in black, ginger, and green. Entered in pattern book during or after 1939.
Backstamp(s): Shelley 1925-1940
Shapes: Regent

13090 Fishbones' - this is the term used for this pattern by the factory worker. Hand painted designs in black, red, and blue. Entered in pattern book during or after 1939.
Backstamp(s): Shelley 1925-1940
Shapes: Regent

13091 **Honeysuckle** border. Entered in pattern book during or after 1939.
Backstamp(s): Shelley 1925-1940
Shapes: Regent

13092 Broad band of blue flowers and green leaves on a white ground. Narrow yellow band below patterned band. Yellow shading fading to white inside cup. Blue edges and yellow ring handle. Entered in pattern book during or after 1939.
Backstamp(s): Shelley 1940-1966
Shapes: Regent

Blue flowers and yellow band 13092 Regent shape cup and saucer. £40-50; $80-100

13093 Apple Blossom. Entered in pattern book during or after 1939.
Backstamp(s): Shelley 1940-1966
Shapes: Regent

13094 **Pine Tree and Heather**. Entered in pattern book during or after 1939.
Backstamp(s): Shelley 1940-1966
Shapes: Perth

13095 **Pine Tree and Heather**. Green swirls inside cup and on saucer. Entered in pattern book during or after 1939.
Backstamp(s): Shelley 1940-1966
Shapes: Perth

13096 **Gold Blossom**. Entered in pattern book during or after 1939.
Backstamp(s): Shelley 1940-1966
Shapes: Ely

13097 Gold print and gold border on fawn ground. Entered in pattern book during or after 1939.
Backstamp(s): Shelley 1925-1940
Shapes: Ripon

13098 **Hedgerow**. Green. Entered in pattern book during or after 1939.
Backstamp(s): Shelley 1940-1966
Shapes: Chester, Gainsborough

13099 **Hedgerow**. Pink. Entered in pattern book during or after 1939.
Backstamp(s): Shelley 1940-1966
Shapes: Chester, Gainsborough

13100 **Gold Blossom**. Entered in pattern book during or after 1940.
Backstamp(s): Shelley 1940-1966
Shapes: Gainsborough, Mocha

13101 **Gold Blossom**. Gold pattern on ivory ground inside cup and on saucer. Gold scrolled pattern outside cup on ivory ground. Dark blue band round middle of saucer. Gold edges, foot and handle. Entered in pattern book during or after 1940.
Backstamp(s): Shelley 1925-1940
Shapes: Gainsborough, Mocha

Right:
Gold Blossom 13101 Gainsborough shape cup and saucer. £40-50; $80-100

13105 **Melody**. Chintz. Red, pink, yellow, and blue flowers on a mint green chintz background inside cup and centre of saucer. Dark coloured outside cup and body of saucer.
Backstamp(s): Shelley 1925-1940.
Shapes: Henley

Melody 13105 Henley shape cup and saucer. £60-80; $100-120

13106 **Gold Vine** and **Floral Spray**. Entered in pattern book during or after 1940.
Backstamp(s): Shelley 1925-1940
Shapes: Cambridge

13108 Hand painted flowers. Colour ground inside cup and on saucer. Entered in pattern book during or after 1940.
Backstamp(s): Shelley 1925-1940
Shapes: Chester

13109 Floral sprays inside cup and centre of saucer. Colour ground outside cup and on saucer. Entered in pattern book during or after 1940.
Backstamp(s): Shelley 1925-1940
Shapes: Henley

13110 Floral sprays inside cup and centre of saucer. Blue ground outside cup and on saucer. Entered in pattern book during or after 1940.
Backstamp(s): Shelley 1925-1940; Shelley 1940-1966
Shapes: Henley

13111 Floral sprays inside cup and centre of saucer. Peach ground outside cup and on saucer. Entered in pattern book during or after 1940.
Backstamp(s): Shelley 1925-1940
Shapes: Henley

13112 Maroon band. Gold print on ivory ground. Entered in pattern book during or after 1940.
Backstamp(s): Shelley 1925-1940
Shapes: Gainsborough

13113 **Open Rose**. Entered in pattern book during or after 1940.
Backstamp(s): Shelley 1925-1940
Shapes: Gainsborough

13114 **Dark Rose**. Entered in pattern book during or after 1940.

Pattern	Description & Shapes
	Backstamp(s): Shelley 1925-1940 **Shapes:** Gainsborough
13115	**Primrose**. Entered in pattern book during or after 1940. **Backstamp(s)**: Shelley 1925-1940 **Shapes:** Chester, Gainsborough
13116	Blue and ivory. Hand painted pattern on ivory. Entered in pattern book during or after 1940. **Backstamp(s)**: Shelley 1925-1940 **Shapes:** Cambridge
13117	**Dark Rose**. Entered in pattern book during or after 1940. **Backstamp(s)**: Shelley 1925-1940 **Shapes:** Ely
13118	**Gold Orchid**. Entered in pattern book during or after 1940. **Backstamp(s)**: Shelley 1925-1940 **Shapes:** Gainsborough
13119	**Dark Rose**. Outside cup and saucer have yellow and gold border. They have bunches of pink roses, blue flowers, and green foliage, which is repeated outside the cup. Gold edges. Entered in pattern book during or after 1940. **Backstamp(s)**: Shelley 1925-1940 **Shapes:** Chester, Gainsborough

Dark Rose 13119 Chester shape cup and saucer. £55-75; $75-95

13120	**Dark Rose**. Entered in pattern book during or after 1940. **Backstamp(s)**: Shelley 1925-1940 **Shapes:** Chester
13121	Ratauds **Rose**. Entered in pattern book during or after 1940. **Backstamp(s)**: Shelley 1925-1940 **Shapes:** Chester, Henley
13122	Warwick Savage **Rose**. Entered in pattern book during or after 1940. **Backstamp(s)**: Shelley 1925-1940 **Shapes:** Chester, Henley
13123	**Rose**. Entered in pattern book during or after 1940. **Backstamp(s)**: Shelley 1925-1940 **Shapes:** Chester, Kent
13124	**Lowestoft**. Small sprays of pink, blue, and yellow flowers with green leaves on a white ground. Entered in pattern book during or after 1940. **Backstamp(s)**: Shelley 1925-1940 **Shapes:** Henley
13125	**Gold Star**. **Backstamp(s)**: Shelley 1925-1940 **Shapes:** Mocha
13126	**Gold Orchid**. Entered in pattern book during or after 1940. **Backstamp(s)**: Shelley 1925-1940; Shelley 1940-1966 **Shapes:** Mocha
13127	**Gold Star**. Entered in pattern book during or after 1940. **Backstamp(s)**: Shelley 1925-1940; Shelley 1940-1966 **Shapes:** Mocha
13128	**Gold Star**. Entered in pattern book during or after 1940. **Backstamp(s)**: Shelley 1925-1940 **Shapes:** Mocha
13129	**Anemone**. Entered in pattern book during or after 1940. **Backstamp(s)**: Shelley 1925-1940 **Shapes:** Henley
13133	**Melody**. Chintz. Red, pink, yellow, and blue flowers on a mint green chintz background. Gold edges, foot and handle. Entered in pattern book during or after 1940. **Backstamp(s)**: Shelley 1925-1940 **Shapes:** Ascot, Ely, Ripon

Melody 13133 Ripon shape cup and saucer. £60-80; $100-120

Melody Ripon shape cup and saucer. £60-80; $100-120

13136	Pink flowers and wattle. Entered in pattern book during or after 1940. **Backstamp(s)**: Shelley 1925-1940 **Shapes:** Regent
13137	Band of green and grey leaves on a white ground outside cup and on saucer. Shaded greenish-yellow below band on cup, inside cup, middle of saucer, and plate. Entered in pattern book during or after 1940. **Backstamp(s)**: Shelley 1940-1966 **Shapes:** Oxford

Right:
Grey and green leaves 13137 Oxford shape cup, saucer, and plate. £40-50; $80-100

13138	Hand painted pink, grey, and green pattern. Entered in pattern book during or after 1940. **Backstamp(s)**: Shelley 1925-1940 **Shapes:** Regent
13139	Hand painted brown and yellow pattern. Entered in pattern book during or after 1940. **Backstamp(s)**: Shelley 1925-1940 **Shapes:** Oxford
13140	Leaves. Entered in pattern book during or after 1940. **Backstamp(s)**: Shelley 1925-1940 **Shapes:** Essex, Perth
13141	Leaves. Entered in pattern book during or after 1940. **Backstamp(s)**: Shelley 1925-1940 **Shapes:** Essex, Perth
13142	Leaves. Entered in pattern book during or after 1940. **Backstamp(s)**: Shelley 1925-1940 **Shapes:** Essex, Perth
13143	Floral print. Entered in pattern book during or after 1940. **Backstamp(s)**: Shelley 1925-1940 **Shapes:** Essex, Perth
13144	Floral print. Entered in pattern book during or after 1940. **Backstamp(s)**: Shelley 1925-1940 **Shapes:** Essex, Perth

Hand painted flowers and leaves 13144 Perth shape cup and saucer. £40-50; $80-100

Pattern	Description & Shapes

13145 **Mallard Ducks in Flight**. Outside cup has three ducks in flight against a backdrop of grass and trees. Blue-green swirls inside cup and main body of saucer. Centre of saucer has grass and flowers. Ivory background. Blue-green ring handle on Cambridge. Entered in pattern book during or after 1940.
Backstamp(s): Shelley 1925-1940
Shapes: Cambridge, Essex

Mallard Ducks in Flight 13145 Essex cup and saucer. £40-50; $80-100

13146 Floral sprays and panels. Entered in pattern book during or after 1940.
Backstamp(s): Shelley 1925-1940
Shapes: Gainsborough

13147 Floral sprays. Entered in pattern book during or after 1940.
Backstamp(s): Shelley 1925-1940
Shapes: Gainsborough

13148 Floral sprays.
Backstamp(s): Shelley 1925-1940
Shapes: Gainsborough

13149 Floral sprays. Entered in pattern book during or after 1940.
Backstamp(s): Shelley 1925-1940
Shapes: Gainsborough

13150 **Gold Star**. Entered in pattern book during or after 1940.
Backstamp(s): Shelley 1925-1940
Shapes: Gainsborough

13152 Purple **Symphony**. Entered in pattern book during or after 1940.
Backstamp(s): Shelley 1925-1940
Shapes: Ely

13153 Chrome **Symphony**. Entered in pattern book during or after 1940.
Backstamp(s): Shelley 1925-1940
Shapes: Ely

13154 Beige **Symphony**. Entered in pattern book during or after 1940.
Backstamp(s): Shelley 1925-1940
Shapes: Ely

13155 Turquoise **Symphony**. Entered in pattern book during or after 1940.
Backstamp(s): Shelley 1925-1940
Shapes: Ely

13156 **Willow**. Pale pink. Entered in pattern book during or after 1940.
Backstamp(s): Shelley 1925-1940
Shapes: Unknown

13157 Dresden **Floral Spray**. Entered in pattern book during or after 1940.
Backstamp(s): Shelley 1925-1940
Shapes: Gainsborough

13158 **Tudor Wreath**. Entered in pattern book during or after 1940.
Backstamp(s): Shelley 1925-1940
Shapes: Gainsborough

13159 **Ning Poo**. Entered in pattern book during or after 1940.
Backstamp(s): Shelley 1925-1940
Shapes: Kent

13160 Gold pattern. Entered in pattern book during or after 1940.
Backstamp(s): Shelley 1925-1940
Shapes: Perth

13161 Gold pattern. Entered in pattern book during or after 1940.
Backstamp(s): Shelley 1925-1940
Shapes: Henley

13162 Gold pattern. Entered in pattern book during or after 1940.
Backstamp(s): Shelley 1925-1940
Shapes: Cambridge

13163 Gold pattern. Entered in pattern book during or after 1940.
Backstamp(s): Shelley 1925-1940
Shapes: Ripon

13164 Leaves. Entered in pattern book during or after 1940.
/120 Gold edges.
Backstamp(s): Shelley 1925-1940
Shapes: Perth

13165 **Blue Pansy Chintz**. Entered in pattern book during or after 1940.
Backstamp(s): Shelley 1925-1940
Shapes: Henley

13166 **Blue Pansy Chintz**. Entered in pattern book during or after 1940.
Backstamp(s): Shelley 1925-1940
Shapes: Ely

13167 Butchers **Pekin**. Entered in pattern book during or after 1940.
Backstamp(s): Shelley 1925-1940
Shapes: Gainsborough

13168 Butchers **Pekin**. Entered in pattern book during or after 1940.
Backstamp(s): Shelley 1925-1940
Shapes: Gainsborough

13169 Plain colour with gold edges. Entered in pattern book during or after 1940.
/B Blue
/F Fawn
/G Green
/P Pink.
Backstamp(s): Shelley 1925-1940
Shapes: Tall Oleander

13170 Plain colour with gold edges. Entered in pattern book during or after 1940.
/B Blue
/G Green
/P Pink
/Y Yellow.
Backstamp(s): Shelley 1925-1940
Shapes: Oleander

13171 **Forget-me-nots**. Entered in pattern book during or after 1940.
Backstamp(s): Shelley 1925-1940
Shapes: Tall Oleander

13172 **Floral Spray**. Entered in pattern book during or after 1940.
Backstamp(s): Shelley 1925-1940
Shapes: Tall Oleander

13173 **Lowestoft**. Small sprays of pink, blue, and yellow flowers with green leaves on a white ground. Entered in pattern book during or after 1940.
Backstamp(s): Shelley 1925-1940
Shapes: Dainty

13174 **Lowestoft**. Small sprays of pink, blue, and yellow flowers with green leaves on a white ground. Entered in pattern book during or after 1940.
Backstamp(s): Shelley 1925-1940
Shapes: Dainty

13175 **Dresden**. Entered in pattern book during or after 1940.
Backstamp(s): Shelley 1925-1940
Shapes: Dainty

13176 **Carnation**. Entered in pattern book during or after 1940.
Backstamp(s): Shelley 1925-1940
Shapes: Dainty

13177 **Open Rose** and **Horseshoe Chintz**. Entered in pattern book during or after 1940.
Backstamp(s): Shelley 1925-1940
Shapes: Dainty

13178 **Dresden** and **Daisy Chintz**. Entered in pattern book during or after 1940.
Backstamp(s): Shelley 1925-1940
Shapes: Dainty

13179 **Blue Symphony**. Entered in pattern book during or after 1940.
Backstamp(s): Shelley 1925-1940
Shapes: Ely

13180 **Green Symphony**. Entered in pattern book during or after 1940.
Backstamp(s): Shelley 1925-1940
Shapes: Ely

13181 Brown and orange pattern. Entered in pattern book during or after 1940.
Backstamp(s): Shelley 1925-1940
Shapes: Ely

13182 Green and pink pattern. Entered in pattern book during or after 1940.
Backstamp(s): Shelley 1925-1940
Shapes: Ely

13183 **Open Flower**. Entered in pattern book during or after 1940.
Backstamp(s): Shelley 1925-1940
Shapes: Ely

13184 White and gold spots. Entered in pattern book during or after 1940.
Backstamp(s): Shelley 1925-1940
Shapes: Ely

13185 Roses, gold print, and panels. Entered in pattern book during or after 1940.
Backstamp(s): Shelley 1925-1940
Shapes: Henley

13186 Roses, gold print, and panels. Entered in pattern book during or after 1940.
Backstamp(s): Shelley 1925-1940
Shapes: Henley

13187 Floral sprays on ivory panels. Entered in pattern book during or after 1940.
Backstamp(s): Shelley 1925-1940
Shapes: Gainsborough, Henley

13188 **Gold Star** and **Spot** inside cup. **Gold Orchid** outside cup. Entered in pattern book during or after 1940.
Backstamp(s): Shelley 1925-1940
Shapes: Henley

13189 Hand painted gold pattern and white spots on blue border. Brown print below border. Entered in pattern book during or after 1940.
Backstamp(s): Shelley 1925-1940
Shapes: Henley

13190 **Gold Jungle**. Entered in pattern book during or after 1940.
Backstamp(s): Shelley 1925-1940
Shapes: Gainsborough, Ripon

13191 **Gold Star, Spots,** and **Gold Orchid** inside cup. Gold print outside cup. Gold edges, foot, and handle. Entered in pattern book during or after 1940.
Backstamp(s): Shelley 1925-1940
Shapes: Gainsborough

13192 **Floral Spray**. Entered in pattern book during or after 1940.
Backstamp(s): Shelley 1925-1940
Shapes: Gainsborough

13193 **Floral Spray**. Entered in pattern book during or after 1940.
Backstamp(s): Shelley 1925-1940
Shapes: Gainsborough

13194 Green bands and gold pattern. Entered in pattern book during or after 1940.
Backstamp(s): Shelley 1925-1940
Shapes: Gainsborough

13195 **Floral Spray**. Entered in pattern book during or after 1940.
Backstamp(s): Shelley 1925-1940
Shapes: Gainsborough

13196 **Englands Charm**. Country scene. Pink flowers in the foreground, probably heather, with woods in the background. Swathe of pink flowers inside cup below rim. Fawn ground. Entered in pattern book during or after 1940.
Backstamp(s): Shelley 1925-1940
Shapes: Ripon

13197 **Lowestoft**. Small sprays of pink, blue, and yellow flowers with green leaves on a white ground. **Gold Bead** border. Gold

Pattern	Description & Shapes
	edges. Entered in pattern book during or after 1940. **Backstamp(s)**: Shelley 1925-1940 **Shapes:** Gainsborough
13198	**Gold Border**, **Open Rose** and **Gold Bead** patterns. Entered in pattern book during or after 1940. **Backstamp(s)**: Shelley 1925-1940 **Shapes:** Gainsborough
13199	**Green Symphony**. Entered in pattern book during or after 1940. **Backstamp(s)**: Shelley 1925-1940 **Shapes:** Gainsborough
13200	Gold pattern on fawn ground. Entered in pattern book during or after 1940. **Backstamp(s)**: Shelley 1925-1940 **Shapes:** Bristol
13202	**White Daisy Chintz**. Entered in pattern book during or after 1940. **Backstamp(s)**: Shelley 1925-1940 **Shapes:** Chester, Henley
13203	**Blue Daisy Chintz**. Chintz. White daisies and blue leaves on a lighter blue ground. Gold edges. Blue line inside Chester cup. Entered in pattern book during or after 1940. **Backstamp(s)**: Shelley 1940-1966 **Shapes:** Cambridge, Chester
13204	**Blue Daisy Chintz**. White daisies and blue leaves on a lighter blue ground. Blue inside cup. Blue foot. Gold edges. Entered in pattern book during or after 1940. **Backstamp(s)**: Shelley 1940-1966 **Shapes:** Ely, Ripon
13205	**Green Daisy Chintz**. White daisies and green leaves on a lighter green ground. Patterned on outer part of saucer and upper half of outside cup. Pale green band outside cup below chintz, centre of saucer, and inside cup. Gold trim. Entered in pattern book during or after 1940. **Backstamp(s)**: Shelley 1940-1966 **Shapes:** Henley

Green Daisy Chintz 13205 Henley shape cup and saucer. £70-90; $120-150

Pattern	Description & Shapes
13206	**Green Daisy Chintz**. White daisies and green leaves on a lighter green ground. Gold edges. Green line inside Cambridge cup. Entered in pattern book during or after 1940. **Backstamp(s)**: Shelley 1940-1966 **Shapes:** Cambridge, Chester
13207	**Green Daisy Chintz**. White daisies and green leaves on a lighter green ground. Green inside cup. Green foot. Gold edges. Entered in pattern book during or after 1940. **Backstamp(s)**: Shelley 1940-1966 **Shapes:** Ely, Ripon
13208	**Ducks In Flight**. Entered in pattern book during or after 1940. **Backstamp(s)**: Shelley 1940-1966 **Shapes:** Oleander
13209	**Primroses And Trees**. Entered in pattern book during or after 1940. **Backstamp(s)**: Shelley 1940-1966 **Shapes:** Oleander
13210	**Basket of Flowers**. Entered in pattern book during or after 1940. **Backstamp(s)**: Shelley 1940-1966 **Shapes:** Oleander
13211	**Daisy and Rock Plant**. Entered in pattern book during or after 1940. **Backstamp(s)**: Shelley 1940-1966 **Shapes:** Gainsborough
13212	**Old Borgfelts Vase** border. Entered in pattern book during or after 1940. **Backstamp(s)**: Shelley 1940-1966 **Shapes:** Gainsborough
13213	**Poppy Wreath**. Entered in pattern book during or after 1940. **Backstamp(s)**: Shelley 1940-1966 **Shapes:** Gainsborough
13214	**Festoon Rose** and **Green Ribbon and Bow**. Entered in pattern book during or after 1940. **Backstamp(s)**: Shelley 1940-1966 **Shapes:** Gainsborough
13215	**Ovington**. Brown print. Enamelled in pink, green, and yellow. Ginger edges, handle and foot. Entered in pattern book during or after 1940. **Backstamp(s)**: Shelley 1940-1966 **Shapes:** Gainsborough
13216	**Ovington**. Enamelled in green and black on black Green edges, handle and foot. Entered in pattern book during or after 1940. /Y Enamelled in yellow, plain edges. **Backstamp(s)**: Shelley 1940-1966 Ovington **Shapes:** Gainsborough, Mocha
13217	**Old Bramble**. Entered in pattern book during or after 1940. **Backstamp(s)**: Shelley 1940-1966 **Shapes:** Oleander
13218	**Daisy and Wildflower**. Entered in pattern book during or after 1940. **Backstamp(s)**: Shelley 1940-1966 **Shapes:** Oleander
13219	**Wildflower** border. Entered in pattern book during or after 1940. **Backstamp(s)**: Shelley 1940-1966 **Shapes:** Gainsborough
13220	**Key, Rose, and Bead**. Entered in pattern book during or after 1940. **Backstamp(s)**: Shelley 1940-1966 **Shapes:** Gainsborough
13221	**Festoon and Rose Wreath**. Entered in pattern book during or after 1940. **Backstamp(s)**: Shelley 1940-1966 **Shapes:** Ely
13222	**Key, Rose, and Laurel**. Entered in pattern book during or after 1940. **Backstamp(s)**: Shelley 1940-1966 **Shapes:** Gainsborough
13223	**Pink Buttercup**. Entered in pattern book during or after 1940. **Backstamp(s)**: Shelley 1940-1966 **Shapes:** Oleander
13224	**Yellow Buttercup**. Entered in pattern book during or after 1940. **Backstamp(s)**: Shelley 1940-1966 **Shapes:** Oleander
13225	**Rose Sprays**. Entered in pattern book during or after 1940. **Backstamp(s)**: Shelley 1940-1966 **Shapes:** Henley
13226	**Border, Bead, and Spray of Flowers**. Entered in pattern book during or after 1940. **Backstamp(s)**: Shelley 1940-1966 **Shapes:** Gainsborough
13227	**Flower** and pieces of **Chippendale/ Ovington** pattern. Entered in pattern book during or after 1940. **Backstamp(s)**: Shelley 1940-1966 **Shapes:** Gainsborough
13228	**Chippendale**. Previously named **Ovington**. Entered in pattern book during or after 1940. **Backstamp(s)**: Shelley 1940-1966 **Shapes:** Gainsborough
13229	**Tree Pattern**. Entered in pattern book during or after 1940. **Backstamp(s)**: Shelley 1940-1966 **Shapes:** Henley
13230	**Floral Sprays and Panel**. Entered in pattern book during or after 1940. **Backstamp(s)**: Shelley 1940-1966 **Shapes:** Gainsborough
13231	**Hedgerow**. Entered in pattern book during or after 1940. **Backstamp(s)**: Shelley 1940-1966 **Shapes:** Henley
13232	**Floral Spray**. Entered in pattern book during or after 1940. **Backstamp(s)**: Shelley 1940-1966 **Shapes:** Oleander
13233	**Floral Spray**. Entered in pattern book during or after 1940. **Backstamp(s)**: Shelley 1940-1966 **Shapes:** Oleander
13234	Hulmes **Rose Spray**. Entered in pattern book during or after 1940. **Backstamp(s)**: Shelley 1940-1966 **Shapes:** Cambridge, Dorothy, Oleander
13235	Hulmes **Rose Spray**. Pink roses and yellow flowers with green foliage on a white ground. Pink edges. Entered in pattern book during or after 1940. **Backstamp(s)**: Shelley 1940-1966 **Shapes:** Devon, Dorothy, Gainsborough, Henley, Victor

Rose Spray 13235 Dorothy shape cup and saucer. £40-50; $80-100

Pattern	Description & Shapes
13236	**Gold Vine** and **Dark Rose**. Entered in pattern book during or after 1940. **Backstamp(s)**: Shelley 1940-1966 **Shapes:** Gainsborough
13237	**Single Rose**. Entered in pattern book during or after 1940. /DB Dark blue band. **Backstamp(s)**: Shelley 1940-1966 **Shapes:** Gainsborough
13238	**Dresden** with green band. Entered in pattern book during or after 1940. /PB Blue band. **Backstamp(s)**: Shelley 1940-1966 **Shapes:** Gainsborough
13239	**Open Rose**. Entered in pattern book during or after 1940. /PB Blue band. **Backstamp(s)**: Shelley 1940-1966 **Shapes:** Gainsborough
13240	Hulmes **Rose**. Small posies of pink roses, blue and white flowers with green leaves on a white ground. Green edges and handle. Entered in pattern book during or after 1940. /P Pink edges and handle. **Backstamp(s)**: Shelley 1940-1966

Pattern	Description & Shapes
	Shapes: Dainty
13241	**Daisy** print inside cup on a white ground. Coloured outside cup and on saucer. Coloured edges and handle. Entered in pattern book during or after 1940. /B Blue /F Fawn /G Green /P Pink. **Backstamp(s)**: Shelley 1940-1966 **Shapes:** Dainty

Daisy print 13241/P Dainty shape cup and saucer. £70-80; $140-160

13242 **Open Rose** outside cup, base of inside cup, and centre of saucer. Coloured inside cup and main part of saucer. Gold edges, foot and handle. Entered in pattern book during or after 1940.
/CE Yellow inside cup
/F Fawn inside cup
/G Green inside cup, mauve handle
/GG Green inside cup, yellow handle
/P Pink inside cup, green handle
T/ Blue inside cup
Backstamp(s): Shelley 1940-1966
Shapes: Dainty

13243 **Lowestoft**. Small sprays of pink, blue, and yellow flowers with green leaves on a white ground outside cup and centre of saucer. Green inside cup and main part of saucer. Gold edges. Mauve foot and handle. Entered in pattern book during or after 1940.
Backstamp(s): Shelley 1940-1966
Shapes: Chester, Henley

13244 Hulmes **Rose and Yellow Flower**. Floral bouquet on white ground outside cup. Pink, mauve, and yellow flowers with green foliage. Sprig in centre of saucer on white ground. Blue outside cup and body of saucer. Gold edges. Entered in pattern book during or after 1940.
Backstamp(s): Shelley 1940-1966
Shapes: Chester, Henley

13245 Hulmes **Rose**. Floral bouquet on white ground of outside cup. Pink, white, blue, and yellow flowers with green foliage. Sprig in centre of saucer on white ground. Peach outside cup and body of saucer. Gold edges. Pale green handle. Entered in pattern book during or after 1940.
Backstamp(s): Shelley 1940-1966
Shapes: Chester

Rose 13245 Chester shape cup and saucer. £55-75; $75-95

13246 Hulmes **Rose and Yellow Flower**. Entered in pattern book during or after 1940.
Backstamp(s): Shelley 1940-1966
Shapes: Chester

13247 **Pink Rose**. Sprays of pink roses and green foliage on white ground of outside cup. Pale green band inside cup below rim. Pale green line encircles outside cup approximately half way between the rim and the base. Saucer has a broad band of rose sprays between two bands of pale green. Gold edges. Pale green handle and foot.
Backstamp(s): Shelley 1940-1966
Shapes: Chester

Pink Rose 13247 Chester shape cup and saucer. £55-75; $75-95

13248 **Lowestoft**. Small sprays of pink, blue, and yellow flowers with green leaves on a white ground between blue bands. Gold edges. Pink foot and handle. Entered in pattern book during or after 1940.
Backstamp(s): Shelley 1940-1966
Shapes: Cambridge, Chester, Devon

Left:
Rose and Yellow Flower 13244 Chester shape cup and saucer. £55-75; $75-95

13249 **Dark Rose**. Entered in pattern book during or after 1940.
Backstamp(s): Shelley 1940-1966
Shapes: Chester, Devon, Henley

13250 Hulmes **Rose and Yellow Flower**. Entered in pattern book during or after 1940.
Backstamp(s): Shelley 1940-1966
Shapes: Devon, Henley

13251 Hulmes **Rose**. Entered in pattern book during or after 1940.
Backstamp(s): Shelley 1940-1966
Shapes: Devon

13252 Hulmes **Rose**. Entered in pattern book during or after 1940.
Backstamp(s): Shelley 1940-1966
Shapes: Atlantic

13253 **Carnation**. Pink carnations, blue flowers and green leaves outside cup and centre of saucer on white ground. Pink inside cup and body of saucer. Green handle. Entered in pattern book during or after 1940.
Backstamp(s): Shelley 1940-1966
Shapes: Henley, Perth, Victor

13254 Butchers **Crocus**. Blue outside cup and on saucer. Blue crocus inside cup, with yellow, pink, orange, and green flowers and leaves on white ground. Blue edges, foot and handle. Entered in pattern book during or after 1940.
/S3 Green outside cup, foot and handle
/S9 Pink outside cup, foot and handle
/S12 Yellow outside cup, orange foot and handle
/S16 Orange outside cup, foot, and handle.
Backstamp(s): Shelley 1940-1966
Shapes: Henley

Crocus 13254/S9 Henley shape cup and saucer. £40-50; $80-100

13255 Enterprise **Tulip**. Entered in pattern book during or after 1940.
Backstamp(s): Shelley 1940-1966
Shapes: Dainty

13256 Warwick Savage **Rose**. Entered in pattern book during or after 1940.
Backstamp(s): Shelley 1940-1966
Shapes: Henley

13257 Hulmes **Rose** at the base of the outside cup and the centre of the saucer. Pink and white roses with other flowers, mainly in blue and yellow, with green foliage. The upper section of the outside cup is pale blue. The lower section covering the base and the outside cup are white. A blue line separates the pale blue and white on the outside of the cup. A blue line also encircles the outside cup approximately half way between the rim and the base. Foot is blue. The centre of the saucer has a white ground. The rest of it is pale blue. Gold edges. Entered in

pattern book during or after 1940. /S16 Yellow.
Backstamp(s): Shelley 1940-1966
Shapes: Chester

Rose 13257/S10 Chester shape cup and saucer. £55-75; $75-95

Rose 13257/S10 pattern inside Chester shape cup

Rose 13257/S16 Chester shape cup and saucer. £55-75; $75-95

13258 Hulmes **Rose and Blue Flower**. Entered in pattern book during or after 1940.
Backstamp(s): Shelley 1940-1966
Shapes: Henley

13259 Hulmes **Rose and Blue Flower**. Entered in pattern book during or after 1940.
Backstamp(s): Shelley 1940-1966
Shapes: Perth

13260 Hulmes **Rose** inside cup on white ground. One spray of flowers. Pink rose with tiny yellow and blue flowers with green leaves. Yellow outside cup and on saucer. Yellow handle. Entered in pattern book during or after 1940.
Backstamp(s): Shelley 1940-1966
Shapes: Henley

13261 Butchers **Crocus**. Entered in pattern book during or after 1940.
Backstamp(s): Shelley 1940-1966
Shapes: Devon

13262 Butchers **Rose** inside cup on white ground. One spray of flowers. Pink rose with tiny yellow and blue flowers with green leaves. Pale blue outside cup and on saucer. Darker blue edges and handle. Entered in pattern book during or after 1940.
Backstamp(s): Shelley 1940-1966
Shapes: Cambridge

13263 **Castle**. Green castles and oriental type trees inside and outside cup as well as on saucer. White ground. Paler green edges, foot and handle. Entered in pattern book during or after 1940.
Backstamp(s): Shelley 1940-1966
Shapes: Gainsborough

13264 **Castle**. Turquoise castles and oriental type trees inside and outside cup as well as on saucer. White ground. Paler turquoise edges, foot and handle. Entered in pattern book during or after 1940.
Backstamp(s): Shelley 1940-1966
Shapes: Gainsborough

13265 **Castle**. Pale blue castles and oriental type trees inside and outside cup as well as on saucer. White ground. Pale blue edges, foot and handle. Entered in pattern book during or after 1940.
Backstamp(s): Shelley 1940-1966
Shapes: Gainsborough

13266 **Castle**. Red-brown castles and oriental type trees inside and outside cup as well as on saucer. White ground. Paler pink edges, foot and handle. Entered in pattern book during or after 1940.
Backstamp(s): Shelley 1940-1966
Shapes: Gainsborough

Castle 13266 Gainsborough shape cup, saucer, and plate. £40-60; $90-110

13267 **Anemone and Daisy**. Entered in pattern book during or after 1940.
Backstamp(s): Shelley 1940-1966
Shapes: Henley

13268 **Poppy**. Entered in pattern book during or after 1940.
Backstamp(s): Shelley 1940-1966
Shapes: Henley

13269 **Hydrangea**. Entered in pattern book during or after 1940.
Backstamp(s): Shelley 1940-1966
Shapes: Cambridge

13270 **May Blossom**. Entered in pattern book during or after 1940.
Backstamp(s): Shelley 1940-1966
Shapes: Bristol

13271 **Fruit Basket**. Entered in pattern book during or after 1940.
Backstamp(s): Shelley 1940-1966
Shapes: Chester

13272 **Cameo Dancing**. Figure in black on dark yellow ground. Entered in pattern book during or after 1940.
Backstamp(s): Shelley 1940-1966
Shapes: Bristol, Henley

13273 **Festoon and Rose Wreath**. Entered in pattern book during or after 1940.
Backstamp(s): Shelley 1940-1966
Shapes: Ely, Kent

13274 **Wildflower** border. Entered in pattern book during or after 1940.
Backstamp(s): Shelley 1940-1966
Shapes: Chester, Gainsborough

13275 **Dark Rose**. Entered in pattern book during or after 1940.
Backstamp(s): Shelley 1940-1966
Shapes: Cambridge, Henley

13276 **Englands Charm**. Country scene. Pink flowers in the foreground, probably heather, with woods in the background. Entered in pattern book during or after 1940.
Backstamp(s): Shelley 1940-1966
Shapes: Henley

13277 **Heather**. Countryside scene with pink heather, trees, bridge, and river. Entered in pattern book during or after 1940.
Backstamp(s): Shelley 1940-1966
Shapes: Henley

13278 **Melody**. Chintz. Red, pink, yellow, and blue flowers on a mint green chintz background inside cup and centre of saucer. Mottled outside cup and main part of saucer. Gold edges, foot and handle. Entered in pattern book during or after 1940.
Backstamp(s): Shelley 1940-1966
Shapes: Henley

13279 **Green Daisy Chintz**. White daisies and green leaves on a lighter green ground inside cup and centre of saucer. Pale green outside cup and main body of saucer. Gold edges. Entered in pattern book during or after 1940.
Backstamp(s): Shelley 1940-1966
Shapes: Henley

13280 **Blue Daisy Chintz**. White daisies and blue leaves on a lighter blue ground inside cup and centre of saucer. Pale blue outside cup and main body of saucer. Gold edges. Entered in pattern book during or after 1940.
Backstamp(s): Shelley 1940-1966
Shapes: Cambridge, Henley

13281 Mottled outside cup and main part of saucer. White inside cup and centre of saucer. Gold edges. Entered in pattern book during or after 1939.
Backstamp(s): Shelley 1925-1940
Shapes: Henley, Ripon

13282 **Heather**. Entered in pattern book during or after 1940.
Backstamp(s): Shelley 1940-1966
Shapes: Henley

13283 **Englands Charm**. Entered in pattern book during or after 1940.
Backstamp(s): Shelley 1940-1966
Shapes: Henley

13284 **Dresden** and **Daisy Chintz**. Entered in pattern book during or after 1940.
Backstamp(s): Shelley 1940-1966
Shapes: Dainty

13285 **Ducks In Flight**. Entered in pattern book during or after 1940.
Backstamp(s): Shelley 1940-1966
Flight
Shapes: Oleander

13286 **Festoon Rose** and **Green Ribbon and Bow**. Entered in pattern book during or after 1940.
Backstamp(s): Shelley 1940-1966
Shapes: Gainsborough

Pattern	Description & Shapes
13287	**Rose**. Entered in pattern book during or after 1940. **Backstamp(s)**: Shelley 1940-1966 **Shapes:** Ripon
13288	**Rose**. Mottled colour outside cup and main part of saucer. Rose sprays inside cup and centre of saucer on a white ground. Gold edges, foot and handle. Entered in pattern book during or after 1940. /B Blue /BL Black /G Green /M Maroon. **Backstamp(s)**: Shelley 1940-1966 **Shapes:** Ripon

Rose 13288/M Ripon shape cup and saucer. £40-50; $80-100

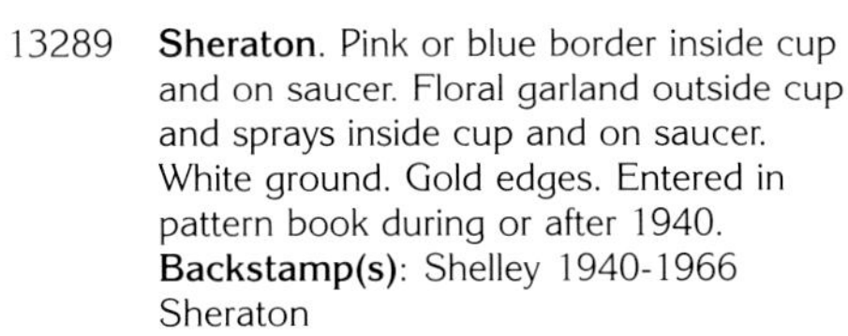

13289 **Sheraton**. Pink or blue border inside cup and on saucer. Floral garland outside cup and sprays inside cup and on saucer. White ground. Gold edges. Entered in pattern book during or after 1940.
Backstamp(s): Shelley 1940-1966 Sheraton
Shapes: Gainsborough

Georgian 13360 Henley shape cup and saucer. £35-45; $50-70

Sheraton 13289 coffee pot. $180-200; $250-300

Sheraton 13289 Gainsborough shape cup and saucer. £40-50; $50-100

13290	**Sheraton**. Green and gold border inside cup and on saucer. Floral garland outside cup and sprays inside cup and on saucer. White ground. Gold edges. Entered in pattern book during or after 1940. **Backstamp(s)**: Shelley 1940-1966 **Shapes:** Gainsborough, Mocha

Sheraton 13290 Gainsborough shape cup and saucer. £40-50; $50-100

13291	**Sheraton**. Blue and gold border inside cup and on saucer. Floral garland outside cup and sprays inside cup and on saucer. White ground. Gold edges. **Backstamp(s)**: Shelley 1940-1966 Sheraton **Shapes:** Gainsborough, Mocha
13292	Hulmes **Rose**. Entered in pattern book during or after 1940. **Backstamp(s)**: Shelley 1940-1966 **Shapes:** Ripon
13293	Hulmes **Rose**. Entered in pattern book during or after 1940. **Backstamp(s)**: Shelley 1940-1966 **Shapes:** Ripon
13294	Pink with green handle. Entered in pattern book during or after 1940. **Backstamp(s)**: Shelley 1940-1966 **Shapes:** Dainty, Oleander
13295	Blue with pink handle. Entered in pattern book during or after 1940. **Backstamp(s)**: Shelley 1940-1966 **Shapes:** Dainty, Oleander

Blue and pink 13295 Dainty shape cup, saucer, and plate. £30-40; $60-80

13296	Pale green with pink handle. Entered in pattern book during or after 1940. **Backstamp(s)**: Shelley 1940-1966 **Shapes:** Dainty, Oleander

Green and pink 13296 Dainty shape cup and saucer. £30-40; $60-80

13297	Puce with fawn handle. Entered in pattern book during or after 1940. **Backstamp(s)**: Shelley 1940-1966 **Shapes:** Dainty, Oleander
13298	Peach with puce handle. Entered in pattern book during or after 1940. **Backstamp(s)**: Shelley 1940-1966 **Shapes:** Dainty, Oleander
13299	Fawn with blue handle. Entered in pattern book during or after 1940. **Backstamp(s)**: Shelley 1940-1966 **Shapes:** Dainty, Oleander
13300	**Floral**. Entered in pattern book during or after 1940. **Backstamp(s)**: Shelley 1940-1966 **Shapes:** Dainty, Oleander
13301	**Floral**. Entered in pattern book during or after 1940. **Backstamp(s)**: Shelley 1940-1966 **Shapes:** Dainty, Oleander
13302	**Crochet**. Pastel or white ground. Grey lacy border on edge of saucer, around centre of the saucer, rim of outside, and

outside cup. Pink, blue, yellow, and amber flowers on outer band and centre of saucer. Also **outside cup**. Gold edges, foot and handle. Entered in pattern book during or after 1940.
Backstamp(s): Shelley 1940-1966
Shapes: Gainsborough

Crochet 13302 Gainsborough shape cup and saucer. £40-50; $80-100

13303 **Crochet**. Grey lacy border on edge of saucer, around centre of the saucer, rim of outside, and outside cup. Pink, blue, yellow, and amber flowers on outer band and centre of saucer. Also inside and outside cup.
Pastel or white ground inside cup and on saucer. Pattern **outside cup** on white ground. Entered in pattern book during or after 1940.
Backstamp(s): 1940-1966
Shapes: Henley, Richmond

Crochet 13303 Henley shape cup and saucer. £40-50; $80-100

Crochet 13303 Richmond shape cup and saucer. £40-50; $80-100

Crochet coffee pot. £150-200; $200-250. 13643 Richmond shape creamer and sugar. £30-40; $50-60

13304 **Georgian**. Maroon border pattern. Pink, blue, white, and mauve posies. White ground. Gold edges. Entered in pattern book during or after 1940.
Backstamp(s): Green Shelley 1940-1966
Shapes: Henley

13305 **Georgian**. Green border pattern. Pink, blue, white, and mauve posies. White ground. Gold edges. Entered in pattern book during or after 1940.
Backstamp(s): Green Shelley 1940-1966
Shapes: Henley

13306 **Georgian**. Blue border pattern. Pink, blue, white, and mauve posies. White ground. Gold edges. Entered in pattern book during or after 1940.
Backstamp(s): Green Shelley 1940-1966
Shapes: Henley

13307 **Crochet**. Entered in pattern book during or after 1940.
Backstamp(s): Shelley 1940-1966
Shapes: Gainsborough

13308 **Blue Daisy**. Entered in pattern book during or after 1940.
Backstamp(s): Shelley 1940-1966
Shapes: Cambridge, Henley

13309 **Blue Pansy**. Entered in pattern book during or after 1940.
Backstamp(s): Shelley 1940-1966
Shapes: Henley

13310 **Dark Rose**. Entered in pattern book during or after 1940.
Backstamp(s): Shelley 1940-1966
Shapes: Ripon

13311 **Open Rose**. Entered in pattern book during or after 1940.
Backstamp(s): Shelley 1940-1966
Shapes: Ripon

13312 **Royalty**. Plain coloured outside cup and main body of saucer. Inside cup and centre of saucer, pink roses, green and brown leaves on an ivory ground. Gold foot and handle. Gold edges. Entered in pattern book during or after 1940.
Backstamp(s): Shelley 1940-1966
Shapes: Ripon

13313 **Heather**. Entered in pattern book during or after 1940.
Backstamp(s): Shelley 1940-1966
Shapes: Ripon

13314 **Englands Charm**. Entered in pattern book during or after 1940.
Backstamp(s): Shelley 1940-1966
Shapes: Ripon

13315 **Green Daisy**. White daisies and green leaves on a lighter green ground inside cup and centre of saucer. Pale green outside cup and on saucer. Gold edges, foot and handle. Entered in pattern book during or after 1940.
Backstamp(s): Shelley 1940-1966
Shapes: Ripon

13316 **Blue Daisy**. Chintz. White daisies and blue leaves on a lighter blue ground inside cup and centre of saucer. Pale blue outside cup and on saucer. Gold edges, foot and handle.
Backstamp(s): Shelley 1940-1966
Shapes: Ripon

13317 **Melody**. Entered in pattern book during or after 1940.
Backstamp(s): Shelley 1940-1966
Shapes: Henley, Ripon

13318 Plain colour. Entered in pattern book during or after 1940.
Backstamp(s): Shelley 1940-1966
Shapes: Oleander

13319 **Carnation**. Entered in pattern book during or after 1940.
Backstamp(s): Shelley 1940-1966
Shapes: Oleander

13320 **Rose and Yellow Flower**. Entered in pattern book during or after 1940.
Backstamp(s): Shelley 1940-1966
Shapes: Oleander

13321 Enterprise **Tulip**. Entered in pattern book during or after 1940.
Backstamp(s): Shelley 1940-1966
Shapes: Oleander

13322 Hulmes **Rose**. Entered in pattern book during or after 1940.
Backstamp(s): Shelley 1940-1966
Shapes: Oleander

13323 Rataulds **Dresden**. Blue. Entered in pattern book during or after 1940.
Backstamp(s): Shelley 1940-1966
Shapes: Oleander

13324 Rataulds **Dresden**. Orange. Entered in pattern book during or after 1940.
Backstamp(s): Shelley 1940-1966
Shapes: Oleander

13325 **Forget-me-nots**. Entered in pattern book during or after 1940.
Backstamp(s): Shelley 1940-1966
Shapes: Henley, Victor

13326 Rataulds **Dresden**. Pink. Entered in pattern book during or after 1940.
Backstamp(s): Shelley 1940-1966
Shapes: Henley, Victor

13327 **Royalty**. Broad border of pink roses, green, and brown leaves. Fawn foot and handle. Gold edges. Entered in pattern book during or after 1940.
Backstamp(s): Shelley 1940-1966
Shapes: Henley, Victor

13328 Hulmes **Rose and Yellow Flower**. Entered in pattern book during or after 1940.
Backstamp(s): Shelley 1940-1966
Shapes: Henley, Victor

13329 Hulmes **Rose and White Flower**. Entered in pattern book during or after 1940.
Backstamp(s): Shelley 1940-1966
Shapes: Henley, Victor

13330 Hulmes **Rose and Yellow Flower**. Yellow inside cup and on saucer. Pink rose with flowers and foliage outside cup on an ivory ground. Gold edges, foot (Henley) and handle. Entered in pattern book during or after 1940.
Backstamp(s): Shelley 1940-1966
Shapes: Henley, Perth, Victor

Rose and Yellow Flower 13330 Perth shape cup and saucer. £40-50; $80-100

Pattern	Description & Shapes
13331	**Melody**. Chintz. Red, pink, yellow, and blue flowers on a mint green chintz background inside cup and centre of saucer. Fawn outside cup and on saucer. Gold edges, foot and handle. Entered in pattern book during or after 1940. **Backstamp(s)**: Shelley 1940-1966 **Shapes:** Footed Oleander
13332	**Blue Daisy**. Entered in pattern book during or after 1940. **Backstamp(s)**: Shelley 1940-1966 **Shapes:** Footed Oleander
13333	**Green Daisy**. Chintz. White daisies and green leaves on a lighter green ground inside cup and centre of saucer. Pale green outside cup and on saucer. Gold edges, foot and handle. Entered in pattern book during or after 1940. **Backstamp(s)**: Shelley 1940-1966 **Shapes:** Footed Oleander
13334	**Vine**. Entered in pattern book during or after 1940. **Backstamp(s)**: Shelley 1940-1966 **Shapes:** Footed Oleander
13335	Butchers **Dark Rose**. Entered in pattern book during or after 1940. **Backstamp(s)**: Shelley 1940-1966 **Shapes:** Low Oleander
13336	Hulmes **Rose and White Flower**. Entered in pattern book during or after 1940. **Backstamp(s)**: Shelley 1940-1966 **Shapes:** Low Oleander
13337	Butchers **Crocus**. Outside cup and main part of saucer are pale lavender. Blue crocus inside cup and centre of saucer, with yellow, pink, orange, and green flowers and leaves on white ground. Gold edges. Pale green handle. **Backstamp(s)**: Shelley 1940-1966 **Shapes:** Low Oleander

Butchers **Crocus** 13337/S14 Oleander shape cup and saucer. £40-50; $80-100

13338	Hulmes **Rose and Yellow Flower**. Entered in pattern book during or after 1940. **Backstamp(s)**: Shelley 1940-1966 **Shapes:** Low Oleander
13339	**Lowestoft**. Entered in pattern book during or after 1940. **Backstamp(s)**: Shelley 1940-1966 **Shapes:** Low Oleander
13340	Warwick Savage **Rose Spray**. Entered in pattern book during or after 1940. **Backstamp(s)**: Shelley 1940-1966 **Shapes:** Low Oleander
13341	**Rose and Daisy** and Butchers **Dresden**. Entered in pattern book during or after 1940. **Backstamp(s)**: Shelley 1940-1966 **Shapes:** Footed Oleander, Victor
13342	Century **Daisy** and Butchers **Dresden**. Entered in pattern book during or after 1940. **Backstamp(s)**: Shelley 1940-1966 **Shapes:** Footed Oleander, Victor
13343	**Rose and Daisy** and **Lowestoft**. Entered in pattern book during or after 1940. **Backstamp(s)**: Shelley 1940-1966 **Shapes:** Footed Oleander, Victor
13344	Century **Daisy** and Hulmes **Rose and Yellow Flower**. Entered in pattern book during or after 1940. **Backstamp(s)**: Shelley 1940-1966 **Shapes:** Footed Oleander, Mocha, Victor
13344	Century **Daisy** and **Sheraton**. Entered in pattern book during or after 1940. **Backstamp(s)**: Shelley 1940-1966 **Shapes:** Footed Oleander, Victor
13345	**Curtain Border** and **Crochet**. Entered in pattern book during or after 1940. **Backstamp(s)**: Shelley 1940-1966 **Shapes:** Gainsborough, Victor
13346	**Curtain Border** and **Crochet**. Entered in pattern book during or after 1940 for export to South America. **Backstamp(s)**: Shelley 1940-1966 **Shapes:** Mocha
13347	**Basket Festoon** and **Sheraton**. Entered in pattern book during or after 1940. **Backstamp(s)**: Shelley 1940-1966 **Shapes:** Gainsborough
13348	Davies **Woodland**. Blue, pink, and yellow flowers, green foliage, and trees set into a woodland landscape. Gold edges. Blue handle and foot. **Backstamp(s)**: Shelley 1940-1966 Woodland **Shapes:** Dainty, Dorothy, Richmond

Woodland 13348 Richmond shape cup and saucer. £40-50; $80-100

13349	**Basket Festoon** and **Open Rose**. Entered in pattern book during or after 1940. **Backstamp(s)**: Shelley 1940-1966 **Shapes:** Footed Oleander
13350	**Rose and Daisy** and **Dark Rose**. Entered in pattern book during or after 1940. **Backstamp(s)**: Shelley 1940-1966 **Shapes:** Footed Oleander
13351	Print inside cup. Plain colour outside cup and on saucer. Entered in pattern book during or after 1940. **Backstamp(s)**: Shelley 1940-1966 **Shapes:** Footed Oleander
13352	**Crackle**. Pink, blue, mauve, and amber flowers and green foliage on a black and white crackle background. Gold edges. Entered in pattern book during or after 1940. **Backstamp(s)**: Shelley 1925-1940 **Shapes:** Cambridge, Ripon
13353	**Rock Garden**. Chintz. Rockery plants set amongst grey stones. Pink, blue, yellow, and whiter flowers with green foliage. Patterned inside cup with plain colour outside cup and on saucer. Gold edges, foot and handle. Entered in pattern book during or after 1940. **Backstamp(s)**: Shelley 1940-1966 Rock Garden **Shapes:** Footed Oleander
13354	**Rock Garden**. Chintz. Rockery plants set amongst grey stones. Pink, blue, yellow, and whiter flowers with green foliage. Gold edges. Entered in pattern book during or after 1940. **Backstamp(s)**: Shelley 1940-1966 Rock Garden **Shapes:** Ripon
13355	**Rock Garden**. Chintz. Rockery plants set amongst grey stones. Pink, blue, yellow, and whiter flowers with green foliage. Items divided into a band of pattern with a band of plain colour below it. Gold edges. Entered in pattern book during or after 1940. **Backstamp(s)**: Shelley 1940-1966 Rock Garden **Shapes:** Henley
13356	**Rock Garden**. Chintz. Rockery plants set amongst grey stones. Pink, blue, yellow, and whiter flowers with green foliage. Patterned inside cup and middle of saucer. Plain colour outside cup and on saucer. Gold edges, foot and handle. Later production runs placed the chintz litho outside cup and all over saucer. Entered in pattern book during or after 1940. **Backstamp(s)**: Shelley 1940-1966 Rock Garden **Shapes:** Footed Oleander
13357	**Rock Garden**. Chintz. Rockery plants set amongst grey stones. Pink, blue, yellow, and whiter flowers with green foliage. Patterned outside cup and on saucer. Plain colour inside cup. Gold edges. Entered in pattern book during or after 1940. **Backstamp(s)**: Shelley 1940-1966 Rock Garden **Shapes:** Low Oleander
13358	**Blue Daisy**. Chintz. White daisies and blue leaves on a lighter blue ground. Blue inside cup. Blue foot. Gold edges, foot and handle. Entered in pattern book during or after 1940. **Backstamp(s)**: Shelley 1940-1966 **Shapes:** Henley
13359	**Rock Garden**. Chintz. Rockery plants set amongst grey stones. Pink, blue, yellow, and whiter flowers with green foliage. Patterned outside cup and on saucer. Gold edges. **Backstamp(s)**: Shelley 1940-1966 Rock Garden

Pattern	Description & Shapes
	Shapes: Chester, Henley, Victor
13360	**Georgian**. Green border pattern. Pink, blue, and mauve posies. White ground. Gold edges. Entered in pattern book during or after 1940. **Backstamp(s)**: Green Shelley 1940-1966. Georgian. **Shapes:** Gainsborough, Henley, Mocha

Georgian 13360 Henley shape cup and saucer. £35-45; $50-70

13361 **Georgian**. Maroon border pattern. Pink, blue, white, and mauve posies. White ground. Gold edges. Gold foot and handle on Ripon. Entered in pattern book during or after 1940.
Backstamp(s): Green Shelley 1940-1966. Georgian.
Shapes: Gainsborough, Ripon

Georgian 13361 Ripon shape cup and saucer. £40-50; $80-100

13362 **Georgian**. Green border pattern. Pink, blue, and mauve posies. White ground. Gold edges, foot and handle. Entered in pattern book during or after 1940.
Backstamp(s): Green Shelley 1940-1966. Georgian.
Shapes: Chester, Gainsborough

13363 **Georgian**. Maroon border pattern. Pink, blue, white, and mauve posies. White ground. Gold edges. Gold foot and handle on Ripon. Entered in pattern book during or after 1940.
Backstamp(s): Green Shelley 1940-1966. Georgian.
Shapes: Gainsborough, Ripon

13364 **Sheraton**. Pink and gold border inside cup and on saucer. Floral garland outside cup and sprays inside cup and on saucer. White ground. Gold edges, foot and handle. Entered in pattern book during or after 1940.
Backstamp(s): Green Shelley 1940-1966
Shapes: Gainsborough

13365 **Sheraton**. Green and gold border inside cup and on saucer. Floral garland outside cup and sprays inside cup and on saucer. White ground. Gold edges, foot and handle. Entered in pattern book during or after 1940.
Backstamp(s): Green Shelley 1940-1966
Shapes: Gainsborough

13366 **Sheraton**. Blue and gold border inside cup and on saucer. Floral garland outside cup and sprays inside cup and on saucer. White ground. Gold edges, foot and handle. Entered in pattern book during or after 1940.
Backstamp(s): Green Shelley 1940-1966
Shapes: Gainsborough

13367 **Maytime**. Chintz. Red, pink, yellow, and blue flowers on a mint green chintz background inside cup and centre of saucer. Pale green outside cup and body of saucer. Gold edges, foot and handle. Entered in pattern book during or after 1940.
Backstamp(s): Shelley 1925-1940
Shapes: Footed Oleander

Maytime 13367/S11 Footed Oleander shape cup and saucer. £80-100; $150-200

Georgian 13361 Tea set, twelve place, forty-one pieces. £600-900; $1,500-2,000

13368 **Maytime**. Chintz. Border of red, pink, yellow, and blue flowers on a mint green chintz background. Gold edges. Entered in pattern book during or after 1940.
Backstamp(s): Shelley 1925-1940
Shapes: Henley

13369 **Maytime**. Chintz. Red, pink, yellow, and blue flowers on a mint green chintz background outside cup and on saucer. Plain colour inside cup. Gold edges, foot and handle. Entered in pattern book during or after 1940.
Backstamp(s): Shelley 1925-1940
Shapes: Ripon

13370 **Daffodil Time**. Springtime scene with a host of daffodils in yellow, white, and amber. Mauve crocuses. Grass and woods in the background. Group of daffodils and crocuses inside cup. Gold edges. Pale yellow handle. Similar to 0295. Entered in pattern book during or after 1940.
Backstamp(s): Shelley 1940-1966
Shapes: Cambridge, Dainty, Henley, New Cambridge, Richmond, Victor

Daffodil Time 13370 Cambridge shape cup and saucer. £40-£50; $75-85

13371 **Crochet**. Pastel or white ground. Grey lacy border on edge of saucer, around centre of the saucer, rim of outside and outside cup. Pink, blue, yellow, and amber flowers on outer band and centre of saucer. Also **outside cup**. Gold edges, foot and handle. Entered in pattern book during or after 1940.
Backstamp(s): Shelley 1940-1966
Shapes: Gainsborough

Crochet 13371 Gainsborough shape cup and saucer. £40-50; $80-100

Crochet 13371/S15 Ripon shape cup and saucer. £40-50; $80-100

Pattern	Description & Shapes
13372	Ivory **Summer Glory**. Chintz. Blue, white, and deep pink flowers on a chintz ground. Gold edges, foot and handle. Also called **Pink Clover**. **Backstamp(s)**: Shelley 1940-1966 Summer Glory **Shapes:** Ripon

Crochet pin dish. £20-30; $30-40

13373 Ivory **Summer Glory**. Chintz. Blue, white, and deep pink flowers on a chintz ground. Chintz band on upper half of outside cup – approximately to base of handle. Area of outside cup below chintz plain colour. Chintz and plain colour separated by a fawn line. Gold edges.
Backstamp(s): Shelley 1940-1966 Summer Glory
Shapes: Henley

13374 Ivory **Summer Glory**. Chintz. Blue, white, and deep pink flowers on a chintz ground inside cup. Outside cup and saucer are a plain colour. Gold edges, foot and handle.
Backstamp(s): Shelley 1940-1966 Summer Glory
Shapes: Footed Oleander

Ivory **Summer Glory** 13374 Footed Oleander shape cup and saucer. £70-90; $120-150

13375 Ivory **Summer Glory**. Chintz. Blue, white, and deep pink flowers on a chintz ground. Gold edges and line inside cup.
Backstamp(s): Shelley 1940-1966 Summer Glory
Shapes: Cambridge

13376 Ivory **Summer Glory**. Chintz. Blue, white, and deep pink flowers on a chintz ground. Ivory outside cup. Gold edges, foot and handle.
Backstamp(s): Shelley 1940-1966 Summer Glory
Shapes: Ripon

13377 Pink **Summer Glory**. Chintz. Blue, white, and deep pink flowers on a chintz ground. Ivory outside cup. Gold edges, foot and handle.
Backstamp(s): Shelley 1940-1966 Summer Glory
Shapes: Ripon

Pink **Summer Glory** 13377 Ripon shape cup and saucer. £70-90; $120-150

13378 **Summer Glory**. Chintz. Blue, white, and deep pink flowers on a chintz ground. Chintz border on upper part of outside cup. Area of outside cup below chintz plain colour. Gold edges.
Backstamp(s): Shelley 1940-1966 Summer Glory
Shapes: Henley

13379 Pink **Summer Glory**. Chintz. Blue, white, and deep pink flowers on a chintz ground inside cup. Outside cup and saucer are a plain colour. Gold edges, foot and handle.
Backstamp(s): Shelley 1940-1966 Summer Glory
Shapes: Footed Oleander

Pink **Summer Glory** 13379 Footed Oleander shape cup and saucer. £70-90; $120-150

13380 Pink **Summer Glory**. Chintz. Blue, white, and deep pink flowers on a chintz ground. Gold edges and line inside cup., Chester: chintz on inside and line on outside.
Backstamp(s): Shelley 1940-1966 Summer Glory
Shapes: Cambridge, Chester

13381 Pink **Summer Glory**. Chintz. Blue, white, and deep pink flowers on a chintz ground.
Backstamp(s): Shelley 1940-1966 Summer Glory
Shapes: Ripon

13382 **Melody**. Chintz. Red, pink, yellow, and blue flowers on a mint green chintz background. Gold edges, foot and handle.
Backstamp(s):
Shapes: Ripon

13383 **Blue Daisy**. Chintz. White daisies and blue leaves on a lighter blue ground. Gold edges.
Backstamp(s): Shelley 1940-1966
Shapes: Carlisle

Blue Daisy 13383 Carlisle shape cup and saucer. £70-90; $120-150

13384 **Green Daisy**. Chintz. White daisies and green leaves on a lighter green ground. Gold edges.
Backstamp(s): Shelley 1940-1966
Shapes: Ripon

13385 **Rock Garden**. Chintz. Rockery plants set amongst grey stones. Pink, blue, yellow, and whiter flowers with green foliage. Patterned outside cup and on saucer. Plain colour inside cup. Gold edges, foot and handle.
Backstamp(s): Shelley 1940-1966 Rock Garden
Shapes: Ripon

Rock Garden 13385 Ripon shape cup and saucer. £70-90; $120-150

Pattern	Description & Shapes
13386	**Maytime**. Chintz. Red, pink, yellow, and blue flowers on a mint green chintz background outside cup and on saucer. Plain colour inside cup. Gold edges, foot and handle. Entered in pattern book during or after 1940. **Backstamp(s)**: Shelley 1925-1940 **Shapes:** Ripon
13387	Ratauds **Regal**. Maroon and yellow scrolled border. Pink, blue, white, and yellow flowers with green foliage on a white ground. Flowers also inside cup. Gold edges. Entered in pattern book during or after 1940. **Backstamp(s)**: Shelley 1940-1966 Regal **Shapes:** Chester, Gainsborough
13388	Ratauds **Regal**. Green and yellow scrolled border. Pink, blue, white, and yellow flowers with green foliage on a white ground. Flowers also inside cup. Gold edges. Entered in pattern book during or after 1940. **Backstamp(s)**: Shelley 1940-1966 Regal **Shapes:** Chester, Gainsborough
13389	Ratauds **Regal**. Blue and yellow scrolled border. Pink, blue, white, and yellow flowers with green foliage on a white ground. Flowers also inside cup. Gold edges. Entered in pattern book during or after 1940. **Backstamp(s)**: Shelley 1940-1966 Regal **Shapes:** Chester, Gainsborough, Mocha
13390	Ratauds **Regal**. Maroon and yellow scrolled border. Pink, blue, white, and yellow flowers with green foliage on a white ground. Flowers also inside cup. Gold edges, foot and handle. Entered in pattern book during or after 1940. **Backstamp(s)**: Shelley 1940-1966 Regal **Shapes:** Chester, Gainsborough
13391	Ratauds **Regal**. Green and yellow scrolled border. Pink, blue, white, and yellow flowers with green foliage on a white ground. Flowers also inside cup. Gold edges, foot and handle. Entered in pattern book during or after 1940. **Backstamp(s)**: Shelley 1940-1966 Regal **Shapes:** Chester, Gainsborough
13392	Ratauds **Regal**. Blue and yellow scrolled border. Pink, blue, white, and yellow flowers with green foliage on a white ground. Flowers also inside cup. Gold edges, foot and handle. Entered in pattern book during or after 1940. **Backstamp(s)**: Shelley 1940-1966 Regal **Shapes:** Chester, Gainsborough
13393	**Virginian Leaf**. Entered in pattern book during or after 1940. **Backstamp(s)**: Shelley 1940-1966 **Shapes:** Gainsborough, Mocha
13394	Tree pattern. Entered in pattern book during or after 1940. **Backstamp(s)**: Shelley 1940-1966 **Shapes:** Gainsborough
13395	Ratauds **Dubarry**. Maroon border. Pink, yellow, and blue flowers with green leaves. Gold edges. Entered in pattern book during or after 1940. **Backstamp(s)**: Shelley 1940-1966 Dubarry **Shapes:** Cambridge, Chester, Gainsborough, Henley, Mocha, Ripon
13396	Ratauds **Dubarry**. Green border. Pink, yellow, and blue flowers with green leaves. Gold edges. **Backstamp(s)**: Shelley 1940-1966 Dubarry **Shapes:** Cambridge, Chester, Gainsborough, Henley, Mocha, Ripon
13397	Ratauds **Dubarry**. Blue border. Pink, yellow, and blue flowers with green leaves. Gold edges. Entered in pattern book during or after 1940. **Backstamp(s)**: Shelley 1940-1966 Dubarry **Shapes:** Cambridge, Chester, Gainsborough, Henley, Mocha, Ripon
13398	Ratauds **Dubarry**. Maroon border. Pink, yellow, and blue flowers with green leaves. Gold edges. Entered in pattern book during or after 1940. **Backstamp(s)**: Shelley 1940-1966 Dubarry **Shapes:** Cambridge, Chester, Gainsborough, Henley, Mocha, Ripon
13399	Ratauds **Dubarry**. Green border. Pink, yellow, and blue flowers with green leaves. Gold edges. Entered in pattern book during or after 1940 **Backstamp(s)**: Shelley 1940-1966 Dubarry **Shapes:** Cambridge, Chester, Gainsborough, Henley, Mocha, Ripon
13400	Ratauds **Dubarry**. Blue border. Pink, yellow, and blue flowers with green leaves. Gold edges. Entered in pattern book during or after 1940. **Backstamp(s)**: Shelley 1940-1966 Dubarry **Shapes:** Cambridge, Chester, Gainsborough, Henley, Mocha, Ripon
13401	Ratauds red **Duchess**. Blue, pink, and yellow bunch of flowers on base of outside cup. Broad patterned border inside cup. Border is mainly red and gold. Outside cup has a bunch of flowers on a white ground with a gold ring around the cup. Gold trim. Entered in pattern book during or after 1940. **Backstamp(s)**: 1940-1966 Duchess **Shapes:** Cambridge, Chester, Gainsborough, Henley, Mocha, Ripon
13402	Ratauds green **Duchess**. Blue, pink, and yellow bunch of flowers on base of outside cup. Broad patterned border inside cup. Border is mainly green and gold. Outside cup has a bunch of flowers on a white ground with a gold ring around the cup. Gold trim. Entered in pattern book during or after 1940. **Backstamp(s)**: 1940-1966 Duchess **Shapes:** Cambridge, Chester, Gainsborough, Henley, Mocha, Ripon
13403	Ratauds blue **Duchess**. Blue, pink, and yellow bunch of flowers on base of outside cup. Broad patterned border inside cup. Border is mainly blue/turquoise and gold. Outside cup has a bunch of flowers on a white ground with a gold ring around the cup. Gold trim. Entered in pattern book during or after 1940. **Backstamp(s)**: Shelley 1940-1966 **Shapes:** Cambridge, Chester, Gainsborough, Henley, Mocha, Ripon
13404	Ratauds maroon **Duchess**. Blue, pink, and yellow bunch of flowers on base of outside cup. Broad patterned border inside cup. Border is mainly maroon and gold. Outside cup has a bunch of flowers on a white ground with a gold ring around the cup. Gold trim. Entered in pattern book during or after 1940. **Backstamp(s)**: Shelley 1940-1966 **Shapes:** Cambridge, Chester, Gainsborough, Henley, Mocha, Ripon

Maroon **Duchess** 13404 Gainsborough shape cup and saucer. £40-50; $80-100

13405	Ratauds green **Duchess**. Blue, pink, and yellow bunch of flowers on base of outside cup. Broad patterned border inside cup. Border is mainly green and gold. Outside cup has a bunch of flowers on a white ground with a gold ring around the cup. Gold trim. Entered in pattern book during or after 1940. **Backstamp(s)**: Shelley 1940-1966 **Shapes:** Cambridge, Chester, Gainsborough, Henley, Mocha, Ripon
13406	Ratauds blue **Duchess**. Blue, pink, and yellow bunch of flowers on base of outside cup. Broad patterned border inside cup. Border is mainly blue and gold. Outside cup has a bunch of flowers on a white ground with a gold ring around the cup. Gold trim. Entered in pattern book during or after 1940. **Backstamp(s)**: Shelley 1940-1966 **Shapes:** Cambridge, Chester, Gainsborough, Henley, Mocha, Ripon
13407	**Rock Garden**. Chintz. Rockery plants set amongst grey stones. Pink, blue, yellow, and whiter flowers with green foliage. Patterned inside cup and centre of saucer. Plain colour outside cup and on saucer. Gold edges, foot and handle. Entered in pattern book during or after 1940. **Backstamp(s)**: Shelley 1940-1966 Rock Garden **Shapes:** Henley

Rock Garden 13407 Henley shape cup and saucer. £70-90; $120-150

Right:
Dubarry 13395 and 13397 Gainsborough shape cup and saucer. £40-50; $80-100

Pattern	Description & Shapes
13408	**Maytime**. Chintz. Patterned inside cup and centre of saucer. Plain colour outside cup and on saucer. Gold edges, foot and handle. Entered in pattern book during or after 1940. **Backstamp(s)**: Shelley 1940-1966 **Shapes:** Henley
13409	Ivory **Summer Glory**. Chintz. Blue, white, and deep pink flowers on a chintz ground inside cup and centre of saucer. Outside cup and main body of saucer plain colour. Entered in pattern book during or after 1940. **Backstamp(s)**: Shelley 1940-1966 Summer Glory **Shapes:** Henley
13410	Pink **Summer Glory**. Chintz. Blue, white, and deep pink flowers on a chintz ground inside cup and centre of saucer. Outside cup and main body of saucer plain colour. Entered in pattern book during or after 1940. **Backstamp(s)**: Shelley 1940-1966 Summer Glory **Shapes:** Henley
13411	**Daffodil Time**. Patterned inside cup and centre of saucer. Plain colour outside cup and on saucer. Gold edges, foot and handle. Entered in pattern book during or after 1940. **Backstamp(s)**: Shelley 1940-1966 **Shapes:** Henley
13412	**Melody**. Chintz. Red, pink, yellow, and blue flowers on a mint green chintz background inside cup. Mint green outside cup and on saucer. Gold edges, foot and handle. Entered in pattern book during or after 1940. **Backstamp(s)**: Shelley 1940-1966. **Shapes:** Footed Oleander, Mocha

Melody 13412 Footed Oleander shape cup and saucer. £70-90; $120-150

13413	**Blue Daisy**. Chintz. White daisies and blue leaves on a lighter blue ground inside cup and centre of saucer. Pale blue outside cup and on saucer. Gold edges, foot and handle. Entered in pattern book during or after 1940. /P **Blue Pansy** chintz. **Backstamp(s)**: Shelley 1940-1966 **Shapes:** Footed Oleander

Right:
Blue Daisy 13413 Footed Oleander shape cup and saucer. £70-90; $120-150

13414	**Green Daisy**. Chintz. White daisies and green leaves on a lighter green ground inside cup and centre of saucer. Pale green outside cup and on saucer. Gold edges, foot and handle. Entered in pattern book during or after 1940. **Backstamp(s)**: Shelley 1940-1966 **Shapes:** Footed Oleander
13415	**Rock Garden**. Chintz. Rockery plants set amongst grey stones. Pink, blue, yellow, and whiter flowers with green foliage. Patterned inside cup with pale peachy-yellow outside cup and on saucer. Gold edges, foot and handle. Entered in pattern book during or after 1940. /S9 pink **Backstamp(s)**: Shelley 1940-1966 Rock Garden **Shapes:** Footed Oleander
13415	**Rock Garden**. Chintz. Rockery plants set amongst grey stones. Pink, blue, yellow, and whiter flowers with green foliage. Patterned inside cup with pale yellow outside cup and on saucer. Gold edges, foot and handle. Entered in pattern book during or after 1940. /S9 pink **Backstamp(s)**: Shelley 1940-1966 Rock Garden **Shapes:** Footed Oleander
13416	**Maytime**. Chintz. Patterned inside cup. Pink outside cup and on saucer. Gold edges, foot and handle. Entered in pattern book during or after 1940. **Backstamp(s)**: Shelley 1940-1966 **Shapes:** Footed Oleander
13417	Ivory **Summer Glory**. Chintz. Blue, white, and deep pink flowers on a chintz ground inside cup. Salmon outside cup and on saucer. Gold edges, foot and handle. Entered in pattern book during or after 1940. **Backstamp(s)**: Shelley 1940-1966 Summer Glory **Shapes:** Footed Oleander
13418	Pink **Summer Glory**. Chintz. Blue, white, and deep pink flowers on a chintz ground inside cup. Mauve outside cup and on saucer. Gold edges, foot and handle. Entered in pattern book during or after 1940., Mocha: chintz on saucer and on outside of cup. /S7 Yellow. **Backstamp(s)**: Shelley 1940-1966 Summer Glory **Shapes:** Footed Oleander, Mocha

13419	**Heather**. Countryside scene with pink heather, trees, bridge, and river. Gold edges. Pale green handle. Entered in pattern book during or after 1940. **Backstamp(s)**: Shelley 1940-1966 Heather **Shapes:** Cambridge, New Cambridge, Perth, Vincent

Heather 13419 New Cambridge shaped cup and saucer. £40-50; $80-100

Heather 13419 Vincent shaped cup and saucer. £30-45; $40-65.

13420	**Englands Charm**. Country scene. Pink flowers in the foreground, probably heather, with woods in the background. Swathe of pink flowers inside cup below rim. Gold edges. Green handle. Entered in pattern book during or after 1940. **Backstamp(s)**: Shelley 1940-1966 **Shapes:** Cambridge
13421	**Royalty**. Broad border of pink roses, green and brown leaves on a pale green ground. Gold edges. Pale green handle. Entered in pattern book during or after 1940. **Backstamp(s)**: Shelley 1940-1966; Royalty **Shapes:** Henley
13422	Ratauds **Pink Rose**. Gold edges. Pink handle. Entered in pattern book during or after 1940. **Backstamp(s)**: Shelley 1940-1966; Royalty **Shapes:** Henley
13423	Warwick Savage **Rose**. Gold edges. Blue handle. Entered in pattern book during or after 1940. /D Dark **Rose** **Backstamp(s)**: Shelley 1940-1966; Royalty **Shapes:** Henley
13424	**Roses, Pansies, and Forget-me-nots**. Floral sprays on a white ground. Pale

Pattern	Description & Shapes
	blue edge and handle. Entered in pattern book during or after 1940. **Backstamp(s)**: Shelley 1940-1966 **Shapes:** Canterbury, Carlisle, Dainty, Ludlow, Oleander, Richmond, Tall Dainty

Roses, Pansies, and Forget-Me-Nots 13424 Dainty shape cup and saucer. £50-60; $110-130

Roses, Pansies, and Forget-Me-Nots 13424 Ludlow shape cup and saucer. £50-60; $110-130

Roses, Pansies and Forget-Me-Nots 13424 Richmond shape cup and saucer. £50-60; $110-130

13425 **Rose and Red Daisy** or **Rose Spray**. Pink roses and red daisies with green leaves. Rose spray also inside cup. Pink edges and handle. Entered in pattern book during or after 1940.
Backstamp(s): Shelley 1940-1966; Rose and Red Daisy
Shapes: Dainty, Tall Dainty, Ludlow, Richmond

Rose Spray 13425 Dainty shape cup and saucer. £70-80; $140-160

13426 **Rose** or **Rosebud**. Pale and deep pink roses with green leaves. Pale green edges and handle. Entered in pattern book during or after 1940.
Backstamp(s): Shelley 1940-1966 Rosebud
Shapes: Canterbury, Dainty, Henley, Ludlow, Stratford

Rosebud 13426 Dainty shape cup and saucer. £70-80; $140-160

Rosebud 13426 Henley shape cup and saucer. £50-60; $110-130

13427 **Begonia**. Yellow and pink begonias with brown stems and green leaves. Yellow begonia inside cup. Pale blue edges and handle. Entered in pattern book during or after 1940.
Backstamp(s): Shelley 1940-1966
Shapes: Dainty, Footed Oleander, Lincoln, Low Oleander, Ludlow, Tall Dainty

Begonia 13427 Dainty shape cup and saucer. £70-80; $140-160. Large teapot. £120-150; $240-300. High comport. £95-120; $180-230. Covered muffin dish. £95-120; $180-230. Condiment set. £75-120; $150-200. Sandwich tray. £25-30; $45-55

Begonia 13427 Footed Oleander shape cup and saucer. £50-60; $110-130

Begonia 13427 Low Oleander shape cup and saucer. £55-75; $75-95

Begonia Bute shape cup and saucer. £40-£50; $75-85

Begonia Lincoln shape cup and saucer. £50-60; $110-130

Begonia Ludlow shape cup and saucer. £50-60; $110-130

Pattern	Description & Shapes
13428	**Stocks**. Mauve, pink, and white stocks with green leaves. Pink edges and handle. Entered in pattern book during or after 1940. **Backstamp(s)**: Shelley 1940-1966 Stocks **Shapes:** Dainty, Dorothy, Footed Oleander, Ludlow, Oleander, Snowdrop, Richmond, Tall Dainty

Stocks 13428 Dorothy shape cup and saucer. £50-60; $110-130

Stocks 13428 Ludlow shape cup and saucer. £50-60; $110-130

Stocks 13428 Oleander shape cup and saucer. £55-75; $75-95

13429	**Blossom**. Branches of blossom in shades of pink with green leaves. Small area of yellow behind blossoms. White ground. Green edges and handle. Entered in pattern book during or after 1940. **Backstamp(s)**: Shelley 1940-1966 **Shapes:** Ludlow, Oleander, Dainty, Dorothy, Richmond

Blossom 13429 Dainty shape cup and saucer. £70-80; $140-160

Blossom 13429 Dorothy shape cup and saucer. £70-80; $140-160

13430	**Primrose**. Pale green edges and handle. Entered in pattern book during or after 1940. **Backstamp(s)**: Shelley 1940-1966 Primrose **Shapes:** Dainty, Dorothy, Perth, New Cambridge, Stratford

Primrose 13430 Dainty shape cup and saucer. £70-80; $140-160

Primrose 13430 Teapot. £125-150; $250-300. New Cambridge shape cup and saucer. £40-50; $80-100

Primrose 13430 Dorothy shape cup and saucer. £35-45; $60-80

Primrose 13430 Oleander shape cup and saucer. £70-80; $140-160

Pattern	Description & Shapes
13431	Small Hulmes **Rose**. Pale pink outside cup and main part of saucer. Ivory inside cup and centre of saucer. Roses outside cup. Rose spray inside cup and centre of saucer. Gold edges, foot and handle. Entered in pattern book during or after 1940. /S18 Green outside cup and main part of saucer. **Backstamp(s)**: Shelley 1940-1966 **Shapes:** Ripon

Right:
Rose 13431/S18 Ripon shape cup and saucer. £70-80; $140-160

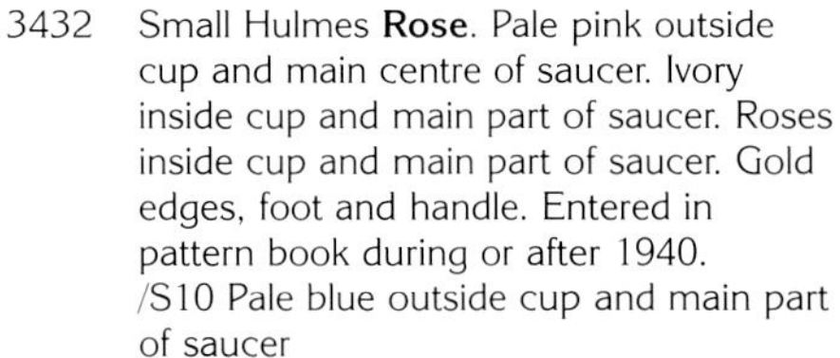

13432	Small Hulmes **Rose**. Pale pink outside cup and main centre of saucer. Ivory inside cup and main part of saucer. Roses inside cup and main part of saucer. Gold edges, foot and handle. Entered in pattern book during or after 1940. /S10 Pale blue outside cup and main part of saucer /S16 Yellow outside cup and centre of saucer. **Backstamp(s)**: Shelley 1940-1966 **Shapes:** Ripon

Rose 13432/S9 Ripon shape cup and saucer. £70-80; $140-160

Rose 13432/S10 Ripon shape cup and saucer. £70-80; $140-160

Rose 13432/S16 Ripon shape cup and saucer. £70-80; $140-160

13433	Hulmes **Dark Rose**. Gold edges. Entered in pattern book during or after 1940. **Backstamp(s)**: Shelley 1940-1966 **Shapes:** Ripon
13434	Hulmes **Rose and Yellow Flower**. Pink outside cup and main part of saucer. Pink rose with flowers and foliage inside cup and centre of saucer on a white ground. Gold edges, foot and handle. Entered in pattern book during or after 1940. **Backstamp(s)**: Shelley 1940-1966 **Shapes:** Footed Oleander

Rose and Yellow Flower 13434 Footed Oleander shape cup and saucer. £70-80; $140-160

13435	Enterprise **Tulip**. Peach outside cup and main part of saucer. Pink tulip with flowers and foliage inside cup and centre of saucer on a white ground. Gold edges, foot and handle. Entered in pattern book during or after 1940. **Backstamp(s)**: Shelley 1940-1966 **Shapes:** Footed Oleander

Tulip 13435 Footed Oleander shape cup and saucer. £70-80; $140-160

Pattern	Description & Shapes
13436	Hulmes **Rose**. Pink roses and small blue flowers with green foliage inside cup and on saucer. Green ground. Gold line outside cup approximately halfway between rim and base. Gold edges, foot and handle. Entered in pattern book during or after 1940. **Backstamp(s)**: Shelley 1940-1966 **Shapes:** Henley, Oleander

Rose 13436 Henley shape cup and saucer. $40-65; £30-45

13437	**Dresden**. Pattern inside cup and centre of saucer on a white ground. Blue outside cup and main part of saucer. Gold edges, foot and handle. Entered in pattern book during or after 1940. **Backstamp(s)**: Shelley 1940-1966 **Shapes:** Oleander
13438	**Dresden**. Pattern inside cup and centre of saucer on a white ground. Orange outside cup and main part of saucer. Gold edges, foot and handle. Entered in pattern book during or after 1940. **Backstamp(s)**: Shelley 1940-1966 **Shapes:** Oleander
13439	**Rose and Red Daisy**. Pattern inside cup and centre of saucer on an ivory ground. Colour ground outside cup and main part of saucer. Gold edges, foot and handle. Entered in pattern book during or after 1940. **Backstamp(s)**: Shelley 1940-1966 **Shapes:** Ripon
13440	Hulmes **Rose and White Flower**. Pattern inside cup and in centre of saucer. Colour ground outside cup and main part of saucer. Gold edges, foot and handle. Entered in pattern book during or after 1940. **Backstamp(s)**: Shelley 1940-1966 **Shapes:** Ripon
13441	**Blue Rock**. Tiny blue flowers and green leaves. Litho inside cup. Plain colour outside cup and on saucer. Gold edges, foot and handle. Entered in pattern book during or after 1940. **Backstamp(s)**: Shelley 1940-1966 **Shapes:** Footed Oleander, Ripon
13442	**Heather**. Green outside cup and outer band of saucer. Countryside scene with pink heather, trees, bridge, and river inside cup and on saucer centre on a white background. Gold edges, handle and foot. Entered in pattern book during or after 1940. **Backstamp(s)**: Shelley 1940-1966 **Shapes:** Henley

Right:
Heather 13442 Henley shape cup and saucer. $40-65; £30-45

13443	**Woodland**. Blue, pink, and yellow flowers, green foliage and trees set into a woodland landscape. Entered in pattern book during or after 1940. **Backstamp(s)**: Shelley 1940-1966 **Shapes:** Ripon
13444	**Green Daisy**. Chintz. White daisies and green leaves on a lighter green ground inside cup and centre of saucer. Green outside cup and main body of saucer. Gold edges, foot and handle. Note in pattern book: 'DON'T DO THIS PATTERN'. **Backstamp(s)**: Shelley 1940-1966 **Shapes:** Henley, Ripon
13445	**Blue Daisy**. Chintz. White daisies and blue leaves on a lighter blue ground inside cup and centre of saucer. Blue outside cup and main body of saucer. Gold edges, foot and handle. Note in pattern book: 'DON'T DO THIS PATTERN'. **Backstamp(s)**: Shelley 1940-1966 **Shapes:** Henley, Ripon
13446	**Melody**. Chintz. Red, pink, yellow, and blue flowers on a mint green chintz background inside cup and centre of saucer. Dark coloured outside cup and body of saucer. Note in pattern book: 'DON'T DO THIS PATTERN'. **Backstamp(s)**: Shelley 1925-1940. **Shapes:** Henley, Ripon

Melody 13446 Henley shape cup and saucer. £70-80; $120-150

13447	Enamelled turquoise polka dots on white ground. Gold dontil edge outside cup and on saucer. Gold edges, foot and handle. **Backstamp(s)**: Shelley 1940-1966 **Shapes:** Henley
13448	**Sheraton**. Green and gold border inside cup and on saucer. Floral garland outside cup and sprays inside cup and on saucer. White ground. Gold edges, foot and handle. **Backstamp(s)**: Shelley 1940-1966 Sheraton **Shapes:** Gainsborough

Sheraton 13448 Gainsborough shape cup and saucer. £40-50; $50-100

13449	**Sheraton**. Blue and gold border inside cup and on saucer. Floral garland outside cup and sprays inside cup and on saucer. White ground. Gold edges, foot and handle. **Backstamp(s)**: Shelley 1940-1966 Sheraton **Shapes:** Gainsborough, Mocha
13450	**Green Daisy**. Chintz. White daisies and green leaves on a lighter green ground. Gold edges. Green foot and handle. **Backstamp(s)**: Shelley 1940-1966 **Shapes:** Cambridge, Henley

Green Daisy 13450 Henley shape cup and saucer. £70-90; $120-150

Pattern	Description & Shapes
13451	**Blue Daisy**. Chintz. White daisies and blue leaves on a lighter blue ground. Blue edges, foot and handle. **Backstamp(s)**: Shelley 1940-1966 **Shapes:** Cambridge, Henley
13452	**Maytime**. Small pink flowers in varying shades of pink with brown branches and green foliage. Inside cup pale fawn. Dull yellow foot (Henley) and handle. Gold edges. **Backstamp(s)**: Shelley 1940-1966 **Shapes:** Cambridge, Henley

Maytime 13452 Henley shape cup and saucer. £80-100; $150-200

13453 **Melody**. Chintz. Red, pink, yellow, and blue flowers on a mint green chintz background. S3 has pale green outside cup. Pale green, yellow, pink or blue trim and handle.
Backstamp(s): 1925-1940, 1940-1966 Melody
Shapes: Henley, Richmond

Melody 13453/S3 Henley shape cup and saucer. £70-80; $120-150

13454 **Rock Garden**. Chintz. Rockery plants set amongst grey stones. Pink, blue, yellow, and whiter flowers with green foliage. Pale green outside cup. Green edges and handles.
Backstamp(s): 1940-1966 Rock Garden
Shapes: Henley, Richmond

Right:
Rock Garden 13454 Henley shape cup and saucer. £70-80; $120-150

13455 Ivory **Summer Glory**. Chintz. Blue, white, and deep pink flowers on a chintz ground. Inside cup is pale blue. Blue handle. Blue foot on Henley. Gold edges.
Backstamp(s): Shelley 1940-1966 Summer Glory
Shapes: Cambridge, Henley, New Cambridge, Regent

Ivory **Summer Glory** 13455/20 Cambridge shape cup and saucer. £70-£80; $130-150

13456 Pink **Summer Glory**. Chintz. Blue, white, and deep pink flowers on a chintz ground. Inside cup is pale green. Green handle. Green foot on Henley. Gold edges.
Backstamp(s): Shelley 1940-1966 Summer Glory
Shapes: Cambridge, Henley, New Cambridge

Ivory and pink **Summer Glory** pin/bonbon dishes. £30-40; $50-60

Right:
Pink **Summer Glory** 13456 Henley shape cup and saucer. £70-80; $130-150

13457 **Crochet**. Pastel or white ground. Grey lacy border on edge of saucer, around centre of the saucer, rim of outside, and outside cup. Pink, blue, yellow, and amber flowers on outer band and centre of saucer. Also **outside cup**. Gold edges, foot and handle.
Backstamp(s): Shelley 1940-1966
Shapes: Ripon

13458 **Begonia**. Gold edges, foot and handle.
Backstamp(s): Shelley 1940-1966
Shapes: Henley, Ripon

Begonia 13458 Henley shape cup and saucer. £40-50; $50-100

13459 **Stocks**. Mauve, pink, and white stocks with green leaves inside cup and centre of saucer on ivory ground. Plain colour outside cup and body of saucer. Gold edges, foot and handle.
Backstamp(s): Shelley 1940-1966
Shapes: Ripon

13460 **Blossom**. Branches of blossom in shades of pink with green leaves inside cup and centre of saucer with small area of yellow behind blossoms on white ground. Plain colour outside cup and body of saucer. Gold edges, foot and handle.
Backstamp(s): Shelley 1940-1966
Shapes: Ripon

Blossom 13460 Ripon shape cup and saucer. £40-50; $80-100

Blossom 13460 Ripon shape cup and saucer. £40-50; $80-100

13461 **Primrose**. Burgundy outside cup and on saucer. Primrose spray inside cup and centre of saucer.
Was also produced with **Rose Spray** inside cup and centre of saucer.
Backstamp(s): Shelley 1940-1966
Shapes: Ripon

Right:
Primrose 13461 Ripon shape cup and saucer. £70-80; $140-160

13462 Enterprise **Tulip**. Bouquet of pink, blue, lilac, and yellow flowers with green foliage on a white ground. Tulip spray inside cup. Pale blue handle. Gold edges.
Backstamp(s): Shelley 1940-1966
Shapes: Dorothy, Victor

13463 Colour ground outside cup and main part of saucer. White inside cup and centre of saucer. Gold edges, foot and handle.
Backstamp(s): Shelley 1940-1966
Shapes: Ripon

13464 **Roses, Pansies, and Forget-me-nots**. Floral sprays on a white ground. Blue border. Gold edges.
Backstamp(s): Shelley 1940-1966
Shapes: Chester, Richmond

13465 **Rose and Red Daisy**. Maroon border. Gold edges.
Backstamp(s): Shelley 1940-1966
Shapes: Chester, Richmond

13466 **Rose**. Green border. Gold edges.
Backstamp(s): Shelley 1940-1966
Shapes: Chester, Henley

13467 **Begonia**. Maroon and yellow border inside cup and on saucer. Yellow and pink begonias with brown stems and green leaves. Begonias also inside cup. White ground. Gold edges.
Backstamp(s): Shelley 1940-1966
Shapes: Chester

13468 **Stocks**. Mauve, pink, and white stocks with green leaves. Maroon border on cup and on saucer. White ground. Gold edges and handle.
Backstamp(s): Shelley 1940-1966
Shapes: Chester, Richmond

13469 **Blossom**. Branches of blossom in shades of pink with green leaves. Small area of yellow behind blossoms. Maroon border on cup and on saucer. White ground. Gold edges and handle.
Backstamp(s): Shelley 1940-1966
Shapes: Chester, Henley

13470 **Primrose**. Green border. Gold edges.
Backstamp(s): Shelley 1940-1966
Shapes: Richmond

13471 **Rose Sprays**. Green border. Gold edges.
Backstamp(s): Shelley 1940-1966
Shapes: Henley

13472 **Open Rose**. Blue border. Gold edges.
Backstamp(s): Shelley 1940-1966
Shapes: Henley

13473 **Dark Rose**. Blue border. Gold edges.
Backstamp(s): Shelley 1940-1966
Shapes: Cambridge

13474 **Georgian**. Green edges.
Backstamp(s): Shelley 1940-1966
Shapes: Oleander

13475 **Rose and Red Daisy**. Blue edges.
Backstamp(s): Shelley 1940-1966
Shapes: Dainty

13476 **Roses, Pansies, and Forget-me-nots**. Floral sprays on a white ground. Blue border inside cup. Gold edges.
Backstamp(s): Shelley 1940-1966
Shapes: Footed Oleander

13477 **Blossom**. Maroon border inside cup. Gold edges.
Backstamp(s): Shelley 1940-1966

Shapes: Footed Oleander, Henley, Richmond

13478 **Primrose**. Green border inside cup. Gold edges.
Backstamp(s): Shelley 1940-1966
Shapes: Richmond

13479 **Rose and Red Daisy** and **Georgian**. Maroon border inside cup.
Backstamp(s): Shelley 1940-1966
Shapes: Gainsborough

13480 **Rose**. Blue edges and handle.
Backstamp(s): Shelley 1940-1966
Shapes: Dainty

13481 **Rose Sprays**. Green edges and handle.
Backstamp(s): Shelley 1940-1966
Shapes: Dainty

Rose Sprays 13481 Dainty shape cup and saucer. £70-80; $140-160

13482 **Begonia**. Red border on edge of saucer and inside cup. Yellow and pink begonias with brown stems and green leaves inside cup. Pink begonia **outside cup**. Gold edges.
Backstamp(s): Shelley 1940-1966
Shapes: Footed Oleander

Begonia 13482 Footed Oleander shape cup and saucer. £55-75; $75-95

13483 **Stocks**. Mauve, pink, and white stocks with green leaves. Maroon border on cup and on saucer. White ground. Gold border inside cup, edges and handle.
Backstamp(s): Shelley 1940-1966
Shapes: Footed Oleander

13484 **Rose Sprays**. Green border inside cup. Gold edges.
Backstamp(s): Shelley 1940-1966
Shapes: Oleander

13485 Coloured and gold **Patches** outside cup and on saucer interspersed with sprays of **Roses and Red Daisies**. One spray inside cup. Gold dontil edges, foot and

handle.
/2 Peach.
Backstamp(s): Shelley 1940-1966
Shapes: Ely, Gainsborough, Henley, Ripon

13486 Plain colours. Gold dontil edges. Gold foot and handle.
Backstamp(s): Shelley 1940-1966
Shapes: Ely

13487 Plain colour. Bubbly gold edges. Gold foot and handle.
Backstamp(s): Shelley 1940-1966
Shapes: Ely, Ripon

Yellow and gold 13487/S1 Ely shape cup and saucer. £70-80; $140-160

13488 Plain colours. Gold dontil edges. Gold foot and handle.
Backstamp(s): Shelley 1940-1966
Shapes: Henley, Richmond

13489 **Roses, Pansies, and Forget-me-nots**. Floral sprays on a white ground. Blue edges and handle.
Backstamp(s): Shelley 1940-1966
Shapes: Dainty

13490 **Patches** and **Georgian**. Gold dontil edges. Gold foot and handle.
Backstamp(s): Shelley 1940-1966
Shapes: Ripon

13491 **Rose**. Pink edges and handle.
Backstamp(s): Shelley 1940-1966
Shapes: Dainty

13492 **Wreath** or **Hedgerow**.
Hedgerow: Pink, blue, yellow, and orange flowers with green foliage on a white ground. Gold edges.
Backstamp(s): Shelley 1940-1966 Hedgerow
Shapes: Gainsborough, Regent, Richmond

Hedgerow 13492 Gainsborough shape cup and saucer. £40-50; $80-100

Hedgerow 13492 Richmond shape cup and saucer. £40-50; $80-100

13493 **Begonia**. Yellow and pink begonias with brown stems and green leaves outside cup and on saucer on pink ground. Ivory inside cup. Gold edges, foot and handle.
Backstamp(s): Shelley 1940-1966
Shapes: Ely, Ripon

Begonia 13493 Ripon shape cup and saucer. £40-50; $80-100

1
3494 **Primrose**. Patterned outside cup and on saucer on blue ground. Gold edges, foot and handle.
Backstamp(s): Shelley 1940-1966
Shapes: Ely

13495 **Blossom**. Patterned outside cup and on saucer on puce ground. Gold edges, foot and handle.
Backstamp(s): Shelley 1940-1966
Shapes: Ely

13496 **Stocks**. Mauve, pink, and white stocks with green leaves outside cup and on saucer on green ground. Ivory inside cup. Gold edges, foot and handle.
Backstamp(s): Shelley 1940-1966
Shapes: Ely, Gainsborough, Ripon

13497 Polka Dots. Raised, coloured polka dots on a white ground. Gold dontil border on rim of cup and on saucer. Gold edges, foot and handle.
/A Turquoise
/B Blue
/C Green
/D Coral/red
/E Black
/G Green
/Y Yellow.
Backstamp(s): Shelley 1940-1966
Shapes: Coffee Cans, Henley

Polka Dots 13497/A Henley shape cup and saucer. £60-75; $85-100

Polka Dots 13497/B seven-piece sandwich/cake set. £70-80; $140-160

Polka Dots 13497/D Henley shape cup and saucer. £60-75; $85-100

Pattern **Description & Shapes**

13498 **Patches** and **Georgian** patterns inside cup and main part of saucer. Floral sprays outside cup. Gold edges, foot and handle.
/S40 Pink.
Backstamp(s): Shelley 1940-1966
Shapes: Gainsborough

Patches and **Georgian** 13498/S40 Gainsborough shape cup and saucer. £40-50; $80-100

13499 **Panel** and **Rose and Red Daisy**. Gold dontil edge. Gold foot and handle.
Backstamp(s): Shelley 1940-1966
Shapes: Gainsborough, Henley, Ripon

13500 **Rose**. Laurel border inside cup. Pink edges and handle.
Backstamp(s): Shelley 1940-1966
Shapes: Victor

13501 **Dark Rose**. Pink roses and green foliage on a white ground. Blue scroll border. Border also inside cup. Dark blue edges. Pale blue handle.
Backstamp(s): Shelley 1940-1966
Shapes: Perth, Victor

Dark Rose 13501 Perth shape cup and saucer. £40-50; $80-100

13502 **Dark Rose**. Pink roses and green foliage on a white ground. Green border. Dark green edges and handle.
Backstamp(s): Shelley 1940-1966
Shapes: Victor

13503 **Open Rose**. Large bunch of flowers that includes pink, white, and orange roses with green foliage on a white ground. Green scroll border inside cup and on saucer. Green edges. Pale green foot (Ely) and handle.
/D **Dark Rose**.
Backstamp(s): Shelley 1940-1966
Shapes: Ely, Perth, Ripon, Victor

13504 **Motif**. Large pink, blue, and yellow flowers with green and grey leaves. Laurel border inside and outside cup as well on saucers and plates. White ground. Pale green edges and handle.
Hulmes **Rose and White Flower** substituted from 29 October 1946.
Backstamp(s): Shelley 1940-1966
Shapes: Perth, Victor

Motif 13504 Perth shape cup and saucer. £40-50; $80-100

13505 **Motif**. Large pink, blue, and yellow flowers with green and grey leaves. Pink and brown border inside and outside cup as well on saucers and plates. White ground. Pink edges and handle.
Hulmes **Rose and Yellow Flower** substituted from 29 October 1946.
Backstamp(s): Shelley 1940-1966
Shapes: Victor

13506 **Blossom**. Maroon border inside cup. Gold edges, foot and handle.
Backstamp(s): Shelley 1940-1966
Shapes: Henley

13507 **Roses, Pansies, and Forget-me-nots**. Floral sprays on a white ground. Pink, scalloped edges. Pink handle.
Backstamp(s): Shelley 1940-1966
Shapes: Dainty

13508 **Roses, Pansies, and Forget-me-nots** and **Blue Scroll**. Floral sprays on a white ground. Blue edges, foot (Ely) and handle.
Backstamp(s): Shelley 1940-1966
Shapes: Ely, Victor

13509 **Rose and Red Daisy**. Pink edges, foot (Ely) and handle.
/A Laurel border with green edges.
Backstamp(s): Shelley 1940-1966
Shapes: Richmond, Victor

13510 **Rose**. Pink edges and handle.
Backstamp(s): Shelley 1940-1966
Shapes: Ely, Victor

13511 **Begonia**. Green edges and handle.
Backstamp(s): Shelley 1940-1966
Shapes: Ely, Richmond, Victor

13512 **Stocks**. Mauve, pink, and white stocks with green leaves. Flowers also inside cup. Green leafy border. White ground. Gold edges and handle. Gainsborough: Green foot and handle.
/L Old Laurel border.
/P Pink Laurel border, pink edges and handle.
Backstamp(s): Shelley 1940-1966
Shapes: Gainsborough, Victor

13513 **Blossom**. Branches of blossom in shades of pink with green leaves. Small area of yellow behind blossoms. Flowers also inside cup. Green border on cup and on saucer. White ground. Green edges, foot and handle.
/L Old Laurel border.
Backstamp(s): Shelley 1940-1966
Shapes: Ely, Perth, Victor

13514 **Primrose**. Green and pink scroll border. Green edges and handle.
Backstamp(s): Shelley 1940-1966
Shapes: Victor

13515 **Rose Sprays**. Green and pink Laurel border. Pink edges and handle.
Backstamp(s): Shelley 1940-1966
Shapes: New Cambridge, Victor

Rose Sprays 13515 New Cambridge shape cup and saucer. £40-50; $80-100

13516 **Sheraton** border. Gold edges.
Backstamp(s): Shelley 1940-1966
Shapes: Ely, Gainsborough

13517 **Primrose** and **Panels**. Gold edges, foot and handle.
Backstamp(s): Shelley 1940-1966
Shapes: Gainsborough

13518 **Roses, Pansies, and Forget-me-nots**. Floral sprays on a white ground. One sprig inside cup. Blue scroll border and gold edges. Pale foot and handle.
Backstamp(s): Shelley 1940-1966
Shapes: Richmond

13519 **Rose and Red Daisy** or **Rose Spray**. Pink roses and red daisies with green leaves. Rose spray also inside cup. Pink

Right:
Blossom 13513 Ely shape cup and saucer. £40-50; $80-100

edges and handle. Dark pink border inside and outside cup as well as on saucer
Backstamp(s): Shelley 1940-1966; Rose and Red Daisy
Shapes: Henley, New Cambridge

Rose and Red Daisy 13519 New Cambridge shape cup and saucer. £40-50; $80-100

13520 **Rose**. Small sprigs of pink roses and green leaves on a white ground. One sprig inside cup. Strawberry pink swathed border outside cup, on saucer, and plate. Pink print border inside cup. Gold edges. Pink foot and handle.
Backstamp(s): (*Are there no backstamps associated with Rose? Thanks.)
Shapes: Henley

13521 **Begonia**. Red, lacy border inside and outside cup as well as outer edge of saucer. Yellow and pink begonias with brown stems and green leaves. Yellow begonia inside cup. Gold edges. Pale green handle and foot.
Backstamp(s): Shelley 1940-1966
Shapes: Chester, Richmond

13522 **Stocks**. Mauve, pink, and white stocks with green leaves inside cup. Green edges and handle.
Backstamp(s): Shelley 1940-1966
Shapes: Cambridge, Richmond

13523 **Blossoms**. Pink blossoms, brown stems, and green leaves against a yellow patch. Green small scroll border inside cup. Large green scroll border outside cup, edge of saucer, and plate. White ground. Gold edges. Pale green foot and handle.
Backstamp(s): Shelley 1940-1966
Shapes: Henley

13524 **Primrose**. Curls border. Gold edges. Green foot and handle.
Backstamp(s): Shelley 1940-1966
Shapes: Richmond

13525 **Rose Sprays**. Green Laurel border. Gold edges. Pink foot and handle, or ring handle (Regent).
Backstamp(s): Shelley 1940-1966
Shapes: Henley, Regent

13526 **Ivy Leaves**.
Backstamp(s): Shelley 1940-1966
Shapes: Gainsborough

13527 **Acanthus Leaf**.
Backstamp(s): Shelley 1940-1966
Shapes: Gainsborough

13528 **Roses, Pansies, and Forget-me-nots**. Floral sprays on a white ground inside cup. Blue scroll border inside cup. Pale blue outside cup and on saucer. Gold edges, foot and handle.
Backstamp(s): Shelley 1940-1966
Shapes: Footed Oleander

Roses, Pansies, and Forget-me-Nots 13528/S10 Footed Oleander shape cup and saucer. £40-50; $80-100

13529 **Rose and Red Daisy**. Pink roses and red daisies with green leaves inside cup. Maroon border inside cup. Pink outside cup and on saucer. Gold edges, foot and handle.
Backstamp(s): Shelley 1940-1966
Shapes: Footed Oleander

13530 **Rose**. Pink outside cup and on saucer. Gold edges, foot and handle.
Backstamp(s): Shelley 1940-1966
Shapes: Footed Oleander

13531 **Begonia**. Green outside cup and on saucer. Gold edges, foot and handle.
Backstamp(s): Shelley 1940-1966
Shapes: Footed Oleander

13532 **Stocks**. Mauve, pink, and white stocks with green leaves.
Plain colour outside cup and on saucer. Green border inside cup. Gold edges, foot and handle.
/S3 green
/S20 mauve.
Backstamp(s): Shelley 1940-1966
Shapes: Footed Oleander

13533 **Blossom**. Branches of blossom in shades of pink with green leaves inside cup with small area of yellow behind blossoms on white ground.
/S3 green
/S20 pink.
Backstamp(s): Shelley 1940-1966
Shapes: Footed Oleander

Stocks 13532/S20 Footed Oleander shape cup and saucer. £40-50; $80-100

Right:
Stocks 13540 Perth shape cup and saucer. £50-70; $90-100

Blossom 13533/S20 Footed Oleander shape cup and saucer. £40-50; $80-100

13534 **Primrose**. Yellow primroses, small blue flowers, and green leaves inside cup on a white ground. Green border inside cup. Pale green outside cup and on saucer. Gold edges, foot and handle.
Backstamp(s): Shelley 1940-1966
Shapes: Footed Oleander

13535 **Rose Sprays**. Green outside cup and on saucer. Gold edges, foot and handle.
Backstamp(s): Shelley 1940-1966
Shapes: Footed Oleander

Rose Sprays 13535 Footed Oleander shape cup and saucer. £70-80; $140-160

13536 **Gold Star** and **Panels**.
Backstamp(s): Shelley 1940-1966
Shapes: Gainsborough

13537 **Begonia**.
Backstamp(s): Shelley 1940-1966
Shapes: Gainsborough, Mocha

13538 **Blossoms**.
Backstamp(s): Shelley 1940-1966
Shapes: Gainsborough

13539 **Blossoms**.
Backstamp(s): Shelley 1940-1966
Shapes: Regent, Victor

13540 **Stocks**. Mauve, pink, and white stocks with green leaves inside cup. Green

Pattern	Description & Shapes
	edges and handle. Pink edges and handle. /S Salmon edges and handle. **Backstamp(s)**: Shelley 1940-1966 **Shapes:** Perth, Regent, Victor
13541	**Begonia**. **Backstamp(s)**: Shelley 1940-1966 **Shapes:** Regent, Victor
13542	**Old Bow**. **Backstamp(s)**: Shelley 1940-1966 **Shapes:** Henley
13543	**Canadian Wild Flowers**. Same as **Lowestoft**. **Backstamp(s)**: Shelley 1940-1966 **Shapes:** Henley
13544	**Harebell**. Harebells inside and outside cup. Saucer has broad garland of harebells. Saucer and outside cup have a scroll border. Gold edges. Pale blue handle and foot. **Backstamp(s)**: Shelley 1925-1940 **Shapes:** Chester, Henley, Richmond

Harebell 13544 Chester shape cup and saucer. £70-80; $140-160

13545	**Bridal Rose**. Also sometimes labelled **Rose Spray**. Pale and deep pink rose sprays with green leaves. Pale pink edges and handle. **Backstamp(s)**: Shelley 1940-1966 Rose Spray **Shapes:** Canterbury, Gainsborough, Henley, Dainty, Ludlow, Ovide, Richmond

Bridal Rose or **Rose Spray** 13545 Dainty shape cup and saucer. £70-80; $80-160

13546	**Blue Rock**. Tiny blue flowers and green leaves. Scroll border. Gold edges. Green foot and handle. **Backstamp(s)**: Shelley 1940-1966 **Shapes:** Gainsborough
13547	**Gold Motif** and **Patches**. Gold edges, foot (Henley and Gainsborough) and handle. **Backstamp(s)**: Shelley 1940-1966 **Shapes:** Gainsborough, Henley, Queen Anne

Bridal Rose or **Rose Spray** 13545 Ludlow shape cup and saucer. £50-60; $120-160

13548	**Gold Print**. **Backstamp(s)**: Shelley 1940-1966 **Shapes:** Ripon
13549	White spots on colour ground. **Backstamp(s)**: Shelley 1940-1966 **Shapes:** Mocha
13550	**Chinese Gold** and **Gold Shamrock** border. Exotic bird on a deep blue ground. **Backstamp(s)**: Shelley 1940-1966 **Shapes:** Mocha, Ripon
13551	**Chinese Gold**. **Backstamp(s)**: Shelley 1940-1966 **Shapes:** Ripon
13552	**Gold Jungle**. **Backstamp(s)**: Shelley 1940-1966 **Shapes:** Gainsborough
13553	**Rose**. **Backstamp(s)**: Shelley 1940-1966 **Shapes:** Gainsborough
13554	**Montrose**. Ivory panels on a maroon and gold patterned background. **Georgian** flower sprays on the ivory panels, outside cup and centre of saucer. Flower spray inside cup on white ground. Gold edges, foot and handle. **Backstamp(s)**: Shelley 1940-1966 Montrose **Shapes:** Chester, Gainsborough, Ripon

Montrose 13554 Ripon shape cup and saucer. £50-60; $120-160

13555	**Rose Spray**. **Backstamp(s)**: Shelley 1940-1966 **Shapes:** Chester, Gainsborough, Mocha
13556	**Georgian** and **Gold Jungle**. **Backstamp(s)**: Shelley 1940-1966 **Shapes:** Gainsborough
13557	**Georgian**. **Backstamp(s)**: Shelley 1940-1966 **Shapes:** Chester, Gainsborough
13558	**Dubarry** and **Rose**. **Backstamp(s)**: Shelley 1940-1966 **Shapes:** Chester, Gainsborough
13559	**Rose Spray**. **Backstamp(s)**: Shelley 1940-1966 **Shapes:** Gainsborough
13560	**Double Rose Spray**. **Backstamp(s)**: Shelley 1940-1966 **Shapes:** Gainsborough
13561	**Rose and Red Daisy**. **Backstamp(s)**: Shelley 1940-1966 **Shapes:** Gainsborough
13562	**Rose and Red Daisy**. /B Blue Curl border. **Backstamp(s)**: Shelley 1940-1966 **Shapes:** Gainsborough
13563	**Rose and Red Daisy**. Small, blue Curl border. **Backstamp(s)**: Shelley 1940-1966 **Shapes:** Gainsborough
13564	**Roses, Pansies, and Forget-me-nots**. **Backstamp(s)**: Shelley 1940-1966 **Shapes:** Gainsborough
13565	**Rose and Red Daisy**. **Backstamp(s)**: Shelley 1940-1966 **Shapes:** Gainsborough
13566	**Rose Spray**. **Backstamp(s)**: Shelley 1940-1966 **Shapes:** Gainsborough
13567	Colour ground with different colour handle. **Backstamp(s)**: Shelley 1940-1966 **Shapes:** Dainty
13568	**Georgian**. Backstamp(s): **Shelley 1940-1966** **Shapes:** Gainsborough
13569	Cutout motifs and spots on a colour ground. /24 Black ground, coral spots /36 Green ground, white spots /41 Maroon ground, turquoise spots /66 Red ground, white spots. Backstamp(s): **Shelley 1940-1966** **Shapes:** Mocha
13570	**Patches** and **Georgian**. Backstamp(s): **Shelley 1940-1966** **Shapes:** Gainsborough
13571	**Patches** and **Rose Spray**. Backstamp(s): **Shelley 1940-1966** **Shapes:** Gainsborough
13572	**Patches** and **Rose Spray**. Backstamp(s): **Shelley 1940-1966** **Shapes:** Ripon
13573	Cutout motifs, sprigs and white spots on a colour ground. Backstamp(s): **Shelley 1940-1966** **Shapes:** Mocha
13574	Maroon with raised white spots outside cup and on saucer. Ivory inside cup and centre of saucer. Gold dontil edges. Gold foot and handle. Backstamp(s): **Shelley 1940-1966** **Shapes:** Henley
13575	**Rose and Red Daisy** and **Green Laurel Border**. Maroon bands. Gold edges. **Backstamp(s):** Shelley 1940-1966 **Shapes:** Gainsborough
13576	Colour ground with cut out pattern of leaves, spots, and gold lines. Gold handle. /63 Silver lines. **Backstamp(s):** Shelley 1940-1966 **Shapes:** Mocha
13577	Wreath of Leaves. Gold edges, foot and handle. /G Green leaves /P Purple leaves. **Backstamp(s):** Shelley 1940-1966

Pattern	Description & Shapes
	Shapes: Gainsborough
13578	Davies **Woodland**. Blue, pink, and yellow flowers, green foliage and trees set into a woodland landscape. Gold edges. Water green handle. **Backstamp(s)**: Shelley 1940-1966 Woodland **Shapes:** Cambridge, Henley, Richmond
13579	Hand painted leaves. Gold edges and handle. /G Green leaves /P Purple leaves. **Backstamp(s)**: Shelley 1940-1966 **Shapes:** Ely
13580	Hand painted and gilded leaves. Gold dontil edges. Gold handle. /G Green leaves /P Purple leaves. **Backstamp(s)**: Shelley 1940-1966 **Shapes:** Unknown
13581	**Rose Spray**. Green edges and handle. **Backstamp(s)**: Shelley 1940-1966 **Shapes:** Dainty
13582	**Orchid** and **Jungle** patterns. Outside cup is ivory with a gold ring about half way down. Inside cup and on saucer have upper band of gold Orchid pattern, and the cup base and on saucer centre are ruby red with the Jungle pattern in gold. Gold edges, foot and handle. **Backstamp(s)**: Shelley 1940-1966 **Shapes:** Gainsborough
13583	**Gold Jungle** on maroon ground with **Curtain** print on ivory. Gold edges and handle. **Backstamp(s)**: Shelley 1940-1966 **Shapes:** Henley, Mocha
13584	Green and gold vine leaves, tendrils, and grapes. White ground. Gold edges, foot and handle., Ely: Gold line inside cup. /G Malachite green /P Purple. **Backstamp(s)**: Shelley 1940-1966 **Shapes:** Ely, Gainsborough

Grapes and vine leaves 13584 Ely shape cup and saucer. £50-60; $120-160

13585	Plain colour. **Backstamp(s)**: Shelley 1940-1966 **Shapes:** Dainty, Richmond
13586	**Primrose Chintz**. Chintz. Yellow primroses on blue chintz ground. Very pale pink edges, foot and handle. **Backstamp(s)**: Shelley 1940-1966 Primrose Chintz **Shapes:** Dainty, Richmond, Henley, Cambridge
13587	**Primrose Chintz**. Chintz. Yellow primroses on blue chintz ground. Pink edges, foot and handle. **Backstamp(s)**: Shelley 1940-1966 **Shapes:** Henley

Primrose Chintz 13587 Henley shape cup and saucer. £70-80; $80-160

13588	**Primrose Chintz**. Chintz. Yellow primroses on blue chintz ground inside cup. Pale blue outside cup and on saucer. Gold edges, foot and handle. **Backstamp(s)**: Shelley 1940-1966 **Shapes:** Footed Oleander

Primrose Chintz 13588 Footed Oleander cup and saucer. £70-80; $80-160

13589	**Primrose Chintz**. Chintz. Yellow primroses on blue chintz ground. Gold edges, foot and handle. **Backstamp(s)**: Shelley 1940-1966 **Shapes:** Ripon
13590	**Harebell**. Blue flowers and green leaves. Pale blue trim and handle. **Backstamp(s)**: Shelley 1940-1966 **Shapes:** Dainty, Dorothy, Footed Oleander, Henley, New Cambridge, Oleander, Oleander double handle cup

Harebell 13590 Footed Oleander shape cup and saucer. £50-60; $120-160B

Blue Rock 13591 Dainty shape cup, saucer, and plate. £60-80; $90-160

Harebell 13590 Henley shape cup and saucer. £50-60; $120-160

Harebell 13590 Oleander shape cup and saucer. £50-60; $120-160

Harebell large teapot. £180-200; $250-300

13591	**Blue Rock**. Tiny blue flowers and green leaves. Spray also inside cup. Pale blue trim and handle. Blue foot on Henley. **Backstamp(s)**: Shelley 1940-1966 Harebell **Shapes:** Bute, Cambridge, Canterbury, Dainty, Dorothy, Henley, Ludlow, New Cambridge, Richmond, Stratford, Tall Dainty

Blue Rock 13591 Dorothy shape cup and saucer. £40-50; $80-100

Blue Rock 13591 Ludlow shape cup and saucer. £50-60; $80-130

Blue Rock 13591 New Cambridge shape cup and saucer. £40-50; $80-100

Blue Rock 13591 Stratford shape cup and saucer. £50-60; $80-130

Pattern	Description & Shapes
13592	**Harebell**. Blue flowers and green leaves. Flowers also inside cup. Pale blue edges and handle. Blue foot on Henley. **Backstamp(s)**: Shelley 1940-1966 **Shapes:** Gainsborough, Henley, Richmond
13593	**Blue Rock**. Tiny blue flowers and green leaves. Flowers also inside cup. Scroll border inside cup, outside cup, and on saucer. Gold edges. Pale blue handle. **Backstamp(s)**: Shelley 1940-1966 **Shapes:** Gainsborough, Henley, Richmond
13594	**Melody**. Chintz. Pattern inside cup and centre of saucer. Colour ground outside cup and main part of saucer. Gold edges and handle. Pattern changed to **Maytime** in July 1964. **Backstamp(s)**: Shelley 1940-1966 **Shapes:** Henley
13595	**Primrose Chintz**. Pattern inside cup and centre of saucer. Colour ground outside cup and main part of saucer. Gold edges. Pattern changed to **Blue Pansy** in July 1964. **Backstamp(s)**: Shelley 1940-1966 **Shapes:** Henley
13596	**Blue Rock**. Tiny blue flowers and green leaves inside cup. Scroll border inside cup. Pale blue outside cup and on saucer. Gold edges, foot and handle. **Backstamp(s)**: Shelley 1940-1966 **Shapes:** Footed Oleander

Blue Rock 13596/S10 Footed Oleander shape cup and saucer. £50-60; $80-130

Pattern	Description & Shapes
13597	**Harebell**. Harebells inside cup. Colour ground outside cup and on saucer. Gold edges, foot and handle. **Backstamp(s)**: Shelley 1925-1940 **Shapes:** Footed Oleander
13598	Pink with spots. Gold inside cup and centre of saucer. Gold dontil edges. Gold foot and handle. /G Green spots /R Red spots /T Turquoise spots /14B Dark blue spots /48G Green spots. **Backstamp(s)**: Shelley 1925-1940 **Shapes:** Ripon
13599	Hand pained gold leaves on a fawn ground. Gold edges, foot and handle. **Backstamp(s)**: Shelley 1925-1940 **Shapes:** Gainsborough
13600	Sgraffito pattern of white, cutout leaves and tendrils on a colour ground. Silver edges. /G Green and gold edges /R Red and gold edges. **Backstamp(s)**: Shelley 1925-1940 **Shapes:** Mocha
13602	Coral spots on colour ground. Gold dontil edges. /B Blue /P Pink. **Backstamp(s)**: Shelley 1925-1940 **Shapes:** Ely
13603	Pink Leaf with spots. Gold dontil edges. Gold handle. **Backstamp(s)**: Shelley 1925-1940 **Shapes:** Ely
13604	**Dubarry**. Pink, yellow, and blue flowers with green leaves, maroon band, and gold trim on a white ground. **Backstamp(s)**: Shelley 1925-1940 **Shapes:** Gainsborough
13605	Ratauds **Regal**. Maroon and yellow scrolled border. Pink, blue, white, and yellow flowers with green foliage on a white ground inside cup. Maroon outside cup and on saucer. Gold edges, foot and handle. **Backstamp(s)**: Shelley 1940-1966 **Shapes:** Gainsborough
13606	Ratauds **Regal**. Green and yellow scrolled border. Pink, blue, white, and yellow flowers with green foliage on a white ground inside cup. Green outside cup and on saucer. Gold edges, foot and handle. **Backstamp(s)**: Shelley 1940-1966 **Shapes:** Gainsborough
13607	Ratauds **Regal**. Blue and yellow scrolled border. Pink, blue, white, and yellow flowers with green foliage on a white ground inside cup. Black outside cup and on saucer. Gold edges, foot and handle. /42 Blue outside cup and on saucer. **Backstamp(s)**: Shelley 1940-1966 **Shapes:** Gainsborough
13608	Ratauds maroon **Duchess**. Blue, pink, and yellow bunch of flowers inside cup and centre of saucer. Maroon outside cup and main part of saucer. Gold edges, foot and handle. **Backstamp(s)**: Shelley 1940-1966 **Shapes:** Gainsborough
13609	Ratauds green **Duchess**. Blue, pink, and yellow bunch of flowers inside cup and centre of saucer. Green outside cup and main part of saucer. Gold edges, foot and handle. **Backstamp(s)**: Shelley 1940-1966 **Shapes:** Gainsborough
13610	Ratauds blue **Duchess**. Blue, pink, and yellow bunch of flowers inside cup and centre of saucer. Black outside cup and main part of saucer. Gold edges, foot and handle. /42 Blue outside cup and on saucer. **Backstamp(s)**: Shelley 1940-1966 **Shapes:** Gainsborough
13611	**Dubarry**. Pink, yellow, and blue flowers with green leaves, maroon band, and gold trim on a white ground inside cup and middle of saucer. Maroon outside cup and on saucer. Gold edges, foot and handle. **Backstamp(s)**: Shelley 1940-1966 **Shapes:** Gainsborough
13612	**Dubarry**. Pink, yellow, and blue flowers with green leaves, green band, and gold trim on a white ground inside cup and middle of saucer. Green outside cup and on saucer. Gold edges, foot and handle. **Backstamp(s)**: Shelley 1940-1966 **Shapes:** Gainsborough
13613	**Dubarry**. Pink, yellow, and blue flowers with green leaves, blue band, and gold trim on a white ground inside cup and middle of saucer. Black outside cup and on saucer. Gold edges, foot and handle. /42 Blue outside cup and on saucer. **Backstamp(s)**: Shelley 1940-1966 **Shapes:** Gainsborough
13614	**Panels**. Flowers sprays and gilding. Gold edges, foot and handle. **Backstamp(s)**: Shelley 1940-1966 **Shapes:** Gainsborough

Pattern	Description & Shapes

13616 **Vine Leaf**. Green and gold vine leaves, tendrils, and grapes. Pattern also inside cup. White ground. Gold edges, foot and handle.
/G Apple green
/R Red
/P Purple.
Backstamp(s): Shelley 1940-1966
Shapes: Gainsborough

Vine Leaf 13616 Gainsborough shape cup and saucer. £40-50; $80-100

13617 **Gold Shamrock**.
Backstamp(s): Shelley 1940-1966
Shapes: Gainsborough

13618 Pale green ground with darker green handle.
/9 Pink handle
/10 Blue handle.
Backstamp(s): Shelley 1940-1966
Shapes: Dainty

Green 13618 Dainty shape cup and saucer. £70-80; $140-160

13619 **Laurel Sprays**. Gold leaves and coloured spots.
/A Green print and pink spots
/B Blue print and pink spots
/C Pink print and green spots.
Backstamp(s): Shelley 1940-1966
Shapes: Ely

13620 Alternating gold and white panels outside cup and on saucer. Ivory inside cup and centre of saucer. Gold edges and handle.
/S1 Fawn inside cup and centre of saucer
/S3 Green inside cup and centre of saucer
/S9 Pink inside cup and centre of saucer
/S10 Blue inside cup and centre of saucer.
Backstamp(s): Shelley 1940-1966
Shapes: Ludlow

Gold and white panels 13620 Ludlow shape cup and saucer. £60-70; $110-150

13621 **Rose Sprays**. Hand painted with gold leaves.
Backstamp(s): Shelley 1940-1966
Shapes: Ludlow, Mocha

13622 **Vine Leaves**. Gilding on stem and grapes.
/G Green leaves
/P Purple leaves
/R Red leaves.
Backstamp(s): Shelley 1940-1966
Shapes: Ludlow, Mocha

13623 **Surrey Scenery**. Pink or blue print on white ground. Country scene showing woman on a wooden bridge over a stream, fields, hedges, trees, and thatched cottages. Pink or blue edges.
Backstamp(s): Shelley 1940-1966
Surrey Scenery
Shapes: Oleander

Pink **Surrey Scenery** 13623 Oleander shape cup and saucer. £50-60; $80-130

Blue **Surrey Scenery** 13623 Oleander shape cup and saucer. £50-60; $80-130

13624 **Serenity**.
Backstamp(s): Shelley 1940-1966
Shapes: Gainsborough

13625 **Blue Rock**. Tiny blue flowers and green leaves outside cup and centre of saucer on a white ground. Buttery-yellow inside cup and main part of saucer. Blue edges, foot and handle.
Backstamp(s): Shelley 1940-1966
Shapes: Dainty, Richmond

13626 **Stocks**. Mauve, pink, and white stocks with green leaves outside cup and centre of saucer on ivory ground. Green inside cup and body of saucer. Pink edges, foot/foot line and handle.
Backstamp(s): Shelley 1940-1966
Shapes: Dainty, Richmond

Stocks 13626 Richmond shape cup and saucer. £50-60; $80-130

13627 **Bramble**. Green edges.
Backstamp(s): Shelley 1940-1966
Shapes: Gainsborough

13628 **Crochet**. Pastel or white ground. Grey lacy border inside cup. Pink, blue, yellow, and amber flowers inside cup and centre of saucer. Black outside cup and body of saucer. Gold edges, foot and handle.
/4 Apple Green outside cup; light Green inside
/41 Maroon outside cup, pink inside
/42 Blue outside cup; pale blue inside
/B Black outside cup, ivory inside.
Backstamp(s): Shelley 1940-1966
Shapes: Gainsborough

Crochet 13628/B Gainsborough shape cup and saucer. £40-50; $80-100

Pattern	Description & Shapes

13629 **Basket Festoon**. Print and edges in blue. Also see 9297 **Basket of Flowers.**
Backstamp(s): Shelley 1940-1966
Shapes: Dainty

Basket Festoon 13629 Dainty shape cup and saucer. £70-80; $140-160

13630 **English Rose**. Red rosebuds with green stems and leaves on a white ground outside cup and centre of saucer. Pale green inside cup and main part of saucer. Gold edges.
Backstamp(s): Shelley 1940-1966
Shapes: Gainsborough

English Rose 13630/S3 Gainsborough shape cup and saucer. £40-50; $80-100

13631 **Rose**. Pale and deep pink roses with green leaves. Gold green edges.
Backstamp(s): Shelley 1940-1966
Shapes: Gainsborough

13632 **English Rose**. Green edges and handle.
Backstamp(s): Shelley 1940-1966
Shapes: Gainsborough

13633 Plain colour outside cup and on saucer. White inside cup. Gold edges and handle.
Backstamp(s): Shelley 1940-1966
Shapes: Cambridge, Dainty, Henley, Richmond, Ripon, Stratford

13634 Davies **Blue Floral Sprays**. Blue edges, foot and handle.
Backstamp(s): Shelley 1940-1966
Shapes: Carlisle, Regent, Richmond

Blue Floral Sprays 13634 Richmond shape cup and saucer. £50-60; $80-130

13635 Alternating gold and colour panels outside cup and on saucer. Ivory inside cup and centre of saucer. Gold dontil edges. Gold handle.
Backstamp(s): Shelley 1940-1966
Shapes: Ludlow

13636 **Friars Cragg, Keswick**. Gold edges, foot and handle.
Backstamp(s): Shelley 1940-1966
Shapes: Ripon

13637 **Castle**. Black print. Green castles and oriental type trees inside and outside cup as well as on saucer. White ground. Gold edges.
Backstamp(s): Shelley 1940-1966
Shapes: Gainsborough

13638 **Castle**. Black print. Purple castles and oriental type trees inside and outside cup as well as on saucer. White ground. Purple edges.
Backstamp(s): Shelley 1940-1966
Shapes: Gainsborough

13639 Green and gold leaves on a white ground. Gold edges.
/A Ivory and gold
/B Bronze green and gold
/R Red and gold
/CG Chrome green and gold
/G Apple green and gold
/H Grey green and gold
/P Purple and gold
/12 Brown and gold.
Backstamp(s): Shelley 1925-1940
Shapes: Gainsborough, Mocha

13640 **English Rose**. Pattern inside cup. Black outside cup and on saucer. Gold edges, foot and handle.
Backstamp(s): Shelley 1940-1966
Shapes: Gainsborough

13641 Rataud's red **Duchess**. Blue, pink, and yellow bunch of flowers. Broad patterned border inside cup. Border is mainly red and gold. Outside cup has a bunch of flowers on a white ground with a gold ring around the cup. Gold trim. Entered in pattern book during or after 1940.
Backstamp(s): 1940-1966 Duchess
Shapes: Gainsborough

Pink 13633/S9 Stratford shape cup and saucer. £55-75; $75-95

13642 Sgraffito pattern of white, cutout motifs.
Backstamp(s): **Shelley 1940-1966**
Shapes: Gainsborough, Ripon

13643 **Crochet**. Pastel or white ground. Grey lacy border on edge of saucer, around centre of the saucer, rim of outside and outside cup. Pink, blue, yellow, and amber flowers on outer band and centre of saucer. Also **outside cup**. Gold edges, foot and handle.
Backstamp(s): Shelley 1940-1966
Shapes: Gainsborough, Mocha, Richmond

13644 **Burns Cottage**. Gold edges, foot and handle.
Backstamp(s): Shelley 1940-1966
Shapes: Ripon

13645 **Melody**. Chintz. Red, pink, yellow, and blue flowers on a mint green chintz background inside cup. Mint green outside cup and on saucer. Green edges and handle.
Backstamp(s): Shelley 1940-1966.
Shapes: Gainsborough, Footed Oleander

Melody cake stand. £70-100; $120-140

13646 **Rock Garden**. Chintz. Rockery plants set amongst grey stones. Pink, blue, yellow, and whiter flowers with green foliage. Patterned inside cup with pale peachy-yellow outside cup and on saucer. Green edges and handle.
Backstamp(s): Shelley 1940-1966 Rock Garden
Shapes: Footed Oleander, Gainsborough

13647 **Maytime**. Chintz. Patterned inside cup. Pink outside cup and on saucer. Pink edges and handle.
Backstamp(s): Shelley 1940-1966
Shapes: Footed Oleander, Gainsborough

13648 Ivory **Summer Glory**. Chintz. Blue, white, and deep pink flowers on a chintz ground inside cup. Salmon outside cup and on saucer. Ginger edges, foot and handle.
Backstamp(s): Shelley 1940-1966
Shapes: Footed Oleander, Gainsborough

13649 Pink **Summer Glory**. Chintz. Blue, white, and deep pink flowers on a chintz ground inside cup. Mauve outside cup and on saucer. Green edges, foot and handle.
Backstamp(s): Shelley 1940-1966
Shapes: Footed Oleander, Gainsborough

13650 **Primrose Chintz**. Yellow primroses on blue chintz ground inside cup. Pale blue outside cup and on saucer. Darker blue edges and handle.
Backstamp(s): Shelley 1940-1966
Shapes: Dainty, Footed Oleander, Gainsborough, Windsor

Primrose Chintz 13650 Gainsborough cup and saucer. £80-100; $150-220

Pattern	Description & Shapes
13651	**Spring Bouquet**. Broad border of flowers that includes white lilies, bluebells, purple asters, orange chrysanthemums, small pink flowers, small orange flowers, green leaves. White ground. Gold edges. **Backstamp(s)**: Shelley 1940-1966 **Shapes:** Dainty, Gainsborough, Richmond, Windsor

Spring Bouquet 13651 Gainsborough shape cup and saucer. £40-50; $80-100

Spring Bouquet 13651 Richmond shape cup, saucer, and plate. £40-50; $80-100

13652	**Hunting Scenes**. Hand painted. Gold edges, foot and handle. **Backstamp(s)**: Shelley 1940-1966 **Shapes:** Ripon
13653	Hand painted leaves and gilding. Gold dontil edges. Gold foot. Produced for Festival of Britain, 1951. /B Blue leaves /P Purple leaves. **Backstamp(s)**: Shelley 1940-1966 **Shapes:** Gainsborough
13654	**Anne Hathaways Cottage**. Gold edges, foot and handle. **Backstamp(s)**: Shelley 1940-1966 Anne Hathaways Cottage, Stratford Upon Avon (on saucers) **Shapes:** Ripon
13655	**Simplicity** and **Bridal Wreath**. **Backstamp(s)**: Shelley 1940-1966 **Shapes:** Gainsborough
13656	**Mountain Ash**. Produced for Festival of Britain, 1951. **Backstamp(s)**: Shelley 1940-1966 **Shapes:** Gainsborough, Mocha
13657	**Old Ireland**. Landscape. Thatched cottage next to a winding road. Pink heather in the foreground. Mountains in the distance. Small birds in flight. Tree to the right of the scene. Heather and trees inside cup. No cottage on plate. Pale green edges and handle. **Backstamp(s)**: Shelley 1940-1966 **Shapes:** New Cambridge, Richmond
13665	Green **Dubarry**. **Backstamp(s)**: Shelley 1940-1966 **Shapes:** Cambridge, Chester, Gainsborough, Henley, Ripon
13666	Blue **Dubarry**. **Backstamp(s)**: Shelley 1940-1966 **Shapes:** Cambridge, Chester, Gainsborough, Henley, Ripon
13667	Colour bands with gold print on ivory ground. /B Blue /G Green /P Purple. **Backstamp(s)**: Shelley 1940-1966 **Shapes:** Gainsborough
13668	**Wild Flowers**. Flowers include bluebells, pink and yellow flowers, and green leaves. Blue, pink or green trim and handles. **Backstamp(s)**: Shelley 1940-1966 Wild Flowers **Shapes:** Dainty, New Cambridge, Footed Oleander, Lincoln, Oleander, Cambridge, Regent, Henley

Old Ireland 13657 New Cambridge shape cup and saucer. £40-50; $80-100

Old Ireland 13657 Richmond shape cup and saucer. £40-50; $50-100

13658	**Gold Bridal Wreath**. Produced for Festival of Britain, 1951. /A **Brown Muff** pattern. **Backstamp(s)**: Shelley 1940-1966 **Shapes:** Gainsborough
13659	**Vine Leaf**. Produced for Festival of Britain, 1951. **Backstamp(s)**: Shelley 1940-1966 **Shapes:** Gainsborough
13663	**Hedgerow**. **Backstamp(s)**: Shelley 1940-1966 **Shapes:** Chester, Oleander
13664	Green **Duchess**. **Backstamp(s)**: Shelley 1940-1966 **Shapes:** Cambridge, Chester, Gainsborough, Henley, Ripon

Wild Flowers 13668 beaker/mug. £60-70; $100-120

Wild Flowers 13668 Henley shape cup and saucer. £40-50; $80-100

Wild Flowers 13668 Henley shape tea-for-two. £250-300; $450-550

Wild Flowers 13668 large teapot. £200-250; $320-370. Sugar and creamer. £40-50; $80-100

Wild Flowers 13668 small teapot. £120-150; $200-230. Small size sugar and creamer. £40-50; $60-70

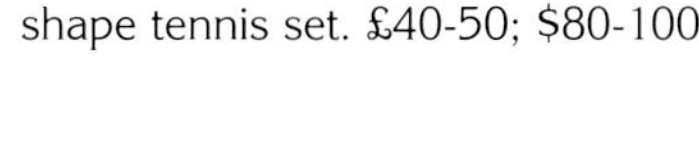

Wild Flowers 13668 Richmond shape tennis set. £40-50; $80-100

Right:
Wild Flowers 13668 snack tray. £40-50; $80-100. Pin tray /bon-bon dish. £30-50; $60-100

Wild Flowers 13668 Lincoln shape cup and saucer. £40-50; $80-100

13669 **Old Mill**. Landscape that includes red-roofed mill house, water mill, green and brown trees, blue water. Water scene also inside cup. White ground. Gold edges. Pale blue handle and foot on Richmond.
Backstamp(s): Shelley 1940-1966 Old Mill
Shapes: Cambridge, New Cambridge, Richmond

Old Mill 13669 large teapot. £150-170; $280-350. New Cambridge shape cup and saucer. £40-50; $80-100

Wild Flowers 13668 New Cambridge shape cup and saucer. £40-50; $80-100

Wild Flowers 13668 Oleander shape cup and saucer. £40-50; $80-100

13670 **Jonquil**. Yellow daffodils and green leaves. White ground. Green trim and handle.
Backstamp(s): Shelley 1940-1966
Shapes: Richmond

13671 **Rambler Rose**. Large pink roses and green foliage on white ground. Rose sprig inside cup. Gold edges. Pale green handle.
Backstamp(s): Shelley 1940-1966
Shapes: Dainty

Rambler Rose 13671 Dainty shape cup and saucer. £70-80; $140-160

Pattern	Description & Shapes
13672	White spots on colour ground. **Backstamp(s)**: Shelley 1940-1966 **Shapes:** Oleander
13673	**Chippendale**. Previously named **Ovington**. **Backstamp(s)**: Shelley 1940-1966 **Shapes:** Gainsborough
13675	Broad and narrow gold bands. **Backstamp(s)**: Shelley 1940-1966 **Shapes:** Gainsborough
13676	Broad gold and narrow black bands. **Backstamp(s)**: Shelley 1940-1966 **Shapes:** Coffee Can, Gainsborough
13677	**Daffodil**. Brown print. Yellow daffodils and green and brown leaves on a white ground. Bud spray inside cup. Gold edges. Green foot and handle on Richmond. **Backstamp(s)**: Shelley 1940-1966 **Shapes:** Avon, Richmond

Daffodil 13677 Avon shape cup and saucer. £40-50; $80-100

Daffodil 13677 Richmond shape cup and saucer. £40-50; $80-100

13678	**Wild Flowers**. Flowers inside cup include bluebells, pink and yellow flowers, and green leaves. Pastel coloured outside cup. Flowers include bluebells, pink and yellow flowers, and green leaves. /SI Fawn /S3 Green /S9 Pink /S10 Blue /S15 Peach /S16 Orange /S20 Mauve /S22 Grey. **Backstamp(s)**: Shelley 1940-1966 **Shapes:** Oleander, Stratford

Right:
Wild Flowers 13678 Stratford shape cup and saucer. £40-50; $80-100

13679	**Old Mill**. Landscape that includes red-roofed mill house, water mill, green and brown trees, blue water. Water scene also inside cup. White ground. Gold edges, foot and handle. **Backstamp(s)**: Shelley 1940-1966 **Shapes:** Ripon
13680	**Heather**. Countryside scene with pink heather, trees, bridge, and river. Gold edges, foot and handle. **Backstamp(s)**: 1940-1966 Heather **Shapes:** Ripon

Heather 13680 Ripon shape cup and saucer. £40-50; $80-100

13681	**Daffodil Time**. Springtime scene with a host of daffodils in yellow, white, and amber. Mauve crocuses. Grass and woods in the background. Group of daffodils and crocuses inside cup. Gold edges, foot and handle. **Backstamp(s)**: Shelley 1940-1966 **Shapes:** Ripon
13683	Plain colour. Gold edges. **Backstamp(s)**: Shelley 1940-1966 **Shapes:** Richmond
13684	**Gold Bridal Wreath**. Gold orange blossom and leaf border against broad, ivory band; white below ivory and centre of saucer and plate. Gold trim. Entered in pattern book during or after 1956., Gainsborough has pattern inside cup, outside cup is white with gold ring approximately halfway between rim and foot. Windsor has white inside cup with gold ring below rim. **Backstamp(s)**: Shelley 1940-1966 Bridal Wreath **Shapes:** Gainsborough, Windsor
13685	**Golden Harvest**. Outside cup and on saucer gold wheat ear and leaves print on pale green or ivory, broad band. White ground below green/ivory band, centre of saucer, and plate. Gold trim. **Backstamp(s)**: Shelley 1940-1966 **Shapes:** Gainsborough, Windsor
13686	**Wild Flowers**. Flowers include bluebells, pink and yellow flowers, and green leaves. **Curly Border**. Gold edges. **Backstamp(s)**: Shelley 1940-1966

	Shapes: Gainsborough
13687	Maroon border band on ivory ground. /B Blue band /G Green band /P Purple band. **Backstamp(s)**: Shelley 1940-1966 **Shapes:** Gainsborough
13688	**Marguerite**. Chintz. White daisies and green leaves on a lighter green ground. Ivory inside cup. Yellow edges, foot and handle. **Backstamp(s)**: Shelley 1940-1966 Marguerite **Shapes:** Henley, Richmond
13689	**English Rose** and **Laurel Border**. **Backstamp(s)**: Shelley 1940-1966 **Shapes:** Henley
13690	**Countryside**. Chintz. Blue, yellow, pink, and purple flowers with green leaves on an ivory ground. Pale green inside cup. Darker green edges, foot and handle. **Backstamp(s)**: Shelley 1940-1966 **Shapes:** Henley

Countryside 13690 Henley shape cup and saucer. £80-120; $150-200.

13691	**Blossom** and **Laurel Border**. **Backstamp(s)**: Shelley 1940-1966 **Shapes:** Dorothy
13692	**English Rose**. Gold edges, foot and handle. **Backstamp(s)**: Shelley 1940-1966 **Shapes:** Gainsborough
13693	**Marguerite**. Chintz. White daisies and green leaves on a lighter green ground inside cup. Orange outside cup and on saucer. Gold edges, foot and handle. **Backstamp(s)**: Shelley 1940-1966 Marguerite **Shapes:** Footed Oleander
13694	**Marguerite**. Chintz. White daisies and green leaves on a lighter green ground outside cup and on saucer. Ivory inside cup. Gold edges, foot and handle. **Backstamp(s)**: Shelley 1940-1966

Marguerite 13694 Ripon shape cup and saucer. £40-50; $80-100

Pattern	Description & Shapes
	Marguerite **Shapes:** Ripon
13695	Sgraffito pattern. White, cutout leaves, tendrils, and cross hatching on a black ground. White edges. Gold foot and handle. **Backstamp(s)**: Shelley 1925-1940 **Shapes:** Ripon
13696	**Marguerite**. Chintz. White daisies and green leaves on a lighter green ground inside cup. Colour ground outside cup. Gold edges. **Backstamp(s)**: Shelley 1940-1966 **Shapes:** Henley
13697	Sgraffito pattern. White, cutout motifs. Gold handle. **Backstamp(s)**: Shelley 1925-1940 **Shapes:** Ripon
13698	**Wine Grape**. Green leaves and purple bunches of grapes on green vine. White ground. Gold edges. **Backstamp(s)**: Shelley 1940-1966 Wine Grape **Shapes:** Richmond, Gainsborough

Wine Grape 13698 Gainsborough shape cup and saucer. £40-50; $80-100

Pattern	Description & Shapes
13699	**Grape Vine**. **Backstamp(s)**: Shelley 1940-1966 **Shapes:** Cambridge
13700	**Countryside**. Chintz. Blue, yellow, pink, and purple flowers with green leaves on an ivory ground inside cup. Pink outside cup and on saucer. Gold edges and handle. **Backstamp(s)**: Shelley 1940-1966 **Shapes:** Footed Oleander
13701	**Countryside**. Chintz. Blue, yellow, pink, and purple flowers with green leaves on an ivory ground. Gold edges and handle. **Backstamp(s)**: Shelley 1940-1966 **Shapes:** Ripon
13702	**Sheraton**. Green and gold border inside cup and on saucer. Floral garland outside cup and sprays inside cup and on saucer. White ground. Gold edges. **Backstamp(s)**: Shelley 1940-1966 **Shapes:** Gainsborough
13703	Ratauds blue **Duchess**. Blue, pink, and yellow bunch of flowers inside cup. Broad patterned border inside cup. Border is mainly blue/turquoise and gold. Bunch of flowers on a white ground outside cup with a gold ring around the cup. Gold edges. **Backstamp(s)**: Shelley 1940-1966 **Shapes:** Gainsborough
13704	**Duchess** and **Bluebell**. Green edges and handle. **Backstamp(s)**: Shelley 1940-1966 **Shapes:** Richmond, Stratford
13705	**Dubarry** and Hulmes **Rose**. Pink edges and handle. **Backstamp(s)**: Shelley 1940-1966 **Shapes:** Richmond, Stratford
13706	**Swirls**. Shaded lines and bands on white ground inside cup and on saucer. Band on foot outside cup. Handle left white. /B Blue /D Grey /F Fawn /G Green /P Pink. **Backstamp(s)**: Shelley 1940-1966 **Shapes:** Regent
13707	**Old Mill**. Landscape that includes red-roofed mill house, water mill, green and brown trees, blue water on a white ground. Pattern inside cup and centre of saucer. Green outside cup and main part of saucer. Gold edges. **Backstamp(s)**: Shelley 1940-1966 **Shapes:** Henley
13708	**Old Ireland**. Landscape. Thatched cottage next to a winding road. Pink heather in the foreground. Mountains in the distance. Small birds in flight. Tree to the right of the scene. Heather and trees inside cup. No cottage on plate. Pale green edges and handle. **Backstamp(s)**: Shelley 1940-1966 **Shapes:** New Cambridge, Richmond
13709	**Glorious Devon**. Blue print on white ground inside cup and centre of saucer. Devonshire country scene showing woman on a wooden bridge over a stream, fields, hedges, trees, and thatched cottages. Pale blue outside cup and main part of saucer. Gold edges. **Backstamp(s)**: Shelley 1940-1966 **Shapes:** Henley
13710	**English Rose**. Gold edges, foot and handle. **Backstamp(s)**: Shelley 1940-1966 **Shapes:** Ripon
13711	**Spring Bouquet**. Pattern inside cup and centre of saucer. Pink outside cup and on saucer. Gold edges. /42 Blue outside cup. **Backstamp(s)**: Shelley 1940-1966 **Shapes:** Henley
13712	**Dubarry**. Pattern inside cup and centre of saucer. Green outside cup and on saucer. Gold edges. **Backstamp(s)**: Shelley 1940-1966 **Shapes:** Henley
13713	**Hedgerow**. Pattern inside cup and centre of saucer. Orange outside cup and on saucer. Gold edges. **Backstamp(s)**: Shelley 1940-1966 **Shapes:** Henley
13714	**Rose and Red Daisy**. Pattern inside cup. Pink outside cup and on saucer. Gold edges. **Backstamp(s)**: Shelley 1940-1966 **Shapes:** Henley
13715	**Blue Rock**. Pattern inside cup. Tiny blue flowers and green leaves. Blue outside cup. **Backstamp(s)**: **Shapes:** Henley
13716	**Harebell**. Pattern inside cup. Fawn outside cup and on saucer. **Backstamp(s)**: Shelley 1940-1966 **Shapes:** Henley
13717	**Georgian** and **Rose and Red Daisy**. Pattern inside cup. Blue outside cup and on saucer. Gold edges and handle. **Backstamp(s)**: Shelley 1940-1966 **Shapes:** Stratford
13718	**Begonia**. Pattern inside cup. Orange outside cup and on saucer. Gold edges and handle. **Backstamp(s)**: Shelley 1940-1966 **Shapes:** Stratford
13719	**Rose and Red Daisy**. Pattern inside cup. Green outside cup and on saucer. Gold edges and handle. **Backstamp(s)**: Shelley 1940-1966 **Shapes:** Stratford
13720	**Duchess** and Warwick Savage **Floral Sprays**. Pattern inside cup. Pink outside cup and on saucer. Gold edges and handle. **Backstamp(s)**: Shelley 1940-1966 **Shapes:** Stratford
13721	**Primrose**. Pattern inside cup. Mauve outside cup and on saucer. Gold edges and handle. **Backstamp(s)**: Shelley 1940-1966 **Shapes:** Stratford
13722	**Primrose**. Pattern inside cup. Salmon outside cup and on saucer. Gold edges and handle. **Backstamp(s)**: Shelley 1940-1966 **Shapes:** Stratford
13723	**Stocks**. Pattern inside cup. Green outside cup and on saucer. Gold edges and handle. **Backstamp(s)**: Shelley 1940-1966 **Shapes:** Stratford
13724	Warwick Savage **Floral Sprays**. Pattern inside cup. Salmon outside cup and on saucer. Gold edges and handle. **Backstamp(s)**: Shelley 1940-1966 **Shapes:** Stratford
13725	Warwick Savage **Rose and Red Daisy**. Pink edges and handle. **Backstamp(s)**: Shelley 1940-1966 **Shapes:** Dainty
13726	Warwick Savage **Tulip and Rose**. Blue edges and handle. **Backstamp(s)**: Shelley 1940-1966 **Shapes:** Dainty
13727	Warwick Savage **Floral**. Green edges and handle. **Backstamp(s)**: Shelley 1940-1966 **Shapes:** Dainty
13728	Warwick Savage **Tulip and Rose**. Orange edges and handle. **Backstamp(s)**: Shelley 1940-1966 **Shapes:** Dainty
13729	Warwick Savage **Rose and Floral**. Gold edges. Pink handle. **Backstamp(s)**: Shelley 1940-1966 **Shapes:** Cambridge, Henley, Richmond
13730	Warwick Savage **Rose and Floral**. Laurel border. Gold edges. Green handle. **Backstamp(s)**: Shelley 1940-1966 **Shapes:** Cambridge
13731	Warwick Savage **Rose and Floral**. Curly border. Gold edges. Green handle. **Backstamp(s)**: Shelley 1940-1966 **Shapes:** Cambridge
13732	Warwick Savage **Tulip and Rose**. Sprays of small blue tulips, pink roses, orange and pink flowers with green foliage on a white ground. Spray also inside cup. Blue scroll border along all edges. Gold edges. Pale blue handle. **Backstamp(s)**: Shelley 1940-1966 **Shapes:** New Cambridge, Warwick

Tulip and Rose 13732 New Cambridge shape cup and saucer. £40-50; $80-100

Pattern	Description & Shapes
13733	**Wine Grape**. Gold edges. **Backstamp(s)**: Shelley 1940-1966 **Shapes:** Cambridge, Gainsborough
13734	**Thistle**. Pink thistle flowers and green foliage on white ground outside cup and centre of saucer on a white ground. Blue inside cup and main part of saucer and plate. White handle. **Backstamp(s)**: Shelley 1940-1966 **Shapes:** Richmond, Ludlow, Warwick

Thistle 13734/S28 Ludlow shape cup and saucer. £60-80; $90-140

Pattern	Description & Shapes
13735	**Violets**. Pattern outside cup and centre of saucer. Lavender inside cup and main part of saucer. **Backstamp(s)**: Shelley 1940-1966 **Shapes:** Richmond, Ludlow, Warwick
13736	**Lily of the Valley**. Pattern outside cup and centre of saucer. Bronze green inside cup and main part of saucer. **Backstamp(s)**: Shelley 1940-1966 **Shapes:** Richmond, Ludlow, Warwick
13737	**Pansy**. Pattern outside cup and centre of saucer. Green inside cup and main part of saucer. **Backstamp(s)**: Shelley 1940-1966 **Shapes:** Richmond, Ludlow, Warwick
13738	**Thistle**. **Backstamp(s)**: Shelley 1940-1966 **Shapes:** Richmond
13739	**Violets**. **Backstamp(s)**: Shelley 1940-1966 **Shapes:** Richmond
13740	**Lily of the Valley**. **Backstamp(s)**: Shelley 1940-1966 **Shapes:** Richmond
13741	**Pansy**. **Backstamp(s)**: Shelley 1940-1966 **Shapes:** Richmond
13742	**Autumn Leaves**. **Backstamp(s)**: Shelley 1940-1966 **Shapes:** Richmond
13743	Polka Dots. Raised, coloured polka dots on a white ground. Gold edges, foot and handle. /A Turquoise /B Blue /C Green /D Coral /E Black /P Pink. **Backstamp(s)**: Shelley 1940-1966 **Shapes:** Coffee Can, Henley
13744	**Countryside Chintz**. Pattern inside cup. Pink outside cup. **Backstamp(s)**: Shelley 1940-1966 **Shapes:** Henley
13745	**Primrose**. Pale mauve inside cup and body of saucer. Primroses on a white ground outside cup and centre of saucer. Pale green edges and handle. **Backstamp(s)**: Shelley 1940-1966 **Shapes:** Dainty, Richmond, Ripon

Primrose 13745 Dainty shape cup and saucer. £70-80; $140-160

Pattern	Description & Shapes
13746	**Wild Flowers**. Flowers inside cup and centre of saucer include bluebells, pink and yellow flowers, and green leaves. Green edges, foot and handle. S3 green S5 blue S9 pink S16 orange **Backstamp(s)**: Shelley 1940-1966 **Shapes:** Ripon, Richmond
13747	**Rambler Rose**. Large pink roses and green foliage on a pale pink ground outside cup and main part of saucer. Green inside cup and centre of saucer. Gold edges. Entered in pattern book during or after 1964. **Backstamp(s)**: Shelley 1940-1966 **Shapes:** Ripon
13748	Polka Dots. Raised, coloured polka dots on a paler ground. Coloured edges and handle. /B blue /C green /D coral dots pink handle /G green /T turquoise /Y yellow. **Backstamp(s)**: Shelley 1940-1966 **Shapes:** Dainty

Polka Dots 13748/C Dainty shape cup and saucer. £70-80; $140-160

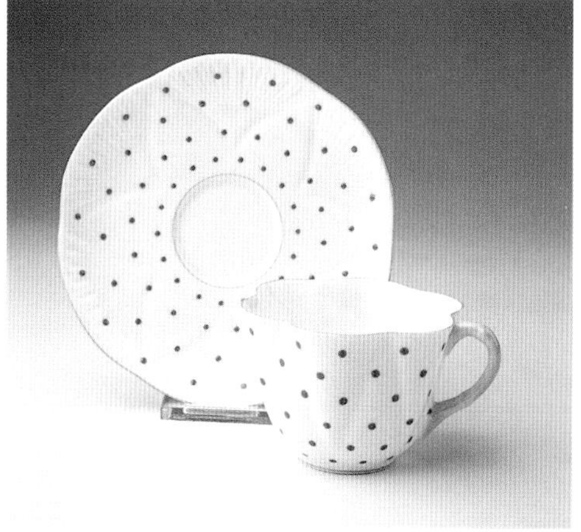

Polka Dots 13748/D Dainty shape cup and saucer. £70-80; $140-160

Polka Dots 13748/G Dainty shape cup and saucer. £70-80; $140-160

Pattern	Description & Shapes
13749	**Charm**. Small green flowers on a white ground. **Backstamp(s)**: Shelley 1940-1966 **Shapes:** Richmond

Charm 13749 Richmond shape cup, saucer, and plate. £40-50; $80-100

Pattern	Description & Shapes
13750	**Trent**. Broad and narrow lines. Gold edges. /P Platinum edges. **Backstamp(s)**: Shelley 1940-1966 Trent **Shapes:** Gainsborough, Ripon
13751	No details. **Backstamp(s)**: Shelley 1940-1966 **Shapes:** Dainty
13752	**Charm**. Small flowers on a white ground. /B Blue /G Green /M Maroon /Y Yellow. **Backstamp(s)**: Shelley 1940-1966 **Shapes:** Dainty, Footed Dainty
13754	Plain colours. Platinum edges. **Backstamp(s)**: Shelley 1940-1966 **Shapes:** Dainty
13755	Plain colours. Gold edges. **Backstamp(s)**: Shelley 1940-1966 **Shapes:** Henley

Charm 13756 Richmond shape cup, saucer, and plate. £40-50; $80-100

13756	**Charm** with **Crochet** border. Small maroon flowers on a white ground. **Backstamp(s)**: Shelley 1940-1966 Charm **Shapes:** Richmond

Charm 13756 Teapot. £150-170; $200-250. Richmond shape sugar and creamer. £40-50; $80-100

13757	**Charm** with **Crochet** border. Small blue flowers on a white ground. **Backstamp(s)**: Shelley 1940-1966 Charm **Shapes:** Richmond
13758	**Charm** with **Crochet** border. Small yellow flowers on a white ground. **Backstamp(s)**: Shelley 1940-1966 Charm **Shapes:** Richmond
13759	**Rambler Rose**. Pattern inside cup and centre of saucer. Pink outside cup and main part of saucer. Gold edges, foot and handle. **Backstamp(s)**: Shelley 1940-1966 **Shapes:** Gainsborough
13760	**Rambler Rose**. Pattern inside cup. Fawn outside cup and on saucer. Gold edges, foot and handle. **Backstamp(s)**: Shelley 1940-1966 **Shapes:** Footed Oleander
13761	Green inside cup. Pink outside cup and on saucer. **Backstamp(s)**: Shelley 1940-1966 **Shapes:** Dorothy, Richmond, Stratford
13762	Orange inside cup. Grey outside cup and on saucer. **Backstamp(s)**: Shelley 1940-1966 **Shapes:** Dorothy, Richmond, Stratford
13763	Pink inside cup. Blue outside cup and on saucer. **Backstamp(s)**: Shelley 1940-1966 **Shapes:** Dorothy, Richmond, Stratford
13764	Orange inside cup. Green outside cup and on saucer. **Backstamp(s)**: Shelley 1940-1966 **Shapes:** Dorothy, Richmond, Stratford
13765	Pink inside cup. Grey outside cup and on saucer. **Backstamp(s)**: Shelley 1940-1966 **Shapes:** Dorothy, Richmond, Stratford
13766	Green inside cup. Mauve outside cup and on saucer. **Backstamp(s)**: Shelley 1940-1966 **Shapes:** Dorothy, Richmond, Stratford
13767	**Charm**. Pattern outside cup and on saucer. Small flowers on a white ground. Colour ground inside cup. /B Blue flowers, blue inside cup /G Green flowers, green inside cup /M Maroon flowers, salmon inside cup /Y Yellow flowers, orange inside cup. **Backstamp(s)**: Shelley 1940-1966 **Shapes:** Dorothy, Regent, Richmond
13768	**Forget-me-nots**. **Backstamp(s)**: Shelley 1940-1966 **Shapes:** Dainty, Richmond
13769	**Fruit Design**. Fruit centre on an ivory ground inside cup. Maroon outside cup and on saucer. Gold edges, foot and handle. **Backstamp(s)**: Shelley 1940-1966 **Shapes:** Gainsborough
13770	Fruit centre with apples, grapes, and leaves on an ivory ground inside cup. Pale blue outside cup and on saucer. Gold edges, foot and handle. **Backstamp(s)**: Shelley 1940-1966 **Shapes:** Gainsborough
13774	**Pole Star**. Mauve outside cup. Saucer is mauve with a white centre. Stars **outside cup** and one in centre of saucer. Mauve foot and handle. /S27 Turquoise outside cup and on saucer /S28 Turquoise outside cup and on saucer on Warwick **Backstamp(s)**: Shelley 1940-1966 **Shapes:** Richmond, Warwick, Ludlow
13775	**Wild Flowers**. Flowers inside cup include bluebells, pink and yellow flowers, and green leaves. Blue outside cup and on saucer. Gold edges, foot and handle. **Backstamp(s)**: Shelley 1940-1966 **Shapes:** Footed Oleander, Henley, Oleander

Wild Flowers 13775 Footed Oleander shape cup and saucer. £60-70; $100-120

Wild Flowers 13775 Henley shape cup and saucer. £40-50; $80-100

13776	**Elegant**. Gold band. **Backstamp(s)**: Shelley 1940-1966 **Shapes:** Gainsborough
13777	**Harmony**. Pink inside cup. **Backstamp(s)**: Shelley 1940-1966 **Shapes:** Richmond
13778	**Lyric**. Dark pink and grey feathers, grey snowflakes on a pale pink ground outside cup and main part of saucer. Two feathers inside cup on white ground. White centre of saucer and plate. White edges. Green handle. Entered in pattern book during or after 1955/1956. **Backstamp(s)**: Shelley 1940-1966 Lyric **Shapes:** Richmond
13779	**Rhythm**. Green inside cup. Green foot. Pink handle. **Backstamp(s)**: Shelley 1940-1966 **Shapes:** Richmond

Pole Star 13774/S28 Warwick shape cup and saucer. £45-75; $85-95

Pattern	Description & Shapes
13781	**Fruit Centre**. Jade green or amber outside cup and on saucer. Fruit decoration inside cup. Gold edges, foot and handle. **Backstamp(s)**: Shelley 1940-1966 **Shapes:** Gainsborough

Fruit Centre 13781/A4 Gainsborough cup and saucer. £90-95; $150-170

Fruit Centre 13781/A4 pattern inside Gainsborough cup.

Fruit Centre 13781/A41 Gainsborough cup and saucer. £90-95; $150-170

Fruit Centre 13781/A41 pattern inside Gainsborough cup.

Fruit Centre 14208/S10 Boston shape cup and saucer. £90-95; $150-170

Fruit Centre 14208/S10 pattern inside Boston shape cup.

13782	**Caprice**. Pastel blue, yellow, and grey leaves on a white ground. Leaves also inside cup. Gold edges. **Backstamp(s)**: Shelley 1940-1966 Caprice **Shapes:** Gainsborough, Henley, Richmond
13783	**Serenity**. **Backstamp(s)**: Shelley 1940-1966 **Shapes:** Gainsborough, Henley, Richmond

Right:
Serenity 13783 Henley shape coffee set. £200-250; $400-500

13784	**Rambler Rose**. **Backstamp(s)**: Shelley 1940-1966 **Shapes:** Richmond
13785	**Daffodil**. **Backstamp(s)**: Shelley 1940-1966 **Shapes:** Richmond
13786	**Primrose**. Sprays on mauve ground outside cup and on saucer. Gold edges, foot and handle. **Backstamp(s)**: Shelley 1940-1966 **Shapes:** Richmond

Primrose 13786 Richmond shape cup and saucer. £40-50; $80-100

13787	**Stocks**. Mauve, pink, and white stocks with green leaves. Gold edges. **Backstamp(s)**: Shelley 1940-1966 **Shapes:** Ripon
13788	**English Lakes**. Lakeland scene with mountains and trees. Pattern inside cup. Gold trim. Pale green handle and foot. **Backstamp(s)**: Shelley 1940-1966 English Lakes **Shapes:** Cambridge, Dainty, Richmond

English Lakes 13788 Richmond shape cup and saucer. £40-50; $80-100

Pattern	Description & Shapes
13789	**Golden Harvest**. **Backstamp(s)**: Shelley 1940-1966 **Shapes:** Ripon, Windsor
13790	**Chantilly**. Signed **H. Pardoe**. **Backstamp(s)**: Shelley 1940-1966 **Shapes:** Gainsborough, Henley, Richmond
13791	**Serenity** border. Green ferns and **Snow Crystals** on a white ground. Platinum trim. **Backstamp(s)**: Shelley 1940-1966 Serenity **Shapes:** Cambridge, Gainsborough, Windsor

Serenity 13791 Gainsborough shape demitasse cup and saucer. £40-50; $80-100

13792 **Wine Grape**. Green leaves and purple bunches of grapes on green vine. Scattered **Grey Crystals**. White ground. Green edges and handle.
Backstamp(s): Shelley 1940-1966
Shapes: Dainty, Stratford

13793 **Yellow Wild Flower** and **Grey Crystals**. Sprays of small yellow and grey flowers and foliage on a white ground. One spray also inside cup. Yellow edges and handle.
Backstamp(s): Shelley 1940-1966
Shapes: Dainty, Ludlow, Stratford

Yellow Wild Flower and **Grey Crystals** 13793 Ludlow shape cup and saucer. £50-60; $110-130

13794 Groups of three spots on colour ground.
Backstamp(s): Shelley 1940-1966
Shapes: Mocha

13795 **Lowestoft**.
Backstamp(s): Shelley 1940-1966
Shapes: Dainty

13796 Universal **Rose Floral** and **Bluebell**.
Backstamp(s): Shelley 1940-1966
Shapes: Dainty, Henley, Ripon

13797 Ratauds **Yutoi**.
Backstamp(s): Shelley 1940-1966
Shapes: Dainty, Henley, Ripon

13798 Davies **Rose Trellis.** Pink, yellow, and blue roses and foliage on a grey trellis. Yellow edges and handle.
Backstamp(s): Shelley 1940-1966
Shapes: Dainty

Rose Trellis 13798 Dainty shape cup and saucer. £70-80; $140-160

13799 **Rose** Roses in shades of pink with yellow and blue flowers, green foliage. White ground. Pink edges and handle.
Backstamp(s): Shelley 1940-1966
Shapes: Dainty

13800 Universal **Rose Bud** and **Stocks**.
Backstamp(s): Shelley 1940-1966
Shapes: Dainty

13801 Plain colours.
/81 Pink
/82 Grey
/83 Green
/84 Mustard
/85 Pink
/86 Mushroom.
Backstamp(s): Shelley 1940-1966
Shapes: Mocha

13802 Plain colours with enamelled white spots.
/81 Pink
/82 Grey
/83 Green
/84 Mustard
/85 Pink
/86 Mushroom.
Backstamp(s): Shelley 1940-1966
Shapes: Mocha

13803 **Rhythm** and **Grey Crystals**.
Backstamp(s): Shelley 1940-1966
Shapes: Dainty, Regent

13804 **Harmony**.
Backstamp(s): Shelley 1940-1966
Shapes: Regent

13805 **Lyric** and **Grey Crystals**. Dark pink and grey feathers, grey snowflakes. Two feathers inside cup. White ground.
Backstamp(s): Shelley 1940-1966 Lyric
Shapes: Regent

13807 **Chantilly**.
Backstamp(s): Shelley 1940-1966
Shapes: Oleander

13808 **Chantilly**. Entered in pattern book during or after 1955.
Backstamp(s): Shelley 1940-1966
Shapes: Ripon

13809 **Forget-me-nots** and **Grey Crystals**. Entered in pattern book during or after 1955.
Backstamp(s): Shelley 1940-1966
Shapes: Henley, Richmond

13810 **Wild Flowers**. Flowers between grey bands include bluebells, pink and yellow flowers, and green leaves. Entered in pattern book during or after 1955.
Backstamp(s): Shelley 1940-1966
Shapes: Henley, Richmond

13811 **Blue Rock**. Litho between blue bands. Tiny blue flowers and green leaves. Blue foot and handle. Entered in pattern book during or after 1955
Backstamp(s):
Shapes: Henley, Richmond

13812 **Primrose Spray** and **Bluebell**. Entered in pattern book during or after 1955.
Backstamp(s): Shelley 1940-1966
Shapes: Henley, Richmond

13813 **Rambler Rose**. Entered in pattern book during or after 1955.
Backstamp(s): Shelley 1940-1966
Shapes: Ripon

13814 **Hedgerow** and **Bluebell**. Entered in pattern book during or after 1955.
Backstamp(s): Shelley 1940-1966
Shapes: Dainty, Ludlow, Stratford

13815 **Rose and Pansy** and **Grey Crystals**. Entered in pattern book during or after 1955.
Backstamp(s): Shelley 1940-1966
Shapes: Dainty, Ludlow, Stratford

13816 Green **Charm**. Green bands. Entered in pattern book during or after 1955.
Backstamp(s): Shelley 1940-1966
Shapes: Henley

13817 Blue **Charm**. Blue bands. Entered in pattern book during or after 1955.
Backstamp(s): Shelley 1940-1966
Shapes: Henley

13818 Yellow **Charm**. Orange bands. Entered in pattern book during or after 1955.
Backstamp(s): Shelley 1940-1966
Shapes: Henley

13819 Maroon **Charm**. Pink bands. Entered in pattern book during or after 1955.
Backstamp(s): Shelley 1940-1966
Shapes: Henley

13820 **Thistle**. Pink thistle flowers and green foliage on a white ground. Thistle spray also inside cup. Pink edges and handle. Entered in pattern book during or after 1955
Backstamp(s): Shelley 1940-1966
Shapes: Dainty, Ludlow, New Cambridge

Thistle 13820 Dainty shape cup and saucer. £70-80; $140-160

Thistle 13820 Ludlow shape cup and saucer. £60-70; $120-140

Thistle 13820 New Cambridge shape cup and saucer. £50-60; $90-120

Pattern	Description & Shapes
13821	**Violets**. Violets and leaves on cup and on saucer. Lavender edges and handle. Entered in pattern book during or after 1955 **Backstamp(s)**: Shelley 1940-1966 Violets **Shapes:** Dainty, Dainty Tennis Set, Ludlow, Stratford

Violets 13821 Dainty shape cup and saucer. £70-80; $140-160

Violets 13821 Ludlow shape cup and saucer. £60-70; $120-140

Violets 13821 Stratford shape cup and saucer. £60-70; $120-140

Violets Bute shape cup and saucer. £45-£55; $80-90

13822	**Lily of the Valley**. Tiny white lilies against broad lily leaves on a white ground. Green edges and handle. Entered in pattern book during or after 1955 **Backstamp(s)**: Shelley 1940-1966 Lily of the Valley **Shapes:** Dainty, Ludlow, Tall Dainty

Lily of the Valley 13822 Dainty shape cup and saucer. £70-80; $140-160

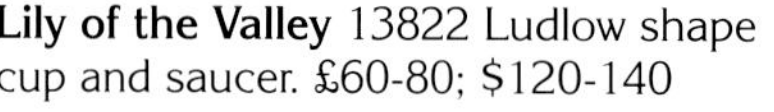

Lily of the Valley 13822 Ludlow shape cup and saucer. £60-80; $120-140

Lily of the Valley Bute shape cup and saucer. £40-£50; $75-85

13823	**Pansy.** Pansies outside cup and on saucer. One bud with foliage inside cup. Pansies in white and shades of mauve through to deep purple with green foliage. Yellow edges and handle. Entered in pattern book during or after 1955. **Backstamp(s)**: Shelley 1940-1966 **Shapes:** Dainty, Ludlow, New Cambridge, Stratford

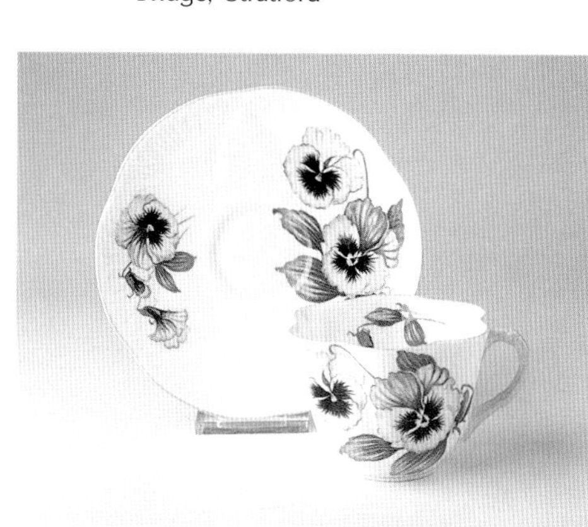

Pansy 13823 Dainty shape cup and saucer. £70-80; $140-160

Pansy 13823 Ludlow shape cup and saucer. £60-80; $120-140

Pansy 13823 Stratford shape cup and saucer. £60-80; $120-140

Pattern	Description & Shapes
13824	Shaded inside cup and base outside cup. Entered in pattern book during or after 1955. /A Blue /P Pink /FB Black. **Backstamp(s)**: Shelley 1940-1966 **Shapes:** Regent
13825	**Serenity** and **Harmony**. Entered in pattern book during or after 1955. **Backstamp(s)**: Shelley 1940-1966 **Shapes:** Richmond
13826	**Lyric**. Dark pink and grey feathers, grey snowflakes. Two feathers inside cup. Grey crochet border white ground. Gold edges. Entered in pattern book during or after 1955. **Backstamp(s)**: Shelley 1940-1966 Lyric **Shapes:** Henley, Richmond

Lyric 13826 Henley shape cup and saucer. £40-50; $80-100

13827	**Serenity** border. Entered in pattern book during or after 1955. **Backstamp(s)**: Shelley 1940-1966 **Shapes:** Richmond
13828	**English Lakes**. Entered in pattern book during or after 1955. **Backstamp(s)**: Shelley 1940-1966 **Shapes:** Henley
13829	**Thistle**. Pink outside cup and on saucer. Entered in pattern book during or after 1955. **Backstamp(s)**: Shelley 1940-1966 **Shapes:** Footed Oleander, Stratford
13830	**Violets**. Mauve outside cup and on saucer. Entered in pattern book during or after 1955. **Backstamp(s)**: Shelley 1940-1966 **Shapes:** Footed Oleander, Stratford
13831	**Pansy**. Yellow outside cup and on saucer. Entered in pattern book during or after 1955. **Backstamp(s)**: Shelley 1940-1966 **Shapes:** Footed Oleander, Stratford

Pansy 13831/S16 Footed Oleander shape cup and saucer. £40-50; $80-100

13832	**Lily of the Valley**. Tiny white lilies against broad lily leaves on a white ground inside cup. Pale green outside cup and on saucer. Gold edges, foot and handle. Entered in pattern book during or after 1955. **Backstamp(s)**: Shelley 1940-1966 **Shapes:** Footed Oleander, Stratford

Lily of the Valley 13832/S3 Footed Oleander shape cup and saucer. £60-80; $120-140

13833	**Chantilly**. Colour ground outside cup and on saucer. Entered in pattern book during or after 1955. /S3 Green /S9 Pink /S10 Blue /S16 Orange. **Backstamp(s)**: Shelley 1940-1966 **Shapes:** Stratford
13834	**Forget-me-nots** and mauve flowers from Warwick Savage **Floral Sprays**. Entered in pattern book during or after 1955. **Backstamp(s)**: Shelley 1940-1966 **Shapes:** Dainty
13835	**English Lakes**. Entered in pattern book during or after 1955. **Backstamp(s)**: Shelley 1940-1966 **Shapes:** Ripon
13836	**Spring Bouquet**. Pattern outside cup and main part of saucer. Pale blue inside cup and centre of saucer. White edges. Entered in pattern book during or after 1955. **Backstamp(s)**: Shelley 1940-1966 **Shapes:** Henley
13837	**Hedgerow**. Pattern outside cup and main part of saucer. Orange inside cup and centre of saucer. White edges. Entered in pattern book during or after 1955. **Backstamp(s)**: Shelley 1940-1966 **Shapes:** Henley
13838	**Rambler Rose**. Pattern outside cup and main part of saucer. Green inside cup and centre of saucer. White edges. Entered in pattern book during or after 1955. **Backstamp(s)**: Shelley 1940-1966 **Shapes:** Henley
13839	**Lyric**. Dark pink and grey feathers, grey snowflakes on a pale pink ground outside cup and main part of saucer. Two feathers inside cup on white ground. White centre of saucer and plate. White edges. Grey foot and handle. Entered in pattern book during or after 1955/1956. **Backstamp(s)**: Shelley 1940-1966 Lyric **Shapes:** Richmond
13840	**Thistle**. Entered in pattern book during or after 1955/1956. **Backstamp(s)**: Shelley 1940-1966 **Shapes:** Oleander
13841	**Violets**. Entered in pattern book during or after 1956. **Backstamp(s)**: Shelley 1940-1966 **Shapes:** Oleander
13842	**Pansy**. Entered in pattern book during or after 1956. **Backstamp(s)**: Shelley 1940-1966 **Shapes:** Oleander
13843	**Lily of the Valley**. Entered in pattern book during or after 1956. **Backstamp(s)**: Shelley 1940-1966 **Shapes:** Oleander
13844	**Pole Star**. Plain colour outside cup and on saucer with a white centre. Stars **outside cup** and one in centre of saucer. Coloured foot and handle. Entered in pattern book during or after 1956. /S9 Pink /S11 Nile Green /S15 Peach /S16 Orange /S27 Mushroom /S28 Drakes Neck Green /S31 Pink **Backstamp(s)**: Shelley 1940-1966 **Shapes:** Richmond
13845	**Autumn Leaves**. Green leaves only. Entered in pattern book during or after 1956. **Backstamp(s)**: Shelley 1940-1966 **Shapes:** Richmond
13846	**Harmony**. Entered in pattern book during or after 1956. **Backstamp(s)**: Shelley 1940-1966 **Shapes:** Richmond
13847	**Pole Star** with pink leaves from **Autumn Leaves**. Entered in pattern book during or after 1956. **Backstamp(s)**: Shelley 1940-1966 **Shapes:** Richmond
13848	**Drifting Leaves**. Combination of **Autumn Leaves** and **Pole Star** patterns.

Pattern	Description & Shapes
	Green leaves and grey stars on an ivory ground. Platinum edges. Entered in pattern book during or after 1956., Gainsborough: Pattern inside cup and platinum ring outside cup, approximately halfway between rim and foot. **Backstamp(s)**: Shelley 1940-1966; Drifting Leaves **Shapes:** Gainsborough, Richmond

Drifting Leaves 13848 Gainsborough shape cup and saucer. £40-50; $80-100

13849 **Charm**. Small maroon flowers on a white ground. Pink edges and handle.
Backstamp(s): Shelley 1940-1966
Shapes: Canterbury Miniature

13850 **Snow Crystals**. Outside cup is black with white snow crystals. Saucer is white with gold snow crystals. Gold edges and handle. Produced from for 1956.
/S11 Orange outside cup with gold snow crystals and handle.
/S74/ Grey outside cup white snow crystals; platinum instead of gold.
Backstamp(s): Shelley 1940-1966
Shapes: Dainty

Snow Crystals 13850 Dainty shape cup and saucer. £60-75; $85-100

Right:
Snow Crystals 13850/74 Dainty shape cup and saucer. £60-75; $85-100

13851 **Green Trousseau**. Gold orange blossom and leaf border against broad, pale green band; white below green and centre of saucer and plate. Gold trim. Entered in pattern book during or after 1956., Gainsborough has pattern inside cup, outside cup is white with gold ring approximately halfway between rim and foot., Windsor has white inside cup with gold ring below rim. Entered in pattern book during or after 1956.
Backstamp(s): Shelley 1940-1966 Sylvan Green Trousseau
Shapes: Gainsborough, Windsor

13852 **Rose Trousseau**. Gold orange blossom and leaf border against broad, pale pink band; white below pink and centre of saucer and plate. Gold trim. Entered in pattern book during or after 1956., Gainsborough has pattern inside cup, outside cup is white with gold ring approximately halfway between rim and foot., Windsor has white inside cup with gold ring below rim. Entered in pattern book during or after 1956.
Backstamp(s): Shelley 1940-1966 Rose Trousseau
Shapes: Gainsborough, Windsor

13853 **Dubarry**. Entered in pattern book during or after 1956.
Backstamp(s): Shelley 1940-1966
Shapes: Gainsborough, Ripon

13854 **Lily of the Valley**. Entered in pattern book during or after 1956.
Backstamp(s): Shelley 1940-1966
Shapes: Gainsborough, Ripon

13855 **Rambler Rose**. Entered in pattern book during or after 1956.
Backstamp(s): Shelley 1940-1966
Shapes: Gainsborough

13856 **Violets**. Purple and mauve violets with green leaves against a golden yellow ground. Black outside cup and on saucer. Gold edges, foot and handle. Entered in pattern book during or after 1956.
Backstamp(s): Shelley 1940-1966
Shapes: Gainsborough

Violets 13856 Gainsborough shape cup and saucer. £40-60; $80-120

13857 **Stocks**. Mauve, pink, and white stocks with green leaves inside cup on white ground. Pink outside cup and on saucer. Gold edges.
Backstamp(s): Shelley 1940-1966
Shapes: Gainsborough

13858 **Chantilly**. Entered in pattern book during or after 1956.
Backstamp(s): Shelley 1940-1966
Shapes: Gainsborough

13859 **Daffodil**. Yellow daffodils with green leaves against a golden yellow ground. Chrome green outside cup and on saucer. Gold edges, foot and handle. Entered in pattern book during or after 1956.
Backstamp(s): Shelley 1940-1966
Shapes: Gainsborough

Daffodil 13859/39 Gainsborough shape cup and saucer. £40-50; $80-100

13860 **Thistle**. Pink thistles and green foliage against a golden yellow ground. Maroon outside cup and on saucer. Gold edges, foot and handle. Entered in pattern book during or after 1956.
Backstamp(s): Shelley 1940-1966
Shapes: Gainsborough

Thistle 13860/41 Gainsborough shape cup and saucer. £40-60; $80-120

Opposite page, bottom left:
Thistle 13860/41 pattern inside Gainsborough shape cup

Pattern **Description & Shapes**

13861 **Pansy**. Mauve shaded pansies on a golden yellow ground inside cup. Blue outside cup and on saucer. Gold edges, foot and handle.
Backstamp(s): Shelley 1940-1966
Shapes: Gainsborough

Pansy 13861/42 Gainsborough shape cup and saucer. £40-60; $80-120

13862 Green **Charm**. Entered in pattern book during or after 1956.
Backstamp(s): Shelley 1940-1966
Shapes: Miniature

13863 Yellow **Charm**. Entered in pattern book during or after 1956.
Backstamp(s): Shelley 1940-1966
Shapes: Miniature

13864 Blue **Charm**. Entered in pattern book during or after 1956.
Backstamp(s): Shelley 1940-1966
Shapes: Miniature

13865 Universal **Rose and Floral**. Entered in pattern book during or after 1956.
Backstamp(s): Shelley 1940-1966
Shapes: Miniature

13866 **Crocus**. Entered in pattern book during or after 1956.
Backstamp(s): Shelley 1940-1966
Shapes: Miniature

13867 Hulmes **Rose Sprays**. Entered in pattern book during or after 1956.
Backstamp(s): Shelley 1940-1966
Shapes: Miniature

13868 **Yutoi**. Entered in pattern book during or after 1956.
Backstamp(s): Shelley 1940-1966
Shapes: Miniature

13869 Plain colour with gold edges.. Entered in pattern book during or after 1956.
Backstamp(s): Shelley 1940-1966
Shapes: Mocha

13870 **Celeste Trousseau**. Entered in pattern book during or after 1956.
Backstamp(s): Shelley 1940-1966
Shapes: Gainsborough

13871 **Blue Symphony**. Entered in pattern book during or after 1956.
Backstamp(s): Shelley 1940-1966
Shapes: Stirling

13872 **Golden Willow**. Entered in pattern book during or after 1956.
Backstamp(s): Shelley 1940-1966
Shapes: Stirling

13873 **Green Leaves** and **Pole Star**. Entered in pattern book during or after 1956.
Backstamp(s): Shelley 1940-1966
Shapes: Stirling

13874 **Green Leaves** and **Pole Star**. Entered in pattern book during or after 1956.
Backstamp(s): Shelley 1940-1966
Shapes: Stirling

13875 **Green Leaves** and **Pole Star**. Entered in pattern book during or after 1956.
Backstamp(s): Shelley 1940-1966
Shapes: Stirling

13876 **Pink Leaves** and **Pole Star**. Entered in pattern book during or after 1956.
Backstamp(s): Shelley 1940-1966
Shapes: Stirling

13877 **Pink Leaves** and **Pole Star**. Entered in pattern book during or after 1956.
Backstamp(s): Shelley 1940-1966
Shapes: Stirling

13878 Sgraffito pattern. White, cutout crosses.
Backstamp(s): Shelley 1925-1940
Shapes: Ripon

13879 **Symphony**. Entered in pattern book during or after 1956.
Backstamp(s): Shelley 1940-1966
Shapes: Stirling

13880 **Rhythm**. Entered in pattern book during or after 1956.
Backstamp(s): Shelley 1940-1966
Shapes: Stirling

13881 **Fantasy**. Entered in pattern book during or after 1956.
Backstamp(s): Shelley 1940-1966
Shapes: Stirling, Windsor

13882 **Hibiscus.** Yellow hibiscus flowers on cup, saucer, and inside cup. Pale green handle. Entered in pattern book during or after 1956.
Backstamp(s): Shelley 1940-1966
Shapes: Dainty, Richmond

Hibiscus 13882 Dainty shape cup and saucer. £60-75; $85-100

13883 **Oleander**. Pink oleander flowers and green leaves on a white ground. Flowers also inside cup. Pink edges and handle. Entered in pattern book during or after 1956.
Backstamp(s): Shelley 1940-1966
Shapes: Dainty, Footed Oleander, Ludlow, Richmond

Oleander 13883 Dainty shape cup and saucer. £70-80; $140-160

Oleander 13883 Footed Oleander shape cup and saucer. £50-70; $90-120

Oleander 13883 Ludlow shape cup and saucer. £60-80; $120-140

Pattern	Description & Shapes
13884	**Easter Lily**. Entered in pattern book during or after 1956. **Backstamp(s)**: Shelley 1940-1966 **Shapes:** Dainty
13885	**Morning Glory**. Blue morning glories and green leaves. One bloom inside cup. Blue trim and handle. **Backstamp(s)**: Shelley 1940-1966 **Shapes:** Dainty, Ludlow, Richmond

Morning Glory 13885 Ludlow shape cup and saucer. £60-80; $120-140

Morning Glory 13885 Oleander shape cup and saucer. £70-80; $140-160

13886 **Campanula**. Purple flowers and green leaves. Mauve edges and handle. White ground. Entered in pattern book during or after 1956., Miniature Dainty is not stamped with this pattern number, but I include it here as it is so rare it must be mentioned!

Campanula 13886 Dainty shape cup and saucer. £70-80; $140-160

Campanula 13886 Ludlow shape cup and saucer. £60-80; $120-140

Backstamp(s): Shelley 1940-1966
Shapes: Dainty, Ludlow, Miniature Dainty, Ovide, Tall Dainty

13887 **Pole Star**. Plain colour outside cup. Outside cup colour as et out below. Saucer has a white centre. Stars outside cup and one in centre of saucer. Coloured foot and handle. Gold edges. Entered in pattern book during or after 1956.
/S9 Pink
/S15 Peach
/S16 Orange
/S26 Lavender
/S27 Mushroom
/S28 Drakes Neck Green
/S29 Green.
Backstamp(s): Shelley 1940-1966
Shapes: Richmond, Cambridge

13888 **Symphony**. Entered in pattern book during or after 1956.
Backstamp(s): Shelley 1940-1966
Shapes: Stirling

13889 **Contemporary**. Entered in pattern book during or after 1956.
Backstamp(s): Shelley 1940-1966
Shapes: Gainsborough, Stirling

13890 **Fantasy**. Entered in pattern book during or after 1956.
/S15 Peach
/S16 Orange
/S26 Lavender
/S28 Drakes Neck Green
/S29 Green
/S31 Pink
/S34 Hazelnut.
Backstamp(s): Shelley 1940-1966
Shapes: Stirling

13892 **Evergreen**. Entered in pattern book during or after 1957.
Backstamp(s): Shelley 1940-1966
Shapes: Stirling

13893 **Pastoral**. Pink and grey flowers and foliage on a white ground. Platinum edges. Entered in pattern book during or after 1957.
Backstamp(s): Shelley 1940-1966
Shapes: Stirling, Unnamed Shape

Pastoral 13893 unnamed shape cup and saucer. £70-80; $140-160

13894 **Charm**. Small flowers with black and grey leaves and stems on a white ground on large panels. Plain colour on small panels, edges, and handle. Entered in pattern book during or after 1957.
/S3 Green
/S10 Blue
/S16 Yellow
/S31 Maroon flowers, pink panels.
Backstamp(s): Shelley 1940-1966
Shapes: Queen Anne

Charm 13894/S16 Queen Anne shape cup and saucer. £70-80; $140-160

Left:
Charm 13894/S31 Queen Anne shape cup and saucer. £70-80; $140-160

Pattern Description & Shapes

13895 **Pole Star**. Plain colour inside cup, on small panels outside cup, on saucer, and plate. Stars on large panels outside cup, on saucer, and plate. Gold or platinum edges. Entered in pattern book during or after 1957.
/S15 Peach
/S16 Orange
/S27 Mushroom
/S28 Drakes Neck Green
/S29 Green
/S31 Pink.
Backstamp(s): Shelley 1940-1966
Shapes: Low Queen Anne

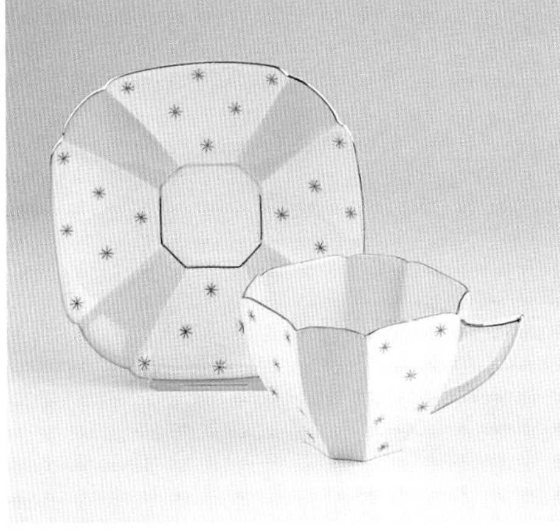

Pole Star 13895/S15 Queen Anne shape cup and saucer. £70-80; $140-160

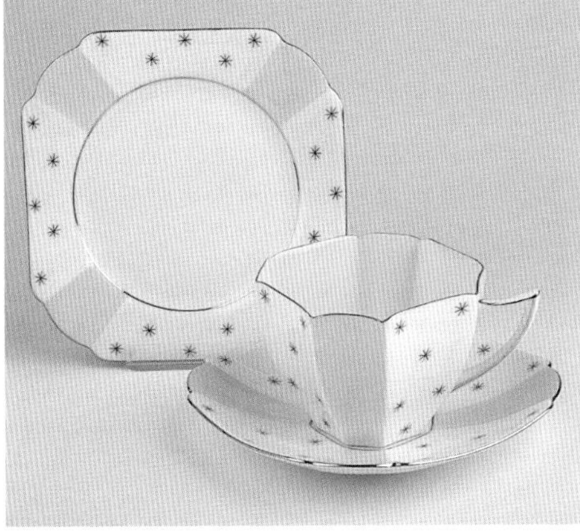

Pole Star 13895/S16 Queen Anne shape cup, saucer, and plate. £70-80; $140-160

Pole Star 13895/S27 Queen Anne shape cup and saucer. £70-80; $140-160

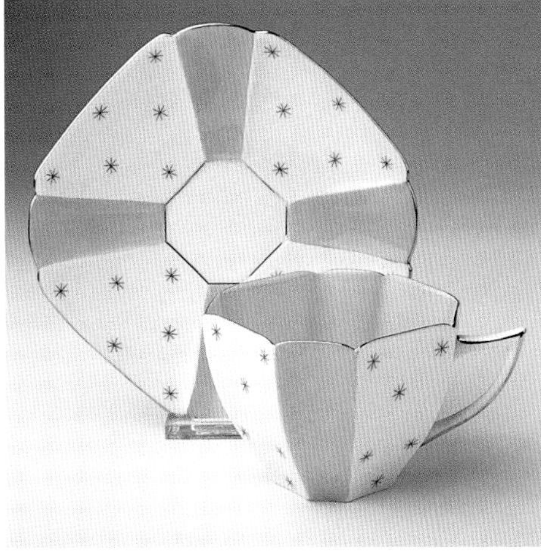

Pole Star 13895/S28 Queen Anne shape cup and saucer. £70-80; $140-160

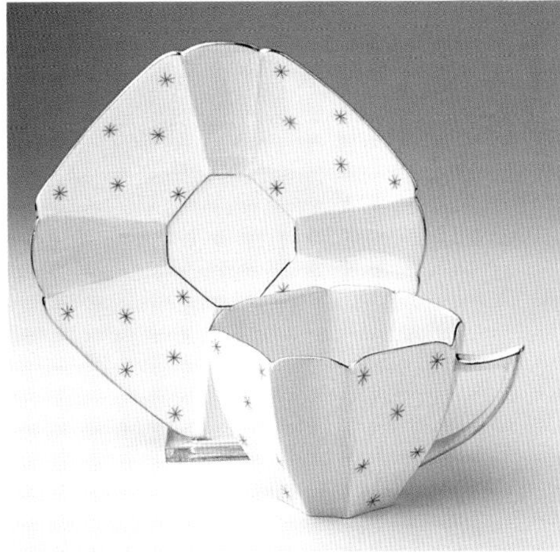

Pole Star 13895/S29 Queen Anne shape cup and saucer. £70-80; $140-160

13896 **Enchantment**. Entered in pattern book during or after 1957.
Backstamp(s): Shelley 1940-1966
Shapes: Stirling

13897 White spots on colour ground. Entered in pattern book during or after 1957.
/S32 Grey
/S33 Blue
/S34 Hazelnut
/S35 Jade
/S36 Old Gold
/S37 Salmon.
Backstamp(s): Shelley 1940-1966
Shapes: Stirling

13898 **Fantasy**. Entered in pattern book during or after 1957.
Backstamp(s): Shelley 1940-1966
Shapes: Stirling

13899 **Crochet** and **Chantilly**. Entered in pattern book during or after 1957.
Backstamp(s): Shelley 1940-1966
Shapes: Gainsborough, Richmond

13900 **Rambler Rose**. Entered in pattern book during or after 1957.
Backstamp(s): Shelley 1940-1966
Shapes: Dainty

13901 Band with shaded ground. Entered in pattern book during or after 1957.
/B Blue
/G Green
/P Pink.
Backstamp(s): Shelley 1940-1966
Shapes: Regent

13904 **Charm**. Small flowers on a white ground. Entered in pattern book during or after 1957.
/B Blue
/G Green
/M Maroon
/Y Yellow.
Backstamp(s): Shelley 1940-1966 Charm
Shapes: Richmond

13905 **Rambler Rose**. Entered in pattern book during or after 1957.
Backstamp(s): Shelley 1940-1966
Shapes: Westminster Miniature

13906 **Bramble**. Entered in pattern book during or after 1957.
Backstamp(s): Shelley 1940-1966
Shapes: Westminster Miniature

13907 **Wine Grape**. Entered in pattern book during or after 1957.
Backstamp(s): Shelley 1940-1966
Shapes: Westminster Miniature

13908 Blackberries and Anemones. Large pink anemones with yellow centres, green leaves, and blackberries on a white ground. Gold edges.
Backstamp(s): Shelley 1940-1966
Shapes: Westminster Miniature

13909 Pink, green, and blue spots. Entered in pattern book during or after 1957.
Backstamp(s): Shelley 1940-1966
Shapes: Dainty

13910 Colour ground with white centre of saucer. Entered in pattern book during or after 1957.
/S3 Green
S10 Blue.
Backstamp(s): Shelley 1940-1966
Shapes: Henley

13911 **Pastoral**. Entered in pattern book during or after 1957.
Backstamp(s): Shelley 1940-1966
Shapes: Stirling

13912 **Enchantment**. Entered in pattern book during or after 1957.
Backstamp(s): Shelley 1940-1966
Shapes: Stirling

13913 **Evergreen**. Entered in pattern book during or after 1957.
Backstamp(s): Shelley 1940-1966
Shapes: Stirling

13914 **Fantasy**. Entered in pattern book during or after 1957.
Backstamp(s): Shelley 1940-1966
Shapes: Stirling

13915 **Lowestoft**. Entered in pattern book during or after 1957.
Backstamp(s): Shelley 1940-1966
Shapes: Westminster Miniature

13916 **Lowestoft**. Entered in pattern book during or after 1957.
Backstamp(s): Shelley 1940-1966
Shapes: Westminster Miniature

13917 **Lyric**. Entered in pattern book during or after 1957.
Backstamp(s): Shelley 1940-1966
Shapes: Westminster Miniature

13918 **Harmony** and **Grey Crystals**. Entered in pattern book during or after 1957.
Backstamp(s): Shelley 1940-1966
Shapes: Westminster Miniature

13919 **Chantilly** and **Pole Star**. Entered in pattern book during or after 1957.
Backstamp(s): Shelley 1940-1966
Shapes: Westminster Miniature

13920 **Symphony** and **Roses, Pansies, and Forget-me-nots**. Entered in pattern book during or after 1957.
Backstamp(s): Shelley 1940-1966
Shapes: Dainty, Ludlow, Stratford

13921 **Symphony** and **Roses, Pansies, and Forget-me-nots** with **Laurel Border**. Entered in pattern book during or after 1957.
Backstamp(s): Shelley 1940-1966
Shapes: Ely

13922 **Columbine**. Flowers and leaves in pink,

Pattern	Description & Shapes
	yellow, blue, maroon, grey, and green. White ground. Gold edges. Entered in pattern book during or after 1957. **Backstamp(s)**: Shelley 1940-1966 **Shapes:** Gainsborough, Stirling, Windsor

Columbine 13922 Windsor shape cup, saucer, and plate. £60-75; $85-100

13923	Dainty pattern as for 051. Entered in pattern book during or after 1957. /B **Dainty Brown** /G **Dainty Green** /P **Dainty Pink** /S28 **Dainty Blue**. **Backstamp(s)**: Shelley 1940-1966 **Shapes:** Ludlow
13924	**Bridal Rose**. Entered in pattern book during or after 1957. /S3 Green /S9 Pink /S10 Blue /S16 Orange. **Backstamp(s)**: Shelley 1940-1966 **Shapes:** Ripon
13925	**Rhythm**. Entered in pattern book during or after 1957. **Backstamp(s)**: Shelley 1940-1966 **Shapes:** Stirling
13926	**Lyric**. Dark pink and grey feathers, grey snowflakes. Two feathers inside cup. Black handle. Entered in pattern book during or after 1957. **Backstamp(s)**: Shelley 1940-1966 Lyric **Shapes:** Stirling
13927	**Harmony**. Entered in pattern book during or after 1957. **Backstamp(s)**: Shelley 1940-1966 **Shapes:** Stirling
13928	**Symphony**. Entered in pattern book during or after 1957. **Backstamp(s)**: Shelley 1940-1966 **Shapes:** Stirling
13929	**Snow Crystals**. Outside cup and saucer are ivory with grey snow crystals. Inside cup various colours as below. Entered in pattern book during or after 1957. /S10 Blue /S34 Hazelnut /S39 Lemon yellow /S40 Green /S41 Lilac /S42 Grey. **Backstamp(s)**: Shelley 1940-1966 **Shapes:** Richmond, Stirling

Right:
Snow Crystals 13929/S39 Stirling shape cup and saucer. £70-80; $140-160

13930	**Hedgerow**. Entered in pattern book during or after 1957. **Backstamp(s)**: Shelley 1940-1966 **Shapes:** Henley, Stirling
13931	Colour inside cup. Entered in pattern book during or after 1957. /S10 Blue /S34 Hazelnut /S39 Lemon yellow /S40 Green /S41 Lilac /S42 Grey. **Backstamp(s)**: Shelley 1940-1966 **Shapes:** Stirling
13932	**Rambler Rose**. Entered in pattern book during or after 1957. **Backstamp(s)**: Shelley 1940-1966 **Shapes:** Ripon
13933	**Crochet**. Entered in pattern book during or after 1957. /S30 Green /S34 Hazelnut /S39 Lemon yellow /S41 Lilac. **Backstamp(s)**: Shelley 1940-1966 **Shapes:** Footed Dainty
13934	**Charm**. Entered in pattern book during or after 1957. /S3 Green outside cup, green **Charm** inside cup /S10 Blue outside cup, blue **Charm** inside cup /S16 Orange outside cup, yellow **Charm** inside cup /S31 Maroon outside cup, maroon **Charm** inside cup **Backstamp(s)**: Shelley 1940-1966 **Shapes:** Footed Dainty
13935	**Rose and Daisy**. Coloured print. White ground. Coloured edges and handle. Entered in pattern book during or after 1958. /B Blue /P Pink /G Green. **Backstamp(s)**: Shelley 1940-1966 **Shapes:** Low Queen Anne

Rose and Daisy 13935/G Queen Anne shape cup, saucer, and plate. £70-80; $140-160

13936	**Fantasy**. Black and grey swirled lines on a white ground outside cup and on saucer and plate. Plain colour inside cup, on edges and handle. Entered in pattern book during or after 1958. /S10 Blue /S34 Hazelnut /S37 Salmon /S39 Lemon Yellow /S40 Green /S41 Lilac. **Backstamp(s)**: Shelley 1940-1966 **Shapes:** Dainty, Queen Anne

Fantasy 13936/S37 Dainty shape cup and saucer. £60-75; $85-100

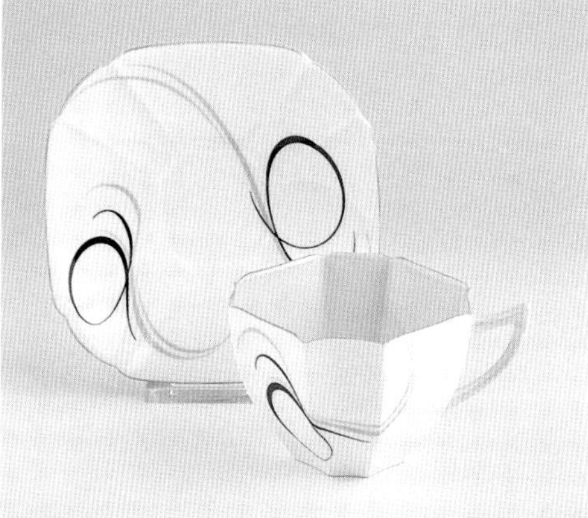

Fantasy 13936/S40 Queen Anne shape cup and saucer. £70-80; $140-160

13937	**Snow Crystals**. Plain colour on small panels outside cup, on saucer, and plate. Snow crystals on large panels outside cup, on saucer, and plate. White inside cup and centre of saucer. Edges and handle according to colour variation. Entered in pattern book during or after 1958. /S10 Blue /S34 Hazelnut /S37 Salmon /S39 Lemon Yellow /S40 Green /S41 Lilac. **Backstamp(s)**: Shelley 1940-1966 **Shapes:** Queen Anne

Opposite page, bottom left:
Snow Crystals 13937/S37 Queen Anne shape cup and saucer. £70-80; $140-160

Pattern Description & Shapes

13938 Colour spots on large panels. Plain colour on small panels. Entered in pattern book during or after 1958.
/B Blue
/G Green
/P Pink
/T Turquoise.
Backstamp(s): Shelley 1940-1966
Shapes: Queen Anne

13939 **Violets**. Pattern inside cup. Lilac outside cup and on saucer. Entered in pattern book during or after 1958.
Backstamp(s): Shelley 1940-1966
Shapes: Footed Dainty

13940 **Primrose**. Pattern inside cup. Green outside cup and on saucer. Entered in pattern book during or after 1958.
Backstamp(s): Shelley 1940-1966
Shapes: Footed Dainty

13941 **Pastoral**. Pattern inside cup. Salmon outside cup and on saucer. Entered in pattern book during or after 1958.
/22 Grey outside cup.
Backstamp(s): Shelley 1940-1966
Shapes: Footed Dainty

13942 **Evergreen**. Pattern inside cup. Green outside cup and on saucer. Entered in pattern book during or after 1958.
Backstamp(s): Shelley 1940-1966
Shapes: Footed Dainty

13943 **Snow Crystals**. Pastel colour outside cup and on saucer. White inside cup with gold snow crystals. Gold edges, foot and handle. Entered in pattern book during or after 1958.
/S10 Blue
/S34 Hazelnut
/S40 Green
/S41 Lilac.
Backstamp(s): Shelley 1940-1966
Shapes: Footed Dainty

Snow Crystals 13943/S10 Footed Dainty shape cup and saucer. £60-75; $85-100

13944 **Golden Harvest**. Entered in pattern book during or after 1958.
/S2 Ivory
/S10 Blue
/S34 Hazelnut
/S41 Lilac.
Backstamp(s): Shelley 1940-1966
Shapes: Footed Dainty

13945 **Lyric** and **Grey Crystals**. Dark pink and grey feathers, grey snowflakes on a white ground on large panels. Plain colour on small panels, edges and handle. Entered in pattern book during or after 1958.
/S10 Blue
/S34 Hazelnut
/S37 Salmon
/S39 Yellow
/S40 Green
/S41 Lilac
Backstamp(s): Shelley 1940-1966 Lyric
Shapes: Queen Anne

13946 **Harmony**. Entered in pattern book during or after 1958.
/S10 Blue
/S34 Hazelnut
/S37 Salmon
/S39 Yellow
/S40 Green
/S41 Lilac
Backstamp(s): Shelley 1940-1966 Lyric
Shapes: Queen Anne

13947 **Enchantment**. Entered in pattern book during or after 1958.
/S3 Green
/S16 Orange.
Backstamp(s): Shelley 1940-1966 Lyric
Shapes: Queen Anne

13948 **Campanula**. Entered in pattern book during or after 1958.
Backstamp(s): Shelley 1940-1966 Lyric
Shapes: Queen Anne

13948 **Morning Glory** and **Grey Crystals**. Entered in pattern book during or after 1958.
Backstamp(s): Shelley 1940-1966 Lyric
Shapes: Queen Anne

13950 **Crochet**. Grey, lacy border on edge of saucer, around centre of the saucer, and rim of outside cup. Pink, blue, yellow, and amber flowers on centre of saucer. Also inside cup. White ground inside cup. Pastel ground inside cup and body of saucer. Entered in pattern book during or after 1958.
/S3 Green
/S10 Blue
/S30 Green
/S31 Pink
/S34 Hazelnut
/S39 Lemon yellow
/S40 Green
/S41 Lilac.
Backstamp(s): 1940-1966
Shapes: Footed Dainty

Crochet 13950/S34 Footed Dainty shape cup and saucer. £60-75; $85-100

Crochet 13950/S39 Footed Dainty shape cup and saucer. £60-75; $85-100

13951 **Lyric**. Dark pink and grey feathers, grey snowflakes inside cup. Pink on panels outside cup and on saucer. Gold edges. Entered in pattern book during or after 1958.
Backstamp(s): Shelley 1940-1966
Shapes: Footed Dainty

13952 **Primrose** and **Crochet**. Yellow primroses with green foliage on an ivory ground inside cup. Grey crochet border inside cup. Plain colour outside cup and on saucer. Gold edges. Entered in pattern book during or after 1958.
/S3 Green
/S10 Blue
/S30 Green
/S31 Pink
/S34 Hazelnut
/S39 Lemon yellow
/S41 Lilac.
Backstamp(s): Shelley 1940-1966
Shapes: Footed Dainty

Primrose 13952/S3 Footed Dainty shape cup and saucer. £60-75; $85-100

13953 **Chantilly**. Signed **H. Pardoe**. Entered in pattern book during or after 1958.
Backstamp(s): Shelley 1940-1966
Shapes: Dainty, Richmond, Stirling

13954 **Rose and Daisy**. Entered in pattern book during or after 1958.
Backstamp(s): Shelley 1940-1966
Shapes: Ludlow

13955 **Field Flowers**. Pink, blue, and mauve flowers with green leaves. Pink trim.
Backstamp(s): Shelley 1940-1966 Field Flowers
Shapes: Henley, Richmond

13956 **Basket and Festoon**. Entered in pattern book during or after 1958.
Backstamp(s): Shelley 1940-1966
Shapes: Ludlow

Pattern	Description & Shapes
13957	**Fuchsia**. Entered in pattern book during or after 1958. **Backstamp(s)**: Shelley 1940-1966 **Shapes:** Cambridge
13958	**Fuchsia**. Entered in pattern book during or after 1958. **Backstamp(s)**: Shelley 1940-1966 **Shapes:** Ripon
13959	**Georgian**. Entered in pattern book during or after 1958. /S15 Peach /S16 Orange /S27 Mushroom /S28 Drakes Neck Green /S29 Green /S31 Pink. **Backstamp(s)**: Shelley 1940-1966 **Shapes:** Stirling
13960	**Patches**. Entered in pattern book during or after 1958. **Backstamp(s)**: Shelley 1940-1966 **Shapes:** Gainsborough
13961	Dainty pattern as for 051. Entered in pattern book during or after 1958. /B **Dainty Brown** /G **Dainty Green** /M **Dainty Mauve** /P **Dainty Pink** /Y **Dainty Yellow** /S28 **Dainty Blue**. **Backstamp(s)**: Shelley 1940-1966 **Shapes:** Dainty
13962	Universal **Pyrethrum**. Entered in pattern book during or after 1958. **Backstamp(s)**: Shelley 1940-1966 **Shapes:** Atholl
13963	**Enchantment**. Entered in pattern book during or after 1958. **Backstamp(s)**: Shelley 1940-1966 **Shapes:** Atholl
13964	**Hibiscus**. Yellow hibiscus flowers and green foliage on a white ground inside cup. Yellow outside cup and on saucer. Gold edges, foot and handle. **Backstamp(s)**: Shelley 1940-1966 **Shapes:** Atholl

Hibiscus 13964/S16 Atholl shape cup and saucer. £60-75; $85-100

13965	**Bridal Rose**. Entered in pattern book during or after 1958. /A **Rose Bud**. **Backstamp(s)**: Shelley 1940-1966 **Shapes:** Atholl
13966	**Roses, Pansies, and Forget-me-nots**. Entered in pattern book during or after 1958. **Backstamp(s)**: Shelley 1940-1966 **Shapes:** Atholl
13967	**Campanula**. Entered in pattern book during or after 1958. **Backstamp(s)**: Shelley 1940-1966 **Shapes:** Atholl
13968	**Ivory Trousseau**. Entered in pattern book during or after 1958. **Backstamp(s)**: Shelley 1940-1966 Trousseau **Shapes:** Gainsborough
13969	**Wine Grape**. Entered in pattern book during or after 1959. **Backstamp(s)**: Shelley 1940-1966 **Shapes:** Richmond
13970	**Violets**. Entered in pattern book during or after 1959. **Backstamp(s)**: Shelley 1940-1966 **Shapes:** Dainty
13971	**Trousseau**. Entered in pattern book during or after 1959. **Backstamp(s)**: Shelley 1940-1966 **Shapes:** Richmond
13972	**Autumn Leaves** and **Blue Scroll Border**. Entered in pattern book during or after 1959. **Backstamp(s)**: Shelley 1940-1966 **Shapes:** Richmond
13973	**Drifting Leaves** and **Lyric**. Gold edges. Entered in pattern book during or after 1959. **Backstamp(s)**: Shelley 1940-1966 **Shapes:** Richmond
13975	**Golden Harvest**. Entered in pattern book during or after 1959. **Backstamp(s)**: Shelley 1940-1966 **Shapes:** Gainsborough, Richmond
13976	**Pink and Yellow Rose**. Entered in pattern book during or after 1959. **Backstamp(s)**: Shelley 1940-1966 **Shapes:** Dainty
13977	**Wild Anemone**. Pink, blue, and mauve flowers with green leaves. Green trim. Henley has green foot and handle. Entered in pattern book during or after 1959. **Backstamp(s)**: Shelley 1940-1966 Wild Anemone **Shapes:** Dainty, Dainty Beaker, Ludlow, Richmond

Wild Anemone 13977 Ludlow shape cup and saucer. £60-70; $100-120

Wild Anemone 13977 muffin dish. £90-100; $150-180

13978	**Wild Anemone**. Entered in pattern book during or after 1959. **Backstamp(s)**: Shelley 1940-1966 **Shapes:** Richmond
13979	Universal **Debonair**. Entered in pattern book during or after 1959. **Backstamp(s)**: Shelley 1940-1966 **Shapes:** Dainty
13980	**Pompadour**. Pink, blue, and yellow flowers with a maroon border. Gold trim. Entered in pattern book during or after 1959. **Backstamp(s)**: Shelley 1940-1966 **Shapes:** Henley

Pompadour 13980 Henley shape cup and saucer. £50-70; $80-120

13981	**English Pansy**. Entered in pattern book during or after 1959. **Backstamp(s)**: Shelley 1940-1966 **Shapes:** Dainty
13982	**Field Flowers**. Entered in pattern book during or after 1959. **Backstamp(s)**: Shelley 1940-1966 **Shapes:** Dainty, Richmond
13983	**Chantilly**. Entered in pattern book during or after 1959. **Backstamp(s)**: Shelley 1940-1966 **Shapes:** Dainty, Richmond
13984	**Wisteria**. Entered in pattern book during or after 1959. **Backstamp(s)**: Shelley 1940-1966 **Shapes:** Gainsborough
13985	**Rose Border**. Entered in pattern book during or after 1959. /42 Blue /53 Pink. **Backstamp(s)**: Shelley 1940-1966 **Shapes:** Ripon
13986	**Rose Border**. Entered in pattern book during or after 1959. /28 Blue /53 Pink. **Backstamp(s)**: Shelley 1940-1966 **Shapes:** Ludlow
13987	**Wild Anemone**. Pink, blue, and mauve

Wild Anemone 13987/S30 Atholl shape cup and saucer. £60-70; $100-120

Pattern	Description & Shapes

flowers with green leaves inside cup on a white ground. Pale green outside cup and on saucer. Gold edges, foot and handle. Entered in pattern book during or after 1959.
Backstamp(s): Shelley 1940-1966 Field Flowers
Shapes: Atholl

13988 **Georgian**. Entered in pattern book during or after 1959.
Backstamp(s): Shelley 1940-1966
Shapes: Queen Anne

13989 **Wild Flowers**. Entered in pattern book during or after 1959.
Backstamp(s): Shelley 1940-1966
Shapes: Queen Anne

13990 **Pyrethrum**. Entered in pattern book during or after 1959.
Backstamp(s): Shelley 1940-1966
Shapes: Queen Anne

13991 **Basket of Flowers** and **Pompadour**. Entered in pattern book during or after 1959.
Backstamp(s): Shelley 1940-1966
Shapes: Footed Oleander

13992 **Georgian**, **Dainty Blue** and **Rose and Daisy**. Entered in pattern book during or after 1959.
Backstamp(s): Shelley 1940-1966
Shapes: Footed Oleander

13993 **Jonquil**. Entered in pattern book during or after 1959.
Backstamp(s): Shelley 1940-1966
Shapes: Richmond

13994 **Violets**. Entered in pattern book during or after 1959.
Backstamp(s): Shelley 1940-1966
Shapes: Richmond

13995 **Wine Grape**. Entered in pattern book during or after 1959.
Backstamp(s): Shelley 1940-1966
Shapes: Ripon

13996 **Vine Leaves**. Entered in pattern book during or after 1959.
Backstamp(s): Shelley 1940-1966
Shapes: Ripon

13997 Universal **Debonair**. Entered in pattern book during or after 1959.
Backstamp(s): Shelley 1940-1966
Shapes: Dainty, Richmond

13998 **Mauve and Yellow Flowers** and German pattern number 553. Entered in pattern book during or after 1959.
Backstamp(s): Shelley 1940-1966
Shapes: Dainty

13999 **Blue and Pink Sprays** from German pattern number 553. Entered in pattern book during or after 1959.
Backstamp(s): Shelley 1940-1966
Shapes: Dainty

14000 **Stork Pattern**. Entered in pattern book during or after 1959.
/G Green
/M Mauve.
Backstamp(s): Shelley 1940-1966
Shapes: Dainty

14001 **Pink Flowers** from German pattern number 553. Pink outside cup and on saucer. Entered in pattern book during or after 1959.
Backstamp(s): Shelley 1940-1966
Shapes: Footed Dainty

14002 Blue pieces from German pattern number 553. Blue outside cup and on saucer. Entered in pattern book during or after 1959.
Backstamp(s): Shelley 1940-1966
Shapes: Footed Dainty

14003 Yellow pieces from German pattern number 553. Green outside cup and on saucer. Entered in pattern book during or after 1959.
Backstamp(s): Shelley 1940-1966
Shapes: Footed Dainty

14004 Mauve pieces from German pattern number 553. Mauve outside cup and on saucer. Entered in pattern book during or after 1959.
Backstamp(s): Shelley 1940-1966
Shapes: Footed Dainty

14005 **Chantilly** and pieces from German pattern number 553. Pink outside cup and on saucer. Entered in pattern book during or after 1959.
Backstamp(s): Shelley 1940-1966
Shapes: Ludlow

14006 **Anemone**. Pink and blue flowers with green leaves. Gold trim. Entered in pattern book during or after 1959.
Backstamp(s): Shelley 1940-1966 Anemone
Shapes: Richmond, Windsor

14007 **Winter Cherry**. Entered in pattern book during or after 1959.
Backstamp(s): Shelley 1940-1966
Shapes: Richmond

14007 **Blue Iris**. Entered in pattern book during or after 1959.
Backstamp(s): Shelley 1940-1966
Shapes: Bute, Dainty, Richmond, Windsor

14009 **Syringa**. Ivory Syringa flowers with green foliage on a white ground. Gold edges. Entered in pattern book during or after 1959.
Backstamp(s): Shelley 1940-1966
Shapes: Bute, Richmond, Windsor

14010 **Golden Broom**. Yellow and orange flowers with green leaves. White ground. Gold edges. Entered in pattern book during or after 1959.
Backstamp(s): Shelley 1940-1966 Golden Broom
Shapes: Bute, Gainsborough, Ludlow, Windsor

Golden Broom 14010 Gainsborough shape cup and saucer. £40-50; $80-100

Golden Broom 14010 Ludlow shape cup and saucer. £60-80; $120-140

14011 **American Brooklime**. Tiny blue flowers and green leaves on white ground. Gold edges. Entered in pattern book during or after 1959.
Backstamp(s): Shelley 1940-1966
Shapes: Bute, Windsor

14012 **Scilla**. Entered in pattern book during or after 1959.
Backstamp(s): Shelley 1940-1966
Shapes: Bute, Windsor

14013 **Celandine**. Yellow flowers and green leaves on a white ground. Gold edges.
Backstamp(s): Shelley green mark for 1940-1966.
Shapes: Bute, Windsor

14014 **Woodland**. Entered in pattern book during or after 1959.
Backstamp(s): Shelley 1940-1966
Shapes: Ripon

14015 **Charm**. Entered in pattern book during or after 1959.
/B Blue **Charm,** blue inside cup
/G Green **Charm,** green inside cup
/M Maroon **Charm,** pink inside cup
/Y Yellow **Charm,** lemon yellow inside cup
Backstamp(s): Shelley 1940-1966
Shapes: Ludlow

14016 Plain colours. Entered in pattern book during or after 1959.
/S3 Green
/S10 Blue
/S31 Pink
/S39 Lemon yellow
/S40 Green
/S41 Lilac.
Backstamp(s): Shelley 1940-1966
Shapes: Ludlow

14017 **Lyric**. Dark pink and grey feathers, grey snowflakes inside cup and main part of saucer. Green outside cup and centre of saucer. Green edges and handle. Entered in pattern book during or after 1959.
Backstamp(s): Shelley 1940-1966 Lyric
Shapes: Ludlow

14018 **Harmony**. Entered in pattern book during or after 1959.
Backstamp(s): Shelley 1940-1966
Shapes: Ludlow

14019 **Roses, Pansies, and Forget-me-nots**. Entered in pattern book during or after 1959.
Backstamp(s): Shelley 1940-1966
Shapes: Ludlow

14020 **Rose Bud**. Entered in pattern book during or after 1959.
Backstamp(s): Shelley 1940-1966
Shapes: Ludlow

14021 **Chantilly**. Entered in pattern book during or after 1960.
Backstamp(s): Shelley 1940-1966
Shapes: Richmond

14022 **Hedgerow**. Pink, blue, yellow, and orange flowers with green foliage on a white ground. Gold edges. Entered in pattern book during or after 1960.
Backstamp(s): Shelley 1940-1966 Hedgerow
Shapes: Richmond

14023 **Wine Grape**. Entered in pattern book during or after 1960.
Backstamp(s): Shelley 1940-1966
Shapes: Richmond

14024 **Maroon Princess**. Inside cup maroon **Dubarry** panels. **Chantilly** flower sprays inside and outside cup as well on saucer and plate. White ground. Gold edges. Entered in pattern book during or after 1960.
Backstamp(s): Shelley 1940-1966 Maroon Princess
Shapes: Richmond

14025 **Green Princess**. Inside cup green **Dubarry** panels. **Chantilly** flower sprays inside and outside cup as well on saucer and plate. White ground. Gold edges. Entered in pattern book during or after

Pattern	Description & Shapes
	1960. **Backstamp(s)**: Shelley 1940-1966 Green Princess **Shapes:** Richmond
14026	**Blue Princess**. Inside cup blue **Dubarry** panels. **Chantilly** flower sprays inside and outside cup as well on saucer and plate. White ground. Gold edges. Entered in pattern book during or after 1960. **Backstamp(s)**: Shelley 1940-1966 Blue Princess **Shapes:** Richmond
14027	**Maroon Empress**. Combination of **Duchess** and **Georgian** patterns. Pink roses, blue, yellow, and mauve flowers with green foliage. Flowers also inside cup. Border of maroon and yellow sections. White ground. Gold edges. Entered in pattern book during or after 1960. **Backstamp(s)**: Shelley 1940-1966 Maroon Empress **Shapes:** Richmond
14028	**Green Empress**. Combination of **Duchess** and **Georgian** patterns. Pink roses, blue, yellow, and mauve flowers with green foliage. Flowers also inside cup. Border of green and yellow sections. White ground. Gold edges. Entered in pattern book during or after 1960. **Backstamp(s)**: Shelley 1940-1966 Green Empress **Shapes:** Richmond
14029	**Blue Empress**. Combination of **Duchess** and **Georgian** patterns. Pink roses, blue, yellow, and mauve flowers with green foliage. Flowers also inside cup. Border of blue and yellow sections. White ground. Gold edges. Entered in pattern book during or after 1960. **Backstamp(s)**: Shelley 1940-1966 Blue Empress **Shapes:** Richmond

Blue Empress 14029 Richmond shape cup and saucer. £60-70; $100-120

Pattern	Description & Shapes
14030	**Chinese Garden**. Entered in pattern book during or after 1960. **Backstamp(s)**: Shelley 1940-1966 **Shapes:** Richmond
14031	**Gold Laurel Wreath (Bridal Wreath)**. Entered in pattern book during or after 1960. **Backstamp(s)**: Shelley 1940-1966 **Shapes:** Gainsborough, Stirling, Windsor
14032	**Wind Flower**. Entered in pattern book during or after 1960. **Backstamp(s)**: Shelley 1940-1966 Wind Flower **Shapes:** Dainty, Richmond, Ludlow, Windsor
14033	**Golden Broom**. Yellow and orange flowers with green leaves. White ground. Similar to 0439. Entered in pattern book during or after 1960. **Backstamp(s)**: Shelley 1940-1966 **Shapes:** Dainty, Richmond, Ludlow, Windsor
14034	Narrow red border. Gold print. Entered in pattern book during or after 1960. **Backstamp(s)**: Shelley 1940-1966 **Shapes:** Windsor
14035	**Cornflower**. Entered in pattern book during or after 1960. **Backstamp(s)**: Shelley 1940-1945 **Shapes:** Richmond
14036	**Dainty Black** and **Rambler Rose**. Entered in pattern book during or after 1960. **Backstamp(s)**: Shelley 1940-1945 **Shapes:** Richmond
14038	**Blue Paisley Chintz**. Paisley pattern Gold edges, foot and handle. Entered in pattern book during or after 1960. **Backstamp(s)**: Shelley 1940-1966 Paisley **Shapes:** Ripon
14039	**Briar Rose**. Entered in pattern book during or after 1960. **Backstamp(s)**: Shelley 1940-1945 Briar Rose **Shapes:** Ripon
14042	**Blue Paisley Chintz**. Paisley pattern. Pale blue foot and handle. Blue edges. Also see 0397. Entered in pattern book during or after 1960. **Backstamp(s)**: Shelley 1940-1966 **Shapes:** Footed Oleander, Henley
14043	**Lowestoft Chintz**. Entered in pattern book during or after 1960. **Backstamp(s)**: Shelley 1940-1966 **Shapes:** Footed Oleander
14044	No known details. Entered in pattern book during or after 1960. **Backstamp(s)**: Shelley 1940-1945 **Shapes:** Footed Oleander
14045	**Jonquil**. Entered in pattern book during or after 1960. **Backstamp(s)**: Shelley 1940-1945 **Shapes:** Atholl
14046	**Crochet**. Green bands. Entered in pattern book during or after 1960. **Backstamp(s)**: Shelley 1940-1945 **Shapes:** Windsor
14047	**Crochet**. Pink bands. Entered in pattern book during or after 1960. **Backstamp(s)**: Shelley 1940-1945 **Shapes:** Windsor
14048	**Crochet**. Blue bands. Entered in pattern book during or after 1960. **Backstamp(s)**: Shelley 1940-1945 **Shapes:** Windsor
14049	**Roses, Pansies, and Forget-me-nots**. Entered in pattern book during or after 1960. **Backstamp(s)**: Shelley 1940-1945 **Shapes:** Dainty, Richmond
14050	**Roses, Pansies, and Forget-me-nots**. Entered in pattern book during or after 1960. **Backstamp(s)**: Shelley 1940-1945 **Shapes:** Dainty
14051	**Rose Bud**. Entered in pattern book during or after 1960. **Backstamp(s)**: Shelley 1940-1945 **Shapes:** Dainty
14052	**Rose Bud**. Entered in pattern book during or after 1960. **Backstamp(s)**: Shelley 1940-1945 **Shapes:** Dainty
14053	**Pole Star**. Plain colour outside cup. Outside cup colour as et out below. Saucer has a white centre. Stars outside cup and one in centre of saucer. Coloured foot and handle. Lemon gold edges. Entered in pattern book during or after 1960. /S9 Pink /S15 Peach /S16 Orange /S26 Lavender /S27 Mushroom /S28 Drakes Neck Green /S29 Green. **Backstamp(s)**: Shelley 1940-1966 **Shapes:** Windsor
14054	**Old Ireland**. Entered in pattern book during or after 1960. **Backstamp(s)**: Shelley 1940-1945 **Shapes:** Ripon
14055	**Celandine**. Yellow flowers and green leaves. Pale green trim and handle. Entered in pattern book during or after 1960. **Backstamp(s)**: Shelley 1940-1966. **Shapes:** Dainty, Ludlow

Celandine 14055 Dainty shape cup and saucer. £60-75; $85-100

Celandine 14055 Ludlow shape cup and saucer. £60-80; $90-110

Pattern	Description & Shapes
14056	**Hibiscus**. Entered in pattern book during or after 1960. **Backstamp(s)**: Shelley 1940-1945 **Shapes:** Dainty
14057	**Thistle**. Entered in pattern book during or after 1960. **Backstamp(s)**: Shelley 1940-1945 **Shapes:** Dainty
14058	**Harebell**. Blue flowers and green leaves on white ground. Entered in pattern book during or after 1960. **Backstamp(s)**: Shelley 1940-1966 **Shapes:** Dainty, Henley, Richmond
14059	**Lily of the Valley**. Entered in pattern book during or after 1960. **Backstamp(s)**: Shelley 1940-1945 **Shapes:** Dainty
14060	**American Brooklime**. Tiny blue flowers and green leaves on white ground. Pale blue edges and handle. Entered in pattern book during or after 1960. **Backstamp(s)**: Shelley 1940-1966 **Shapes:** Dainty

American Brooklime 14060 Dainty shape cup and saucer. £60-75; $85-100

14061 **Scilla**. Blue flowers and green leaves. Spray also inside cup. Pink or gold edges. Pink or blue handle. Similar to 0437. Entered in pattern book during or after 1960.
Backstamp(s): Shelley 1940-1966
Shapes: Dainty, Ludlow

Scilla 14061 Ludlow shape cup and saucer. £70-80; $130-160

14062 **Blue Iris**. Entered in pattern book during or after 1960.
Backstamp(s): Shelley 1940-1945
Shapes: Dainty

14063 **Syringa**. Ivory Syringa flowers with green foliage on a white ground. Green edges and handle. Entered in pattern book during or after 1960.
Backstamp(s): Shelley 1940-1966
Shapes: Dainty

Syringa 14063 Dainty shape cup and saucer. £60-80; $120-140

14064 **Lily of the Valley**. Green outside cup and on saucer. Entered in pattern book during or after 1960.
Backstamp(s): Shelley 1940-1945
Shapes: Richmond

14065 Blue band with gold printed border below it. Entered in pattern book during or after 1960.
Backstamp(s): Shelley 1940-1945
Shapes: Windsor

14066 **Black Greek Key**. Entered in pattern book during or after 1960.
Backstamp(s): Shelley 1940-1945
Shapes: Gainsborough

14067 **Paradise**. Entered in pattern book during or after 1960.
Backstamp(s): Shelley 1940-1945 Paradise
Shapes: Windsor

14068 **Caribbean**. Gold and black feathers on a white ground inside cup, outside cup, and on saucer. Lower half of cup is pale blue as is outside part of saucer. White and blue separated by gold ring. Gold edges. Entered in pattern book during or after 1960.
Backstamp(s): Shelley 1940-1966
Shapes: Windsor

Caribbean 14068/S43 Windsor shape cup and saucer. £60-80; $90-120

Caribbean 14068/S43 bread and butter/cake plate. £30-40; $50-70

14069 **Pastoral**. Pink and grey flowers and foliage on a grey ground outside cup and on saucer. White inside cup. Dark grey edges, foot and handle. Entered in pattern book during or after 1960.
Backstamp(s): Shelley 1940-1966 Pastoral
Shapes: Richmond

Pastoral 14069 Richmond shape cup and saucer. £60-80; $90-120

14070 **Pansy Chintz**. Entered in pattern book during or after 1961.
Backstamp(s): Shelley 1940-1945
Shapes: Henley

14071 **Pansy Chintz**. Green outside cup and on saucer. Entered in pattern book during or after 1961.
Backstamp(s): Shelley 1940-1945
Shapes: Footed Oleander

14072 **Briar Rose**. Pink inside cup. Entered in pattern book during or after 1961.
Backstamp(s): Shelley 1940-1945
Shapes: Henley

14073 **Blue Paisley Chintz**. Paisley pattern. Pale green inside cup. Green edges, foot and handle. Entered in pattern book during or after 1961.
Backstamp(s): Shelley 1940-1966
Shapes: Henley

14074 **Fruit Centre** and **Laurel Border**. Entered in pattern book during or after 1961.
Backstamp(s): Shelley 1940-1945
Shapes: Footed Oleander

14075 **Heavenly**. Sprigs of flowers and garland border. Colour edges. Entered in pattern book during or after 1961.
/B **Heavenly Blue**
/M **Heavenly Mauve**
/P **Heavenly Pink**.
Backstamp(s): 1940-1966
Shapes: Dainty

Heavenly Blue 14075/B Dainty shape cup and saucer. £70-80; $140-160

Pattern	Description & Shapes
14076	**Melody**. Entered in pattern book during or after 1961. **Backstamp(s)**: Shelley 1940-1945 **Shapes:** Richmond
14077	**Classic**. Entered in pattern book during or after 1961. /4 Green /40 Pink /41 Maroon /42 Blue. **Backstamp(s)**: Shelley 1940-1945 **Shapes:** Windsor
14078	**Empire**. Entered in pattern book during or after 1961. /4 Green /40 Pink /41 Maroon /42 Blue. **Backstamp(s)**: Shelley 1940-1945 **Shapes:** Windsor
14079	**Rambler Rose**. Entered in pattern book during or after 1961. **Backstamp(s)**: Shelley 1940-1945 **Shapes:** Dainty
14080	**Thistle**. Entered in pattern book during or after 1961. **Backstamp(s)**: Shelley 1940-1945 **Shapes:** Cambridge, Windsor
14081	**Fiesta**. Entered in pattern book during or after 1961. **Backstamp(s)**: Shelley 1940-1945 Fiesta **Shapes:** Windsor
14082	**Gaiety**. Entered in pattern book during or after 1961. **Backstamp(s)**: Shelley 1940-1945 Gaiety **Shapes:** Windsor
14083	**Blue Rock** and **Blue Scroll Border**. Entered in pattern book during or after 1961. **Backstamp(s)**: Shelley 1940-1945 Gaiety **Shapes:** Windsor
14084	**Stocks** and **Blue Scroll Border**. Mauve, pink, and white stocks with green leaves. White ground. Green border. Green edges, foot and handle. Entered in pattern book during or after 1961. **Backstamp(s)**: Shelley 1940-1966 **Shapes:** Windsor
14085	**Syringa**. Green outside cup and on saucer. Entered in pattern book during or after 1961. **Backstamp(s)**: Shelley 1940-1945 **Shapes:** Windsor
14086	**Anemone**. Green outside cup and on saucer. Entered in pattern book during or after 1961. **Backstamp(s)**: Shelley 1940-1945 **Shapes:** Windsor
14087	**Celandine**. Ivory outside cup and on saucer. Entered in pattern book during or after 1961. **Backstamp(s)**: Shelley 1940-1945 **Shapes:** Windsor
14088	**Scilla**. Blue outside cup and on saucer. Entered in pattern book during or after 1961. **Backstamp(s)**: Shelley 1940-1945 **Shapes:** Windsor
14089	**Blue Iris**. Pink outside cup and on saucer. Entered in pattern book during or after 1961. **Backstamp(s)**: Shelley 1940-1945 **Shapes:** Windsor
14090	**Elegance**. Entered in pattern book during or after 1961. **Backstamp(s)**: Shelley 1940-1945 **Shapes:** Dainty
14091	**Ashford**. Entered in pattern book during or after 1961. **Backstamp(s)**: Shelley 1940-1945 **Shapes:** Oleander
14092	**Paradise**. Black and gold feathers on white ground outside cup and on saucer. Colour ground inside cup. Gold edges. Entered in pattern book during or after 1961. /S3 Green /S10 Blue /S31 Pink /S34 Hazelnut /S39 Lemon yellow /S40 Green /S41 Lilac. **Backstamp(s)**: Shelley 1940-1966 **Shapes:** Dainty

Paradise 14092/S34 Dainty shape cup and saucer. £60-75; $85-100

Pattern	Description & Shapes
14093	**Trousseau**. Entered in pattern book during or after 1961. **Backstamp(s)**: Shelley 1940-1945 **Shapes:** Windsor
14094	**Golden Harvest**. Entered in pattern book during or after 1961. **Backstamp(s)**: Shelley 1940-1945 **Shapes:** Windsor
14095	**Bridesmaid**. Entered in pattern book during or after 1961. **Backstamp(s)**: Shelley 1940-1945 Bridesmaid **Shapes:** Gainsborough, Windsor
14096	**Golden Rose**. Entered in pattern book during or after 1961. **Backstamp(s)**: Shelley 1940-1945 Golden Rose **Shapes:** Windsor
14097	**Daphne**. Water green outside cup and on saucer. Entered in pattern book during or after 1961. **Backstamp(s)**: Shelley 1940-1945 **Shapes:** Windsor
14098	**Bridal Wreath** on black band. Entered in pattern book during or after 1961. **Backstamp(s)**: Shelley 1940-1945 **Shapes:** Mocha, Windsor
14099	**Bridesmaid**. Entered in pattern book during or after 1961. **Backstamp(s)**: Shelley 1940-1945 Bridesmaid **Shapes:** Windsor
14100	**Sycamore**. Black, grey, and yellow leaves on a white ground. Spray also inside cup. Platinum border inside cup, edges of saucer, plate foot, and stroke on handle. Entered in pattern book during or after 1961. **Backstamp(s)**: Shelley 1940-1966 Sycamore **Shapes:** Bute, Mocha, Windsor

Sycamore 14100 Windsor shape cup, saucer, and plate. £60-80; $90-100

Pattern	Description & Shapes
14101	**Sylvan**. Entered in pattern book during or after 1961. **Backstamp(s)**: Shelley 1940-1945 **Shapes:** Bute, Gainsborough, Windsor
14102	**Mayfair**. Entered in pattern book during or after 1961. **Backstamp(s)**: Shelley 1940-1945 **Shapes:** Unknown
14103	**Green Peony**. Gold peonies with gold and grey leaves on broad, pale green band outside cup and on saucer. Ivory below green. Gold line separates green and ivory. Gold and grey peony spray inside cup on ivory ground. Gold trim. Entered in pattern book during or after 1961. **Backstamp(s)**: Shelley 1940-1966 **Shapes:** Windsor
14104	**Rose Peony**. Gold peonies with gold and grey leaves on broad, pale pink band outside cup and on saucer. Ivory below pink. Gold line separates pink and ivory. Gold and grey peony spray inside cup on ivory ground. Gold trim. Entered in pattern book during or after 1961. **Backstamp(s)**: Shelley 1940-1966 Rose Peony **Shapes:** Windsor
14105	Hulmes **Dresden Rose**. Entered in pattern book during or after 1961. **Backstamp(s)**: Shelley 1940-1966 Dresden Rose **Shapes:** Ludlow
14106	**Forget-me-nots**. Entered in pattern book during or after 1961 on comports. **Backstamp(s)**: Shelley 1940-1966 **Shapes:** Dainty
14107	**Rosalie**. Entered in pattern book during or after 1961. **Backstamp(s)**: Shelley 1940-1966 Rosalie **Shapes:** Windsor
14108	**Trousseau**. Entered in pattern book during or after 1961. **Backstamp(s)**: Shelley 1940-1966 **Shapes:** Windsor
14109	**Cameo Rose**. Green. Entered in pattern book during or after 1961. **Backstamp(s)**: Shelley 1940-1966 **Shapes:** Windsor

Sycamore 14100 Windsor shape coffee pot.

Pattern	Description & Shapes
14110	**Cameo Rose**. Pink. Entered in pattern book during or after 1961. **Backstamp(s)**: Shelley 1940-1966 **Shapes:** Windsor
14111	**Cameo Rose**. Blue. Entered in pattern book during or after 1961. **Backstamp(s)**: Shelley 1940-1966 **Shapes:** Windsor
14112	**Acanthus**. Entered in pattern book during or after 1961. **Backstamp(s)**: Shelley 1940-1966 **Shapes:** Dainty
14113	**Golden Wheat**. Entered in pattern book during or after 1961. **Backstamp(s)**: Shelley 1940-1966 **Shapes:** Dainty, Oleander
14114	**Shamrocks**. Shamrock sprigs on white ground. Sprig also inside cup. Green edges and handle. Entered in pattern book during or after 1961. **Backstamp(s)**: Shelley 1940-1966 Shamrock **Shapes:** Bute, Dainty, Ludlow

Shamrocks 14114 Ludlow shape cup and saucer. £60-80; $120-140

14115	**Paradise**. Entered in pattern book during or after 1961. **Backstamp(s)**: Shelley 1940-1966 **Shapes:** Dainty, Footed Dainty
14116	**Bridesmaid**. Similar to 0441. Entered in pattern book during or after 1961. **Backstamp(s)**: Shelley 1940-1966 **Shapes:** Dainty
14117	**Grey Mist**. Entered in pattern book during or after 1961. **Backstamp(s)**: Shelley 1940-1966 **Shapes:** Richmond
14118	**Glamis**. Entered in pattern book during or after 1961. **Backstamp(s)**: Shelley 1940-1966 **Shapes:** Windsor
14119	**Margaret Rose**. Entered in pattern book during or after 1961. **Backstamp(s)**: Shelley 1940-1966 **Shapes:** Richmond
14120	**Lady Eleanor**. Entered in pattern book during or after 1961. **Backstamp(s)**: Shelley 1940-1966 **Shapes:** Richmond
14121	**Lady Eleanor**. Ivory. Entered in pattern book during or after 1961. **Backstamp(s)**: Shelley 1940-1966 **Shapes:** Richmond
14122	**Lady Eleanor**. Pink. Entered in pattern book during or after 1961. **Backstamp(s)**: Shelley 1940-1966 **Shapes:** Richmond
14123	**Lady Eleanor**. Blue. Entered in pattern book during or after 1961. **Backstamp(s)**: Shelley 1940-1966 **Shapes:** Richmond
14124	**Silver Sawn**. Pink. Entered in pattern book during or after 1961. **Backstamp(s)**: Shelley 1940-1966 **Shapes:** Windsor
14125	**Tapestry Rose Chintz**. Grey roses and foliage on a yellow ground outside cup and on saucer. Ivory inside cup. Gold edges, foot and handle. Entered in pattern book during or after 1961. **Backstamp(s)**: Shelley 1940-1966 Tapestry Rose **Shapes:** Ripon

Tapestry Rose Chintz 14125 Ripon shape cup and saucer. £80-90; $160-200

14126	**Tapestry Rose Chintz**. Grey roses and foliage on a yellow ground. Entered in pattern book during or after 1961. **Backstamp(s)**: Shelley 1940-1966 **Shapes:** Footed Oleander
14127	**Gold and Grey Wheat**. Entered in pattern book during or after 1962. **Backstamp(s)**: Shelley 1940-1966 **Shapes:** Footed Oleander
14128	**Rosalie**. Pink roses and grey foliage on a white ground. Gold edges. Entered in pattern book during or after 1962. **Backstamp(s)**: Shelley 1940-1966 **Shapes:** Ripon
14129	**Bridesmaid**. Entered in pattern book during or after 1962. **Backstamp(s)**: Shelley 1940-1966 **Shapes:** Ripon
14130	**Chantilly**. Entered in pattern book during or after 1962. **Backstamp(s)**: Shelley 1940-1966 **Shapes:** Ripon
14131	**Ferndown**. Pink edges and handle. Garlands of leaves and stems around centre of outside cup and on saucer. Leaves are brown, grey, yellow, and pink. Entered in pattern book during or after 1962. **Backstamp(s)**: Shelley 1940-1966 **Shapes:** Dainty

Ferndown 14131 Dainty shape cup and saucer. £60-75; $85-100

14133	**Acanthus**. Broad burgundy border outside cup, on saucer, and plate. Ivory below border. Gold acanthus print on burgundy and ivory join. Gold ring inside cup. Gold edges. Entered in pattern book during or after 1962. **Backstamp(s)**: Shelley 1940-1966 **Shapes:** Windsor

Acanthus 14133/89 Windsor shape cup, saucer, and plate. £60-80; $100-160

14134	Rococo. Grey and turquoise. Entered in pattern book during or after 1962. **Backstamp(s)**: Shelley 1940-1966 **Shapes:** Unknown
14135	Rococo. Grey. Entered in pattern book during or after 1962. **Backstamp(s)**: Shelley 1940-1966 **Shapes:** Unknown
14136	Kendal Grey Leaf border. Entered in pattern book during or after 1962. **Backstamp(s)**: Shelley 1940-1966 **Shapes:** Unknown
14137	**Melrose**. Entered in pattern book during or after 1962. **Backstamp(s)**: Shelley 1940-1966 **Shapes:** Windsor
14138	**Serenity** and **Grey Crystals**. Entered in pattern book during or after 1962. **Backstamp(s)**: Shelley 1940-1966 **Shapes:** Dainty
14139	**Caprice**. Entered in pattern book during or after 1962. **Backstamp(s)**: Shelley 1940-1966 **Shapes:** Dainty
14140	**Rhythm**. Entered in pattern book during or after 1962. **Backstamp(s)**: Shelley 1940-1966 **Shapes:** Dainty
14141	**Symphony**. Entered in pattern book during or after 1962. **Backstamp(s)**: Shelley 1940-1966 **Shapes:** Dainty
14142	**Pole Star**. Grey stars. Green edges and handle. Entered in pattern book during or after 1962. **Backstamp(s)**: Shelley 1940-1966 **Shapes:** Dainty
14143	**Snow Crystals**. Blue edges and handle. Entered in pattern book during or after 1962. **Backstamp(s)**: Shelley 1940-1966 **Shapes:** Dainty
14144	**Harmony**. Entered in pattern book during or after 1962. **Backstamp(s)**: Shelley 1940-1966 **Shapes:** Dainty
14145	**Lyric**. Dark pink and grey feathers, grey snowflakes. Pink edges and handle. Entered in pattern book during or after 1962. **Backstamp(s)**: Shelley 1940-1966 Lyric **Shapes:** Dainty
14146	**Georgian** with bluebells. Entered in

Pattern	Description & Shapes
	pattern book during or after 1962. **Backstamp(s)**: Shelley 1940-1966 **Shapes:** Dainty
14147	**Acanthus**. Entered in pattern book during or after 1962. **Backstamp(s)**: Shelley 1940-1966 **Shapes:** Windsor
14148	**Snow Crystals**. Entered in pattern book during or after 1962. **Backstamp(s)**: Shelley 1940-1966 **Shapes:** Dainty
14149	**Golden Rose**. Entered in pattern book during or after 1962. **Backstamp(s)**: Shelley 1940-1966 **Shapes:** Windsor
14150	Black. Entered in pattern book during or after 1962. **Backstamp(s)**: Shelley 1940-1966 **Shapes:** Mocha
14151	**Syringa**. Pattern outside cup and centre of saucer. Green inside cup and main part of saucer. Entered in pattern book during or after 1962. **Backstamp(s)**: Shelley 1940-1966 **Shapes:** Richmond
14152	**Celandine**. Pattern outside cup and centre of saucer. Orange inside cup and main part of saucer. Entered in pattern book during or after 1962. **Backstamp(s)**: Shelley 1940-1966 **Shapes:** Richmond
14153	**American Brooklime**. Tiny blue flowers and green leaves on white ground outside cup and centre of saucer. Pastel colour inside cup and main part of saucer. Entered in pattern book during or after 1962. /S41 mauve edges and handle /S43 green inside cup. **Backstamp(s)**: Shelley 1940-1966 American Brooklime **Shapes:** Richmond
14154	**Scilla**. Pattern outside cup and centre of saucer. Blue inside cup and main part of saucer. Entered in pattern book during or after 1962. **Backstamp(s)**: Shelley 1940-1966 **Shapes:** Richmond
14155	**Blue Iris**. Pattern outside cup and centre of saucer. Ivory inside cup and main part of saucer. Entered in pattern book during or after 1962. **Backstamp(s)**: Shelley 1940-1966 **Shapes:** Richmond
14156	**Thistle**. Pink thistle and green foliage inside cup and main part of saucer. Thistle outside cup and centre of saucer on a white ground. Green edges, foot and handle. Entered in pattern book during or after 1962. **Backstamp(s)**: Shelley 1940-1966 **Shapes:** Richmond

Thistle 14156 Richmond shape cup and saucer. £70-80; $140-160

14157	**Margaret Rose**. Entered in pattern book during or after 1962. **Backstamp(s)**: Shelley 1940-1966 **Shapes:** Footed Oleander, Low Oleander
14159	**Pansy**. Entered in pattern book during or after 1962. **Backstamp(s)**: Shelley 1940-1966 **Shapes:** Oleander, Richmond
14160	**Bridesmaid**. Entered in pattern book during or after 1962. **Backstamp(s)**: Shelley 1940-1966 **Shapes:** Dainty
14161	**Acanthus**. Entered in pattern book during or after 1962. **Backstamp(s)**: Shelley 1940-1966 **Shapes:** Windsor
14162	**Empire**. Entered in pattern book during or after 1962. **Backstamp(s)**: Shelley 1940-1966 **Shapes:** Mocha
14163	**Wild Anemone**. Entered in pattern book during or after 1962. **Backstamp(s)**: Shelley 1940-1966 Wild Anemone **Shapes:** Bute
14164	**Crochet**. Entered in pattern book during or after 1962. **Backstamp(s)**: Shelley 1940-1966 **Shapes:** Ripon
14165	**Heavenly Blue**. Entered in pattern book during or after 1962. **Backstamp(s)**: Shelley 1940-1966 **Shapes:** Ripon
14166	**Freesia**. Pink, purple, and yellow freesias and green leaves on white ground. Spray also inside cup. Broad, fawn band on edge of saucer and plate. Fawn foot. Gold edges. Entered in pattern book during or after 1963. **Backstamp(s)**: Shelley 1940-1966 Freesia **Shapes:** Windsor

Freesia large shell shape dish in original box. £60-80; $100-130

14167	**Honeysuckle**. Entered in pattern book during or after 1962. **Backstamp(s)**: Shelley 1940-1966 **Shapes:** Windsor
14168	**Blue Poppy**. Blue poppies and green leaves. White ground. Blue edges and handle. Entered in pattern book during or after 1962. **Backstamp(s)**: Shelley 1940-1966 Blue Poppy **Shapes:** Dainty, Ludlow, Richmond

Blue Poppy 14168 Ludlow shape cup and saucer. £60-80; $100-120

14169	**Castle**. Green. Entered in pattern book during or after 1962. **Backstamp(s)**: Shelley 1940-1966 **Shapes:** Ripon
14170	**Basket**. Entered in pattern book during or after 1962. **Backstamp(s)**: Shelley 1940-1966 **Shapes:** Ripon
14171	**Freesia**. Pink, purple, and yellow freesias and green leaves. White ground. Green edges and handle. Entered in pattern book during or after 1962. **Backstamp(s)**: Shelley 1940-1966 **Shapes:** Dainty, Footed Oleander

Freesia 14171 Footed Oleander shape cup and saucer. £70-80; $140-160

14172	**Honeysuckle**. Entered in pattern book during or after 1962. **Backstamp(s)**: Shelley 1940-1966 **Shapes:** Dainty
14173	**Daffodil Spray**. Entered in pattern book during or after 1962. **Backstamp(s)**: Shelley 1940-1966 **Shapes:** Richmond
14174	**Melody**. Chintz. Red, pink, yellow, and blue flowers on a mint green chintz background. Mint green inside cup. Gold edges. Entered in pattern book during or after 1962. **Backstamp(s)**: Shelley 1940-1966 Melody **Shapes:** Richmond
14175	**Maytime**. Entered in pattern book during or after 1962. **Backstamp(s)**: Shelley 1940-1966 **Shapes:** Henley
14176	**Bramble**. Pink bramble flowers, green leaves, brown stems, against smaller grey leaves outside cup and middle of saucer. Spray also inside cup. White ground. Gold trim. Yellow band on saucer and

Pattern	Description & Shapes

plate. Yellow foot and handle. Entered in pattern book during or after 1962.
Backstamp(s): Shelley 1940-1966
Shapes: Windsor

14177 **Margaret Rose**. Entered in pattern book during or after 1962.
Backstamp(s): Shelley 1940-1966
Shapes: Oleander

14178 Platinum bands. Entered in pattern book during or after 1962.
Backstamp(s): Shelley 1940-1966
Shapes: Gainsborough

14179 Gold roses and scrolls pattern on coloured ground. White band at base of outside cup and white centre of saucer. Gold edges and handle. Entered in pattern book during or after 1962.
/41 Maroon
/42 Blue.
Backstamp(s): Shelley 1940-1966
Shapes: Mocha, Windsor

14180 Gold motif on colour ground. Entered in pattern book during or after 1963.
/40 Pink
/83 Green.
Backstamp(s): Shelley 1940-1966
Shapes: Mocha, Windsor

14181 Gold motif. Entered in pattern book during or after 1963.
Backstamp(s): Shelley 1940-1966
Shapes: Windsor

14182 Green band with white below it. Gold pattern on the green band. Gold line separating green from white. Gold edges. Entered in pattern book during or after 1963.
Backstamp(s): Shelley 1940-1966
Shapes: Windsor

14183 Gold motif. Peach band. Entered in pattern book during or after 1963.
Backstamp(s): Shelley 1940-1966
Shapes: Windsor

14184 **Tapestry Rose**. Chintz. Entered in pattern book during or after 1963.
Backstamp(s): Shelley 1940-1966
Shapes: Henley

14185 **Viscount**. Maroon. Entered in pattern book during or after 1963.
Backstamp(s): Shelley 1940-1966
Shapes: Carlisle

14186 **Viscount**. Blue. Entered in pattern book during or after 1963.
Backstamp(s): Shelley 1940-1966
Shapes: Carlisle

14187 **Flowers of Gold**. Gold tulips, roses, and other flowers and foliage on a white ground. Gold edges. Entered in pattern book during or after 1963.
Backstamp(s): Shelley 1940-1966
Shapes: Dainty

Flowers of Gold 14187 Dainty shape cup and saucer. £60-75; $85-100

14188 **Bramble**. Entered in pattern book during or after 1963.
Backstamp(s): Shelley 1940-1966
Shapes: Dainty

Bramble 14188 Dainty shape cup and saucer. £70-80; $140-160

14189 **Pyrethrum**. Entered in pattern book during or after 1963.
Backstamp(s): Shelley 1940-1966
Shapes: Dainty

14190 **Fantasy**. Entered in pattern book during or after 1963.
Backstamp(s): Shelley 1940-1966
Shapes: Windsor

14191 **Freesia**. Pink, purple, and yellow freesias and green leaves. White ground. Gold edges. Entered in pattern book during or after 1963.
Backstamp(s): Shelley 1940-1966
Shapes: Windsor

14192 **Flowers of Gold**. Pattern inside cup. Green outside cup and on saucer. Entered in pattern book during or after 1963.
Backstamp(s): Shelley 1940-1966
Shapes: Carlisle

14193 **Flowers of Gold**. Pattern inside cup. Pink outside cup and on saucer. Entered in pattern book during or after 1963.
Backstamp(s): Shelley 1940-1966
Shapes: Carlisle

14194 **Flowers of Gold**. Pattern inside cup. Dark green outside cup and on saucer. Entered in pattern book during or after 1963.
Backstamp(s): Shelley 1940-1966
Shapes: Carlisle

14195 **Tapestry Rose**. Chintz. Entered in pattern book during or after 1963.
Backstamp(s): Shelley 1940-1966
Shapes: Henley

14196 **Black Chintz**. Entered in pattern book during or after 1963.
Backstamp(s): Shelley 1940-1966
Shapes: Ripon

14197 **Wild Apple**. Entered in pattern book during or after 1963.
Backstamp(s): Shelley 1940-1966
Shapes: Dainty, Tall Dainty

14198 **Blue Harlequin**. Band of overlapping blue and grey diamonds. White ground. Entered in pattern book during or after 1963.
Backstamp(s): Shelley 1940-1966 Blue Harlequin
Shapes: Avon Coffee, Bristol

14199 **Pink Harlequin**. Band of overlapping pink and grey diamonds. White ground. Entered in pattern book during or after 1963.
Backstamp(s): Shelley 1940-1966 Pink Harlequin
Shapes: Bristol

14200 **Cleopatra**. Band of vertical panels decorated with abstracts and stylised leaves. Grey, green, pink brown, and black on a white ground. Entered in pattern book during or after 1963.
Backstamp(s): Shelley 1940-1966 Cleopatra
Shapes: Bristol

14201 **Osterley**. Entered in pattern book during or after 1963.
Backstamp(s): Shelley 1940-1966
Shapes: Carlisle

14202 **Rose Spray**. Entered in pattern book during or after 1963.
Backstamp(s): Shelley 1940-1966
Shapes: Tall Dainty

14203 **Stocks**. Mauve, pink, and white stocks with green leaves. White ground. Entered in pattern book during or after 1963.
Backstamp(s): Shelley 1940-1966
Shapes: Tall Dainty

14204 **Roses, Pansies, and Forget-me-nots**. Entered in pattern book during or after 1963.
Backstamp(s): Shelley 1940-1966
Shapes: Tall Dainty

14205 **Freesia**. Pink, purple, and yellow freesias and green leaves. White ground. Entered in pattern book during or after 1963.
Backstamp(s): Shelley 1940-1966
Shapes: Tall Dainty

14206 **Wind Flowers**. Entered in pattern book during or after 1963.
Backstamp(s): Shelley 1940-1966
Shapes: Tall Dainty

14207 **Regal**. Entered in pattern book during or after 1963.
Backstamp(s): Shelley 1940-1966 Regal
Shapes: Windsor

14208 **Fruit Centre**. Plain coloured outside cup and on saucer. Fruit decoration inside cup, with peaches, berries, and leaves. Gold edges, foot and handle. Entered in pattern book during or after 1963.
/S3 Green with **Apple**
/S9 Pink with **Apple**
/S10 Blue with **Peach**
/S16 Orange with **Peach.**
Backstamp(s): Shelley 1940-1966
Shapes: Boston, Lincoln

14209 **Briar Rose Chintz**. Pink outside cup and on saucer. Entered in pattern book during or after 1963.
Backstamp(s): Shelley 1940-1966 Regal
Shapes: Boston

14210 **Melody**. Chintz. Red, pink, yellow, and blue flowers on a mint green chintz background. Entered in pattern book during or after 1963. Replaced with **Green Paisley Chintz** in 1964.
Backstamp(s): Shelley 1940-1966.
Shapes: Boston, Lincoln

Green Paisley Chintz 14210 Lincoln shape cup and saucer. £80-90; $160-190

Pattern	Description & Shapes
14211	**Tapestry Rose**. Chintz. Orange outside cup and on saucer. Entered in pattern book during or after 1963. **Backstamp(s)**: Shelley 1940-1966 Regal **Shapes:** Boston
14212	**Blue Daisy**. Chintz. White daisies and blue leaves on a lighter blue ground. Patterned inside cup. Pale blue outside cup and on saucer. Gold trim. Entered in pattern book during or after 1963. **Backstamp(s)**: Shelley 1940-1966 **Shapes:** Boston
14213	**Rock Garden**. Chintz. Rockery plants set amongst grey stones. Pink, blue, yellow, and whiter flowers with green foliage. Patterned inside cup. Peach outside cup and on saucer. Gold edges. Entered in pattern book during or after 1963. **Backstamp(s)**: Shelley 1940-1966 Rock Garden **Shapes:** Boston
14214	**Blue Paisley Chintz**. Paisley pattern inside cup. Lilac outside cup and on saucer. Gold edges. Entered in pattern book during or after 1963. **Backstamp(s)**: Shelley 1940-1966. **Shapes:** Boston
14215	**Maytime Chintz**. Pattern inside cup. Pink outside cup and on saucer. Entered in pattern book during or after 1963. **Backstamp(s)**: Shelley 1940-1966. **Shapes:** Boston
14216	**Green Daisy**. Chintz. White daisies and green leaves on a lighter green ground. Patterned inside cup. Pale green outside cup and on saucer. Gold trim. Entered in pattern book during or after 1963. **Backstamp(s)**: Shelley 1940-1966 **Shapes:** Boston
14217	**Marguerite**. Chintz. Chintz. White daisies and green leaves on a lighter green ground. Patterned inside cup. Yellow outside cup and on saucer. Gold edges. Entered in pattern book during or after 1963. **Backstamp(s)**: Shelley 1940-1966 **Shapes:** Boston, Lincoln

Marguerite 14217 Lincoln shape cup and saucer. £80-90; $160-190

14218	**Primrose Chintz**. Pattern inside cup. Blue outside cup and on saucer. Entered in pattern book during or after 1963. **Backstamp(s)**: Shelley 1940-1966 **Shapes:** Boston
14219	**Black Chintz**. Pattern inside cup. Peach outside cup and on saucer. Entered in pattern book during or after 1963. Changed to **Floral Chintz** from October 1964. **Backstamp(s)**: Shelley 1940-1966 **Shapes:** Boston
14220	**Georgian Chintz**. Pattern inside cup. Lavender outside cup and on saucer. Entered in pattern book during or after 1963. **Backstamp(s)**: Shelley 1940-1966 **Shapes:** Boston
14221	**Violets**. Entered in pattern book during or after 1963. **Backstamp(s)**: Shelley 1940-1966 **Shapes:** Tall Dainty
14222	**Syringa**. Entered in pattern book during or after 1963. **Backstamp(s)**: Shelley 1940-1966 **Shapes:** Tall Dainty
14223	**Begonia**. Entered in pattern book during or after 1963. **Backstamp(s)**: Shelley 1940-1966 **Shapes:** Tall Dainty
14224	**Fiesta**. Entered in pattern book during or after 1963. **Backstamp(s)**: Shelley 1940-1966 Fiesta **Shapes:** Richmond
14225	**Gaiety**. Entered in pattern book during or after 1963. **Backstamp(s)**: Shelley 1940-1966 **Shapes:** Richmond
14226	**Flowers of Gold**. Entered in pattern book during or after 1964. **Backstamp(s)**: Shelley 1940-1966 **Shapes:** Henley, Ripon
14227	**Blue Sprays**. Entered in pattern book during or after 1964. **Backstamp(s)**: Shelley 1940-1966 **Shapes:** Dainty
14228	**Purple Sprays**. Entered in pattern book during or after 1964. **Backstamp(s)**: Shelley 1940-1966 **Shapes:** Dainty
14229	**Bridesmaid** and **Melrose** border. Entered in pattern book during or after 1964. **Backstamp(s)**: Shelley 1940-1966 **Shapes:** Windsor
14230	**Pansy Chintz**. Entered in pattern book during or after 1964. **Backstamp(s)**: Shelley 1940-1966 **Shapes:** Ripon
14231	**Heavenly**. Sprigs of flowers and garland border. Colour edges. Entered in pattern book during or after 1964. /B **Heavenly Blue** /M **Heavenly Mauve** /P **Heavenly Pink**. **Backstamp(s)**: 1940-1966 **Shapes:** Ripon
14232	**Roses, Pansies, and Forget-me-nots**. Entered in pattern book during or after 1964. **Backstamp(s)**: Shelley 1940-1966 **Shapes:** Ripon
14233	**Blue Rock**. Tiny blue flowers and green leaves. Gold edges. Entered in pattern book during or after 1964. **Backstamp(s)**: Shelley 1940-1966 **Shapes:** Ripon
14234	**Rose Spray**. Entered in pattern book during or after 1964. **Backstamp(s)**: Shelley 1940-1966 **Shapes:** Ripon
14235	**Pastoral**. Entered in pattern book during or after 1964. **Backstamp(s)**: Shelley 1940-1966 Pastoral **Shapes:** Dainty, Richmond
14236	**Georgian Chintz**. Entered in pattern book during or after 1964. **Backstamp(s)**: Shelley 1940-1966 **Shapes:** Richmond
14237	**Primrose**. Lilac outside cup and on saucer. Entered in pattern book during or after 1964. **Backstamp(s)**: Shelley 1940-1966 **Shapes:** Richmond
14238	**Lily of the Valley**. Entered in pattern book during or after 1964. **Backstamp(s)**: Shelley 1940-1966 **Shapes:** Richmond, Tall Dainty
14239	**Freesia**. Pink, purple, and yellow freesias and green leaves inside cup on white ground. Green outside cup and on saucer. Gold edges. Entered in pattern book during or after 1964. **Backstamp(s)**: Shelley 1940-1966 **Shapes:** Richmond
14240	**Harebell**. Blue flowers and green leaves inside cup on white ground. Blue outside cup and on saucer. Gold edges. Entered in pattern book during or after 1964. **Backstamp(s)**: Shelley 1940-1966 **Shapes:** Richmond
14241	**Crochet** and **Georgian**. Entered in pattern book during or after 1964. **Backstamp(s)**: Shelley 1940-1966 **Shapes:** Richmond
14242	**Blue Poppy**. Blue poppies and green leaves on a white ground. Peach outside cup and on saucer. Peach edges. Entered in pattern book during or after 1964. **Backstamp(s)**: Shelley 1940-1966 **Shapes:** Richmond
14243	Gold **Fleur De Lys** on a white ground. Gold edges. **Backstamp(s)**: Shelley 1940-1966 **Shapes:** Carlisle, Dainty, Richmond

Fleur De Lys 14243 Carlisle shape cup and saucer. £90-95; $150-170

14244	**American Brooklime**. Tiny blue flowers and green leaves on white ground inside cup and on plate. Peach outside cup and on saucer. Entered in pattern book during or after 1964. **Backstamp(s)**: Shelley 1940-1966 **Shapes:** Boston
14245	**Blue Rose**. Blue roses on a white ground inside cup. Peach outside cup and on saucer. Gold edges. Entered in pattern book during or after 1964. **Backstamp(s)**: Shelley 1940-1966 **Shapes:** Boston, Lincoln

Blue Rose 14245 Lincoln shape cup and saucer. £90-95; $150-170

Pattern	Description & Shapes
14246	**Primrose Spray**. Pattern inside cup. Orange outside cup and on saucer. Entered in pattern book during or after 1964. **Backstamp(s)**: Shelley 1940-1966 **Shapes:** Boston
14247	**Pink and Yellow Roses**. Pattern inside cup. Orange outside cup and on saucer. Entered in pattern book during or after 1964. **Backstamp(s)**: Shelley 1940-1966 **Shapes:** Boston
14248	**Bridesmaid**. Pink roses on a white ground inside cup. Pink outside cup and on saucer. Gold edges. Entered in pattern book during or after 1964. **Backstamp(s)**: Shelley 1940-1966 **Shapes:** Boston, Lincoln

Bridesmaid 14248 Lincoln shape cup and saucer. £90-95; $150-170

14249 **Thistle**. Pattern inside cup. Pale pink outside cup and on saucer. Gold edges, foot and outer part of handle. Entered in pattern book during or after 1964.
Backstamp(s): Shelley 1940-1966
Shapes: Boston

Thistle 14249/S9 Boston shape cup and saucer. £90-95; $150-170

14250 **Lily of the Valley**. Pattern inside cup. Pale green outside cup and on saucer. Gold edges, foot and outer part of handle. Entered in pattern book during or after 1964.
Backstamp(s): Shelley 1940-1966
Shapes: Boston

14251 **Harebell**. Blue flowers and green leaves inside cup on white ground. Plain colour outside cup and on saucer. Gold edges. Entered in pattern book during or after 1964.
/S3 pale green
Backstamp(s): Shelley 1940-1966
Shapes: Boston, Lincoln

Harebell 14251/S3 Lincoln shape cup and saucer. £60-80; $90-110

14252 **Campanula**. Purple flowers and green leaves on a white ground inside cup. Lilac outside cup and on saucer. Gold edges. Entered in pattern book during or after 1964.
Backstamp(s): Shelley 1940-1966
Shapes: Boston, Lincoln

Campanula 14252/S41 Lincoln shape cup and saucer. £60-80; $90-110

14253 **Violets**. Pattern inside cup. Lilac outside cup and on saucer. Entered in pattern book during or after 1964.
Backstamp(s): Shelley 1940-1966
Shapes: Boston

14254 **Wild Flowers**. Flowers inside cup include bluebells, pink and yellow flowers, and green leaves. Pale blue outside cup and on saucer. Gold edges. Entered in pattern book during or after 1964.
Backstamp(s): Shelley 1940-1966
Shapes: Boston, Lincoln

Right:
Wild Flowers 14254 Lincoln shape cup and saucer. £60-80; $90-110

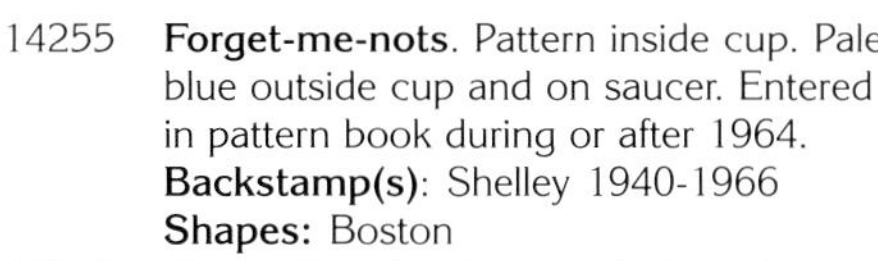

14255 **Forget-me-nots**. Pattern inside cup. Pale blue outside cup and on saucer. Entered in pattern book during or after 1964.
Backstamp(s): Shelley 1940-1966
Shapes: Boston

14256 Plain colour. Gold edges. Entered in pattern book during or after 1964.
Backstamp(s): Shelley 1940-1966
Shapes: Richmond

14257 Plain colour. Platinum edges. Entered in pattern book during or after 1964.
Backstamp(s): Shelley 1940-1966
Shapes: Ripon, Windsor

14258 **Columbia**. Horizontal blue sections with grey pedestal and grey foliage. Grey scroll pattern surrounds each blue section. White ground. Platinum edges. Entered in pattern book during or after 1964.
Backstamp(s): Shelley 1940-1966 Columbia
Shapes: Carlisle

14259 **Blenheim**. Horizontal burgundy sections with grey pedestal and grey foliage. Grey scroll pattern surrounds each burgundy section. White ground. Gold edges. Entered in pattern book during or after 1964.
Backstamp(s): Shelley 1940-1966 Blenheim
Shapes: Avon Coffee, Carlisle

Blenheim 14259 Avon Coffee shape cup, saucer, and plate. £60-80; $90-110

Blenheim 14259 Carlisle shape cup and saucer. £60-80; $90-110

Pattern	Description & Shapes
14260	**Meissenette**. Blue print. Fruit, leaves, flowers, and tendrils. White ground. Entered in pattern book during or after 1964. **Backstamp(s)**: Shelley 1940-1966 **Shapes:** Dainty

Meissenette 14260 Dainty shape cup and saucer. £60-75; $85-100

14261 **Plain colour. Gold edges. Entered in pattern book during or after 1964.**
/S50 Blue
/S51 Fawn
/S52 Pink
/S55 Yellow
/S56 Green
/S57 Blue.
/**Backstamp(s)**: Shelley 1940-1966
Shapes: Avon Coffee

14262 **Primrose Spray**. Entered in pattern book during or after 1964.
Backstamp(s): Shelley 1940-1966
Shapes: Carlisle

14263 **Briar Rose Chintz**. Entered in pattern book during or after 1964.
Backstamp(s): Shelley 1940-1966
Shapes: Ripon

14264 **Maytime Chintz**. Entered in pattern book during or after 1964.
Backstamp(s): Shelley 1940-1966
Shapes: Ripon

14265 **Marguerite Chintz**. Entered in pattern book during or after 1964.
Backstamp(s): Shelley 1940-1966
Shapes: Ripon

14266 **Blue Pansy Chintz**. Entered in pattern book during or after 1964.
Backstamp(s): Shelley 1940-1966
Shapes: Ripon

14267 **Rock Garden**. Chintz. Rockery plants set amongst grey stones. Pink, blue, yellow, and white flowers with green foliage. Gold edges. Entered in pattern book during or after 1964.
Backstamp(s): Shelley 1940-1966 Rock Garden
Shapes: Carlisle, Ripon

Rock Garden 14267 Carlisle shape cup and saucer. £70-90; $140-180

14268 **Blue Daisy**. Chintz. White daisies and blue leaves on a lighter blue ground. Patterned outside cup and on saucer. Gold trim, foot and handle. Entered in pattern book during or after 1964.
Backstamp(s): Shelley 1940-1966
Shapes: Ripon

Blue Daisy 14268 Ripon shape cup and saucer. £70-90; $140-180

14269 **Green Daisy**. Chintz. White daisies and green leaves on a lighter green ground. Patterned outside cup and on saucer. Gold trim, foot and handle. Entered in pattern book during or after 1964.
Backstamp(s): Shelley 1940-1966
Shapes: Ripon

14270 **Tapestry Rose Chintz**. Entered in pattern book during or after 1964.
Backstamp(s): Shelley 1940-1966
Shapes: Ripon

14271 **Blue Paisley Chintz**. Paisley pattern. Gold edges. Entered in pattern book during or after 1964.
Backstamp(s): Shelley 1940-1966
Shapes: Ripon

14272 **Green Paisley Chintz**. Paisley pattern. 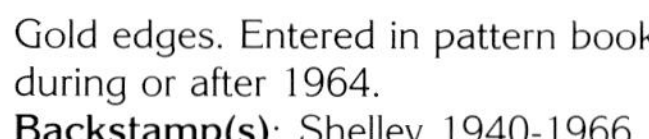 Gold edges. Entered in pattern book during or after 1964.
Backstamp(s): Shelley 1940-1966
Shapes: Ripon

14273 **Georgian Chintz**. Entered in pattern book during or after 1964.
Backstamp(s): Shelley 1940-1966
Shapes: Ripon

14274 **Floral Chintz**. Entered in pattern book during or after 1964.
Backstamp(s): Shelley 1940-1966
Shapes: Ripon

14275 **Golden Laurel**. Entered in pattern book during or after 1964.
Backstamp(s): Shelley 1940-1966
Shapes: Ripon

14276 **Rambler Rose**. Large pink roses and green foliage on a pale pink ground outside cup and main part of saucer. Yellow inside cup and centre of saucer. Gold edges. Entered in pattern book during or after 1964.
Backstamp(s): Shelley 1940-1966
Shapes: Ripon

14277 Hulmes **Rose** on colour ground. Entered in pattern book during or after 1964.
/S3 Green
/S9 Pink
/S10 Blue
/S16 Yellow.
Backstamp(s): Shelley 1940-1966
Shapes: Ripon

14278 **Georgian Chintz**. Entered in pattern book during or after 1964.
Backstamp(s): Shelley 1940-1966
Shapes: Ripon

14279 Details unknown. Entered in pattern book during or after 1964.
Backstamp(s): Shelley 1940-1966
Shapes: Windsor

14280 **Fiord**. Geometric pattern in shades of blue and mauve. White ground. Entered in pattern book during or after 1964.
Backstamp(s): Shelley 1940-1966 Fiord
Shapes: Stirling

14281 **Naples**. Entered in pattern book during or after 1964.
Backstamp(s): Shelley 1940-1966
Shapes: Avon

14282 **Apollo**. Entered in pattern book during or after 1964.
Backstamp(s): Shelley 1940-1966
Shapes: Avon

14283 **Aegean**. Broad border of vertical stripes in black, shades of blue and brown.

Aegean 14283 Avon shape cup and saucer. £40-50; $80-100

Right:
Green Paisley Chintz 14272 Ripon shape cup and saucer. £70-90; $140-180. **Blue Paisley Chintz** 14038 Ripon shape cup and saucer. £70-90; $140-180

Pattern	Description & Shapes

White ground. White ground. Entered in pattern book during or after 1964.
Backstamp(s): Shelley 1940-1966
Shapes: Avon

14284 **Red Tapestry Rose**. Entered in pattern book during or after 1964.
Backstamp(s): Shelley 1940-1966
Shapes: Ripon

14285 **Trousseau**. Entered in pattern book during or after 1965.
Backstamp(s): Shelley 1940-1966
Shapes: Ripon

14286 **Bluebell Wood**. Bluebells at the foot of trees. Hills in the background. Rock and bluebells inside cup. White ground. Gold edges, blue foot (Richmond) and handle. Entered in pattern book during or after 1965.
Backstamp(s): Shelley 1940-1966 Bluebell Wood
Shapes: Richmond, Ripon

Bluebell Wood 14286 Richmond shape cup and saucer. £50-70; $80-110

14287 **Loch Lomond**. Outside cup and on saucer, trees, grass, pink heather, and rocks on the banks of the lake against a mountain backdrop. Inside cup, rocks, green grass, and pink heather. White ground. Gold edges, pale green foot (Richmond) and handle. Dainty has pink handle. Entered in pattern book during or after 1965.
Backstamp(s): Shelley 1940-1966 Loch Lomond
Shapes: Dainty, Richmond

Loch Lomond 14287 Dainty shape cup and saucer. £70-80; $140-160

Loch Lomond 14287 Richmond shape cup and saucer. £60-70; $100-120

Loch Lomond 14287 unverified shape cup and saucer. £80-100; $120-160

14288 Plain colour. Entered in pattern book during or after 1965.
/S47 Blue
/S48 Maroon
/S53 Green
/72 Black.
Backstamp(s): Shelley 1940-1966
Shapes: Carlisle

14289 **Queen Elizabeth**. Turquoise band on ivory ground. Entered in pattern book during or after 1965.
Backstamp(s): Shelley 1940-1966
Shapes: Gainsborough

14290 Multi-coloured spots. Entered in pattern book during or after 1965.
Backstamp(s): Shelley 1940-1966
Shapes: Dainty

14291 **Scroll Border**. Entered in pattern book during or after 1965.
Backstamp(s): Shelley 1940-1966
Shapes: Carlisle

14292 **Gold Grecian Scroll**. Entered in pattern book during or after 1965.
Backstamp(s): Shelley 1940-1966
Shapes: Carlisle, Mocha

14293 **Lilac** or **Lilac Time**. Lilacs with green foliage and small pink flowers on a white ground. Lilac sprig also inside cup. Purple edges. Mauve foot (Richmond) and handle. Entered in pattern book during or after 1965.
Backstamp(s): Shelley 1940-1966 Lilac; Lilac Time
Shapes: Dainty, Richmond

14294 **Black Grecian Scroll**. Entered in pattern book during or after 1965.
Backstamp(s): Shelley 1940-1966
Shapes: Carlisle, Mocha

14295 **Corfu**. Entered in pattern book during or after 1965.
Backstamp(s): Shelley 1940-1966
Shapes: Carlisle

14296 **Stocks**. Mauve, pink, and white stocks with green leaves. White ground. Pink saucer. Entered in pattern book during or after 1965.
Backstamp(s): Shelley 1940-1966
Shapes: Avon

14297 **Freesia**. Pink, purple, and yellow freesias and green leaves on a white ground. Yellow saucer. Entered in pattern book during or after 1965.
Backstamp(s): Shelley 1940-1966
Shapes: Avon

14298 **Thistle**. Green saucer. Entered in pattern book during or after 1965.
Backstamp(s): Shelley 1940-1966
Shapes: Avon

14299 **Blue Poppy**. Blue poppies and green leaves on a white ground. Blue saucer. Entered in pattern book during or after 1965.
Backstamp(s): Shelley 1940-1966
Shapes: Avon

14300 **Apollo**. Entered in pattern book during or after 1965.
Backstamp(s): Shelley 1940-1966
Shapes: Avon

14301 **Aegean**. Broad border of vertical stripes in black, shades of blue and brown. White ground. White ground. Gold trim. Entered in pattern book during or after 1965.
Backstamp(s): Shelley 1940-1966
Shapes: Avon

14302 **Pink Rose**. Pattern inside cup and centre of saucer. Maroon outside cup and main part of saucer. Entered in pattern book during or after 1965.
Backstamp(s): Shelley 1940-1966
Shapes: Carlisle

14303 **Pink Rose**. Pattern inside cup and centre of saucer. Colour outside cup and main part of saucer. Entered in pattern book during or after 1965.
Backstamp(s): Shelley 1940-1966
Shapes: Carlisle

14304 Davies **Tulip**. Pattern inside cup and centre of saucer. Green outside cup and main part of saucer. Entered in pattern book during or after 1965.
Backstamp(s): Shelley 1940-1966
Shapes: Carlisle

14305 **Rural England**. Entered in pattern book during or after 1965.
Backstamp(s): Shelley 1940-1966
Shapes: Ripon

14306 **Jacobean**. Entered in pattern book during or after 1965.
Backstamp(s): Shelley 1940-1966
Shapes: Unknown

14307 **Hathaway**. In production from 1964 to c. 1965. Cup with Hathaway litho and olive green saucer.
Backstamp(s): 1940-1966
Shapes: Avon

Hathaway 14307 Avon shape cup and saucer. £55-75; $75-95

Pattern	Description & Shapes
14308	**Mosaic**. Entered in pattern book during or after 1965. **Backstamp(s)**: Shelley 1940-1966 **Shapes:** Avon
14309	**Chequers**. Entered in pattern book during or after 1965. **Backstamp(s)**: Shelley 1940-1966 **Shapes:** Avon
14310	**Bramble**. Entered in pattern book during or after 1965. **Backstamp(s)**: Shelley 1940-1966 **Shapes:** Carlisle
14311	**Honeysuckle**. Pink and yellow honeysuckle sprays with green foliage on a white ground. Gold edges. Entered in pattern book during or after 1965. **Backstamp(s)**: Shelley 1940-1966 **Shapes:** Avon, Carlisle, Dainty

Honeysuckle 14311 Avon shape cup and saucer. £55-75; $75-95

Pattern	Description & Shapes
14312	**Freesia**. Pink, purple, and yellow freesias and green leaves. White ground. Gold edges. Entered in pattern book during or after 1965. **Backstamp(s)**: Shelley 1940-1966 **Shapes:** Carlisle
14313	**Stocks**. Mauve, pink, and white stocks with green leaves. White ground. Entered in pattern book during or after 1965. **Backstamp(s)**: Shelley 1940-1966 **Shapes:** Carlisle
14314	**Blue Poppy**. Blue poppies and green leaves. White ground. Gold edges. Entered in pattern book during or after 1965. **Backstamp(s)**: Shelley 1940-1966 **Shapes:** Carlisle
14315	**Lilac**. Entered in pattern book during or after 1965. **Backstamp(s)**: Shelley 1940-1966 **Shapes:** Carlisle
14316	**Meisenette**. Entered in pattern book during or after 1965. **Backstamp(s)**: Shelley 1940-1966 **Shapes:** Carlisle
14317	**Grecian Scroll**. Entered in pattern book during or after 1966. **Backstamp(s)**: Shelley 1940-1966 **Shapes:** Carlisle
14318	**Shelbourne**. Entered in pattern book during or after 1966. **Backstamp(s)**: Shelley 1940-1966 **Shapes:** Carlisle
14319	**Rose**. Entered in pattern book during or after 1966. **Backstamp(s)**: Shelley 1940-1966 **Shapes:** Dainty
14320	**Yutoi**. Entered in pattern book during or after 1966. **Backstamp(s)**: Shelley 1940-1966 **Shapes:** Dainty
14321	**Moss Rose**. Entered in pattern book during or after 1966. **Backstamp(s)**: Shelley 1940-1966 **Shapes:** Dainty
14322	**Summer Bouquet**. Entered in pattern book during or after 1966. **Backstamp(s)**: Shelley 1940-1966 **Shapes:** Dainty
14323	**Country Gardens**. Entered in pattern book during or after 1966. **Backstamp(s)**: Shelley 1940-1966 **Shapes:** Dainty
14324	**Eglantine**. Entered in pattern book during or after 1966. **Backstamp(s)**: Shelley 1940-1966 **Shapes:** Dainty
14325	**Sycamore**. Entered in pattern book during or after 1966. **Backstamp(s)**: Shelley 1940-1966 **Shapes:** Dainty
14326	**Blackberry**. Entered in pattern book during or after 1966. **Backstamp(s)**: Shelley 1940-1966 **Shapes:** Dainty
14327	**Rural England**. Entered in pattern book during or after 1966. **Backstamp(s)**: Shelley 1940-1966 **Shapes:** Richmond
14328	**Cascade**. Entered in pattern book during or after 1966. **Backstamp(s)**: Shelley 1940-1966 **Shapes:** Carlisle, Mocha
14329	**Lady Jane**. Similar to **Lady Eleanor**. Entered in pattern book during or after 1966. **Backstamp(s)**: Shelley 1940-1966 **Shapes:** Richmond
14330	**Blue Poppy**. Blue poppies and green leaves on white ground inside cup and centre of saucer. Colour outside cup and body of saucer. Gold edges, foot and handle. Entered in pattern book during or after 1966. /S10 Blue /S15 Peach. **Backstamp(s)**: Shelley 1940-1966 **Shapes:** Boston, Lincoln

Blue Poppy 14330 Lincoln shape cup and saucer. £80-100; $120-160

Blue Poppy 14330/S15 Lincoln shape cup and saucer. £80-100; $120-160

Pattern	Description & Shapes
14331	**Gold Grecian Scroll**. Entered in pattern book during or after 1966. **Backstamp(s)**: Shelley 1940-1966 **Shapes:** Carlisle, Mocha
14332	**Blue Primrose**. Entered in pattern book during or after 1966. **Backstamp(s)**: Shelley 1940-1966 **Shapes:** Ripon
14333	**Pink Glory**. Entered in pattern book during or after 1966. **Backstamp(s)**: Shelley 1940-1966 **Shapes:** Ripon
14334	**Yellow Marguerite**. Entered in pattern book during or after 1966. **Backstamp(s)**: Shelley 1940-1966 **Shapes:** Ripon
14335	**Black Maytime**. Entered in pattern book during or after 1966. **Backstamp(s)**: Shelley 1940-1966 **Shapes:** Ripon
14336	**Black Maytime**. Pale green outside cup. Entered in pattern book during or after 1966. **Backstamp(s)**: Shelley 1940-1966 **Shapes:** Boston
14337	**Yellow Marguerite**. Yellow outside cup. Entered in pattern book during or after 1966. **Backstamp(s)**: Shelley 1940-1966 **Shapes:** Boston
14338	Blue **Primrose Chintz**. Blue outside cup. Entered in pattern book during or after 1966. **Backstamp(s)**: Shelley 1940-1966 **Shapes:** Boston
14339	Pink **Primrose Chintz**. Lilac outside cup. Entered in pattern book during or after 1966. **Backstamp(s)**: Shelley 1940-1966 **Shapes:** Boston
14340	**Swansea Rose**. Lilac outside cup. Entered in pattern book during or after 1966. **Backstamp(s)**: Shelley 1940-1966 **Shapes:** Boston
14341	**Rural England**. Entered in pattern book during or after 1966. **Backstamp(s)**: Shelley 1940-1966 **Shapes:**

Pattern	Description & Shapes
Dainty White	Plain white. **Backstamp(s)**: All **Shapes:** Dainty
Spano Lustre	**Spano Lustre** Iridescent glaze. Gold edges and handle. **Backstamp(s)**: Wileman Foley 1890-1910; Shelley 1912-1925 **Shapes:** Dainty

Dainty White Dainty shape: large square dessert bowl, £40-50, $60-80; set of six small, square dessert bowls, £60-70, $80-100; comport/footed cake plate, £50-70, $80-100; hors d'oeuvre dish, £50-70, $80-100; large teapot and stand/trivet, £100-120, $150-200; small teapot and stand/trivet, £60-80, $90-120; large sugar and creamer, £40-50, $60-70; small sugar and creamer on tray, £50-60, $70-80; cup, saucer, and plate, £30-40, $50-60; tall cup, saucer, and plate, £30-40, $50-60; mug/beaker, £30-40, $50-60; double egg cup, £30-40, $50-60; egg cup, £20-30, $30-40; milk jug, £40-50, $50-60; pin tray/bon-bon dish, £20-30, $30-40.

Regency Tall Dainty shape coffee set on gold coloured stand. £160-180; $200-250

Summer-time	Roses. Pink, white, yellow, and purple roses with green foliage on a white ground. Gold edges and handle. No pattern number on the pieces I have seen. **Backstamp(s)**: Shelley 1940-1966 Summer-time **Shapes:** Mocha
Regency	**Regency**. Dainty White with gold edges and handles. **Backstamp(s)**: All; carmine-coloured twin-turreted castle mark "Shelley Castle China England" with the Late Foley mark for 1910-1916 **Shapes:** Dainty, Tall Dainty

Dainty White Dainty shape: large teapot, £100-120, $150-200; sugar and creamer, £40-50, $50-60; cup and saucer, £25-35; $45-55; faience tray, £100-120, $150-170.

Spano Lustre Dainty shape demitasse cup and saucer. £30-40; $50-60

Nairobi	**Nairobi**. Various tropical fish on a white ground outside cup and on saucer. Pale green inside cup. Black handle. Pale green foot. **Backstamp(s)**: Shelley 1940-1966; Roland Ward Nairobi Kenya **Shapes:** Mocha, Richmond

Right:
Nairobi Richmond shape breakfast cup and saucer. £80-100; $120-$150

Bibliography

Books

Davenport, Chris. *Shelley Pottery The Later Years*. England: Deanprint Ltd, 1997.
Eberle, Linda and Susan Scott. *The Charlton Standard Catalogue of Chintz*. Second edition. Canada: The Charlton Press, 1997.
Hill, Susan. *The Shelley Style*. England: Warwick Printing Company, 1997.
Knight, Richard and Susan Hill. *Wileman*. England: Jazz Publications, 1995.
Watson, Howard and Pat Watson. *Collecting Art Deco Ceramics*. London: Kevin Francis, 1993.
Watkins, Chris, William Harvey, and Robert Senft. *Shelley Potteries*. London: Barrie & Jenkins, 1994.

Articles

Shelley Group Magazine. United Kingdom, Various Issues, 1999-2002.

Index